Readings in
Labor Market Analysis

ECONOMIC SERIES
Under the Editorship of
Clark W. Reynolds
Stanford University

Readings in Microeconomics, Second Edition
edited by William Breit, *University of Virginia*
and Harold M. Hochman, *The Urban Institute, Washington, D. C.*

Readings in Labor Market Analysis
edited by John F. Burton, Jr., Lee K. Benham,
William M. Vaughn, III, and Robert J. Flanagan
All of the University of Chicago

Modern Political Arithmetic
Bruce F. Davie and Bruce F. Duncombe
Georgetown University

Readings in Macroeconomics, Second Edition
edited by M. G. Mueller
University of Glasgow

Economic Analysis and Industrial Structure
Douglas Needham
State University of New York, Brockport

Readings in the Economics of Industrial Organization
edited by Douglas Needham
State University of New York, Brockport

Readings in the History of Economic Theory
edited by Ingrid H. Rima
Temple University

Readings in Labor Market Analysis

Edited by
John F. Burton, Jr.
Lee K. Benham
William M. Vaughn, III
Robert J. Flanagan
All of the University of Chicago

HOLT, RINEHART AND WINSTON, INC.
New York   Chicago   San Francisco   Atlanta
Dallas   Montreal   Toronto   London   Sydney

Copyright © 1971 by Holt, Rinehart and Winston, Inc.
All rights reserved
Library of Congress Catalog Card Number: 73-132530
SBN cloth: 03-086215-9
SBN paper: 03-077020-3
Printed in the United States of America
1 2 3 4 006 9 8 7 6 5 4 3 2 1

Editor's Foreword

Labor economics was created primarily out of historical necessity. Institutional alterations of the market structure by private pressures and public policy have continually tended to precede analysis of their economic implications. It is not surprising, therefore, that most courses on the subject have until recently constituted a curious mixture of collective bargaining history, constitutional law, Keynesian employment theory, and anecdotes. This volume, in the tradition of the present series of economics textbooks, begins to remedy this problem by providing the reader with a set of articles and excerpts from the best available analytical literature. Step by step the selections offer the basic theoretical tools, methodology, and empirical analysis essential for a complete understanding of key aspects of labor market behavior. It becomes possible to analyze labor supply functions, decisions concerning investment in human capital, information costs, migration, and the reflection of market adjustment mechanisms in the behavior of occupational, interindustry, and racial and geographical wage differentials, as well as the role of unions in the creation of wage differentials. In addition, the public policy implications of minimum wage legislation are presented objectively, giving all sides of the theoretical debate in addition to the best existing empirical evidence on the issue.

By taking an explicitly microeconomic approach to the subject, rather than an industrial relations or macroeconomic approach, the editors have been purposefully selective. This permits the student to go in depth into problems of market adjustment at the level of individual, firm, occupation, and industry without sacrificing detail yet with the retention of generality. He is thus enabled to develop his own use of the tools of labor theory for the analysis of new problems, illustrating both the power and the limitations of existing doctrine. This selectivity has meant, however, that certain topics of keen social concern have had to be understressed, such as the relationship between employment and population growth, private versus efficiency pricing of labor units, income distribution, the welfare implications of monopsony in labor markets, full employment policy and structural unemployment, and the estimation of labor demand functions (a branch of production theory). These issues merit full treatment in future compendia. In the meantime this volume fills a major gap in the literature on labor economics by integrating theory, methodology, and empirical research with frank commentary by the editors on those hypotheses which remain unconfirmed as well as those areas where theory has yet to catch up with the real world.

Stanford, California
March 1971

—*Clark W. Reynolds*

Preface

How are wages and other working conditions determined? How do workers choose their occupations and employers? How do employers choose among their employees when layoffs are necessary?

Research on these and other questions related to the pricing and allocation of labor continues to follow two traditions. The economic approach emphasizes the role of market forces and therefore applies the tools of microeconomic or price theory to the problems. The industrial relations approach emphasizes the importance of institutions, such as trade unions, and therefore applies concepts such as bargaining theory in its analysis of the questions.[1] There have been efforts to ally these two approaches, but with few exceptions the liaison has been uneasy or unsuccessful.

In this volume, we make no attempt to mend or paper-over the breach between the economic and industrial relations approaches. We are concerned with the central economic problems of the labor sector—how labor services are priced and allocated—and in our view the economic approach is clearly the most useful for these problems. We do, however, consider institutions such as laws and unions when they impinge on the predominant role of economic forces in allocating resources.

The pricing and allocation of labor resources can readily be analyzed by the tools of price theory; and, more important, the predictions of price theory for

---

[1] Most industrial relations research, although it is frequently allocated to the jurisdiction of "labor economics," is really concerned with a different set of topics than resource allocation and pricing, for example, the development of union structure, the regulation of the industrial relations system, and the intricacies of dispute settlement. In these areas, the industrial relations approach can be of considerable value.

labor market operations can generally be tested rigorously against available data—a feature uncharacteristic of many of the industrial relations theories. Therefore, the articles included have been chosen to provide a three-stage approach to an understanding of labor market behavior. First, the theoretical articles provide the tools of analysis and yield the behavioral predictions for each of the major topics covered. Second, the methodological exchange—as well as sections of several theoretical and empirical articles—considers the problems of devising valid tests of the predictions. Finally, the empirical articles provide the evidence thus far available on the operation of the labor market.

This three-stage approach is reflected in the organization of the volume. The basic competitive theory of wage determination, from which all other theoretical extensions or qualifications proceed, is outlined in the two selections in Part I. In Part II, a debate is presented which isolates several crucial methodological issues. Part III examines two topics in supply and demand. Part IIIA considers the factors that govern the decision to work and the amount of work offered. Part IIIB, on monopsony, introduces a qualification to the competitive theory of demand necessary when the number of buyers of labor is limited, and presents some evidence on its empirical importance. Assuming the worker has decided to work, he must choose an occupation and an employer. The theoretical considerations governing occupational choice are covered in Part IV, while the theory and evidence on the mechanisms through which an occupation or an employer or a location can be changed during a worker's lifetime are covered in Parts V and VI. The result of the economic forces covered in the first six parts, the pattern of wage differentials and consequent allocation of labor, is discussed in Part VII. Finally, Part VIII covers the theoretical and empirical impact of one type of government policy on the labor market.

Our purpose is to familiarize advanced undergraduate or graduate students with the analytical tools of labor economists and to provide a sampling of important applications of these tools. We assume that our readers have already absorbed at least an intermediate-level course in price theory. But only a minimal amount of mathematical knowledge is required to read the selections. The value (measured in convenience utils) of this volume to students ultimately depends on the opportunity cost of their time and the efficiency of college reserve book rooms. The former seems quite high in most universities, while the latter—despite the best efforts of some of our favorite librarians—seems quite low. We also believe the value of the volume is enhanced because, with only three exceptions, the texts of the readings are reprinted in their entirety. (In a few cases, cross references extraneous to this volume have been deleted.)

We follow the tradition of anthologists in despairing of the problem of selection which we faced. By restricting the volume to articles on the microeconomic topics of pricing and allocation of labor among markets, we have had to omit interesting topics that are more extensively macroeconomic, such as unemployment, the functional distribution of income, the determination of the general wage level, and related policy issues. And even within our general microeconomic jurisdiction, we have omitted such topics as the distribution of earnings and the production function approach to the demand for labor because these areas are still relatively unsettled in the literature.

Each of the editors feels that there are important omissions, but each has a different list. The empirical literature in particular provides a number of close substitutes for many of the articles included here. Some guidance to these substitutes and to existing gaps in our knowledge is provided in the introductory material to each part. Ultimately, this volume represents what one group of labor economists views as a selection of basic readings, based on their experiences as graduate students at four universities and as teachers at a fifth and on their perusal of the lists of readings assigned for advanced undergraduate and basic graduate courses in labor economics at ten leading universities.

We would like to express our appreciation to the authors of these selections for their initial analyses, and our thanks to both the authors and their publishers for permission to reprint. In particular, we thank H. Gregg Lewis for his advice and for taking time to excerpt his book *Unionism and Relative Wages in the United States*, and Mary T. Hamilton for updating the tables in the article, "Postwar Movements of Wage Levels and Unit Labor Costs," which she coauthored with Albert Rees.

Chicago, Illinois
March 1971

John F. Burton, Jr.
Lee K. Benham
William M. Vaughn, III
Robert J. Flanagan

Contents

Editor's Foreword		*v*
Preface		*vii*
Part I	The Basic Theory of the Labor Market	1
1.	The Supply of Factors of Production *by Milton Friedman*	3
2.	The Demand for Labour *by K. W. Rothschild*	21
Part II	The Method of Labor Market Analysis	33
3.	On Choice in Labor Markets *by Simon Rottenberg*	37
4.	On Choice in Labor Markets: Comment *by Robert J. Lampman*	53
5.	On Choice in Labor Markets: Reply *by Simon Rottenberg*	61
Part III	Special Topics in Supply and Demand	67
A.	Aggregate Supply	71
6.	Hours of Work and Hours of Leisure *by H. Gregg Lewis*	71
7.	Labor-Force Participation and Unemployment: A Review of Recent Evidence *by Jacob Mincer*	79

8.	A Theory of the Allocation of Time by Gary S. Becker	106

B. Monopsony — 126

9.	Monopsonistic Conditions by K. W. Rothschild	126
10.	Concentration and Monopsony in Labor Markets by Robert L. Bunting	132
11.	The Baseball Players' Labor Market by Simon Rottenberg	140

Part IV Human Capital — 157

12.	Investment in Human Capital: Effects on Earnings by Gary S. Becker	159
13.	Investment in Human Capital: Rates of Return by Gary S. Becker	178
14.	Investment in Human Capital: A Comment by R. S. Eckaus	197
15.	On-the-Job Training: Costs, Returns, and Some Implications by Jacob Mincer	201

Part V Information — 231

16.	Information in the Labor Market by George J. Stigler	233
17.	Information Networks in Labor Markets by Albert Rees	245

Part VI Labor Mobility — 251

18.	The Costs and Returns of Human Migration by Larry A. Sjaastad	253
19.	Voluntary Labor Mobility in the U.S. Manufacturing Sector by John E. Parker and John F. Burton, Jr.	266

Part VII Wage Differentials — 275

A. Interindustry Wage Differentials — 281

20.	Wage Differentials: Theory and Measurement by Melvin W. Reder	281
21.	The Relation of Differential Wage Movements and the Redistribution of Labour Among Industries by the Organization for Economic Co-operation and Development	310
22.	Concentration and Labor Earnings by Leonard W. Weiss	344

B. Occupational Wage Differentials — 362

23.	Present Values of Lifetime Earnings for Different Occupations by Bruce W. Wilkinson	362

24.	Training Lags and the Cobweb Pattern in Engineering *by Richard B. Freeman*	378
C.	Geographical Wage Differentials	393
25.	Migration, Location and Remuneration of Medical Personnel: Physicians and Dentists *by Lee Benham, Alex Maurizi, and Melvin W. Reder*	393
26.	Hourly Earnings Differentials by Region and Size of City *by Victor R. Fuchs*	413
D.	Racial Wage Differentials	421
27.	Discrimination and Occupational Wage Differences in the Market for Unskilled Labor *by David P. Taylor*	421
E.	Union Impact on Wage Differentials	437
28.	Marshall and Friedman on Union Strength *by Lloyd Ulman*	437
29.	Unionism and Relative Wages in the United States *by H. Gregg Lewis*	458
30.	Unionism, Concentration, and Wage Changes: Toward a Unified Theory *by Harold M. Levinson*	477
31.	Changes in Wage Dispersion *by Albert Rees and Mary T. Hamilton*	484
32.	The Effects of Unions on Resource Allocation *by Albert Rees*	489
Part VIII	**Government Policy—Minimum Wage Laws**	497
33.	The Economics of Minimum Wage Legislation *by George J. Stigler*	501
34.	The Minimum Wage and Poverty *by Jacob J. Kaufman and Terry G. Foran*	508

PART I
THE BASIC THEORY OF THE LABOR MARKET

Central to the study of the labor market is the theory of the competitive labor market. Central to the theory of the competitive labor market are numerous buyers and sellers in the market, ease of entry and exit, mobility of resources, lack of collusion, the existence of sufficient information, and so on. Under these conditions, the aggregate supply and demand for each type of labor are the result of the decisions of many individuals and firms, and these two forces determine the price (or wage) of labor. Differences in wages among occupations and sectors, in turn, allocate workers to their most productive uses. To understand the theory of the labor market, then, it is necessary to understand the competitive forces that affect the supply of and demand for various types of labor. The selections in Part I reflect this objective.

The first reading, Milton Friedman's "The Supply of Factors of Production," discusses the forces that affect the short-run and long-run aggregate supply of labor, and the supply of labor to various occupations. The unique characteristics of labor as a factor of production are also discussed and evaluated. Further elaboration on some of these concepts of supply is found in Part IIIA, Aggregate Supply, and Part IV, Human Capital. With the first selection, these parts provide a representative picture of the supply side of the labor market.

On the demand side of the labor market, we include K. W. Rothschild's "The Demand for Labor," a short analysis of the factors that affect the demand for labor under conditions of perfect competition. As Rothschild notes, the law of diminishing marginal productivity of factors of production is central to the theory of the demand for labor. Applied to the factor labor, this law states that ceteris paribus, adding successive increments of labor to other factors of production will eventually result in reduced returns per unit of labor. This condition is sufficient to explain the downward-sloping demand curve for labor. Rothschild also discusses some of the qualifications that have to be made in the interest of realism.

Virtually no empirical work is included on demand in the labor market. For such work the reader is referred to certain aspects of the "production function" literature. Probably the best place to begin is still with Paul H. Douglas' classic *The Theory of Wages*.[1] It is worth

---

[1] (New York: Crowell-Collier and Macmillan, Inc., 1954).

noting, however, that considering the importance of this topic, we are surprised at the unsettled state of the empirical literature.[2]

Although in Part I we present the supply and demand sides of the market, we do not present a selection which combines them in a market which sets wages or allocates labor. This task is left for an instructor or for consideration in a supplementary textbook. The related topic of equilibrium in the labor market is considered in some of the articles on wage differentials in Part VII.

The basic theory of the labor market is by itself a useful analytical device. Later parts of the volume add the refinements needed when certain competitive assumptions are relaxed (as in Part IIIB, on monopsony) or when institutional considerations are introduced (as in Part VIII, on minimum wages). The end result of these extensions, hopefully, is a more general theory of the labor market.

---

[2] For a survey of the "production function" literature see Marc Nerlove, "Recent Empirical Studies of the CES and Related Production Functions," in Murray Brown *et al., The Theory and Empirical Analysis of Production* (New York: National Bureau of Economic Research, Inc., 1967), pp. 55–136.

1
The Supply of
Factors of Production

Milton Friedman

The Factors of Production

Our discussion of demand for factors of production was in highly abstract terms; we did not consider the specific character of the factors of production or give them names. The reason is that on the demand side, there seems no empirical classification of factors that has such special importance as to deserve being singled out; the classification that is useful will vary from problem to problem. On the demand side, the chief consideration in classifying factors is substitution in production. A single factor consists of units that are regarded as perfect substitutes in production; different factors consist of units that are not perfect substitutes. For some problems, it will be desirable to separate out many different factors of production; for others, only a few.

It has traditionally been supposed that

Reprinted from Milton Friedman, *Price Theory: A Provisional Text* (Chicago: Aldine Publishing Company, 1962; revised edition, 1966); copyright © 1962 by Aldine Publishing Company, pp. 199–225.

conditions of supply give a more substantial and empirically significant basis for distinguishing among factors of production in specific terms. The classical economists distinguished three main factors of production: land, capital, and labor. Land they regarded as a permanent non-reproducible resource fixed in amount, the supply of which was therefore perfectly inelastic to the economy as a whole. Capital they regarded as a reproducible resource, the amount of which could be altered through deliberate productive action, so its supply was not perfectly inelastic. Indeed, in the main, they tended to regard it as highly elastic. Labor, like capital, they regarded as reproducible and expansible, and, indeed, as supplied to the economy in the long-run at constant cost, yet to be distinguished from capital because of its dual status as a productive resource and an ultimate consumer.

This particular tripartite division was doubtless a consequence of the particular social problems that were important at the time the classical theory was developed and the social structure in which the industrial revolution occurred in England. There may still be some problems for which it is important to distinguish land from other resources, but for most problems it hardly seems important to do so. In most contexts now important, land, in any economically relevant sense, is indistinguishable from other forms of capital. The productive power of the soil can be produced at a cost by drainage, fertilization and the like, and is clearly not permanent. Land rent, even in the customary meaning of the term, has become a much smaller fraction of total income in advanced countries in the course of time.

From a broad viewpoint, there is much to be said for regarding all sources of productive power as capital. Much of the productive power of what we call labor is clearly the product of deliberate investment; and is produced in the same sense as machinery or buildings. Human productive power is substitutable for non-human productive power, and can be produced in place of the latter at a cost. Indeed, one of the striking features of capitalist development is the tendency for a larger and larger fraction of total investment to take the form of human capital. What is designated as "property" income is in general a smaller fraction of total income —despite the much greater absolute amount of physical capital—the more advanced the society. It is a smaller fraction in the United States, for example, than in Burma or India, probably also than in France or Great Britain, and probably also in the United States today than a hundred years ago.

Even though we recognize that all sources of productive services can be regarded as capital, our social and political institutions make it desirable to recognize that there is an important distinction for many problems between two broad categories of capital—human and non-human capital. We can explore the significance of this distinction by examining Marshall's discussion of the special "peculiarities" of labor which in his view justify distinguishing it from other factors. He lists five peculiarities:

1. "The worker sells his work, but retains capital in himself."
2. "The seller of labor must deliver it himself."
3. "Labor is perishable."
4. "The sellers of it are often at a disadvantage in bargaining."
5. A "great length of time [is] required for providing additional supplies of specialized ability."

As Marshall recognizes, the first two of these peculiarities stand on a rather different footing than the others. Labor is perishable in the sense that the depreciation of the source of labor services (the human being) depends primarily on time rather than on rate of use, so if today's labor services are not used they cannot very readily be stored and there is not a correspondingly larger amount available tomorrow. But this is equally true of much non-human capital— of the services of a bridge or a road or a machine that deteriorates primarily with time, or, economically speaking, of an automobile, whose physical characteristics can be preserved but whose economic value cannot because of obsolescence.

Again, the bargaining disadvantage is by no means always on the side of labor, as Marshall points out and as experience has amply demonstrated since. Insofar as there is any systematic difference on this score, it would seem to be an indirect effect of item (1). Since non-human capital can be bought and sold, it is easier to borrow on such capital than it is to borrow on prospective earning power, and it is possible to get funds by selling some of it, whereas this is not possible with human capital. More generally, a "bargaining" problem of any kind arises only when the market is not competitive; and indeed, strictly speaking, only when it is competitive on neither the selling nor the buying side. But then the bargaining advantage depends on which party is the monopolist, or if both are, on their relative monopoly power, and it is hard to see that this depends intimately on whether the resource in question is or is not labor.

Again, item (5) is at most a question of degree. A great length of time is required for other kinds of capital: the Suez and Panama Canals and the investments involved in the early stages of the radio, aviation, and television industries come readily to mind.

Items (1) and (2) are on a different footing, since they derive from the basic institutional character of our society. These peculiarities would disappear only in a slave society and there only for the slaves. The fact that human capital sources cannot in our society be bought or sold means, as was noted above, that human capital does not provide as good a reserve against emergencies as non-human capital. In consequence, the larger the fraction of any given total income that comes from human capital, the greater we should expect to be the desire to save. In the second place, this fact reduces the scope of market forces in investment in human capital. The individual who invests in a machine can own the machine and so be sure that he gets the return from his investment. The individual who invests in another individual cannot get this kind of assurance. Individuals have incentives to invest in themselves or their progeny that they do not have to invest in machines. Thus there may readily be either underinvestment or overinvestment in human relative to non-human capital.

Finally, the fact that human capital sources cannot be bought and sold is the basic reason for Marshall's second peculiarity: it is only for this reason that the seller of labor must deliver it himself. But this means that non-pecuniary considerations become relevant to the use of human capital in a way that they do not for non-human capital. The owner of land, for example, has no reason to be concerned whether the land is used in a way that is "pleasant" or "unpleasant" or the owner of a horse whether the horse is used in work that it "enjoys" or does not "enjoy," provided both types of work involve the same effect of the land's or the horse's subsequent productivity. The owner of labor-power, on the other hand, does have reason to be concerned. He is required, as it were, to make a tie-in contract: his sale of labor-power is tied-in with the "purchase" of the conditions of work, the pleasantness of the task, etc., etc.

These special considerations applying to human capital affect its supply in ways that deserve further consideration, so we shall turn to a consideration of the supply of labor in general in the short and long run, and then of the supply of labor in different occupations. Similar consideration is not required for the other factors.

The Supply of Labor as a Whole

Labor is, of course, not homogeneous; an hour of labor of a ditch-digger is not equal to an hour of labor of an airplane pilot. Yet, as always, we can think of constructing a supply curve for labor in general by taking for granted some structure of wage rates and adopting some convention for adding together different kinds of labor. For example, we may define our assumed structure of wage rates in terms of fixed ratios of wages, and then convert actual hours of labor into "equivalent" hours by using these ratios. If we suppose the wage rate of the pilot to be fixed at 10 times the wage rate of the ditch-digger, we can regard one hour of the pilot's labor as equivalent to 10 ditch-digger hours. In this way, we can conceive of the total number of equivalent hours of labor supplied as a function of some index number of the structure of wage rates, say the rate for the ditch-digger, recognizing that at each such rate, the total supply consists in fact of so many hours of ditch-digger's labor, so much of the pilot's labor, etc. And, as always, in following this procedure, we are not supposing that the structure of relative wage rates is in fact determined outside the economic system or is independent of the level of wage rates; we are simply dividing up our problems and considering them one by one.

It seems desirable to distinguish between two kinds of supply curves of labor in general: the supply of labor for a given population of given capacities—the short-run supply of labor—and the supply of labor without such restrictions—the long-run supply of labor. The second clearly involves a "theory" of population.

The Short-Run Supply of Labor

Our given conditions obviously mean that the short-run supply of labor for *all* purposes is perfectly inelastic: 24 hours times the number of people is the available daily supply of labor if we neglect the corrections for different qualities of labor. But clearly, the problem that we are interested in is the supply of labor, not for all purposes, but for use through the market. So the problem we are concerned with is essentially the factors that determine the fraction of the total labor power that is offered for sale on the market.

In our modern society, this fraction is relatively small, so there is considerable room for variation in it. Something less than half the total population is classified as "in the labor force," and these individuals devote only a minor part of their total time to market activities—perhaps one-fourth. Moreover the fraction has undoubtedly varied considerably over time and from country to country.

Perhaps the most widely accepted hypothesis about the short-run supply curve of labor is that it is backward bending above some wage rate, as in Figure 1.1. Each point on this curve is to be interpreted as showing the *maximum* quantity offered at the given price, which is why the negatively sloped segment is said to be "backward bending" rather than "forward-falling." A

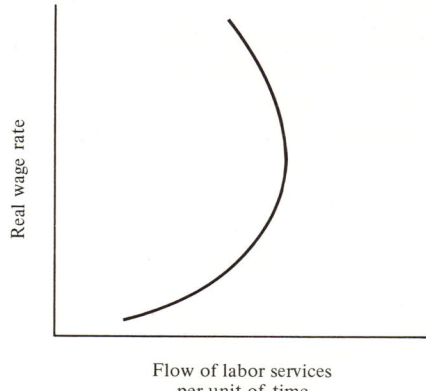

FIGURE 1.1

variety of empirical evidence points to this conclusion. In the first place, as the real wage rate has increased secularly over long periods of time in advanced countries, the average number of hours a week has tended to decline and the fraction of children in the labor market to decrease. The fraction of women has not behaved so systematically, but probably increased. Yet all in all, if such observations over a long period of time were regarded as being on the supply-curve, they would produce a backward bending segment. Additional evidence is furnished by experience in underdeveloped countries, where it seems to be common experience that beyond a fairly low level, an increase in wage rate per hour will reduce the number of hours worked. The natives act as if they wanted a certain sum of money almost regardless of how long they have to work for it; if they can get that sum in fewer hours, they will work fewer hours.

The theoretical explanation offered for the backward bending segment of the supply curve is that a rise in the real wage rate arising from an increased demand for labor has two effects: (1) It makes leisure more expensive, since the cost of an hour of leisure is the wage that could be earned in that hour. This is the substitution effect, and by itself would tend to raise the number of hours worked. (2) If the individual were to work the same number of hours, the rise in the real wage rate increases his real income, which would lead him to want to purchase more of various kinds of goods, including leisure. This is the income effect, and by itself would tend to reduce the number of hours worked unless leisure is an inferior good. The argument, then, is that beyond some point the income effect dominates the substitution effect. It shows up in people working fewer hours, in the withdrawal of supplementary workers (children, wives, etc.) from the labor force, etc. This way of putting it also makes it clear that much depends on the relative value attached to goods purchased with money through the market relative to goods that can be acquired through nonmarket activity. In a primitive society, the initial low wage rate at which the income effect becomes dominant reflects a lack of familiarity with market goods and a limited range of tastes. As tastes develop and knowledge spreads, the point at which the income effect dominates tends to rise.

An objection sometimes raised to an analysis like the above is that individuals cannot determine for themselves the number of hours they work; this is an institutional datum which the individual must take or leave. This objection is almost entirely specious. In the first place, we have seen that much of the adjustment may take the form of the fraction of the people in the labor force. In the second place, even at any given time, a particular individual has some leeway. He can work overtime or not, take off more or less time during the year, choose the kind of occupation or employer that offers the number of hours of work he wants, etc. But neither of these is the basic fallacy. The important point is that the individual is like the perfect competitor: to each individual separately, the number of hours of work per week may be fixed, yet the level at which it is fixed is the result of the choices of the individuals as a group. If at any moment this level of hours is, say, larger than on the average people prefer at the given wage rate, this means that any employer who makes them shorter, who adjusts them to the workers' preferences, will make employment with him more attractive than employment with others. Hence he can attract the better people or attract people at a lower wage rate. Employers thus have an incentive to adjust working conditions and hours to the preferences of the workers. (In our earlier terminology, because of the tie-in character of the transaction, employers are sellers of conditions of work as well as buyers of labor.) Competition in this way does permit individuals in effect to determine for themselves the number of hours they work.

Although the supply curve under discussion is a short-run curve, in the sense that it holds population constant, we have been talking in terms of the effect of alternative levels of real wage-rates each of which is regarded as permanent, i.e., is expected to continue. Clearly, the reaction to a higher wage rate expected to be temporary and then to revert to a lower level will tend to be very different than the reaction to a higher wage rate expected to be permanent. The temporarily higher wage rate would seem more likely to bring forth an increased quantity of labor from a fixed population than a permanently higher one, since there would be strong temptation to take advantage of the opportunity while it lasts and to buy the leisure later.

An interesting case in point is the experience in the United States during World War II, when both the fraction of the population in the labor force and the average number of hours worked per week were substantially higher than during the pre-war period. At first glance, it seems that this increase cannot reflect a response to a higher real wage rate expected to be temporary: money wages rose sharply but so did prices, both openly and indirectly through deterioration in the quality of products, so that average money wages per unit of time divided by an index of prices of consumer goods corrected for quality deterioration may not have risen at all and may even have fallen. Some economists have rationalized this apparent conflict between a constant real wage and an increased quantity of labor supplied by introducing the notion of a "money illusion," namely that suppliers of labor react to nominal money wage rates, not to real wage rates, and that they would behave differently if, say, all nominal prices and wages were doubled.

It is not, however, necessary to introduce a *deus ex machina* such as a money illusion to explain this phenomenon. It can readily be rationalized on the grounds that the apparent failure of real wages to rise is itself an illusion for two reasons. First, many additional persons who entered the labor market would not have been hired previously at the prevailing real wage rate; the real wage rate they could get increased even though average wage rates did not. Indeed, it is possible for the real wage rate to have increased in the relevant sense for every individual separately, yet for the average to have remained unchanged.[1] Second, people may very well have thought that the rise in prices of consumer goods during the war was temporary and that after the war prices would return to their pre-war level. Any part of their wages saved should be deflated by the expected post-war, not the war-time, price level; but if this were done it would be seen that real wages, as evaluated by their recipients, were higher than would be indicated by deflating by current prices alone. This second force is especially important, if, as has been argued, part of the increase in labor supplied is to take advantage of a temporary opportunity. This would mean that laborers would have planned to save an abnormally large part of any increase in income, which would make the expected future price level particularly important. This interpretation is indirectly supported by a number of facts, in particular by the abnormally high fraction of income saved during the war period and the extent to which such savings were accumulated in the form of assets fixed in nominal value (government bonds, cash, etc.) rather than as equity securities or real goods. Of course, the expectations about the future price level were, in the event, disappointed, but a mistaken prediction of the future is in a very different class than an illusion about the present.

The Long-Run Supply of Labor

If we turn to the problem of the long-run supply of labor, we must analyze the effect of the real wage rate on the size of the population and the qualities and skills it possesses. We need, that is, a theory of population and a theory of investment in the human agent. It is clear that these two are not unrelated: additional labor power can be produced either by increasing the number of laborers or by investing more capital in each laborer. For simplicity, we shall phrase the following discussion in terms of the size of population, though much of it also applies to investment in the human agent.

To begin with, the theory of population was regarded as an essential element of economic theory, and the Malthusian theory of population was a cornerstone of classical economic theory. In its crudest form, the Malthusian doctrine was that labor is a form of capital which, like other capital, can be produced at a cost; that it is produced under conditions of constant cost, the level of this constant cost being the

---

[1] To illustrate this possibility, suppose there is no variation possible in the number of hours worked by a laborer if he works; the wage rate at which labor of type A can initially get employment is $1 an hour; labor of type B, $.50 an hour; there are 50 laborers of type A and 50 of type B; the laborers of type A are willing to work at $1 an hour; laborers of type B are unwilling to work at $.50 an hour. Initially, then, only labor of type A will be working and the average wage rate will be $1 an hour. Let the (real) wage rate offered for labor of type A go up to $1.25 an hour and for labor of type B to $.75 an hour. Suppose that at these wage rates, laborers of both types are willing to work and that both work the same number of hours. The average wage rate will still be $1 an hour, yet the wage rate that is relevant to the supply of labor has risen for every worker separately.

minimum standard of living consistent with preservation. If the wage provides a standard of living above this level, marriages will tend to occur earlier, the birth rate to rise, the death rate to fall, and the population tend to increase; and conversely. In this form, the theory leads to a perfectly elastic long-run supply curve of labor, as in Figure 1.2, where $0W$ is the wage rate that provides the minimum standard of living.

Even in this crude form, the theory is consistent with much observed evidence, some available to Malthus and more experienced since his time. Some extreme examples are furnished by the Philippines and Puerto Rico. The large amount of capital invested in the Philippines by the United States over the period of a half-century has been accompanied by an approximate tripling of the population with little or no change in the average standard of living. Similarly, a major effect of increased U.S. assistance to Puerto Rico, especially since 1933, has been a very rapid rise in population. Numerous other examples could be cited.

At the same time, if $0W$ is interpreted as essentially a technologically-determined datum, the experience of most countries in the Western world contradicts the crude Malthusian theory. In such countries, the real wage has risen dramatically in the last century-and-a-half. True, population has also risen, but by nothing like the extent that would have been required to wipe out the gain in average real income.

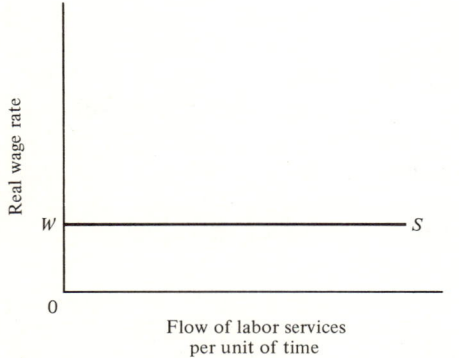

FIGURE 1.2

This apparent contradiction of the Malthusian theory led to its rejection by economists and, indeed, essentially to the exclusion of population theory from economics. Population, it was said, depends primarily on a host of non-economic considerations which are not within our competence or field of interest. For our purposes, we shall take population for granted, and leave the explanation of population change to demographers, sociologists, and the like. More recently, economists have renewed their interest in population theory and have become again concerned with reintegrating the theory of population with economic theory—a development that is to be encouraged.

One way of working toward a theory of population that is consistent with experience in the Western world and at the same time is coherent with economic theory as a whole is to re-examine the Malthusian theory and interpret it in a more sophisticated fashion. Instead of taking the essence of the Malthusian theory to be the existence of a technologically-determined cost of production of human beings, we can regard its essence as being the notion that the production of human beings is to be regarded as if it were a deliberative economic choice determined by the balancing of returns and costs. From this point of view, children are to be regarded in a dual role: they are a consumption good, a way of spending one's income to acquire satisfaction, an alternative to purchasing automobiles or domestic service or other goods; and they are a capital good produced by economic activity, an alternative to producing machines or houses or the like.

Viewed as a consumption good, the amount produced will be determined by the relative cost of children versus other consumer goods, the income available for all uses, and the tastes and preferences of the individuals in question. Non-economic forces enter the picture primarily in determining these tastes and preferences. Viewed as a capital good, the amount produced will be determined by the returns that this capital good is expected to earn relative to other capital goods, and the relative costs of producing this and alternative capital goods. A major difference between this and other capital goods is the possibility of appropriating the returns by the individual who makes the initial capital investment. The fact that children are, in this sense, a joint product means that the two sets of considerations need to be combined: the returns from the children as capital goods may be taken as reducing their costs as consumer goods. Were it not for this factor, it is pretty clear that gross underinvestment in human capital would be almost inevitable in a free society.

From this broader point of view, $0W$ in Figure 1.2 is not to be regarded as a technologically-determined datum but as a rather complex resultant of the factors just discussed—a phenomenon that was already emphasized in Malthus' time in the description of $0W$ as a "conventional" minimum, with emphasis on the possibility of raising it by altering people's tastes and values.

Along these lines, the failure of population to increase in the Western world as fast as crude Malthusian theory suggested may have reflected simply a rise in the costs of children relative to the return from them, and need not even have involved a change of tastes. A number of factors that presumably operated in this direction come to mind: (1) The cost of raising children is clearly greater in the city than in rural areas, and economic development in the Western world involved extensive shifts to cities. (2) Returns from children as capital goods are also lower in the city than in the country, because they are in general less valuable at early ages, and, moreover, the mores in the city are such that they are likely to cease contributing the returns from their productive use to the family at an earlier age. (3) The loosening family ties that came as a concomitant of industrialization made the children less valuable as a means of providing unemployment and old-age security. (4) With growing real income, the aspect of children as consumer's goods became more important than as factors of production— that is, the services yielded by children as a consumer's good are a superior good. But this meant sending children to school longer and keeping them out of the labor market longer, which reduced the positive return to parents from children, increased the cost involved and made children more expensive relative to other consumer goods. This list is not intended to be exhaustive but rather to be suggestive. Clearly some counterbalancing items need to be included as well.

The modified Malthusian doctrine may be consistent not only with historical developments in the Western world but also with many currently observed phenomena. For example, the higher birth rate in the country than in the city is clearly consistent with the considerations cited above. Indeed, from this point of view, the tendency for a net migration from the country to the city in the United States can be interpreted very differently than is generally the case. It is usually interpreted as reflecting a disequilibrium position in the process of correction, but with so much friction that the corrective process proceeds slowly or "too slowly," so the return to the farmer is on the average below its long-run equilibrium value relative to the return to the city dweller. The alternative interpretation suggested by the above analysis is that rural areas have a comparative advantage in the production of human capital as well as of food; that people in rural areas are involved, as it were, in two industries that are pursued jointly—the production of food and of human capital—and that they engage in net exports of both to the city. On this interpretation, the net flow of population from country to city is no evidence of disequilibrium but of equilibrium, and part of the return to rural families are the returns they get either in pecuniary or nonpecuniary form from their children.

Another observed phenomenon that may fit this analysis is the strong tendency for the number of children produced per family to be smaller in "higher" socio-economic classes than in "lower" socio-economic classes (higher among professional and business people, for example, than among unskilled workers). Yet it is not clear whether there is a tendency within socio-economic classes for the number of children to be lower the higher the income. Items (3) and (4) above indicate one way in which these phenomena can be explained. Because of different taste and opportunities, the relative costs of children are different in different socio-economic classes. Perhaps the major factor is that in the higher classes, the child is likely to stay in school longer and, of great importance, to get a kind of education which must be privately paid for, whereas in the lower classes, education is more likely to be publicly paid for or earned by the child himself. Thus children are more expensive relative to other consumer goods the higher the socio-economic class. But these factors may not operate within socio-economic classes, so it would not be surprising to find that the higher the income within such a class, the larger the number of children.

Again, indirect evidence for such an interpretation is provided by the relation between the birth rate and general economic conditions, and by the effects of special subsidies provided by state action for children. Both Hitler and Mussolini introduced such subsidies, and various family allowance schemes, for example, the current French scheme, involve such a subsidy. There seems some evidence that such schemes have in fact had a significant effect on the rate of population growth.

This analysis can by no means be regarded as well established, or even well defined. But it does seem one of the more promising directions in which an economic theory of population is capable of being developed.

The Supply of Labor In Different Occupations

In discussing the supply curve of labor in general, we have taken for granted the structure of wage rates for labor of different kinds—relative wages in different occupations. This structure of wages is itself determined by the relative demand for and supply of labor of different kinds. The reason we have been putting it aside and are able to analyze it separately is because the major forces determining the supply curves of labor in particular occupations can be regarded as largely, though of course not entirely, independent of those determining the total supply of labor.

At any given time, there will exist some structure of relative wage rates (or average earnings) in different occupations. It is useful to regard this structure as the result of three kinds of forces or phenomena producing differentials between wage rates in different occupations:

1. *Factors other than wage rates that affect the attractiveness of different occupations to individuals in a position to choose among them:* Even if there were perfect competition, perfect and costless mobility, and all members of the population had identical abilities, money wage rates in different occupations would by no means be equal. Some occupations are less attractive than others and will therefore have to offer a higher wage than others if they are to attract people to them. Given differences in tastes, the precise set of differentials that will arise in this way depends not only on the characteristics of the occupations but also on the conditions of demand. If the demand for an occupation is relatively small, it may be possible to staff it entirely with people who regard it as more attractive than other occupations, in which case the wage rate would, on this score alone, be relatively low; if, on the other hand, the demand is relatively large, it can be met only by attracting people into the occupation who regard other occupations as more attractive, in which case the wage rate would have to be relatively high. Differentials in wage rates which arise from this set of forces may be termed *equalizing differences*.

2. *Factors that produce non-competing*

groups: For a variety of reasons, not all people are in a position to choose freely—not even once during their lifetime—among occupations. The existence of such barriers to the staffing of particular occupations produces a series of partly sheltered, though not entirely unrelated, markets, and inhibits the operation of the forces discussed above. Differences in natural ability can be classified under this heading, although they could perhaps also be classified under the preceding one. Differentials in wage rates arising from this set of forces may be termed *differences arising from non-competing groups.*

3. *Incomplete adjustment to changes in demand or supply:* The immediate effect on wage rates of any change in the demand for or supply of labor of various kinds may be very different from its ultimate effect. This is a market in which it may take a long time for the ultimate effect to be felt—for the immediate effect to produce reactions that will lead to a new equilibrium. At any time, therefore, some part of the differences in wage rates may be regarded as attributable to incompleteness of adjustment. Of course, what comes under this heading depends on one's viewpoint, on the conditions that are being held constant for the purpose in hand, since by "adjustment" we mean adjustment to some given set of conditions. If this given set of conditions defines market demand and supply curves, the existing position involves full adjustment to them, and nothing comes under this heading. The longer the run, which means the narrower and more ultimate the set of conditions taken as given, the more comes under this heading. Differentials in wage rates arising from incompleteness of adjustment may be termed *transitional differences.*

Equalizing Differences In Wage Rates

To simplify the discussion of the supply of labor in different occupations, let us concentrate on two particular occupations, say A and B. We can then summarize the conditions of supply for these occupations as in Figure 1.3. The vertical axis shows the wage rate in A relative to the wage rate in B, both being expressed in some common and convenient form, say per hour. The horizontal axis shows the number of man-hours supplied in A relative to the number in B. The curve then shows the maximum relative number of man-hours that would be supplied at various relative wage rates.

This method of summarizing supply conditions is not, of course, perfectly general, and implies something about the conditions of supply. For it might be that the relative number of man-hours supplied depends not only on the relative wage rate but also on the absolute wage rates—for example, that the relative supply would be different at wage rates of $3 in A and $1.50 in B than at wage rates of $6 in A and $3 in B. However, this kind of effect is not something we are going to be able to say much about, and its neglect is more than compensated for by the convenience of the above mode of summarizing supply conditions. Of course, the supply curve is only valid for given "other" conditions; in particular, for given alternative employment opportunities.

If all individuals had identical tastes and abilities, they would, given the same information, evaluate identically the relative merits of different occupations. The result would be that a supply curve like that in Figure 1.3 would be horizontal: there would be some relative wage rate that would be

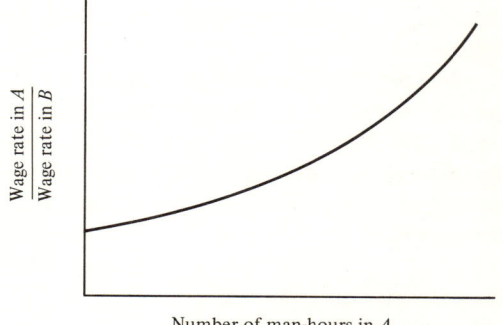

FIGURE 1.3

regarded by all as making the two occupations equally attractive. At any higher relative wage rate, all would go into A; at any lower relative wage rate, all would go into B. Differences in tastes, abilities, or information about the two occupations will lead to differences among individuals in the relative wage rates regarded as making the two occupations equally attractive and will introduce a slope into the curve, as in Figure 1.3.

We can organize our discussion most conveniently by classifying the factors affecting the supply curve into three categories: (a) those that determine the relative pecuniary attractiveness of the two occupations; (b) the variability of income in the two occupations; (c) non-pecuniary differences among the occupations. A major reason for this particular breakdown is that the factors in the first category affect all individuals (at least, all of equal ability) alike and so should affect mainly the height of the supply curve; they are almost the only factors that would have to be taken into account in a "slave" society, and their counterparts are relevant in drawing the supply curve of the services of non-human capital for one use or another. The second and third categories introduce the factors that become important because of the peculiarities attached to human capital.

(a) Factors Capable of Actuarial Evaluation. Consider a slave owner deciding whether to specialize and train his slaves to pursue occupation A or occupation B. This decision may not, of course, be irrevocable; an individual trained for A may be able at a later date to shift to B, but generally only at considerable cost. In making his decision, the slave owner would want to know much more than the wage rate per hour in the two occupations: A, for example, might be seasonal, B not seasonal, which might make the expected number of hours of work per year lower in A than in B; A might be more affected by cyclical movements than B, so the expected number of years of work would be lower in A than in B; A might be an occupation requiring great physical strength, so that the number of years during which an individual could be employed in A might be lower than in B, which might be a sedentary occupation; A might require a longer period of training; and so on and on.

The effect of all such factors can be summarized in the expected net returns from each occupation for any given wage rate and for each age of the worker, as in Figure 1.4. The net return for any occupation and year depends, of course, on precisely what are regarded as occupational expenses and so deducted from gross returns. A literal slave owner would regard the cost of feeding, housing, and clothing the slaves as an occupational expense; he would be interested only in the excess of earnings over this sum. Thanks to the dual nature of human beings in our society—as factors of production and as ultimate consumers to satisfy whose wants production is carried on—it is impossible or nearly impossible to distinguish the part of a man's consumption that is to be regarded as an occupational expense (required to maintain him as a productive resource) from final consumption.[2] Perhaps the best procedure is to deduct only those occupational expenses that are clearly special to a particular occupation, and to regard the minimum expenses beyond this that are necessary to maintain the human being as a factor of production as the same in all occupations. This treatment accounts for the initial segment of zero net returns in Figure 1.4, which is intended to display the features of a "typical" pattern of lifetime returns. The subsequent segment of negative returns refers to the period of training, when special outlays—for tuition fees, books,

---

[2] One of the ways of rationalizing the personal exemption and credit for dependents under the income tax is as an allowance for occupational expenses of this kind. Similarly, the pressure for an "earned income credit" derives from the recognition that all expenses are deducted in computing taxable income from non-human capital, but not in computing taxable income from human capital.

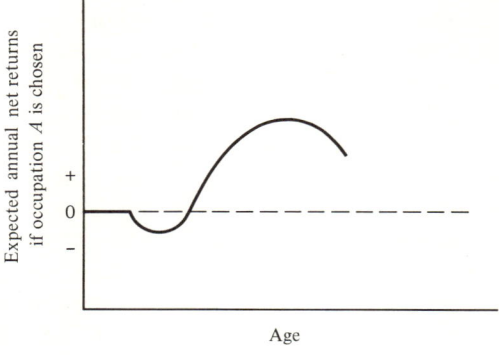

FIGURE 1.4

equipment, etc.—are likely to exceed any positive returns. Thereafter, in general net returns rise to a peak and subsequently decline. In addition to the more obvious occupational expenses, it is clear that income taxes should also be deducted in computing net returns.

Since the figures plotted are *expected* net returns, they conceal wide differences among the returns to different individuals and are affected by the likelihood of unemployment. Similarly, the declining segment in part reflects not only a possible decline in the productivity of the active worker with age, but also the smaller probability that an individual will be actively earning income as he grows older because of voluntary retirement, retirement or idleness forced by ill health, or death. Note also that the vertical axis shows the returns if occupation A is *chosen* and not from the practice of occupation A. It therefore includes earnings from other occupations that may be followed instead of A by people who choose A initially. The reason for this is that one factor affecting the attractiveness of different occupations is precisely the relative value that training for an occupation has in carrying on other occupations.

While the shape of the curve in Figure 1.4 is reasonably typical, it will of course differ from occupation to occupation in detail. The amount of capital investment varies widely and with it the age at which expected earnings become positive. The peakedness of the curve and the age at which the peak is reached likewise vary widely.

The simple average level of lifetime earnings is not, of course, adequate to summarize the attractiveness of a particular lifetime earnings pattern, even to the impersonal slave-owner, in a world in which the interest rate is not zero, the timing of the returns matters also. For example, suppose the lifetime earnings patterns for A and B are as in Figure 1.5 and that both have the same average level. A is then clearly the more attractive financially, since the excess earnings in A in early years could be invested at interest and so yield a sum not available in B. To take account of this effect, we can compute the present capital value of the expected net returns in each occupation. Let $E_1\ E_2, \ldots$ be the expected annual returns in years 1, 2, ... and r be the interest rate. Then $V = \dfrac{E_1}{1+r} + \dfrac{E_2}{(1+r)^2} + \cdots$ is the capital value in year zero of the stream of expected returns.

It will be recalled that the lifetime earning curves and so the capital values were computed for particular wage rates. To summarize the effect of the category of factors now under consideration, we can ask what relative wage rate would make the capital values in the two occupations equal. Suppose this were a wage rate 1.4 times as high in A as in B. We could then say that at this rate the two occupations would be equally attractive financially or actuarially, and that if actuarial attractiveness were the only con-

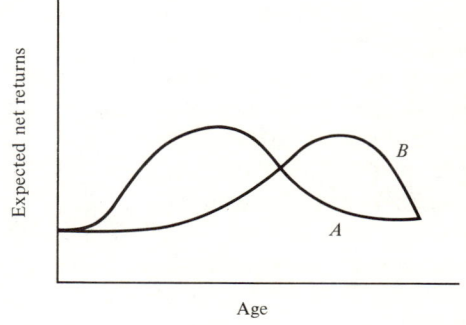

FIGURE 1.5

sideration, the supply curve would be a horizontal line at a relative wage rate of 1.4, as in Figure 1.6.

We have already listed many of the factors that will affect the relative wage rate that will make two occupations equally attractive financially: seasonal and cyclical variability of employment, length of training, direct cost of training, direct occupational expenses subsequent to training, tax structure, length of working life in an occupation, temporal pattern of earnings over the course of a working lifetime, etc. There are doubtless many others that might be important for one or another particular occupation, so that a complete statement is impossible. A self-contained analytical apparatus for taking such factors into account is both possible and desirable; a self-contained and complete list of the empirical factors to be taken into account is not.

(b) *Variability of Returns.* As already noted, the average net returns that enter into the capital values defined above conceal differences of return from individual to individual. These differences are of little importance to the slave-owner—at least if we assume him to own enough slaves—since they will tend to cancel out and so he can concentrate on the expected return. To the individual in our society choosing an occupation, they cannot so easily be put to one side. He will want to know not only the present capital value of expected returns but also the distribution of returns—or more compactly, the probability distribution of present capital values. Occupations *A* and *B,* for example, may be equally attractive financially, yet *A* may be an occupation like, say movie acting, offering a small chance of a very high reward together with a large chance of a small reward, while *B* may be an occupation like typing, offering reasonable certainty of a particular return with no great chance of wide departures in either direction.

The effect of this variability depends, of course, on the tastes of individuals with respect to risk or uncertainty. If we accept the expected utility theory of choice, the wage-rates that will render two occupations equally attractive to an individual will be those that will equate the expected utility from them rather than the expected money return or capital value.

If all people had the same tastes with respect to uncertainty, the effect of different variability of returns would be to raise or lower the height of a supply curve like the horizontal one in Figure 1.6 for *A* and *B* at a relative wage rate of 1.4 for *A*. If, for example, *A* offered a small chance of a large return while *B* offered only moderate variability, and if people in general preferred the former kind of uncertainty to the latter, the effect of variability would be to reduce the height of the curve from 1.4 to a lower number, say 1.3, the difference measuring, as it were, the price people are willing to pay to get the kind of uncertainty they like. For example, it is probably true that more people prefer the kind of variability ascribed above to movie acting to the kind ascribed to typing, and in consequence it is my guess that the average returns to movie actors—account being taken of failures as well as of successes—is less than the average returns to typists.

Of course, people do not all have the same tastes. Some will prefer the kind of variability just attributed to *A,* some the kind attributed to *B.* The former will be attracted to *A* at a wage rate below 1.4, the latter only at a higher wage rate, so the

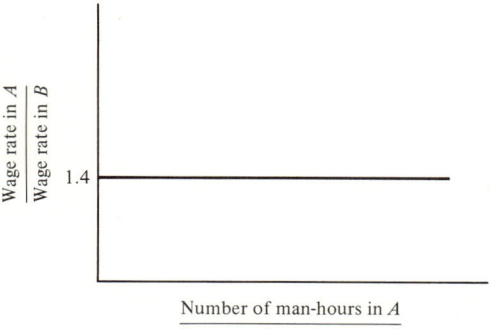

FIGURE 1.6

supply curve will be given a positive slope as in Figure 1.7. If $0A$ exceeds unity, it would be reasonable to say that on balance people prefer the kind of variability offered by A, and conversely.

(c) **Non-Pecuniary Advantages.** In addition to the factors affecting the money returns from different occupations, there are many other factors that affect their attractiveness to any given individual—the kind of work involved, the location at which it is carried on, the social prestige attached to it, and so on. Like variability of income, some such factors may be evaluated pretty much alike by most people; in this case, their effect is to shift the supply curve upward or downward. Insofar as people differ in their evaluation of non-pecuniary advantages and disadvantages, the effect is to impart a slope to the supply curve. Perhaps the extreme case of difference is if some prefer occupation A over B and others B over A, no matter what the relative pecuniary returns. In this case, the supply curve will be perfectly inelastic.

If there were no differences in tastes or abilities, and an essentially perfect market, all supply curves would be perfectly elastic and relative wage rates would be determined completely by conditions of supply; conditions of demand would determine only the number in each occupation. In this case, all differences in return would be equalizing, and equalizing to all individuals. That is, the structure of wage rates would be such that each individual would be indifferent which occupation be pursued; there would then be no "rents." At the other extreme, at which individuals are swayed exclusively by non-pecuniary considerations and there are wide differences in tastes, supply curves would be completely inelastic and relative wage rates would be determined by conditions of demand. All wages would, as it were, be price-determined instead of price-determining and so be "rents."

In the more general case, in which there are differences in tastes and abilities but they do not completely determine the choice of occupations, supply curves will be positively sloped. In this case, differences in return will be equalizing *only at the margin*. Some individuals will be receiving a rent in the sense that they would be willing to pursue their occupation at a lower total return, though even these will be on the margin in the sense that they regard the additional return from working a little longer or harder as just compensating for the additional costs involved in doing so. There is, that is, an extensive margin and an intensive one. An increase in demand will tend to push the extensive margins outward by attracting more individuals into the occupation. Its effect on the intensive margin is less certain for the reasons discussed above in connection with the backward bending short-run supply curve of labor in general.

(d) **The Effect of Income Taxes.** It seems worth singling out for special attention the effect of income taxes, first, because they have so greatly increased in importance in recent years; second, because there is such general misunderstanding of their role and such widespread belief that they cannot be "shifted"; third, because they are omitted from the list of factors discussed explicitly by Friedman and Kuznets.[3]

As already noted, the relevant figure for the individual to compare in judging the

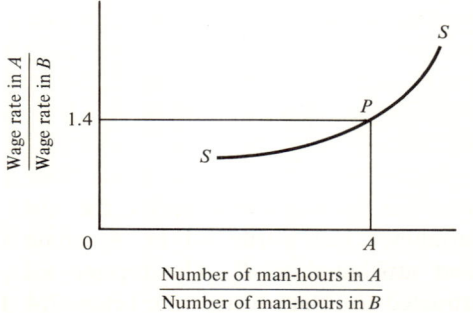

FIGURE 1.7

[3] Milton Friedman and Simon Kuznets, *Income from Independent Professional Practice* (New York: National Bureau of Economic Research, 1945).

relative attractiveness of two occupations is return after taxes, not return before taxes. It has frequently been argued that income taxes do not affect this choice because a larger income before taxes means also a larger income after taxes, and hence if one occupation is more attractive than the other before taxes, it will be more attractive after taxes. Unfortunately, this is not true, partly because the base of the tax is not the same as the figure that is relevant in considering net pecuniary return, partly because the tax base cannot take account of non-pecuniary factors.

Consider first a straight proportional income tax with no exemptions. Even this tax will affect the relative returns in different occupations. The most obvious reason will be if the tax base does not permit the deduction of all expenses regarded as occupational expenses in choosing between occupations and these differ from occupation to occupation. But even if the tax base is the same in this sense as the return relevant to the choice among occupations, it is almost sure to differ in other senses. For example, let one occupation yield a return that varies from year to year for any given individual and is sometimes negative, whereas another yields the same income during each year of work. Unless the tax provides for a subsidy (a negative payment) when net income is negative, the tax burden will be heavier on the first occupation than on the second, so that at a relative wage rate that would make the present capital value of the two occupations equal before taxes, the capital value will be smaller in the first occupation after allowance for taxes. This particular effect is by no means a curiosity; it arises especially between occupations that require training and those that do not, since in the former the return is, as we saw earlier, likely to be negative during earlier years. In these cases, the neglect of negative incomes is the same as not permitting the expenses of training to be deducted in computing taxable income.

The effects so far considered could in principle be eliminated by proper definition of the base. But this is hardly possible if two occupations differ in non-pecuniary attractiveness, so that a higher monetary return is required in one than in the other to make them equally attractive. In this case, it would take a higher relative return with the tax than without it to make the two occupations equally attractive. In effect, the non-pecuniary advantages of the lower-paid occupation is not subject to the tax, so that one way to avoid the tax is to engage in occupations with large non-pecuniary advantages.

The introduction of an exemption and of progressive rates has additional effects. An occupation in which an individual's income fluctuates from year to year will tend to be more heavily taxed for a given present value before tax than one in which it is constant from year to year. Here again, changes in the tax law to provide "averaging" of income might eliminate this effect, but no changes can very well eliminate a comparable effect when the variability is between people. Suppose that occupation A and B promise in advance the same average income before tax, but in A income varies more from individual to individual than in B. Then with a progressive tax schedule, average income after tax will be lower in A than in B. The progressive tax accentuates the effect of the non-pecuniary advantages mentioned above, for with such a tax, the ratio of incomes after tax will be lower than before tax.

It follows that the existence of an income tax does affect the choice of occupations and so the allocation of resources among different uses. Indeed, if all differences in income were equalizing, in the sense that supply curves of the kind we have been drawing were horizontal, an income tax would have no redistributive effects at all, no matter how steeply graduated. Relative wages after tax would be the same with a steeply graduated tax as with a flat tax. The reason is that people would leave occupations specially affected by the steeply graduated tax (occupations that are highly paid to compensate for extreme non-pecuniary disadvantages, or that offer highly variable returns, etc.) and enter those less affected by it until this pattern of relative wage rates was attained. The same relative wage rates after tax would, of course, mean higher wage rates before tax in the occupations affected by the steeply graduated tax, and this would curtail the quantity demanded to match the reduced quantity supplied.

More generally, differences in taste will produce a positively sloping supply curve, so that the form of tax will affect the relative wage rates. The reduction in numbers employed in the occupations specially affected by the steeply graduated tax would be produced by the exodus (or better the failure to enter) of those who had the least attachment to these occupations on non-pecuniary grounds. The final result would be a lower relative wage after tax than with a flat tax, though, of course, a higher relative wage before tax.

It is clear that this analysis of the income tax parallels the usual analysis of excise taxes. And indeed, it seems likely that corresponding to any given income tax, there is, in principle, some set of excise taxes on final services that would have precisely the same allocative and distributive effects.

Differences Arising from Noncompeting Groups

In order for differences in return to be predominantly equalizing—that is, produced by the factors discussed in the preceding section—it is clearly necessary that many individuals be in a position to choose freely between the occupations in question. Now to a very large extent this is the case, and, accordingly many existing differences in wage rates can be regarded as equalizing differences. But there is considerable evidence that not all differences in return can be so regarded. In particular, differences in return between such broad classes of occupations as professional and nonprofessional seem considerably larger than can be explained in terms of differences in costs, non-pecuniary advantages or disadvantages, and the like.

The additional factor that enters in such cases is a barrier of some kind or other to entry into the better-paid occupations. Only some individuals are free to choose these occupations; they constitute, in Cairnes' happy term, a "noncompeting group." Many different causes may give rise to barriers to entry and so to the establishment of noncompeting groups, and it may be desirable to list some of the more important.

(1) *Deliberate restrictions on entry.* Immigration restrictions, for example, make American workers a noncompeting group relative to workers in other countries. Within the country, the requirement of a license to practice an occupation—as in medicine, law, and the like—may be a means of deliberately restricting entry. The granting of licenses is generally placed in the hands of people currently in the occupation and they have an understandable incentive to restrict entry. Again, trade union power to force an employer to pay no less than an agreed wage is a means of restricting entry into the occupation.

Restrictions of this kind are extremely numerous in detail and have been growing in recent decades. But, however vexatious, I would judge that except perhaps for the immigration restrictions they have not been of major empirical importance; almost surely they have not been as important as some of the other barriers to be mentioned.

(2) *Geographic immobility.* This is often cited as a cause of differences in return, particularly for alleged differences between North and South and country and city. It seems doubtful, however, that, except for particular and isolated cases, it is of any major importance in the United States. Census figures show quite extraordinary movements of people. During the 1940's, for example, the movement within the United States quite dwarfed in magnitude the forced movements of population in Europe, both those forced by the Nazis and those forced by the Soviets. And it must be recalled that

it is not necessary for everyone to move. Mobility at the margin is enough.

(3) *Differences in ability.* It is somewhat arbitrary whether to regard differences in ability as creating noncompeting groups or to combine them with differences in taste and regard them as giving rise to equalizing differences. It is clear that they will produce differences in returns as between individuals greater than is required to compensate for differences in costs incurred and the like; in effect, one individual is more units of labor power than another, more human capital. The effect on wage rates in identifiable occupations arises because different occupations will tend to be staffed—or to require —different average levels of ability. Of course, there is no objective standard of "higher" and "lower" abilities that will be respected by the market: whether a particular type of ability will be highly remunerated depends entirely on whether the demand for it is high relative to the supply available.

Some examples may perhaps show why it is difficult to distinguish differences in "ability," in the economically relevant sense, from differences in "taste," and why it is tempting to include them with the factors giving rise to equalizing differences. Is the relatively high compensation of a deep-sea diver to be regarded as a reward for the scarce ability of being willing to work under water and in dangerous circumstances or for the nonpecuniary disadvantages of the trade? What of the stunt-artist? The physician? Obviously there is a large area where "ability" and "tastes" merge.

(4) *Socio-economic stratification of the society.* In many countries it is still true and in most countries it was true not so long ago that perhaps the major source of internal barriers to entry was posed by the stratification of the population into social classes. In general, the learned professions and certain other occupations have been freely open only to members of the upper classes, and so on down the line. Of course, stratification was never complete—there was always some possibility of upward mobility—but the hindrances in the path of such mobility sufficed to maintain wide differentials in rate of return.

This kind of strictly social stratification has never been as important in this country as in most others and it has clearly been decreasing greatly over time, in large measure because of the wide availability of education. Its decreasing importance is clearly revealed in the behavior of relative wages in clerical and manual professions. Literacy was at one time sufficiently rare to give rise to a noncompeting group; it clearly is so no longer. In consequence, there has been a long-term downward trend in the ratio of earnings in clerical pursuits to earnings in manual pursuits. From being considerably higher paid, clerical pursuits are probably now in general lower paid. On a higher level, the same phenomenon is repeating itself in the ratio of the salary of college teachers to the salary of high school teachers: this ratio has been declining steadily over time.

The difficulty or impossibility of having a good capital market for investment in human capital is a major reason why social and economic position can affect the alternatives open to a young man in choosing his career. The possibility of getting expensive training depends on the ability of a parent or benefactor to finance it, or the willingness and capacity of the young man to "work his way through," and even then, on the ability of the young man's family to do without the earnings he might otherwise get during his training. These factors remain important for certain careers and doubtless are one of the most important source of differences in earnings attributable to noncompeting groups.

(5) *Color* might have been included under the preceding heading but it seems better to separate it out for special treatment. Clearly, Negroes have not been in the same position as whites to choose among occupations. They have not had the same possibility of getting training and education, partly because of the lessened availability

of public facilities, partly because of discrimination in private institutions. But the effect of color is much more complicated than this. Because of the prejudices of both customers and fellow workers, being a Negro involves having a lower economic productivity in some occupations and so color has the same effect on earnings as a difference in ability. As a result, the stratification of the population by color has clearly been one of the most potent forces producing non-equalizing differences in return in the United States.

Transitional Differences in Return

This heading requires very little discussion. Clearly the supply of labor of a particular kind is likely to be much less elastic in the short run than in the long run, so any change in demand is likely to have much sharper effects initially than ultimately. Perhaps the only point that needs fuller illustration is the point made at the outset that what we call a transitional difference depends on our point of view. Consider the changes in the ratio of clerical to manual earnings noted above. The excess of clerical earnings a century or so ago could have been regarded as transitional from a sufficiently broad point of view, since high clerical earnings were leading (along with other factors) to the provision of education and to increased prestige of white-collar work. These, in the course of several generations, would reduce or erase the excess. Yet it is clear that for many problems this is a much broader point of view than is desirable.

2
The Demand for Labour

K. W. Rothschild

The Nature of the Demand for Labour

We buy consumption goods because we *want* them; because we want to eat, to be clothed, and to get some enjoyment. The demand for such goods is therefore ruled by two factors: the utility of the goods to the buyer and his purchasing power. In certain cases the demand for labour is of the same nature, viz., when we hire somebody's personal services, be it those of a domestic servant or those of the family doctor. But in the vast majority of cases workers are not employed because their work satisfies any wants of the employer, but because he hopes to obtain a profit by selling their output to the public. Normally, therefore, the demand for labour is a 'derived' demand, dependent not only on the conditions in the particular labour market, but also on the conditions prevailing in the market for this labour's produce. Our assumption of perfect competition, therefore, really involves that both in the labour market and in the commodity market a homogeneous unit is supplied and demanded by such a large number of people—employers and employees in the first case, sellers and consumers in the second—that not one of them, by his own isolated action, can affect the current wage or price. (Or, in other words, everybody in the market will regard current prices and wages as given.)

The employer, then, who is faced with the question whether he should engage more workers will ask: 'Will the additional workers add more to my receipts than I have to pay them in wages?' If the answer is in the affirmative he will employ more workers, because by doing so he will increase his profits. In other words, with wage and prices taken as unalterable data, the entrepreneur, in deciding the number of workers he should employ, will fix his attention on the additional output obtained from an additional,

Reprinted from K. W. Rothschild, *The Theory of Wages.* 2nd ed. (London: Routledge & Kegan Paul, Ltd., 1954; reprinted by Augustus M. Kelley, Publishers, New York, 1967), pp. 15–35.

or 'marginal' worker. If the value of his additional, his 'marginal', output is greater than his wage, then, and only then, will he be employed. In order, therefore, to obtain an idea of the nature and shape of the individual firm's demand curve for labour, we must find out the relationship between 'marginal productivity' (which term we shall use from now onwards to denote the increase in value of the total output caused by the marginal worker) and the number of workers employed.

This relationship is primarily governed by a well-known economic tendency: the Law of Diminishing Returns. This law states that if one (or more) factor of production remains fixed while increasing amounts of other factors are applied to it, then the returns per unit of the variable factors will increase up to a point and then diminish. This law, which is a static law and assumes technical knowledge as given, is most clearly illustrated by imagining a given piece of land with an increasing number of men and machinery applied to it. It is obvious that after an optimum point has been reached, additional men and machinery will only be able to increase output to a diminishing extent.

The same will be true for a factory or for a whole industry if we assume for the moment that the amount of land and machinery used by each employer is given. Up to a point the employment of additional men will mean a more than proportionate increase in output as the division of labour is improved and better use is made of the machinery. But after that point additional men will only bring decreasing increments to the total output. This may take the form of the additional men doing auxiliary work of a less productive nature, or doing the same work as the others but causing an all round decline in output per head because of the overcrowding of space and machinery that will follow.

This Law of Diminishing Returns then shows us that under static conditions the demand schedule of the employer for labour will be of the same nature as the demand schedule of the individual consumer for finished goods: the lower the wage the greater the number of men demanded.[1] To illustrate this, here is an artificial marginal productivity schedule of one firm working under perfectly competitive conditions.

[1] It will be clear that equilibrium can only be reached in that part of the marginal productivity schedule where marginal productivity is declining. Up to the point where marginal productivity increases, expansion will always be profitable. For if it is worth while to employ n workers at the wage a, then it will be *a fortiori* worth while to employ $(n + 1)$ workers if this means an increase in the output of each of them.

TABLE 2.1

1	2	3	4	5 $[(3) \times (4)]$
Number of men employed	Total output per day	Marginal output	Price per unit s.	Marginal productivity s.
10*	200	—	2	—
11	218	18	2	36
12	235	17	2	34
13	250	15	2	30
14	263	13	2	26
15	273	10	2	20
16	280	7	2	14
17	283	3	2	6
etc.				

* We assume that up to this point increasing returns prevail.

The Demand for Labour

TABLE 2.2

1	2	3	4	5 [(3) × (4)]
Number of men employed	Total output per day	Marginal output per man	Price per unit	Marginal productivity per man
			s.	s.
100	2000	—	2	—
110	2180	18	1/11½	35/3
120	2350	17	1/11	32/7
130	2500	15	1/10	27/6
140	2630	13	1/9	23/7
150	2730	10	1/8½	17/1
160	2800	7	1/8	11/8
170	2830	3	1/7½	4/11

In the case of this example the employer will engage 11 workers, if the current day wage is 36s., 12 workers, if it falls below 34s., 13 workers if it falls below 30s., etc.[2]

In order to obtain the demand conditions for labour of the whole industry—and this is really the more important case—we have to add up the demand schedules of the individual firms, thus again obtaining the 'normal' law of demand. But when we deal with the industry as a whole another factor enters which reinforces the tendency for the demand price for labour to decrease as the number of workers to be employed increases. For an expansion of output in the whole industry will not leave the price of the commodity unaffected. It will have to fall in order to induce buyers to take up the additional supplies. Thus marginal productivity for the industry as a whole will decline not only because marginal output declines but also because with a larger labour force each unit of output has to be sold at a lower price.

To illustrate this industrial marginal productivity schedule let us imagine an industry consisting of ten firms, all working under the same production conditions as the one pictured in Table 2.1. Their total output at any level of employment will then simply be ten times the output of each individual firm. But marginal productivity per man will fall at a steeper rate for the industry as a whole than for the individual firm because the general expansion in output leads to a fall in price.

It will be seen from this table that if employment is to expand so that, for instance, 13 workers are engaged in *each* of the ten firms and not just in one, the day wage would have to fall below 27s. 6d. as compared with 30s. in the previous case.

Elasticity of Demand

Having established the *direction* of change in the demand for labour following a change

[2] In diagrammatic terms, and assuming a continuous marginal productivity schedule, we obtain the following picture:

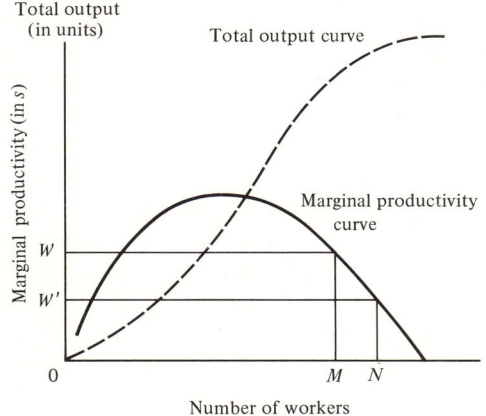

At a wage rate OW, OM men will be employed; if the wage-rate falls to OW¹ employment will increase to ON.

in the wage-rate, we must now give some attention to the *degree* the demand will increase or decrease for any given fall or rise in wages. In other words, we have now to introduce a concept familiar to every student of economics: the elasticity of demand. We call the demand for labour elastic (or greater than 1) when a small change in the wage-rate calls for a proportionately greater change in the amount of labour demanded; and we call the demand inelastic (or smaller than 1) when the increase or decrease in the amount demanded is proportionately less than the (small) fall or rise in wage rates. A special case is that of unit elasticity, where a small change in the wage-rate will lead to an exactly proportionate and (opposite) change in the amount of labour demanded. An important corollary which follows directly from the definition of elasticity is that under conditions of elastic demand a fall in wages will lead to such an increase in employment that the total wage bill will increase, while a rise in wage rates will lead to a reduction in the wage bill. The opposite will be true under conditions of inelastic demand, while unit elasticity means that a change in the wage-rate will affect employment in such a way that the total wage bill after the change in wages is the same as before.[3]

Under our present assumptions, viz., that the supply of the factors of production other than labour is given, the elasticity of demand for a particular type of labour will obviously be determined by two forces: the technical conditions of production and the elasticity of demand for the commodities produced by that labour force. This follows at once from our Table 2.2, where the demand schedule for labour, the marginal productivity column, is the product of the marginal output schedule (dependent on the technical conditions of production) and the price schedule for the finished commodity (dependent on the elasticity of demand for that commodity).

Short-term and Long-term Demand Conditions

Since technical conditions and demand elasticity for the final commodity vary considerably from industry to industry, the elasticities of demand for different types of labour will cover a wide range. But for every demand schedule it will usually be true that it becomes more elastic the longer the period that has elapsed since the wage-rate changed.

In other words, elasticity of demand is not independent of the time factor, and generally the short-term demand is less elastic than the long-term demand. This is caused both by the technical and the price factors. In the short run, capital equipment is of a more or less rigidly fixed nature, designed for a certain output capacity which in turn requires a certain number of workers narrowly defined by technical factors. This means that the course of marginal productivity which we have pictured before in tabular and diagrammatic form, rising smoothly and continuously up to a certain point and then falling off gradually, is only applicable to the long run when enough time has elapsed to change and reorganize the equipment in such a way as to give the best combination with different sizes of the labour force. In the short run, where such new combinations cannot be carried out in view of the fixed nature of equipment, the shape

---

[3] A numerical illustration of the meaning of elasticity of demand may be taken from the schedule of Table 2.1. There, a fall in the wage-rate from 36s. to 34s., will lead to an expansion in employment from 11 workers to 12. This means that a reduction in wages of approximately 5½ per cent leads to a proportionately greater change in employment, viz., an expansion of 9 per cent. Demand at this point is, therefore, elastic and the fall in the wage-rate will cause the total wage bill to rise from 396s. (11 × 36) to 408s. (12 × 34).

On the other hand, a change in the wage-rate from 30s. to 26s., which is equivalent to a reduction of slightly more than 13 per cent., will increase employment only by less than 8 per cent., from 13 to 14. Demand at this point is, therefore, inelastic and the wage bill at the lower wage-rate is only 364s. (14 × 26) as compared with 390s. (13 × 30) at the higher rate.

of the marginal productivity curve will be different. Up to the point of capacity output the marginal productivity of additional workers will be approximately constant. For there will be idle machines, and new men can be put to work on them under more or less the same conditions as apply to the men already working in the factory. As soon, however, as output reaches capacity there will be a sharp and sudden drop in marginal productivity because the technical design of the factory (the number and nature of machines, etc.) will not allow additional men to be applied as fruitfully as before.[4]

An illustration of these short-term conditions can be given by a variation of the long-term example given above in Table 2.1.

TABLE 2.3

Number of men employed	Total output per day	Marginal output	Price per unit s.	Marginal productivity s.
8	160	20	2	40
9	180	20	2	40
10	200	20	2	40
11	210	10	2	20
12	220	10	2	20
13	230	10	2	20

The plant in our example has been built for an output capacity which requires 10

[4] The question as to what determines capacity output is not free of ambiguities and depends on such questions as the length of the working day and the practicability of second and third shifts. If, for instance, a second shift is possible but less productive than a first, marginal productivity will remain constant up to the full output of shift one, then drop suddenly and again continue at a constant (but lower) level up to the full output of shift two.

The capacity level of output (under one-shift working) can also be overstepped by introducing overtime. This will, however, necessitate the payment of higher overtime rates so that at the capacity level the wage-rate will go up suddenly. Alternately this can also be represented as a sudden fall in marginal productivity, in so far as one shilling's worth of additional labour will now produce less than before.

workers. Up to this point every worker can be put to work under identical conditions so that their marginal productivity remains constant at 40s. Beyond that point only inferior production facilities can be offered and marginal productivity will fall to 20s. At full capacity working[5] then the short-term demand schedule will be completely inelastic within the range of 20s. and 40s. Wage changes within this range would leave the employment situation unaffected.[6]

These technical conditions making for an inelastic short-term demand schedule are reinforced by the fact that consumers' demand for consumption goods also tends to be less elastic in the short run than in the long run. Long-standing commitments and force of habit make it difficult for the consumer to readjust his purchases instantaneously to every change in price. It will need some time until he will react in a noticeable degree to a changed price structure.

This inelastic nature of competitive short-run demand conditions is, perhaps, to some extent responsible for the very stiff attitude of employers and trade unions in wage ne-

[5] And only this interests us here as we are dealing with perfect competition. . . .
[6] The diagrammatic presentation of this case looks as follows:

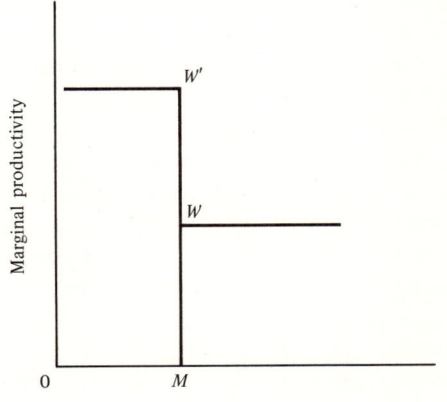

OM is the number of workers corresponding to the capacity output. In the short run the demand for labour will be completely inelastic between the levels MW and MW¹.

gotiations. For, in this period, a rise in wages cannot be followed by a considerable reduction in the number of employed if the equipment is to be used at all; because to rearrange plant and production processes is a slow business. This will mean that the rise in wages will lead to a rise in the wage bill which, if the rise in wage rates is considerable, may well eat into profits, interest, depreciation charges, and other overhead costs. And in the short period, while capital cannot be transformed, there will be no escape from such a situation. The inelastic nature of short-term demand will also induce the trade unions to resist strongly any pressure towards lowering wages. For this would mainly mean that less is paid to all the workers while the increase in employment due to the fall of wages would, during this period, be very small. If we remember that under modern conditions, with capital equipment having a life extending over many years, the 'short period' may be very long indeed, it will be clear that such wage negotiations will be hotly contested; for, during that period at least, they will have an important influence on how the industry's product is shared between capital and labour. This argument, however, does not apply to depression periods, when the existence of idle resources makes the short-term demand more elastic. But in such times the fight for the determination of the wage level is likely to assume bitter forms for other reasons. . . .

As time passes, the demand for labour will tend to become more elastic. As depreciation funds accumulate and part of the capital equipment comes up for replacement, its form can be so changed as to allow its effective combination with a larger or smaller proportion of labour according to whether wages have fallen or risen. The extent to which this is possible will depend on the technical conditions of production; there will also be other factors, such as new inventions, expected market conditions, behaviour of competitors, and other dynamic elements, which will probably have a far more potent influence on investment decisions than changes in wage levels.[7] But some response will be possible, and that will mean that the long-term marginal output will not fall so steeply as the short-term one. Also, in the long run, the demand for the finished product will become more elastic as people adjust their spending policy to the new price level.

If we allow for still more time to pass, then we can also take into account, still assuming that the *total* supply of capital remains unchanged, that capital leaves high-wage industries and moves to low-wage industries. The consequence will be that additional labour in the low-paid industry can be combined with additional capital which will prevent marginal productivity from dropping off quickly. Similarly, if capital leaves the high-paid industry, the loss of marginal product due to a decline in the number of workers will be reduced. This will give the very-long-term demand of an industry for labour considerable elasticity and will set a limit to the extent to which wages in one industry can be permanently held above or pressed below the average level in other industries.[8]

At this point we must discuss an important problem, which might have occurred to the reader at several stages of our argument. So far we have always spoken of the demand of one industry for a special type of labour. But can the above analysis also be applied to labour as a whole? There is no doubt that the fathers of the marginal productivity theory were mainly thinking in terms of labour as a whole. But the more one tries to go into this difficult problem the more one realizes the inadequacy of this approach. Firstly, to speak of the 'marginal productivity' of labour in general raises considerable difficulties. These, however, could perhaps be overcome by choosing the proper

---

[7] There are also indications that it is not so much *changes* in wages as the *absolute level* of wages which has a decisive influence on the decision to substitute capital for labour.

[8] This becomes at once clear when we illustrate

units for measuring labour supply. But even if we get round this stumbling-block, we come to a more difficult problem. When we dealt with a change in wages in one industry only, we were justified in assuming that the rise or fall in money wages was equivalent to a proportionate rise or fall in real wages. For the general price level is unlikely to be noticeably affected by what happens in one industry. But when *all* wages are altered this is no longer true. The changes in money wages will have an appreciable effect on the price level. Until we have investigated more fully the nature of these repercussions, we shall not be able to estimate the effect of a general change in money wages on real wages and employment.

Thirdly, even if we neglect this monetary complication and deal with changes in real wages only, there remains the difficulty that with such a *general* change the assumption of 'other things remaining equal' must break down. If all workers get higher wages and if short-term demand for labour is inelastic, then the share of wages in the national income will go up. That will mean that capitalists will have to cut down either consumption or the supply of new capital, or both.[9] At any rate, it is no longer permissible to assume that the amount of capital will remain the same, except in the very short period. Nor is it likely that a general change in real wages will leave the supply of labour unaffected. We see, therefore, that we must first deal with these problems before we can try to find out the effects of changes in the real wages of labour in general.

Is the Marginal Productivity Theory Determinate?

The foregoing paragraphs show clearly that in wage theory questions arise which can by no means be answered with the aid of the marginal productivity theory alone. If we remember that this theory leaves out such important points as the effect of wage

short-period and long-period demand graphically.

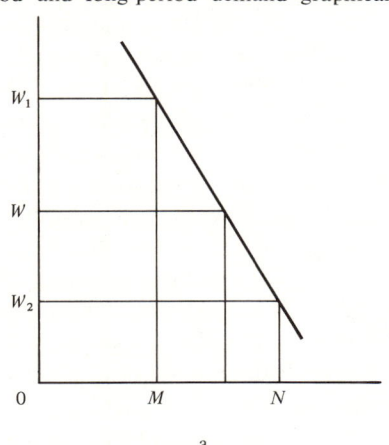

a

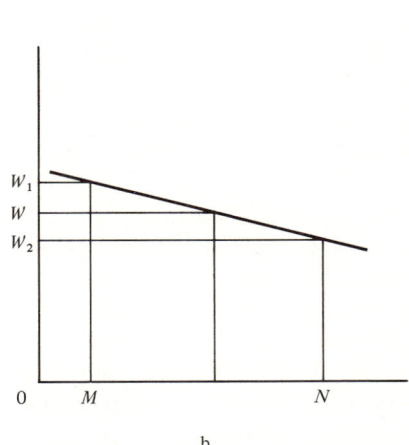

b

[Part a of this figure] represents the inelastic short-period demand curve, while part b represents the long-period demand curve, allowing for changes in the form of equipment, and the flow of capital from or to other industries. Let OW be the average wage level in all industries, and let us assume that OM and ON are the minimum and maximum level of employment that can be employed with the industry's capital equipment. Then the maximum and minimum point to which wages can be forced—OW_1 and OW_2—will be considerably farther from the average wage in the short run than in the long run.

Once again the reader is warned that these conclusions rest on the assumption of perfect competition. They do not apply, or do not apply fully, to conditions of monopoly or large-scale unemployment. To these conditions we shall return later.

[9] This assumes that the rise in wages is not due to technical progress which raises marginal productivity and the national income.

changes on the supply of labour, monopoly, bargaining strength, etc., it will become clear why we claimed in the previous chapter that the marginal productivity theory, like its forerunners, cannot be regarded as a complete theory of wages. Rather, it is an analysis of the nature of the demand for labour. To base on this analysis alone, as has been done only too frequently, sweeping generalizations as to the futility of trade unions, or the impossibility of pressing wages below the 'right' amount, only betrays the same lack of imagination for the complexity of the real world as has been criticized in the classical wage theories.

On the other hand, whenever the assumptions of the marginal productivity theory are fairly representative of actual circumstances in a specific case, it will be of immediate value in interpreting the wage situation there. Thus, if we have a large number of employers strongly competing with each other for a given amount of labour,[10] then we should assume that the workers will just get that wage which equals their marginal productivity and which will keep them all employed. If they tried to raise wages beyond that level, some would become unemployed. Whether the wage bill would rise or fall would depend on the elasticity of demand.

Here, however, a certain question arises. Even if we assume that all the assumptions of the marginal productivity theory are met in a certain case, does that necessarily mean that there is only one rigidly defined wage level at which all men will be employed? In other words, is the marginal productivity theory absolutely determinate, or is there a range of indeterminateness within which wages can be pushed upwards or downwards without affecting the employment situation?

Apart from the case of an inelastic short-run demand curve which we have discussed earlier, there are two other cases which have to be mentioned in this connection. The first, which was discovered by Edgeworth, is perhaps more of theoretical than of practical interest. Edgeworth noted that a certain range of indeterminateness can occur as soon as we give up the assumption of a continuous demand curve for labour. With the normal continuous downward-sloping demand curve—which is adopted not so much because of its correspondence with reality, but because of the great mathematical and graphical conveniences connected with it—the slightest change in the wage-rate will affect the level of employment. This is, however, only possible because the continuous demand curve assumes that labour can be added or subtracted in infinitesimally small units. In reality, since labour consists of indivisible human beings who have to be employed for certain time intervals, at least one hour, but often for minimum periods of a day, week, month, or even a year, demand is not perfectly continuous.

But when demand is discontinuous and labour can only be engaged or disengaged in certain 'lumps', then the marginal productivity of a given number of workers is no longer one definite quantity but breaks up into two limiting quantities—the internal margin and the external margin. If we have a group of 100 workers, the internal margin will be given by the loss of income which would follow the removal of the 100th man, while the external margin will be equal to the addition to income that would result from the 101st worker. Thus, in the example given in Table 2.1, the marginal productivity of 12 workers is characterized by an internal margin of 34s., and an external margin of 30s.

The internal margin, then, will set the upper limit and the external margin the lower limit within which the wage has to settle to keep the given number of men employed. If the wage rises above the internal margin it will be worth the employer's while to dismiss some men, and their competition for jobs will bring wages down. If the wage falls below the external margin employers will try to expand employment, and their competitive bidding for the limited labour force will push wages up. But be-

---

[10] Capital supply and technical knowledge are also assumed as given.

tween these two limits the wage can be changed either way without affecting employment.

When the labour force is very large and can be engaged for very short time intervals, then the range between the internal and external margin is likely to be very small (until it becomes zero in the case of the continuous demand curve). But when the number of workers in a certain field is comparatively small or if they can only be engaged for considerable periods (take, for instance, the case of company lawyers), then this range of indeterminateness within which the wage has to be fixed by a process of bargaining or mere chance, may be quite considerable.

The second case, where it can be shown that the marginal productivity theory does not provide a uniquely determined solution —even if its major assumptions are accepted—is the one usually known under the name 'The economy of high wages'. The fundamental idea behind this case is of considerable importance in many fields of economic theory. Static equilibrium theory tries to find those positions in which a given system will tend to come to rest. Small deviations from these positions will set into motion economic forces which will tend to restore the equilibrium position. But there is no guarantee that there is always just one equilibrium. There may very well be several equilibrium positions. In that case a change which, seen from the old equilibrium level, may seem to make for disequilibrium and instability, may after the lapse of some time react in such a way on some of the other data of the economic system that a *new* equilibrium is reached which might be just as stable as the old one.

'The economy of high wages' is an example of such a new equilibrium. With a given number of workers and a given supply of capital, the marginal productivity theory seems to fix quite uniquely (if we disregard the Edgeworth case) the equilibrium wage. Any attempt to raise the wage above that level, or press it below it, would set in motion economic forces, viz., competition among the workers or employers, which would sooner or later bring the wage back to its old level. If this does not happen instantaneously, however, i.e., if the wage stays higher for some time, then, the high-wage economists say, something different may happen. The higher wage and the higher standard of living that goes with it will increase the productivity of the workers. This will, of course, also increase marginal productivity and more workers will be employed at any given wage than before. In the end, because of this increased demand, the same number of workers may be employed at the higher wage as were originally employed at the lower wage. The old equilibrium has been replaced by a new equilibrium.[11]

It should be noted that this really shows that the solution offered by the margin productivity theory is not always unique, and not that we have forgotten the basic assumption 'other things remaining equal'. The

---

[11] In diagrammatic terms the 'economy of high wages' can be represented [as below].

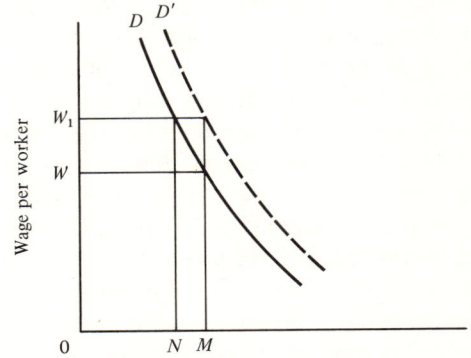

The given number of workers OM will all be employed at the 'equilibrium' wage OW. If the wage is raised to OW_1 employment will fall to ON. But the higher standard of living caused by the higher wage level may so increase productivity that the demand curve for labour shifts from D to D^1. Then, all OM men will be employed at OW_1 which now becomes the 'equilibrium' wage.

The argument works also in the other direction. If wages are pressed below the equilibrium for some time, productivity may fall to such an extent that in the end *only* at this lower wage will all the workers be employed.

marginal productivity theory states that there is *one* wage, and one wage only, at which a given number of men will be employed, so long as capital supply and productivity (dependent on technical knowledge and the demand for the final commodity) do not change. The wage is regarded as a function of the number of men, capital supply, and productivity. The theorem of the 'economy of high wages' shows, however, that we cannot assume that productivity is an independent variable uniquely determining a certain wage level. It is itself a function of the wage level, both cause and effect of wage changes. Therefore, there is more than one equilibrium position, and the marginal productivity theory cannot tell us which equilibrium combination of wages and productivity is the 'proper' one.

There is no doubt that the principle of the 'economy of high wages' is of considerable practical importance. Thus, it is widely held that the fixing of minimum wages in the 'sweated' industries so increased the productivity of the workers (by improving their standard of living and by forcing the employers to pay more attention to the proper organization of production) that the large-scale unemployment which had been expected in many circles did not materialize. But, of course, there are limits to the extent to which wages can be raised on this principle. On the whole, we should expect a law of diminishing returns to operate here. As long as workers live on a very low standard, a certain increase in their wages should produce quite a considerable effect on their output. As their standard increases and becomes more satisfactory in every respect, the same increase will lead only to very small additions in output and finally to none at all.[12]

On the whole, therefore, attempts to raise wages in order to raise productivity are likely to be more successful among the low paid workers or among colonial people. Nevertheless, the strain and intensity of modern large-scale production methods make the application of this principle a practical proposition even among the better-paid workers. Only workers who can afford certain 'semi-luxuries', like better and quicker forms of transport, better housing, holidays and entertainments, will be able to stand up fully to the nerve-racking atmosphere of modern factory life.

Differences in Efficiency

So far we have spoken of the demand for a certain type of labour without taking into account that labour is by no means a perfectly homogeneous factor of production. Workers are human beings with their numerous individual differences, and one person is rarely a perfect substitute for another one. How does this affect our analysis?

First of all, in many cases we shall find that what we have called 'one type of labour' can be conveniently split up into different groups of labour, all engaged at the same task, but with varying levels of skill. We can then break up our demand curve for, say, boot and shoe operatives, into separate demand curves for 'highly skilled', 'skilled', 'semi-skilled', etc., workers. For each of these groups a separate demand curve, based on the marginal productivity schedule of that group, can be drawn up and will determine the wage for a given number of men.

Since all these groups are, however, engaged in operations which are to a considerable extent interchangeable, their wage-rates will be interdependent. As we can always assume that the more skilled, more efficient workman can at least achieve the same output as the one in the group below him, it is clear that his wage will be the upper limit to which the wage of the lower group can rise. For if employers engage only so many skilled men at a certain wage and not more, they will be even less prepared to take on any semi-skilled men at

---

[12] It should be noted that we are here only concerned with the increase in output due to the better physical standard of the workers. Higher wages may also make the worker more contented or may have other *psychological* effects which may react favourably on output.

that wage. The latters' wage-rate will, therefore, lie below the skilled rate. Similarly, the semi-skilled wage-rate will not fall below the rate paid to the group immediately below it. As soon as their wages touched this lower level, semi-skilled men would at once be engaged to replace the unskilled men who, in order to find employment, would have to work at a lower wage.

Thus we see that if we split up a non-homogeneous type of labour into a hierarchy of equi-efficient groups we obtain a scale of interdependent wage-rates. The wages of each group will depend on the numbers in that group and their marginal productivity, but they cannot rise above or fall below the wages paid to the neighbouring groups. This interdependence exists also for the most efficient and the least efficient group, though in these cases one of the neighbouring groups is missing. If the wages of the highest group rose while the wage-rates of all the other groups remained unchanged, a point would be reached when employers would prefer to substitute cheaper, less skilled labour for the very expensive, highly skilled workers. Thus the wages of the lower groups in the hierarchy will set a limit to the level to which the top-group can rise. And in a similar way a fall in the wages of the lowest group will come to an end by a large-scale substitution of these unskilled men for their more skilled, but considerably more expensive colleagues.[13]

But even this reduction of a large labour group into smaller and more homogeneous groups does not completely solve the problem of differences in efficiency. For in these smaller groups we shall still be faced with noticeable differences of personal efficiency. How do they affect the wage-rate?

Here a difference must be made according to the method of wage payments used. If the workers are paid by results no special difficulty arises. For differences in personal efficiency will be looked after more or less automatically[14] by variations in the actual weekly earnings of the workers.

With time rates the position is different. Here, too, we could imagine a system whereby the wage-rate for a given number of men is determined by the marginal productivity of the 'average' man, while the actual wage paid to each particular man would to some extent vary according to his personal efficiency. Such a system is, indeed, not infrequent in some of the salaried jobs where a certain salary *range* rather than a fixed salary is offered for a given job. But in most of the cases where time wages are paid such a system is impracticable. Not only would it be difficult to assess differences in personal efficiency among a large number of workers, but modern methods of collective bargaining and a widespread feeling in favour of 'equalitarian justice' among human beings make the payment of standard wages a necessity. This will mean that, if a given number of men is to be employed, the wage will have to be equal to the marginal productivity of the *least* efficient man; for if the wage rose beyond this level it would not pay to employ this man and he would

---

[13] Interdependence of wage-rate is, of course, not limited to different types of workers in the same industry. To some extent *all* wage-rates are interdependent, for, since all the produce of labour competes in the last resort for the consumer's shilling, every commodity, and therefore every type of labour, is to some extent a substitute for all the other commodities, or for all types of labour. An isolated wage-increase in one labour group would, therefore, sooner or later be brought to an end by an increase in the demand for the produce of other types of labour.

This universal interdependence of wage-rates is at the basis of the general equilibrium theory of wages where *every* change in one wage-rate is shown to have repercussions on all the other wage-rates. Since, however, these repercussions are usu-

ally small and spread over a wide field—except in the special case which we have just discussed in the text—the explanatory value of the complex general equilibrium structure is not very great. We have, therefore, kept in the main to the more usual partial equilibrium analysis.

[14] Most 'payment by result' methods are in reality a time wage with some sort of bonus for increased output. The adjustment of earnings to personal efficiency is, therefore, usually not perfect.

be dismissed. But the marginal productivity of the more efficient men will now be greater than the wage, and on each of them an employer will be able to make an extra profit. It is, therefore, clear that employers will be rather keen to get the more productive rather than the less productive men. Wages, however, being fixed for the whole group, they will not be able to compete for them by offering higher wages. So competition will take other forms, and the more efficient workers will obtain certain non-monetary advantages such as more leisure, more congenial work, etc. In particular, they will obtain steadier employment, since it will be the less efficient workers who will be dismissed first in a depression. Thus, if we take into account not only money wages but other advantages as well, we see that under competition differences in efficiency will to some extent find expression in differences in reward, even if standard wages are paid.

Do Employers Know the Marginal Productivity of Their Workers?

In conclusion we must say a few words about this question which must have worried quite a number of readers. Is a theory not blatantly remote from reality, they would argue, if it regards as the driving force behind employers' demand a factor whose very name is probably Greek to most of them?

Now, two things must be said in answer to this. Firstly, even if an employer had never heard of 'marginal productivity' this will not prevent him from thinking in terms of the marginal analysis. As long as he reasons something like this: 'How much on balance is this man going to bring me in and how much will he add to my costs? Is it worth while to take him on?' he is, in fact, behaving as the theory expects.

But this still assumes that he can estimate the marginal productivity of an additional man. He may not be able to do this; he may only think in terms of average productivity, or may just run his business 'by intuition'. Even then the marginal productivity theory will show us his demand schedule for labour if he tries, 'intuitively', to maximize his profits. To the extent that he succeeds in this aim, wages will approach the marginal productivity level. Inertia, ignorance, and habit may cause divergencies, but as long as competition is fully at work, wages will tend towards the point indicated by the theory.

PART II
THE METHOD OF LABOR MARKET ANALYSIS

Of what value is the labor market theory developed in the preceding readings by Milton Friedman and K. W. Rothschild? It is tempting to mesh labor market theory with the economic theory for the product market, to vary the assumptions concerning these markets (such as the number of buyers and sellers in each), to specify a goal for the economy (such as maximizing consumer welfare), and, finally, to draw conclusions about the most desirable way to organize the economy. The theory which integrates the examination of various specific markets is known as general equilibrium theory and has a variant known as welfare economics, which is concerned with the maximization of consumer welfare. The welfare-maximizing solution, known as the Pareto optimum, coincides with the equilibrium solution of the economic model known as pure-and-perfect competition. The assumptions of the competitive model are well defined—for example, many sellers and buyers in each market, and no government interference with market solutions;[1] and the model can be used to condemn any real-world phenomenon which violates these assumptions because of the deleterious impact of the violation on consumer welfare. Condemned phenomena include unions, producer monopolies, and minimum wage laws.

The use of the welfare economics approach to draw policy prescriptions has been criticized from several sources because of the attributes of the competitive economic model. Joseph Schumpeter has attacked the notion that consumer welfare is maximized by having the largest possible number of firms in each industry.[2] He argues that this conclusion resulted from the competitive model's inappropriate reliance on static equilibrium analysis. He feels that a more appropriate model is a dynamic one which could capture changes in production methods and products. These elements, Schumpeter asserts, are ignored by the competitive model, but in the long run are the most important sources of increased consumer welfare. Moreover, the sources of change are large firms, not small, Schumpeter states; and he concludes that the competitive model provides misguided implications for policy makers. Another criticism of the competitive theory has been made by Neil W. Chamberlain and James W. Kuhn, who argue that the model seeks only to maximize the welfare of indi-

---

[1] This statement would be qualified in the presence of externalities in which case some form of government intervention may be required to increase consumer welfare.

[2] Joseph Schumpeter, *Capitalism, Socialism and Democracy,* 2nd ed. (New York: Harper & Row, Publishers, 1947).

viduals in their role as consumers and ignores their role as producers.[3] If the model were reformulated to consider the welfare flowing from both roles, some institutions such as unions now might be considered appropriate. A third criticism of the competitive model is that its value to policy makers is questionable whenever its conditions are violated in more than one market. Richard G. Lipsey and Kelvin Lancaster have demonstrated that there is no a priori rule that "more competitive" conditions are preferable to "less competitive" conditions in a given market, so long as all other markets are not perfectly competitive.[4]

These are some of the difficulties of using economic theory—including labor market theory—to provide policy guidance. But there is an even more fundamental difficulty. We have implicitly assumed that it is correct to move from theory—as an abstraction of the real world—to real world policies. Milton Friedman, in his essay "The Methodology of Positive Economics," has demonstrated the incorrectness of this approach.[5] He distinguishes between "positive" and "normative" economics. The former concerns "what is," that is, the "facts" of economics; whereas the latter combines positive economics with the values of the policy maker to arrive at a "normative" judgment as to "what ought to be." Many have misused economic theory by not building on "facts," but by moving directly from theory to policy, Friedman asserts.

What do we mean by "facts" in economics? Essentially, we mean hypotheses which have been validated by comparing their predictions with experience. If we have a hypothesis which says if A happens, then B will follow, that hypothesis tentatively can be accepted as valid only if we find factual evidence or data which does not contradict that prediction. We do not determine the validity of a hypothesis by evaluating the reality of its assumptions. In fact, the validity of the assumptions for the study of a particular problem is indicated by correspondence between the predictions and experience. There may be subsidiary and legitimate roles for assumptions in a theory; but even if its assumptions are less "realistic," as long as its predictions are more accurate, theory I is more valid than theory II.

The confusion over the role of assumptions in establishing the validity of a theory has long plagued the labor economics field, and one of the best-known controversies is presented here.[6] A considerable number of critics have attacked the reality of the assumptions

---

[3] *Collective Bargaining,* 2nd ed. (New York: McGraw-Hill, Inc., 1965), pp. 323–339.

[4] "The General Theory of the Second Best," *Review of Economic Studies,* vol. 24 (1956), pp. 11–32.

[5] In *Essays in Positive Economics* (Chicago: University of Chicago Press, 1953), pp. 3–43.

[6] For an earlier controversy, see Richard A. Lester, "Shortcomings of Marginal Analysis for Wage-Employment Problems," *American Economic Review,* vol. 36 (March 1946), pp. 63–82 and Fritz Machlup, "Marginal Analysis and Empirical Research," *American Economic Review,* vol. 36 (September 1946), pp. 519–528.

of labor market theory, including the notions that workers have substantial knowledge of labor market opportunities and considerable mobility. Simon Rottenberg properly concludes that this attack on economic theory is irrelevant if the theory provides verified hypotheses about how the labor market operates. But Rottenberg slips into another trap of which the theory tester must be wary. As Robert J. Lampman points out, Rottenberg transforms the competitive hypotheses into nonrefutable predictions. And an hypothesis incapable of refutation is of no use in understanding how the economy operates because it reduces to a tautology.

Part II sets the tone for the balance of this book. We hope to demonstrate how the basic theory of the labor market can be refined and extended and translated into testable hypotheses. Our quest is to determine the extent to which labor market theory is useful because it provides hypotheses which have been verified and the extent to which we do not have an adequate explanation for the operation of the labor market. Whether or not we have an extensive body of positive economics for the labor market is crucial when we must deal with policy questions in normative economics such as the wisdom of minimum wage laws, which we will consider in the final part.

3
On Choice in Labor Markets

Simon Rottenberg

A voluminous literature reporting on empirical research on labor markets has been published in recent years. Some of this literature has contributed much to understanding of the limitations on fruitful use in *real* markets of the *theory* of worker behavior in labor markets. Some of it, however, has charged the theory with errors it does not contain. This paper proposes to examine conventional theory and the nature of the criticism which has been made of it.[1]

Reprinted from the *Industrial and Labor Relations Review,* Vol. 9, No. 2, January, 1956, pp. 183–199. Copyright © 1956 by Cornell University. All rights reserved.

[1] The large volume of research on labor markets in the last decade and a half has been motivated by the belief that economic theory is an unsatisfactory instrument for understanding resource allocation and compensation in labor markets.

"Since 1940 there has been considerable interest in the movement of labor within a local labor market. This interest grew out of a dissatisfaction with the traditional assumptions of economic theory about the movement of workers from one job to another in response to differences in wage

The Classical Theory

Criteria for choice among alternatives in labor markets and the consequences of choice were discussed by Adam Smith in some detail in a classic chapter, "Of Wages and Profit in the Different Employments of Labour and Stock."[2] A number of economists who wrote in the early and middle parts of the nineteenth century—among them Senior, McCulloch, and Mill—developed the subject, interpreting Smith here, revising him there, and describing more up-to-date versions of labor market behavior.

Smith summarized the theory of the labor market in this way:

rates." Charles A. Myers, "Labor Mobility in Two Communities," in E. W. Bakke *et al., Labor Mobility and Economic Opportunity* (Cambridge, Mass., and New York: The Technology Press and John Wiley and Sons, Inc., 1954), p. 68.

[2] Adam Smith, *An Inquiry into the Nature and Causes of the Wealth of Nations,* Modern Library edition (New York: Random House, 1937), Book I, chap. 10.

The whole of the advantages and disadvantages of the different employments of labour and stock must, in the same neighborhood, be either perfectly equal or continually tending to equality. If, in the same neighbourhood, there was any employment evidently either more or less advantageous than the rest, so many people would crowd into it in the one case, and so many would desert it in the other, that its advantages would soon return to the level of the other employments. This at least would be the case in a society where things were left to follow their natural course, where there was perfect liberty, and where every man was perfectly free both to choose what occupation he thought proper, and to change it as often as he thought proper. Every man's interest would prompt him to seek the advantageous, and to shun the disadvantageous employment.[3]

The theory has two parts. One relates to the nature of occupational choice: "every man" will pursue his interest and this will "prompt him to seek the advantageous, and to shun the disadvantageous employment." The other relates to the consequences of this behavioral choice system: "the whole of the advantages and disadvantages" of all employments will be equal or will tend toward equality. Any disparity in net advantage will cause persons to redistribute themselves. Greater numbers in the relatively more advantaged employments, and fewer in the relatively disadvantaged, will tend to restore equality of net advantage in all.

Inequalities may occur in the short run, while the process of adjustment works itself out; in this period, net advantage will be only "tending to equality." Inequalities may also occur when things are not left at perfect liberty and men are not free to choose among alternative employments. Otherwise, in Smith's system, net advantage will be equal in all employments.

It is of primordial importance to understand that the early economists said that it was *"the whole of the advantages and disadvantages"* in all employments that would be equal. This is so apparent from their writings that there should be no confusion about it. They did *not* say *wages* are equal in all employments. Smith, who knew the economy of his time in remarkable detail, despite the rudimentary state of the statistical arts, knew that wages were different in various employments and explicitly enumerated the causes of difference. Wages would vary, he said, with the ease or hardship, the cleanliness or dirtiness, the honorableness or dishonorableness of the employment; with the easiness and cheapness or the difficulty and expense of its learning; with its constancy or inconstancy; with the small or great trust which is reposed in the worker; and with the probability or improbability of success in the employment.

Those who followed Smith added other causes of difference; when we search for what is common to all, we find that it is the influence which the circumstances of different employments have upon the numbers who will make themselves available in them. Thus, if men prefer an agreeable employment to a disagreeable one, they will tend to move into the former and away from the latter; increasing numbers in the one and diminishing numbers in the other will have opposite effects upon wages in the two employments; when the differential in wages is just large enough to overcome the difference in the agreeableness-property of the two, movement between them ceases, because men are now indifferent in choice and this just-sufficient differential persists.

Occupations equal in other respects would tend to be equal in price, but occupations *unequal* in other respects would be *unequal* in price. Just as price differentials compensate for differentials in other qualities so differentials in other qualities compensate for differentials in price. Thus occupational choice was understood by the economists to be made with reference to the total complex of attributes which attach to jobs.

This is, of course, a description of the process which operates in free labor markets. The classical economists knew, however, that real world markets are not al-

---

[3] *Ibid.*, p. 99.

ways free. In the second part[4] of his chapter "Of Wages and Profit in the Different Employments of Labour and Stock," Smith discussed the restrictions on "perfect liberty" in real markets. Here, he dealt with three types of circumstances in the labor markets of his time in which men were distributed among occupations by other criteria than relative net advantage. First, some persons who were disposed to enter a trade were prevented from entering it. Second, some were encouraged to enter a trade that they would otherwise not be disposed to enter. Third, some were obstructed from moving from one employment to another.

Differences in wages among employments thus can be of two classes. They can be "compensating," in which case they are a function of differences in the nonwage qualities of different jobs. Or they can be "real," in which case they are a function of restrictions on freedom of occupational choice.

The classical thesis respecting the distribution of workers among employments was only a specific application of the general principle which the classical economists understood to govern the distribution of all resources among uses. This is what Kenneth Boulding calls the principle of "equal advantage"—which operates to move resources "from the low-advantage locations where there are 'too many' to the high-advantage locations where they are 'too few.' "[5]

In the ensuing discussion, criticisms of the classical theory of the labor market, as made in recent labor market studies, are presented in paraphrased form and subjected to analysis.[6]

[4] *Ibid.*, p. 118 ff.
[5] K. E. Boulding, "Toward a General Theory of Growth," *The Canadian Journal of Economic and Political Science,* August 1953, p. 338.
[6] In addition to paraphrasing the criticism, I have drawn specific references from the recent literature of the labor market. That part of the literature which is consistent with conventional doctrine is not discussed at all. For a review of the critical literature, the reader is referred to Herbert S. Parnes, *Research on Labor Mobility* (New York: Social Science Research Council, 1954).

Relative Prices and Occupational Choice

1. *Economists in the classical tradition say that men make occupational choices in terms of relative prices in different occupations. If we ask people why they have chosen to enter their crafts or why they have (or have not) made job changes, we find that most workers make choice decisions with reference to the "human relations" factors which attach to jobs or for "personal reasons," for example, and that the structure of wages plays a very small role in the choice process.*[7]

We must distinguish here between the early classical economists and their neoclassical successors. The classical economists did not say that choice was made with reference to price alone. They did not formu-

[7] An example of this criticism can be found in Richard A. Lester, *Hiring Practices and Labor Competition* (Princeton: Industrial Relations Section, Princeton University, 1954), p. 96 ff. "Accepted theory is based primarily on interfirm mobility of labor and on job applications and acceptances differentiated according to relative levels of compensation . . . paid by companies. . . . The wage-mobility focus of traditional theory is too narrow. Some of the important relationships are more varied, indirect, and subtle than the theory assumes. . . . In view of the character of the employment process in most of the interviewed firms, traditional theory appears to give a misleading impression of precision and unique solutions. . . . In resource allocation, economic theory assumes price to be the indicator and governor. Relative wage changes are presumed to be the mechanism for bringing about the proper redistribution of labor."

Professors Myers and Maclaurin found, in their study of the Fitchburg labor market, that "In terms of total inter-factory moves, differences in wage rates were not an important cause of movement." Charles A. Myers and Rupert Maclaurin, *The Movement of Factory Workers* (New York: John Wiley and Sons, Inc., 1943), p. 19.

Generalizing from a number of labor market studies, Clark Kerr has written, "Two processes, among others, are going on all the time in our economy: wage rates are changing and individuals are moving among jobs. The two processes may or may not be closely connected." Clark Kerr, "Labor Markets: Their Character and Consequences," *American Economic Review,* May 1950, p. 278 ff.

late hypothetical models; the world of their theory was the real world as they perceived it. Abstraction from complex reality was a later innovation in the methodology of economics. The simple case, which could be dealt with precisely and mathematically and in which functional relationships could be drawn between pairs of variables, was a contribution of more recent times. Even Marshall, who used the analytical and expository technique of *ceteris paribus* much and with great care, is the despair of young students who hunger for neat solutions, for Marshall is full of "ifs" and "buts" and qualifying clauses.[8]

Labor Market of Classical Economics

In the labor markets of Adam Smith and the economists who followed him, workers made occupational choice in terms of comparative total net advantages, not in terms of comparative wages. McCulloch saw, for example, that some workers might prefer low-wage, healthful employment to high-wage, unhealthful employment. "The agreeableness and healthiness of their employments," he said, "seem to be the principal cause of the redundant numbers, and consequent low wages, of workmen in ordinary field labor."[9] Adam Smith said that the price of labor in inconstant employments must compensate for the "anxious and desponding moments" which the casual worker suffers when he thinks of the instability of his situation. This is the same as saying that workers consider instability as well as price in making choice. Nassau Senior, on the other hand, maintained that steady, regular labor is disliked by workers and that "the opportunities for idleness afforded by an occupation of irregular employment" will cause the long-period earnings of irregular employment to be less than the common average of regular employments. Though Smith and Senior pursued the principle to opposite judgments, what is relevant for us is that neither saw workers choosing solely in terms of relative price. For one, choice was made in terms of relative price and relative instability; for the other, it was made in terms of relative opportunity for idleness. For neither was choice made in terms of relative price, standing alone.

Examples from Senior and Mill

Examples can be multiplied almost without end, but reference will be made only to a few more. Employment in the slave trade, Senior wrote, implies "fatigue, hardship, and danger, public execration, and, if a slave trader can be supposed to reflect on the nature of his occupation, self reproach."[10] Earnings in this employment must be great, therefore, to compensate for the odium which attaches to it. This clearly means that the decision whether to accept employment in the slave trade depends upon price *and* the odious character of the trade.

A father, Senior said again, does not "have his child nursed in the country at 2s. a-week till he is eight years old, and then [have him] removed to a farm-yard or a cotton-mill" and he does not reflect that "in giving him a more expensive education he is engaging in a speculation which is

---

[8] Marshall wrote of his own work: "Though urged by the late Professor Walras about 1873 to publish [his, Marshall's, diagrammatic illustrations of economic problems], he had declined to do so because he feared that if separated from all concrete study of actual conditions, they might seem to claim a more direct bearing on real problems than they in fact had. He began, therefore, to supply some of the requisite limitations and conditions." Contributed by Marshall to a German compilation, *Portraits and Short Lives of Leading Economists,* and quoted by J. M. Keynes, "Alfred Marshall, 1842–1924," in A. C. Pigou, ed., *Memorials of Alfred Marshall* (London: Macmillan Co., Ltd., 1925), p. 21.

[9] J. R. McCulloch, *A Treatise on the Circumstances Which Determine the Rate of Wages and the Condition of the Labouring Classes,* 2d ed. (London: G. Routledge and Co., 1854), p. 55.

[10] Nassau W. Senior, *An Outline of the Science of Political Economy,* Library of Economics edition (London: George Allen and Unwin Ltd., 1938), p. 202.

likely to be unprofitable," because, "with all men, except a few outcasts, one of the greatest sources of immediate gratification" is to witness a son's daily improvement.[11] Just as relative price is not the exclusive criterion of occupational choice for adults in the classical system, it is not the exclusive criterion of the occupational choices which parents make for their offspring.

Mill writes of the handloom weavers who cling to their craft "in spite of the scanty remuneration which it now yields" because they have "freedom of action" in this employment, and he quotes Mr. Muggeridge's report to the Handloom Weavers Inquiry Commission:

He can play or idle as feeling or inclination lead him; rise early or late, apply himself assiduously or carelessly, as he pleases, and work up at any time, by increased exertion, hours previously sacrificed to indulgence or recreation. There is scarcely another condition of any portion of our working population thus free from external control. . . . The weaver will stand by his loom while it will enable him to exist, however miserably.[12]

Thus Mill indicated that the handloom weaver did not choose his employment in terms of wages, but preferred lower to higher wage employment, because it was otherwise attractive to him and the wage difference was not sufficiently large to overcome this attraction.

Senior spoke of the choice between employment as a Manchester weaver or spinner or work as an agricultural laborer, carpenter, or coal heaver as depending not only upon the weekly wage in each occupation, but also upon the opportunities for employment of wives and children. Even here, he pointed out, choices must be seen in net terms. From the gain in earnings of secondary income earners in the family must be subtracted certain costs: "the wife is taken from her household labours," "the moral inconveniences" are great, "the infant children suffer from the want of material attention and those who are older from the deficiency of religious, moral, and intellectual education, and childish relaxation and amusement."[13]

Thus, it is clear that total net advantage and not price alone is the touchstone of occupational choice and change in the theory of the economists, and it is total net advantage and not price alone that is said to be equal in all employments.

Price-Quantity Curves

Latter-day economists, who have developed more elegant systems of analysis than the classicists, *do* use price as the instrument for allocating labor among alternative uses, and their supply curves are drawn to relate quantity to price. Price-quantity curves are drawn, however, upon other-things-equal assumptions, but since economists are not repetitively explicit about this, it is sometimes forgotten.

Quantity is related to price in formal economic analysis for several reasons. First, price is continuously quantifiable; other qualities which attach to occupations may not be quantifiable at all or may be discontinuous. Second, preference patterns related to price are consistent; preference patterns related to other qualities are not. Other things being equal, all persons prefer a higher price for their services to a lower one; but all individuals do not, for example, prefer security to risk. Some are timid and others are gamblers by nature. Third, the analytical model which assumes that behavioral choices are related to price, *ceteris paribus,* gives tolerably good predictive results. Everywhere there is massive aggregative evidence that people move from low-income areas to high, and from areas of thin opportunity, where long-run earnings are likely to be low, to thick opportunity areas, where long-run earnings are likely to be high. Irishmen move to Scotland, Mexi-

---

[11] *Ibid.*, pp. 205–206.
[12] John Stuart Mill, *Principles of Political Economy* (London: George Routledge and Sons, Ltd., 1895), p. 266.

[13] Nassau W. Senior, *Three Lectures on the Rate of Wages* (London: John Murray, 1830), pp. 8–9.

cans to the United States, Southerners to the North, rural people to the towns, and Europeans to the New World; net flows are not in the opposite directions.

Despite this, it is not inconsistent with the classical model for another attribute than price to operate as an allocating instrument. If, for example, an employer finds that he is losing his workers to other employers because, given the structure of other differentials, the difference between the wage he pays and the wage paid by the others draws the workers away, he has a variety of tactics open to him to induce them to say. He may offer more wages, or better housing, or superior schooling for the workers' children, or less obnoxious foremen, or more security, or a more acceptable system of advancement to better jobs. But, though tactical choices are open in great variety, there is only a single strategy and this is to reduce the differential of total net advantage between employment with others and employment with him. This is all the classical economists said; they did not say the price differential itself must be changed. Any choice of method made by an employer is consistent with their understanding of the system by which workers are distributed among occupations.

While the employer may contrive any tactic to make employment in his enterprise relatively more attractive, he will usually find that the supply of labor is more elastic to a nonmoney price and that it will be usually cheaper, therefore, to increase the wage he pays than to improve the quality of the employment in some other way. This is so because preferences are diverse among men, and money is a more efficient instrument of exchange than any other commodity. Consider, for example, the employer who wants to attract workers to an occupation. Assume two choices are open to him: he may pay more wages or he may "pay" free gifts of spirituous beverages. Those who have a strong preference for spirits over other commodities may be indifferent to the "currency" in which they are paid; if they received money payments, they would, in any case, exchange it for spirits. Others, who prefer liquor less, will seek to exchange it for other things which they prefer more. The latter persons will suffer some inconvenience in seeking out others willing to make an exchange, and it will be necessary to compenaste for this inconvenience by paying more in spirits than would have been necessary to pay in money. The inconvenience effect applies especially to the class of cases where nonmoney payments are made in commodities which workers can acquire easily through normal purchase. It applies somewhat less to cases where payments are made in nonmarketed "commodities" like plant ventilation, for which only imperfect substitutes (such as respiratory masks which filter out dust fragments) are purchasable. It is inapplicable only for nonmarketed "commodities" which are not at all substitutable by marketed goods, such as decent and compassionate supervisors.

Complexity of Motivation

Real life is complex, and the behavior of men has diverse motivations. If many variables affect a result, however, it does not mean that a particular one is without influence. As Lionel Robbins has remarked, the thermometer reading in his room in winter is affected by the opening of his window, as well as by the intensity of the fire in the grate. It may be uncomfortably cold in the room with the window open, but Robbins is surely right to say that the room will be warmer if there is a fire. For some purposes, it is useful to hold other things constant and examine the consequences of differentiation in a single variable. This is what Robbins does when he remarks that his room will be warmer if the fire is high. It is what the economist does when he says workers will choose a high wage in preference to a low one. Robbins does not say that the temperature of the room is a unique function of the efficiency of the fire; the economists do not say that occupational choice is a unique function of relative price.

Complex motivation in real life does not destroy the truism of simple motivational behavior in the abstract neoclassical model of the labor market. Other things equal, it can be a correct description of real life behavior to say that workers make job choices with reference to relative prices.

The Test of Meaningfulness

If the model is to be meaningful, it must be correct and also useful. It is *correct,* other things equal, if workers prefer higher prices to lower; it is incorrect, if workers prefer lower prices to higher, or if workers are indifferent toward price and make random choices as between higher and lower prices. It is *useful* if from among the multiple motivations which influence worker occupational choice, a significant one has been selected against which to examine choice.

How can we know if the model is meaningful? Following Friedman,[14] we may attempt to ascertain this by seeing whether workers do distribute themselves among employments consistently with the distribution which a theory constructed upon the model tells us to expect. If behavior conforms to these expectations more frequently than to those generated by some alternative theory, then the model is meaningful.[15]

---

[14] Milton Friedman, *Essays in Positive Economics* (Chicago: University of Chicago Press, 1953), Part I, "The Methodology of Positive Economics."
[15] There is some confusion in the literature of the labor market on the nature of theory. The ordinary form which theory takes is that of a postulated functional relationship between variables, one dependent and at least one independent, which has the power to give predictions at some level of generalization and which is testable. If the machine lacks generalized predictive power, it is not a theory, but only an apparatus for describing unique phenomena or, at best, a taxonomic tool for distinguishing likes and unlikes. If it has the power to predict, but results are functions of "too many" variables, it *is* theory but lacks the capacity to be manipulated; it is therefore useless and there is nothing to do with it but keep it in storage in a kind of intellectual

Elements in Job Attractiveness

Some of the recent literature takes the position that wage differentials have little to do with job choice. Workers are asked why they leave jobs, why they take jobs, why they change jobs. They reply that a constellation of considerations influences their decisions, that alternative wages are only one component of this constellation, and that other factors than alternative wages

---

warehouse. With "too many" independent variables, a theory has no capacity to be verified; its goodness cannot be tested.

The model (the postulated functional relationship between variables) need not be realistic to give good results. "Bohr's theory of the atom, with its circulating electrons, was at first taken to be a faithful picture of the objective reality. It was only later that it came to be realized that *any other picture* [italics supplied] will do equally well, provided it leads to the same mathematical equations. And the modern Schroedinger atom, with its waves in multidimensional space, presents us with a picture which is frankly incredible." J. W. N. Sullivan, *The Limitations of Science* (New York: Viking Press, 1949), p. 157.

To draw another example from the physical sciences, John Dalton, the Manchester schoolmaster, found regularity in the chemical composition of various substances. "[He] now cast about for an *explanation* of the composition of matter. . . . He made the assumption . . . [of] the famous *atomic hypothesis. If the truth of this hypothesis be granted,* the laws of chemical combination may be deduced directly, and are made intelligible. . . . It is . . . important to note that the hypothesis is nothing more than a *mentally constructed and quite imaginary* mechanism, accounting for the facts. *We must be under no illusion that our pictorial conception is representative of the actual machinery of nature* [italics supplied]. Whether there are such things as atoms, and whether the atomic hypothesis is actually in accordance with nature, we have no real knowledge whatever. . . . It must be carefully borne in mind that *all we know* is that certain chemical processes take place *as if* the hypothesis were true." F. W. Westaway, *Scientific Method* (New York: Hillman-Curl, Inc., 1937), pp. 240–241.

Or consider the process of "continuous creation." "Where does the created material come from? It does not come from anywhere. Material simply appears—it is created. At one time the various atoms composing the material do not exist, and at a later time they do. This may seem

weigh more heavily on choice. Such choice criteria are consistent, however, with conventional doctrine, which permits choice to be made in terms, let us say, of the cleanliness or dirtiness of jobs. In the classical system, a worker may choose a job because it is clean and reject another because it is dirty. The classicists only argue that other things equal, the clean job will carry a lower wage than the dirty job and that the difference in the wage will be only enough to compensate for the cleanliness properties of the two jobs, if workers are permitted to move freely between jobs.

Occupational choice in terms of relative wages is made only in a framework in which other job properties are given. If a dirty occupation is expanding and must attract workers from a clean occupation, then the wage differential between the two must be, for a time, larger than when the distribution of workers between the two is in equilibrium. It can be seen that given other job properties, choice will be made in terms of relative wages, if one asks whether workers can be attracted to otherwise unattractive employments by offering very, very high wages. There surely is some wage high enough to

move workers. The principle that relative wages are meaningful in job choice can be proved by arguing the case of the extremely high wage. The economists' position is simply this: that workers will be indifferent between clean and dirty occupations, if the wage differential is just sufficient to compensate for differential cleanliness; that they will prefer the clean job, if the wage differential is less than this; that they will prefer the dirty job, if the wage differential is more than this. It does not matter whether we say that they choose jobs in terms of cleanliness properties, *wages being given,* or that they choose jobs in terms of relative wages, *cleanliness properties being given.* In either case, we say the same thing.

The money wage becomes the determinant of choice only when other attributes are compared. This does not say that choice is made only in terms of relative prices.

Responses to Questions on Job Choice

The trade of common informer cannot be made more agreeable short of revising the values of our culture, but given the odium which attaches to the trade, a price can be attached to it, such that some are willing to engage in it. They are paid "at a rate quite disproportioned to the quantity of work they do. They are paid not so much for encountering toil as for being pelted and hissed."[16] Ask a man why he does not become an informer and he will answer that it will make him unpopular with his fellows, but we cannot be led by this to the judgment that price is irrelevant to his choice. At some price differential between the informer's trade and others, he will accept work of this kind. Men do act as informers. The relevance of price to choice is not nullified by the response that the trade is eschewed because of the odium in which it is held. If the informer's wage becomes very high, and this same man does enter the trade, he will answer, when asked why

---

a very strange idea, and I agree that it is, *but in science it does not matter how strange an idea may seem so long as it works—that is to say, so long as the idea can be expressed in precise form and so long as its consequences are found to be in agreement with observation.*" [italics supplied] Fred Hoyle, *The Nature of the Universe* (New York: Harper and Brothers, 1950), pp. 123–124.

"Sometimes palpably fictitious theories have been more fruitful in producing new discoveries than perfectly correct but quite abstract formulae." A. D. Ritchie, *Scientific Method* (London: Kegan Paul, Trench, Trubner & Co., Ltd., 1923), p. 159.

In economics, as in the physical sciences, the consistency of the model with observed experience is not the measure of the goodness of a theory; it is the predictive results that count. I think that Professor Reynolds, for example, is on the wrong road when he writes, "A proper test of competitive labor market theory would require factual evidence sufficient to test the key assumptions of this theory." Lloyd G. Reynolds, *The Structure of Labor Markets* (New York: Harper and Brothers, 1951), p. 207.

[16] Nassau W. Senior, *Industrial Efficiency and Social Economy* (New York: Henry Holt, 1928), Vol. 2, p. 248.

he accepted the job, "Because the price is high." The values of this worker may not have changed at all, but one response has reference to the odious character of the work and the other to its high price. No appropriate inference on the weights attached by workers to different qualities in jobs can be drawn from the replies to questions about motivations for job-taking and job-changing.

Another example may be helpful. Consider a worker with a given criteria system. If he rejects an offer of work in Greenland, he will explain his choice by saying, "It's too cold up there." If he accepts the offer, he will explain by saying, "They're paying good money." When he said, "It's too cold," what he really intended was, "It's too cold, for the money they're paying"; and, when he said, "They're paying good money," what he really intended was "They're paying good *enough* money, even for the cold I will experience in Greenland."

Two things can be inferred from this example. First, job choices are not made in single-motivational terms; and, second, responses couched in single-motivational terms have other motivations implicitly embedded within them. The same man, with the same criteria system, is here seen to respond differently. The relative importance he attaches to wages and warmth has not changed, but his replies have. His response is determined by the *whole* complex of circumstances that confront him, all taken together.[17]

Knowledge and Ignorance in Job Choice

2. *If workers are to make job choices with reference to the comparative net advantages in different employments, they must have knowledge of the qualities which attach to jobs. Frequently, however, they make choices in conditions of ignorance, and the most extreme case is the one in which the worker moves from unemployment to a job or from a job to unemployment. In these cases, comparison is not possible.*[18]

---

[17] Much of the recent research in labor markets has precisely involved the methodology of putting questions to samples of workers and inferring their criteria systems from their responses. See Parnes, *op. cit.*, p. 147 ff. This methodology was [mistakenly, I think] thought to be appropriate by a group of economists who met at Harvard in 1948, under the auspices of the Committee on Labor Market Research of the Social Science Research Council. "[Do] wage rates have a marked influence on workers' job choices [?] The direct approach to this problem is to interview workers who have recently changed jobs concerning their reasons for leaving the previous job and for taking the present job." Lloyd G. Reynolds, *Research on Wages:* Report of a Conference held on February 21–22, 1948, at the Littauer Center, Harvard University (New York: Social Science Research Council, 1948, mimeo.), p. 20.

Professor Myers seems to support the view expressed in this paper. He says, "The answer [to the question of 'what workers want in jobs'] will depend on what they already enjoy in their work." "Labor Mobility in Two Communities," p. 75.

[18] Professor Reynolds says, "[Workers'] knowledge of wage and nonwage terms of employment in other companies is very meager," *The Structure of Labor Markets*, p. 213.

Professor Parnes says, "There are at least three different circumstances in which workers voluntarily terminate employment. A worker may quit a job because he has found another which is more attractive to him; because of dissatisfaction with his present job and the hope that he will find a more satisfying one; or with no intention of seeking other work. Only separations of the first type are clearly relevant in research intended to test empirically the premises of traditional economic theory relating to labor mobility." Parnes, *op. cit.*, p. 149. Paraphrasing the findings of the Myers and Schultz study of the Nashua labor market, Professor Parnes reports that "fully a third [of the sampled workers] had not 'chosen' the job in any real sense, but had either drifted into it or had taken it because they could find no other." *Ibid.*, p. 156. Parnes believes that the evidence that workers possess incomplete knowledge of alternatives weakens the analytical power of economic theory. "Unless workers have reasonably accurate and complete knowledge of the extent and nature of employment opportunities, there is no basis for assuming a purposeful movement of workers among jobs, and the foundation for the entire theoretical analysis is weakened. The evidence on this point is not reassuring. The average manual worker seems to have very limited knowledge of job opportunities in the labor market and even less information regarding the specific characteristics of jobs in establishments other than his own." *Ibid.*, p. 187.

Comparisons by Unemployed Workers

It seems to be a plausible proposition that even unemployed workers assess alternatives and choose among them. Consider a worker who is unemployed and who is offered a job with properties x, y, and z. Is comparison possible here? It is, and it is comparison with a dual facet.

The worker makes, first, a comparison between a continued status of unemployment and the job offered. He would not, under all circumstances, accept the job. If it were offered, for example, at a wage of one penny per year, he would prefer unemployment. A "job" with full leisure at zero income would be preferred to a job with less leisure at a one-penny-per-annum wage. The wage differential would not be sufficient to compensate for the relatively less advantageous nonwage properties of the penny-per-annum job.

The worker makes, secondly, a comparison between the net advantages of the job offered and the net advantages of other jobs not offered and not known in any specific sense, but which are known in some expectational sense. This only says that the choice is made in conditions of uncertainty. Most economic choices are made in conditions of uncertainty; we have only to look at business mortality rates to verify this fact. But this does not mean that choice cannot be made in any other way than randomly. The worker knows the properties of the job offered to him; he estimates the properties of other jobs which he expects may become available; and he compares the two and chooses whether to accept the first or wait for another.[19] Assume that the worker quits his job (about whose properties he has knowledge) but has no other job immediately available to him. He may move to unemployment, but still be available for other employment. In the same way as has already been discussed, there is a comparison made and choice is possible. The choice here is between a known job and an unknown, expected job whose properties are estimated. If the worker moves from a known job to "out-of-the-labor-force status" and is not available for work, again he compares and chooses. Here, the properties of the known job were not sufficiently advantageous to compensate for the attractions of leisure.

The notion that when unemployed workers take jobs "because they are unemployed," choice is made by them outside a framework of comparison is, thus, not correct. An unemployed worker can be expected to reject work at a very low wage or, what is the same thing, work at a very high wage which is so hazardous that he has perfect certainty that it will cause his death. Unemployed workers, thus, do not take "any" job or "the first job offered." Persistent unemployment will be preferred to some jobs. If the "first job offered" is taken, it is because the worker, having made an estimate, decides that all things considered, he is better off with it than he would be if he continued to be unemployed and waited for a next offer.

"Pushes" and "Pulls"

Some writers have attempted to distinguish between "pushes" and "pulls" to explain worker behavior in the labor market.[20] If a worker is discharged or demoted, or if something else distasteful to him transpires

---

[19] By omitting the possibility of estimation in uncertainty, I think that Professor Reynolds underestimates the number of alternatives by which workers consider, in some implicit sense, that they are confronted. He says of New Haven workers, "The decision to take or to keep a job usually depends on a comparison between the characteristics of the job and the worker's minimum standards, rather than on a comparison of the job with other known alternatives." *The Structure of Labor Markets,* p. 212.

[20] See, for example, Clark Kerr. "There is some real question how effective a wage structure can be in distributing labor in any event. Wages are only one of several important considerations which repel workers from some jobs and attract them to others. The push of unemployment, for example, is often more effective than the pull of higher wages." "Labor Markets: Their Character and Consequences," p. 288.

in his present place, he is said to be "pushed" to make a change. If he is offered or becomes aware of a higher wage or otherwise superior position elsewhere, he is said to be "pulled" to make a change.

Because "pushed" workers move to other jobs more frequently and because a disproportionately large number of new job-takers are of this class, they may appear to be more actively engaged in calculating net advantage among alternatives than those who are "pulled." But appearance may be deceptive. It may be only that differential rates of movement for "pushed" and "pulled" workers reflect different magnitudes for the two classes in the net advantages of present and new situations. The average difference between the net advantage of their present position and that of a new situation may be very much larger for "pushed" workers than the average difference between the two for workers who are merely "pulled." If this is so, we should expect a higher rate of movement between jobs by "pushed" workers, even if the propensity to calculate and compare were equal for the two classes.

If choices are rational, they are made in terms of the worker's assessment of difference between two situations. It is not the fact that he is badly off, by any absolute measure, in his present place that causes him to move; it is rather that he is badly off relative to what he estimates his position will be after moving. If he believes that he can improve his lot by going elsewhere, he will go; if he does not, he will stay. What is important to his decision is difference; to understand the nature of choice in labor markets, we must look at response to difference.

The comparison of estimated alternatives is made in a context of more or less correct understanding of the "going rate" in different employments, of the "worth" of the worker's services, or of the availability of alternative opportunities. There is verification of this behavioral pattern in the empirical studies themselves, which show that quits are more frequent in times and places of expanding employment than in those of constant or diminishing employment.

The unemployed worker who sets a minimum standard for jobs which he will find acceptable is making a choice with respect to the comparative attractiveness of alternatives. In substance, the worker is saying, "For work of this kind, I shall not accept a wage of less than X cents per hour; because I believe that if I wait, I shall find this price." Seen in this way, the case of the minimum standard turns out to be a specific variation of the general case of calculation and choice on the basis of comparative net attractiveness. Even if, as the empirical studies have found, "workers' knowledge of job alternatives is fragmentary and imperfect,"[21] movement of workers can equalize earnings in equal employments. Some will overestimate the relative value of a new job and will move more rapidly and frequently than they would if they had full knowledge. Some will underestimate and will move less rapidly and frequently than they would if they had full knowledge. If over and underestimation is randomly distributed among workers, the differences will cancel, and movement will tend to be just that required to equalize net advantage. This may be a sensible expectation of what happens in the labor market.

Uncertainty and Job Selection

Estimates made in uncertainty may lead, of course, to some wrong directional movement. Even if the cancelling-out process which is here suggested does operate in labor markets, therefore, and appropriate allocation of labor among uses is finally achieved, economists will still be interested in enlarging knowledge and diminishing uncertainty, because the more certain are the conditions within which choice is made, the smaller will be the number of moves necessary to reach the optimum.

Empirical research has found that work-

---

[21] George P. Schultz, "Recent Research on Labor Mobility," in *Proceedings, Industrial Relations Research Association,* Boston, 1951, p. 116.

ers who leave a present employment with another specific employment already arranged move to higher gross weekly earnings positions more often than do workers who leave without a specific alternative arranged. From this the conclusion has been drawn that the classical understanding of the nature of worker behavioral choice is more consistent with reality in the former case than in the latter. In both cases, however, workers may well be searching for greater advantage. The conclusion we can appropriately draw from the evidence is that choice in a context of less uncertainty is more successful than choice in a context of more uncertainty. This is only like saying that the incidence of mortality of firms with certain futures is less than the incidence of mortality of firms with uncertain futures. We cannot infer from differential mortality rates differential motivations or differential behavioral patterns.

We can say that uncertainty retards optimum resource distribution in the cases of both firms and workers and hinders equation of net advantages in different uses, but this is all. We cannot say that uncertainty prevents these tendencies or that it leads to nonoptimum distribution and nonequivalence.

The retarding process operates in two ways. First, movement between occupations is more frequent in conditions of uncertainty than in conditions of certainty; second, each movement is less complete than it otherwise would be. But long-distance movement can occur by a chain of short-distance moves. Equivalence of new advantage in positions *A* and *Z* can be achieved without specific movement between them, if only there is movement from *A* to *B,* from *B* to *C,* etc. An examination of the pattern of internal migration in the United States will show precisely this kind of movement. Just as not every worker need move for equivalence to occur, not every moving worker need make a full move. It is only necessary that movement tend to be from less to more advantageous employments.

Desire of Workers for Security

3. *Workers value security highly. They prefer present employment at lower prices to other employment at higher, because moving will diminish their security. Therefore, workers are unresponsive to differentials in prices in alternative employments.*[22] *Workers are especially insecure in periods of less than full employment, and especially in these periods, price differentials will not move them to change jobs. Therefore, the classical doctrine is especially deficient for an understanding of behavior at time of cyclical troughs.*

Surely, workers give attention to security, along with price, in making job decisions. The security attribute is one of the comparative components, along with price, upon which workers make choices. Workers who have acquired security of tenure or who are employed by firms which are expected to be successful in the future may prefer to stay at a lower wage, rather than moving to other employments at a higher wage. But this is no proof that actual behavior of workers is at variance with the classicists' perception. The economists realized that workers *do* give weight to the expected duration of employment in making behavioral choices.

Adam Smith listed as one of the causes of variableness in wages the constancy or inconstancy of employment. Paraphrasing him, Nassau Senior spoke of the London porter, who works inconstantly and thus must be paid more to induce him to pursue that calling than the hodman, whose work is more severe but can "always find a market for his services." Their discussion was of prices in different employments in relationship to the qualities of casualness or regularity that attach to different jobs. But, in principle, the classic proposition was that other things equal, a lower wage attaches (will attract workers) to regular employment than to irregular employment; it requires no revision to read it as saying that

[22] " 'Oldtimers' were . . . frequently unwilling to risk the security of their present positions by moving." Myers and Maclaurin, *op. cit.,* pp. 50–51.

a worker will accept a lower wage in a secure employment in preference to one somewhat larger wage in an insecure (or less secure) employment. The important role played by seniority rules, in recent years, for rationing dismissals and promotive vacancies among workers merely puts a new face on Adam Smith's point that a constant employment will be preferred to an inconstant one. In his day, workers were willing to pay a price for the short-run security of constant employment; in ours, they are willing to pay a price for the long-run security of seniority status. Just as inconstancy could be paid for by a higher wage then, the loss of seniority status can be paid for now. There is some earnings difference that will induce even very long-service workers to take up new employment.

Choice is not made by workers in terms of instantaneous earnings differences, and it was not understood by the economists that it would be. It was "obvious" to Senior that "the labourer's situation does not depend on the amount which he receives at any one time, but on his average receipts during a given period—during a week, a month, or a year; and that the longer the period taken, the more accurate will be the estimate."[23] He saw, too, that the number of competitors in the medical and legal professions was diminished, not only by the high cost of learning these arts, but also because, for a period of some years of apprenticeship or study, the earnings of practitioners are very low.[24]

Thus it is consistent with the theory that in periods of less than full employment, the relative hourly wage should be less important in motivating job changes than in periods of full employment. A sensible worker accepts a "low" wage in present employment, at the trough of the cycle, because he has a low estimation of his future earnings prospects if he should leave to search for an alternative. A comparison of long-run earnings in different employments (one known and others estimated) diminishes the influence of hourly wages upon choice in trough periods. In periods of cyclical peak, on the other hand, when opportunities for work elsewhere are many, the expectation of long-run earnings in other employment is high, and hourly wage rates weigh more heavily upon choice.

It is even consistent with the theory that in conditions of layoffs in particular labor markets, workers move from "better" previous employment to a "worse" present one. The worker who makes a job choice must be thought to calculate net advantage in long-run rather than instantaneous terms. He may, therefore, choose a secure employment at a lower wage over an insecure employment at a higher wage, even in periods of full employment. Just so, in times of unemployment he accepts a job with reference to his calculation of long-run prospects, and this may lead him to conclude that a lower wage job than he has held is still for him the more advantageous one.

---

[23] *Three Lectures on the Rate of Wages,* p. 7. Professors Reynolds and Shister wrote, "Economists have tended to assume that even when a worker has a job he will keep his eyes continuously open for something better and will be willing to switch to a superior job at the drop of a hat." Lloyd G. Reynolds and Joseph Shister, *Job Horizons* (New York: John Wiley and Sons, Inc., 1949), p. 45.

If a "superior job" means merely a job paying a higher wage, then two things need to be said. (1) The classical economists did not assume such behavior; and (2) the neoclassical economists may have assumed such behavior, but this assumption was not intended to be descriptive of real life. The usefulness of the abstraction from the real world in which the assumption appears depends not upon its "realism" but upon the degree of conformity of predictions derived from the abstraction with observable experience. If, on the other hand, "superior job" means one which is, on balance, superior, *all things con-sidered,* then it seems indeed to be sensible to assume that a worker "*will* be willing to switch." Any other assumption has the worker making choices according to the rule that he shall be disadvantaged. It is doubtful that many workers are guided by such a rule.

[24] *An Outline of the Science of Political Economy,* p. 207.

Rationality of Worker Behavior

4. Workers do not act rationally in labor markets. They do not make comparisons of net advantage in alternative employments. They do not even examine the evidence which is available to them. Their decisions stem more from habit than from rational calculation.[25]

The idea that choice is made in terms of relative net advantage does not imply that comparison and calculation by workers be explicit. Professor Machlup's driver decided whether to pass a truck on the highway without explicitly solving some formidable equations.[26] In some implicit sense, of course, he did solve them. That his solution might not have been correct we know from the incidence of highway accidents, but in event of a mishap most observers would say that the driver had "miscalculated." Few, if any, would assume he had made no calculation of the situation.

Calculation in labor markets occurs in the same way; wrong choices (miscalculations) are not infrequent.[27]

Meaning of Rational Choice

When we assume that workers choose rationally among employment alternatives, we mean that they make choice decisions which are consistent with their goals. If the goal is A, choice which leads to the achievement of A is rational; choice which leads to the achievement of B, when the chooser believes it leads to A, is also rational. Choice is irrational, if the goal is A, and the choice leads to B, when the chooser believes it leads to B. Choice is random, when there is no goal (when there is indifference among ends) and selection is made as though it depended upon the turn of a coin.

If, therefore, workers' goals are to maximize net advantage and if they make choices which they believe will maximize net advantage, they are making rational choices. They may miscalculate and come to wrong decisions, but wrong decisions are not irrational decisions and do not destroy the classical thesis.

It may be said that the qualities which attach to jobs are so large in number and so diverse that calculated comparison of jobs is not possible. To this there are two answers. First, though comparison is difficult, comparison occurs; we know this because we know that choices are made and that the pattern of choice does not distribute people randomly in the economy but puts them more or less where they are wanted. Second, comparison is diverse among individuals. The qualities of an employment do not attach to it in any intrinsic, objective

---

[25] Myers and Maclaurin found in Fitchburg, for example, "There were large groups of employees . . . who had become sufficiently habituated to their working environment so that they were not interested in moving to another concern that promised immediate payment of better wages for comparable types of work. *Op. cit.,* pp. 49–50.

[26] Fritz Machlup, "Marginal Analysis and Empirical Research," *American Economic Review,* September 1946, pp. 534–535.

[27] The notion that *explicit* calculation must occur, if there is to be comparison, seems to be held by Professor Parnes, who has written, "In many voluntary job changes the worker simply is not in a position to make a conscious comparison of the advantages of alternative jobs." Parnes, *op. cit.,* p. 158, n. 11. "A good deal of voluntary movement—perhaps most of it—is not the product of deliberate and careful comparison of alternative job opportunities, but rather the result of workers' leaving jobs that are distasteful in order to cast around for others which they hope will be more satisfactory." *Ibid.,* pp. 161–162.

Reynolds and Shister suggest that theory assumes explicit calculation. "[In the economic theory of job choices], the worker is regarded as behaving like a scientist, carefully gathering all of the relevant facts, and then choosing the job which promises the greatest net advantage." *Job Horizons,* p. 80.

Professor Shister elsewhere describes the actual process of job choice in this way: "Most workers who are changing jobs take the first one they find if it meets certain *absolute* standards that they have developed. The evaluation of the new job is not based on drawing comparisons with other jobs." *Economics of the Labor Market* (New York: J. B. Lippincott Company, 1949), p. 395. Of first-job taking, he says, "Workers gaining full-time employment for the first time do not indulge in rational comparisons involving net economic advantage." *Ibid.,* p. 398.

sense. An occupation has qualities only as workers perceive them, and their perceptions are diverse. Some will think dirtiness very disagreeable; others will think it only somewhat disagreeable. Some will have a preference for security; others for risk. If John Doe believes that, wages aside, job *A* is only slightly preferable to *B,* Richard Roe may believe it is preferable by far. Doe, who, let us say, was on the margin of moving to *B,* can be induced to move by a small differential in wages; a large differential will be necessary to move Roe.

It is because there is variation among workers in the evaluation of jobs that we have an upward sloping supply curve of labor of a craft and the possibility of equalization of net advantage by adjusting relative wages, with only fractional response by workers to a changing wage structure.

It is not correct, of course, to conclude that workers do not behave as the economists assume they do because we find cases in which workers sometimes move from employments that pay well to those that pay badly. It cannot be said that in these cases workers made no comparison or that they chose irrationally. The choice may be simply incorrect, but still rational, and as has been suggested, wrong choices only slow down the process of advantage equalization. Or it may not be incorrect at all, for a high wage is preferable to a low wage only in other-things-equal circumstances and other things may not have been equal. Depending upon circumstances, workers may maximize net advantage by moving to a new occupation which pays more, less, or the same rate, and any one of the three can be consistent with the classical doctrine.

Habit and Calculated Comparison

The apparent persistence of wage differentials in similar employments in a labor market does not necessarily mean that calculated comparison does not occur. What seem to be similar employments may not be similar at all in the worker's perception of them, and there also may be errors in observation. What appears to be "the same kind of work" may really be different when account is taken of all the qualities considered by workers in making occupational choice. Some of these are surely so subtle that they escape detection.

The distinction between choice from habit and choice based upon calculation is not clear-cut, and what seems to be habitual behavior may be consistent with calculated behavior. Senior remarked, for example, that "ten [English mechanics] go to America for one who will venture to France," although their wage gain would be greater, if they went to France.[28] This can be interpreted as pursuit of the habitual idiom, but it can also be seen as calculated avoidance of the real cost of assimilating an unhabitual one.

If there are persistent price differentials in truly similar employments, it may only be because adjustment is not quickly brought about. McCulloch said on this point:

It often happens that, owing to an attachment to the trade, or the locality in which they have been bred, or the difficulty of learning other trades, individuals will continue, for a lengthened period, to practice their peculiar trades, or will remain in the same district, when other trades in that district and the same trades in other districts, yield better wages to those engaged in them. But how slowly soever, wages, taking everything into account, are sure to be equalized in the end.[29]

Conclusions

If we accept the argument that workers make employment choices without respect to wages, or in ignorance or randomly, we are then confronted with some questions. How shall we explain, for example, the massive evidence that the geographical movement of workers is from low, long-run

[28] *An Outline of the Science of Political Economy,* p. 222.
[29] *A Treatise on the Circumstances Which Determine the Rate of Wages and the Condition of the Labouring Classes,* pp. 67–68.

earnings opportunities to high? Or how shall we explain why occupations requiring rare talent or long and arduous training for their successful performance carry a higher price than those requiring talents possessed by many and skills that are come by easily?

Can we sensibly believe that gross behavior which is consistent with the conventional theory is the result of accidental circumstance and random choice? It seems unlikely that this should be so. The economic theory of the labor market is logically defensible and gives good gross predictive results, if allowance is made for the time necessary for the allocational process to work itself out. Where it has been said to contain errors, it seems to be for these reasons:

1. Empirical research has sought to test the theory by measuring the *assumptions* of the abstract and simple neoclassical model of worker behavior against the complicated motivational system of real workers, rather than by measuring the predictive *results* derived from the use of the analytical apparatus against observed experience.
2. Wrong inferences about the valuation of job qualities by workers have been drawn from responses to interview questions.
3. Exposition intended to characterize whole and general universes have been interpreted to apply to the unique individuals of which they are composed.
4. Disbelief exists that predictions from simple models can give good results in complicated real worlds.
5. The part of the theory which was relevant to free markets was applied to markets in which there are constraints on choice.
6. It was believed that conditions of certainty (of perfect knowledge) are necessary to rational choice.
7. The theory was incorrectly thought to assume uniformity and instantaneity, or at least rapidity, in response behavior among workers.
8. It was thought that rational choice required conscious and explicit calculation.

4
On Choice in Labor Markets: Comment

Robert J. Lampman

In a recent issue of this journal Professor Simon Rottenberg undertook a defense of classical wage theory in the form of a critique of recent empirical labor market studies.[1] Asserting that the empiricists[2] have attributed to the classicists errors which the latter did not commit, he appeals to the nature of theory to quiet the empiricists and to elevate the classicists.

It is the thesis of this comment that the standard for judging theories, namely, verification, called up by Professor Rottenberg is, if fully applied to classical wage theory,

Reprinted from the *Industrial and Labor Relations Review,* Vol. 9, No. 4, July, 1956, pp. 629–636. Copyright © 1956 by Cornell University. All rights reserved.

[1] "On Choice in Labor Markets," Vol. 9, No. 2 (January 1956), pp. 183–199 [Reading 3 in this text, to which all page references in parentheses in this reading refer—Eds.].

[2] For a review of the findings of the "empiricists" see Herbert S. Parnes, *Research on Labor Mobility* (New York: Social Science Research Council, 1954).

not a defense but an indictment of that theory.

A brief restatement of the controversy will be helpful. Researchers into the facts challenge the *realism* of classical wage theory, by offering the following findings: (1) worker responses to questionnaires indicate that wage differences play a very small role in the choice process; (2) workers are often ignorant of job alternatives; (3) workers value security highly and hence are unresponsive to wage differences; (4) workers do not seem to calculate net advantages or act rationally in choosing among jobs.

In Professor Rottenberg's view, these findings leave classical wage theory undefiled. The findings have to do, he points out, with the assumptions and not with the predictions of classical theory. The test of a theory is not in the realism or factual accuracy of its assumptions. The crucial question, rather, is whether the theory has "generalized predictive power." A theory is a good one if, regardless of the realism of its

53

"model," its predictions are realized. Rottenberg refers rather obliquely to the question of verifiability, suggesting in a footnote that if ". . . a theory has no capacity to be verified, its goodness cannot be tested."[3] He holds, in general, that the predictions of classical wage theory are in fact verified in the contemporary scene.[4]

Now let us move in to take a closer look at the controversy, keeping in mind the general question: Is the classical wage theory a "good" theory? The standard suggested for judging theories is verifiability. We propose to examine these questions in order: (1) What is a verifiable prediction? (2) Does classical wage theory, as interpreted by Professor Rottenberg, contain a set of verifiable predictions? (3) Do the empiricists have any verifiable predictions? and (4) How can verifiable predictions help with policy questions?

(1) What is a verifiable prediction?

Positivism is a philosophy of the laboratory which emphasizes the distinction between "logical truth" and "empirical truth." Operationalism is the method which, by definition, is the only way to establish empirical truth. In the positivistic system there are three possible responses to any proposition about the empirical world. One is to classify it as empirically not disproved. (Short of this are statements which are in principle testable, though not yet tested.) The second possibility is to find it empirically disproved. The third response which may be given is: no answer concerning its disproof is possible.

Propositions to which the third response must be given may be referred to as nonverifiable or nonoperational propositions. The term "nonverifiable propositions" applies to all definitional propositions (this is a tree), all axiomatic propositions (2 + 2 = 4), and all value statements (oh, what a nice party!).

In order for a proposition to be verifiable, it must be set up as involving an observable operation; that is, both the "if" and the "then" must be observable[5] and independent of the prediction. It must be possible for some set of empirical findings to disprove the prediction.[6]

The empirical truth of a prediction does not depend on the realism or factual accuracy of the conventional assumptions which may or may not have lain behind the framing of the "if-then" proposition. The "usefulness" of the *conventions* (or as Professor Rottenberg would call them, the "models"),[7]

---

[3] Footnote 15, pp. 189–190 [p. 57—Eds.]. In the same footnote he states that in "ordinary form" theory is testable.

[4] In another context Rottenberg states: "The usefulness of theory derives from the capacity of abstract, simple, and unrealistic models to yield results which are highly predictive of real phenomenal experience. Much of the criticism of theory derives from the belief—which I think false—that simple models cannot be used to explain complex phenomena or from the failure to understand that results that are drawn from these models are only tendential." Discussion on "Labor in a Developing Economy," Papers and Proceedings of the American Economic Association, *American Economic Review,* Vol. 45, No. 2 (May 1955), pp. 191–196.

[5] As Professor Machlup puts it, "In principle we want both Assumed Change and Deduced Change to be capable of being compared with recorded data so that the correspondence between the theory and the data can be checked." Fritz Machlup, "The Problem of Verification in Economics," *Southern Economic Journal,* Vol. 22, No. 10 (July 1955), p. 4.

[6] "For a proposition to be testable by some physical operation, it must predict that certain observations will *not* occur, so that, if they do, the proposition is refuted." Donald F. Gordon, "Operational Propositions in Economic Theory," *Journal of Political Economy,* Vol. 63, No. 2 (April 1955), p. 150. Also relevant here is: ". . . since a hypothesis can be definitely refuted or 'falsified' but not definitely confirmed or 'verified', some logicians have urged that we speak only of 'falsifiable', not verifiable propositions." Machlup, *loc. cit.,* p. 4.

[7] Professor Machlup offers the following alternative designations for such assumptions: heuristic assumptions, basic postulates, useful fictions, procedural rules, definitional assumptions, self-evident propositions, axioms, a priori truths, tru-

which may be simply hunches or wild imaginings about worker, entrepreneur, or consumer motives and behavior, is measured only by whether or not they lead to verifiable predictions having some interest.

In any event, there is no point in examining the realism of the conventions if we are interested in empirical testing. The introduction of more "realistic" conventions will not establish the prediction as verifiable.[8]

---

isms, tautologies, definitions, rigid laws, resolutions, working hypotheses, ideal types, heuristic mental constructs, indisputable facts of experience, facts of immediate experience, data of introspective observation, private empirical data, typical behavior patterns. He notes that Einstein referred to such assumptions in physical science as "free creations of the human mind." *Loc. cit.,* pp. 9 and 16.

[8] Perhaps the most widely remarked nonverifiable proposition in economics is that having to do with income redistribution. Whether or not taking money from the rich and giving it to the poor will increase total consumer satisfactions is nonverifiable and not subject to disproof so long as there is no independently observable indication of satisfactions, which are originally conceived as uniquely and subjectively experienced phenomena. In "Making Utility Predictions Verifiable," *Southern Economic Journal,* Vol. 22, No. 3 (January 1956), pp. 360–366, the present author discusses this issue. It is argued there that the nonverifiability characteristic is fully shared by utility maximization predictions which do not involve interpersonal comparison. Ways to rewrite these predictions to make them verifiable by introducing independent, observable indicators of total utility are suggested.

Following this example a little further, the empirical truth of the prediction, "*if* we take from the rich and give to the poor, *then* total consumer satisfactions will be increased" is not affected by findings that individual consumers do not behave rationally, are ignorant of alternatives, do not buy cheaper articles having higher quality.

Now it seems to me that there is a rather complete analogy between the controversy about income redistribution and the controversy about wage theory to which Professor Rottenberg is a party. In both controversies nonverifiable predictions are offered. Some critics of these predictions, finding they are unable to prove or disprove them, direct their empirical investigations toward the conventions about the essential nature of the data (consumer and worker behavior). In neither case

(2) Are the predictions of classical wage theory verifiable?

Careful reading of Professor Rottenberg's article suggests that classical theory of the allocation of labor from the supply side may be paraphrased this way. First, there is a convention entered about workers' essential nature. This is the assumption that workers in choosing among jobs seek to maximize net advantage. Second is what we may label a low-level prediction, namely, that a single worker, *if* given a choice between two jobs, *then* will choose that one which offers him the higher net satisfaction. Third is the higher-level (higher in the sense that aggregation is involved) prediction: *if* all workers are free to choose among all jobs, *then* the result will be that all jobs will have equal net advantages, as evaluated by those holding the jobs.[9]

In the article discussed here Professor Rottenberg devotes a good deal of his attention to the low-level prediction. Quite rightly, from a positivist point of view, he points out that the empirical truth (or lack of it) in this prediction is unaffected by findings of fact about the convention. On these grounds he dismisses the findings that workers are motivated by nonwage considerations, are ignorant, and irrational.[10]

He then offers a series of predictions consistent with the convention. (1) If a worker is offered two jobs identical in all respects

---

can such findings alter the goodness of the prediction since it is, as stated, nonverifiable anyway. In the positivist system, investigations of the realism of the conventions amount to beating a dead horse.

[9] Logically, for this to happen, there must be competitive conditions on the demand side and workers must have equal attractiveness to employers, although their preferences in types of work may differ.

[10] He also argues that the classicists were not unaware of the "real" essential nature of worker behavior and that it is hard to prove that workers are in fact irrational. This all strikes me as quite aside from the main drift of his article and seems even to contradict his principal thesis.

except that one offers a higher wage, he will prefer or choose the one having a higher wage (pp. 42–43). (2) If a worker is offered a "dirty job" which pays a wage differential over a "clean job" just sufficient to overcompensate for differential "cleanliness," then the worker will choose the "dirty job"[11] (p. 44).

Similarly, Professor Rottenberg offers up a list of higher-order predictions which he regards as consistent with the classical convention.[12] (1) If workers have free choice, the result will be that the net advantages of all jobs are equalized[13] (p. 47). (2) If workers are allowed free choice, then the result will be that ". . . people are placed more or less where they are wanted" (p. 50). (3) If workers are allowed free choice, then the result will be that ". . . geographic movement of workers is from low long-run earnings opportunities to high" (p. 51). (4) If workers are allowed free choice, then occupations requiring rare talent will carry a high price (p. 52). (5) If workers are allowed free choice, then occupations requiring long and arduous training will carry a high price (p. 52).

Are these predictions drawn from Professor Rottenberg's article verifiable? One of the elementary rules of operationalism is that a prediction must be disprovable by some possibly observable set of facts. Has this rule been observed?

Consider the second lower-order prediction. We enter the convention that workers seek to maximize net advantage. This suggests the prediction that if a worker is offered a "dirty job" which pays a wage differential over a "clean job" just sufficient to overcompensate for differential "cleanliness," then the worker will choose the "dirty job." Is this a verifiable prediction? How can an objective observer tell whether any given wage differential is "just sufficient"? If the worker chooses the "dirty" job, the wage differential is sufficient; if he does not, then the wage differential is not sufficient. It cannot possibly be proved wrong by any empirical examination of actual choices.[14] Professor Rottenberg firmly states that the calculation of "sufficient" wage differentials is completely subjective. He writes:

The qualities of an employment do not attach to it any intrinsic, objective sense. An occupation has qualities only as workers perceive them, and their perceptions are diverse. . . . Depending upon circumstances, workers may maximize net advantage by moving to a new occupation which pays more, less, or the same

---

[11] He suggests by example that we may substitute for "dirty job" the job of informer, work in Greenland, insecure work, etc.

[12] Sometimes he writes as if these are statements of undisputed fact concerning what *does* happen.

[13] This appears in his discussion of worker ignorance. He suggests that some may overestimate and some may underestimate the advantages of moving, with the result being that the net advantages of jobs are equalized. Thus, even though the low-order prediction may not be realized, the higher-order one is.

[14] The prediction, while nonverifiable in its present form, could be redrawn to be verifiable by taking it out of the subjective and introducing an independent objective indicator of "dirtiness." An operational proposition here requires hypothesizing stability of tastes or preferences. On this latter point see Gordon, *loc. cit.* Also, it should be noted that the implicit proposition that all workers prefer higher wages to lower wages is explicit in the original classical model, but is asserted to be consistent with it by Professor Rottenberg.

Of interest here are some comments by Professor Milton Friedman on interpretation of size distribution of income data. He urges that such data should be analyzed with a view to gaining predictive power over the movement of people. A "higher" income is then, by definition, one that results in movement to it. Thus, the fact that farmers move is incontestable evidence that their incomes are low and "any income measure that suggests the reverse is wrong." Further, "The test of our results is whether the computed incomes do or do not enable us to predict the reactions of individuals when they are faced with a choice between situations differing in respect of items that do not have a straight-forward market price." "Comments," *Studies in Income and Wealth,* Vol. 13 (New York: National Bureau of Economic Research, 1952), pp. 56–60.

rate, and anyone of the three can be consistent with the classical doctrine (p. 51).

How about the higher-order predictions? Are they verifiable? Number 1 is that free choice by workers will result in (or at least tend toward) equalization of net advantages of all jobs. Here the question is: how can these subjectively experienced totals of net advantages be objectively measured? Without such measurement no empirical findings could possibly disprove the prediction. Hence, it has no empirical content. It is enlightening to alter the prediction radically. For example, suppose we predict that if all workers are assigned jobs by lot, then this will result in equalization of net advantages of all jobs. How could this be empirically disproved?

Higher-order prediction number 2 seems somewhat out of place, since it deals with demand conditions perhaps more than with supply. How would we know whether workers were or were not placed "more or less where they are wanted?" Is this a quantifiable matter? Suppose we alter it to read "if workers' choices among jobs are severely restricted by trade union (or government) rules, then they will be placed more or less where they are wanted." Could this prediction be disproved?

Prediction number 3 is a rather different kettle of fish. It is that if workers have free choice, then "geographic movement of workers is from low long-run earning opportunities to high."[15] Now here we are on more solid ground with a prediction that could possibly be disproved by empirical findings. Two comments may be entered. If workers have *limited* choice, this may also be true.[16] Also, if it were found to be false, it would be consistent for Professor Rottenberg to claim that the classical model is not thereby discredited, since the latter points to subjectively experienced net advantages rather than long-run earnings opportunities. Here we could set up the following verifiable proposition, assuming stability of preferences: if the earnings differential of place A over place B is widened, then the additional flow of workers from B to A will exceed the additional flow from A to B.

Prediction 4 is probably verifiable, but has a hiatus in it, because it introduces a variable not hitherto entered in the article, namely, the talent of workers and also, implicitly, demand conditions. Professor Rottenberg states this as if it were a well-established point that the rarer the talent required the higher the price. A moment's reflection will suggest that this is not always true.

The same general comments made in connection with predictions 3 and 4 apply to prediction 5.

There is confusion in Professor Rottenberg's discussion of the higher-order predictions. While early in the article he mentions that the realism of the convention or model is not at issue, in the latter section he leads the reader to believe that that is the issue in his mind. He seems to suggest that verification of a prediction consistent with a convention serves to establish the factual inaccuracy of some other convention. Thus, he argues:

Can we sensibly believe that gross behavior which is consistent with the conventional theory is the result of accidental circumstance and random choice? It seems unlikely that this should be so. The economic theory of the labor market is logically defensible and gives good gross predictive results, if allowance is made

---

[15] This is apparently the proposition that set off the empirical studies. Note that C. A. Myers cites J. R. Hicks in such a way as to indicate that his statement of the theory is the dragon he originally set out to slay. The Hicks quote is ". . . differences in net economic advantages, chiefly differences in wages, are the main causes of migration." *Labor Mobility and Economic Opportunity*, E. W. Bakke, et al. (New York: Wiley, 1954), p. 68. The Hicks citation is from *The Theory of Wages* (London: Macmillan, 1932), p. 76.

[16] This point is expanded below in discussion of question 4.

for the time necessary for the allocation process to work itself out (p. 52).

He seems to be saying that the classical convention is the only "useful" convention in wage theory.[17]

The point here is that you cannot discredit one convention by establishing that another convention is useful in casting up predictions which are verifiable or even verified. Both the empiricists and Professor Rottenberg are guilty of this unfair tactic. The only way to discredit the convention of the empiricists (that workers are ignorant, non-responsive to wage differentials, etc.) is to set up verifiable predictions consistent with the convention and then find them empirically "untrue." This leads us to the next question.

(3) Do the empiricists have any verifiable predictions?

The controversy between Rottenberg and the empiricists is quite unfruitful, since it produces no meeting of minds on what the predictions to be tested are. Rottenberg says predictions consistent with his model are not proved untrue by findings of the empiricists. This does not establish, however, the empirical truth of his predictions nor the exclusive merit of his convention. As argued above, many of his predictions are, in the form he presents them, nonverifiable. Others are not exclusively identified with his model.

Similarly, the fact that the empiricists have failed to establish empirical untruth in the classical predictions does not do any violence to predictions consistent with the empiricists' conventions. Professor Rottenberg has not talked about either the possible lower-order or higher-order predictions which have been drawn and in some cases tested by the empiricists. Space will not permit an exhaustive discussion of these predictions, but one or two may be stated. (1) If workers have free choices in the absence of unions, there will be substantial and persisting differences in pay and perquisites for identical work in the same market areas.[18] (2) If wage differentials among occupations (or regions, industries, or skill levels) are substantially narrowed by collective bargaining, there will be no additional difficulty in finding workers to fill the higher-paying jobs.[19]

(4) How can verifiable predictions help with policy questions?

We have asserted that most of the predictions offered by Professor Rottenberg as consistent with the classical convention are nonverifiable. This means, perhaps, in his own language, that the theory is ". . . not a theory, but only an apparatus for describing unique phenomena, or at best, a taxonomic tool for distinguishing likes and unlikes" (p. 43, fn. 15). However, in the controversial context it has normative connotations. When we say that leaving workers free to choose (i.e. free from union and government interference) will maximize net advantage and contribute to the most efficient allocation of labor there is at least a strong presumption that we are arguing in favor of free choice on the ground that it is "better" than restricted choice. The nonverifiability of the predictions and the "persuasive" terms of "maximum net advantage"

---

[17] This is rather like arguing that since there is a rational pattern observed in nature, there must be a rational God who planned it all; or like saying that since predictions consistent with a certain atomic model are verified, it must be that other models are factually wrong. He also confuses the issue by reference to logical defensibility of the theory. Logical tests have nothing to do with verifiability, either forward or backward. The big question is not: how do workers choose jobs? Rather it is: is it "useful" to pretend that they choose jobs in a way that we are not sure they do? Methodologically, it would be all right to enter the convention that workers behave like eggplants. If this gives rise to verifiable predictions that are useful, then the convention is "useful," but it does not prove that workers *are* eggplants.

[18] See Lloyd G. Reynolds, *The Structure of Labor Markets* (New York: Harper, 1951), p. 216. On regional differences, see p. 246.
[19] *Ibid.*, p. 234; also p. 264.

and "most efficient" allocation mark it as a value judgment.[20]

As a value judgment it is in the same class as the statement, "Oh, what a nice party!" It is saying, in effect: "If we let workers choose,[21] they will get what they want (and we'll call that maximum net advantage); and whatever employers and workers agree upon on the basis of voluntary offerings, we will call the most efficient allocation of labor; and the whole thing altogether we'll call 'Oh, what a nice party!'" If we are all agreed that this is what is meant by a nice party, then the controversy may be only on how to go about establishing conditions of free choice. But along comes someone else saying, "No, a nice party is when groups of workers get together with groups of employers and set rules (or governments do) which restrict freedom of choice by individuals."[22] Now the first group responds, "No, that can't be a nice party because it isn't the conditions we have identified as such." The second group replies, "Can you prove it isn't a nice party? Also, can you prove the nice things you predict will follow from free choice do actually happen in any factual case? Can you prove exactly how far workers are moved from the maximum of net advantages by a particular restriction on choice?"

It is a flat out-and-out value judgment question. You pays your money and you takes your choice. In making this choice, it will be helpful to know more about how much each choice "costs." These "costs" can be appraised by intuition, by prophetic insight, or by the testing of verifiable predictions which relate to the alternative market arrangements. No constructive purpose is served by offering value judgments under the guise of scientific procedure.

Confusion between treating the classical wage theory as predictive and normative is widespread. While Professor Rottenberg treats it as predictive without normative aspects, Professor Reynolds treats it as normative without predictive power. The latter sets up the predictions of classical theory as his norms:

... Competitive reasoning is clearly helpful in defining what one means by optimum matching of individual abilities and job requirements. . . . While it is possible in principle to describe what is meant by 'a competitive wage structure,' there seems to be no way of determining how far a particular wage structure deviates from the competitive norm. The concept thus seems to have little operational usefulness for public policy.[23]

The overriding policy issue is what kind of labor market do we want? Which forms

[20] "Orthodox theory of economic behavior is not a study of human behavior at all. It is incorrect to call it a theory for it does not seek to explain behavior. It should rather be called a *system* of behavior; the sole purpose of the system being the provision of a criterion for being 'economically better off.'" I. M. D. Little, *A Critique of Welfare Economics* (Oxford: Clarendon Press, 1950), p. 51.

[21] Some writers in the field of welfare economics would simply identify free choice as the basic value involved here and let it go at that.

[22] For a good analysis of alternate structurings of the labor market see Clark Kerr, "The Balkanization of Labor Markets," in *Labor Mobility and Economic Opportunity,* pp. 92–110.

[23] *The Structure of Labor Markets,* p. 224. Also see p. 268 wherein he asserts that a competitive market offers "the best way" to allocate labor but is at the same time "an impossible ideal." He finds that the competitive model does not help him decide the crucial question of whether collective bargaining and government intervention are improving or worsening the wage structure (pp. 249ff). In our context it is most extraordinary for Reynolds to say, "It is not a basic objection to say that the competitive norm is not empirically observable" (p. 259). His proposal for judging alternative market arrangements is to observe how closely they approximate equalization of net attractiveness of jobs. This is to be facilitated by a nationwide job evaluation in terms of job disutilities. This is the index of job "dirtiness" Professor Rottenberg needs. Reynolds also notes that workers ". . . want administrative equalization of job attractiveness rather than equalization through the painful and uncertain process of mobility" (p. 260). This means they want the "nice party" at the lowest possible admission price.

of employer, union, and government intervention are tolerable or desirable?[24] In order to help in answering this question scholars need to point the way to consideration of consequences which are identifiable as close to or far away from one goal or a set of goals. Clear thinking requires that we set out clear distinctions between goals, ways to seek the goals, and ways to measure the degree of attainment of those goals.[25]

---

[24] "The necessity for maximum utilization of all our resources in recent years has forced us to ask more insistently than in the past whether our method of free movement of labor based on employer and worker choices directed toward individual advantage can be retained as a basic procedure for manpower allocation. . . . To this point in our history we have not had to answer that question with facts. On the whole we have observed the results and found them satisfying. A categorical 'yes' based on faith and evangelistic fervor was enough." E. Wight Bakke, *Labor Mobility and Economic Opportunity*, p. 6.

[25] Verifiability is not the only standard which can be called up in judging theories. Nor is it a sufficient standard to use in seeking to resolve a controversy. For one thing, there are great problems in practice of testing predictions which are verifiable in principle. See Machlup, *loc. cit.*, pp. 18–21. But also compare Gordon, *loc. cit.*, for a somewhat contradictory point of view.

5
On Choice in Labor Markets: Reply

Simon Rottenberg

Professor Lampman has clearly thought hard and long on the methods by which knowledge makes progress and truths are established and has written a formidable defense for his thesis.

His criticism of my paper is of three orders. I shall deal with them in what seems to me to be the inverse rank of their importance.

First, he finds, here and there, imprecision of language. My statement, for example, that "occupations requiring rare talent will carry a high price" should have had appended, to have been completely correct, *ceteris paribus*; or it might have been phrased, "if the demand is the same in two occupations, one of which requires rare talent and the other requires only talents that are common, the price will be higher in the former." Truncated expressions occur very often, simply because it is inconvenient to be repetitively explicit; and it seems better to expect that qualifying phrases will be understood, although they are unexpressed. We usually think it sufficient to say, "Taxi fares in New York are a function of distance." We do not add, "if the meter is not set wrong," because we think this will be understood, and indeed, it usually is. This criticism is, in any case, highly peripheral to Professor Lampman's central argument.

Second, somewhat less peripheral and more important, but still not central, are his comments on two points: "(4) How can verifiable predictions help with policy questions?" and "(3) Do the empiricists have any verifiable predictions?"

I start with his question (4). There is a difference between an explanation of what is and an explanation of what ought to be. There is a difference, that is to say, between a positive science and an ethical system. Economics has its contribution to make to an understanding of that part of social behavior which is its subject of study, if it is manipulated as a positive science. It is help-

Reprinted from the *Industrial and Labor Relations Review*, Vol. 9, No. 4, July, 1956, pp. 636–641. Copyright © 1956 by Cornell University. All rights reserved.

ful in making policy decisions, but it cannot determine them.

I ask Professor Lampman to assume with me for the moment that it can be verifiably predicted that a rise in the earnings of narcotics peddlers relative to earnings in other trades will cause people to move in to the narcotics peddling trade. Let us also agree for the moment that if all people freely choose their trades, including this one, human resources will be optimally distributed among uses, in the sense that output will be smaller if some are forced to move to other trades.

If these propositions are true, it does not follow that narcotics peddling should not be prohibited by law. He and I would probably agree that it should be, under most circumstances. But this has nothing to do with economics. If we agree, it is because we hold roughly the same ethical values.

Consider another case. If a coal seam is depleted, we may predict that after a time, a coal town will shrink in size and people will move off to seek their fortune where the income outlook is better. We may even be prepared to say that this is a good thing, judged on the criteria of productivity and output. But we are not really in a position to say that *on other criteria,* which override those with respect to which economists have special competence, the community should not subsidize the coal town residents, so that they may stay where they are. On the other criteria we have nothing special to offer; our advice is no better than that of other informed people.

Economics, as an analytical system, can do no more than predict the consequences of policies. It says nothing conclusive about what policies ought to be adopted, because it says nothing about the consequences that ought to be desired. As Lionel Robbins puts it, "Economics is neutral as between ends."[1] It is, of course, a good thing for economists to participate in policy making; but when they do (except as they operate within limits appropriate to their special competence), they are acting only as citizens. It is a good thing only because it is good for the whole citizenry to participate in the decision-making processes of a democratic society.

I hope I may be permitted to incorporate here by reference John Neville Keynes' "Grounds for Recognising a Distinct Positive Science of Political Economy," rather than repeating its argument.[2]

I turn now to Lampman's question (3). I do not deny that the empiricists have verifiable predictions, but they are predictions derived inductively from phenomena which they have observed or believe they have observed and, therefore, they lack the capacity for general use which is the property of predictions derived from theoretical systems. They are of the order: "I have observed regularities in Paducah, Tacoma, Kenosha, Augusta, and Altoona; I therefore predict that I shall find the same phenomena in Flagstaff and Bay City."

See, for example, the second prediction which Professor Lampman draws from Professor Reynolds' book: "If wage differentials among occupations (et cetera) are substantially narrowed by collective bargaining, there will be no additional difficulty in finding workers to fill the higher paying jobs." Suppose I ask Professor Lampman: "If the differential between the earnings of engineers and messengers were reduced to one penny per year, should we not expect that the number who invest in engineering training would diminish?" I think he would answer, "Yes, we should expect this." Or see the obverse side of the prediction: "If wage differentials among occupations (et cetera) are substantially widened by collective bargaining, there will be no less difficulty in finding workers to fill the higher paying jobs." Suppose now I ask Professor Lampman: "If the

---

[1] *The Nature and Significance of Economic Science,* 2d edition (London: Macmillan and Company, Ltd., 1949), p. 147.

[2] *The Scope and Method of Political Economy,* 4th edition (New York: Kelley & Millman, Inc., 1955), p. 46 ff.

salaries of teachers were, say, tripled, while others remained unchanged, should we not expect school administrators to have less difficulty in filling their vacancies?" Again, I think he would answer, "Yes."

If my surmise is correct, he might reconcile his answers and the prediction he derives from the Reynolds' observations by saying that what was found to be true by Reynolds can not be transformed to a general expression which would cover the engineer-messenger and teacher cases. But the transformation that Professor Lampman made can be interpreted to have the characteristics of covering these cases. If his general formulation of the prediction is not correct, what form shall we correctly give it? Can a generalized prediction be constructed at all from empirical observations which have specific and concrete dimensions?

Perhaps the trouble lies only in lack of precision. Suppose we give a defined meaning to the word "substantially" ("substantially" means thirty cents per hour) and insert a reference to length of run. The prediction then takes the following form: In a New England factory city in 1946–8 (and other places) it was observed and it is, therefore, predicted for all places that if (the) wage differential(s) between (say, two) occupations (et cetera) is narrowed by thirty cents per hour by collective bargaining, there will be no additional difficulty in finding workers to fill the higher-paying jobs in the following six months. The statement has lost its generality completely. What if the differential is narrowed by fifty cents? What if the run is one year? We have no prediction that will help us now. Phrased precisely, the statement has little to say.

I cannot believe that inductive processes in labor market research promise much progress. If the conventional theories are believed to give bad results, what needs to be done is to devise another theory, derive predictions from it, and submit them to the test of verification. If behavior in the real world conforms more often and more closely to these predictions than to those of conventional theory, then a better theory will have been discovered and we shall have advanced a bit.

I take the liberty here again of inserting by reference Keynes' Chapter VI, "On the Method of Specific Experience in Political Economy" and his Chapter VII, "On the Deductive Method in Political Economy."[3] The former closes with a paragraph which contains the sentence:

The prevalance of a low type of inductive reasoning in the treatment of economic questions is one of the most fertile sources of economic fallacy.

I come now, thirdly, to what I think is the core of his criticism, which is contained in his "(2) Are the predictions of classical wage theory verifiable?" It is here that he introduces the main arguments in support of the central thesis of his comment, "the standard for judging theories, namely, verification, called up by Professor Rottenberg is, if fully applied to classical wage theory, not a defense but an indictment of that theory."

I am constrained to say, in the beginning, that I think he is wrong, and I shall try to explain why I do.

From what is the Lampman thesis drawn? Rottenberg, Professor Lampman says, has written two "lower-order predictions" (about the behavior of individuals) and five "higher-order predictions" (about the behavior of aggregates of individuals), which he says derive from labor market theory. Many of these predictions are nonverifiable. Therefore, on the test of verifiability, the theory is defective.

I ask Professor Lampman to suppose that I am a careless worker. I have available to me a theoretical system from which a very large number of predictions about behavior in real labor markets can be derived. Let us suppose (without admitting it) that this reservoir contains many predictions which

[3] *Ibid.*, p. 172 ff.

are verifiable and a few which are not, and that because I am careless, I take out only those that are not. What would have been indicted—the theory or Rottenberg's exposition of it? The conclusion that the theory is defective needs still another step, which Professor Lampman did not take, which would establish that Rottenberg has drawn a representative sample of predictions from the reservoir.

But this is only a parenthetical comment based, for the sake of the argument, on the assumption that I had actually written seven *predictions,* which Professor Lampman enumerates. I did not, and this is the main reason why his thesis falls; what he calls "predictions" are not all predictions. He has sought to test the goodness of the theory by examining the verifiability of things that are not to be verified.

Economic theory or any facet of it (e.g. the economic theory of the labor market) has, as one of its characteristics, the property of being a kind of logical system, whose proof requires the exercise of logical processes and only the exercise of logical processes. I will draw an analogy from geometry.[4] From the straight-line axiom, "Through any two points there is one and only one straight line," we can derive the statement, "Two straight lines can intersect in only one point." We do not appeal to empirical experience to verify this statement. We see that it is true, because if two straight lines had two points in common, they would coincide and be only one line. We see that it is true, not by reference to experience, but by logical reference to the straight-line axiom. That is to say, "Two straight lines can intersect in only one point" is not a prediction in the sense that we speak of predictions derived from theory which need to be verified to test the theory's goodness.

Let me caution that I have not here backed away from the methodological proposition which appears in my paper and which, I take it, Professor Lampman also agrees to, that the appropriate test of a theory's goodness is the empirical verification of the predictions that can be made from it. I am saying only that we must not confuse the logical mechanics of a theory and its predictions. A theory can be logically true and proven and still be a bad theory—bad in the sense that its predictions are, say, almost always wrong.

Professor Lampman arrives at a wrong conclusion because he treats as though they were predictions the logical statements of economics and its conventions. He, therefore, seeks verifiability for nonpredictive, but only logically consequential, statements.

The statement that net advantages are equal in all employments is derived logically from the conventions that workers maximize net advantage, employers maximize returns, and all are free to pursue their objectives, in the same way that the statement that two straight lines can intersect in only one point is derived logically from the convention that only one straight line can be drawn through any two points. Neither is a prediction; their proofs lie in logical and not in empirical experience.

Nor are the two "lower-order predictions" really predictions. What Professor Lampman calls "lower-order predictions" are really amplifications of the convention. The convention is that workers, in choosing among jobs, seek to maximize net advantage. What does this mean? It means, for example, that if a worker is offered two jobs identical in all respects except that one offers a higher wage, he will prefer or choose the one having a higher wage; etc. This is the way the "lower-order predictions" should be read. Since they are part of the conventions of the theory, their verification or an examination of their capacity to be verified becomes superfluous and methodologically wrong. Economics has little to say, in fact, about the behavior of individuals. The explanation of what individuals do falls really in the province of psychology. The job of economics is to explain the behavior of aggregates of individuals, in which there is room for nonuniformities among individuals to

---

[4] That I should resort to geometry for an analogy was suggested to me by Professor Milton Friedman.

cancel themselves out, and this is the area in which it has power.

What then are the *predictions* that can be derived from labor market theory? They refer to two classes of phenomena: the distribution of workers among employments and the price of labor in different employments. Expressed generally, they are the following: *ceteris paribus,* if the relative price of labor in an employment changes, it is predicted that the supply of labor to it will change directly and the demand for labor in it will change inversely; and *ceteris paribus,* if the supply of labor to an employment or the demand for labor in it change, it is predicted that the price of labor in it will change inversely to the change in supply and directly to the change in demand. These are the predictions in their simplest form. Labor market theory also permits predictions of a more complex order by specifying that degrees of change are functions of the elasticities of slope of the relevant schedules.

An infinite number of applied predictions flow out of these general predictive expressions. A number of them appeared inferentially in my paper [Reading 3, p. 37—Eds.], where I said, "Everywhere there is massive aggregate evidence that people move from low-income areas to high and from areas of thin opportunity, where long-run earnings are likely to be low, to thick opportunity areas, where long-run earnings are likely to be high. Irishmen move to Scotland, Mexicans to the United States, Southerners to the North, rural people to the towns, and Europeans to the New World; net flows are not in the opposite directions." This says that if income is lower in Ireland than in Scotland, it is predicted that the net movement of people will be to Scotland. Two predictions appear earlier in this reply: if the difference in earnings for engineers and messengers falls away to almost zero, it is predicted that fewer people will invest in engineering training; and if teachers' and narcotics peddlers' earnings rise, relative to others, people will move into the teaching and narcotics peddling trades. It can be easily seen that predictions of this kind can be multiplied without end.

Predictions as to the behavior of the relative prices of labor in different employments are of this order: if a large number of skilled European artisans migrate to southern Brazil, it is predicted that artisans' wages will fall, relative to others; if women are permitted to work in an employment which had previously been closed to them, it is predicted that wages in this employment will fall relatively; if the United States closes its doors to immigrants, having previously accepted them in large numbers, it is predicted that the price of common labor will rise relatively; if illegal Mexican entrants are effectively prohibited from crossing the Rio Grande, it is predicted that the price of labor in south Texas agriculture will rise relatively; (it is predicted that) "when all can write, the work of copying, which used to earn higher wages than almost any kind of manual labour, will rank (in earnings) among unskilled trades";[5] it is predicted that if the occupations of head heaters and rollers in iron works are skilled and responsible occupations, require great physical strength and involve much discomfort, the wages in them will be (relatively) very high.[6] It can be seen that predictions of this kind can also be multiplied without end.

I submit, finally, that all of these predictions are capable of being verified, as are the innumerable others of which they are merely illustrative; therefore, that the theorems from which they are derived are conceivably refutable and operationally meaningful; and that Professor Lampman's thesis that "the standard for judging theories, namely, verification, . . . is, if fully applied to classical wage theory not a defense but an indictment of that theory," is not tenable.

I think I have discussed the heart of his comment and I want to commend him for the atmosphere of high principle in which it was composed.

[5] Alfred Marshall, *Principles of Economics,* 8th edition (London: MacMillan and Co., Ltd., 1938), p. 682.
[6] *Ibid.*, p. 684.

PART III
SPECIAL TOPICS IN SUPPLY AND DEMAND

A. Aggregate Supply

As Milton Friedman's selection in Part I indicates, traditional economic theory views labor supply at the household level and, with suitable modifications, at the aggregate level as being responsive to changes in the real wage rate. Friedman analyzed this response by using traditional consumption theory, which views leisure as a good (the same as apples, bananas, and cats), in other words, as something to be desired. The price of leisure, for example an hour's leisure, is the wage rate. Given a wage rate, the consumer allocates his time between work and leisure, and these two activities exhaust his time. According to consumer choice theory, a change in the wage rate produces both an income effect and a substitution effect. As a result of an increase in the wage rate, leisure is more expensive (assuming all other prices remain constant) and, for this reason, less leisure is demanded. Hence, the substitution effect of a wage increase leads to an increase in the number of hours worked (assuming, of course, that leisure is a normal good). However, as a result of the real wage increase, the worker finds himself with an increased income for any number of hours worked. As a consequence of this income effect, he purchases more of all normal goods, including leisure. Hence, the income effect leads to a reduction in the number of hours worked. A problem is obvious: the net change in labor activity as a result of a change in the real wage rate cannot be deduced from theory. The problem can only be resolved with empirical evidence, which is the approach of the articles by Lewis and Mincer.

Reading 6, "Hours of Work and Hours of Leisure," by H. Gregg Lewis, examines the long-run trend in hours of leisure. In the United States the evidence through 1955 suggests that there has been an increase in the number of hours of leisure, associated with a decrease in the number of hours worked. The fact that the long-run trends in real property income and in real wage rates were positive during this period implies that on balance the income effect of an increase in the real wage rate was stronger than the substitution effect. Lewis notes that although the dominance of the income effect has manifested itself primarily in a shortened workweek, increases in other forms of leisure such as a smaller fraction of lifetime years in the labor force, more holidays not worked, longer vacations, fewer working days in a week, shorter working days, and (to a minor extent) more frequent rest periods during the working hours are also evident. The effects of legislation on hours worked (Fair Labor Standards Act, Adamson Act) are examined along with the influences of the income tax, the federal old-age insurance program, and interest rates. It is noted that these "institutional phenomena" may hinder the measurement of the pure relationship between hours worked and changes in the income variables. But Lewis suggests that, with limited exceptions, over the long run the effects of these institutional factors probably have been negligible.

Evidence on a related topic is presented by Jacob Mincer in "Labor Force Participation and Unemployment: A Review of Recent Evidence." This reading considers changes in the size of the labor force in response to changes in cyclical fluctuations in aggregate labor demand. Again the analysis proceeds from traditional economic theory. In this context, the substitution effect is embodied in the "discouraged worker" hypothesis (as unemployment increases, some workers drop out of the labor force in the belief that no work is available); while the income effect is embodied in the "additional worker" hypothesis (as unemployment increases, family income declines, inducing other members to enter the labor force to supplement the family income). Mincer agrees with those who have found the labor supply increasingly responsive to employment conditions. He attributes this development mainly to the growth of the female labor force and the relative decline in importance of the very old and the very young in the labor force. He qualifies, however, the strength of this response and notes possible biases in earlier works. Furthermore, his article suggests that unemployment compensation and social security may be contributing to the growth of an intermittent labor force, and that both programs probably weaken or create lags in both the discouraged and added worker effects. The references at the end of his article form an excellent bibliography for further reading in this area.

The last article in Part IIIA presents an alternative way to analyze the household's decision about the number of hours to spend in the labor force. Gary S. Becker places the labor supply decision in the middle of a more general theory as to how households allocate their time. The theory recognizes that consumption of commodities requires time and that enjoyment of time often requires commodities. Commodities such as sleep, which require many hours and relatively few goods, are "high-time" commodities. Other commodities such as eating lobsters, which usually requires a low amount of time per dollar of the good, are less time-intensive. In this theory, the labor hours the household supplies are determined simultaneously with the household's total consumption decisions. The effect of a change in the real wage rate under this theory is basically the same as in the traditional income-substitution analysis, but the range of predictions is greater. An increase in the wage rate makes time-intensive commodities more expensive, and this added cost alone leads to more hours of work supplied (the old substitution effect). The income effect of the wage increase, however, leads to an increased consumption of both types of commodities. Hence, once again the net effect of wage increases on hours of labor supplied is uncertain and depends on the tastes and preferences of the household in question. Implications of this form of analysis in explaining several observed labor market phenomena are mentioned by Becker.

Omitted from Part IIIA is any discussion of long-run aggregate labor supply. As Friedman noted in Reading 1, long-run supply can be increased "either by increasing the number of laborers or by investing more capital in each laborer." The latter method has already been briefly discussed and is treated in greater detail in Part IV. The former method, increasing the number of laborers, involves a discussion of population theory, which we have had to omit for reasons of space. Interested readers may consult Gary S. Becker's article "An Economic Analysis of Fertility"[1] or Richard A. Easterlin's *Population, Labor Force and Long Swings in Economic Growth: The American Experience.*[2]

B. Monopsony

Our second special topic in supply and demand is monopsony. Literally, monopsony is a market situation in which there is only one buyer. In our case, in a strict sense, monopsonistic conditions exist when there is only one buyer of labor who confronts the positive sloping aggregate labor supply curve. However, in the labor market, the term monopsony often is used in a more general sense to refer to any buyer who faces anything but an infinitely elastic supply curve. The important fact is that because the monopsonist operates in a labor market with a positively sloping supply curve, his decision to purchase more labor has some effect on the wage level. In traditional monopsony theory, the employer realizes that the marginal cost and the average cost of an additional worker differ, and he reacts to the former cost. He hires less labor and pays this labor a lower wage than he would in a competitive situation. The result is that under monopsonistic conditions resources are less efficiently allocated than under competitive conditions.

The misallocation of resources is not the only reason for the interest in monopsony theory. From a policy point of view it can be shown that if monopsonistic conditions prevail, then a "correct" minimum wage results in better resource allocation. The same result holds for a "correct" set of union wage demands. Whether these institutional arrangements improve or worsen the operation of the labor market in fact is an empirical question.

The first selection on monopsony is an excerpt from K. W. Rothschild's *The Theory of Wages*. It describes succinctly the theory of monopsony. Furthermore, it extends the analysis to related topics such as the discriminating monopsonist and whether concentration of employers in an area leads to monopsony. For further elaboration of this theory the reader is referred to virtually any labor economics

---

[1] A Conference of the Universities—National Bureau Committee for Economic Research, *Demographic and Economic Change in Developed Countries* (Princeton, N.J.: Princeton University Press, 1960).

[2] (New York: National Bureau of Economic Research, Inc., 1968).

textbook or elementary price theory book.[3] We omit any discussion of whether monopsony constitutes exploitation of the worker, since he is paid less than the value of his marginal product.[4] (We will note, however, that Gary S. Becker's analysis of on-the-job training, included in Part IV, yields the prediction that the marginal product of a worker will normally exceed his wage, if he has received specific investment.)

The second selection in this section, chapter 1 from Robert Bunting's *Employer Concentration in Local Labor Markets,* represents virtually the only available empirical work on monopsony. But, as Bunting himself admits in this excerpt, his work is not a direct test for monopsony in the United States. Rather it is an examination of whether employment in local labor markets is concentrated in a limited number of employers. It is generally assumed that monopsony power in labor markets is associated with high concentration of employees among employers, but this critical assumption remains untested. Despite Bunting's findings that there was, as of 1948, little evidence of employer concentration in local labor markets, the main message emerging from this selection may be that further empirical research on the topic of monopsony is needed desperately.

The final article in Part IIIB is Simon Rottenberg's "The Baseball Players' Labor Market." Although many of the institutional arrangements that Rottenberg describes have changed since 1956 (and as of this writing others such as the reserve clause may be changing further), these changes detract little from the basic import of the article. Rottenberg describes how institutional arrangements, contracts, and agreements among the major league club owners have created a monopsonistic market for baseball players' services. Furthermore, he asks whether the objectives of the owners might be better achieved through a modified competitive market for players' services. The questions raised in this article and the answers given go far beyond the baseball players' market and, for that matter, beyond the theory of monopsony.

---

[3] One interesting interpretation is found in Martin Bronfenbrenner, "Potential Monopsony in Labor Markets," *Industrial and Labor Relations Review,* vol. 9 (July 1956), pp. 577–588.

[4] Discussions of the topic can be found in K. W. Rothschild, *The Theory of Wages* (New York: Augustus M. Kelley, Publishers, 1967), pp. 103–105; and Allan Cartter, *Theory of Wages and Employment* (Homewood, Ill.: Richard D. Irwin, Inc., 1959), pp. 65–70.

A. AGGREGATE SUPPLY

6
Hours of Work and Hours of Leisure

H. Gregg Lewis

In this paper *the shorter work week* is a synonym for *the declining trend in the fraction of a worker's lifetime devoted to market (labor force or breadwinning) activities* or, equivalently, for *the increasing fraction devoted to non-market (leisure) activities*. The problem of explaining this long-run trend, however, is but one of many problems that fall under the heading "the per capita demand for leisure" or "the per capita supply of hours of work." There are in addition other "time series" variations (seasonal and cyclical, for example) in hours of work as well as many types of cross-sectional "differentials" in hours of work that also demand explanations consistent with that for the long-run trend.

This paper reports some of the exploratory work of a research project on some of

Reprinted from *Proceedings of the Ninth Annual Meeting,* edited by L. Reed Tripp (1957), pp. 196–206, by permission of the Industrial Relations Research Association.

these hours of work problems that we[1] have undertaken in the Labor Economics Workshop at the University of Chicago. We hope to provide both improved estimates of some of the main differentials in hours of work per head and more satisfying explanations of these differentials. Because our work is still in its early stages, however, this paper will deal mainly with the analytical tools with which we are working on the long-run trend data.

Our approach is orthodox: mainly the theory of the demand for leisure viewed as a consumption good. Let us review quickly the main elements of this theory. Assume a two-commodity world—leisure (time) and "wage goods"—and, to begin with, abstract from the problem of the allocation of a worker's consumption of leisure over his lifetime. Each worker, facing a given market price of leisure in terms of wage goods (real

[1] My associates are Miss Ethel Jones and Mr. Jeremiah German.

wage rate per hour) and with a given real property income, is viewed as allocating his total income[2] between leisure and wage goods in such a way as to maximize his utility.

Thus given the worker's tastes, his consumption of leisure and thus his hours of work supplied, both measured in hours per unit period of time, depend upon his estimates of his long-run or permanent real wage rate and real property income prospects. His demand function for leisure (or labor supply function) has the familiar properties: the substitution effect of a rise in the real wage rate is a reduced consumption of leisure per head (increased hours of work supplied per head); the income effect of a rise in the real wage rate or in real property income is an increased rate of consumption of leisure per head (reduced supply of hours per head) if leisure is a normal commodity. Market or group demand functions for leisure also have these properties though they may also depend upon the distribution of tastes, real wage rates, and real property income.

Now let us put this theory to work on the problem of the long-run trend. Assume, I think reasonably, that tastes for leisure are very stable in the long run. In the United States in the last half century both the real wage rate per hour and real property income per head have had strong upward trends. Thus each successive generation has been able to estimate higher real wages and real property income prospects than its predecessors. The rise in real wage rate prospects tends on the one hand to produce substitution effects raising the hours of work supplied per head and, on the other hand, income effects lowering the hours of work supplied per head (if leisure is a normal commodity) and the rise in real property income prospects also tends to produce income effects in the same direction. It is apparent that if this theory is to be consistent with the long-run data, leisure must be a normal commodity; one, indeed, for which the long-run income effects outweigh the long-run substitution effects.

That hours of work on the average for the economy as a whole have tended to change relatively slowly and smoothly is quite consistent with this theory, for the hours of labor supplied per head are made to depend chiefly upon long-run or permanent real wage rate and real property income prospects which will tend to be relatively little affected by short-run ("transitory") variations in real wage rate and real property income.

I have said nothing thus far about the *demand* for hours of work per head—that is, about employers' preferences (arising either from the employers' personal tastes or from technological considerations) regarding the hours of labor per capita of their employees. Assume to begin with that at each real wage rate employers are completely indifferent with respect to the hours of work schedules of their employees, though, of course, they are not indifferent with respect to the total of the man-hours of all of their employees taken together. Thus at any given real wage rate, the demand schedule of each employer and, indeed, of all employers together will be infinitely elastic with respect to the hours of work *per employee* and to all other aspects of the hours of work schedules of employees (such as the timing of the hours during the day or week and the like).

Given this assumption about employers' preferences regarding the hours of work schedules of their employees, the equilibrium market real wage rate must be the same for

---

[2] His real property income plus his real earnings calculated at a zero rate of consumption of leisure time. Furthermore, this total real income should be interpreted as long run or "permanent" income in the sense used by Friedman and Kuznets; see their *Income from Independent Professional Practice* (New York: National Bureau of Economic Research, 1945), pp. 325–338 and 352–364. See also Friedman's *A Theory of the Consumption Function* (to be published by the National Bureau) chapters II and III for further discussion of the distinction between "permanent" and "transitory" components of income and consumption.

all employers. In particular there will be no "equalizing" real wage rate differentials compensating for the non-pecuniary disadvantages of the hours of work schedules provided by some employers relative to those provided by others, for, indeed, there will be no such non-pecuniary advantages or disadvantages.

For explaining the global facts on the long-run trend of hours of labor in this country (and for understanding many of the cross-section differentials in hours of work as well), it would only complicate the theory, I believe, without substantial gain in interpreting the data, to bring into the theory employer demand schedules for hours of work per employee that are not infinitely elastic.

There are some observed phenomena, however, that cannot be explained with so simple a theory: premium rates for overtime, for night work, and for work on Sundays and holidays, for example. Suppose, therefore, that employers do have preferences, even strong ones, for some hours of work schedules for their employees over other schedules and that therefore they are prepared to offer higher wage rates (premium rates) per hour to employees to induce them to conform to the preferred schedules. Nevertheless it may still be true that these employer preferences will not produce equalizing wage rate differentials. Significant equalizing differentials will appear only if in their absence the number of workers supplying their labor services to employers in particular hours of work schedule categories were not equal to the number demanded by employers for these categories at the going real wage rate.

The crucial test of the importance of employers' preferences in the analysis of hours of work per head data is in the size of equalizing premium rates for hours of work schedules less preferred by employees and in the proportion of the labor force working at these rates. I submit that on this test employers' preferences have played only a minor role in the long-run trend of hours of work in this country. It is probably true that a larger proportion of the total man-hours worked per year in the U. S. is now paid at premium rates than in 1900, though it is questionable that the proportion would be substantially higher than in 1900 in the absence of such legislation as the Fair Labor Standards Act.[3] The main fact, however, is clear: the fraction of total man-hours that is worked at premium rates is relatively small.

Let me summarize the preceding discussion in the language of a supply-demand model: On the supply side there is a stable, negatively inclined long-run schedule relating average hours of work per head to the average real wage rate. On the demand side there is, to a first approximation, an infinitely elastic schedule involving the same variables. With the long-run growth of the economy, the demand schedule has moved upward along the real wage rate axis tracing out the observed hours of work-real wage rate points on the stable long-run supply schedule (except during periods of substantial unemployment or effective legislation affecting hours of work per head when the points are off the supply schedule).

The explanation most commonly given for the "shorter work week," particularly by laymen, is legislation imposing on employers absolute maxima on hours of work schedules (chiefly for women and children) or penalty rates for overtime per day or per week. It is certainly consistent with the approach that I have taken in this paper that drastic legislation could reduce hours of work drastically, particularly in the short run.

[3] I suspect that the term *penalty* rate is at least as accurate descriptively for the last decade and a half as the term *premium* rate: employers pay these rates in significant part not to recruit workers reluctant to work longer hours without a special price incentive, but because the public and, perhaps, to some extent unions have sought to restrain workers from working as many hours as they would like and employers would offer them at prevailing wage rates, in order to ration employment generally or particular attractive union employment opportunities.

I will be very surprised to find that the historical data contain convincing evidence, however, that hours of legislation prior to the Fair Labor Standards Act did more than create slight downward bumps in the long-run trend in average hours worked per person for the economy as a whole. Legislation in particular areas, such as the Adamson Act for the railroad industry, was undoubtedly effective in some instances in reducing hours of work per head by amounts somewhat greater than can be explained by the long-run rise of real wages, but all of the earlier legislation taken together surely covered effectively at any one time only a relatively small fraction of the adult population.

The Fair Labor Standards Act, on the other hand, has covered approximately two-fifths of the labor force, including almost all wage and salary workers in the manufacturing, mining, communications, and public utilities industries, and more than half of the employees in wholesale trade and finance, insurance, and real estate. Furthermore, three rather crude pieces of evidence make me suspect that careful study of the wages and hours data will show that in the industries covered by the Act it has had significant effects particularly during the 1940's. First, the drop in average hours worked per man-week from 1929 to 1942 in manufacturing industries appears to have been at an unusually large rate compared to the average rate for the first three decades of the century, though the period 1929 to 1942 was certainly not one to brighten long-run wage rate prospects of wage earners. The drop from 1929 (48 hours per week) to 1942 (42 hours per week) was at the rate of approximately 4.5 hours or 10 percent per decade; the drop from 1900 (55 to 60 hours per week) to 1929 was at the rate of approximately 2.5 to 4 hours or 5 to 7.5 percent per decade.[4]

Second, the decline in average hours worked per week per employee in manufacturing industries from 1942 to 1955 (38 hours per week[5]) was at the rate of 3 hours or 7.5 percent per decade, lower than for 1929 to 1942, though the period was marked in general by high levels of employment and a substantial increase in real wage rates. Furthermore, Table 6.1 below shows that the decline in hours per week during this period tended to be smaller for manufacturing and other industries covered by the Act, than for industries largely uncovered by the Act.

Third, the sample surveys of the labor force made monthly by the Bureau of the Census, reported in the *Current Population Reports,* consistently have shown that a very high proportion of the labor force employed in manufacturing industries work 40 hours a week, neither more nor less; in other industries the concentration at 40 hours per week generally has been substantially smaller.

What about the effects of unions on hours of work? We need to distinguish here between their effects on the hours of work of

---

[4] 1942 was the first year after the Act was passed in which the lowness of average hours worked per week cannot easily be attributed to substantial unemployment rather than effectiveness of the Act. Indeed, by 1942 the unusually high level of demand for labor during World War II may already have pushed hours of work somewhat beyond the level they would have had in peace time. Furthermore, the Bureau of Labor Statistics figures for average hours per week per head in the last decade and a half probably overestimate average hours (on a basis comparable to 1929) because the B. L. S. figures are for hours "paid for" rather than for hours worked. For these reasons I have reduced the B. L. S. figure for 1942 from 42.9 to 42.0.

The data on actual hours worked per week in manufacturing industries before the 1930's are of uncertain quality. The figure I have used for 1929 is that of the National Industrial Conference Board covering 25 manufacturing industries. Most estimates for 1900 are between 55 and 60.

[5] The B. L. S. figure for average hours worked per week in manufacturing for 1955 was 40.7. I have reduced this to 38 because of the inclusion in the B. L. S. figure of approximately two to three hours "paid for" that in 1929 would not have been paid for and thus not counted as hours worked.

TABLE 6.1 AVERAGE HOURS OF WORK PER WEEK PER EMPLOYED PERSON BY INDUSTRY—1942 AND 1955

Industry	Average Hours of Work per Week per Employee		Change from 1942 to 1955	
	1942	1955	Hours	Percent
A. Largely covered by Fair Labor Standards Act				
Manufacturing	42.9	40.7	−2.2	−5.1
Metal mining	43.6	42.2	−1.4	−3.2
Petroleum and natural gas*	42.6*	40.6	−2.0*	−4.7*
Telephone*	41.9*	39.6	−2.3*	−5.5*
Wholesale trade*	42.2*	40.6	−1.6*	−3.8*
Electric utilities*	41.6*	41.2	−0.4*	−1.0*
B. Largely uncovered by Act				
Class I railroads	46.9	41.9	−5.0	−10.7
Local railways and buses	48.0	43.1	−4.9	−10.2
Retail trade	41.6	39.0	−2.6	−6.3
Hotels, year-round	45.3	41.5	−3.8	−8.4
Laundries	43.3	40.3	−3.0	−6.9
Cleaning and dyeing	43.4	39.5	−3.9	−9.0
Non-metallic mining and quarrying*	46.0*	44.5	−1.5*	−3.3*
Building construction*	38.4*	36.1	−2.3*	−6.0*
Agriculture	55.5	46.5	−9.0	−16.2

Sources and explanations: For all industries except agriculture the data are those of the Bureau of Statistics (1942 and 1943 data from the *Handbook of Labor Statistics,* 1947 edition; 1955 data from the *Monthly Labor Review,* October 1956). All of the B. L. S. data for the period covered in the table, and particularly those for 1955, overestimate hours of work because of their inclusion of "time paid for but not worked." If the B.L.S. data were corrected for this error, the changes from 1942 to 1955 would be made somewhat larger than shown in the table. Although the corrections would differ from industry to industry, it seems unlikely that they would be substantially larger on the average for "covered" industries than for "uncovered."

The 1942 figure for agriculture is from the Bureau of the Census *Labor Force Bulletin,* No. 6; the 1955 figure is from the *Current Population Reports,* Series P–50, No. 67 and is adjusted to include employed persons with a job but not at work.

* For these industries the figure in the "1942" column is that for 1943 because inspection of the data indicated that the 1942 figure might still be low because of incomplete recovery from the Depression. Notice that these industries predominantly are in the "covered" category.

the employees they represent in collective bargaining and their effects on hours generally in the economy. I am firmly convinced that some unions in the United States, though by no means all of them, have won for their members real wages significantly higher than these employees otherwise would have received. However, even the strongest of these unions surely have won real wage increases that total at most only a small fraction of the general rise in real wages in the United States in the last half century.

These union-won wage increases like the much larger long-run general wage increases will tend to reduce the hours supplied per union member. Furthermore, some unions among the strong ones may reduce hours per head to an even greater extent in order to ration relatively attractive unionized employment opportunities among workers. For both of these reasons I expect that the data will show that some differences in hour of work among industries and occupations are attributable to unionism.

The economic role of unions in the long-run decline of average hours worked per head in the economy as a whole, on the other hand, is surely a minor one. It is not necessary to argue that the union-won wage increases have been at the expense of non-union labor, but only that unions at all times in the last half century have represented a minority of the labor force, until recently a quite small minority, and that even the strongest unions have won wage increases that are relatively small compared to the general rise in real wages.

I close this brief survey of the factors bearing upon the long-run decline in hours of work per head with a short consideration of the income tax. By lowering the relative price of leisure (the real wage rate after tax) the income tax tends to produce a substitution effect: reduced hours per head. It is not so clear that the tax tends also to produce the income effects that we associate with a long-run decline in real wages (say by moving backward in our history). This would be true if the government were to spend the tax receipts buying goods to be "dumped in the ocean."

On the other hand, if the tax receipts were used to command resources to produce much wanted services for the community, then to a first approximation there will be no income effect for the community as a whole, but only a substitution effect. In this case the tax will cause hours worked per head to be lower at the real wage *before* tax than otherwise would be true.

It follows that if the truth is somewhere in between, say half of the tax receipts are wasted, the hours of work supplied per head will be lower than otherwise would be expected at the real wage rate *less half of the tax*. Only in the first case in which the tax receipts are used entirely to waste resources will the income and substitution effects of the tax have approximately the ratio they have in the long-run growth of the economy. In all other cases the substitution effect will be disproportionately important and thus the tax will tend to bend the trend of hours of work downward.

Until the last decade and a half the income tax surely must have had only small effects on the long-run movement of hours of work per head. In the last fifteen years, however, the income tax has risen to a level at which it may very well be producing substitution effects accelerating the secular decline of hours of work.

Thus far my comments have dealt mainly with the long-run decline in the over-all fraction of an average worker's lifetime devoted to market activities. I turn now to some aspects of the "form" of this decline.

First, let us go back to the theory of the individual worker's demand for leisure. He has to determine not only the fraction of his life that he will devote to leisure activities but also the distribution of his consumption of leisure over his lifetime. Because of the phenomena of aging and of learning by experience, the marginal cost of leisure will tend to vary from one age to another. In particular, it is characteristic of persons in almost all pursuits that, if they live long enough, they will reach an age after which the productivity increasing effects of experience are more than offset by the productivity decreasing effects of growing old. Thus the marginal cost of leisure will tend to be relatively low in old age.

Two other factors also work to make the real marginal cost of leisure relatively low in old age. One is the interest rate. The other, important only in recent years, is the Federal Old Age Insurance program. This program from the beginning has contained in one form or another an "earnings test" under which insurance benefits are a negatively inclined function of income earned during benefit years. The earnings test tends to make the real marginal cost of leisure time less than the real wage rate per hour.

The rising long-run trend of the real wage rate in the United states is a factor working in the opposite direction partially offsetting the interest rate factor.

Now assume that leisure time is a commodity for which workers have no time preference.⁶ Then if the marginal cost of present leisure in terms of future leisure were unity, the individual worker would plan to consume his leisure at a constant rate over his lifetime. We observe, however, that the marginal cost of leisure tends to be relatively low in old age—the marginal cost of present (in youth) leisure in terms of future (in old age) leisure tends to be greater than unity. Under these circumstances the worker will plan to distribute his consumption of leisure disproportionately toward his old age.

Available data indicate that the disproportionately high rate of consumption of leisure time in old age shows itself mainly in retirement from the labor force. Thus the long-run decline in "hours of work" will be registered in part in a decline in labor force participation. This expectation is confirmed by Census data which show a decline of approximately eight to ten percent since 1900 in the proportion of the United States adult male population in the labor force (or if not in the labor force, in school).

It is apparent that future leisure is not a perfect substitute for present leisure, for if that were true, then on the preceding line of reasoning the shorter work week would have taken *only* the form of reduced labor force participation. In fact, of course, the work "week" has fallen also for those in the labor force and this decline has taken several forms. I turn now to examine this variety.

First, why is it that for the great majority of adult males the working hours tend to be bunched rather than spread out over the "waking" hours of the day? That "mixing business and pleasure tends to spoil both" goes far toward explaining the phenomenon. It is apparent, however, that mixing the two does not completely spoil both, for a good many factory workers do have rest periods, office workers coffee breaks, and business managers and professional workers their long lunch "hour." Casual observation indicates, indeed, that there is more mixing of pleasure with business among salaried workers and the self-employed who do not work on a fixed schedule of hours than among hourly-rated "factory" workers who "punch a time clock." This can be rationalized as the result of the higher cost of mixing leisure with work for those whose work activities are highly complementary than for those whose working hours need not be meshed closely with those of fellow workers.

The preceding line of reasoning does not explain, however, why males consume leisure time in larger proportion "at home" than "at work." Hence assume not only that leisure time is not homogeneous by place of consumption, but also that "at home" leisure is preferred to "at work" leisure.⁷ The mixing of "at home" leisure with "at home" work, moreover, will tend to be expensive for most workers because of the travel involved. Thus both the tendency to mix little leisure with work and the tendency to consume leisure at home can be explained as the result of the preference for "at home" leisure over "at work" leisure and the minimizing of the travel costs involved in consuming leisure away from one's place of work.

Furthermore, there are likely to be differences among workers in their relative preferences for "at home" leisure over "at work" leisure that will be correlated with the facilities offered in work places for the

---

⁶ By "no time preference" I do not mean a constant rather than a diminishing marginal rate of substitution of present for future leisure, but that the marginal rate of substitution is unity at a rate of consumption of present leisure equal to that for future leisure.

⁷ I mean by lack of *homogeneity* among two kinds of leisure, that there is a diminishing rather than constant marginal rate of substitution of one for the other. A *preference* for one kind of leisure over another means that at equal rates of consumption of the two the rate at which one is substituted for the other is less than one unit of the more preferred to one unit of the less preferred.

consumption of leisure. Thus is it really surprising that professors, for example, tend to consume more leisure time in their university surroundings than factory and mine workers do in factories and mines?

Both of the alternate hypotheses advanced to explain the "bunching" of hours of work during the day imply that the relative costs of any considerable mixing of pleasure and business during the day are high and the returns in satisfaction relatively low, particularly for "factory and mine" workers. This implication is supported by the long-run trend data which indicate that the fraction of the increased consumption of leisure per head since 1900 taken in the form of rest periods, coffee breaks, and the like has been small, probably no larger than five percent.

The preference for "at home" leisure over "at work" leisure together with the minimizing of the costs of travel and of travel time has another implication: that the reduction in hours of work per head since 1900 would have come about through reducing the number of days worked per year rather than the number of hours worked per day. In fact, however, about half of the reduction came from reduced hours per day. These long-run data suggest that individuals not only are not indifferent between non-consecutive and consecutive leisure time—between 14 hours of leisure distributed equally over the days of the week and 14 hours allotted to a single day, but also that there may be a slight preference for the former over the latter. That this preference is slight is indicated by: (1) about half of the reduction in hours of work per head did come about through fewer days per year; (2) the "non-working" days of the week are consecutive (Saturday and Sunday[8]); and (3) vacations of two weeks or more are now quite common.

The shortening of the work week thus has come about in a variety of ways: a smaller fraction of lifetime years in the labor force; more holidays not worked; longer vacations; fewer working days in the week;[9] shorter working days; and to a minor extent, more frequent rest periods during the working hours. The relative cost and taste factors that underlie the division of workers' leisure over their lifetimes, I believe, tend to be quite stable. Thus I hazard the prediction that in the next half century the proportions in which increased consumption of leisure per head is divided among these forms will differ fairly little from the proportions observed in the last fifty years.

[8] That Sundays and holidays are preferred over other days for the consumption of leisure is confirmed by the premium rates commonly paid for work on these days and the relatively small fraction of the labor force that does work on these days. The same kind of evidence confirms the preference for day work over night work. If workers actually preferred to work at night, employers would not have to pay night shift premiums.

[9] Notice in this connection that the alternatives are not simply, for example, five days *vs.* four days. A four and three-quarter day "week" for example can be obtained by having a four day week, say, every fourth week and five-day weeks the rest of the time. It is very clear, indeed, that additional "holidays" are a means of reducing the number of "days per week" in a gradual fashion without resort to "half-days" of work.

7
Labor-Force Participation and Unemployment: A Review of Recent Evidence

Jacob Mincer

Introduction

After three decades of research and occasionally animated controversy, the short-run behavior of the labor force is still not well understood.[1] We are not clear about the causes of monthly movements of as many as three million people in and out of the labor force, nor do we fully understand the huge seasonal swing in the labor force and the year-to-year variation in the seasonal. In the postwar years this variation amounted to a difference of two to four million people between the winter low and summer high. The net annual changes in the labor force were much milder, but these also varied from a quarter of a million to one and a half million during this period.

Reprinted by permission of the publisher and author from *Prosperity and Unemployment*, edited by Robert Aaron Gordon and Margaret S. Gordon, John Wiley & Sons, Inc. Copyright 1966, pp. 73–112.

[1] The research reported in this paper is an outgrowth of a larger study of unemployment differentials in the United States, supported in part by a grant from the Ford Foundation.

Relative to the size of the labor force and the population, these net annual fluctuations are small. Yet analytical interest has centered primarily on these nonseasonal net changes in the labor force rather than on the much bigger seasonal and gross (into and out of the labor force) movements. The reason is not hard to find. In the quest for diagnosis of unemployment and inflation problems it is important to know what are the labor-force responses, if any, to the short-run "cyclical" fluctuations in aggregate demand.

When the issue was first raised, after the Great Depression, the income and substitution effects of standard demand theory, as applied to the worker's allocation of time, were pitted against one another as separate and opposing theories under the labels "additional" and "discouraged" workers, respectively. It was soon realized, however, that these two effects may coexist in life, as they do in theory. Additional workers may enter the labor market to bolster declining family income in a recession, but at the same time some unemployed workers may give up the apparently hopeless job search and withdraw from the labor market, whereas potential labor-force entrants or re-entrants may be inhibited from even starting to look for jobs. Thus the question is not which of the tendencies is the true one but which is stronger.

This is an empirical question. Until recently the weight of evidence, emerging largely from the researches of Clarence Long [1], suggested that, except for periods of war mobilization when the labor force expands and severe depression during which it probably shrinks, the labor force neither receives clear-cut net gains nor suffers net losses under the pressure of cyclically high effective demand or cyclically high unemployment.

Recently, new studies have addressed themselves to the old question, attacking various bodies of data with modern analytical tools. Although the conclusions reached by some of these studies are best described as agnostic, a growing number give unqualified support to the notion that the labor force, as measured, responds positively even to the relatively mild fluctuations characteristic of the postwar period.

In what follows I shall examine (a) the recent empirical studies of the relation between labor-force participation and employment conditions, (b) the recent empirical record bearing on the question, (c) the concept of "disguised" unemployment, and (d) some relevant implications of recent labor-force trends.

Review of Recent Research

The studies under review fall into three distinct categories, determined by the kinds of data used. Each analysis specializes either in (a) monthly gross-flow data, (b) cross-section area comparisons of labor markets, or (c) time-series data.

Gross-change Analyses

Gross-change data, derived from the monthly Current Population Survey, offer potentially the richest insights into labor-force behavior. The employment status of individuals—consisting of three categories, employed, unemployed, and out of the labor force—is presented in the current month with information on the employment status of the same individuals in the preceding month. This reveals the anatomy of any monthly net change in the labor force; a net increase (or reduction) in the size of a given labor force can be traced to its component flows into and out of employment. As mentioned before, these data show a huge amount of labor-force turnover even in periods of relative stability.

The major advantage of the data for our problem is that they permit the separate identification of the added-worker and discouraged-worker phenomena in the gross flows. The disadvantage of the data lies in the difficulty of reliably establishing inferences about net changes. This is because response errors, which in other data tend to be offsetting, are additive in the gross-change data, leading to large errors and biases.[2]

Hansen [2] examined the monthly gross-change data for the period 1948 through 1959. His focus was not, however, on labor-force changes but on the effects of labor-force flows on the observed level of unemployment.[3] He found that gross additions to unemployment by labor-force entrants and re-entrants increased in recession periods but that the same happened, and at about the same rate, to withdrawals of unemployed from the labor force. On balance, therefore, the observed increase in unemployment during recession periods was neither enlarged by the increased influx of additional workers nor reduced by the increased labor-force withdrawals of the unemployed.

These findings do not provide evidence

---

[2] For a discussion of these issues, see Robert B. Pearl, "Gross Change in the Labor Force: A Problem in Statistical Measurement," *Employment and Earnings*, April 1963.

[3] This aspect was the major issue in the Woytinsky-Humphrey debate in the late 1930's.

on the total response of the labor force, since movements into and out of employment are not shown. It is likely, for example, that in recessions the flow from out of the labor force to employment diminishes. Of course, the opposite flow from employment to out of the labor force is also likely to decrease. But if the latter flow decreases less than the former, Hansen's results would imply a shrinking of the labor force during recessions.

In a more comprehensive analysis of gross-change data Altman [3] distinguishes the effects of gross flows on the size of the labor force from the effects on the observed size of unemployment. However, he restricts himself to an analysis of the labor force of married women for the period from 1955 to 1962. His findings on the cyclical flows between unemployment and out of the labor force are similar to Hansen's, but he establishes the reality of additional and discouraged workers a bit more clearly. There is a positive correlation between gross additions to the labor force of married women and the unemployment rate of married men. There is also a positive correlation between reductions in the labor force of married women and their own unemployment rate.

Concerning net effects, Altman suggests a slight dominance of the added worker in affecting the unemployment rate simultaneously with a small net discouragement effect on the size of the labor force during recessions. He also suggests possible differences in early and later stages of the cycle. These are interesting possibilities, but although the noise in the data is not fatal to the findings on gross changes it makes conclusions about net effects much less secure.[4]

Cross-section Analyses

Comparisons during a given observation period of different family units in surveys, or of population groups in different areas, have also been utilized for exploring the determinants of labor-force participation. The empirical procedure now commonly used consists of estimating from these cross sections the parameters of a single equation relating labor-force rates of a given population group in the various areas to a set of independent variables. The major variables, based on price-theory considerations, are family income and the wage rate (or full-time earnings) of the individuals in the group. A simple statistical model is

$$M = a + b_1 Y + b_2 W + e \quad (1)$$

where M is the labor-force rate, Y, the family income, W, the wage rate, and e, a set of other variables of possible interest, such as family size, education, or geographic area. In this model b_1 is an estimate of the income effect, expected to be negative, and b_2 is an estimate of the substitution effect,[5] expected to be positive. If Y and W are averages of groups in labor markets they are likely to approximate "normal" or "long-run" levels of income and wage rate, and the coefficients b_1 and b_2 measure long-run effects. Define variables y_t and w_t as short-run deviations of family income and personal wages, respectively, from their "normal," "full-employment" levels. Their inclusion in equation (1) makes possible a specific exploration of effects of short-term changes in economic conditions on participation rates. Equation (1) becomes:

$$M = a + b_1 Y + b_2 W \\ + c_1 y_t + c_2 w_t + e \quad (2)$$

The coefficient c_1 can be interpreted as the added-worker effect (per unit of cyclical income change) and c_2 as the discouraged-worker effect (per unit of wage change). Strictly speaking, this interpretation is valid only if Y and W, as measured, do not show

---

[4] In his study Altman explores a number of other questions, not directly relevant to the present review. His work illustrates the promise the gross-change data hold out and the great need for improving their quality.

[5] Provided the full-time earnings W have been included in family income Y. For a full discussion of the theoretical and econometric considerations see the author's "Labor Force Participation of Married Women" [12].

any cyclical variations. If Y and W are affected by cyclical fluctuation, c_1 and c_2 do not tell the whole story. Parts of the cyclical effects are then contained in the b_1 and b_2 coefficients.

Separate estimates of c_1 and c_2 are difficult to obtain in the cross section.[6] However, an indirect estimate of the net cyclical effects on labor-force participation may be obtained under the additional assumption that the cyclical deviations y_t and w_t are negative functions of the relevant unemployment rate u in the area. Then equation (2) can be written as

$$M = a + b_1 Y + b_2 W + b_3 u + e \quad (3)$$

If all these assumptions hold, the sign of b_3 represents the direction of the net response of the labor force to cyclical differentials in labor-market conditions among the areas.[7] Whether such an interpretation is valid depends on the nature of the inter-area differentials in unemployment rates. As we shall see, these need not reflect only, or even primarily, cyclical differences.

Two recent studies use model (1) in the form of equation (3), with a few variables added, for the specific purpose of explaining the net effects of employment conditions on participation rates. One is the study of Bowen and Finegan [6], the other of Cain, to which reference has already been made. Because the methodology, data, and results are very similar in the two studies, this discussion does not distinguish between them, except as indicated.

The results obtained by Bowen and Finegan and the comparable findings of Cain are impressive in that a strong net negative sensitivity of labor force to unemployment (a negative coefficient b_3) is apparent for all major population groups in the Census years 1940, 1950, and 1960.[8] For the whole labor force a combined estimate of the regression coefficient b_3 in 1960 was -0.68, suggesting a 1-percentage-point increase in the unemployment rate is associated, on the average, with 2/3 of a percentage point decrease in the total labor-force participation rate.[9]

To anticipate later findings, the pattern of differential sensitivities, which they found in the age-sex cross sections, is qualitatively comparable with that found in time series. But the cross-section estimates of the net response of the labor force to unemployment are higher in total and in male subgroups than the corresponding estimates obtained from time series (see Table 7.1, next section). These high estimates also assert the existence of relationships in cross sections which are not visible in time series. For example, the significant effect of unemployment on the prime labor force of males (age 25–54) shown in the cross section is not detectable in time series.

The time-series parameters purport to measure short-run cyclical labor-force responses. Do the cross-section parameters represent incorrect estimates of the time-series relationship or do they provide somewhat different kinds of information than time-series estimates? The answer is both, to some degree.

A purely statistical exaggeration of the negative size and significance of the regression coefficients may result from spurious correlation. Recall that the independent variable U/L is the unemployment rate in

---

[6] In my study (*op. cit.*), I was able to estimate the effects of transitory family income (coefficient c_1) in addition to the long-run parameters b_1 and b_2. The negative sign of c_1 supported the existence of the additional-worker effect. I was not concerned in that study with coefficient c_2. However, I did attempt a very indirect estimate of the net cyclical effect and concluded that it seemed negligible. In his recent study of the subject, Glen Cain [4] points out that in this attempt I used one of the several estimates of c_1 which biased the test in favor of the additional-worker hypothesis. After recomputing an average estimate of c_1, Cain concludes that my test supports the net-discouragement hypothesis.

[7] This formal argument is explicit in Cain [5]. Bowen and Finegan [6] leave the coefficient b_3 open to interpretation.

[8] See their summary Table 4-7 and Table 4-10 in [6].

[9] *Ibid.*, p. 154.

the area (of the whole labor force in Bowen and Finegan, of the male labor force in Cain), and the dependent variable L_i/P_i is the labor-force rate of the particular population group i. Now, if job opportunities are the only variable, aside from those already included in the regression, which similarly affects the sizes of the total and component labor forces in the area, a smaller U in the numerator of the independent variable will be associated with a larger L in the denominator of the independent variable and with a larger numerator of the dependent variable, correctly showing a negative correlation. To the extent, however, that factors other than job opportunities and those listed in the regression create similar differences in (total and component) labor forces across areas they will again cause the numerator of the dependent and denominator of the independent variables to move in the same direction, creating some degree of "spurious" negative correlation and biasing the negative coefficients toward higher values.[10] It is possible, at this level of conjecture, to think of positive spuriousness as well. Autonomous shifts of labor supply of particular groups could create a positive correlation between U and L. It is unlikely, however, that such shifts would be random with respect to areas.

One factor amenable to investigation which might create a certain amount of negative spuriousness is the seasonal component of the unemployment rate. During the Census week, as at any other time, this component must vary from one area to another across the United States. Because the seasonal component of the labor force is inversely related, except in the summer months, to the seasonal component of unemployment,[11] this is a likely source of upward bias in the observed partial correlation and regression coefficients. An attempt to ascertain the magnitude of this bias suggests that it is likely to be small, though perhaps not negligible.[12]

The substantive question about the cross-section estimates relates to their interpretation. Do they represent responses to short-run (cyclical) variations in job opportunities or are they more appropriately recognized as long-run responses to long-run differences? Such responses are likely to be stronger in area cross sections than in aggregate time series. Migration to better job opportunities is an alternative to dropping out of the labor force, an alternative that is not available in the aggregate when conditions worsen.

If area differences in unemployment represent, in large part, short-run variations in job opportunities, the *levels* of unemployment in the various areas in, say, 1960, should be positively correlated with *changes* in these rates from 1959 or from 1958 to 1960. However, I found no correlation with changes from 1959 or from 1958.[13] At the same time, there was a strong correlation ($r = +.8$) between unemployment levels in 1957 and in 1964 in the same areas. The correlation between 1950 and 1960 was not much smaller. The conclusion must be that the unemployment rates in the areas do not

---

[10] This suggests that a cleaner analysis would utilize U/P, rather than U/L as the unemployment variable. The correlation that was studied is: $r [L_i/P_i, (U/P)(P/L)]$. We are interested in $r (L_i/P_i, U/P)$, but even if this were zero, the correlation that was observed would be negative if extraneous factors create a covariation between L_i/P_i and L/P.

[11] That net discouragement is a fact in seasonal movements has been overlooked. Seasonal behavior illustrates the ubiquity of the phenomenon, as well as the inappropriateness of the term.

[12] The coefficient of determination between the 1960 Census week unemployment rates for the Non-Southern SMSA's and the annual average rates in the corresponding areas (as shown in Table D-5, pp. 243–245, of the 1965 *Manpower Report of the President*) was about 0.70, despite the many noncomparabilities in the two sets of data. If at least half the "unexplained variation" is due to these measurement errors, the proportion of the seasonal component in the variance of the unemployment across areas could not have exceeded 15 per cent.

[13] Data are from the source listed in the preceding footnote.

reflect short-run, transitory components in Y and W of Model (1). Rather, they represent long-run structural differences among areas to which participation adjusts.

More evidence in favor of this interpretation is provided by the experience in the depressed areas. In 17 major depressed areas (as classified in 1961) the total labor force declined by 6.3 per cent between 1953 and 1960, whereas the national civilian labor force increased by 11.1 per cent.[14] Again, between 1957 and 1963, the aggregate work force in the 12 major depressed areas declined by about 6 per cent compared with an increase of nearly 8 per cent in all areas.[15]

How much of this response is migration and how much labor-force withdrawal is not clear. That migration may be important is readily apparent from the fact that there is a negative correlation between the relatively stable SMA levels of unemployment (1960 and 1957 were tried alternatively) and the rates of population growth between 1950 and 1960 in these areas. To illustrate:[16] the 20 SMA's with slowest population growth (eight actually declined) were mainly depressed areas, with an average unemployment rate of 8.5 per cent in 1960, whereas almost all of the 20 fastest growing SMA's had unemployment rates below the national average. Migration, being selective, raises the labor-force rates in the receiving areas (and these have low unemployment rates) and lowers them in the areas of out-migration (which have high unemployment rates), even *within* age groups.

I conclude that the findings in the cross-section analyses constitute evidence largely in favor of a hypothesis that prolonged depressed employment conditions in an area tend to shrink the area's labor-force rates. If migration is relevant, this shrinking should

---

[14] Statement by Walter Heller before the Joint Economic Committee, *Hearings on the Economic Report of the President*, 87th Congress (Washington, Government Printing Office, 1961).
[15] *Manpower Report of the President*, March 1964, p. 33.
[16] Data from Population Census, 1950, 1960.

be weaker when areas of potential immigration are also depressed. This may be the reason for the relatively low 1940 levels of the partial correlation and regression coefficients in the Bowen-Finegan regressions and for the dramatic increases in them afterward. If so, the parameters based on recent cross-section data may even overestimate the effects of a severe depression. Although the differential pattern of age-sex group labor-force behavior is qualitatively comparable in cross section and time series (see Table 7.1), I conclude that the application of cross-section sensitivity parameters to the fluctuations we have experienced in the postwar period may strongly overestimate the response.

Time-Series Analyses

Several recent studies undertake a direct attack on time series to explore effects of short-run variations in employment demand on the size of the labor force.

Dernburg and Strand [7] apply multiple regression and simultaneous equations to the analysis of monthly data covering the period 1947 through 1962. Their basic equation is

$$\left(\frac{L}{P}\right)_t = a_m + a_1 \left(\frac{E}{P}\right)_t + a_2 \left(\frac{X}{P}\right)_{t+2} + a_3 \left(\frac{1}{P}\right)_t + e_{t1}$$

$(L/P)_t$ is the adult civilian labor-force participation ratio in month t, $(E/P)_t$ is the percentage of the adult civilian noninstitutional population employed in month t, and $(X/P)_{t+2}$ is the ratio of new unemployment-compensation exhaustions to the adult civilian noninstitutional population two months after t.

Variations in E/P are supposed to represent short-run variations in employment opportunities, and X/P the relevant variations in income prospects. The sign of a_1 is expected to be positive, reflecting the discouraged-worker effect. The sign of a_2 is also expected to be positive, reflecting the added-worker effect. The presumption is that the prospect of loss of income due to the exhaustion of unemployment compensation causes secondary workers in the family to enter the labor force.[17]

The following estimates were obtained (1) for the whole period and (2) for the shorter period 1953–1962:[18]

$$\left(\frac{L}{P}\right)_t = a_m + \underset{(.0308)}{.8715} \left(\frac{E}{P}\right)_t$$
$$+ \underset{(.641)}{12.347} \left(\frac{X}{P}\right)_{t+2} \quad (1)$$
$$- \underset{(419.4)}{3492.2} \left(\frac{1}{P}\right)_t + e_{t1}$$
$$R^2 = 0.8138 \qquad S_u = 0.00227$$

$$\left(\frac{L}{P}\right)_t = a_m + \underset{(.0367)}{.9490} \left(\frac{E}{P}\right)_t$$
$$+ \underset{(.735)}{12.699} \left(\frac{X}{P}\right)_{t+2} \quad (2)$$
$$- \underset{(695.4)}{5326.1} \left(\frac{1}{P}\right)_t + e_{t1}$$
$$R^2 = 0.8766 \qquad S_u = 0.00206$$

The results appear to be a striking confirmation of both the discouraged- and added-worker effects. An auxiliary simultaneous equation, which relates the exhaustion ratio to the employment ratio, permits an estimate of the total, that is, the net effect of changes in the employment ratio on the labor-force ratio. The net coefficient is positive, showing a dominant discouragement effect, that is, a clear procyclical behavior of the labor force. The size of the net coefficient is interpreted to mean that over the period 1947–1962 a fall in employment of 100 was on balance associated with withdrawal from the labor force of 38 workers.

Although the substantive meaning of the results seems clear and reasonable, some of the statistical coefficients pose difficulties. Thus I read the coefficient of X/P as saying that, other things being equal, the prospect of one additional exhaustion of unemployment-compensation benefits (say, by a family head) pushes as many as 12(!) wives or relatives into, or deters them from leaving, the labor force. If X/P does not mean what it says, it must be a proxy for some other variable which is at work.

Another doubt is raised by the over-all amazingly good predictability of labor-force size, even on a monthly basis, as shown by the remarkably small standard error of estimate (S_u). Translated into numbers of people, this standard error amounts to about 140,000–160,000, a figure that is *smaller* than the average sampling standard error of month-to-month changes in the labor force.[19]

These doubts are further increased by the following consideration: Suppose that X/P is indeed a proxy, namely for the unemployment-population ratio U/P. A multiple regression of $(L/P)_t$ on $(E/P)_t$ and $(U/P)_t$ would produce a perfect fit in which each partial regression coefficient is equal to unity. But U/P is not the same as X/P. Moreover, X/P has a lead of two months, whereas the tautological regression requires a concurrent figure. To check on these reasonable objections, I correlated U/P with X/P on a concurrent basis and then with X/P leading one quarter.[20] The lead boosted the correlation from +.8 to over +.9! This comes dangerously close to fulfilling the requirements of the tautological model. Admittedly, neither the multiple correlation nor the regression coefficients are literally equal to unity in the empirical regressions. But the coefficient at E/P is close, whereas the coefficient at X/P

---

[17] No direct evidence is provided on the notion that the entry of secondary earners is more sensitive to this state of unemployment experience than to the initial job loss and income decline of the family. Longer-run trends are supposed to be captured by the variable $1/P$. Seasonals are eliminated by dummy variables in the regression.

[18] Standard errors of regression coefficients are in parentheses. R^2 is the multiple coefficient of determination. S_u^2 is the residual variance.

[19] BLS, *Monthly Report on the Labor Force,* January 1965, p. 47.

[20] I used mid-quarterly months, that is, four months each year, for this test.

TABLE 7.1 LABOR FORCE-EMPLOYMENT REGRESSION STATISTICS, TOTAL AND SUBGROUPS, 1947–1964

	Quarterly, 1947–1964 (Tella)		Quarterly, 1947–1963 (Cooper and Johnston)			Cross Section 78 SMSA's, 1960 (Bowen and Finegan)		Monthly, 1947–1962 (Dernburg and Strand)	Labor-Force Participation Rate, 1955
	b_{le} (1)	r_{le}^2 (2)	b_{ue} (3)	r_{ue}^2 (4)	b_{le} (5)	b_{lu} (6)	b'_{le} (7)	b_{le} (8)	(9)
Males									
14–19	+.36	.36	−.42	.09	+.58	−1.94	+.80	+.70	49.5
20–24	+.46	.67	−.54	.55	+.46	—	—	+.26	90.8
25–34	+.20	.40	−.77	.81	+.23			—	97.7
35–44	+.07	.06	−1.00	.82	.00	−.24	+.20	—	98.1
45–54	+.14	.16	−.82	.65	+.18			+.07	96.5
55–64	+.46	.60	−.76	.08	+.24	−.66	+.45	−.31	87.9
65 and over	+.74	.60	−.12	.00	+.88	−1.62	+.83	+.74	39.6
All Males	+.40*	.64*	−.65	.39	+.35			+.36	83.6
Females									
14–19	+.40	.20	−.26	.05	+.74	−.73†	+.75†	+.93	29.9
20–24	+.44	.20	−.41	.03	+.59	—	—	+.42	46.0
25–34	+.52	.36	—	—	—			+.46	34.9
35–44	+.51	.44	−.29	.00	+.71	−.57†	+.52†	+.57	41.6

	(1)	(2)	(3)	(4)	(5)	(6)	(7)	(8)	(9)
45–54	+.69	.45	−.06	.00	+.94			+.68	43.8
55–64	+.63	.43	−.26	.00	+.74			+.83	32.5
65 and over	+.70	.50	−.01	.00	+.99			+.86	10.6
All Females	+.62*	.66*	−.28	.08	+.72	−.76‡	+.67‡	+.70	34.8
All	+.39§	.43§	−.62	.50	+.38	−.68	+.53	+.45	58.7

* Based on annual data, 1948–1962, Tella [10].

† Single women only.

‡ Married women only.

§ Monthly data, 1947–1962, Dernburg and Strand [7], equation (1b).

Column

1. Partial regression coefficient of L/P on E/P shown in Tella [10], Table 1, p. 74.
2. Partial coefficient of determination of L/P on E/P, calculated by formula:

$$r^2 = \frac{t^2}{t^2 + \text{d.f.}}$$

where t is the ratio of the regression coefficient to its standard error, and d.f. is the number of degrees of freedom.

3. Partial regression coefficient of U/P on E/P, Cooper and Johnston [11], Table 5, p. 138.
4. Partial coefficient of determination, calculated as in Column 2.
5. Implicit partial regression coefficient of L/P on E/P, calculated.
6. Statistically significant partial regression coefficients of L/P on U/L as shown in Bowen and Finegan [6], Table 4-10, p. 154.
7. Rough estimate of implicit partial regression coefficient of L/P on E/P, calculated by formula:

$$b'_{le} = 1 + \frac{1}{b_{lu} \cdot (P/L) - 1}$$

8. Net effect of employment calculated by Dernburg and Strand [8] from simultaneous equations.
9. *Manpower Report of the President*, March 1964, Table A-2, p. 196.

is about half the value that would be obtained if X/P were a strict fraction of U/P.[21] However, this does not dispel the doubts: the random component in X/P differs from that in U/P, and creates "errors in variables" effects that bias the regression coefficients downward.

Having confessed to all these doubts, I do not propose to reject the Dernburg-Strand findings. Their message may be a correct one, but I do not see how one can reliably extract that message from their equations.[22] It might be argued that because it is the inclusion of the income variable X/P into the equation that creates most of the insecurity in interpreting the multiple regressions perhaps restriction of the equation to E/P would be a safer though cruder approach. It foregoes the ambition of detecting each of the separate income and substitution effects, but it would, at least descriptively,[23] indicate the net outcome.

Dernberg and Strand show the result of doing this in equation (1b):

$$\left(\frac{L}{P}\right)_t = a'_m + \underset{(.0373)}{.3902} \left(\frac{E}{P}\right)_t$$
$$- \underset{(740.2)}{2341.0} \left(\frac{1}{P}\right)_t + e'_{t1}$$
$$R^2 = 0.405 \qquad S_u = 0.0041$$

[21] U/P is over 20 times the size of X/P.
[22] In a subsequent, as yet unpublished paper, Dernburg and Strand [8] apply similar procedures to population age-sex subgroups. Their findings are largely consistent with those in the first paper, and less vulnerable to statistical doubts. This is because in the sequel they relate *particular* group labor-force ratios to the *aggregate* employment and exhaustion ratio. I am grateful to Professor Dernburg for making the manuscript available to me.
[23] If the relation between cyclical movements of the income and substitution variables is stable over the period, this approach is not misleading, even in a structural sense. Thus a regression of the workweek on wage rates yields a net structural relation so long as we are willing to assume that in the long run income (properly defined) is a constant multiple of wage rate.

Once again the triumph of the discouraged worker seems to be established for the period 1947–1962, on a monthly basis.[24]

This descriptive "net outcome" approach was followed by Tella [9, 10] and by Cooper and Johnston [11]. Tella relates trend-adjusted labor-force-population ratios to employment-population ratios of the same population group, first for men and women separately on an annual basis from 1948–1962 [9]. In a second paper [10] he extends this analysis to 14 age-sex groups, on a quarterly basis, from the end of 1947 to the middle of 1964. In the quarterly analysis the employment variable is lagged one quarter in order to avoid bias due to the presence of the same sampling error in the two variables. In each case the military is included in the labor force, employment, and population figures. Cooper and Johnston [11] used the same quarterly data to relate trend-adjusted unemployment-population ratios $(U/P)_t$ to employment-population ratios $(E/P)_t$. The (U, E) regressions can be translated into (L, E) regressions, and conversely, by means of the following identities:

$$b_{ue} \equiv b_{le} - 1 \quad \text{and}$$
$$\frac{b_{ue}^2}{r_{ue}^2} \equiv \frac{b_{le}^2}{r_{le}^2} - (1 + 2b_{ue})$$

where b_{ue} is the relevant (partial or simple) regression coefficient of U/P on E/P, b_{le} is the relevant (partial or simple) regression coefficient of L/P on E/P, and r^2 with corresponding subscripts is the relevant coefficient of determination.

Table 7.1 brings together the regression estimates of the net effect of employment variation on the size of the total labor force and its age-sex subgroups. Additional statistics of interest are shown in Table 7.2. It is important to note that in each case labor

[24] Interestingly, the partial regression coefficient of (E/P) which measures the net outcome is very close to that obtained by the full analysis involving two simultaneous equations (.3902 versus .3715). (*Cf.* note 25).

force of a group was related to its own employment. Columns 1, 5, 7, and 8 are conceptually comparable estimates of the net effect b_{le}. They differ, of course, in terms of data and of methodology, as already described and as noted in the table, but nevertheless there is a fair amount of agreement in the results. There is a net positive sensitivity to employment conditions in totals and in all groups with the exception of the primary male labor force, age 25–55, but even this group is positively sensitive in the cross section, as mentioned. There is further agreement on the greater sensitivity of females as a group compared with males as a group. Finally, the extreme age groups are more sensitive than the middle-age groups. The single most important conclusion is that, in time-series, *labor-force sensitivity to employment conditions is a characteritsic of the secondary labor force.*

It is true, of course, that most of the males 20–24 and many of the other workers in the "secondary" labor force are not secondary in any sense. The results, however, suggest that differences in behavior among age-sex groups are likely to be attributable to the differential proportions of secondary workers in the groups. The rank correlations between the average labor-force participation rates in the groups (Column 9, Table 7.1) [page 86] and the "employment-sensitivity" coefficients were +.85, +.80, and +.65, when compared with columns 8, 5, and 1, respectively.

Proceeding to the differences among the results of the studies, there are several noteworthy features:

1. The cross-section sensitivity estimates exceed the corresponding time-series estimates in the male group and therefore in total, but not in the female groups. As noted, the cross-section sensitivity also extends to the primary labor force of males. These differences from the time-series estimates again suggest the role of migration in the inter-area labor-force adjustments. Employment-connected migration is likely to be a family decision based largely on the employment situation of the primary worker.[25]

2. The estimates in Columns 1 and 5 are based on the same quarterly data. However, Tella (Column 1) lagged the employment variable one quarter, which reduced the sizes of his coefficients in all groups, except males 55–64.[26] Indeed, the coefficients in Column 5 are those that Tella would have obtained, if he had run a coincident rather than lagged regression.

3. The regression coefficients in the Cooper–Johnston (U, E) regression (Column 3) do not convey any different information from those obtained by an (L, E) regression of the same data. Strength of the net discouragement effect is measured by the extent to which the absolute size of the negative b_{ue} coefficient is less than unity. This difference is precisely equal to the coefficient b_{le}, by definition.[27]

This approach, however, produces low correlation coefficients in contrast to the high ones produced by (L, E) regressions.

The (L, E) partial correlation coefficients (Column 2) move together with the regression coefficients in column 1, suggesting that labor-force behavior is most predictable in those groups in which sensitivity to employment is highest. This seems puzzling, for the groups with highest sensitivity are groups with the lowest degree of labor-force attachment (Column 9) and with greatest degree

---

[25] According to *Manpower Report of the President,* March 1964, pp. 33–34, outmigration from areas of high unemployment during the 1950's occurred almost entirely among men in the 24–44 age group.

[26] According to Tella, this group's labor-force rate shows an exceptionally good fit with the employment variable lagged one and two quarters.

[27] $\dfrac{\text{Cov }(L, E)}{\text{Var }(E)} = \dfrac{\text{Cov }(U, E)}{\text{Var }(E)} + 1$

90 Special Topics in Supply and Demand

TABLE 7.2 LABOR-FORCE ATTACHMENT, VARIATION, AND SENSITIVITY TO EMPLOYMENT, 1947–1964, QUARTERLY

	Labor-Force Participation Rate, 1955 (1)	Total Variation (2)	Residual Variation (3)	Labor-Force Turnover (4)	"Uncorrected" Sensitivity Coefficient (5)	"Corrected" Sensitivity Coefficient (6)	
						(a)	(b)
Males							
14–19	49.5	3.83	1.15	1.45	+.58	+.28	+.32
20–24	90.8	1.93	1.06	1.09	+.46	+.37	+.25
25–34	97.7	.64	.38	1.00	+.23	+.17	0
35–44	98.1	.31	.30	1.01	0	0	0
45–54	96.5	.43	.39	1.02	+.18	+.14	0
55–64	87.9	.97	.62	1.03	+.24	−.16	0
65 and over	39.6	5.64	.79	1.23	+.88	+.40	+.30
All Males					+.35	+.17	+.25
Females							
14–19	29.9	1.54	.91	1.60	+.74	+.41	+.30
20–24	46.0	1.31	.97	1.38	+.59	−.15	−.06
25–34	34.9	1.28	.58	1.34	—	0	0
35–44	41.6	2.40	.48	1.27	+.71	0	+.35
45–54	43.8	5.07	.71	1.23	+.94	+.72	+.68
55–64	32.5	4.64	.65	1.28	+.74	+.26	+.38
65 and over	10.6	.78	.47	1.52	+.99	+.60	+.80
All Females					+.72	+.33	+.50
All					+.38	+.19	+.29

Column
1   See Column 9 in Table 7.1.
2   Quarterly standard deviation of labor-force participation rates, uncorrected for trend, derived from Tella [10], Table 1, p. 74.
3   Standard error of estimate from regression of labor-force participation rates on employment ratio and time, Tella, *ibid*.
4   Ratio of number working some time during 1955 to average weekly size of labor force. G. Bancroft, *The American Labor Force*, Table 10, p. 16.
5   Regression coefficients in Column 5, Table 7.1.
6   Same coefficients adjusted by procedure described in text.
    6(a) utilizes the employment-population ratio of males (age 25–64) as the cyclical index of demand.
    6(b) utilizes the (BLS) employment-population ratio as the cyclical index.

of instability, as measured by their variances (Table 7.2, Column 2) [above]. These groups have much greater scope for labor-force decisions than the primary labor force. Many of these decisions are subject to factors other than and additional to the current general state of the labor market. We would therefore expect these parts of the labor force to be the least predictable *in the sense that even after the regression larger unexplained variation remains in these groups compared with the others*. This is shown by the residual variances from Tella's regressions in Column 3, Table 7.2.

The differences between the squared correlation coefficients in the (L, E) and the equivalent (U, E) regressions arise from the fact that fluctuations in the labor force exceed the fluctuations in unemployment in the secondary-worker groups, whereas the converse is true in the primary labor-force group.[28]

An Error Model

There remains the likelihood of upward biases in the sensitivity estimate, the b_{le} regression coefficients. Tella's lag procedure is designed to reduce biases, and it does reduce the b_{le} coefficients (Column 1 compared with Column 5 in Table 7.1) by a sizable amount in many of the groups. It is not clear, however, how effective such a makeshift is.

The general problem is posed by the procedure of correlating the labor force of a group with *its own* employment. First, since E_i is a part of L_i, any sampling response and other measurement errors in E_i will be duplicated in L_i, spuriously biasing the regression coefficients toward unity.[29] Second, specific groups may experience (a) employment-demand fluctuations independent of the over-all state of the market and (b) specific labor-supply fluctuations which result in employment fluctuations of the group.[30] If our purpose is to estimate the response of the group to the general cyclical state of demand, both phenomena create upward biases in the estimated coefficients b_{le}.

Formally, let E_i, the employment of a particular group i, consist of components

$$E_i = E_c + E_{sd} + E_{ss} + e$$

and

$$U_i = U_c + U_{sd} + U_{ss} + u$$

so that

$$L_i = L_c + L_{sd} + L_{ss} + (e + u)$$

Subscript c indicates the general cyclical component, sd the component resulting from specific demand fluctuation, ss the specific supply fluctuations, and e, u the measurement errors.

For simplicity, assume that (1) all components of E and U, except those with the same subscripts, are independent, and

(2) Cov $(E_c, U_c) < 0$
(3) Cov $(E_{sd}, U_{sd}) < 0$
(4) Cov $(E_{ss}, U_{ss}) > 0$[31]
(5) Cov $(e, u) = 0$

Then

$$b_{le} = \frac{\text{Cov}(L_c, E_c) + \text{Cov}(L_{sd}, E_{sd}) + \text{Cov}(L_{ss}, E_{ss}) + \text{Cov}(e+u, e)}{\text{Var}(E)}$$

Call the "true" cyclical regression coefficient $b(L_c, E_c) = b_c$, and the ratio Var $(E_c)/$ Var $(E) = k$. Then

$$b_{le} = kb_c + \frac{\text{Cov}(L_{sd}, E_{sd}) + \text{Cov}(L_{ss}, E_{ss})}{\text{Var}(E)} + \frac{\text{Var}(e)}{\text{Var}(E)}$$

Now, by lagging E one quarter, we are likely to eliminate most of the "error of measurement bias" Var $(e)/$Var (E), since in the lagged regression this term becomes [Cov (e_t, e_{t-1})]/Var (E). The lag probably also reduces the remaining terms. But it does not provide the desired estimate b_c, though it probably comes close to it.

---

[28] Since predicting L from E means no more than predicting U, the residual must be the same in both regressions. However, the squared correlation coefficients are different:

$$r_{le}^2 = 1 - \frac{S^2}{S_l^2} \qquad r_{ue}^2 = 1 - \frac{S^2}{S_u^2}$$

where S^2 is residual variance. Hence

$$\frac{1 - r_{le}^2}{1 - r_{ue}^2} = \frac{S_u^2}{S_l^2}$$

Tests of statistical significance, keeping in mind that the null hypothesis is $\beta_{le} = 0$ and $\beta_{ue} = -1$, respectively, must yield the same results, even though the correlation coefficients look different.

The Cooper-Johnston and Tella procedures are not exactly equivalent because of the lag in Tella's regression. Moreover, the implicit standard errors are much larger in the former, because of a rather strong correction for auto-correlation. Aside from this, it should be clear that the (U, E) regressions overestimate the standard errors, just as the (L, E) regressions underestimate them.

[29] The (U, E) approach provides no escape, since its regression coefficient will be *lowered*, in absolute value, to the same extent: biased toward zero.

[30] Also resulting in a positive correlation between employment and unemployment. The summer seasonal is the best example. However, the phenomenon need not be only seasonal.

[31] Cf. note 39.

The equation can be further rewritten

$$b_{le} = kb_c + (1-k) + \frac{\text{Cov}(U_{sd}, E_{sd}) + \text{Cov}(U_{ss}, E_{ss})}{\text{Var}(E)}$$

By assumptions (3) and (4), the two terms in the numerator on the right-hand side have opposing signs. Which predominates is not clear, but the fraction is likely to be small. Let us neglect it for the purpose of a rough estimating procedure. Hence

$$b_{le} = kb_c + (1-k)$$

Note that k is the proportion of the variance of employment in a group E_i attributable to the general demand situation. It follows that a correlation of E_i with an appropriate aggregate employment demand index C will produce an estimate of k. The coefficient of determination $r^2(E_i, C)$ measures the proportion of variance E_i accounted for by C.

In view of the findings that labor-force behavior of the primary labor force is not cyclically sensitive, its employment fluctuations can serve as a good cyclical index of employment demand. Using the quarterly data to correlate the total employment ratio with the employment ratio of the "core" group of males (25–64), I obtained an $r^2 = .77$. Applying this estimate of k to the appropriate regression coefficient in Column 5, Table 7.1, which is $b_{le} = .38$, the corrected coefficient b_c is calculated from:

$$.38 = .77b_c + .23, \text{ so } b_c = .19$$

Similar correlations of the core group employment ratio with employment ratios of age-sex subgroups provided the means for a downward adjustment of all the coefficients of Column 5, Table 7.1. The corrected estimates are shown in Table 7.2, Column 6 (a), next to the uncorrected ones (Table 7.2, Column 5). An alternative set of corrected estimates was obtained by the same procedure, using the nonagricultural BLS employment series as the numerator of the cyclical index. Results are shown in Column 6 (b).

It seems clear that net labor-force sensitivity to employment demand in time series has been, perhaps quite strongly, overestimated by the regression procedures or the application of cross-section parameter estimates.

The Annual Record: Preliminary Findings

Considerations of errors and biases, analyzed in the preceding section, suggest a direct approach in which labor-force behavior of a group should be related to some index of the demand for labor which is statistically independent of the particular labor-force measurements. In this section I report such a preliminary survey of year-to-year movements, a subject to which previous studies gave only brief attention.[32] The description that follows raises many questions but provides some insights into the major cyclical and other responses of the labor force during the post-war experience.

Figure 7.1 shows the contrasting labor-force behavior of primary (males 25–65) and secondary (all other) labor-force groups, and provides a comparison of variation in the latter group's labor-force rate with that of several cyclical labor-market indicators. These include: the primary group employment-population ratio, the nonagricultural employment-population ratio, the workweek of production workers in manufacturing, the quit rate in manufacturing (adjusted for trend), first differences in hourly earnings in manufacturing, and the NICB help-wanted advertising index.

The general conformity of movement is positive and is best described by noting that, of the 17 year-to-year movements, the direction of change in the secondary labor force differs only four times from the quit rate, the primary employment-population ratio, and the nonagricultural employment-population ratio. Aside from the 1947–1948 difference in the quit rate, the periods with divergent movements were: 1951–1953, 1956–1957, and 1961–1962.

---

[32] Tella [9].

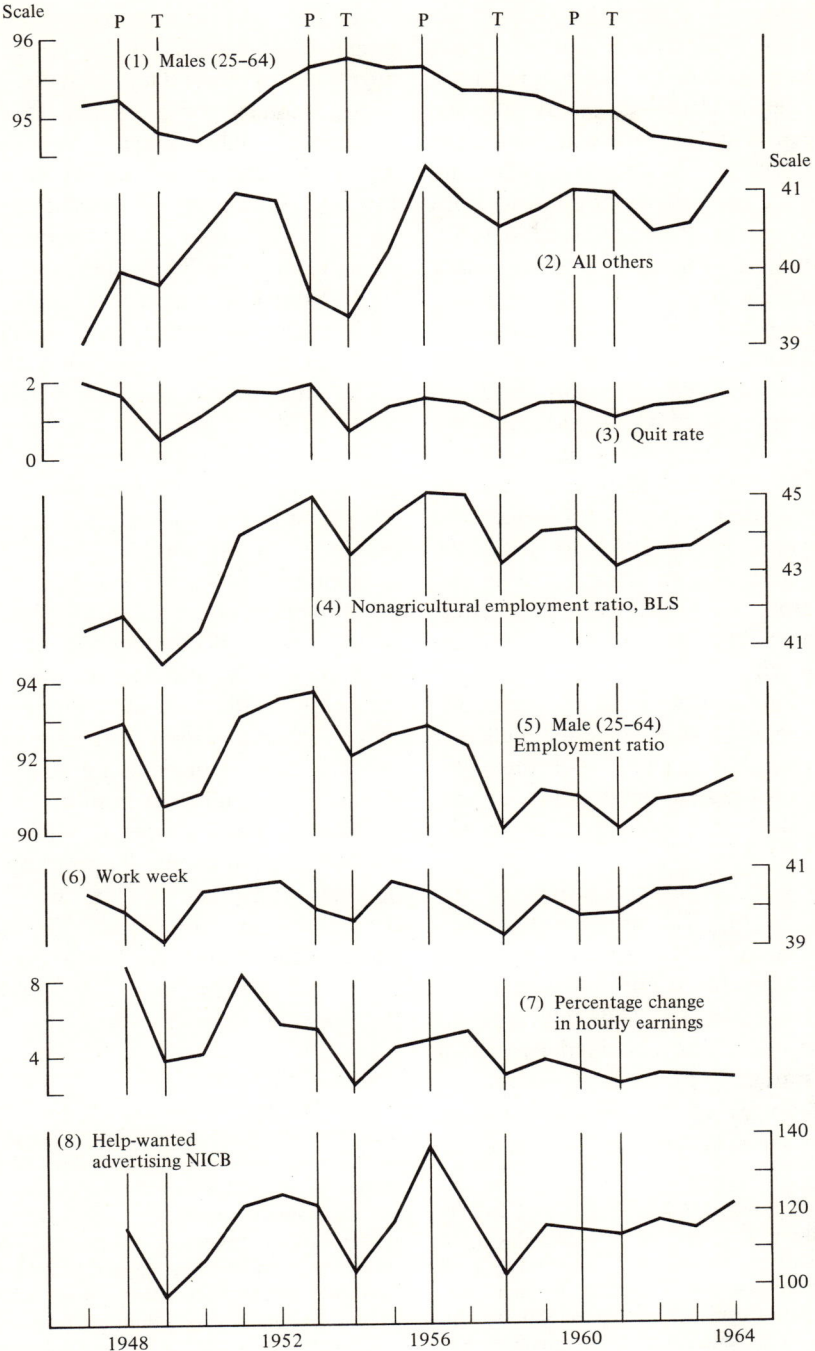

FIGURE 7.1 Labor-force rates and cycle indexes.

The differences are as instructive as the similarities. The 1948 peak and the 1949 trough are repeated in the labor-force rate. The differences in 1951–1953 are affected by the Korean War. There was a substantial influx of secondary workers in 1950 and 1951 during the early phase of the war. With the reduction of war effort and truce in 1953, there was an increasing outflow of secondary workers from the labor force, while the primary civilian labor force increased in size. This substitution repeats the post-World War II pattern between 1945 and 1947.[33]

The cycle troughs of 1954 and 1958 are duplicated in the secondary labor force. From 1956 to 1957 the labor-force rate declines sharply while demand indicators are level or decline. From 1961 to 1962 the labor force continues to decline, while demand indicators are moving up. Thereafter, the labor force resumes conformity, though at a lower level.

Perhaps significantly, both of these differential episodes follow federal increases in minimum wages,[34] coupled with the 1961 extension of coverage to retail trade, an important employer of many secondary workers.[35]

Proceeding to a disaggregation of the labor force, Figure 7.2 presents five sex-groups and Figure 7.3 portrays the behavior of the older labor force (65 and over) and the young group (14–24). The young group is shown for males and classified by school enrollment status.

Several features of the annual variation portrayed in these charts call for comment.

1. The cyclical conformity of the disaggregated groups is not as clear as in the aggregate of secondary workers. Evidently, disaggregation brings to the fore the "autonomous" labor-force components (L_{sd} and L_{ss} in the error model) and magnifies the importance of the measurement errors ($e + u$). However, the differential behavior of subgroups is interesting and suggestive.

2. Nonwhite females (Figure 7.2) exhibit peaks of participation *inverse* to the business cycle. It would seem that in this group the additional-worker effect dominates. This is clear in the case of adult women, as in the example of the 35–44 age group. This finding is important on theoretical grounds and in conjunction with other evidence. In my study of labor-force participation of women I interpreted the additional-worker effect as an alternative to dissaving, asset decumulation, or increasing debt in family attempts to maintain consumption in the face of unemployment and other income losses.[36] I argued, consequently, that such behavior should be particularly discernible in families at low levels of wealth, particularly in view of capital market imperfections. Supporting evidence in that study and in the work of Cain strengthens this inference.[37] In the present context this means *the "additional worker" is more likely to be a low-income person than the "discouraged worker."*

---

[33] See Long [1], Appendix Tables B-1 and B-2. A similar very interesting pattern is observable each year in the seasonal movements: married women decrease their labor-force participation each summer when children return home from school, and many of the latter enter the labor market. See Altman [9], Table 3, p. 33.

[34] From 40 to 75¢ in 1950, from 75¢ to $1.00 in 1956, and from $1.00 to $1.25 in 1961, to be increased in two steps.

[35] Cf. the findings by Albert Rees in this volume on the employment effects of recent minimum wage increases.

[36] Mincer [12], p. 75 ff.

[37] Cain [5], pp. 13–14, reports that cross-section area multiple regressions relating labor-force rates of nonwhite married women show little net response to unemployment in 1950, and a negative, but very small, response in 1960. He argues that in the case of nonwhite wives, the income effect (inducing work in this context) appears stronger than the substitution effect (discouraging work) relative to the case of white wives.

Cain found a similar differential pattern in the parameters of long-run income and wage variables. These long-run income and wage parameter estimates from the cross section help to explain a long-standing puzzle, the much milder upward secular trend in labor-force participation of non-white compared to white women. See Cain [4] and Long's comments on Mincer [12].

FIGURE 7.2 Labor-force rates by color and sex.

3. Secular declines in participation dominate the pattern of labor-force behavior of older men. The declines are perhaps, on average, steeper in bad than in good times (Figure 7.3), but the particularly strong drop from 1951 to 1952 and the continued strong decline *after* the 1958 recession are not in consonance with general short-run demand fluctuations. The decline since 1958 may reflect a more-than-cyclical erosion of job opportunities, and the 1961 minimum wage increase and extension may have played a part in it.

All such factors were reinforced and possibly dominated by the changing retirement provisions of OASDI. The Social Security Act of 1935 made receipt of pension conditional on cessation of work. Subsequent amendments enabled beneficiaries to earn up to a certain minimum a month without reduction in pensions, or above the minimum with certain fractional reductions. These provisions were liberalized in the postwar period. The monthly minimum was raised to $50 in 1950, to $75 in 1952, and to $100 in 1958. These changes were followed by declines in participation of older males (Figure 7.3) at times when demand indexes (Figure 7.1) show upward movements.

Presumably, the result of such changes is that wage earners are allowed to take intermittent or part-time work without loss of benefits or with only small losses. This may bring some people back from complete retirement into intermittent participation, but it also strengthens the incentives of others to retire. The opposing effects, illustrated by data on work experience of men 65 and over, indicate a steep drop in their proportion of full-time job holding and increase in part-time and part-period work.[38] Evidently the net effect was to reduce the average weekly participation rate, and by more than participation on an annual basis: the participation rate dropped from 45.8 in 1950 to 28.4 in 1963, and the proportion working some time during the year dropped from 49.3 in 1950 to 37.6 in 1963.[39]

Of course, the downward trend in labor-force rates of older people has been influenced by increasing levels of benefit payments. The important point about the liberalization of penalty provisions is that it affects both the trend and the short-run flexibility of the older labor force.

Recent studies of the Social Security Administration[40] show that OASDI benefits may also have reduced the labor force of the 62–64 year group when in 1961 these benefits were made available to retired persons in this age range. The total number availing themselves has grown to 600,000 in 1963, so that 28 per cent of men in this age group now receive benefits.

In view of these figures, it would seem that the accelerated drop in the labor-force rate of men in the age group 55–64 since 1961 (from 87.3 in 1961 to 85.6 in 1964) is in part attributable to these provisions.[41]

The studies referred to show further effects of OASDI incentives. In the over-65 age group larger proportions of beneficiaries than nonbeneficiaries among those well

---

[38] *Monthly Labor Review,* LXXXVIII (January 1965), p. 10.

[39] *Manpower Report of the President,* March 1965, and Special Labor Force Reports, Annual Work Experience Surveys, of the Bureau of Labor Statistics.

[40] *Social Security Bulletins,* June 1964 and August 1964.

[41] This illustrates why the term substitution effect is more appropriate than the so-called discouragement effect: labor supply responds not to one market-wage prospect but, in general, to a real-wage differential. The same effect can be produced on labor supply by raising or lowering the alternative real income or the market wage. The example illustrates the fact that encouragement in one sector helps to create or to strengthen discouragement from another.

Thus labor-supply elasticity is not zero even in the primary groups throughout the range of the wage (real-wage differential) variable. It may appear to be almost zero in the normally observed range of variation (such as the mild business cycle), but a bigger change in the wage differential, in either direction, tends to produce a visible response.

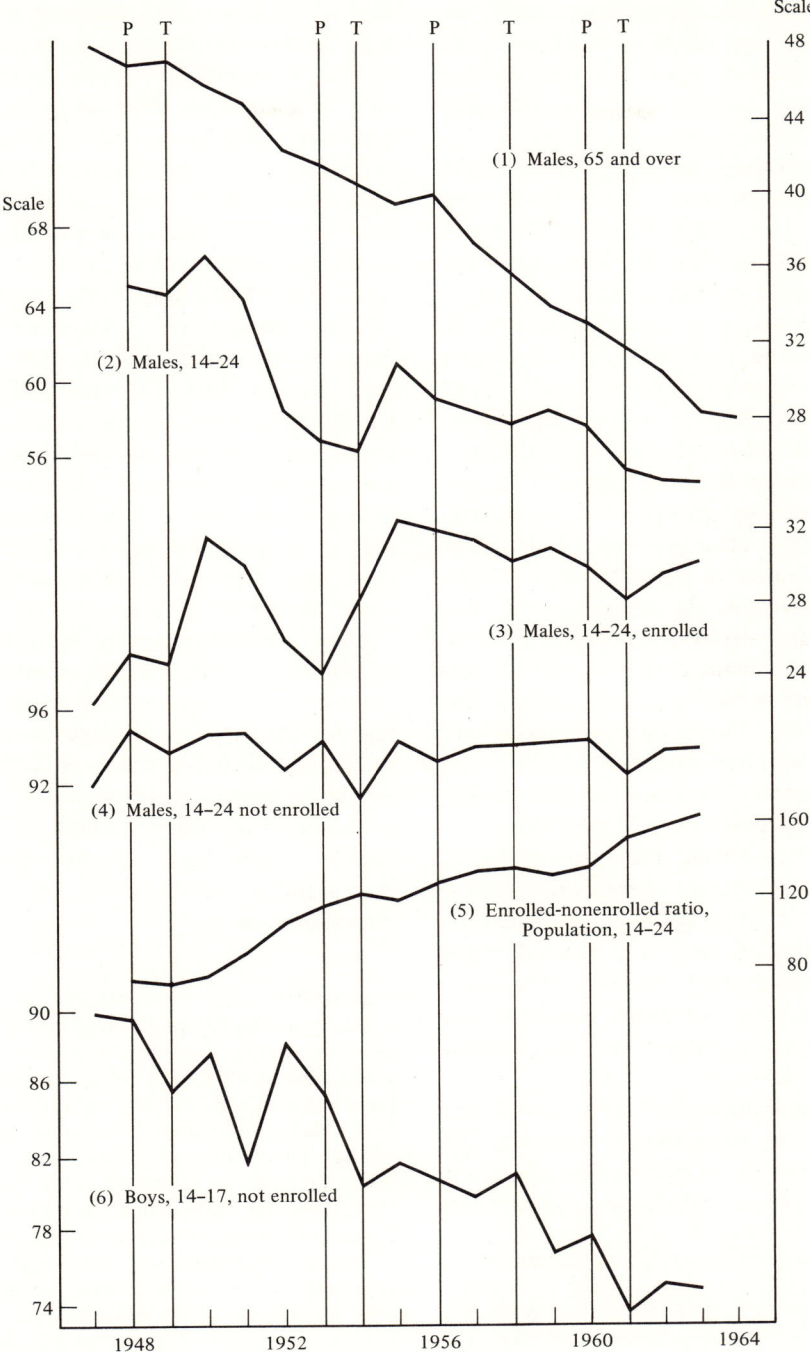

FIGURE 7.3 Labor-force rates of the old and the young.

enough to work are not working or not planning to work. Among those working, a majority of beneficiaries work intermittently or part-time, but most nonbeneficiaries work full time.

Most interesting, in conjunction with the unemployment situation, is the finding that although in 1951 22 per cent of the retired claimed layoffs as a cause of retirement only 8 per cent made this claim in 1963.[42]

The latter finding is, *prima facie,* not consistent with the view that high unemployment was the major cause of continued and perhaps accelerated labor-force withdrawal of older men. However, an isolated pair of survey responses is not a sufficient statistic; more evidence is needed. One could argue that although a clear response to expansion and liberalization of OASDI (and private) pension provisions is demonstrated, such responses are stronger in periods of depressed employment. It is probably true that the real-wage differential has changed from *both* directions. Developments on each side need to be explored further.

4. Labor-force participation of teenagers and young people (14–24) continued its secular decline during the postwar period. Changing employment conditions seem to be reflected in the behavior of the labor force of enrolled and not-enrolled youth, shown separately in Figure 7.3. The labor-force fluctuations are more pronounced in the enrolled group, whose average participation rate is lower.[43]

The data indicate not only labor-force withdrawals in recession periods but also relative increases in school enrollment at such times (Figure 7.3), an interesting reflection of changing opportunity costs during the business cycle.[44]

The downward trend in the labor-force rate of youngsters does not seem to accelerate. However, throughout the period, the subgroup whose participation continuously and most sharply declined is the 14–17-year-old not-enrolled. Its participation rate fell from 88 per cent in 1952 to 74 per cent in 1963. This group had severe declines during three cyclical downturns, as well as from 1950 to 1951, 1955 through 1957, and 1960 to 1961. The latter (also a cyclical decline) and two former declines coincided with federal increases in minimum wages and the extension of coverage. This group experienced a sharp increase in unemployment at the end of the 1950's, but there has been no further marked change since 1960.[45]

Supporting evidence for the probable role of minimum wages in the labor-market experience of this group is provided in a regression analysis of teenage unemployment by Arnold Katz, in which he finds that the employment-population ratio of boys age 14–19 who are out of school has been adversely affected by increases in minimum wages and the increased size of the teenage population group.[46]

---

[42] At the same time, compulsory retirement age was quoted by 22 per cent recently, compared to 11 per cent in 1951, poor health by 35 per cent compared to 41 per cent earlier, and preference for leisure by 17 per cent compared to 3 per cent in 1951. *Social Security Bulletin,* August 1964, Table 5, p. 6.

[43] This abstracts from summer months, as the data by enrollment status are based on October figures. Inclusion of summer months would greatly augment the fluctuations in the enrolled group.

[44] In a recent study of chronically depressed areas, it was found that virtually all boys of high school age (16 and 17) attend school, and most of the young men aged 14 to 24 who are not in the labor force are at school. See Bureau of Labor Statistics, *The Structure of Unemployment in Areas of Substantial Labor Surplus,* Study Paper No. 23 in Joint Economic Committee, *Study of Employment, Growth, and Price Levels* (Washington: Government Printing Office, 1960), p. 16.

Similar countercyclical effects on enrollment were found in longer time series by Beverly Duncan, "Dropouts and the Unemployed," *Journal of Political Economy,* LXXIII (April 1965), 121–134.

[45] *Manpower Report of the President,* March 1965, Table B-8.

[46] The regression was run separately for the 14–17 and 18–19 age groups. The population coefficient was more reliable and the minimum wage coefficient less reliable in the second group.

The factor of population size has been receiving increased attention, particularly in connection with the growth of the teenage group. However, the population explosion has been blamed for sins it does not perpetrate without accomplices. The population factor, *by itself*, need not increase unemployment or decrease labor-force participation. In the absence of strong barriers to downward wage flexibility, an increased population group of teenagers will exert a downward pressure on their wages only to the extent of the inelasticity of substitution between less experienced and more experienced workers. Some and perhaps even a sizeable degree of wage decline is unlikely to produce labor-force withdrawal, *without going to school,* at this stage in life. Minimum wages, however, can effectively block entry to jobs for many of these youngsters. If their way back to school is blocked for reasons of low productivity (or "ability" or any other term indicating disadvantages), all these factors *interact* to lock a growing number of them out of the labor market and out of school as well.

5. Labor-force behavior of the primary labor force, particularly of males 25–54, is quite insensitive to demand fluctuations. A very gentle decline, however, has been perceptible since the midfifties. It appears that this decline primarily involves nonwhite males. On further inspection the development is narrowed down to unmarried nonwhite males in this age group. In both color groups unmarried men had lower and decreasing participation rates as well as higher and increasing unemployment rates during the last decade. However, the proportion of married men in this age group is much higher among whites than among nonwhites. Marital status is not unresponsive to economic conditions. The proportion of married white males in this group increased somewhat between 1950 and 1960, but the opposite is true of nonwhites. Slight as they have been, these trends suggest a more-than-cyclical deterioration in the low-income "marginal" groups.

To sum up: positive cycle sensitivity (net "discouragement" effect) is readily discernible in the annual behavior of the secondary labor force. So is the added-worker response in some of the low-income subgroups. But powerful trend factors and institutional changes continue to dominate the behavior of labor-force groups. Much more attention should be paid to these factors and changes.[47]

Disguised Unemployment

Because the recorded size of the labor force is lower in times of slack than it would have been under conditions of full employment, it follows that the observed unemployment count understates the magnitude of manpower loss created by the recession.

Calculation of this deficit, called "hidden" or "disguised" unemployment, utilizes the regression equations which relate labor-force ratios to employment or unemployment ratios. Full-employment levels are fixed for the independent variables in some conventionally arbitrary way, such as a 4 per cent rate of unemployment, and the hypothetical size of the labor force that would be obtained under these conditions is estimated from the equation. The difference between the estimated full-employment labor force and the actually reported labor force constitutes hidden unemployment. Addition of hidden to observed unemployment yields the "manpower gap," or "adjusted" unemployment.

Now, if this addition is to measure the total "manpower loss," the assumed level of "full-employment unemployment" should be subtracted from reported unemployment; that is, the manpower loss in reported unemployment is its *cyclical* component, not total unemployment. Otherwise, full employment must be defined by a zero unemployment level. The relative importance of disguised unemployment in this corrected manpower gap would, of course, loom much larger.

[47] An exploratory analysis of trends is presented in the author's "Economic Factors in Labor Force Participation," to be published in the *International Encyclopedia of the Social Sciences.*

Estimates of hidden unemployment, without this correction, were calculated in several of the studies quoted earlier. The resulting estimates do, of course, differ from one equation to another, and they depend on the definition of full employment. The numbers are not small: by way of illustration, the numbers quoted run as high as three million in 1962 (under the prevailing 4 per cent assumption).[48] This is several times larger than the cyclical component of reported unemployment (a little over one million above a 4 per cent rate in 1962).

What are we to make of these numbers? Do they mean, for instance, that recession-caused "waste" in 1962 was a much bigger problem in its disguised than in its undisguised components? In what sense are the two components comparable and additive, as the calculation of the manpower gap implies?

To answer these questions, we must take account of two important aspects of disguised unemployment: (a) the method of its calculation and (b) the fact that it is almost exclusively *concentrated in the secondary labor force.*

It is clear from the method of calculation that, in a cyclical context, the importance of hidden unemployment in a population group is a direct function of the degree of labor-force responsiveness to short-run variations in employment conditions.[49] It is a reflection of short-run supply elasticity with respect to the real-wage differentials, in a broad sense, between labor-market and non-market activities. In addition to pecuniary conditions involved in the market alternative are the ease of finding a job, its locational and other conveniences, and attractiveness of the job content. All these dimensions of the real market-wage rate improve as the market tightens. Thus disguised unemployment indicates potential availability at higher than currently prevailing real-wage conditions. But reported unemployment is, implicitly, and presumably behaviorally, defined in terms of currently prevailing real-wage conditions. The difference is real, though in practice the boundary in attitudes and in survey responses is fuzzy enough to create errors of misclassification. But these work in either direction.

It might be argued that this distinction is not really relevant to the manpower loss concept. If employment (wage) conditions improved to normal levels, the million cyclically unemployed who reported themselves as such would be absorbed into employment and so would the three million previously disguised unemployed. Additivity of reported and disguised unemployment must mean that production would increase proportionately from each source. More precisely, the assumption is that the net marginal products in the two groups are equal to one another when they are employed, and equal to zero when unemployed (one visibly, the other invisibly).

I submit that this assumption must be questioned precisely in view of the differences in supply elasticities. These differences, practically by definition, arise from the greater scope for substitution between market and non-market activities (including leisure) in the disguised group. It is no accident that the disguised unemployed are found mainly in the secondary labor force. This fact simply illustrates the strong inverse correlation, predictable from economic theory, between labor-force sensitivity and degree of labor-force attachment shown in Table 7.1.

Consider a population group whose average participation rate is 40 per cent. This does not mean that 40 per cent of the individuals are almost always in the labor force; the remaining 60 percent almost never. It means rather that the same individuals are sometimes in and sometimes out

---

[48] See Tables 2 and 3 in Dernburg and Strand [7], pp. 387, 388.

[49] The level is also affected by secular trends which the equations fit to the various population groups. No analysis has been applied to explain the trends.

during a period of years. Data on labor-force turnover certainly support this proposition (see Column 4, Table 7.2). Assume then that, on the average, an individual in such a group expects to spend 40 per cent of his time in the labor force. The fact that 60 per cent of his time is spent outside the labor force means that other than "gainful" activities are important. This implies that the opportunity costs of job-searching and job-holding are greater for secondary workers than for primary ones, and that the payoff to job mobility is smaller, since the expected period of employment is shorter. Hence the *net* gain from moving into the labor market and the *net* loss from leaving it due to adverse conditions in the market can be quite small, and certainly much smaller than for the primary groups.[50] Given some scope for timing of their activities, work in the labor market will be preferred at times when search costs are low and job conditions attractive. The fact that many other factors influence timing helps to explain not only the greater sensitivity with respect to employment conditions (higher regression coefficients in Tables 7.1 and 7.2) but also the greater instability (variance, residual variance, and turnover in Table 7.2) in groups within *lower levels* of participation.

It is paradoxical that the optimization of timing labor-force activities creates the illusion of disguised unemployment. The more economical the timing, the larger the number of disguised unemployed! The paradox reflects a myopic preoccupation with GNP. The focus on disguised unemployment as a component of the manpower loss not only misses the broader view of total productivity but also the important fact that a flexible labor force is a source of strength in potentially inflationary situations.

This reasoning seriously questions the comparability and additivity of the two kinds of unemployment from a *total production* and *welfare* point of view. However, it should not be interpreted as denying the existence of "involuntary" labor-force withdrawal. I am simply suggesting that the regression procedures are more likely to catch the kind of behavior I describe in the above model than the classic type of discouraged worker. The latter is perhaps best defined in the words of the *President's Manpower Report:* "Where opportunities are *chronically* limited, some persons give up a fruitless search for work and rely on charity or in other ways subsist without recourse to work . . ."[51] Such cases are most likely to arise as a result of structural displacements, personal adversity, or other barriers to jobs. The business-cycle downturn aggravates such problems, but its effect is unlikely to be an immediate withdrawal from the labor force.[52]

In a series of case studies of plant shutdowns, Wilcock and Franke found that the unemployed continued their labor-force attachment for years.[53] About 10 per cent withdrew from the labor force after two years of search. After three years, 10–20 per cent of them wound up on relief. The process of discouragement and "squeeze out" of the labor force where it exists is not a matter of quick response to mild business-cycle fluctuations as we have known them in the postwar period.

---

[50] This is not to say that non-market activities of primary workers are not productive. In addition to differences in search costs, the marginal rate of substitution between market and non-market activities is weaker for primary than secondary workers. Hence it takes a much greater diminution of the marginal value product of *primary* workers to squeeze them out of the labor market.

[51] *Manpower Report of the President,* March 1964, p. 30. My italics.

[52] According to Altman's study of gross flows, most secondary workers with high labor-force mobility drop out of the labor force before their unemployment extends past five weeks. In contrast, those with stronger attachments do not drop out long after the exhaustion of unemployment benefits.

[53] Richard Wilcock and Walter Franke, *Unwanted Workers: Permanent Layoffs and Long-term Unemployment* (New York: Free Press, 1963).

TABLE 7.3 REPORTED AND "ADJUSTED" UNEMPLOYMENT RATES

Age Group	Male Rates, 1962		Female Rates, 1962		Male Rates, 1964-II		Female Rates, 1964-II	
	Reported (1)	"Adjusted" (2)	Reported (3)	"Adjusted" (4)	Reported (5)	"Adjusted" (6)	Reported (7)	"Adjusted" (8)
14–19	13.4	23.4	13.2	24.8	15.6	18.1	16.1	19.3
20–24	8.9	12.7	9.1	10.0	8.0	9.3	9.1	11.5
25–34	4.5	4.8	6.5	9.6	3.4	3.5	6.0	7.7
35–44	3.6	3.5	5.2	9.0	2.7	2.7	4.9	6.2
45–54	3.9	4.2	4.1	8.4	3.3	3.4	3.8	5.9
55–64	4.6	4.7	3.5	9.2	3.9	4.4	3.7	4.6
65 and over	4.6	12.5	4.1	18.5	4.0	5.6	3.1	5.0
All	5.3	7.0	6.2	11.3	4.7	5.3	6.3	8.0

Sources: Annual rates, 1962, from Dernburg and Strand [8], Tables 7 and 8. Second-quarter rates, 1964, from Tella [10], Table 3, p. 77.

The disguised unemployment which appears in Table 7.3 is probably best described as a part of the "labor-force reserve." There are many reasons why we may want to know a great deal about its size and composition. The procedures which led to the estimates in Table 7.3 are not the most suitable for this purpose.

Some Implications

Trends in Labor-force Flexibility

Only a few years ago, the accepted view of short-run labor-force behavior could best be described in the formula: "zero net cycle elasticity plus small random variation." Recent studies amend this formula (a bit drastically) into: "strong net cycle elasticity plus very small random variation." On the basis of the review described in these pages, I propose as a tentative diagnosis: "some net cycle elasticity plus much residual variation due to other factors."

Because other factors, mainly World War II, demobilization, and the Korean War, dominated labor-market conditions since labor-force surveys were initiated, it is not surprising that labor-force responsiveness to the mild peace-time cycle could not be well discerned in the mid-fifties. The evolving record, as the history of our topic illustrates, does reduce the standard errors somewhat, but this record leads to a hypothesis that the labor force exhibits a *trend toward growing responsiveness,* which is another reason why it is easier to observe it now than in the past.

The result is produced by a combination of long standing trends, the most important of which are the growth of the female labor force and the decreasing degree of labor-force attachment of the young and of older males.

These basic trends are intimately connected with the processes of economic growth. For the present discussion we can take these for granted and look at the consequences. The results can be summarized as: (1) growth of discretionary labor-force participation and (2) weakening of the income effect, that is, of incentives for added-worker behavior.

1. The growing female labor-force participation, the increasing rate and length of schooling among the young, and the growing tendency to combine early retirement with reduced labor-force participation, create a growing class of intermittent or "multiple" job holders.

The manifestations of these developments are observed as increasing proportions of part-time and part-period workers, increased degree of labor-force turnover, and increased proportions of inexperienced workers among the employed and the unemployed—all these phenomena being almost equivalent by definition.[54]

2. The growing level of income, assets, and credit availability diminish the need for emergency help by other family members when main earners become unemployed.[55] Unemployment compensation probably weakens, or rather, creates a lag in both the discouragement and added-worker effects. However, the availability of unemployment compensation and of social security payments may be contributing to the growth of the intermittent labor force.

Unemployment

Labor-force flexibility carries several implications for the study of reported unemployment.

1. The greater the labor-force responsiveness of a group, the lower is the cyclical amplitude and conformity of its unemployment rate to the business cycle. This is be-

---

[54] In nonfarm jobs, the number of voluntary part-time workers more than doubled between 1950 and 1964, while the number of full-time workers increased only 20 per cent. Special Labor Force Report, in *Monthly Labor Review,* LXXXVII (September 1964), p. 1009.

[55] The growing number of women with marketable skills may be producing some added workers on a non-cyclical basis, namely, working wives in depressed areas and wives supporting schooling of their husbands.

cause labor-force withdrawals (largely from unemployment) increase and labor-force entries decrease during the downswing, while labor-force entries increase during the upswing. The conformity is weaker because the flexible labor force is also responsive to factors other than business conditions. A comparison of Columns 3, 4, and 9 in Table 7.1 illustrates these facts.

2. Because labor-force entrants and re-entrants must spend some time in job search, unemployment rates are likely to be higher in groups with higher labor-force turnover. Higher labor-force turnover is, of course, characteristic of secondary labor-force groups. A comparison of turnover rates, participation rates, and sensitivity coefficients (Table 7.2) with unemployment rates (Table 7.3) illustrates this.

3. In view of (1), the unemployment rate of the primary labor force is a better cyclical index than the rates of other sex-age components. It is therefore also likely to be superior, in this respect, to the aggregate unemployment rate.

4. If labor-force responsiveness is growing, we should observe over time an increasing size and inertness in the aggregate unemployment rate. This would be consistent with observed unemployment patterns during the last decade. And if this were the whole story, we could look at the unemployment rate of the primary labor force and, finding that it (mid-1965) is as low as it was before the 1957 recession, conclude that all is well and clear.

However, the growing importance of secondary labor-force groups in the total labor force does not, by itself, imply an increase in the unemployment rates of secondary workers, such as is recently observed among teenagers and, to a much lesser extent, among women. The analysis presented in this paper suggests that, in some proportion, these increases in unemployment rates within the particular groups may be due to growing flexibility within the groups as well as to increases in labor supplies superimposed on downward inflexible wages. If so, the unemployment rate of the primary groups may not be a good index of current conditions. If, as a result of minimum wages, employers tend to substitute experienced for inexperienced workers, the unemployment rate in the primary group may have decreased, in part, *at the expense* of higher rates in other groups.

References

1. Clarence D. Long, *The Labor Force Under Changing Income and Employment* (Princeton: Princeton University Press for the National Bureau of Economic Research, 1958).
2. W. L. Hansen, "Cyclical Sensitivity of the Labor Force," *American Economic Review,* LI (June 1961), 299–309.
3. Stuart Altman, *Unemployment of Married Women,* unpublished Ph.D. Dissertation, University of California at Los Angeles, 1963.
4. Glen G. Cain, *Labor Force Participation of Married Women,* unpublished Ph.D. Dissertation, University of Chicago, 1963.
5. Glen G. Cain, "The Net Effect of Unemployment on Labor Force Participation of Secondary Workers," *Social Systems Research Institute Paper 6408,* University of Wisconsin, October 1964.
6. W. G. Bowen and T. A. Finegan, "Labor Force Participation and Unemployment," in A. M. Ross, ed., *Employment Policy and the Labor Market* (Berkeley: University of California Press, 1965), pp. 115–161.
7. K. Strand and T. Dernburg, "Cyclical Variation in Labor Force Participation," *Review of Economics and Statistics,* XLVI (November 1964), 378–391.
8. T. Dernburg and K. Strand, "Hidden Unemployment," unpublished manuscript, 1965.
9. A. Tella, "The Relations of Labor Force to Employment," *Industrial and Labor Relations Review,* XVII (April 1964), 454–469.

10. A. Tella, "Labor Force Sensitivity to Employment by Age, Sex," *Industrial Relations,* IV (February 1965), 69–83.
11. S. Cooper and D. F. Johnston, "Labor Force Projections 1970–1980," *Monthly Labor Review,* LXXXVIII (February 1965), 129–140.
12. J. Mincer, "Labor Force Participation of Married Women," in Universities-National Bureau Committee for Economic Research, *Aspects of Labor Economics* (Princeton: Princeton University Press for the National Bureau of Economic Research, 1962), pp. 63–97.

8
A Theory of the Allocation of Time

Gary S. Becker

I. Introduction

Throughout history the amount of time spent at work has never consistently been much greater than that spent at other activities. Even a work week of fourteen hours a day for six days still leaves half the total time for sleeping, eating and other activities. Economic development has led to a large secular decline in the work week, so that whatever may have been true of the past, to-day it is below fifty hours in most countries, less than a third of the total time available. Consequently the allocation and efficiency of non-working time may now be more important to economic welfare than that of working time; yet the attention paid by economists to the latter dwarfs any paid to the former.

Fortunately, there is a movement under way to redress the balance. The time spent at work declined secularly, partly because young persons increasingly delayed entering the labour market by lengthening their period of schooling. In recent years many economists have stressed that the time of students is one of the inputs into the educational process, that this time could be used to participate more fully in the labour market and therefore that one of the costs of education is the forgone earnings of students. Indeed, various estimates clearly indicate that forgone earnings is the dominant private and an important social cost of both high-school and college education in the United States.[1] The increased awareness

Reprinted from *The Economic Journal* (Royal Economic Society, September 1965), pp. 493–517, by permission of the publisher and author.

[1] See T. W. Schultz, "The Formation of Human Capital by Education," *Journal of Political Economy* (December 1960), and my *Human Capital* (Columbia University Press for the N.B.E.R., 1964), Chapter IV. I argue there that the importance of forgone earnings can be directly seen, *e.g.,* from the failure of free tuition to eliminate impediments to college attendance or the increased enrolments that sometimes occur in depressed areas or time periods.

of the importance of forgone earnings has resulted in several attempts to economise on students' time, as manifested, say, by the spread of the quarterly and tri-mester systems.²

Most economists have now fully grasped the importance of forgone earnings in the educational process and, more generally, in all investments in human capital, and criticise educationalists and others for neglecting them. In the light of this it is perhaps surprising that economists have not been equally sophisticated about other non-working uses of time. For example, the cost of a service like the theatre or a good like meat is generally simply said to equal their market prices, yet everyone would agree that the theatre and even dining take time, just as schooling does, time that often could have been used productively. If so, the full costs of these activities would equal the sum of market prices and the forgone value of the time used up. In other words, indirect costs should be treated on the same footing when discussing all non-work uses of time, as they are now in discussions of schooling.

In the last few years a group of us at Columbia University have been occupied, perhaps initially independently but then increasingly less so, with introducing the cost of time systematically into decisions about non-work activities. J. Mincer has shown with several empirical examples how estimates of the income elasticity of demand for different commodities are biased when the cost of time is ignored;³ J. Owen has analysed how the demand for leisure can be affected;⁴ E. Dean has considered the allocation of time between subsistence work and market participation in some African economies;⁵ while, as already mentioned, I have been concerned with the use of time in education, training and other kinds of human capital. Here I attempt to develop a general treatment of the allocation of time in all other non-work activities. Although under my name alone, much of any credit it merits belongs to the stimulus received from Mincer, Owen, Dean and other past and present participants in the Labor Workshop at Columbia.⁶

The plan of the discussion is as follows. The first section sets out a basic theoretical analysis of choice that includes the cost of time on the same footing as the cost of market goods, while the remaining sections treat various empirical implications of the theory. These include a new approach to changes in hours of work and "leisure," the full integration of so-called "productive" consumption into economic analysis, a new analysis of the effect of income on the quantity and "quality" of commodities consumed, some suggestions on the measurement of productivity, an economic analysis of queues and a few others as well. Although I refer

---

² On the cause of the secular trend towards an increased school year see my comments, *ibid.*, p. 103.

³ See his "Market Prices, Opportunity Costs, and Income Effects," in *Measurement in Economics: Studies in Mathematical Economics and Econometrics in Memory of Yehuda Grunfeld* (Stanford University Press, 1963). In his well-known earlier study Mincer considered the allocation of married women between "housework" and labour force participation. (See his "Labor Force Participation of Married Women," in *Aspects of Labor Economics* (Princeton University Press, 1962).)

⁴ See his *The Supply of Labor and the Demand for Recreation* (unpublished Ph.D. dissertation, Columbia University, 1964).

⁵ See his *Economic Analysis and African Response to Price* (unpublished Ph.D. dissertation, Columbia University, 1963).

⁶ Let me emphasise, however, that I alone am responsible for any errors.

I would also like to express my appreciation for the comments received when presenting these ideas to seminars at the Universities of California (Los Angeles), Chicago, Pittsburgh, Rochester and Yale, and to a session at the 1963 Meetings of the Econometric Society. Extremely helpful comments on an earlier draft were provided by Milton Friedman and by Gregory C. Chow; the latter also assisted in the mathematical formulation. Linda Kee provided useful research assistance. My research was partially supported by the IBM Corporation.

to relevant empirical work that has come to my attention, little systematic testing of the theory has been attempted.

II. A Revised Theory of Choice

According to traditional theory, households maximise utility functions of the form

$$U = U(y_1, y_2, \cdots, y_n) \quad (1)$$

subject to the resource constraint

$$\Sigma p'_i y_i = I = W + V \quad (2)$$

where y_i are goods purchased on the market, p'_i are their prices, I is money income, W is earnings and V is other income. As the introduction suggests, the point of departure here is the systematic incorporation of non-working time. Households will be assumed to combine time and market goods to produce more basic commodities that directly enter their utility functions. One such commodity is the seeing of a play, which depends on the input of actors, script, theatre and the playgoer's time; another is sleeping, which depends on the input of a bed, house (pills?) and time. These commodities will be called Z_i and written as

$$Z_i = f_i(x_i, T_i) \quad (3)$$

where x_i is a vector of market goods and T_i a vector of time inputs used in producing the ith commodity.[7] Note that, when capital goods such as refrigerators or automobiles are used, x refers to the services yielded by the goods. Also note that T_i is a vector because, e.g., the hours used during the day or on weekdays may be distinguished from those used at night or on week-ends. Each dimension of T_i refers to a different aspect of time. Generally, the partial derivatives of Z_i with respect to both x_i and T_i are non-negative.[8]

In this formulation households are both producing units and utility maximisers. They combine time and market goods via the "production functions" f_i to produce the basic commodities Z_i, and they choose the best combination of these commodities in the conventional way of maximising a utility function

$$\begin{aligned} U &= U(Z_i, \cdots Z_m) \\ &\equiv U(f_1, \cdots f_m) \\ &\equiv U(x_1, \cdots x_m; T_1, \cdots T_m) \end{aligned} \quad (4)$$

subject to a budget constraint

$$g(Z_i \cdots Z_m) = Z \quad (5)$$

where g is an expenditure function of Z_i and Z is the bound on resources. The integration of production and consumption is at odds with the tendency for economists to separate them sharply, production occurring in firms and consumption in households. It should be pointed out, however, that in recent years economists increasingly recognise that a household is truly a "small factory":[9] it combines capital goods, raw materials and labour to clean, feed, procreate and otherwise produce useful commodities. Undoubtedly the fundamental reason for the traditional separation is that firms are usually given control over working time in exchange for market goods, while "discretionary" control over market goods and consumption time is retained by households as they create their own utility. If (presumably different) firms were also given control over market goods and consumption time in exchange for providing utility the separation would quickly fade away in analysis as well as in fact.

The basic goal of the analysis is to find

---

[7] There are several empirical as well as conceptual advantages in assuming that households combine goods and time to produce commodities instead of simply assuming that the amount of time used at an activity is a direct function of the amount of goods consumed. For example, a change in the cost of goods relative to time could cause a significant substitution away from the one rising in relative cost. This, as well as other applications, are treated in the following sections.

[8] If a good or time period was used in producing several commodities I assume that these "joint costs" could be fully and uniquely allocated among the commodities. The problems here are no different from those usually arising in the analysis of multi-product firms.

[9] See, e.g., A. K. Cairncross, "Economic Schizophrenia," *Scottish Journal of Political Economy* (February 1958).

measures of g and Z which facilitate the development of empirical implications. The most direct approach is to assume that the utility function in equation (4) is maximised subject to separate constraints on the expenditure of market goods and time, and to the production functions in equation (3). The goods constraint can be written as

$$\sum_{1}^{m} p_i x_i = I = V + T_w \overline{w} \qquad (6)$$

where p_i is a vector giving the unit prices of x_i, T_w is a vector giving the hours spent at work and $\overline{w}$ is a vector giving the earnings per unit of T_w. The time constraints can be written as

$$\sum_{1}^{m} T_i = T_c = T - T_w \qquad (7)$$

where T_c is a vector giving the total time spent at consumption and T is a vector giving the total time available. The production functions (3) can be written in the equivalent form

$$\left. \begin{array}{l} T_i \equiv t_i Z_i \\ x_i \equiv b_i Z_i \end{array} \right\} \qquad (8)$$

where t_i is a vector giving the input of time per unit of Z_i and b_i is a similar vector for market goods.

The problem would appear to be to maximise the utility function (4) subject to the multiple constraints (6) and (7) and to the production relations (8). There is, however, really only one basic constraint: (6) is not independent of (7) because time can be converted into goods by using less time at consumption and more at work. Thus, substituting for T_w in (6) its equivalent in (7) gives the single constraint[10]

$$\Sigma p_i x_i + \Sigma T_i \overline{w} = V + T \overline{w} \qquad (9)$$

[10] The dependency among constraints distinguishes this problem from many other multiple-constraint situations in economic analysis, such as those arising in the usual theory of rationing (see J. Tobin, "A Survey of the Theory of Rationing," *Econometrica* (October, 1952)). Rationing would reduce to a formally identical single-constraint situation if rations were saleable and fully convertible into money income.

By using (8), (9) can be written as

$$\Sigma (p_i b_i + t_i \overline{w}) Z_i = V + T\overline{w} \qquad (10)$$

with

$$\left. \begin{array}{l} \pi_i \equiv p_i b_i + t_i \overline{w} \\ S' \equiv V + T\overline{w} \end{array} \right\} \qquad (11)$$

The full price of a unit of Z_i (π_i) is the sum of the prices of the goods and of the time used per unit of Z_i. That is, the full price of consumption is the sum of direct and indirect prices in the same way that the full cost of investing in human capital is the sum of direct and indirect costs.[11] These direct and indirect prices are symmetrical determinants of total price, and there is no analytical reason to stress one rather than the other.

The resource constraint on the right side of equation (10), S', is easy to interpret if $\overline{w}$ were a constant, independent of the Z_i. For then S' gives the money income achieved if all the time available were devoted to work. This achievable income is "spent" on the commodities Z_i either directly through expenditures on goods, $\Sigma p_i b_i Z_i$, or indirectly through the forgoing of income, $\Sigma t_i \overline{w} Z_i$, i.e., by using time at consumption rather than at work. As long as $\overline{w}$ were constant, and if there were constant returns in producing Z_i so that b_i and t_i were fixed for given p_i and $\overline{w}$ the equilibrium condition resulting from maximising (4) subject to (10) takes a very simple form:

$$U_i = \frac{\partial U}{\partial Z_i} = \lambda \pi_i \quad i = 1, \cdots m \qquad (12)$$

where λ is the marginal utility of money income. If $\overline{w}$ were not constant the resource constraint in equation (10) would not have any particularly useful interpretation: $S' = V + T\overline{w}$ would overstate the money income achievable as long as marginal wage-rates were below average ones. Moreover, the equilibrium conditions would become more complicated than (12) because marginal would have to replace average prices.

The total resource constraint could be given the sensible interpretation of the maxi-

[11] See my *Human Capital, op. cit.*

mum money income achievable only in the special and unlikely case when average earnings were constant. This suggests dropping the approach based on explicitly considering separate goods and time constraints and substituting one in which the total resource constraint necessarily equalled the maximum money income achievable, which will be simply called "full income."[12] This income could in general be obtained by devoting all the time and other resources of a household to earning income, with no regard for consumption. Of course, all the time would not usually be spent "at" a job: sleep, food, even leisure are required for efficiency, and some time (and other resources) would have to be spent on these activities in order to maximise money income. The amount spent would, however, be determined solely by the effect on income and not by any effect on utility. Slaves, for example, might be permitted time "off" from work only in so far as that maximised their output, or free persons in poor environments might have to maximise money income simply to survive.[13]

Households in richer countries do, however, forfeit money income in order to obtain additional utility, *i.e.*, they exchange money income for a greater amount of psychic income. For example, they might increase their leisure time, take a pleasant job in preference to a better-paying unpleasant one, employ unproductive nephews or eat more than is warranted by considerations of productivity. In these and other situations the amount of money income forfeited measures the cost of obtaining additional utility.

Thus the full income approach provides a meaningful resource constraint and one firmly based on the fact that goods and time can be combined into a single overall constraint because time can be converted into goods through money income. It also incorporates a unified treatment of all substitutions of non-pecuniary for pecuniary income, regardless of their nature or whether they occur on the job or in the household. The advantages of this will become clear as the analysis proceeds.

If full income is denoted by S, and if the total earnings forgone or "lost" by the interest in utility is denoted by L, the identity relating L to S and I is simply

$$L(Z_1, \cdots, Z_m) \equiv S - I(Z_1, \cdots, Z_m) \quad (13)$$

I and L are functions of the Z_i because how much is earned or forgone depends on the consumption set chosen; for example, up to a point, the less leisure chosen the larger the money income and the smaller the amount forgone.[14] Using equations (6) and (8), equation (13) can be written as

$$\Sigma p_i b_i Z_i + L(Z_1, \cdots, Z_m) \equiv S \quad (14)$$

This basic resource constraint states that full income is spent either directly on market goods or indirectly through the forgoing of money income. Unfortunately, there is no simple expression for the average price of Z_i as there is in equation (10). However, marginal, not average, prices are relevant for behaviour, and these would be identical for

---

[12] This term emerged from a conversation with Milton Friedman.

[13] Any utility received would only be an incidental by-product of the pursuit of money income. Perhaps this explains why utility analysis was not clearly formulated and accepted until economic development had raised incomes well above the subsistence level.

[14] Full income is achieved by maximising the earnings function

$$W = W(Z_1, \ldots Z_m) \quad (1')$$

subject to the expenditure constraint in equation (6), to the inequality

$$\sum_{1}^{m} T_i \leq T \quad (2')$$

and to the restrictions in (8). I assume for simplicity that the amount of each dimension of time used in producing commodities is less than the total available, so that (2') can be ignored; it is not difficult to incorporate this constraint. Maximising (1') subject to (6) and (8) yields the following conditions

$$\frac{\partial W}{\partial Z_i} = \frac{p_i b_i \sigma}{1 + \sigma} \quad (3')$$

where σ is the marginal productivity of money income. Since the loss function $L = (S - V) - W$, the equilibrium conditions to minimise the loss is the same as (3') except for a change in sign.

the constraint in (10) only when average earnings, $\overline{w}$, was constant. But, if so, the expression for the loss function simplifies to

$$L = \overline{w}T_c = \overline{w}\Sigma t_i Z_i \quad (15)$$

and (14) reduces to (10). Moreover, even in the general case the total marginal prices resulting from (14) can always be divided into direct and indirect components: the equilibrium conditions resulting from maximising the utility function subject to (14)[15] are

$$U_i = T(p_i b_i + L_i), \quad i = 1, \cdots, m \quad (16)$$

where $p_i b_i$ is the direct and L_i the indirect component of the total marginal price $p_i b_i + L_i$.[16]

Behind the division into direct and indirect costs is the allocation of time and goods between work-orientated and consumption-orientated activities. This suggests an alternative division of costs; namely, into those resulting from the allocation of goods and those resulting from the allocation of time. Write $L_i = \partial L/\partial Z_i$ as

$$L_i = \frac{\partial L}{\partial T_i}\frac{\partial T_i}{\partial Z_i} + \frac{\partial L}{\partial x_i}\frac{\partial x_i}{\partial Z_i} \quad (17)$$

$$= l_i t_i + c_i b_i \quad (18)$$

where $l_i = \frac{\partial L}{\partial T_i}$ and $c_i = \frac{\partial L}{\partial x_i}$ are the marginal forgone earnings of using more time and goods respectively on Z_i. Equation (16) can then be written as

$$U_i = T[b_i(p_i + c_i) + t_i l_i] \quad (19)$$

The total marginal cost of Z_i is the sum of $b_i(p_i + c_i)$, the marginal cost of using goods

[15] Households maximise their utility subject only to the single total resource constraint given by (14), for once the full income constraint is satisfied, there is no other restriction on the set of Z_i that can be chosen. By introducing the concept of full income the problem of maximising utility subject to the time and goods constraints is solved in two stages: first, full income is determined from the goods and time constraints, and then utility is maximised subject only to the constraint imposed by full income.

[16] It can easily be shown that the equilibrium conditions of (16) are in fact precisely the same as those following in general from equation (10).

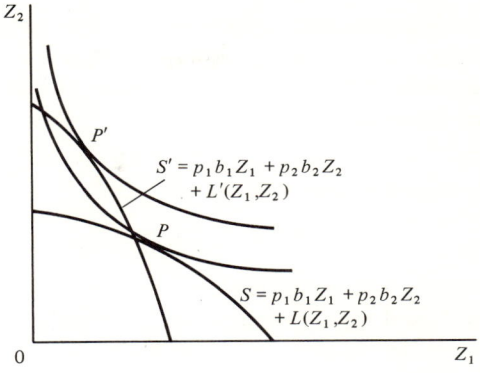

FIGURE 8.1

in producing Z_i, and $t_i l_i$, the marginal cost of using time. This division would be equivalent to that between direct and indirect costs only if $c_i = 0$ or if there were no indirect costs of using goods.

Figure 8.1 shows the equilibrium given by equation (16) for a two-commodity world. In equilibrium the slope of the full income opportunity curve, which equals the ratio of marginal prices, would equal the slope of an indifference curve, which equals the ratio of marginal utilities. Equilibrium occurs at p and p' for the opportunity curves S and S' respectively.

The rest of the paper is concerned with developing numerous empirical implications of this theory, starting with determinants of hours worked and concluding with an economic interpretation of various queueing systems. To simplify the presentation, it is assumed that the distinction between direct and indirect costs is equivalent to that between goods and time costs; in other words, the marginal forgone cost of the use of goods, c_i, is set equal to zero. The discussion would not be much changed, but would be more cumbersome were this not assumed.[17] Finally, until Section IV goods and

[17] Elsewhere I have discussed some effects of the allocation of goods on productivity (see my "Investment in Human Capital: A Theoretical Analysis," *Journal of Political Economy*, special supplement (October 1962), Section 2); essentially the same discussion can be found in *Human Capital*, *op. cit.*, Chapter II [Reading 12 in this text—Eds.].

time are assumed to be used in fixed proportions in producing commodities; that is, the coefficients b_i and t_i in equation (8) are treated as constants.

III. Applications

(a) Hours of Work

If the effects of various changes on the time used on consumption, T_c, could be determined their effects on hours worked, T_w, could be found residually from equation (7). This section considers, among other things, the effects of changes in income, earnings and market prices on T_c, and thus on T_w, using as the major tool of analysis differences among commodities in the importance of forgone earnings.

The relative marginal importance of forgone earnings is defined as

$$\alpha_i = \frac{l_i t_i}{p_i b_i + l_i t_i} \quad (20)$$

The importance of forgone earnings would be greater the larger l_i and t_i, the forgone earnings per hour of time and the number of hours used per unit of Z_i respectively, while it would be smaller the larger p_i and b_i, the market price of goods and the number of goods used per unit of Z_i respectively. Similarly, the relative marginal importance of time is defined as

$$\gamma_i = \frac{t_i}{p_i b_i + l_i t_i} \quad (21)$$

If full income increased solely because of an increase in V (other money income) there would simply be a parallel shift of the opportunity curve to the right with no change in relative commodity prices. The consumption of most commodities would have to increase; if all did, hours worked would decrease, for the total time spent on consumption must increase if the output of all commodities did, and by equation (7) the time spent at work is inversely related to that spent on consumption. Hours worked could increase only if relatively time intensive commodities, those with large γ, were sufficiently inferior.[18]

A uniform percentage increase in earnings for all allocations of time would increase the cost per hour used in consumption by the same percentage for all commodities.[19] The relative prices of different commodities would, however, change as long as forgone earnings were not equally important for all; in particular, the prices of commodities having relatively important forgone earnings would rise more. Now the fundamental theorem of demand theory states that a compensated change in relative prices would induce households to consume less of commodities rising in price. The figure shows the effect of a rise in earnings fully compensated by a decline in other income: the opportunity curve would be rotated clockwise through the initial position p if Z_1 were the more earnings-intensive commodity. In the figure the new equilibrium p' must be to the left and above p, or less Z_1 and more Z_2 would be consumed.

Therefore a compensated uniform rise in earnings would lead to a shift away from earnings-intensive commodities and towards goods-intensive ones. Since earnings and

---

[18] The problem is: under what conditions would

$$\frac{-\partial T_w}{\partial V} = \frac{\partial T_c}{\partial V} = \Sigma t_i \frac{\partial Z_i}{\partial V} < 0 \quad (1')$$

when $\quad \Sigma(p_i b_i + l_i t_i)\frac{\partial Z_i}{\partial V} = 1 \quad (2')$

If the analysis were limited to a two-commodity world where Z_1 was more time intensive, then it can easily be shown that (1') would hold it, and only if,

$$\frac{\partial Z_1}{\partial V} < \frac{-\gamma_2}{(\gamma_1 - \gamma_2)(p_1 b_1 + l_1 t_1)} < 0 \quad (3')$$

[19] By a uniform change of β is meant

$$W_1 = (1 + \beta) W_0(Z_1, \ldots Z_n)$$

where W_0 represents the earnings function before the change and W_1 represents it afterwards. Since the loss function is defined as

$$L = S - W - V$$
$$= W(\hat{Z}) - W(Z),$$

then $L_1 = W_1(\hat{Z}) - W_1(Z)$
$$= (1 + \beta)[W_0(\hat{Z}) - W_0(Z)] = (1 + \beta)L_0$$

Consequently, all opportunities costs also change by β.

time intensiveness tend to be positively correlated,[20] consumption would be shifted from time-intensive commodities. A shift away from such commodities would, however, result in a reduction in the total time spent in consumption, and thus an increase in the time spent at work.[21]

The effect of an uncompensated increase in earnings on hours worked would depend on the relative strength of the substitution and income effects. The former would increase hours, the latter reduce them; which dominates cannot be determined *a priori*.

The conclusion that a pure rise in earnings increases and a pure rise in income reduces hours of work must sound very familiar, for they are traditional results of the well-known labour–leisure analysis. What, then, is the relation between our analysis, which treats all commodities symmetrically and stresses only their differences in relative time and earning intensities, and the usual analysis, which distinguishes a commodity having special properties called "leisure" from other more commonplace commodities? It is easily shown that the usual labour–leisure analysis can be looked upon as a special case of ours in which the cost of the commodity called leisure consists entirely of forgone earnings and the cost of other commodities entirely of goods.[22]

As a description of reality such an approach, of course, is not tenable, since virtually all activities use both time and goods. Perhaps it would be defended either as an analytically necessary or extremely insightful approximation to reality. Yet the usual substitution and income effects of a change in resources on hours worked have easily been derived from a more general analysis which stresses only that the relative importance of time varies among commodities. The rest of the paper tries to go further and demonstrate that the traditional approach, with its stress on the demand for "leisure," apparently has seriously impeded the development of insights about the economy, since the more direct and general approach presented here naturally leads to a variety of implications never yet obtained.

The two determinants of the importance of forgone earnings are the amount of time used per dollar of goods and the cost per unit of time. Reading a book, taking a haircut or commuting use more time per dollar of goods than eating dinner, frequenting a night-club or sending children to private summer camps. Other things the same, forgone earnings would be more important for the former set of commodities than the latter.

The importance of forgone earnings would be determined solely by time intensity only if the cost of time was the same for all commodities. Presumably, however, it varies considerably among commodities and at different periods. For example, the cost of time

---

[20] According to the definitions of earning and time intensity in equations (20) and (21), they would be positively correlated unless l_i and t_i were sufficiently negatively correlated. See the further discussion later on.

[21] Let it be stressed that this conclusion usually holds, even when households are irrational; sophisticated calculations about the value of time at work or in consumption, or substantial knowledge about the amount of time used by different commodities is not required. Changes in the hours of work, even of non-maximising, impulsive, habitual, etc., households would tend to be positively related to compensated changes in earnings because demand curves tend to be negatively inclined even for such households (see G. S. Becker, "Irrational Behavior and Economic Theory," *Journal of Political Economy* (February 1962)).

[22] Suppose there were two commodities Z_1 and Z_2, where the cost of Z_1 depended only on the cost of market goods, while the cost of Z_2 depended only on the cost of time. The goods-budget constraint would then simply be

$$p_1 b_1 Z_1 = I = V + T_w \overline{w}$$

and the constraint on time would be

$$t_2 Z_2 = T - T_w$$

This is essentially the algebra of the analysis presented by Henderson and Quandt, and their treatment is representative. They call Z_2 "leisure," and Z_1 an average of different commodities. Their equilibrium condition that the rate of substitution between goods and leisure equals the real wage-rate is just a special case of our equation (19) (see *Microeconomic Theory* (McGraw-Hill, 1958), p. 23).

is often less on week-ends and in the evenings because many firms are closed then,[23] which explains why a famous liner intentionally includes a week-end in each voyage between the United States and Europe.[24] The cost of time would also tend to be less for commodities that contribute to productive effort, traditionally called "productive consumption." A considerable amount of sleep, food and even "play" fall under this heading. The opportunity cost of the time is less because these commodities indirectly contribute to earnings. Productive consumption has had a long but bandit-like existence in economic thought; our analysis does systematically incorporate it into household decision-making.

Although the formal specification of leisure in economic models has ignored expenditures on goods, cannot one argue that a more correct specification would simply associate leisure with relatively important forgone earnings? Most conceptions of leisure do imply that it is time intensive and does not indirectly contribute to earnings,[25] two of the important characteristics of earnings-intensive commodities. On the other hand, not all of what are usually considered leisure activities do have relatively important forgone earnings: night-clubbing is generally considered leisure, and yet, at least in its more expensive forms, has a large expenditure component. Conversely, some activities have relatively large forgone earnings and are not considered leisure: haircuts or child care are examples. Consequently, the distinction between earnings-intensive and other commodities corresponds only partly to the usual distinction between leisure and other commodities. Since it has been shown that the relative importance of forgone earnings rather than any concept of leisure is more relevant for economic analysis, less attention should be paid to the latter. Indeed, although the social philosopher might have to define precisely the concept of leisure,[26] the economist can reach all his traditional results as well as many more without introducing it at all!

Not only is it difficult to distinguish leisure from other non-work[27] but also even work from non-work. Is commuting work, non-work or both? How about a business lunch, a good diet or relaxation? Indeed, the notion of productive consumption was introduced precisely to cover those commodities that contribute to work as well as to consumption. Cannot pure work then be considered simply as a limiting commodity of such joint commodities in which the contribution to consumption was nil? Similarly,

---

[23] For workers receiving premium pay on the week-ends and in the evenings, however, the cost of time may be considerably greater then.

[24] See the advertisement by United States Lines in various issues of the *New Yorker* magazine: "The S.S. *United States* regularly includes a week-end in its 5 days to Europe, saving [economic] time for businessmen" (my insertion).

[25] For example, *Webster's Collegiate Dictionary* defines leisurely as "characterized by leisure, taking *abundant time*" (my italics); or S. de Grazia, in his recent *Of Time, Work and Leisure*, says, "Leisure is a state of being in which activity is performed for its town sake or as its own end" (New York: The Twentieth Century Fund, 1962, p. 15).

[26] S. de Grazia has recently entertainingly shown the many difficulties in even reaching a reliable definition, and *a fortiori,* in quantitatively estimating the amount of leisure. See *ibid.,* Chapters III and IV; also see W. Moore, *Man, Time and Society* (New York: Wiley, 1963), Chapter II; J. N. Morgan, M. H. David, W. J. Cohen and H. E. Brazer, *Income and Welfare in the United States* (New York: McGraw-Hill, 1962), p. 322, and Owen, *op. cit.,* Chapter II.

[27] Sometimes true leisure is defined as the amount of discretionary time available (see Moore, *op. cit.,* p. 18). It is always difficult to attach a rigorous meaning to the word "discretionary" when referring to economic resources. One might say that in the short run consumption time is and working time is not discretionary, because the latter is partially subject to the authoritarian control of employers. (Even this distinction would vanish if households gave certain firms authoritarian control over their consumption time; see the discussion in Section II.) In the long run this definition of discretionary time is suspect too because the availability of alternative sources of employment would make working time also discretionary.

pure consumption would be a limiting commodity in the opposite direction in which the contribution to work was nil, and intermediate commodities would contribute to both consumption and work. The more important the contribution to work relative to consumption, the smaller would tend to be the relative importance of forgone earnings. Consequently, the effects of changes in earnings, other income, etc., on hours worked then become assimilated to and essentially a special case of their effects on the consumption of less earnings-intensive commodities. For example, a pure rise in earnings would reduce the relative price, and thus increase the time spent on these commodities, *including the time spent at work*; similarly, for changes in income and other variables. The generalisation wrought by our approach is even greater than may have appeared at first.

Before concluding this section a few other relevant implications of our theory might be briefly mentioned. Just as a (compensated) rise in earnings would increase the prices of commodities with relatively large forgone earnings, induce a substitution away from them and increase the hours worked, so a (compensated) fall in market prices would also induce a substitution away from them and increase the hours worked: the effects of changes in direct and indirect costs are symmetrical. Indeed, Owen presents some evidence indicating that hours of work in the United States fell somewhat more in the first thirty years of this century than in the second thirty years, not because wages rose more during the first period, but because the market prices of recreation commodities fell more then.[28]

A well-known result of the traditional labour–leisure approach is that a rise in the income tax induces at least a substitution effect away from work and towards "leisure." Our approach reaches the same result only via a substitution towards time-intensive consumption rather than leisure. A simple additional implication of our approach, however, is that if a rise in the income tax were combined with an appropriate excise on the goods used in time-intensive commodities or subsidy to the goods used in other commodities there need be no change in full relative prices, and thus no substitution away from work. The traditional approach has recently reached the same conclusion, although in a much more involved way.[29]

There is no exception in the traditional approach to the rule that a pure rise in earnings would not induce a decrease in hours worked. An exception does occur in ours, for if the time and earnings intensities (*i.e.*, $l_i t_i$ and t_i) were negatively correlated a pure rise in earnings would induce a substitution towards time-intensive commodities, and thus away from work.[30] Although this exception does illustrate the greater power of our approach, there is no reason to believe that it is any more important empirically than the exception to the rule on income effects.

(b) The Productivity of Time

Most of the large secular increase in earnings, which stimulated the development of the labour–leisure analysis, resulted from an increase in the productivity of working time due to the growth in human and physical capital, technological progress and other

---

[28] See *op. cit.*, Chapter VIII. Recreation commodities presumably have relatively large forgone earnings.

[29] See W. J. Corbett and D. C. Hague, "Complementarity and the Excess Burden of Taxation," *Review of Economic Studies,* Vol. XXI (1953–54); also A. C. Harberger, "Taxation, Resource Allocation and Welfare," in the *Role of Direct and Indirect Taxes in the Federal Revenue System* (Princeton University Press, 1964).

[30] The effect on earnings is more difficult to determine because, by assumption, time intensive commodities have smaller costs per unit time than other commodities. A shift towards the former would, therefore, raise hourly earnings, which would partially and perhaps more than entirely offset the reduction in hours worked. Incidentally, this illustrates how the productivity of hours worked is influenced by the consumption set chosen.

factors. Since a rise in earnings resulting from an increase in productivity has both income and substitution effects, the secular decline in hours worked appeared to be evidence that the income effect was sufficiently strong to swamp the substitution effect.

The secular growth in capital and technology also improved the productivity of consumption time: supermarkets, automobiles, sleeping pills, safety and electric razors, and telephones are a few familiar and important examples of such developments. An improvement in the productivity of consumption time would change relative commodity prices and increase full income, which in turn would produce substitution and income effects. The interesting point is that a very different interpretation of the observed decline in hours of work is suggested because these effects are precisely the opposite of those produced by improvements in the productivity of working time.

Assume a uniform increase only in the productivity of consumption time, which is taken to mean a decline in all t_i, time required to produce a unit of Z_i, by a common percentage. The relative prices of commodities with large forgone earnings would fall, and substitution would be induced towards these and away from other commodities, causing hours of work also to fall. Since the increase in productivity would also produce an income effect,[31] the demand for commodities would increase, which, in turn, would induce an increased demand for goods. But since the productivity of working time is assumed not to change, more goods could be obtained only by an increase in work. That is, the higher real income resulting from an advance in the productivity of consumption time would cause hours of work to *increase*.

Consequently, an emphasis on the secular increase in the productivity of consumption time would lead to a very different interpretation of the secular decline in hours worked. Instead of claiming that a powerful income effect swamped a weaker substitution effect, the claim would have to be that a powerful substitution effect swamped a weaker income effect.

Of course, the productivity of both working and consumption time increased secularly, and the true interpretation is somewhere between these extremes. If both increased at the same rate there would be no change in relative prices, and thus no substitution effect, because the rise in l_i induced by one would exactly offset the decline in t_i induced by the other, marginal forgone earnings ($i_i t_i$) remaining unchanged. Although the income effects would tend to offset each other too, they would do so completely only if the income elasticity of demand for time-intensive commodities was equal to unity. Hours worked would decline if it was above and increase if it was below unity.[32] Since these commodities have probably on the whole been luxuries, such an increase in income would tend to reduce hours worked.

The productivity of working time has probably advanced more than that of consumption time, if only because of familiar reasons associated with the division of labour and economies of scale.[33] Consequently, there probably has been the traditional substitution effect towards and income effect away from work, as well as an income effect away from work because time-intensive commodities were luxuries. The secu-

---

[31] Full money income would be unaffected if it were achieved by using all time at pure work activities. If other uses of time were also required it would tend to increase. Even if full money income were unaffected, however, full real income would increase because prices of the Z_i would fall.

[32] So the "Knight" view that an increase in income would increase "leisure" is not necessarily true, even if leisure were a superior good and even aside from Robbins' emphasis on the substitution effect (see L. Robbins, "On the Elasticity of Demand for Income in Terms of Effort," *Economica* (June 1930)).

[33] Wesley Mitchell's justly famous essay "The Backward Art of Spending Money" spells out some of these reasons (see the first essay in the collection, *The Backward Art of Spending Money and Other Essays* (New York: McGraw-Hill, 1932)).

lar decline in hours worked would only imply therefore that the combined income effects swamped the substitution effect, not that the income effect of an advance in the productivity of working time alone swamped its substitution effect.

Cross-sectionally, the hours worked of males have generally declined less as incomes increased than they have over time. Some of the difference between these relations is explained by the distinction between relevant and reported incomes, or by interdependencies among the hours worked by different employees;[34] some is probably also explained by the distinction between working and consumption productivity. There is a presumption that persons distinguished cross-sectionally by money incomes or earnings differ more in working than consumption productivity because they are essentially distinguished by the former. This argument does not apply to time series because persons are distinguished there by calendar time, which in principle is neutral between these productivities. Consequently, the traditional substitution effect towards work is apt to be greater cross-sectionally, which would help to explain why the relation between the income and hours worked of men is less negatively sloped there, and be additional evidence that the substitution effect for men is not weak.[35]

Productivity in the service sector in the United States appears to have advanced more slowly, at least since 1929, than productivity in the goods sector.[36] Service industries like retailing, transportation, education and health, use a good deal of the time of households that never enter into input, output and price series, or therefore into measures of productivity. Incorporation of such time into the series and consideration of changes in its productivity would contribute, I believe, to an understanding of the apparent differences in productivity advance between these sectors.

An excellent example can be found in a recent study of productivity trends in the barbering industry in the United States.[37] Conventional productivity measures show relatively little advance in barbers' shops since 1929, yet a revolution has occurred in the activities performed by these shops. In the 1920s shaves still accounted for an important part of their sales, but declined to a negligible part by the 1950s because of the spread of home safety and electric razors. Instead of travelling to a shop, waiting in line, receiving a shave and continuing to another destination, men now shave themselves at home, saving travelling, waiting and even some shaving time. This considerable advance in the productivity of shaving nowhere enters measures for barbers' shops. If, however, a productivity measure for general barbering activities, including shaving, was constructed, I suspect that it would show an advance since 1929 comparable to most goods.[38]

(c) Income Elasticities

Income elasticities of demand are often estimated cross-sectionally from the behaviour of families or other units with different incomes. When these units buy in the same market-place it is natural to assume that they face the same prices of goods. If, how-

---

[34] A. Finnegan does find steeper cross-sectional relations when the average incomes and hours of different occupations are used (*see* his "A Cross-Sectional Analysis of Hours of Work," *Journal of Political Economy* (October, 1962)).

[35] Note that Mincer has found a very strong substitution effect for women (see his "Labor Force Participation of Married Women," *op. cit.*).

[36] See the essay by Victor Fuchs, "Productivity Trends in the Goods and Service Sectors, 1929–61: A Preliminary Survey," N.B.E.R. Occasional Paper, October 1964.

[37] See J. Wilburn, "Productivity Trends in Barber and Beauty Shops," mimeographed report, N.B.E.R., September 1964.

[38] The movement of shaving from barbers' shops to households illustrates how and why even in urban areas households have become "small factories." Under the impetus of a general growth in the value of time they have been encouraged to find ways of saving on travelling and waiting time by performing more activities themselves.

ever, incomes differ because earnings do, and cross-sectional income differences are usually dominated by earnings differences, commodities prices would differ systematically. All commodities prices would be higher to higher-income units because their forgone earnings would be higher (which means, incidentally, that differences in real income would be less than those in money income), and the prices of earnings-intensive commodities would be unusually so.

Cross-sectional relations between consumption and income would not therefore measure the effect of income alone, because they would be affected by differences in relative prices as well as in incomes.[39] The effect of income would be underestimated for earnings-intensive and overestimated for other commodities, because the higher relative prices of the former would cause a substitution away from them and towards the latter. Accordingly, the income elasticities of demand for "leisure," unproductive and time-intensive commodities would be understated, and for "work," productive and other goods-intensive commodities over-stated by cross-sectional estimates. Low apparent income elasticities of earnings-intensive commodities and high apparent elasticities of other commodities may simply be illusions resulting from substitution effects.[40]

Moreover, according to our theory demand depends also on the importance of earnings as a source of income. For if total income were held constant an increase in earnings would create only substitution effects: away from earnings-intensive and towards goods-intensive commodities. So one unusual implication of the analysis that can and should be tested with available budget data is that the source of income may have a significant effect on consumption patterns. An important special case is found in comparisons of the consumption of employed and unemployed workers. Unemployed workers not only have lower incomes but also lower forgone costs, and thus lower relative prices of time and other earnings-intensive commodities. The propensity of unemployed workers to go fishing, watch television, attend school and so on are simply vivid illustrations of the incentives they have to substitute such commodities for others.

One interesting application of the analysis is to the relation between family size and income.[41] The traditional view, based usually on simple correlations, has been that an increase in income leads to a reduction in the number of children per family. If, however, birth-control knowledge and other variables were held constant economic theory suggests a positive relation between family size and income, and therefore that the traditional negative correlation resulted from positive correlations between income, knowledge and some other variables. The data I put together supported this interpretation, as did those found in several subsequent studies.[42]

---

[39] More appropriate income elasticities for several commodities are estimated in Mincer, "Market Prices . . .," *op cit.*

[40] In this connection note that cross-sectional data are often preferred to time-series data in estimating income elasticities precisely because they are supposed to be largely free of co-linearity between prices and incomes (see, *e.g.,* J. Tobin, "A Statistical Demand Function for Food in the U.S.A.," *Journal of the Royal Statistical Society,* Series A (1950)).

[41] Biases in cross-sectional estimates of the demand for work and leisure were considered in the last section.

[42] See G. S. Becker, "An Economic Analysis of Fertility," *Demographic and Economic Change in Developed Countries* (N.B.E.R. Conference Volume, 1960); R. A. Easterlin, "The American Baby Boom in Historical Perspective," *American Economic Review* (December 1961); I. Adelman, "An Econometric Analysis of Population Growth," *American Economic Review* (June 1963); R. Weintraub, "The Birth Rate and Economic Development: An Empirical Study," *Econometrica* (October 1962); Morris Silver, *Birth Rates, Marriages, and Business Cycles* (unpublished Ph.D. dissertation, Columbia University, 1964); and several other studies; for an apparent exception, see the note by D. Freedman, "The Relation of Economic Status to Fertility," *American Economic Review* (June 1963).

Although positive, the elasticity of family size with respect to income is apparently quite low, even when birth-control knowledge is held constant. Some persons have interpreted this (and other evidence) to indicate that family-size formation cannot usefully be fitted into traditional economic analysis.[43] It was pointed out, however, that the small elasticity found for children is not so inconsistent with what is found for goods as soon as quantity and quality income elasticities are distinguished.[44] Increased expenditures on many goods largely take the form of increased quality—expenditure per pound, per car, etc.—and the increase in quantity is modest. Similarly, increased expenditures on children largely take the form of increased expenditures per child, while the increase in number of children is very modest.

Nevertheless, the elasticity of demand for number of children does seem somewhat smaller than the quantity elasticities found for many goods. Perhaps the explanation is simply the shape of indifference curves; one other factor that may be more important, however, is the increase in forgone costs with income.[45] Child care would seem to be a time-intensive activity that is not "productive" (in terms of earnings) and uses many hours that could be used at work. Consequently, it would be an earnings-intensive activity, and our analysis predicts that its relative price would be higher to higher-income families.[46] There is already some evidence suggesting that the positive relation between forgone costs and income explains why the apparent quantity income elasticity of demand for children is relatively small. Mincer found that cross-sectional differences in the forgone price of children have an important effect on the number of children.[47]

(d) Transportation

Transportation is one of the few activities where the cost of time has been explicitly incorporated into economic discussions. In most benefit-cost evaluations of new transportation networks the value of the savings in transportation time has tended to overshadow other benefits.[48] The importance of the value placed on time has encouraged experiment with different methods of determination: from the simple view that the value of an hour equals average hourly earnings to sophisticated considerations of the distinction between standard and overtime hours, the internal and external margins, etc.

The transport field offers considerable opportunity to estimate the marginal productivity or value of time from actual behaviour. One could, for example, relate the ratio of the number of persons travelling by aeroplane to those travelling by slower mediums to the distance travelled (and, of course, also to market prices and incomes). Since relatively more people use faster mediums for longer distances, presumably largely because of the greater importance of the saving in time, one should be able to estimate a marginal value of time from the relation between medium and distance travelled.[49]

---

[43] See, for example, Duesenberry's comment on Becker, *op. cit.*

[44] See Becker, *op. cit.*

[45] In *Ibid.*, p. 214 fn. 8, the relation between forgone costs and income was mentioned but not elaborated.

[46] Other arguments suggesting that higher-income families face a higher price of children have generally confused price with quality (see *ibid.*, pp. 214–15).

[47] See Mincer, "Market Prices . . .," *op. cit*. He measures the price of children by the wife's potential wage-rate, and fits regressions to various cross-sectional data, where number of children is the dependent variable, and family income and the wife's potential wage-rate are among the independent variables.

[48] See, for example, H. Mohring, "Land Values and the Measurement of Highway Benefits," *Journal of Political Economy* (June 1961).

[49] The only quantitative estimate of the marginal value of time that I am familiar with uses the relation between the value of land and its commuting distance from employment (see *ibid.*). With many assumptions I have estimated the marginal value of time of those commuting at about 40% of their average hourly earnings. It is not clear whether this value is so low because of errors in these assumptions or because of severe kinks in the supply and demand functions for hours of work.

Another transportation problem extensively studied is the length and mode of commuting to work.[50] It is usually assumed that direct commuting costs, such as train fare, vary positively and that living costs, such as space, vary negatively with the distance commuted. These assumptions alone would imply that a rise in incomes would result in longer commutes as long as space ("housing") were a superior good.[51]

A rise in income resulting at least in part from a rise in earnings would, however, increase the cost of commuting a given distance because the forgone value of the time involved would increase. This increase in commuting costs would discourage commuting in the same way that the increased demand for space would encourage it. The outcome depends on the relative strengths of these conflicting forces: one can show with a few assumptions that the distance commuted would increase as income increased if, and only if, space had an income elasticity greater than unity.

For let Z_1 refer to the commuting commodity, Z_2 to other commodities, and let

$$Z_1 = f_1(x, t) \qquad (22)$$

where t is the time spent commuting and x is the quantity of space used. Commuting costs are assumed to have the simple form $a + l_1 t$, where a is a constant and l_1 is the marginal forgone cost per hour spent commuting. In other words, the cost of time is the only variable commuting cost. The cost per unit of space is $p(t)$, where by assumption $p' < 0$. The problem is to maximise the utility function

$$U = U(x, t, Z_2) \qquad (23)$$

subject to the resource constraint

$$a + l_1 t + px + h(Z_2) = S \qquad (24)$$

If it were assumed that $U_t = 0$—commuting was neither enjoyable nor irksome—the main equilibrium condition would reduce to[52]

$$l_1 + p'x = 0 \qquad (25)$$

which would be the equilibrium condition if households simply attempt to minimise the sum of transportation and space costs.[53] If $l_1 = kS$, where k is a constant, the effect of a change in full income on the time spent commuting can be found by differentiating equation (25) to be

$$\frac{\partial t}{\partial S} = \frac{k(\epsilon_x - 1)}{p''x} \qquad (26)$$

where ϵ_x is the income elasticity of demand for space. Since stability requires that $p'' > 0$, an increase in income increases the time spent commuting if, and only if, $\epsilon_x > 1$.

In metropolitan areas of the United States higher-income families tend to live further from the central city,[54] which contradicts our analysis if one accepts the traditional view that the income elasticity of demand for housing is less than unity. In a definitive study of the demand for housing in the United States, however, Margaret Reid found income elasticities greater than unity.[55] Moreover, the analysis of distance commuted incorporates only a few dimensions of the demand for housing; prin-

---

[50] See L. N. Moses and H. F. Williamson, "Value of Time, Choice of Mode, and the Subsidy Issue in Urban Transportation," *Journal of Political Economy* (June 1963), R. Muth, "Economic Change and Rural–Urban Conversion," *Econometrica* (January 1961), and J. F. Kain, *Commuting and the Residential Decisions of Chicago and Detroit Central Business District Workers* (April 1963).

[51] See Muth, *op. cit.*

[52] If $U_t \neq 0$, the main equilibrium condition would be

$$\frac{U_t}{U_z} = \frac{l_1 + p'x}{p}$$

Probably the most plausible assumption is that $U_t < 0$, which would imply that $l_1 + p'x < 0$.

[53] See Kain, *op. cit.*, pp. 6–12.

[54] For a discussion, including many qualifications, of this proposition see L. F. Schnore, "The Socio-Economic Status of Cities and Suburbs," *American Sociological Review* (February 1963).

[55] See her *Housing and Income* (University of Chicago Press, 1962), p. 6 and *passim*.

cipally the demand for outdoor space. The evidence on distances commuted would then only imply that outdoor space is a "luxury," which is rather plausible[56] and not even inconsistent with the traditional view about the total elasticity of demand for housing.

(e) The Division of Labour Within Families

Space is too limited to do more than summarise the main implications of the theory concerning the division of labour among members of the same household. Instead of simply allocating time efficiently among commodities, multi-person households also allocate the time of different members. Members who are relatively more efficient at market activities would use less of their time at consumption activities than would other members. Moreover, an increase in the relative market efficiency of any member would effect a reallocation of the time of all other members towards consumption activities in order to permit the former to spend more time at market activities. In short, the allocation of the time of any member is greatly influenced by the opportunities open to other members.

IV. Substitution Between Time and Goods

Although time and goods have been assumed to be used in fixed proportions in producing commodities, substitution could take place because different commodities used them in different proportions. The assumption of fixed proportions is now dropped in order to include many additional implications of the theory.

It is well known from the theory of variable proportions that households would minimise costs by setting the ratio of the marginal product of goods to that of time equal to the ratio of their marginal costs.[57] A rise in the cost of time relative to goods would induce a reduction in the amount of time and an increase in the amount of goods used per unit of each commodity. Thus, not only would a rise in earnings induce a substitution away from earnings-intensive commodities but also a substitution away from time and towards goods in the production of each commodity. Only the first is (implicitly) recognised in the labour–leisure analysis, although the second may well be of considerable importance. It increases one's confidence that the substitution effect of a rise in earnings is more important that is commonly believed.

The change in the input coefficients of time and goods resulting from a change in their relative costs is defined by the elasticity of substitution between them, which presumably varies from commodity to commodity. The only empirical study of this elasticity assumes that recreation goods and "leisure" time are used to produce a recreation commodity.[58] Definite evidence of substitution is found, since the ratio of leisure time to recreation goods is negatively related to the ratio of their prices. The elasticity of substitution appears to be less than unity, however, since the share of leisure in total

---

[56] According to Reid, the elasticity of demand for indoor space is less than unity (*ibid.*, Chapter 12). If her total elasticity is accepted this suggests that outdoor space has an elasticity exceeding unity.

[57] The cost of producing a given amount of commodity Z_i would be minimised if

$$\frac{\partial f_i/\partial x_i}{\partial f_i/\partial T_i} = \frac{P_i}{\partial L/\partial T_i}$$

If utility were considered an indirect function of goods and time rather than simply a direct function of commodities the following conditions, among others, would be required to maximise utility:

$$\frac{\partial U/\partial x_i}{\partial U/\partial T_i} \equiv \frac{\partial Z_i/\partial x_i}{\partial Z_i/\partial T_i} = \frac{p_i}{\partial L/\partial T}$$

which are exactly the same conditions as above. The ratio of the marginal utility of x_i to that of T_i depends only on f_i, x_i and T_i, and is thus independent of other production functions, goods and time. In other words, the indirect utility function is what has been called "weakly separable" (see R. Muth, "Household Production and Consumer Demand Functions," unpublished manuscript).

[58] See Owen, *op. cit.*, Chapter X.

factor costs is apparently positively related to its relative price.

The incentive to economise on time as its relative cost increases goes a long way towards explaining certain broad aspects of behaviour that have puzzled and often disturbed observers of contemporary life. Since hours worked have declined secularly in most advanced countries, and so-called "leisure" has presumably increased, a natural expectation has been that "free" time would become more abundant, and be used more "leisurely" and "luxuriously." Yet, if anything, time is used more carefully to-day than a century ago.[59] If there was a secular increase in the productivity of working time relative to consumption time (see Section III(b)) there would be an increasing incentive to economise on the latter because of its greater expense (our theory emphatically cautions against calling such time "free"). Not surprisingly, therefore, it is now kept track of and used more carefully than in the past.

Americans are supposed to be more wasteful of food and other goods than persons in poorer countries, and much more conscious of time: they keep track of it continuously, make (and keep) appointments for specific minutes, rush about more, cook steaks and chops rather than time-consuming stews and so forth.[60] They are simultaneously supposed to be wasteful—of material goods—and overly economical—of immaterial time. Yet both allegations may be correct and not simply indicative of a strange American temperament because the market value of time is higher relative to the price of goods there than elsewhere. That is, the tendency to be economical about time and lavish about goods may be no paradox, but in part simply a reaction to a difference in relative costs.

The substitution towards goods induced by an increase in the relative cost of time would often include a substitution towards more expensive goods. For example, an increase in the value of a mother's time may induce her to enter the labour force and spend less time cooking by using pre-cooked foods and less time on child-care by using nurseries, camps or baby-sitters. Or barbers' shops in wealthier sections of town charge more and provide quicker service than those in poorer sections, because waiting by barbers is substituted for waiting by customers. These examples illustrate that a change in the quality of goods[61] resulting from a change in the relative cost of goods may simply reflect a change in the methods used to produce given commodities, and not any corresponding change in *their* quality.

Consequently, a rise in income due to a rise in earnings would increase the quality of goods purchased not only because of the effect of income on quality but also because of a substitution of goods for time; a rise in income due to a rise in property income would not cause any substitution, and should have less effect on the quality of goods. Put more dramatically, with total income held constant, a rise in earnings should increase while a rise in property income should decrease the quality chosen. Once again, the composition of income is important and provides testable implications of the theory.

One analytically interesting application of these conclusions is to the recent study by Margaret Reid of the substitution between store-bought and home-delivered milk.[62] According to our approach, the cost of inputs into the commodity "milk consumption at home" is either the sum of the price of milk in the store and the forgone

[59] See, for example, de Grazia, *op. cit.,* Chapter IV.
[60] For a comparison of the American concept of time with others see Edward T. Hall, *The Silent Language* (New York: Doubleday, 1959), Chapter 9.

[61] Quality is usually defined empirically by the amount spent per physical unit, such as pound of food, car or child. See especially S. J. Prais and H. Houthakker, *The Analysis of Family Budgets* (Cambridge, 1955); also my "An Economic Analysis of Fertility," *op. cit.*
[62] See her "Consumer Response to the Relative Price of Store versus Delivered Milk," *Journal of Political Economy* (April 1963).

value of the time used to carry it home or simply the price of delivered milk. A reduction in the price of store relative to delivered milk, the value of time remaining constant, would reduce the cost of the first method relatively to the second, and shift production towards the first. For the same reason a reduction in the value of time, market prices of milk remaining constant, would also shift production towards the first method.

Reid's finding of a very large negative relation between the ratio of store to delivered milk and the ratio of their prices, income and some other variables held constant, would be evidence both that milk costs are a large part of total production costs and that there is easy substitution between these alternative methods of production. The large, but not quite as large, negative relation with income simply confirms the easy substitution between methods, and indicates that the cost of time is less important than the cost of milk. In other words, instead of conveying separate information, her price and income elasticities both measure substitution between the two methods of producing the same commodity, and are consistent and plausible.

The importance of forgone earnings and the substitution between time and goods may be quite relevant in interpreting observed price elasticities. A given percentage increase in the price of goods would be less of an increase in commodity prices the more important forgone earnings are. Consequently, even if all commodities had the same true price elasticity, those having relatively important forgone earnings would show lower apparent elasticities in the typical analysis that relates quantities and prices of goods alone.

The importance of forgone earnings differs not only among commodities but also among households for a given commodity because of differences in income. Its importance would change in the same or opposite direction as income, depending on whether the elasticity of substitution between time and goods was less or greater than unity.

Thus, even when the true price elasticity of a commodity did not vary with income, the observed price elasticity of goods would be negatively or positively related to income as the elasticity of substitution was less or greater than unity.

The importance of substitution between time and goods can be illustrated in a still different way. Suppose, for simplicity, that only good x and no time was initially required to produce commodity Z. A price ceiling is placed on x, it nominally becomes a free good, and the production of x is subsidised sufficiently to maintain the same output. The increased quantity of x and Z demanded due to the decline in the price of x has to be rationed because the output of x has not increased. Suppose that the system of rationing made the quantity obtained a positive function of the time and effort expended. For example, the quantity of price-controlled bread or medical attention obtained might depend on the time spent in a queue outside a bakery or in a physician's office. Or if an appointment system were used a literal queue would be replaced by a figurative one, in which the waiting was done at "home," as in the Broadway theatre, admissions to hospitals or air travel during peak seasons. Again, even in depressed times the likelihood of obtaining a job is positively related to the time put into job hunting.

Although x became nominally a free good, Z would not be free, because the time now required as an input into Z is not free. The demand for Z would be greater than the supply (fixed by assumption) if the cost of this time was less than the equilibrium price of Z before the price control. The scrambling by households for the limited supply would increase the time required to get a unit of Z, and thus its cost. Both would continue to increase until the average cost of time tended to the equilibrium price before price control. At that point equilibrium would be achieved because the supply and demand for Z would be equal.

Equilibrium would take different forms depending on the method of rationing. With a literal "first come first served" system the size of the queue (say outside the bakery or in the doctor's office) would grow until the expected cost of standing in line discouraged any excess demand;[63] with the figurative queues of appointment systems, the "waiting" time (say to see a play) would grow until demand was sufficiently curtailed. If the system of rationing was less formal, as in the labour market during recessions, the expected time required to ferret out a scarce job would grow until the demand for jobs was curtailed to the limited supply.

Therefore, price control of x combined with a subsidy that kept its amount constant would not change the average private equilibrium price of Z,[64] but would substitute indirect time costs for direct goods costs.[65] Since, however, indirect costs are positively related to income, the price of Z would be raised to higher-income persons and reduced to lower-income ones, thereby redistributing consumption from the former to the latter. That is, women, the poor, children, the unemployed, etc., would be more willing to spend their time in a queue or otherwise ferreting out rationed goods than would high-earning males.

V. Summary and Conclusions

This paper has presented a theory of the allocation of time between different activities. At the heart of the theory is an assumption that households are producers as well as consumers; they produce commodities by combining inputs of goods and time according to the cost-minimisation rules of the traditional theory of the firm. Commodities are produced in quantities determined by maximising a utility function of the commodity set subject to prices and a constraint on resources. Resources are measured by what is called full income, which is the sum of money income and that forgone or "lost" by the use of time and goods to obtain utility, while commodity prices are measured by the sum of the costs of their goods and time inputs.

The effect of changes in earnings, other income, goods prices and the productivity of working and consumption time on the allocation of time and the commodity set produced has been analysed. For example, a rise in earnings, compensated by a decline in other income so that full income would be unchanged, would induce a decline in the amount of time used at consumption activities, because time would become more expensive. Partly goods would be substituted for the more expensive time in the production of each commodity, and partly goods-intensive commodities would be substituted for the more expensive time-intensive ones. Both substitutions require less time to be used at consumption, and permit more to be used at work. Since the reallocation of time involves simultaneously a reallocation of goods and commodities, all three decisions become intimately related.

The theory has many interesting and even novel interpretations of, and implications about, empirical phenomena. A few will be summarised here.

A traditional "economic" interpretation of the secular decline in hours worked has stressed the growth in productivity of working time and the resulting income and substitution effects, with the former supposedly dominating. Ours stresses that the substitution effects of the growth in productivity of working and consumption time tended to offset each other, and that hours worked

---

[63] In queueing language the cost of waiting in line is a "discouragement" factor that stabilises the queueing scheme (see, for example, D. R. Cox and W. L. Smith, *Queues* (New York: Wiley 1961)).

[64] The social price, on the other hand, would double, for it is the sum of private indirect costs and subsidised direct costs.

[65] Time costs can be criticised from a Pareto optimality point of view because they often result in external diseconomies: *e.g.*, a person joining a queue would impose costs on subsequent joiners. The diseconomies are real, not simply pecuniary, because time is a cost to demanders, but is not revenue to suppliers.

declined secularly primarily because time-intensive commodities have been luxuries. A contributing influence has been the secular decline in the relative prices of goods used in time-intensive commodities.

Since an increase in income partly due to an increase in earnings would raise the relative cost of time and of time-intensive commodities, traditional cross-sectional estimates of income elasticities do not hold either factor or commodity prices constant. Consequently, they would, among other things, be biased downward for time-intensive commodities, and give a misleading impression of the effect of income on the quality of commodities consumed. The composition of income also affects demand, for an increase in earnings, total income held constant, would shift demand away from time-intensive commodities and input combinations.

Rough estimates suggest that forgone earnings are quantitatively important and therefore that full income is substantially above money income. Since forgone earnings are primarily determined by the use of time, considerably more attention should be paid to its efficiency and allocation. In particular, agencies that collect information on the expenditure of money income might simultaneously collect information on the "expenditure" of time. The resulting time budgets, which have not been seriously investigated in most countries, including the United States and Great Britain, should be integrated with the money budgets in order to give a more accurate picture of the size and allocation of full income.

B. MONOPSONY

9
Monopsonistic Conditions

K. W. Rothschild

The Meaning of Monopsony

... we have introduced the fact that the firm very often has some control over the price of its output, because it is a 'single seller', a monopolist. Now we must turn to the analogous case in the labour market, where the firm is very often in the position of a 'single buyer' of labour, is a monopsonist. In other words, we must now do away with the assumption that a firm can obtain any number of workers at a wage-rate fixed by the market. This assumption of an infinite elasticity of supply of labour is at least as unrealistic as that of perfect competition in the sale of commodities.

The fact will be that in the absence of regulated wage-rates a firm's demand for labour will have an effect on its price. This will be true not only in the case of a big monopoly which is the sole purchaser of a certain type of labour. It will be equally true where a large number of small firms, all demanding the same type of labour, are distributed over a wide area. In this case each firm will be able to draw without difficulty on a limited amount of local labour which has been traditionally attached to it. But if employment is to be expected it will not be sufficient to raise wages by a tiny fraction in order to attract workers from competing firms: labour costs may have to go up quite markedly. This may take several forms.

First of all, even where workers in competing firms are ready to move, their lack of knowledge regarding alternative opportunities will often mean that a small increase in wages in one firm will not attract their attention. It may need some expenditure on informative advertising to bring the change to the knowledge of a wider circle or else it may be necessary to raise wages by a noticeable margin. For such good news has a habit of spreading quickly. In both cases the additional labour can be obtained only

---

Reprinted from K. W. Rothschild, *The Theory of Wages*. 2nd ed. (London: Routledge & Kegan Paul, Ltd., 1954; reprinted by Augustus M. Kelley, Publishers, New York, 1967), pp. 94–102.

at a higher cost than was the case before, which means that the supply of labour is not perfectly elastic.

Then, if we assume that the competing firms are in more distant places, even perfect knowledge of all existing opportunities will not suffice to make a fractional increase in wage-rates an effective force. For now workers moving to the expanding firm will have to cover the costs of movement. Thus the wider the area over which the employer has to cast his net in order to obtain additional labour the higher the wages he has to offer in order to cover the costs of movement of the (spatially) marginal worker.

From these examples it will be clear that monopsonistic elements in the labour market, far from being the exception, are very widespread. In fact, what we said about the supply of labour to an *industry* will be largely true for the supply of labour to a firm, once the conditions of perfect competition are absent.

The Effects of Monopsony

In order to be able to appreciate the new element introduced by monopsony let us take two numerical examples illustrating perfect competition and monopsony respectively.

TABLE 9.1

	Perfect Competition				*Monopsony*		
Number of men	Efficiency wage per man s.	Total wage bill s.	Marginal cost of labour s.	Number of men	Efficiency wage per man s.	Total wage bill s.	Marginal cost of labour s.
10	2	20	—	6	1/6	9/–	—
11	2	22	2	7	1/7	11/1	2/1
12	2	24	2	8	1/8	13/4	2/3
13	2	26	2	9	1/9	15/9	2/5
				10	1/10	18/4	2/7
				11	1/11	21/1	2/9
				12	2/–	24/–	2/11
				13	2/1	27/1	3/1

Alternatively, the employer can try to obtain more local labour *of a different kind* at the current wage-rate. Workers, who in other industries earn a lower wage, will generally be prepared to move to the expanding industry if they can obtain a higher wage there. But though in this case the nominal wage-rate does not change, the efficiency wages of the new workers will be higher because they will obtain the same money wage for a lower output.[1]

[1] Their output will be lower because they have been trained in a different industry. If their efficiency were the same as that of the old employees they would not have stayed—in the absence of unemployment, which we still assume—at a lower wage in a different industry.

Under monopsony, as we see, additional men can only be obtained by raising the wage-rate. This, however, means that the marginal cost of labour increases by more than the wage of the marginal worker. For not only has he to be paid a higher wage, but normally the wages of all other workers will have to be raised to the same level, since commonly one rate only is paid for the job. Thus if, in our example, an eleventh worker is employed, labour costs increase by the 1s. 11d. paid to that worker *plus* 10d. consisting of the ten additional pennies which have now to be paid to the original employees. Thus the marginal cost of the eleventh worker is 2s. 9d., a figure which we can obtain directly by comparing the total wage-bill for eleven workers with that for ten workers.

In Chapter II [Reading 2 in this text—Eds.], we said that, on the profit-maximizing principle, an entrepreneur will engage an additional worker if his marginal productivity at least covers his wage. But we can see from [Table 9.1] that under monopsonistic conditions this rule will not yield maximum profits. For employing an extra man adds more to the firm's labour costs than just this man's wages. His employment will, therefore, only be profitable if his marginal productivity also covers these additional costs. Or, to put it more generally, a firm will employ an additional man if the marginal productivity of labour covers the marginal cost of labour. Under perfect competition the marginal cost of labour equals the wage-rate and the more restricted statement of [Reading 2] did therefore apply there. But under monopsonistic conditions the marginal cost of labour will lie above the wage-rate, and equilibrium will therefore be reached at a point where the marginal productivity of labour is greater than the wage-rate.

To see the effects of monopsony more clearly let us now add the marginal productivity schedule of the workers to our example. Let us assume this schedule runs as follows:

TABLE 9.2

Number of Workers	Marginal Productivity
6	2/6
7	2/5
8	2/4
9	2/3
10	2/2
11	2/1
12	2/–
13	1/11

Comparing this table with the perfect competition and monopsony tables it can be seen that in the former case twelve men will be employed at a wage-rate of 2s. each, while in the latter case only eight men will be employed receiving a wage of 1s. 8d. This follows directly from the equalization of marginal productivity and marginal cost of labour.[2]

[2] As in previous cases, a diagrammatic presentation will help to illustrate this example.

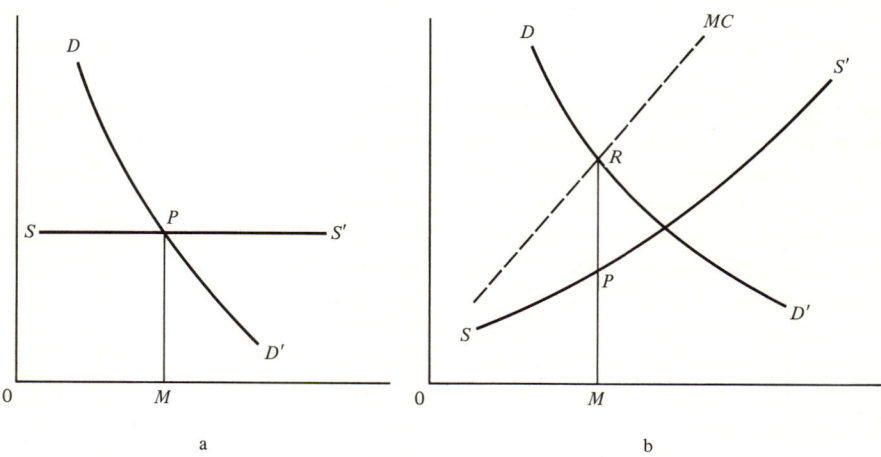

a

b

[In part a of the figure] we have the case of perfect competition, where the perfectly elastic supply curve SS' signifies that all the labour that could be needed by one firm can be obtained at the current wage-rate. Equilibrium will then be reached where the marginal productivity or labour demand schedule DD' cuts SS', and at this point the wage, MP, equals marginal productivity.

[In part b]—monopsony—the rising supply curve signifies that additional workers can only be obtained by raising the wage-rate. MC represents the marginal cost of labour which lies above SS' because

The monopsonist is thus in a position to increase his profits by keeping his labour costs down through a reduction in the number of men he employs. But just because these monopsony profits are made in the labour market, labour is in a stronger position to appropriate a share in them than in the case of monopoly profits. Since monopsony profits arise from the fact that some workers are prepared to offer their services at a lower wage than others, and the monopsonist then keeps the wage at a lower level by not extending employment to the higher wage-group, the position can be cured by making the wage-demands of all workers uniform—at a higher level. This is, indeed, to some extent the purpose of the trade unions' 'common rule' which fixes one wage offer for their entire membership. In this way they create a perfectly elastic supply of labour at the official rate, and it is no longer possible to reduce wages by reducing the number of workers.

In this way a trade union, by removing the monopsonistic framework, may be able to raise wages *and* employment, a rather exceptional case. In our example, if a trade union fixed the wage for all workers at 2*s.*, the marginal cost of labour to the firm would become 2*s.* throughout, and employment would be expanded from eight men to twelve men, while at the same time the wage had risen by 4*d.* from 1*s.* 8*d.* to 2*s.* In fact, in this case trade union action would just restore the conditions of a perfectly competitive market.

It may not always be so easy to get rid of monopsonistic conditions. If monopsony is widespread and has existed for some time, monopsony profits may have disappeared, because the lower wages may have attracted such a large number of firms into the industry that none of them makes any abnormal profits. A mere raising of wages coupled with the introduction of the 'common rule' would not provide a solution in these circumstances. Higher wages would just make the firms unprofitable and unemployment would ensue. In this case the monopsonistic position could only be overcome if these measures were accompanied by a concentration of production in a smaller number of firms which could then work up to full capacity.

Some Further Remarks on Monopsony and Related Topics

So far we have assumed that the employer must pay the higher wage, which has to be offered in order to attract additional workers, to *all* his employees. This may, however, not always be the case. It may be possible to pay the higher wage only to the newcomer, and to continue to pay to the others only that rate which is necessary to keep them in the firm. This case we call 'Discriminating monopsony'.

Under discriminating monopsony the marginal cost of labour will be—as under perfect competition—equal to the wage of the marginal worker. For even though a higher wage may have to be paid to him, this will not lead to an additional increase in costs through the raising of the wages of the original labour force. Going back once more to our numerical example, we can see that our monopsonist, if he can discriminate, i.e., if he can pay to each worker his supply price only, will expand employment to the same level as the competitive firm, viz., to twelve men, where marginal cost, 2*s.*, equals marginal productivity.[3] But though the level of employment in this case will equal that of the competitive firm, the discriminating

---

an additional worker adds to the cost of the original labour force. Profits will be maximized when additional revenue just equals additional cost, i.e., where *DD'* cuts *MC*. At this point *0M* workers, whose marginal productivity is *MR*, will be employed at the wage *MP*.

[3] [In part b of the figure in] footnote 2 the marginal cost of labour for the discriminating monopsonist coincides with the supply curve *SS'*, because employing an additional man just adds his wage to labour costs. Equilibrium will then be reached at the point where *DD'* cuts *SS'* which leads to a greater level of employment than prevails under non-discriminating monopsony.

monopsonist's profits will be considerably greater. For he pays to every worker only the minimum that is necessary to keep him in his job,[4] and this will considerably reduce his labour costs. If we assume in our example that the supply price of the first five workers (not shown in the table) is 1s. 6d., the total wage bill of the discriminating monopsonist will be 19s. 9d. (6 × 1s. 6d. + 1s. 7d. + 1s. 8d · · · + 2s.). But that of the perfect competitor will be 24s. (12 × 2s.).

Where an industry is well organized and where workers co-operate closely in large numbers, widespread knowledge of wage conditions and collective bargaining will make monopsonistic discrimination rather unlikely. But where such conditions are absent it can easily arise. An obvious case is that of home workers, with each of whom the employer strikes a separate bargain. But even with office and factory work it can develop where trade unions are weak and where fear of unemployment induces the workers to accept those conditions which they personally regard as the essential minimum.

While perfect monopsonistic discrimination, i.e., discrimination between individual and individual, is probably rare in the more developed countries and industries, the same cannot be said of group discrimination. For the same work, groups which can be clearly distinguished—men and women, men and boys, white and coloured population—may be paid different wages. If an expanding firm, which relied on female labour, has exhausted the local female labour supplies, it will have to raise wages either to attract women from farther afield or to get men, whose supply price will be higher. Even though the wage payable to the men may be higher than that for additional women, the firm might choose male labour, because their higher wages need not be extended to the women already employed. Thus the traditionally maintained monopsonistic discrimination against women will mean that the marginal cost of the extra men may be less than that of the lower-paid extra women.

The fact that the cost of labour is often not independent of the firm's demand for it—that the supply of labour is not infinitely elastic—will induce firms to apply measures which will reduce the necessary rise in wage-rates as far as possible. Just as the monopolistic firm, which has some influence over the price of its products, tries to raise these prices by advertising expenditure, so the monopsonist will try to reduce his labour costs by expenditure, which we may call 'buying costs' of the monopsonist. These buying costs will be directed towards raising the workers' preference for work in that particular firm and thus to reduce the additional amount necessary for attracting more men. Such expenditure will be incurred even where wages are fixed by collective agreement, in order to enable a firm to have the first choice of the available man-power, and thus to pay lower efficiency wages than other firms. Such buying expenditure will usually take the form of an expansion of welfare facilities, such as canteens, bathing facilities, sport and social activities, etc., which will make work more desirable than in factories, where such opportunities do not exist.[5]

A special case, which is closely connected with the idea of monopsony and which may prevent marginal productivity from being equated even with the marginal costs of labour, is that of 'collusion between employers'. So far we have assumed that a firm has either no influence on the wage-rate at all (perfect competition), or is aware that its own demand for labour will have an effect on the wages it has to pay (monopsony). But if there is a relatively small number of

---

[4] That is, he pays to each worker his transfer cost only, and appropriates all 'rent' that would normally go to labour.

[5] Such welfare expenditure may also be caused through other factors, such as legislation, trade union pressure, and the advertising effect which such conditions have on a socially-minded public opinion. . . .

firms all competing for the same type of labour, they may become aware that a rise in the demand of one firm will affect the wages which *all* the firms have to pay. If one firm offers higher wages in order to attract additional workers from neighbouring firms, then they, too, will have to raise wages simply to maintain their labour force.

Under such conditions a strong desire will arise among employers to prevent any competitive bidding for labour. This may lead to open agreement banning such action, but more frequently it will take the form of tacit agreements and of the creation of a business morale, which regards the raising of wages in order 'to snatch away' one's competitor's workers as 'bad form' and 'spoiling the labour market'. And even the firm that would be prepared to disregard this social pressure may hesitate to increase its immediate profits where marginal productivity lies above marginal costs, if it is afraid that its own improvement in wage-rates would be immediately followed by a defensive rise in the competing firms, so that in the end no additional workers would be forthcoming while higher wages would have to be paid all round.

But once this collusion among employers is present the mechanism which equates marginal productivity and marginal costs will no longer exist. The wage will be kept at the traditional or agreed level even though for each firm it would be profitable to expand employment by attracting labour from neighbouring firms. Wages will only be raised through trade union pressure, and such a rise may in a case like this leave employment unaffected, since it will only close the gap between marginal productivity and the marginal cost of labour, and not raise the latter above the former.[6]

[6] In diagrammatic language the position looks like this:

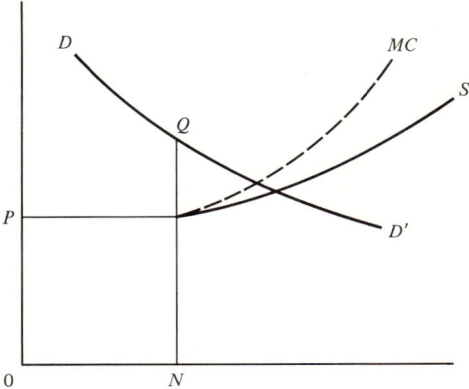

If OP is the 'accepted' wage the firm will employ ON men, because additional workers could only be obtained at higher wages, as indicated by the supply curve PS. But ON men is less than the monopsonistic equilibrium which is given by the intersection of the marginal productivity curve DD' with the marginal cost of labour MC. Since at the employment level ON, marginal productivity NQ is higher than the marginal cost OP, it is clear that wages could be raised to NQ without causing a decline in employment.

10
Concentration and Monopsony in Labor Markets

Robert L. Bunting

1. The Relevance of Concentration to Monopsony

One need not be very familiar with the writings of professional economists to be aware of great differences among them on matters of national labor policy. It is clear that some substantial part of these differences arises from different beliefs about the degree of competition among employers in labor markets. To the extent that this is so, the point at issue is subject to scientific analysis. And to the extent that empirical investigation can resolve the differences, greater consensus among economists can safely be predicted on a wide range of important policy problems: minimum wages, collective bargaining, fair labor standards, and the like.

The conflict in views held by economists with regard to the extent of labor monopsony[1] in the United States seems to be, primarily, a reflection of differences in belief about the structural characteristics of labor markets. On the one hand, there is the view that many markets in the United States are

Reprinted from Robert L. Bunting, *Employer Concentration in Local Labor Markets*, The University of North Carolina Press, 1962, pp. 3–14, by permission of the publisher.

[1] Monopsony is used in this paper as a generic term that covers not only simple monopsony theory as it is commonly given in the economics literature (see Shorey Peterson, *Economics* [1st ed. rev.; New York: Henry Holt and Company, 1954], pp. 641–44) but also the more complicated monopsony-like theories (employers' associations or cartels, wage domination or leadership, labor oligopsony, kinky labor supply curves, etc.) that "assume" that some "profit-maximizing" unit acts as though the supply of labor to itself were less than infinitely elastic. See as illustrations: Adam Smith, *The Wealth of Nations* ("Everyman's Library"; London: J. M. Dent and Sons, Ltd., 1937), I, 57–78; Paul H. Douglas, "Wage Theory and Wage Policy," *International Labour Review*, XXXIX, No. 3 (1939), 319–59; M. Bronfenbrenner, "Applications of the Discontinuous Oligopoly Demand Curve," *Journal of Political Economy*, XLIX (June, 1940), 420–27; K. W. Rothschild, *The Theory of Wages* (Oxford: Basil Blackwell, 1956), pp. 94–105.

"dominated" by one or a few relatively large firms; the expression "the company town" appears frequently in the writings of those who are sympathetic with this view. The contrary notion is that such labor market situations are not widespread, so that most workers in this country sell their services in markets characterized by competitive behavior among firms. The disagreement is obviously similar in many respects to that concerning the amount of product market monopoly in this country.

Until 1946 there were no readily available data which covered a large part of employment in the United States and which provided the distribution of firms by employment size in local labor markets. In that year, however, the Bureau of Old-Age and Survivors Insurance (BOASI) and the Office of Domestic Commerce jointly initiated a new series of bulletins; these bulletins contained county distributions of firms by employment-size categories, as well as industry and wage information. This publication program was continued unaltered through 1948 by which time the data had been improved and extended enough for them to serve as the basis for reasonably accurate estimates of labor market concentration. The purpose of this study is that of providing a set of such estimates for 1948; the hope is that they will contribute to the settlement of the disagreement among economists regarding labor market concentration, and hence labor monopsony, in the United States.

In the preceding paragraphs the words monopsony and concentration have been used rather loosely. It is important to see that they are not identical concepts—that they should not be used interchangeably. Concentration refers to a physical, observable, and describable characteristic of the market: high concentration exists when "a few" employers hire "a large percentage" of the workers in the market; low concentration exists when no single employer, or small group of employers together, hires a "significantly large" percentage of the labor force. The word "monopsony," on the other hand, refers to a condition that exists within the market; it describes the results of a type of market behavior among buyers leading to a wage complex the general level of which is below that which would have prevailed if those employers had been acting competitively. The hypothesis of central importance to this study relates market behavior to market structure: more precisely, it states that monopsony in labor markets is associated with high concentration of employees among employers.

It may be worth while to examine briefly the rationale underlying this hypothesis. Consider what shall be called a "local labor market" in which a certain group of employers are currently acting as buyers of a particular type of labor. The elasticity of supply of labor to this "local labor market" will be high if one condition is met: it is that there be an appreciable number of job opportunities offered by employers outside this "market" which are excellent substitutes in the eyes of the workers concerned. If this condition obtains there will be little incentive for the employers in the "local labor market" to engage in monopsonistic activity, for the high supply elasticity makes it certain that the monopsony gains will be small.

The validity of this analysis is quite independent of the extent to which most of the employment opportunities in this "market" are concentrated in one or a few employers. The point is that monopsonistic behavior can be successful only if what has been referred to as the "local labor market" is the *whole* market, in the sense that it includes all employment opportunities that the workers think of as good alternatives.

Suppose that this condition is satisfied; the local labor market has been defined in such a way that the elasticity of supply of labor to it is "low." The inelasticity of labor supply thus holds out the promise of monopsony gains to the employers. There will be an incentive to the employers to capture these gains, however, only if the costs of capturing them are not excessive. Capturing them necessarily means that the labor-purchasing firms exercise control over the market pressures urging them toward the competitive market position and move instead toward the pure monopsony market position; the more closely this latter position can be approximated, the greater the monopsony returns. Thus the pursuit of monopsony gain requires collective action—action involving tacit or explicit collusion—on the part of the employers. But such organizational activity is difficult—i.e., costly—and the difficulties increase the larger the number of employers concerned.[2] Thus concentration enters the theory as a determinant of the costs of collective action. And the concentration hypothesis—that, *ceteris paribus,* monopsonistic behavior is most likely to be observed where a few employers hire a large percentage of the relevant labor force—becomes the statement that monopsony is most likely to exist, given conditions of labor supply, where the potential net gains are greatest.

A comparative comment is again relevant; the above outline of the theoretical basis for this study closely parallels the theory of product market monopoly. The problems associated with defining the components of labor supply and the geographic extent of the labor market in the monopsony analysis have their counterparts in defining the product components of industry supply and the geographic extent of the product market. Concentration plays an identical role in the monopoly analysis; it is a major determinant of the cost of collective action on the part of sellers. This parallelism may helpfully be continued by pointing out that an important aim of the present study is that of beginning the process of building a body of concentration ratios for labor markets comparable with the established body of concentration data now available to students of product monopoly.[3]

It must immediately be recognized, however, that there is dissatisfaction with the concentration-monopoly hypothesis;[4] further-

---

[2] The labor market models, such as wage leadership, in which tacit collusion appears are almost universally discussed in terms that clearly indicate the assumed presence of concentration. Thus it might seem that the emphasis in the text upon the costliness of this type of behavior is unnecessary and, perhaps, misleading. I believe, however, that this is the correct analytical approach. In any given market situation holding out the possibility of monopsonistic gain, the efficient means of obtaining those gains is through joint action of a straightforward type; the interested employers gather around a table and hammer out a common course of action. This process must involve the achievement of agreement on technical matters—such as the appropriate wage scales for various levels of activity in possibly quite diverse employment situations—as well as perhaps more difficult policy problems having to do with the best means of maximizing monopsony gains. (Should the emphasis be upon short- or long-term gains? How far below the competitive level may wages be pressed before other firms will be enticed into the market?) The point is that effective collective action requires communication and consensus, both of which have real economic costs attached. Bringing tacit collusion into this framework is based on the assumption that these costs do not disappear when less obvious methods of striving for common policies are adopted. Rather, one would expect that they rise, that the costs of obtaining a particular level of monopsony returns in any given set of market circumstances would be greater for those who try to operate under the handicap of indirect means of communication.

[3] It is this aim which dictates the availability of an 84–page table containing much of the basic data analyzed in Chapter III. This table may be procured at no cost by writing to either the author, Robert L. Bunting, Department of Economics and Business Administration, Cornell College, Mount Vernon, Iowa, or to the publishers, The University of North Carolina Press, Chapel Hill, N.C.

[4] Miller has expressed one version of this dissatisfaction in the following fashion: "It is perhaps a sign of the immaturity of the science of economics that the notion should persist that the competitiveness of the economy or of a sector of the economy can ultimately be characterized by some single number or set of numbers." (John Perry Miller, "Measures of Monopoly Power and Concentration: Their Economic Significance" in National Bureau of Economic Research, *Business Concentration and Price Policy,* A Conference of the

more, the empirical efforts to test it have enjoyed neither a large nor unambiguous measure of success.[5] It may be that the theory is deficient—that, for example, other necessary conditions remain unidentified—or, it may be that the empirical tests have been too crude. Whatever the nature of the unsolved problems in the area of product market monopoly, the meaning of this state of affairs for the relatively unexplored empirical area of monopsony is clear: the significance of findings on labor market concentration for the extent to which less-than-competitive wages obtain in labor markets is not known. Labor market concentration measures such as those of this study *may* be excellent indicators of monopsonistic behavior. On the other hand, the measures may be seriously inadequate because they do not encompass some important aspect of structure or because they fail altogether to identify other relevant variables of a nonstructural character.

The point of the above discussion may be summarized briefly: this is a study of concentration in labor markets; the literature clearly indicates the belief of many economists that the degree of concentration is relevant to an analysis of monopsony and that measures such as those presented here point in the right direction; *but,* the relationship between these measures and the type of market behavior referred to as monopsony is imprecisely understood and awaits empirical clarification. Further words of caution concerning this aspect of the measures presented and analyzed in the following pages will not be considered necessary.

2. Concentration Curves, Concentration Ratios, and a Summary of Findings

In the preceding section market structure was related to monopsonistic behavior along these lines: monopsony is most likely to occur in those labor market situations in which a few firms hire a large proportion of the employed workers. The problem that is immediately encountered in the effort to make this statement operational is that of sharpening its imprecise language. How many employers are "a few"? What percentage of the employed force constitutes "a large proportion"?

The correct general answer to this sort of question is clear: "a few" and "a large proportion" are those numbers which lead to the best predictions of monopsonistic behavior. But little empirical work has been done by way of testing the labor market concentration hypothesis, so these numbers are not now known. The appropriate procedure, therefore, would seem to be to choose as many probably relevant measures as possible, compare them, and test them against each other. Thus the processes of testing the theory and refining the measures are interdependent. As pointed out earlier, however, testing the basic hypothesis is beyond the scope of this study; we are concerned here only with a preliminary investigation of the extent and characteristics of concentration.

Universities-National Bureau Committee for Economic Research [Princeton: Princeton University Press, 1955], p. 119.) In the same volume Kaysen takes a similar line of attack, pointing to factors other than concentration which must be taken into account in order to explain product market behavior. Other contributions (George J. Stigler, Tibor Scitovsky, and William Fellner), while generally unhappy with the performance of the concentration hypothesis, tend to view it as the most promising operational device available; they generally place major emphasis on the need for improved concentration measures and more comprehensive empirical tests of these measures.

[5] See, for example, the Richard Ruggles essay ("The Nature of Price Flexibility and the Determinants of Relative Price Changes in the Economy") in *Business Concentration and Price Policy,* pp. 441–95. See also Joe S. Bain, "Relation of Profit Rate to Industry Concentration: American Manufacturing, 1936–1940," *The Quarterly Journal of Economics,* LXV, No. 3 (August, 1951), pp. 293–324; and, for a more recent effort, Victor R. Fuchs, "Integration, Concentration, and Profits in Manufacturing Industries," *The Quarterly Journal of Economics,* LXXV (May, 1961), pp. 278–91.

Ideally, the accomplishment of this more limited aim would involve the presentation of a complete set of concentration measures for each market. This in turn would make it possible to construct a complete set of concentration curves, such as that shown in Figure 10.1—curves providing for each market the cumulative percentage of employment by number of employers, when all employers have been arrayed from largest to smallest.

Such a task would be a large one for most United States labor markets—and especially large for certain of those markets. For example, there were more than 100,000 firms in Cook County, Illinois, at the time of the study, and that county is only a part of the Chicago labor market area. Obtaining firm employment figures, ranking them, and computing employment percentages for all the firms in that metropolitan area would obviously be a sizable task. Thus a choice had to be made between intensive investigation of the concentration curves of a few labor markets and a less intensive examination of those of a larger number. The decision made in this connection tended in the direction of the second alternative; three points—those corresponding with the largest firm, the four largest firms, and the ten largest firms—on the concentration curves of 1774 labor market areas were estimated. It is these estimates that constitute the basic data of this study.[6]

The judgments underlying the decision to look less deeply but more broadly should be stated explicitly. First, there is the belief that ten is a fairly large number in the context of this study: that, in other words, monopsonistic behavior is unlikely to be observed unless something like ten or fewer employers hire the majority of the employees in the market. It is this belief that leads to the widespread use of the numbers three, four, and eight in product market studies. Second, there is the judgment that those markets which rank high in concentration by the three measures presented here would also rank high at points beyond these on the concentration curves. There turns out to be a good deal of support for this belief in the data presented in Chapter III;[7] the same tendency has been observed in product market data.[8] Third, it was felt that the identification and ranking by degree of concentration of a large number of labor market areas has more to offer, at this stage of our understanding of monopsonistic problems, than a more detailed examination of the concentration characteristics of a few areas.

[6] In addition to these, rough overestimates of a fourth point on the concentration curves—that for the thirty largest firms—were made by assuming that those firms which ranked eleven through thirty had the same number of employees as the tenth-ranking firm. These overestimates are used at several points in the study to provide a rough picture of the concentration curves beyond the point of the ten largest employers.

[7] See especially the data of Table 6, in which the rankings of the labor markets at the three measured points are shown to be highly correlated; these rank correlation coefficients indicate a strong tendency for those labor markets showing highest concentration ratios for the single largest employer to have the highest concentration ratios for the four and ten largest employers also. More direct evidence is contained in footnote "a" to that table: estimates of the thirty-largest-firm ratios were found to correlate highly with the ratios for the four largest firms.

[8] See Gideon Rosenbluth in *Business Concentration and Price Policy*, pp. 64–65.

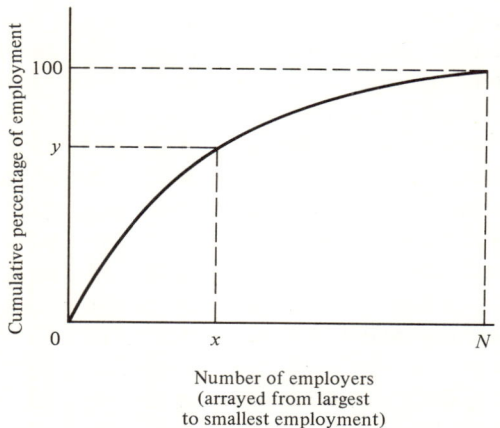

FIGURE 10.1 The Concentration Curve.

The three measures that represent the points on the concentration curves are called "concentration ratios"; for convenience they are expressed as percentages—percentages of the total employed labor force in local labor markets hired by the largest, the four largest, and the ten largest firms located in those markets. To illustrate, consider a labor market in which the largest firm has 100 employees, the three next-largest have a combined total of 150 employees, and the six next-largest firms have a combined total of 150 employees; if there are 1,000 employed workers in the labor market area altogether, the three "concentration ratios" are 10 per cent (for the single largest firm), 25 per cent (for the four largest firms), and 40 per cent (for the ten largest firms). Such percentages were computed for 1,774 local labor market areas, in which approximately 93 per cent of the total employed labor force was located.[9]

Brief reference was made in Section 1 to the fact that this project was made possible by the relatively recent availability of data on firm employment by geographic location. These data are a by-product of the Old-Age and Survivors Insurance Program. Under law, employers covered by this legislation must make quarterly reports to the Bureau of Old-Age and Survivors Insurance; these reports provide employment and wage information upon which workers' retirement and insurance benefits are based. Tabulations based on the first of these reports of 1948, providing covered employment during the pay period ending nearest March 15 of that year, were produced by the bureau for the purpose of publishing the *1948 County Business Patterns*.[10] It was from these tabulations that the numerators of the concentration ratios were obtained.

The denominators of the concentration ratios are estimates of the employed labor forces of the 1,774 labor markets. Geographically speaking, these markets were defined as single counties or small clusters of counties. The 1948 labor force estimates for these counties were made from 1940 and 1950 Census information. The estimating procedure involved the assumption that the changes in sizes of the county labor forces over the ten-year period—as shown by comparison of the two census figures—took place smoothly. That is, estimates of the 1948 labor forces for all markets were made by the "straight-line" method; for example, a county showing labor forces of 70,000 in 1940 and 80,000 in 1950 would be estimated at 78,000 for 1948. It was these estimates, adjusted for the prevailing level of unemployment, that were used as the denominators of the ratios.

These ratios—measures of the relative sizes of the few largest firms in local labor markets—were used to investigate absolute level of concentration prevailing in labor markets and the relationships between concentration and the following: firm size, the size of labor markets (as measured by the number of employed workers), industrial

[9] It should be noted that it is just as reasonable to measure concentration by an alternative method, specifying the least number of firms required to account for, say, 50 per cent of the employed workers in a market. Brief reference to Table 4 will make it clear that the use of such an indicator, even for very low concentration levels of 10 or 20 per cent, would have greatly increased the computational work involved in preparing the measures. Moreover, the evidence referred to in footnote 7 above indicates that such measures would rank labor markets by concentration in much the same way as the one-four-ten largest-firms technique. Rosenbluth's experiments with distributions of firms by industry are quite interesting in this connection also; he shows, for example, high rank correlations between certain industries as ranked by the percentage of employment accounted for by the three largest firms and as ranked by the number of firms required to account for 80 per cent of employment. See, Rosenbluth, *Business Concentration and Price Policy*, pp. 66–69.

[10] U.S. Department of Commerce, *County Business Patterns, First Quarter, 1948: Business Establishments, Employment, and Taxable Pay Rolls, By Industry Groups, Under Old-Age and Survivors Insurance Program* (Washington: U.S. Government Printing Office, 1949).

composition of the labor force, and geographic region. The major findings of the inquiry will be briefly summarized in this same order.

1. The level of employer concentration at the time of this study was not high. Thus, the data show that the four largest firms hired more than 50 per cent of the total employed local force in at least 1.1 per cent but not more than 8.7 per cent of the areas studied; at least 0.3 per cent and not more than 3.7 per cent of the total employed labor force was located in these areas. Comparable percentage limits for the single largest firms in labor markets were (for areas) 0.3–2.3 and (for labor force) 0.1–0.6; for the ten largest firms the percentage limits were (for areas) 2.2–18.7 and (for labor force) 0.9–9.6.

2. Increasing concentration in local labor markets tends to be associated with increasing dominance by the largest firm of the other large firms in the market areas. Thus the largest firm employed 18.8 per cent of the sum of the employment of the ten largest firms, among the bottom-ranking (by concentration) 10 per cent of the areas, and 48.2 per cent among the top-ranking 10 per cent of the areas.

3. There is a tendency for the size of labor markets (as measured by total employment) to decrease as concentration increases. Analysis of various size categories of the areas showed that this tendency derived primarily from a marked inverse relationship among the very large and very small areas; it seemed to be nonexistent among the numerous areas of intermediate labor force size. Both the level of concentration and the inverse size-concentration relationship are consistent with an hypothesis that stresses random factors as the basic explanation of concentration. The lapse in the inverse relationship between concentration and community size, however, is inconsistent with the acceptance of this hypothesis as a complete explanation—that is, the "lapse" indicates the presence of other systematic elements in the data.

4. The investigation of the industry aspects of concentration involved analysis of the industrial composition of the labor forces of both "all firms" and "large firms only" in concentrated areas. With respect to the analysis of the former, there was a clear tendency, among broad industry groups, for "mining" and "manufacturing" to be disproportionately represented; in concentrated areas the percentage of the labor force allocated to these two industry groups was approximately twice as great as in comparable nonconcentrated areas.

The labor force of the *largest firms* in high concentration areas was also disproportionately allocated among industries. Nine industries accounted for 88 per cent of the total employment of the 100 top-ranking firms in the 100 areas of highest concentration; these same nine industries accounted for only 25.8 per cent of the United States total covered (by OASI) employment in 1948. They are (using a finer industry classification system than in the paragraph above): "mining," "textile mill products," "lumber and wood products," "paper and allied products," "chemicals and allied products," "primary metal industries," "machinery, except electrical," "electrical machinery," and "transportation equipment."

These industries had at least this one characteristic in common: they contained disproportionate shares of large firms. They accounted for only 4.8 per cent of the *total* number of "covered" firms, whereas their percentage of "covered" *large* firms (500 employees and over) was 44. Thus it is not surprising that these same industries accounted for disproportionate percentages of the labor forces of the largest firms in non-concentrated areas as well as in concentrated areas—65 per cent, as opposed to 88 per cent (mentioned above) for the high concentration areas.

The importance of the nine industries varied with the size of labor markets. To illustrate: "mining" was relatively more important in small labor markets than in large, "transportation equipment" was more important among large markets than small, and "textiles" showed up as an important industry among labor market areas of all sizes.

5. The data showed concentration to have strong regional characteristics. For example, in a ranking of all labor market areas by concentration, 40 per cent of the labor force of the East South Central region, as compared with only 4 per cent of that of the Pacific region, was contained in areas ranking above the median. Regional variation in concentration seemed to be explainable in terms of industry and community size; that is, regions ranking high in concentration tended to be those containing the nine high concentration industries in effective combination with numerous relatively small labor market areas. There was no evidence of systematic variation that could be imputed to region alone—or to other factors.

The findings listed above have been stated without qualification, as if there were no question about the accuracy of the data from which the indexes of concentration were obtained or whether they measure what ought to be measured. In fact, there are serious problems at the conceptual and operational levels involving both the preparation and interpretation of the ratios. . . .

The "errors" involved in the concentration indexes generally appear to be such as to cancel themselves out—very roughly speaking—insofar as their aggregate effect on the absolute level of concentration is concerned. This statement, however, is based on the assumption that governments and non-profit firms should not be thought of in the same context with profit-oriented employers, who presumably are trying to extract monopsonistic gains from the labor market. If this assumption is dropped and if all units of government (except education) at all levels (federal, state, and local) are considered as a single "firm," concentration rises substantially. The aggregate increase from all sources of error may be as great as 72 per cent for certain of the concentration measures.

It is worth noting, however, that the acceptance of even this drastic estimate of the average error in the measures is consistent with an appraisal of the general level of concentration as being quite low. An increase in all ratios of 72 per cent would put less than 16 per cent (perhaps as little as 5 per cent) of the employed labor force in labor markets in which the four largest firms hire as much as 50 per cent of the labor force.

11
The Baseball Players' Labor Market[1]

Simon Rottenberg

Since its inception in the 1870's, organized baseball has developed a market for baseball players and their services in which there is less than perfect freedom to buy and sell. In this paper I shall discuss analytically a number of market problems which are interesting because of some unusual characteristics of the baseball labor market and the organization of the baseball industry.

In the labor market, monopsony is more frank and explicit and less imperfect than in the more common case, in other industries, of covert antipirating agreements. The nature of the industry is such that competitors must be of approximately equal "size" if any are to be successful; this seems to be a unique attribute of professional competitive sports.

Before passing to the analytical questions, however, I must describe the structure of the industry and the rules of the market. The structure and the rules of the market

---

Reprinted from the *Journal of Political Economy* (June 1956) by permission of The University of Chicago Press. Copyright, 1956, pp. 242–258.

[1] Am indebted to my colleagues and the students of the Department of Economics at the University of Chicago for challenging discussions of this topic which I have had with them. I must lay claim, however, to any errors the paper still contains.

Although I have referred to a large number of different sources in the considerable literature on baseball, I have found no document so valuable by far as the *Hearings before the Subcommittee on Study of Monopoly Power of the Committee on the Judiciary of the House of Representatives* (82d Cong., 1st sess.), Serial No. 1, Part 6: *Organized Baseball* (Washington, D.C.: Government Printing Office, 1952). The materials collected in this volume are massive and are indispensable for the understanding of the economics of this market. The volume will be cited henceforth, for brevity, as "*Celler Hearings,*" after Congressman Emanuel Celler, the committee chairman.

The companion piece to the hearings of the subcommittee is its report, *Organized Baseball: Report of the Subcommittee on Study of Monopoly Power of the Committee on the Judiciary, Pursuant to H. Res. 95, House of Representatives* (82d Cong., 2d sess. [Washington, D.C.: Government Printing Office, 1952]). This document will be referred to henceforth as "*Celler Report.*"

for baseball players and their services are defined in seven documents which constitute the constitutional papers of the baseball industry. These documents are the Constitution of the National League of Professional Baseball Clubs, the Constitution of the American League of Professional Baseball Clubs, the Major League Agreement, the Major League Rules, the Major-Minor League Agreement, the Major-Minor League Rules, and the Agreement of the National Association of Professional Baseball Leagues (the minor leagues).[2]

The documents specify the procedures for their own amendment, and they are amended from time to time. They are enormously complex. This complexity arises, in part, from the ingenuity of club owners and business managers in doing violence to the purposes of the rules while obeying their letter. Let a rule be established proscribing a practice and inhibiting gainful action, and teams find some substitute for it, and an amended rule emerges. Complexity also arises from the effort to compromise inconsistent interests within baseball.

Taken all together, the documents constitute baseball as a collusive combination. The parties to this combination have agreed to be bound by rules that inhibit competition and to enforce these rules by extra-legal sanctions.

The organized baseball industry[3] consists of two major leagues and a number of minor leagues. The number of minor leagues varies from time to time in response to changes in product-market conditions. In 1955 there were thirty-three minor leagues operating.[4]

Most leagues are composed of eight teams, but leagues of other sizes, for example, of six teams, are not uncommon. Sometimes a league begins a season with eight teams and will lose a team or two that do not prosper and are abandoned in midseason.

The major-league season provides for a schedule of 154 games played by each team; 77 games are played at its own home ball park and 77 in those of its opponents. Thus each team plays 22 games with each of the other seven teams in its league, 11 at home and 11 away.

The minor leagues are classified into categories defined by the sum of the populations of the cities of which each is composed. These categories are called Open Classification, AAA, AA, A1, A, B, C, D, and E.[5]

The minor leagues are made up of teams that are either "independent" or are "farm" teams of a major-league team. Farm teams are either owned outright by a major-league team or controlled by "working agreements" which give the major-league club, in return for financial or other assistance, the right to acquire the services of a specified number of players of the minor-league teams. A farm system makes it possible for a major-league team to accumulate a pool of players from which it can make replacements on its own team, and it provides a place where

---

[2] *The Baseball Blue Book, 1955* (Fort Wayne, Ind.: Bureau of the Blue Book, 1955).

[3] This paper is almost exclusively concerned with *organized* baseball. "Organized" baseball refers to the combination bound together by the constitutional documents I have enumerated. Baseball, outside of organized baseball, consists of amateur baseball, in which players receive no compensation for their play; semiprofessional baseball and the industrial leagues (composed of teams representing firms), in both of which a few players are paid for their playing services, but others are not; and a few fully professional leagues and clubs which are independent of organized baseball.

[4] For a record of the number of minor leagues from 1905 to 1951 see *Celler Hearings*, p. 992.

[5] The number of leagues in each category in 1955 was as follows:

Classification	Aggregate Population Requirement	No. of Leagues
Open Classification	10,000,000	1
AAA	3,000,000	2
AA	1,750,000	3
A1	1,450,000	0
A	1,000,000	3
B	250,000	7
C	150,000	8
D	Up to 150,000	9
E	Up to 150,000	0

promising players can be "seasoned" for major-league play.

Of approximately 260 minor-league teams operating in 1955, 155 were farms of the major-league teams, 40 owned outright and 115 controlled by working agreements. Farm teams are not equally distributed among the major-league teams. In 1955, for example, the St. Louis National League team controlled eighteen farm teams, while the Boston and the Chicago American League teams controlled only six farm teams each.[6]

Every team admitted to organized baseball has *"territorial rights"* in the city in which it is located. No team in organized baseball may play in the territory of any other team without the latter's consent.[7] Each team, therefore, monopolizes its own territory within organized baseball, and this monopoly right is a marketable commodity.

An elaborate system of rules has been devised to govern the contractual relationships between players and teams and among teams in the disposition of players' services. This system of rules structures the labor market and imposes restraints upon freedom in the market.

Until he signs his first contract with a team in organized baseball, a player is a *free agent* who may dispose of his services as he wishes, and teams may compete in bidding for him with relative freedom. In the market for free agents, competition is very intense. A star high-school player may have a large number of representatives of different teams prepared to negotiate with him the day after his graduation from school.[8]

When bidding is heavy for the services of a particular free agent, the player is paid a *bonus* for signing a contract with one team rather than another. Bonuses of $100,000 or more to secure a player's signature are not unknown, although they have usually been much smaller.[9] The bonus can be thought of as part of the player's first year's salary or as an income supplement which is distributed over the length of his playing life. The size of the bonus is not the only dimension of bidders' offers. A free agent will also choose among alternative bidders on the basis of his estimates of his lifetime baseball earnings with each bidder, and these estimates are compounded of his estimates of his length of playing life (which may be longer with one team than with another) and his estimates of his average annual earnings.[10]

When a player signs a contract, it must be a *uniform contract,* the terms of which are specified in detail by organized baseball. There is one uniform contract for the major

---

[6] *Baseball Official Guide, 1955* (St. Louis, Mo.: C. C. Spink & Sons, 1955), p. 162.

[7] *Baseball Blue Book, 1955*, p. 712.

[8] The rules do not permit negotiation with a high-school student until the day following his graduation.

[9] In an attempt to reduce the size of bonuses paid to free agents, baseball's rules have recently been changed to impose real costs upon teams contracting bonus players. A bonus player signed to a major-league team, for example, must be kept on the team roster for two years; normally a young player contracted by a major-league team would be sent to the minor leagues for several years of "seasoning." Bonus players, for this purpose, are defined as those who are paid in excess of a stipulated amount for their first year plus an extra sum in compensation for signing their first contracts. To skirt the rule, some teams are said to have paid the player less than this amount but to have employed his father in some nominal capacity at a high salary, although the rules include in their definition of a bonus player payments made to other persons "for the use or benefit" of the player (*Baseball Blue Book, 1955*, pp. 513–14, 613–14, 729).

[10] Players under contract to Team A or its farm system are a non-competing group vis-a-vis players under contract to Team B or its farm system, because of the operation of the "reserve rule" to be discussed below. Average salaries may therefore vary among teams. On July 1, 1950, the mean salaries of the major-league teams ranged from $18,788 for the New York Yankees to $8,031 for the St. Louis Browns (*Celler Hearings*, p. 965). The range of salaries paid by different teams is also different, and a free agent, in computing his prospective earnings with different clubs, can be expected to consider the salary range of each of the bidders for his services and to estimate where, in the whole course of his playing career, he is likely to fall within it.

leagues and another for the minors; the two are very similar. No deviation from the terms of the uniform contract is permitted without the approval of the appropriate executive officer of organized baseball, and deviation is rarely permitted.[11]

The uniform contract provides that, in consideration of the payment of the compensation provided for in the contract, the player "agrees to render skilled services as a baseball player." The team may terminate the player's contract if the player should "fail, in the opinion of the Club's management, to exhibit sufficient skill or competitive ability to . . . continue as a member of the Club's team."

Almost all contracts run for a one-year term. However, the uniform player contract contains a renewal clause, conventionally called the *reserve clause,* which permits the team to renew the contract for the following year at a price which the team may fix—subject, in the major leagues only, to the constraint that the salary in the following year shall not be less than 75 per cent of the salary in the current year. In the minor-league uniform contract there is no constraint at all on the price which the team may fix for the next season's services.

The team with which the player is contracted has exclusive right to the use of his playing services; he may not play baseball elsewhere without its consent. His contract may be assigned by this team to another team, and he is bound to report for play with the assignee team. No other team in organized baseball may employ him.

No team may negotiate with a player already under contract to another team. This is called *tampering* and is prohibited by the rules.[12] If any team wants to secure the services of a player contracted by another, it may negotiate with the team that owns the rights to his services for a purchase, but it may not bid the player away directly by contracting him.

Once a player has signed his first contract in organized baseball, therefore, he is no longer free to dispose of his services. He may withdraw from organized baseball and follow some other calling, but he may not choose freely among bidders for him within baseball.

The market for baseball players has really divided into three markets. One is the market for free agents, in which the player is the seller; another is the market for players who have already signed their first contracts, in which the teams are both the sellers and the buyers; the third is the market for current services of contracted players, in which the player is the seller and the team that holds his contract is the buyer.

Some attempts have been made to enforce in the courts the exclusive right to contracted players' services which is conveyed by the uniform contract. On the principle that involuntary servitude is contrary to public policy, the courts have been reluctant to compel players to fulfil their contracts, to restrain them from performing for others, or to restrain others from employing them, and these attempts have met with little success.[13] Baseball has therefore resorted to extra-legal sanctions to enforce exclusive rights. A player who refuses to play for a team by which he is contracted, or refuses to play for a team to which his contract has been assigned, is suspended; he may not be employed by another team in organized baseball.[14] If he finds employment in baseball outside of organized baseball, he is declared "ineligible" and may not play in organized baseball again until he is restored to eligibility; the length of time after his petition

---

[11] *Baseball Blue Book, 1955,* pp. 509, 609.
[12] *Ibid.,* pp. 511, 611.

[13] On the principle of a case decided in 1852 (*Lumley* v. *Wagner*) a contracted player may be restrained by a court of equity from making his services available to a third party if (1) the player is unique; (2) the contract is definite; (3) there is mutuality; and (4) the contract is not an unreasonable restraint of trade. There is some question whether players' contracts fulfil these conditions (Peter S. Craig, "Monopsony in Manpower," *Yale Law Journal,* March, 1953, p. 590).
[14] *Baseball Blue Book, 1955,* pp. 538, 636.

for re-instatement before he will be permitted to resume play will depend upon the evaluation of the gravity of his offense.[15] A team in organized baseball that employs a suspended or ineligible player will find that other teams will refuse to meet it on the field of play; a team outside of organized baseball that employs him will not be permitted to hire the ball park of a team in organized baseball; players who participate in contests in which an ineligible player takes part themselves become ineligible.[16]

The reserve rule is the heart of the limitation on freedom in the baseball labor market. A number of different defenses have been offered for it, some specious and others somewhat stronger.

The defense most commonly heard is that the reserve rule is necessary to assure an equal distribution of playing talent among opposing teams; that a more or less equal distribution of talent is necessary if there is to be uncertainty of outcome; and that uncertainty of outcome is necessary if the consumer is to be willing to pay admission to the game. This defense is founded on the premise that there are rich baseball clubs and poor ones and that, if the players' market were free, the rich clubs would outbid the poor for talent, taking all the competent players for themselves and leaving only the incompetent for the other teams. It will be seen later that the premise is false.

Most of the revenue of baseball clubs comes from admission receipts.[17] A rich club, therefore, is one located in an area where attendance at baseball games is high; a poor club is one whose attendance is low.

Attendance at baseball games, as a whole, is a function of the general level of income, the price of admission to baseball games relative to the prices of recreational substitutes, and the goodness of substitutes.[18] Attendance at the games of any given team is a positive function of the size of the population of the territory in which the team has the monopoly right to play;[19] the size and convenience of location of the ball park,[20] and the average rank standing of the team during the season in the competition of its league. It is a negative function of the goodness of leisure-time substitutes for base-

---

[15] *Ibid.*, pp. 540, 637.

[16] *Ibid.*

[17] Combined major-league teams' revenue in 1950 was distributed by source as follows:

	Per Cent
Home-game admissions	57.2
Road-game admissions	14.1
Exhibition games	2.8
Radio and television rights	10.5
Concessions (net)	9.2
Other	6.2

Approximately twenty-five cents of each admission price is paid to the visiting team; the remaining admission revenue is kept by the home team (*Celler Report*, p. 6).

[18] The following estimates show some trends related to baseball attendance:

	1929	1954
Expenditures for recreation as a percentage of total personal consumption expenditures	5.5	5.2
Admissions to specified spectator amusements* as a percentage of expenditures for recreation	21.1	14.0
Spectator sports† as a percentage of admissions to specified spectator amusements	7.2	13.0
Professional baseball as a percentage of spectator sports	25.8	25.1‡

* "Specified spectator amusements" are motion-picture theaters; legitimate theaters, opera, and entertainments of non-profit institutions (except athletics); and spectator sports.

† "Spectator sports" are professional baseball, football, and hockey; horse- and dog-race tracks; college football; and "others."

‡ 1950; information not available for 1954.

(Source: U.S. Department of Commerce, *National Income, 1954 Edition: Supplement to the Survey of Current Business* [Washington, D.C.: Government Printing Office, 1954], Table 30, pp. 206 ff.; *Survey of Current Business*, July, 1955, Table 30, p. 19; *Celler Report*, p. 12.)

[19] Metropolitan area population per major-league team in 1950 ranged from 4,277,000 for each of the three teams in the New York area to 898,000 for Cincinnati and 857,000 for each of the two teams in St. Louis (*Celler Report*, p. 99).

[20] Major-league ball parks ranged in seating capacity in 1955 from 27,523 for Washington to 73,811 for Cleveland (*Baseball Blue Book, 1955*, pp. 18 ff.).

ball in the area and of the dispersion of percentages of games won by the teams in the league.[21]

There is, in fact, a wide variation in attendance among teams. In the period 1931–50 the New York Yankees' aggregate paid attendance was 24,270,000, while that of the St. Louis Browns was 4,160,000.[22]

If, it is argued, other things being equal, a team in an area with a large population has larger revenues than teams in less populous areas, then, in a free players' labor market, the former will get the most capable players, there will be wide variation among teams in the quality of play, contests will become certain, and attendance will decline.

The history of baseball seems, at least superficially, to support the position that the purpose of the reserve rule was to achieve balance of playing strength among teams. The first professional baseball league was the National Association of Professional Baseball Players, organized in 1870. It did not survive five seasons of play, and A. G. Mills, who first proposed the reserve rule, is reported to have said of its experience:

> This condition was greatly aggravated by the general practice on the part of the richer clubs of stripping the weaker ones of their best playing talent. Then would follow the collapse of a number of these clubs in mid-season, leaving their players unpaid, while the winning clubs, owing to the disbandment of the weaker ones, would also frequently fall from inability to arrange a paying number of games.[23]

The National Association was succeeded by the National League, which was formed in 1876.

To bring the process of unequal distribution of talent to a halt, it was thought necessary to devise the reserve rule to permit the poorer teams to retain the services of players whom they would otherwise lose to teams prepared to pay higher salaries. If this was the purpose of the reserve rule, there seems to be some question whether it has been successful. A number of different measures suggest themselves for testing the equality of distribution of player ability among teams. A simple test is one which counts the number of times each team has won its league pennant. In the period 1920–51 the New York Yankees led the American League in eighteen years, and the Chicago White Sox in none. In the National League, in the same period, the St. Louis Cardinals won in nine years, the New York Giants in eight, and the Philadelphia Phillies and Boston Braves in one year each.[24]

Clearly, there has been unequal distribution of talent. The Yankees have had better fortune than the others. By offering higher prices for the purchase of players' contracts from other teams, they have acquired players already under contract; by offering higher first-year salaries and prospects for higher professional lifetime earnings, they have induced the better free agents to sign with them; and by investing heavily in a farm system in the minor leagues, they have had access to a large pool of players from which the most capable could be drawn to the Yankees themselves.

By this simple empirical test, it can be seen that the reserve rule has not distributed players among teams perfectly equally; the teams that were prepared to outbid others for players have not been frustrated by the rule. The reason for this result will be shown later. It will also be shown that a market in which freedom is limited by the reserve rule cannot be expected to equalize the distribution of players among teams more than a market in which there is perfect freedom.

---

[21] That is to say, the "tighter" the competition, the larger the attendance. A pennant-winning team that wins 80 per cent of its games will attract fewer patrons than a pennant-winning team that wins 55 per cent of them.

[22] *Ibid.*, p. 100.

[23] *Celler Report*, p. 18, quoting *Spalding's Official Baseball Record, 1915*, p. 47.

[24] *Celler Report*, p. 102. Operationally, perfect equality of distribution of players among teams may be made manifest in the following ways: every game ends in a tie; every team wins exactly half of the games it plays; every team, in an eight-team league, wins the pennant every eighth year.

If the reserve rule does not, in fact, equalize the distribution of players, can it have some other result? By confronting each contracted player with an exclusive bidder, the rule can have the effect of depressing salaries, at least for some players. The relevance of salary levels to the rule was clearly seen in an official release of the National League on September 29, 1879, shortly after the adoption of the reserve rule for the first time.

The financial results of the past season prove that salaries must come down. We believe that players in insisting on exorbitant prices are injuring their own interests by forcing out of existence clubs which cannot be run and pay large salaries except at a large personal loss. ... In view of these facts, measures have been taken by this league to remedy the evil to some extent in 1880.[25]

The "measures" taken were a secret agreement among the members of the league that each might reserve five players who could not be contracted by other teams. Over the years the number of players who might be reserved has been revised upward from time to time until now the major-league teams are permitted to reserve forty players and minor-league teams a smaller number, depending on their league classification.[26]

Two other rules affecting the disposition of players should be mentioned. The *draft* or *selection* rule prevents a player from being held indefinitely in a lower classification league if his services are wanted by a team of a higher classification. After a player in the minor leagues has served a stipulated number of years in the minor leagues,[27] he becomes eligible to be drafted (selected) by teams of higher classifications.[28] A player who is drafted has his contract taken up by the team that drafts him. The team that loses him is paid according to a schedule which appears in the constitutional documents; the price depends upon the league classification of the team from which the player is drafted and the classification of the team that drafts him.[29] Thus the draft is a forced sale at a previously stipulated price. A team of classification A or higher may lose only one player in each season by the draft, irrespective of the number of draft-eligible players it has under reserve; in leagues of lower classification than A any number of eligibles may be drafted from any team. Thus only as many players may be drafted from the higher minor-league teams as there are teams.[30]

An elaborate system of rules has been worked out for determining the priority of selecting teams in the draft process. First choice is given to teams of high league classification and last choice to low-classification teams; for teams of any given league classification, first choice is given to those that stood lowest at the end of the previous season, and last choice is given to those that stood highest. The system appears to give the advantage of first choice to the teams of any classification which need talented players most. The advantage, however, is largely illusory. A minor-league team that holds the contracts of, say, three players, each of whom, if sold, would be worth $40,000, will not be prepared to lose any of them for the substantially lower draft

---

[25] *Celler Hearings*, p. 139, quoting a release published in the *New York Clipper*, October 11, 1879.
[26] A class AAA team, for example, may reserve thirty-eight players, and a class D team, only twenty-one.
[27] For example, this number is five years in the Pacific Coast League (players in this league, and *only* in this league, may opt to sign a contract which exempts them from the draft; in November, 1955, there were only twenty-seven players in this league who had chosen to sign such a contract); four years in AAA leagues; and two years in D leagues (*Baseball Blue Book, 1955*, pp. 521–22).
[28] In November, 1955, 3,184 players were eligible to be drafted, of a total of about 6,900 players reserved by minor-league teams (*Sporting News*, November 23, 1955, p. 5).
[29] If a major-league team drafts a Pacific Coast League player, it must pay the team losing the player $15,000; if a major-league team drafts a class E player, it must pay the team that loses him $1,500; etc. (*Baseball Blue Book, 1955*, p. 521).
[30] *Ibid.*, pp. 768–69.

price. Since it does not know which of the three will be drafted, it will sell them all before the draft dates.[31] It sells, of course, to the highest bidder, without regard to the previous season's rank position of the bidding teams. In the end, therefore, it seems to be true that the players who are left to be drafted are those who are worth about the draft price. If there are bargains to be had, it is because someone miscalculated the market. As a result, few players are actually drafted.[32]

The *waiver*[33] rule limits the freedom of higher-classification teams to dispose of their players to lower-classification teams. A major-league team may freely sell a player's contract to another major-league team of its own league. However, it may not sell the contract to a team of the other major league or to a minor-league team without first asking the other teams of its own league in the first case, and the other teams of both major leagues in the second, to "waive" the player. If one or more of these teams refuses to waive, they say, in effect, that they are prepared to take over the player's contract at a waiver price specified in the rules (currently $10,000).[34]

A major-league player may not have his salary reduced during the season for which he is contracted and may not have it reduced for the following season, if he should stay in the major leagues, to less than 75 per cent of its current season level. A team that claims a player for whom waivers have been requested, therefore, says that the exclusive right to the use and disposition of the player's services is worth $10,000, given the salary costs which his contract attaches to him.

A team that has asked other major-league teams for waivers on a player so that it may assign his contract to a minor-league team may, if it wishes, withdraw its request for waivers if any of the major-league teams express an interest in having the player by filing a claim for him. Negotiations then often ensue, in which the team that owns the player tries to get from the team that wants him a price higher than the waiver price. If the negotiations are successfully consummated, the player's contract is assigned outright between the major-league teams; he does not transfer on waivers. The rationale of the waiver rule is that it seeks to keep a player in the highest league classification for which his services are acceptable,

---

[31] Usually some days are set aside in November of each year for drafting; as soon as drafting by the major league is done, the minor leagues begin their own draft, in which teams in each league classification draft from teams in lower classifications.

[32] In November, 1954, of the several thousand eligibles, thirteen players were drafted by major-league teams and forty-four by minor-league teams. Of the thirteen, only seven spent the full following season in the major leagues, none with distinction.

The rule that only one player may be drafted in each year from the higher-classification minor-league teams has permitted the major-league teams with farm systems to protect their reservoir of players by moving draft eligibles among their teams. For example, in November, 1955, the Montreal Royals, an AAA team which is the property of the Brooklyn Dodgers, had a roster of thirty-three players, of whom thirty-two were draft-eligible. By moving its promising draft-eligible players from its other farm teams to Montreal just before the draft dates, Brooklyn was assured that it would lose only one of them. The others, who were being protected so that Brooklyn would have a pool of talent from which to get replacements for its players in the future, were reshuffled among the Brooklyn farm teams when the period for drafting had expired. This process is repeated each year.

[33] *Baseball Blue Book, 1955*, pp. 529 ff., 749 ff.

[34] A major-league team may "optionally assign" a player whose contract it holds to a minor-league team within three years of the time it has contracted him without asking waivers. An optional assignment is one which gives the assignor team the right to recall the optioned player into its own service. It differs from an "outright" assignment, which transfers, for a consideration, the right to use or dispose of the player's services. The optional assignment is an exception to the waiver rule.

There is also a waiver rule affecting the assignment of minor-league players between minor-league teams of different classifications.

if he is worth the waiver price, and despite the fact that he is worth more than this to a lower-classification team.[35]

Only the bare bones of the market rules of the industry have been described in this paper. Their full texts and the exceptions which the rules permit can be found in the constitutional documents themselves. For our purposes the skeletal description given here suffices.

Very little information is available on player salaries. All contracts are registered with the relevant executive offices of major- and minor-league baseball, but salary information is not made public. The reports of player salaries which appear in the public press are said not to be reliable. Some salary data were divulged, however, by the congressional committee hearings of 1951.

The rules impose a minimum salary in the major leagues of $6,000 per year.[36] No other league has a minimum-salary rule. Neither does any league have a maximum individual player salary rule. All leagues except the two major leagues and the only Open Classification league—the Pacific Coast League—have *team* maximum salary limits.[37]

TABLE 11.1 AVERAGE SALARIES PER PLAYER—MONTH AND MONTHLY SALARY RANGES

League Classification	Mean	Median	Range
AAA	$876	$850	$200–$4,000
AA	639	600	300– 4,200
A	391	350	100– 1,555
D	192	165	80– 1,000

Source: *Celler Hearings*, p. 965.

On July 1, 1950, the range of major-league salaries was from $5,000[38] to $90,000 per year. The mean was $13,288, and the median $11,000.[39] In the minor leagues salaries were very much lower. Average salaries per player-month and monthly salary ranges in that year were reported to be as shown in Table 11.1.

The large variation in players' salaries can be expected to attract many players who are hopeful that they will finally fall in the upper levels of the salary distribution. This will cause the average salary of baseball players to be below the level at which it would lie if the dispersion of salaries were smaller.

Baseball-playing skills, at some level of proficiency, are, of course, widely distributed among the young male population of the United States and some other countries of the Western Hemisphere, and the supply of baseball-playing labor must be very elastic to price. In the lower minor leagues players make themselves available at prices which seem to be less than they could earn in some other employment. A congressional committee heard testimony from one former minor-league player that he accepted his first contract with a class D team in 1941 for a salary of $60 a month and that this was the common beginning wage in that classification at the time.[40] The worth of

---

[35] That this is a "fact" may be demonstrated as follows: any major-league team can purchase a player of whom another major-league team wishes to dispose by offering a higher price for his contract than any minor-league bidder and by offering a price which is high enough so that it pays the team owning the player's contract to sell him to the bidding team rather than to employ him on one of its farm teams. The major-league team could do this if there were no waiver rule. If the waiver rule gives it a claim upon a player superior to that of a minor-league team, it is because the former can claim the player at a lower price than the latter is willing to pay for him.

[36] *Baseball Blue Book, 1955*, p. 543.

[37] For example, $7,000 per month per team in A1 leagues; $750 per month per team in E leagues. Each AAA and AA league may set its own team maximum; they were, for example, in 1951, American Association (AAA), $13,800 per team-month; International League (AAA), 14,000 per team-month (*Celler Hearings*, p. 189; *Baseball Blue Book, 1955*, p. 739).

[38] $5,000 was the minimum established by the rules for major-league players at that time.

[39] *Celler Hearings*, p. 965.

[40] *Ibid.*, p. 349.

these earnings must surely have been reduced by some of the real costs which baseball players incurred. The same witness, for example, told the committee:

> We used to finish a game in the evening, get on our bus, known as Stucker's Steamer. . . . The man who owned the club was named Rex Stucker. And this was an old, beat-up Ford, a bus, in which we had bunks in the back of the bus, and we used to pile all our suitcases, baseball bats and other things in this bus and then leave Sioux City about midnight and travel to Cheyenne, Wyoming. It is about 600 miles away. We were to get there at 4:30 the following afternoon and play a game in Cheyenne, Wyoming, that night. . . . That is a common practice in all minor leagues. . . . That is the common practice to save hotel bills.[41]

There are other disadvantages of life in the minor leagues. A player under contract may have his salary reduced in midseason if he is assigned outright to another team of a lower classification, and he may have his contract terminated without notice.[42] Earnings in the lower minor leagues are so low that, at the end of each season, it is a common practice for class D teams to have a "player's night" to raise money that can be given to the players to permit them to pay the expenses of their transportation to their homes.

If players are willing to sell their services for such a wage and under such circumstances, it is perhaps because they derive very large psychic income from playing the game and because, on the average, the players in the lower leagues overestimate the probability that they will excel in play and be chosen to receive a higher salary with a team of a higher-classification league.

Experience diminishes uncertainty and increases knowledge, however, and players recalculate the probabilities which they assign to the occurrence of events. As they find that they have miscalculated, they withdraw from the market. The president of the association of minor leagues testified:

> The turnover in B, C, and D (leagues) is terrific. . . . Boys may be in there a week or maybe 30 days. The turnover in the lower classifications is awfully heavy. . . . I suppose that a good many class D clubs have a turnover maybe five or six times during the season of almost their complete roster.[43]

Especially in the major leagues players have opportunities for earning supplementary income which would not be available to them if they were not baseball players. They may be paid for speaking engagements or for product indorsements; between seasons, if they are employed as salesmen, say, of insurance or automobiles, they will be more successful because they are players; if they invest in retail or service establishments, they are more likely to prosper; if they play well, they may receive gifts from grateful fans; when they retire from baseball, they may teach at baseball schools; if they are engaged in business ventures, they will be rewarded in proportion to the favor in which they were held by the fans during their baseball careers.

The reserve rule, which binds a player to the team that contracts him, gives a prima facie appearance of monopsony to the market. Once having signed a first contract, a player is confronted by a single buyer who may unilaterally specify the price to be paid for his services. Each team and the players under contract to it appear in a labor market specific to them.[44] This market is distinct from those of other teams. No movement among markets, either of buyers or sellers, is permitted. In each market the team operates as buyer; the players, as sellers. While there is no competition on the buying side,

---

[41] *Ibid.*
[42] The president of the association of minor leagues told the Celler Committee of the no-notice rule: "That inspires the player to hustle a little all the time" (*ibid.*, p. 205).
[43] *Ibid.*, pp. 206, 213.
[44] In the case of farm systems, the system defines the limits of the market; all the teams in the system coalesce into a single buyer for market purposes.

there is intense competition on the sellers' side.

In such a market rational maximizing teams[45] might be expected to behave like discriminating monopsonists. Each player will have his supply price; if he is offered less than this, he will prefer to work at some other occupation. The supply price will vary among individuals. For each of them it ought to be related to how much he can earn in the next best employment outside of baseball, with the appropriate adjustments made for the plaudits of the crowd, for the supplementary income opportunities baseball provides, for the convenience of seasonal employment and the inconvenience of constant travel, and so on. A maximizing team would be expected to pay different salaries to different players, even though they are of the same quality, but only just about the salaries that are necessary to prevent them from withdrawing their services.

Actually, however, teams seem to pay, in the major leagues, much more than this.

Here a paradox emerges. If baseball players have, on the average, no skills other than those necessary to play baseball proficiently, then their next best wage would be relatively low. Why are they paid so much more?

To begin with, it is undoubtedly correct that the player will not be paid more than he is worth to the team, his worth being determined by that part of the team's revenue which is attributable to his capacity to attract patrons to the ball park, net of the price paid for his contract to another team or the cost of his development. Nor will he receive less than his reservation price. The salary he receives, therefore, must fall somewhere between these limits; the question is: Why does it not fall at the bottom of the range?

The answer must be that the player is not without his defenses, even if he is in a monopsonistic market. He may withhold his services, and, in fact, each year there are a few holdouts who refuse to sign contracts providing for salaries that are unacceptable to them. In the end they usually sign, either because they become convinced, after a time, that the team will not offer more or because the team raises its offer. But sometimes players hold out for the full season. These may simply be cases of irrational behavior on the part of the player; though he is able to earn only $5,000 in another employment, he may sometimes refuse to accept $15,000 for playing baseball if he believes he is worth $20,000. But, if, in truth, he is worth $20,000, then it pays the team to offer $16,000. Thus the process by which the salary is fixed assumes the characteristics of bargaining, and the level at which it falls is a function of the shrewdness and guile of the parties in devising their bargaining strategies. Moreover, the teams cannot push the salary "too low" even for those who do sign, because it does not pay to have discontented players. Player performance is determined in part by natural abilities like sharpness of eye, perception of space, and muscular co-ordination but also in part by the effort the player exerts. A player who is

---

[45] The question may be asked whether it is sensible to assume that baseball-team owners are rational maximizers of money quantities. Representatives of organized baseball often say that the owners are interested more in providing opportunities for wholesome sport than they are in turning a profit. It was said in 1951 that ten of the sixteen major-league primary owners had their main business interests outside of baseball, and the Celler Committee heard testimony that, as of July, 1951, of 2,287 officers and directors of minor-league teams, only 291 made their living primarily from baseball. If baseball entrepreneurs get large psychic income from their association with the game, they will be willing to pay a price for engaging in the baseball business. This does not mean necessarily that they will be prepared to take a loss on their baseball operations but only that they are prepared to take a smaller return from baseball investment than their capital would earn in some other use. Still, one major-league property is reported to have sold in recent years for three and a half million dollars and another is said to be up for sale, at this writing, for four million dollars. The most expensive major-league property has been estimated to be worth fifteen million dollars and the average six million dollars. It seems unlikely that people will subject capital of this magnitude to large risk of loss for the pure joy of association with the game.

unhappy about his salary will perhaps not play as well as one who is not.

The solution to the problem of individual salary levels is not, however, completely indeterminate within the limits of the range which has been specified, as it would be in a classic duopoly case. This is so because, while each player has a monopoly of his own services, he is not truly unique, and there are more or less good substitutes for him. His salary is therefore partially determined by the difference between the value productivities and costs of other players by whom he may be replaced.

A rational team will seek to maximize the rent it derives from each player. It will be indifferent between two shortstops, one of whom is worth $30,000 and costs $20,000, and the other of whom is worth $20,000 and costs $10,000. It will prefer the first if it can have him for $19,000; but it will prefer the second if it must pay the first $21,000 to induce him to play. It will be prepared to pay a Babe Ruth a fabulous salary, simply because there are no very good substitutes for him, and he is worth so much more to the team than any other player. But if a Ruth insisted upon receiving his full worth, it would pay to employ in his stead some other person of less skill on whom some positive rent would be earned. The team would keep a Ruth even if he insisted upon receiving his full value only if all other players also insisted upon receiving theirs and if rents were therefore zero for all of them. Since it is incredible that all players should, in fact, exact their full worth, it follows from this analysis that at least some players are exploited.[46]

It has been suggested,[47] however, that, while major-league players, and especially the star players of the major leagues, may be exploited, it does not follow that all players taken together are. The process by which players are brought to the major leagues can be likened to that by which paying oil wells are brought in or patentable inventions discovered. In all these cases there is heavy investment in the discovery of knowledge. When it is discovered, the returns on it are high, but these returns must compensate for the losses incurred on the attempts which failed. In this schematic conception minor-league players who do not qualify for major-league play are like dry wells and research which does not yield a patent. They are paid more than they are worth because they may turn out to be of major-league caliber. To their cost must be added the cost of scouts and try-out camps and other costs of finding players and assessing their capacities. The monopsony gains in the major leagues are merely compensation for investment losses in scouting and in the operation of farm teams, and returns to investment in baseball, like returns to investment in oil and in research, should be no higher than returns to capital used in other ventures. If they were higher, capital would flow from other uses to investment in baseball.

This suggestion has a great deal of analytical merit. Its power is reduced somewhat, however, by the restraints on freedom of entry in the baseball industry. If the returns on oil investments or on investment in research are very much larger than returns on other investment, new entrants are free to search for oil and knowledge. But the rule of "territorial rights," which gives monopoly rights to desirable locations in the product market to teams currently in organized baseball and the system of private sanctions for the enforcement of the rule put serious disabilities upon prospective new entrants into the base-

---

[46] Representatives of organized baseball testified before the Celler Committee that players receive their full value. "If the players are dissatisfied, they are traded to other teams which will pay them more." This belief is, of course, not consistent with the other, also held by baseball representatives, that the reserve rule has the effect of balancing team strength by permitting poorer clubs, which pay less than the richer clubs, to retain players to whom the latter are prepared to pay a higher wage.

[47] I am indebted for the immediately following idea to Professor Gary S. Becker.

ball industry. If, therefore, there are monopoly gains arising from the characteristics of the baseball labor market, they are reinforced by restraints on competition in the product market.

Is it clear that the reserve rule is necessary to achieve more or less equal quality of play among teams? Assume that teams are distributed among locations, as they are in fact, so that the revenues of some are very much larger than those of others. Assume a free players' labor market, in which players may accept the offer of the highest bidder and teams may make offers without restraint.

At first sight, it may appear that the high-revenue teams will contract all the stars, leaving the others only the dregs of the supply; that the distribution of players among teams will become very unequal; that contests will become less uncertain; and that consumer interest will flag and attendance fall off. On closer examination, however, it can be seen that this process will be checked by the law of diminishing returns, operating concurrently with each team's strategic avoidance of diseconomies of scale.

Professional team competitions are different from other kinds of business ventures. If a seller of shoes is able to capture the market and to cause other sellers of shoes to suffer losses and withdraw, the surviving competitor is a clear gainer. But in baseball no team can be successful unless its competitors also survive and prosper sufficiently so that the differences in the quality of play among teams are not "too great."

If the size of a baseball team is thought of as the number of players under contract to it, each player being weighted by some index of his quality, then diseconomies of scale set in at some point when a team too far outstrips its competitors, and they become larger in proportion to the size of the differences.

Two teams opposed to each other in play are like two firms producing a single product. The product is the game, weighted by the revenues derived from its play. With game admission prices given, the product is the game, weighted by the number of paying customers who attend. When 30,000 attend, the output is twice as large as when 15,000 attend. In one sense, the teams compete; in another, they combine in a single firm in which the success of each branch requires that it be not "too much" more efficient than the other. If it is, output falls.

A baseball team, like any other firm, produces its product by combining factors of production. Consider the two teams engaged in a contest to be collapsed into a single firm, producing as output games, weighted by the revenue derived from admission fees. Let the players *of one team* be one factor and all others (management, transportation, ball parks, *and the players of the other team*), another. The quantity of the factor—players—is measured by making the appropriate adjustment for differential qualities among players, so that a man who hits safely in 35 per cent of his times at bat counts as more than one who hits safely only 20 per cent of the time. Given the quantity of the other factors, the total product curve of the factor—players of one team—will have the conventional shape; it will slope upward as the "quantity" of this factor is increased, reach a peak, and then fall. It will not pay to increase this factor without limit. Beyond some point—say, when a team already has three .350 hitters—it will not pay to employ another .350 hitter. If a team goes on increasing the quantity of the factor, players, by hiring additional stars, it will find that the total output—that is, admission receipts—of the combined firms (and, therefore, of its own) will rise at a less rapid rate and finally will fall absolutely. At some point, therefore, a first star player is worth more to poor Team B than, say, a third star to rich Team A. At this point, B is in a position to bid players away from A in the market. A's behavior is not a function of its bank balance. It does what it calculates it is worthwhile to do; and the time comes when, in pursuing the strategy of its own *gains,* it is worthwhile, whatever the size of its cash balance, to forego the services of an expert player and see him employed by another team.

The wealthy teams will usually prefer winning to losing.[48] If they do, they will prefer winning by close margins to winning by wide ones. If their market behavior is consistent with this objective—that is, if they behave like rational maximizers—playing talent will be more or less equally distributed among teams.

It does not require collusion to bring about this result. It is not senseless to expect it to be produced by a free labor market in which each team is separately engaged in gainful behavior. The position of organized baseball that a free market, given the unequal distribution of revenue, will result in the engrossment of the most competent players by the wealthy teams is open to some question. It seems, indeed, to be true that a market in which freedom is limited by a reserve rule such as that which now governs the baseball labor market distributes players among teams about as a free market would.

Players under contract to a team may be used by that team itself, or they may be sold to another team. Each team determines whether to use a player's services itself or to sell him, according to the relative returns on him in the two uses. If the return will be higher from sale, he will be sold, and vice versa. Now, if he can be sold to another team for a price higher than his worth to his present team, it is because he is worth more to the team that buys him than to the team that sells him. It follows that the players will be distributed among teams so that they are put to their most "productive" use;

each will play for the team that is able to get the highest return from his services.[49] But this is exactly the result which would be yielded by a free market. The difference is only that in a market subject to the reserve rule part of the price for the player's services is paid to the team that sells his contract, and part of his value is kept by the team that holds his contract; in the free market the player gets his full value.

If players were not indentured to teams but were free to accept the offers of the highest bidders, would the amount of investment in the training of players and the quality of play fall? In such a market, players will bear a larger proportion of the cost of training, and the wages they receive will have to compensate for this cost. If it pays now, in a monopsonistic market, to invest in training and development, it will also pay to do so in a free market. There will be cases in which players will reject a higher salary in the major leagues in order to remain longer in the minors and acquire skills that will assure even larger earnings in the future, just as medical students, receiving a negative income, now reject factory work at some positive wage.

Are there other alternatives to the reserve rule? Are there some other rules which would tend to produce a more or less equal distribution of playing talent among teams and which would not be defective on some other criterion?

Let there be a free players' market and let the total revenues of all teams in the

---

[48] It should not be thought that wealthy teams will invariably want to assemble a winning combination of players, either in a free market or in a market governed by the reserve rule. A team will seek to maximize the difference between its revenue and its costs. If this quantity is maximized, for any given club, by assembling a team of players who are of lower quality than those of another club in its league, it will pay the former to run behind.

[49] The sale of a player's contract occurs in a market in which the seller is a monopolist and the buyer an oligopsonist. The selling price will be not less than the player's capitalized value to the team that owns his contract (the difference between his average yearly product to it and his average yearly salary, multiplied by the estimated number of remaining years of his playing life and appropriately discounted). It will not be more than his capitalized value to the team for which his product would be higher than for any other team. The price will fall between these limits, at a point determined by bargaining strategies and the player's capitalized value to other would-be buyers.

major leagues be pooled and shared equally by all teams, perhaps after adjusting for differences in operating costs associated with differences in the size of franchise cities. All teams will then be equal in capacity to bid for talent. There will be no incentive, however, for any single team to win or to assemble a winning combination. Win or lose, play badly or well, it will receive its equal slice of pie. It will pay for all teams, taken together, to play well enough, on the average, so that revenue will not fall off faster than costs. But any individual team, by employing only men whose supply prices are low, whatever their quality, can then take advantage of the gains yielded by the expenditures of the others. No team will be willing to spend if it cannot be assured that others will also do so. Each team will therefore tend to buy the cheapest playing services in the market. A rule of equal sharing of revenue leads to the equal distribution of mediocre players among teams and to consumer preference for recreational substitutes.

As another possibility, let teams bid for players and players accept offers, subject only to the constraint that a ceiling is imposed on the salaries that may be paid to individual players. The allocational effects of this rule would appear to depend upon the level of the ceiling. If the maximum salary permitted by the rule is higher than the highest wage paid to any player in a free market, the effect can be nothing but zero. It may appear that if the ceiling is sufficiently lower than this, so that more than one team is prepared to pay the specified maximum price to the highest-salaried player, the rule will begin to have some positive effects, and that, the lower the maximum salary, the larger will be the effects. On closer view, this is seen to be not true. Suppose the maximum is placed at some level, x. Players who would be worth more than x in a free market will then distribute themselves among teams on other criteria than the yearly salary, and teams will bid for players by offering other quantities than price; for example, perquisites or the security of long-term contracts.[50] Teams which, in the absence of a maximum salary rule, would have outbid other would-be buyers of a player's services with cash will outbid them with non-money offers, and the distribution of players among teams will be left unaffected. If complementary rules are devised and successfully enforced (such as rules forbidding the payment of perquisites, contracts for longer than one year, secret understandings, and employment of players' relatives), so that the cash price is the whole price received by the player, those who receive the maximum will tend to accept, among competing bids, those from the teams which paid the highest average salary, for they will then be combined with higher-priced (and better) players, and the probability that they will share in World Series bonus earnings will be higher.[51] Even if players worth the maximum wage or more are distributed randomly (thus, in the long run, equally)

[50] An interesting subsidiary question is: What effect will long-term contracts, rather than one-year contracts, have on player salaries if the market is free and the contracts are enforceable? Players will accept a lower annual salary if they have the security of a long contract, but they will demand a higher annual salary because it will then be impossible for them to accept a higher offer from another team during the life of the contract. Assuming that players estimate their future prospects correctly, those who expect to do well will take only a one-year contract. Teams will be prepared to pay a higher annual salary because they have the security of having a player's services for a long period; but they will pay a lower annual salary because they run the risk that the quality of his play will decline during the life of the contract. If they estimate a player's future correctly, they will sign a long-term contract with those who will do well in the future and a one-year contract with those who will not. On the assumption of correct estimation of the future on both sides of the market, the outcome seems to be that there will be no difference in the annual salary whatever the length of the contract.

[51] Part of the revenues of each annual World Series is distributed to players of the teams which are in the upper half of the major leagues' rank standings at the season's end.

among teams, they will be exploited; the market will not be free for them.

As still another possibility, let there be a free players' labor market and let franchises be distributed so that the size of the product market is equal for all teams. Suppose, for example, that all teams are located in markets whose population is two million. Thus, in the New York area there will be six teams rather than three; in the Chicago area, three rather than two; and so on. If attendance is a unique function of the size of the market, such a distribution of teams may equalize revenues among teams. But, as has already been shown,[52] attendance is a function of several variables. If psychic income is not zero for all team owners, or if it is larger for some than others, and if consumer income levels, the convenience of reaching the ball park, the taste for recreation relative to other objects of expenditure, or the taste for baseball (within recreational expenditures) is not equal among cities, differences in revenues will occur. When they do, a self-generating process begins to operate to increase the magnitude of the differences. If the revenues of Team A are larger than those of Team B for any of the foregoing reasons, despite the equality of market size, Team A is in a position to contract the better players by offering a higher price;[53] Team A then wins more games than B, and its relative attendance and revenues increase. Now it is in a still better position to outbid B for players. Equal division of markets may, however, tend to result in a somewhat more equal distribution of players among teams than unequal division of markets.

Finally, let teams bid for players and let players accept offers, subject to the constraints that a low ceiling is imposed on the number of players that may be under contract to any team and that the control of players in the minor leagues is prohibited. Suppose no team is permitted to contract, directly or indirectly, more than, say, fifteen players.[54] The smaller the number of players each team is permitted to contract, the more equally will talent be distributed among teams. But it must be kept in mind that player limits are inhibitions on freedom to contract and, therefore, inconsistent with market freedom. Like other rules which have been discussed, they lead to exploitation by preventing some players from contracting with a team prepared to pay a higher price for their services; they receive less than they would be worth in a free market uninhibited by rules.

Markets in which the freedom to buy and sell is constrained by the reserve rule or by the suggested alternatives to it do not promise better results than do markets constructed on the postulate of freedom. It appears that free markets would give as good aggregate results as any other kind of market for industries, like the baseball industry, in which all firms must be nearly equal if each is to prosper. On welfare criteria, of course, the free market is superior to the others, for in such a market each worker receives the full value of his services, and exploitation does not occur.

[52] Above, p. 144.
[53] It may, of course, not do so (see n. 48).

[54] The reader is reminded that major-league teams are now permitted by the rules to have an active roster of twenty-five players during the playing season (and, for one year from the date of their discharge from military service, up to five more who have returned from the service); that they may have an additional fifteen players under contract who are out on option to play with minor-league teams, subject to recall; and that they may hold several hundred players indirectly by contracting them to minor-league teams which they own or with which they have working agreements.

PART IV

HUMAN CAPITAL

Waste neither time nor money
But make the best use of both

Ben Franklin

Probably the fastest-growing segment of economics literature is concerned with the economics of education. A significant amount of this literature is being incorporated gradually into the field of labor economics: specifically that portion dealing with human capital, or investment in man.

The concept of human capital is much broader than the one aspect on which we focus. It includes all types of investment that man can make which improve his productivity in market as well as nonmarket activities. Such investments may involve money expended and income foregone during the investment period. The types of investment range from health activities to formal education to on-the-job training. And like other additions to capital, rational investment in man involves current sacrifices which should be compensated by future returns comparable to those realized on other forms of investment. These returns should compensate the individual for the actual cost of the investment (tuition, for instance), for the opportunity costs of the investment (lost income), and for the deferred nature of the payment.

Here we concentrate on investment in on-the-job training rather than on other forms of human capital formation. However, all of the readings in Part IV discuss other forms of investment. In particular, the second Becker selection emphasizes rates of return to education and training and related issues of long-run occupational choice. Later, Sjaastad's article in Part VI discusses the returns from mobility; and Wilkinson's article in Part VII considers the returns from investment in formal education. Readers who wish to pursue the broader topic of the economics of education, especially the returns to formal education, may refer to two basic sources. Mark Blaug has prepared a bibliography of material published through 1966 and also has edited a volume which contains an excellent collection of articles on the economics of education.[1]

Our main concern in Part IV is the implications of on-the-job training for labor market behavior. The classic work in this area is

---

[1] Mark Blaug, *Economics of Education: A Selected Annotated Bibliography* (New York: Pergamon Press, Inc., 1966); and Mark Blaug, ed., *Economics of Education I* (Baltimore: Penguin Books, Inc., 1968).

Gary S. Becker's *Human Capital*. Becker develops the theory of on-the-job training for two types of training: (1) specific training, which raises a worker's marginal productivity more in the firm giving the training than in other firms, and (2) general training, which raises a worker's productivity equally in all firms. Becker argues that under conditions of perfect competition, workers (not firms) will pay for general training, while specific training will be financed largely by employers. These assertions are then related by Becker to several observed phenomena in the labor market. The comment by R. S. Eckaus emphasizes the special assumptions embodied in Becker's analysis. Among the more notable are the notion of perfect competition and the assumption that training can be provided as a product separate from the firm's primary output. Although these assumptions are explicitly made by Becker, Eckaus' comment serves to underlie their importance and demonstrates again the crucial role of empirical information in resolving theoretical disputes about the operation of the labor market.

Part IV concludes with Jacob Mincer's "On-the-Job Training: Costs, Returns, and Some Implications." In this reading, Mincer is, as Mary Jean Bowman notes, Becker's "empirical mind and conscience."[2] Mincer develops a method to estimate the value of the investment in on-the-job training (the magnitude is found to be comparable to the amount invested in formal education). And he also estimates rates of return to on-the-job training and finds them slightly below the return to formal education. Finally, the extent of on-the-job training is related to several aspects of labor market behavior, namely, male-female income differentials and white-Negro income differentials.

These three selections provide a fairly complete picture of the literature on on-the-job training. They also convey implicitly and explicitly the flavor of other writings in the much broader area of human capital. There are indications that this general area will continue to grow as quickly as it has in the last decade. And as Part IV reveals, there is still much room for further empirical research on the narrower topic of on-the-job training.

[2] "The Human Investment Revolution in Economic Thought," in Blaug, ed., *Economics of Education I, op. cit.*, p. 115.

12
Investment in Human Capital: Effects on Earnings[1]

Gary S. Becker

The original aim of this study was to estimate the money rate of return to college and high-school education in the United States. In order to set these estimates in the proper context, a brief formulation of the theory of investment in human capital was undertaken. It soon became clear to me, however, that more than a restatement was called for; while important and pioneering work had been done on the economic return to various occupations and education classes,[2] there had been few, if any, attempts to treat the process of investing in people from a general viewpoint or to work out a broad set of empirical implications. I began then to prepare a general analysis of investment in human capital.

It eventually became apparent that this general analysis would do much more than fill a gap in formal economic theory: it offers a unified explanation of a wide range of empirical phenomena which have either been given *ad hoc* interpretations or have baffled investigators. Among these phenomena are the following: (1) Earnings typically increase with age at a decreasing rate. Both the rate of increase and the rate of retarda-

---

Reprinted from Gary Becker, *Human Capital* (New York: National Bureau of Economic Research, 1964), pp. 7–36. Copyright © 1964, by National Bureau of Economic Research. All Rights Reserved.

[1] This chapter and the one that follows were published in somewhat different form in *Investment in Human Beings*, NBER Special Conference 15, supplement to *Journal of Political Economy*, October 1962, pp. 9–49.

[2] In addition to the earlier works of Smith, Mill, and Marshall, see the brilliant work (which greatly influenced my own thinking about occupational choice) by M. Friedman and S. Kuznets, *Income from Independent Professional Practice*, New York, NBER, 1945; see also H. Clark, *Life Earnings in Selected Occupations in the U.S.*, New York, 1937; J. R. Walsh, "Capital Concept Applied to Man," *Quarterly Journal of Economics*, February 1935; G. Stigler and D. Blank, *The Demand and Supply of Scientific Personnel*, New York, NBER, 1957. In recent years, of course, there has been considerable work, especially by T. W. Schultz; see, for example, his "Investment in Human Capital," *American Economic Review*, March 1961, pp. 1–17.

tion tend to be positively related to the level of skill. (2) Unemployment rates tend to be inversely related to the level of skill. (3) Firms in underdeveloped countries appear to be more "paternalistic" toward employees than those in developed countries. (4) Younger persons change jobs more frequently and receive more schooling and on-the-job training than older persons do. (5) The distribution of earnings is positively skewed, especially among professional and other skilled workers. (6) Abler persons receive more education and other kinds of training than others. (7) The division of labor is limited by the extent of the market. (8) The typical investor in human capital is more impetuous and thus more likely to err than is the typical investor in tangible capital.

What a diverse and even confusing array! Yet all these, as well as many other important empirical implications, can be derived from very simple theoretical arguments. The purpose here is to set out these arguments in general form, with the emphasis placed on empirical implications, although little empirical material is presented....

In this chapter a lengthy discussion of on-the-job training is presented and then, much more briefly, discussions of investment in schooling, information, and health. On-the-job training is dealt with so elaborately not because it is more important than other kinds of investment in human capital—although its importance is often under-rated—but because it clearly illustrates the effect of human capital on earnings, employment, and other economic variables. For example, the close connection between indirect and direct costs and the effect of human capital on earnings at different ages are vividly brought out. The extended discussion of on-the-job training paves the way for much briefer discussions of other kinds of investment in human beings.

1. On-the-Job Training

Theories of firm behavior, no matter how they differ in other respects, almost invariably ignore the effect of the productive process itself on worker productivity. This is not to say that no one recognizes that productivity is affected by the job itself; but the recognition has not been formalized, incorporated into economic analysis, and its implications worked out. I now intend to do just that, placing special emphasis on the broader economic implications.

Many workers increase their productivity by learning new skills and perfecting old ones while on the job. Presumably, future productivity can be improved only at a cost, for otherwise there would be an unlimited demand for training. Included in cost are the value placed on the time and effort of trainees, the "teaching" provided by others, and the equipment and materials used. These are costs in the sense that they could have been used in producing current output if they had not been used in raising future output. The amount spent and the duration of the training period depend partly on the type of training since more is spent for a longer time on, say, an intern than a machine operator.

Consider explicitly now a firm that is hiring employees for a specified time period (in the limiting case this period approaches zero), and for the moment assume that both labor and product markets are perfectly competitive. If there were no on-the-job training, wage rates would be given to the firm and would be independent of its actions. A profit-maximizing firm would be in equilibrium when marginal products equaled wages, that is, when marginal receipts equaled marginal expenditures. In symbols

$$MP = W, \qquad (1)$$

where W equals wages or expenditures and MP equals the marginal product or receipts. Firms would not worry too much about the relation between labor conditions in the present and future, partly because workers would only be hired for one period and partly because wages and marginal products in future periods would be independent of a firm's current behavior. It can therefore legitimately be assumed that workers have unique marginal products (for given amounts of other inputs) and wages in each period, which are, respectively, the maximum productivity in all possible uses and the market wage rate. A more complete set of equilibrium conditions would be the set

$$MP_t = W_t, \quad (2)$$

where t refers to the tth period. The equilibrium position for each period would depend only on the flows during that period.

These conditions are altered when account is taken of on-the-job training and the connection thereby created between present and future receipts and expenditures. Training might lower current receipts and raise current expenditures, yet firms could profitably provide this training if future receipts were sufficiently raised or future expenditures sufficiently lowered. Expenditures during each period need not equal wages, receipts need not equal the maximum possible marginal productivity, and expenditures and receipts during all periods would be interrelated. The set of equilibrium conditions summarized in equation (2) would be replaced by an equality between the *present values* of receipts and expenditures. If E_t and R_t represent expenditures and receipts during period t, and i the market discount rate, then the equilibrium condition can be written as

$$\sum_{t=0}^{n-1} \frac{R_t}{(1+i)^{t+1}} = \sum_{t=0}^{n-1} \frac{E_t}{(1+i)^{t+1}}, \quad (3)$$

when n represents the number of periods, and R_t and E_t depend on all other receipts and expenditures. The equilibrium condition of equation (2) has been generalized, for if marginal product equals wages in each period, the present value of the marginal product stream would have to equal the present value of the wage stream. Obviously, however, the converse need not hold.

If training were given only during the initial period, expenditures during the initial period would equal wages plus the outlay on training, expenditures during other periods would equal wages alone, and receipts during all periods would equal marginal products. Equation (3) becomes

$$MP_0 + \sum_{t=1}^{n-1} \frac{MP_t}{(1+i)^t}$$
$$= W_0 + k + \sum_{t=1}^{n-1} \frac{W_t}{(1+i)^t}, \quad (4)$$

where k measures the outlay on training.

If a new term is defined,

$$G = \sum_{t=1}^{n-1} \frac{MP_t - W_t}{(1+i)^t}, \quad (5)$$

equation (4) can be written as

$$MP_0 + G = W_0 + k. \quad (6)$$

Since the term k only measures the actual outlay on training, it does not entirely measure training costs, for it excludes the time that a person spends on this training, time that could have been used to produce current output. The difference between what could have been produced, MP'_0, and what is produced, MP_0, is the opportunity cost of the time spent in training. If C is defined as the sum of opportunity costs and outlays on training, (6) becomes

$$MP'_0 + G = W_0 + C. \quad (7)$$

The term G, the excess of future receipts over future outlays, is a measure of the return to the firm from providing training; and, therefore, the difference between G and C measures the difference between the return from and the cost of training. Equation (7) shows that the marginal product would equal wages in the initial period only when the return equals costs, or G equals C; it would be greater or less than wages as the return was smaller or greater than costs. Those familiar with capital theory might argue that this generalization of the simple equality between marginal product and wages is spurious because a full equilibrium would require equality between the return from an investment—in this case, made on the job—and costs. If this implied that G equals C, marginal product would equal wages in the initial period. There is much to be said for the relevance of a condition equating the return from an investment with costs, but such a condition does not imply that G equals C or that marginal product equals wages. The following discussion demonstrates that great care is required in the application of this condition to on-the-job investment.

Our treatment of on-the-job training produced some general results—summarized in equations (3) and (7)—of wide applicability, but more concrete results require more specific assumptions. In the following sections two types of on-the-job training are discussed in turn: general and specific.

General Training

General training is useful in many firms besides those providing it; for example, a machinist trained in the army finds his skills of value in steel and aircraft firms, and a doctor trained (interned) at one hospital finds his skills useful at other hospitals. Most on-the-job training presumably increases the future marginal productivity of workers in the firms providing it; general training, however, also increases their marginal product in many other firms as well. Since in a competitive labor market the wage rates paid by any firm are determined by marginal productivities in other firms, future wage rates as well as marginal products would increase in firms providing general training. These firms could capture some of the return from training only if their marginal product rose by more than their wages. "Perfectly general" training would be equally useful in many firms and marginal products would rise by the same extent in all of them. Consequently, wage rates would rise by exactly the same amount as the marginal product and the firms providing such training could not capture any of the return.

Why, then, would rational firms in competitive labor markets provide general training if it did not bring any return? The answer is that firms would provide general training only if they did not have to pay any of the costs. Persons receiving general training would be willing to pay these costs since training raises their future wages. Hence it is the trainees, not the firms, who would bear the cost of general training and profit from the return.[3]

These and other implications of general training can be more formally demonstrated in equation (7). Since wages and marginal products are raised by the same amount, MP_t must equal W_t for all $t = 1, \cdots n - 1$, and therefore

$$G = \sum_{t=1}^{n-1} \frac{MP_t - W_t}{(1 + i)^t} = 0. \qquad (8)$$

Equation (7) is reduced to

$$MP'_0 = W_0 + C, \qquad (9)$$

or

$$W_0 = MP'_0 - C. \qquad (10)$$

In terms of actual marginal product

$$MP_0 = W_0 + k, \qquad (9')$$

or

$$W_0 = MP_0 - k. \qquad (10')$$

The wage of trainees would not equal their opportunity marginal product but would be less by the total cost of training. In other words, employees would pay for general training by receiving wages below their current (opportunity) productivity. Equation (10) has many other implications, and the rest of this section is devoted to developing the more important ones.

Some might argue that a really "net" definition of marginal product, obtained by subtracting training costs from "gross" marginal product, must equal wages even for trainees. Such an interpretation of net pro-

---

[3] Some persons have asked why any general training is provided if firms do not collect any of the returns. The answer is simply that they have an incentive to do so wherever the demand price for training is at least as great as the supply price or cost of providing the training. Workers in turn would prefer to be trained on the job rather than in specialized firms (schools) if the training and work complemented each other (see the discussion in section 2 below).

ductivity could formally save the equality between marginal product and wages here, but not always, as shown later. Moreover, regardless of which interpretation is used, training costs would have to be included in any study of the relation between wages and productivity.

Employees pay for general on-the-job training by receiving wages below what they could receive elsewhere. "Earnings" during the training period would be the difference between an income or flow term (potential marginal product) and a capital or stock term (training costs), so that the capital and income accounts would be closely intermixed, with changes in either affecting wages. In other words, earnings of persons receiving on-the-job training would be net of investment costs and would correspond to the definition of *net* earnings used throughout this paper, which subtracts all investment costs from "gross" earnings. Therefore, our departure with this definition of earnings from the accounting conventions used for transactions in material goods—which separate income from capital accounts to prevent a transaction in capital from *ipso facto*[4] affecting the income side—is not capricious but is grounded in a fundamental difference between the way investment in material and human capital are "written off." The underlying cause of this difference undoubtedly is the widespread reluctance to treat people as capital and the accompanying tendency to treat all wage receipts as earnings.

Intermixing the capital and income accounts could make the reported "incomes" of trainees unusually low and perhaps negative, even though their long-run or lifetime incomes were well above average. Since a considerable fraction of young persons receive some training, and since trainees tend to have lower current and higher subsequent earnings than other youth, the correlation of current consumption with the current earnings of young males[5] would not only be much weaker than the correlation with long-run earnings, but the signs of these correlations might even differ.[6]

Doubt has been cast on the frequent assertion that no allowance is made in the income accounts for depreciation on human capital.[7] A depreciation-type item is deducted, at least from the earnings due to on-the-job training, for the cost would be deducted during the training period. Depreciation on tangible capital does not bulk so large in any one period because it is usually "written off" or depreciated during a period of time designed to approximate its economic life. Hence human and tangible capital appear to differ more in the time pattern of depreciation than in its existence,[8] and the effect on wage income of a rapid

---

[5] The term "young males" rather than "young families" is used because as J. Mincer has shown (in his "Labor Force Participation of Married Women," *Aspects of Labor Economics*, Princeton for NBER, 1962), the labor force participation of wives is positively correlated with the difference between a husband's long-run and current income. Participation of wives, therefore, makes the correlation between a family's current and a husband's long-run income greater than that between a husband's current and long-run income.

[6] A difference in signs is impossible in Friedman's analysis of consumer behavior because he assumes that, at least in the aggregate, transitory and long-run (that is, permanent) incomes are uncorrelated (see his *A Theory of the Consumption Function*, Princeton for NBER, 1957); I am suggesting that they may be *negatively* correlated for young persons.

[7] See C. Christ, "Patinkin on Money, Interest, and Prices," *Journal of Political Economy*, August 1957, p. 352; and W. Hamburger, "The Relation of Consumption to Wealth and the Wage Rate," *Econometrica*, January 1955.

[8] In a recent paper, R. Goode has argued (see his "Educational Expenditures and the Income Tax," in Selma J. Mushkin, ed., *Economics of Higher Education*, Washington, 1962) that educated persons should be permitted to subtract from income a depreciation allowance on tuition payments. Such an allowance is apparently not required for on-the-job training costs or, as seen later, for the indirect costs of education; indeed, one might argue, on the contrary, that too much or too rapid depreciation is permitted on such investments.

---

[4] Of course, a shift between assets with different productivities would affect the income account on material goods even with current accounting practices.

"write-off" of human capital is what should be emphasized and studied.

This point can be demonstrated differently and more rigorously. The ideal depreciation on a capital asset during any period would equal its change in value during the period. In particular, if value rose, a negative depreciation term would have to be subtracted or a positive appreciation term added to the income from the asset. Since training costs would be deducted from earnings during the training period, the economic "value" of a trainee would at first increase rather than decrease with age, and only later begin to decrease. Therefore, a negative rather than a positive depreciation term would have to be subtracted initially.[9]

Training has an important effect on the relation between earnings and age. Suppose that untrained persons received the same earnings regardless of age, as shown by the horizontal line UU in Figure 12.1. Trained persons would receive lower earnings during the training period because training is paid for at that time, and higher earnings at later ages because the return is collected then. The combined effect of paying for and collecting the return from training in this way would be to make the age earnings curve of training persons, shown by TT in Figure 12.1, steeper than that of untrained persons, the difference being greater the greater the cost of, and return from, the investment.

Not only does training make the curve steeper but, as indicated by Figure 12.1, also more concave; that is, the rate of increase in earnings is affected more at younger than at older ages. Suppose, to take an extreme case, that training raised the level of marginal productivity but had no effect on the slope, so that the marginal productivity of trained persons was also independent of age. If earnings equaled marginal product, TT would merely be parallel to and higher than UU, showing neither slope

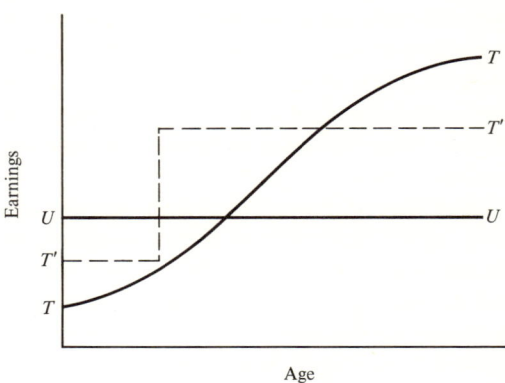

FIGURE 12.1 Relation of Earnings to Age.

nor concavity. Since, however, earnings of trained persons would be below marginal productivity during the training period and equal afterward, they would rise sharply at the end of the training period and then level off (as shown by the dashed line $T'T'$ in Figure 12.1), imparting a concave appearance to the curve as a whole. In this extreme case an extreme concavity appears (as in TT); in less extreme cases the principle would be the same and the concavity more continuous.

Foregone earnings are an important, although neglected, cost of much investment in human capital and should be treated in the same way as direct outlays. Indeed, *all* costs appear as foregone earnings to workers receiving on-the-job training; that is, all costs appear as lower earnings than could be received elsewhere, although direct outlays, C, may really be an important part of costs. The arbitrariness of the division between indirect and direct costs and the resulting advantage of treating total costs as a whole[10] can be further demonstrated by

---

[9] See Chapter VII, section 2 [*Human Capital*] for some empirical estimates of "depreciation" on human capital.

[10] The equivalence between indirect and direct costs applies to consumption as well as to investment decisions. In my paper, *A Theory of the Allocation of Time*, IBM Research Paper RC 1149, March 20, 1964, an analysis incorporating both direct and indirect consumption costs is applied to the choice between work and nonwork, price and income elasticities of demand for goods, the economic function of queues, and several other areas.

contrasting school and on-the-job training. Usually only the direct costs of school training are emphasized, even though opportunity costs are sometimes (as with college education) an important part of the total. A shift from school training to on-the-job training would, however, reverse the emphasis and make all costs appear as foregone earnings, even when direct outlays were important.

Income-maximizing firms in competitive labor markets would not pay the cost of general training and would pay trained persons the market wage. If, however, training costs were paid, many persons would seek training, few would quit during the training period, and labor costs would be relatively high. Firms that did not pay trained persons the market wage would have difficulty satisfying their skill requirements and would also tend to be less profitable than other firms. Firms that paid both for training and less than the market wage for trained persons would have the worst of both worlds, for they would attract too many trainees and too few trained persons.

These principles have been clearly demonstrated during the last few years in discussions of problems in recruiting military personnel. The military offers training in a wide variety of skills and many are very useful in the civilian sector. Training is provided during part or all of the first enlistment period and used during the remainder of the first period and hopefully during subsequent periods. This hope, however, is thwarted by the fact that re-enlistment rates tend to be inversely related to the amount of civilian-type skills provided by the military.[11] Persons with these skills leave the military more readily because they can receive much higher wages in the civilian sector. Net military wages for those receiving training are higher relative to civilian wages during the first than during subsequent enlistment periods because training costs are largely paid by the military. Not surprisingly, therefore, first-term enlistments for skilled jobs are obtained much more easily than are re-enlistments.

The military is a conspicuous example of an organization that both pays at least part of training costs and does not pay market wages to skilled personnel. It has had, in consequence, relatively easy access to "students" and heavy losses of "graduates." Indeed, its graduates make up the predominant part of the supply in several civilian occupations. For example, well over 90 per cent of United States commercial airline pilots received much of their training in the armed forces. The military, of course, is not a commercial organization judged by profits and losses and has had no difficulty surviving and even thriving.

What about the old argument that firms in competitive labor markets have no incentive to provide on-the-job training because trained workers would be bid away by other firms? Firms that train workers are supposed to impart external economies to other firms because the latter can use these workers free of any training charge. An analogy with research and development is often drawn since a firm developing a process that cannot be patented or kept secret would impart external economies to competitors. This argument and analogy would apply if firms were to pay training costs, for they would suffer a "capital loss" whenever trained workers were bid away by other firms. Firms can, however, shift training costs to trainees and have an incentive to do so when faced with competition for their services.[12]

[11] See *Manpower Management and Compensation*, report of the Cordiner Committee, Washington, 1957, Vol. I, Chart 3, and the accompanying discussion. The military not only wants to eliminate the inverse relation but apparently would like to create a positive relation because they have such a large investment in heavily trained personnel. For a recent and excellent study, see Gorman C. Smith, "Differential Pay for Military Technicians," unpublished Ph.D. dissertation, Columbia University, 1964.

[12] Sometimes the alleged external economies from on-the-job training have been considered part of the "infant industry" argument for protection (see

The difference between investments in training and in research and development can be put very simply. Without patents or secrecy, firms in competitive industries cannot establish property rights in innovations, and these innovations become fair game for all comers. Patent systems try to establish these rights so that incentives can be provided to invest in research. Property rights in skills, on the other hand, are automatically vested, for a skill cannot be used without permission of the person possessing it. The property right of the workers in his skills is the source of his incentive to invest in training by accepting a reduced wage during the training period and explains why an analogy with unowned innovations is misleading.

Specific Training

Completely general training increases the marginal productivity of trainees by exactly the same amount in the firms providing the training as in other firms. Clearly some kinds of training increase productivity by different amounts in the firms providing the training and in other firms. Training that increases productivity more in firms providing it will be called specific training. Completely specific training can be defined as training that has no effect on the productivity of trainees that would be useful in other firms. Much on-the-job training is neither completely specific nor completely general but increases productivity more in the firms providing it and falls within the definition of specific training. The rest increases productivity by at least as much in other firms and falls within a definition of general training. A few illustrations of the scope of specific training are presented before a formal analysis is developed.

The military offers some forms of training that are extremely useful in the civilian sector, as already noted, and others that are only of minor use to civilians, i.e., astronauts, fighter pilots, and missile men. Such training falls within the scope of specific training because productivity is raised in the military but not (much) elsewhere.

Resources are usually spent by firms in familiarizing new employees with their organization,[13] and the knowledge thus acquired is a form of specific training because productivity is raised more in the firms acquiring the knowledge than in other firms. Other kinds of hiring costs, such as employment agency fees, the expenses incurred by new employees in finding jobs, or the time employed in interviewing testing, checking references, and in bookkeeping do not so obviously increase the knowledge of new employees, but they too are a form of specific investment in human capital, although not training. They are an investment because outlays over a short period create distributed effects on productivity; they are specific because productivity is raised primarily in the firms making the outlays; they are in human capital because they lose their value whenever employees leave. In the rest of this section reference is mostly to on-the-job specific training even though the analysis applies to all on-the-job specific investment.

Even after hiring costs are incurred, firms usually know only a limited amount about the ability and potential of new employees.

J. Black "Arguments for Tariffs," *Oxford Economic Papers*, June 1959, pp. 205–206). Our analysis suggests, however, that the trouble tariffs are supposed to overcome must be traced back to difficulties that workers have in financing investment in themselves—in other words, to ignorance or capital market limitations that apply to expenditures on education, health, as well as on-the-job training. Protection would serve the same purpose as the creation of monopsonies domestically, namely, to convert general into specific capital so that firms can be given an incentive to pay for training (see the remarks on specific training below and in section 4 of this chapter). Presumably a much more efficient solution would be to improve the capital market directly through insurance of loans, subsidies, information, etc.

[13] To judge from a sample of firms recently analyzed, formal orientation courses are quite common, at least in large firms (see H. F. Clark and H. S. Sloan, *Classrooms in the Factories*, New York, 1958, Chap. IV).

They try to increase their knowledge in various ways—testing, rotation among departments, trial and error, etc.—for greater knowledge permits a more efficient utilization of manpower. Expenditures on acquiring knowledge of employee talents would be a specific investment if the knowledge could be kept from other firms, for then productivity would be raised more in the firms making the expenditures than elsewhere.

The effect of investment in employees on their productivity elsewhere depends on market conditions as well as on the nature of the investment. Very strong monopsonists might be completely insulated from competition by other firms, and practically all investments in their labor force would be specific. On the other hand, firms in extremely competitive labor markets would face a constant threat of raiding and would have fewer specific investments available.

These examples convey some of the surprisingly large variety of situations that come under the rubric of specific investment. This set is now treated abstractly in order to develop a general formal analysis. Empirical situations are brought in again after several major implications of the formal analysis have been developed.

If all training were completely specific, the wage that an employee could get elsewhere would be independent of the amount of training he had received. One might plausibly argue, then, that the wage paid by firms would also be independent of training. If so, firms would have to pay training costs, for no rational employee would pay for training that did not benefit him. Firms would collect the return from such training in the form of larger profits resulting from higher productivity, and training would be provided whenever the return—discounted at an appropriate rate—was at least as large as the cost. Long-run competitive equilibrium requires that the present value of the return exactly equals costs.

These propositions can be stated more formally with the equations developed earlier. According to equations (5) and (7), the equilibrium of a firm providing training in competitive markets can be written as

$$MP'_0 + G\left[\sum_{t=1}^{n-1} \frac{MP_t - W_t}{(1+i)^t}\right] \quad (11)$$
$$= W_0 + C,$$

where C is the cost of training given only in the initial period, MP'_0 is the opportunity marginal product of trainees, W_0 is the wage paid to trainees, and W_t and MP_t are the wage and marginal product in period t. If the analysis of completely specific training given in the preceding paragraph is correct, W would always equal the wage that could be received elsewhere, $MP_t - W_t$ would be the full return in t from training given in 0, and G would be the present value of these returns. Since MP'_0 measures the marginal product elsewhere and W_0 measures the wage elsewhere of trainees, MP'_0 equals W_0. As a consequence G equals C, or, in full equilibrium, the return from training equals costs.

Before claiming that the usual equality between marginal product and wages holds when completely specific training is considered, the reader should bear in mind two points. The first is that the equality between wages and marginal product in the initial period involves opportunity, not actual marginal product. Wages would be greater than actual marginal product if some productivity was foregone as part of the training program. The second is that, even if wages equaled marginal product initially, they would be less in the future because the differences between future marginal products and wages constitute the return to training and are collected by the firm.

All of this follows from the assumption that firms pay all costs and collect all returns. But could not one equally well argue that workers pay all specific training costs by receiving appropriately lower wages initially and collect all returns by receiving wages equal to marginal product later? In terms of equation (11), W_t would equal MP_t, G would equal zero, and W_0 would equal $MP'_0 - C$, just as with general training. Is it more plausible that firms rather than workers pay for and collect and return from training?

An answer can be found by reasoning along the following lines. If a firm had paid for the specific training of a worker who quit to take another job, its capital expenditure would be partly wasted, for no further return could be collected. Likewise, a worker fired after he had paid for specific training would be unable to collect any further return and would also suffer a capital loss. The willingness of workers or firms to pay for specific training should, therefore, closely depend on the likelihood of labor turnover.

To bring in turnover at this point may seem like a *deus ex machina* since it is almost always ignored in traditional theory. In the usual analysis of competitive firms, wages equal marginal product, and since wages and marginal product are assumed to be the same in many firms, no one suffers from turnover. It would not matter whether a firm's labor force always contained the same persons or a rapidly changing group. Any person leaving one firm could do equally well in other firms, and his employer could replace him without any change in profits. In other words, turnover is ignored in traditional theory because it plays no important role within the framework of the theory.

Turnover becomes important when costs are imposed on workers or firms, which are precisely the effects of specific training. Suppose a firm paid all the specific training costs of a worker who quit after completing it. According to our earlier analysis, he would have been receiving the market wage and a new employee could be hired at the same wage. If the new employee were not given training, his marginal product would be less than that of the one who quit since presumably training raised the latter's productivity. Training could raise the new employee's productivity but would require additional expenditures by the firm. In other words, a firm is hurt by the departure of a trained employee because an equally profitable new employee could not be obtained. In the same way an employee who pays for specific training would suffer a loss from being laid off because he could not find an equally good job elsewhere. To bring turnover into the analysis of specific training is not, therefore, a *deus ex machina* but is made necessary by the important link between them.

Firms paying for specific training might take account of turnover merely by obtaining a sufficiently large return from those remaining to counterbalance the loss from those leaving. (The return on "successes"— those remaining—would, of course, overestimate the average return on all training expenditures.) Firms could do even better, however, by recognizing that the likelihood of a quit is not fixed but depends on wages. Instead of merely recouping on successes what is lost on failures, they might reduce the likelihood of failure itself by offering higher wages after training than could be received elsewhere. In effect, they would offer employees some of the return from training. Matters would be improved in some respects but worsened in others, for the higher wage would make the supply of trainees greater than the demand, and rationing would be required. The final step would be to shift some training costs as well as returns to employees, thereby bringing supply more in line with demand. When the final step is completed, firms no longer pay all training costs nor do they collect all the return but they share both with employees.[14]

[14] A. Marshall (*Principles of Economics*, 8th ed., New York, 1949, p. 626) was clearly aware of specific talents and their effect on wages and productivity: "Thus the head clerk in a business has an acquaintance with men and things, the use of which he could in some cases sell at a high price to rival firms. But in other cases it is of a kind to be of no value save to the business in which he already is; and *then his departure would perhaps injure it by several times the value of his salary,* while probably he could not get half that *salary elsewhere.*" (My italics.) However, he overstressed the element of indeterminacy in these wages ("their earnings are determined . . . by a bargain between them and their employers, the terms of which are theoretically arbitrary") because he ignored the effect of wages on turnover (*ibid.*, fn. 2).

The shares of each depend on the relations between quit rates and wages, layoff rates and profits, and on other factors not discussed here, such as the cost of funds, attitudes toward risk, and desires for liquidity.[15]

If training were not completely specific, productivity would increase in other firms as well, and the wage that could be received elsewhere would also increase. Such training can be looked upon as the sum of two components, one completely general, the other completely specific; the former would be relatively larger, the greater the effect on wages in other firms relative to the firms providing the training. Since firms do not pay any of the completely general costs and only part of the completely specific costs, the fraction of costs paid by firms would be inversely related to the importance of the general components, or positively related to the specificity of the training.

Our conclusions can be stated formally in terms of the equations developed earlier. If G is the present value of the return from training collected by firms, the fundamental equation is

$$MP' + G = W + C. \qquad (12)$$

If G' measures the return collected by employees, the total return, G'', would be the sum of G and G'. In full equilibrium the total return would equal total costs, or $G'' = C$. Let a represent the fraction of the total return collected by firms. Since $G = aG''$ and $G'' = C$, equation (12) can be written as

$$MP' + aC = W + C, \qquad (13)$$

or

$$W = MP' - (1 - a)C.^{16} \qquad (14)$$

---

[15] The rate used to discount costs and returns is the sum of a (positive) rate measuring the cost of funds, a (positive or negative) risk premium, and a liquidity premium that is presumably positive since capital invested in specific training is very illiquid (see the discussion in section 2 of Chapter III [Reading 13 in this text—Eds.]).

[16] If G'' did not equal C, these equations would be slightly more complicated. Suppose, for example, $G'' = G + G' = C + n$, $n \geq 0$, so that the present value of the total return would be

Employees pay the same fraction of costs, $1 - a$, as they collect in returns, which generalizes the results obtained earlier. For if training were completely general, $a = 0$, and equation (14) reduces to equation (10); if firms collected all the return from training, $a = 1$, and (14) reduces to $MP'_0 = W_0$; and if $0 < a < 1$, none of the earlier equations is satisfactory.

A few major implications of this analysis of specific training are now developed.

Rational firms pay generally trained employees the same wage and specifically trained employees a higher wage than they could get elsewhere. A reader might easily believe the contrary—namely, that general training would command a higher wage relative to alternatives than specific training does, since, after all, competition for persons with the latter is apt to be weaker than for those with the former. This view, however, overlooks the fact that general training raises the wages that could be received elsewhere while (completely) specific training does not, so a comparison with alternative wages gives a misleading impression of the *absolute* effect on wages of different types of training. Moreover, firms are not too concerned about the turnover of employees with general training and have no incentive to offer them a premium above wages elsewhere because the cost of such training is borne entirely by employees. Firms are concerned about the turnover of employees with specific training, and a premium is offered to reduce their turnover because firms pay part of their training costs.

The part of specific training paid by employees has effects similar to those discussed earlier for general training: it is also paid by a reduction in wages during the training period, tends to make age-earnings profiles steeper and more concave, etc. The part paid by firms has none of these implications,

---

greater than total costs. Then $G = aG'' = aC + an$, and

$$MP' + aC + an = W + C,$$

or

$$W = MP' - [(1 - a)C - an].$$

since current or future wages would not be affected.

Specific, unlike general, training produces certain "external" effects, for quits prevent firms from capturing the full return on costs paid by them, and layoffs do the same to employees. These, however, are external *diseconomies* imposed on the employees or employers of firms providing the training, not external economies accruing to other firms.

Employees with specific training have less incentive to quit, and firms have less incentive to fire them, than employees with no training or general training, which implies that quit and layoff rates are inversely related to the amount of specific training. Turnover should be least for employees with extremely specific training and most for those receiving such general training that productivity is raised less in the firms providing the training than elsewhere (as, say, in schools). These propositions are as applicable to the large number of irregular quits and layoffs that continually occur as to the more regular cyclical and secular movements in turnover; in this section, however, only the more regular movements are discussed.

Consider a firm that experiences an unexpected decline in demand for its output, the rest of the economy being unaffected. The marginal product of employees without specific training—such as untrained or generally trained employees—presumably equaled wages initially, and their employment would now be reduced to prevent their marginal productivity from falling below wages. The marginal product of specifically trained employees initially would have been greater than wages. A decline in demand would reduce these marginal products too, but as long as they were reduced by less than the initial difference with wages, firms would have no incentive to lay off such employees. For sunk costs are sunk, and there is no incentive to lay off employees whose marginal product is greater than wages, no matter how unwise it was, in retrospect, to invest in their training. Thus workers with specific training seem less likely to be laid off as a consequence of a decline in demand than untrained or even generally trained workers.[17]

If the decline in demand were sufficiently great so that even the marginal product of specifically trained workers was pushed below wages, would the firm just proceed to lay them off until the marginal product was brought into equality with wages? To show the danger here, assume that all the cost of and return from specific training was paid and collected by the firm. Any worker laid off would try to find a new job, since nothing would bind him to the old one.[18] The firm might be hurt if he did find a new job, for the firm's investment in his training might be lost forever. If specifically trained workers were not laid off, the firm would lose now because marginal product would be less than wages but would gain in the future if the decline in demand proved temporary. There is an incentive, therefore, not to lay off workers with specific training when their marginal product is only temporarily below wages, and the larger a firm's investment the greater the incentive not to lay them off.

A worker collecting some of the return from specific training would have less incentive to find a new job when temporarily laid off than others would: he does not want to lose his investment. His behavior while laid off in turn affects his future chances of being laid off, for if it were known that he would not readily take another job, the firm could lay him off without much fear of losing its investment.

These conclusions can be briefly summarized. If one firm alone experienced an unexpected decline in demand, relatively few workers with specific training would be laid off, if

[17] A very similar argument is developed by Walter Oi in "Labor as a Quasi-fixed Factor of Production," unpublished Ph.D. dissertation, University of Chicago, 1961. Also, see his article with almost the same title in *Journal of Political Economy*, December 1962.

[18] Actually one need only assume that the quit rate of laid-off workers tends to be significantly greater than that of employed workers, if only because the opportunity cost of searching for another job is less for laid-off workers.

only because their marginal product was initially greater than their wage. If the decline were permanent, all workers would be laid off when their marginal product became less than their wage and all those laid off would have to find jobs elsewhere. If the decline were temporary, specifically trained workers might not be laid off even though their marginal product was less than their wage because the firm would suffer if they took other jobs. The likelihood of their taking other jobs would be inversely related, and therefore the likelihood of their being laid off would be positively related, to the extent of their own investment in training.

The analysis can easily be extended to cover general declines in demand; suppose, for example, a general cyclical decline occurred. Assume that wages were sticky and remained at the initial level. If the decline in business activity were not sufficient to reduce the marginal product below the wage, workers with specific training would not be laid off even though others would be, just as before. If the decline reduced marginal product below wages, only one modification in the previous analysis is required. A firm would have a greater incentive to lay off specifically trained workers than when it alone experienced a decline because laid-off workers would be less likely to find other jobs when unemployment was widespread. In other respects, the implications of a general decline with wage rigidity are the same as those of a decline in one firm alone.

The discussion has concentrated on layoff rates, but the same kind of reasoning shows that a rise in wages elsewhere would cause fewer quits among specifically trained workers than among others. For specifically trained workers initially receive higher wages than are available elsewhere and the wage rise elsewhere would have to be greater than the initial difference before they would consider quitting. Thus both the quit and layoff rate of specifically trained workers would be relatively low and fluctuate relatively less during business cycles. These are important implications that can be tested with the data available.

Although quits and layoffs are influenced by considerations other than investment costs, some of these, such as pension plans, are more strongly related to investments than may appear at first blush. A pension plan with incomplete vesting privileges[19] penalizes employees who quit before retirement and thus provides an incentive—often an extremely powerful one—not to quit. At the same time pension plans "insure" firms against quits for they are given a lump sum—the nonvested portion of payments—whenever a worker quits. Insurance is needed for specifically trained employees because their turnover would impose capital losses on firms. Firms can discourage such quits by sharing training costs and the return with employees, but they would have less need to discourage them and would be more willing to pay for training costs if insurance were provided. The effects on the incentive to invest in one's employees may have been a major stimulus to the development of pension plans with incomplete vesting.[20]

An effective long-term contract would insure firms against quits, just as pensions do and also insure employees against layoffs. Firms would be more willing to pay for all kinds of training—assuming future wages were set at an appropriate level—since a contract, in effect, converts all training into completely specific training. A casual reading of history suggests that long-term contracts have, indeed, been primarily a means of inducing firms to undertake large investments in employees. These contracts are seldom used today in the United States,[21] and while they have declined in importance over time, they were probably always the

[19] According to the as yet unpublished National Bureau study of pensions, most plans have incomplete vesting.
[20] This economic function of incomplete vesting should caution one against conceding to the agitation for more liberal vesting privileges. Of course, in recent years pensions have also been an important tax-saving device, which certainly has been a crucial factor in their mushrooming growth.
[21] The military and the entertainment industry are the major exceptions.

exception here largely because courts have considered them a form of involuntary servitude. Moreover, any enforcible contract could at best specify the hours required on a job, not the quality of performance. Since performance can vary widely, unhappy workers could usually "sabotage" operations to induce employers to release them from contracts.

Some training may be useful not in most firms nor in a single firm, but in a set of firms defined by product, type of work, or geographical location. For example, carpentry training would raise productivity primarily in the construction industry, and French legal training would not be very useful in the United States. Such training would tend to be paid by trainees, since a single firm could not readily colllect the return,[22] and in this respect would be the same as general training. In one respect, however, it is similar to specific training. Workers with training "specific" to an industry, occupation, or country are less likely to leave that industry, occupation, or country than other workers, so their industrial, occupational, or country "turnover" would be less than average. The same result is obtained for specific training, except that a firm rather than an industry, occupation, or country is used as the unit of observation in measuring turnover. An analysis of specific training, therefore, is helpful also in understanding the effects of certain types of "general" training.

Although a discrepancy between marginal product and wages is frequently taken as evidence of imperfections in the competitive system, it would occur even in a perfectly competitive system where there is investment in specific training. The investment approach provides a very different interpretation of some common phenomena, as can be seen from the following examples.

A positive difference between marginal product and wages is usually said to be evidence of monopsony power; just as the ratio of product price to marginal cost has been suggested as a measure of monopoly power, so has the ratio of marginal product to wages been suggested as a measure of monopsony power. But specific training would also make this ratio greater than one. Does the difference between the marginal product and the earnings of major-league baseball players, for example, measure monopsony power or the return on a team's investment? Since teams do spend a great deal on developing players, some and perhaps most of the difference must be considered a return on investment (even if there were no uncertainty about the abilities of different players).[23]

Earnings might differ greatly among firms, industries, and countries and yet there might be relatively little worker mobility. The usual explanation would be that workers were either irrational or faced with formidable obstacles in moving. However, if specific[24] training were important, differences in earnings would be a misleading estimate of what "migrants" could receive, and it might be perfectly rational not to move. For example, although French lawyers earn less than American lawyers, the average French lawyer could not earn the average American legal income simply by migrating to the United States, for he would have to invest in learning English and American law and procedures.[25]

[22] Sometimes firms cooperate in paying training costs, especially when training apprentices (see *A Look at Industrial Training in Mercer County, N. J.*, Washington, 1959, p. 3).

[23] S. Rottenberg ("The Baseball Players' Labor Market," *Journal of Political Economy*, June 1956, p. 254 [Reading 11, pp. 140–155, in this text—Eds.]) argues that the strong restrictions on entry of teams into the major leagues is prima-facie evidence that monopsony power is important, but the entry or threat of new *leagues*, such as have occurred in professional basketball and football, is a real possibility. And, of course, new teams have entered in recent years.

[24] Specific, that is, to the firms, industries, or countries in question.

[25] Of course, persons who have not yet invested in themselves would have an incentive to migrate, and this partly explains why young persons migrate more than older ones. For a further explanation,

In extreme types of monopsony, exemplified by an isolated company town, job alternatives for both trained and untrained workers are nil, and all training, no matter what its nature, would be specific to the firm. Monopsony combined with control of a product or an occupation (due, say, to antipirating agreements) converts training specific to that product or occupation into firm-specific training. These kinds of monopsony increase the importance of specific training and thus the incentive to invest in employees.[26] The effect on training of less extreme monopsony positions is more difficult assess. Consider the monopsonist who pays his workers the best wage available elsewhere. I see no reason why training should have a systematically different effect on the foregone earnings of his employees than of those in competitive firms and, therefore, no reason why specific training should be more (or less) important to him. But monopsony power as a whole, including the more extreme manifestations, would appear to increase the importance of specific training and the incentive for firms to invest in human capital.

2. Schooling

A school can be defined as an institution specializing in the production of training, as distinct from a firm that offers training in conjunction with the production of goods. Some schools, like those for barbers, specialize in one skill, while others, like universities, offer a large and diverse set. Schools and firms are often substitute sources of particular skills. This substitution is evidenced by the shift over time, for instance, in law from apprenticeships in law firms to law schools and in engineering from on-the-job experience to engineering schools.[27]

Some types of knowledge can be mastered better if simultaneously related to a practical problem; others require prolonged specialization. That is, there are complementary elements between learning and work and between learning and time. Most training in the construction industry is apparently still best given on the job, while the training of physicists requires a long period of specialized effort. The development of certain skills requires both specialization and experience and can be had partly from firms and partly from schools. Physicians receive apprenticeship training as interns and residents after several years of concentrated instruction in medical schools. Or, to take an example closer to home, a research economist spends not only many years in school but also a rather extensive apprenticeship in mastering the "art" of empirical and theoretical research. The complementary elements between firms and schools depend in part on the amount of formalized knowledge available: price theory can be formally presented in a course, while a formal statement of the principles used in gathering and handling empirical materials is lacking. Training in a new industrial skill is usually first given on the job, since firms tend to be the first to be aware of its value, but as demand develops, some of the training shifts to schools.

A student does not work for pay while in school but may do so after or before school, or during vacations. His earnings are usually less than if he were not in school since he cannot work as much or as regularly. The difference between what could have been and what is earned (including any value placed on foregone leisure) is an important indirect cost of schooling. Tuition, fees, books, supplies, and unusual transportation and lodging expenses are other, more

---

see the discussion in Chapter III [Reading 13 in this text—Eds.]); also see the paper by L. Sjaastad, "The Costs and Returns of Human Migration," *Investment in Human Beings*, pp. 80–93 [Reading 18 in this text—Eds.].

[26] A relatively large difference between marginal product and wages in monopsonies might measure, therefore, the combined effect of economic power and a relatively large investment in employees.

[27] State occupational licensing requirements often permit on-the-job training to be substituted for school training (see S. Rottenberg, "The Economics of Occupational Licensing," *Aspects of Labor Economics*, pp. 3–20).

direct, costs. *Net* earnings can be defined as the differences between actual earnings and direct school costs. In symbols,

$$W = MP - k, \quad (15)$$

where MP is actual marginal product (assumed equal to earnings) and k is direct costs. If MP_0 is the marginal product that could have been received, equation (15) can be written as

$$\begin{aligned} W &= MP_0 - (MP_0 - MP + k) \\ &= MP_0 - C, \end{aligned} \quad (16)$$

where C is the sum of direct and indirect costs and where net earnings are the difference between potential earnings and total costs. These relations should be familiar since they are the same as those derived for general on-the-job training, which suggests that a sharp distinction between schools and firms is not always necessary: for some purposes schools can be treated as a special kind of firm and students as a special kind of trainee. Perhaps this is most apparent when a student works in an enterprise controlled by his school, which frequently occurs at many colleges.

Our definition of student net earnings may seem strange since tuition and other direct costs are not usually subtracted from "gross" earnings. Note, however, that indirect school costs are implicitly subtracted, for otherwise earnings would have to be defined as the sum of observed and foregone earnings, and foregone earnings are a major cost of high-school, college, and adult schooling. Moreover, earnings of on-the-job trainees would be net of *all* their costs, including direct "tuition" costs. Consistent accounting, which is particularly important when comparing earnings of persons trained in school and on the job, would require that earnings of students be defined in the same way.[28]

Regardless of whether all costs or merely indirect costs are subtracted from potential earnings, schooling would have the same kind of implications as general on-the-job training. Thus schooling would steepen the age-earnings profile, mix together the income and capital accounts, introduce a negative relation between the permanent and current earnings of young persons, and (implicitly) provide for depreciation on its capital. This supports my earlier assertion that an analysis of on-the-job training leads to general results that apply to other kinds of investment in human capital as well.

3. Other Knowledge

On-the-job and school training are not the only activities that raise real income primarily by increasing the knowledge at a person's command. Information about the prices charged by different sellers would enable a person to buy from the cheapest, thereby raising his command over resources; information about the wages offered by different firms would enable him to work for the firm paying the highest. In both examples, information about the economic system and about consumption and production possibilities is increased, as distinct from knowledge of a particular skill. Information about the political or social system—the effect of different parties or social arrangements—could also significantly raise real incomes.[29]

Let us consider in more detail investment in information about employment opportunities. A better job might be found by spending money on employment agencies and situation-wanted ads, by using one's time to examine want ads, by talking to friends and visiting firms, or in Stigler's language by "search."[30] When the new job requires geographical movement, additional time and resources would be spent in mov-

---

[28] Students often have negative net earnings and in this respect differ from most on-the-job trainees, although at one time many apprentices also had negative earnings.

[29] The role of political knowledge is systematically discussed in A. Downs, *An Economic Theory of Democracy*, New York, 1957, and more briefly in my "Competition and Democracy," *Journal of Law and Economics*, October 1958.

[30] See G. J. Stigler, "Information in the Labor Market," *Investment in Human Beings*, pp. 94–105 [Reading 16 in this text—Eds.].

ing.³¹ These expenditures constitute an investment in information about job opportunities that would yield a return in the form of higher earnings than would otherwise have been received. If workers paid the costs and collected the return, an investment in search would have the same implications about age-earnings profiles, depreciation, etc., as general on-the-job training and schooling, although it must be noted that the direct costs of search, like the direct costs of schooling, are usually added to consumption rather than deducted from earnings. If firms paid the costs and collected the return, search would have the same implications as on-the-job specific training.

Whether workers or firms pay for search depends on the effect of a job change on alternatives: the larger the number of alternatives made available by a change, the large (not the smaller) is the fraction of costs that have to be paid by workers. Consider a few examples. Immigrants to the United States have usually found many firms that could use their talents, and these firms would have been reluctant to pay the high cost of transporting workers to the United States. In fact immigrants have almost always had to pay their own way. Even a system of contract labor, which was seen to be a means of protecting firms against turnover, was singularly unsuccessful in the United States and has been infrequently used.³² Firms that are relatively insulated from competition in the labor market have an incentive to pay the costs of workers coming from elsewhere since they have little to worry about in the way of competing neighboring firms. In addition, firms would be willing partly to pay for search within a geographical area because some costs—such as an employment agency's fee—would be specific to the firm doing the hiring since they must be repeated at each job change.

4. Productive Wage Increases

One way to invest in human capital is to improve emotional and physical health. In Western countries today earnings are much more closely geared to knowledge than to strength, but in an earlier day, and elsewhere still today, strength had a significant influence on earnings. Moreover, emotional health increasingly is considered an important determinant of earnings in all parts of the world. Health, like knowledge, can be improved in many ways. A decline in the death rate at working ages may improve earning prospects by extending the period during which earnings are received; a better diet adds strength and stamina, and thus earning capacity; or an improvement in working conditions—higher wages, coffee breaks, and so on—may affect morale and productivity.

Firms can invest in the health of employees through medical examinations, lunches, or avoidance of activities with high accident and death rates. An investment in health that increased productivity to the same extent in many firms would be a general investment and would have the same effect as general training, while an investment in health that increased productivity more in the firms making it would be a specific investment and would have the same effect as specific training. Of course, most investments in health in the United States are made outside firms, in households, hospitals, and medical offices. A full analysis of the effect on earnings of such "outside" investment in health is beyond the scope of this study, but I would like to discuss a relation between on-the-job and "outside" human investments that has received much attention in recent years.

When on-the-job investments are paid by reducing earnings during the investment period, less is available for investments outside the job in health, better diet, schooling,

---

³¹ Studies of large geographical moves—those requiring both a change in employment and consumption—have tended to emphasize the job change more than the consumption change. Presumably money wages are considered to be more dispersed geographically than prices.

³² For a careful discussion of the contract-labor system in the United States, see C. Erickson, *American Industry and the European Immigrant, 1860–1885*, Cambridge, Mass., 1957.

and other factors. If these "outside" investments were more productive, some on-the-job investments would not be undertaken even though they were very productive by "absolute" standards.

Before proceeding further, one point needs to be made. The amount invested outside the job would be related to current earnings only if the capital market was very imperfect, for otherwise any amount of "outside" investment could be financed with borrowed funds. The analysis assumes, therefore, that the capital market is extremely imperfect, earnings and other income being a major source of funds.[33]

A firm would be willing to pay for investment in human capital made by employees outside the firm if it could benefit from the resulting increase in productivity. The only way to pay, however, would be to offer higher wages during the investment period than would have been offered since direct loans to employees are prohibited by assumption. When a firm gives a productive wage increase—that is, an increase that raises productivity—"outside" investments are, as it were, converted into on-the-job investments. Indeed, such a conversion is a natural way to circumvent imperfections in the capital market and the resultant dependence of the amount invested in human capital on the level of wages.

The discussion can be stated more formally. Let W represent wages in the absence of any investment, and let a productive wage increase costing an amount C be the only on-the-job investment. Total costs to the firm would be $\pi = W + C$, and since the investment cost is received by employees as higher wages, π would also measure total wages. The cost of on-the-job training is not received as higher wages, so this formally distinguishes a productive wage increase from other on-the-job investments. The term MP can represent the marginal product of employees when wages equal W, and G the gain to firms from the investment in higher wages. In full equilibrium,

$$MP + G = W + C = \pi. \quad (17)$$

Investment would not occur if the firm's gain was nil ($G = 0$), for then total wages (π) would equal the marginal product (MP) when there is no investment.

It has been shown that firms would benefit more from on-the-job investment the more specific the productivity effect, the greater their monopsony power, and the longer the labor contract; conversely, the benefit would be less the more general the productivity effect, the less their monopsony power, and the shorter the labor contract. For example, a wage increase spent on a better diet with an immediate impact on productivity might well be granted,[34] but not one spent on general education with a very delayed impact.[35]

---

[33] Imperfections in the capital market with respect to investment in human capital are discussed in section 2 of Chapter III [Reading 13 in this text—Eds.].

[34] The more rapid the impact, the more likely it is that it comes within the (formal or de facto) contract period. Leibenstein apparently initially assumed a rapid impact when discussing wage increases in underdeveloped countries (see his "The Theory of Underemployment in Backward Economies," *Journal of Political Economy*, April 1957). In a later comment he argued that the impact might be delayed ("Underemployment in Backward Economies: Some Additional Notes," *Journal of Political Economy*, June 1958).

[35] Marshall (*Principles of Economics*, p. 566) discusses delays of a generation or more and notes that profit-maximizing firms in competitive industries have no incentive to grant such wage increases.

"Again, in paying his workpeople high wages and in caring for their happiness and culture, the liberal employer confers benefits which do not end with his own generation. For the children of his workpeople share in them, and grow up stronger in body and in character than otherwise they would have done. The price which he has paid for labour will have borne the expenses of production of an increased supply of high industrial faculties in the next generation: but these faculties will be the property of others, who will have the right to hire them out for the best price they will fetch: neither he nor even his heirs can reckon on reaping much material reward for this part of the good that he has done."

The effect of a wage increase on productivity depends on the way it is spent, which in turn depends on tastes, knowledge, and opportunities. Firms might exert an influence on spending by exhorting employees to obtain good food, housing, and medical care, or even by requiring purchases of specified items in company stores. Indeed, the company store or truck system in nineteenth century Great Britain has been interpreted as partly designed to prevent an excessive consumption of liquor and other debilitating commodities.[36] The prevalence of employer paternalism in underdeveloped countries has frequently been accepted as evidence of a difference in temperament between East and West. An alternative interpretation suggested by our study is that an increase in consumption has a greater effect on productivity in underdeveloped countries, and that a productivity advance raises profits more there either because firms have more monopsony power or because the advance is less delayed. In other words "paternalism" may simply be a way of investing in the health and welfare of employees in underdeveloped countries.

An investment in human capital would usually steepen age-earnings profiles, lowering reported earnings during the investment period and raising them later on. But an investment in an increase in earnings may have precisely the opposite effect, raising reported earnings more during the investment period than later and thus flattening age-earning profiles. The cause of this difference is simply that reported earnings during the investment period tend to be net of the cost of general investments and gross of the cost of an increase in productive earnings.[37]

The productivity of employees depends not only on their ability and the amount invested in them both on and off the job but also on their motivation, or the intensity of their work. Economists have long recognized that motivation in turn partly depends on earnings because of the effect of an increase in earnings on morale and aspirations. Equation (17), which was developed to show the effect of investments outside the firm financed by an increase in earnings, can also show the effect of an increase in the intensity of work "financed" by an increase in earnings. Thus W and MP would show initial earnings and productivity, C the increase in earnings, and G the gain to firms from the increase in productivity caused by the "morale" effect of the increase in earnings. The incentive to grant a morale-boosting increase in earnings, therefore, would depend on the same factors as does the incentive to grant an increase used for outside investments. Many recent discussions of wages in underdeveloped countries have stressed the latter,[38] while earlier discussions often stressed the former.[39]

[36] See G. W. Hilton, "The British Truck System in the Nineteenth Century," *Journal of Political Economy*, April 1957, pp. 246–247.

[37] If E represents reported earnings during the investment period and MP the marginal product when there is no investment, $E = MP - C$ with a general investment, $E = MP$ with a specific investment paid by the firm, and $E = MP + C$ with an increase in productive earnings.

[38] See Leibenstein, *Journal of Political Economy*, April 1957, and H. Oshima, "Underdevelopment in Backward Economies: An Empirical Comment," *Journal of Political Economy*, June 1958.

[39] For example, Marshall stressed the effect of an increase in earnings on the character and habits of working people (*Principles of Economics*, pp. 529–532, 566–569).

13
Investment in Human Capital: Rates of Return

Gary S. Becker

The most important single determinant of the amount invested in human capital may well be its profitability or rate of return, but the effect on earnings of a change in the rate of return has been difficult to distinguish empirically from a change in the amount invested. For since investment in human capital usually extends over a long and variable period, the amount invested cannot be determined from a known "investment period." Moreover, the discussion of on-the-job training clearly indicated that the amount invested is often merged with gross earnings into a single net earnings concept (which is gross earnings minus the cost of or plus the return on investment).

1. Relation Between Earnings, Costs, and Rates of Return

In this section, some important relations between earnings, investment costs, and rates of return are derived. They permit one to distinguish, among other things, a change in the return from a change in the amount invested. The discussion proceeds in stages from simple to complicated situations. First, investment is restricted to a single period and returns to all remaining periods; then investment is distributed over a known group of periods called the investment period. Finally, it is shown how the rate of return, the amount invested, and the investment period can all be derived from information on net earnings alone.

The discussion is from the viewpoint of workers, and is, therefore, restricted to general investments; since the analysis of specific investments and firms is very similar, its discussion is omitted.

Let Y be an activity providing a person entering at a particular age, called age zero, with a real net earnings stream of Y_0 during the first period, Y_1 during the next period, and so on until Y_n during the last period. The general term "activity" rather than occupation or another more concrete term is used in order to indicate that any kind of

Reprinted from Gary S. Becker, *Human Capital* (New York: National Bureau of Economic Research, 1964), pp. 37–66. Copyright © 1964, by National Bureau of Economics Research. All Rights Reserved.

investment in human capital is permitted, not just on-the-job training but also schooling, information, health, and morale. As in the previous chapter, "net" earnings mean "gross" earnings during any period minus tuition costs during the same period. "Real" earnings are the sum of monetary earnings and the monetary equivalent of psychic earnings. Since many persons appear to believe that the term "investment in human capital" must be restricted to monetary costs and returns, let me emphasize that essentially the whole analysis applies independently of the division of real earnings into monetary and psychic components. Thus the analysis applies to health, which has a large psychic component, as well as to on-the-job training, which has a large monetary component. When psychic components dominate, the language associated with consumer durable goods might be considered more appropriate than that associated with investment goods; to simplify the presentation, investment language is used throughout.

The present value of the net earnings stream in Y would be

$$V(Y) = \sum_{j=0}^{n} \frac{Y_j}{(1+i)^{j+1}},[1] \quad (18)$$

where i is the market discount rate, assumed for simplicity to be the same in each period. If X were another activity providing a net earning stream of $X_0, X_1, \cdots X_n$, with a present value of $V(X)$, the present value of the gain from choosing Y would be given by

$$d = V(Y) - V(X)$$
$$= \sum_{j=0}^{n} \frac{Y_j - X_j}{(1+i)^{j+1}}. \quad (19)$$

Equation (19) can be reformulated to bring out explicitly the relation between costs and returns. The cost of investing in human capital equals the net earnings foregone by choosing to invest rather than choosing an activity requiring no investment. If activity Y requires an investment only in the initial period and if X does not require any, the cost of choosing Y rather than X is simply the difference between their net earnings in the initial period, and the total return would be the present value of the differences between net earnings in later periods. If $C = X_0 - Y_0$, $k_j = Y_j - X_j$, $j = 1, \cdots n$, and if R measures the total return, the gain from Y could be written as

$$d = \sum_{j=1}^{n} \frac{k_j}{(1+i)^j} - C = R - C. \quad (20)$$

The relation between costs and returns can be derived in a different and, for our purposes, preferable way by defining the internal rate of return,[2] which is simply a rate of discount equating the present value of returns to the present value of costs. In other words, the internal rate, r, is defined implicitly by the equation

$$C = \sum_{1}^{n} \frac{k_j}{(1+r)^j}, \quad (21)$$

which clearly implies

$$\sum_{j=0}^{n} \frac{Y_j}{(1+r)^{j+1}}$$
$$- \sum_{0}^{n} \frac{X_j}{(1+r)^{j+1}} = d = 0, \quad (22)$$

since $C = X_0 - Y_0$ and $k_j = Y_j - X_j$. So the internal rate is also a rate of discount equating the present values of net earnings. These equations would be considerably simplified if the return were the same in each

---

[1] The discussion assumes discrete income flows and compounding, even though a mathematically more elegant formulation would have continuous variables, with sums replaced by integrals and discount rates by continuous compounding. The discrete approach is, however, easier to follow and yields the same kind of results. Extensions to the continuous case are straightforward.

[2] A substantial literature has developed on the difference between the income gain and internal return approaches. See, for example, Friedrich and Vera Lutz, *The Theory of Investment of the Firm*, Princeton, 1951, Chap. ii, and the articles in *The Management of Corporate Capital*, Ezra Solomon, ed., Glencoe, 1959.

period, or $Y_j = X_j + k, j = 1, \cdots n$. Thus equation (21) would become

$$C = \frac{k}{r}[1 - (1+r)^{-n}], \qquad (23)$$

where $(1 + r)^{-n}$ is a correction for the finiteness of life that tends toward zero as people live longer.

If investment is restricted to a single known period, cost and rate of return are easily determined from information on net earnings alone. Since investment in human capital is distributed over many periods—formal schooling is usually more than ten years in the United States, and long periods of on-the-job training are also common—the analysis must, however, be generalized to cover distributed investment. The definition of an internal rate in terms of the present value of net earnings in different activities obviously applies regardless of the amount and duration of investment, but the definition in terms of costs and returns is not generalized so readily. If investment were known to occur in Y during each of the first m periods, a simple and superficially appealing approach would be to define the investment cost in each of these periods as the difference between net earnings in X and Y, total investment costs as the present value of these differences, and the internal rate would equate total costs and returns. In symbols,

$$C_j^1 = X_j - Y_j, j = 0, \cdots m - 1,$$

$$C^1 = \sum_0^{m-1} C_j^1 (1+r)^{-j},$$

and

$$C^1 = \frac{k}{r} \frac{(1-(1+r)^{m-1-n})}{(1+r)^{m-1}}. \qquad (24)$$

If $m = 1$, this reduces to equation (23).

Two serious drawbacks mar this appealing straightforward approach. The estimate of total costs requires a priori knowledge and specification of the investment period. While the period covered by formal schooling is easily determined, the period covered by much on-the-job training and other investment is not, and a serious error might result from an incorrect specification: to take an extreme example, total costs would approach zero as the investment period is assumed to be longer and longer.[3]

A second difficulty is that the differences between net earnings in X and Y do not correctly measure the cost of investing in Y since they do not correctly measure earnings foregone. A person who invested in the initial period could receive more than X_1 in period 1 as long as the initial investment yielded a positive return.[4] The true cost of an investment in period 1 would be the total earnings foregone, or the difference between what could have been received and what is received. The difference between X_1 and Y_1 could greatly underestimate true costs; indeed, Y_1 might be greater than X_1 even though a large investment was made in period 1.[5] In general, therefore, the amount invested in any period would be determined not only from net earnings in the same period but also from net earnings in earlier periods.

If the cost of an investment is consistently defined as the earnings foregone, quite different estimates of total costs emerge. Although superficially a less natural and straightforward approach, the generalization from a single period to distributed investment is actually greatly simplified. Therefore, let C_j be the foregone earnings in the

[3] Since

$$C^1 = \sum_0^{m-1} (X_j - Y_j)(1+r)^{-j}, \lim_{m \to n} C^1$$

$$= \sum_0^{n-1} (X_j - Y_j)(1+r)^{-j} = 0,$$

by definition of the internal rate.

[4] If C_0 was the initial investment, r_0 its internal rate, and if the return were the same in all years, the amount

$$X_1^1 = X_1 + \frac{r_0 C_0}{1 - (1+r_0)^{-n}}$$

could be received in period 1.

[5] Y_1 is greater than X_1 if

$$X_1 + \frac{r_0 C_0}{1 - (1+r_0)^{-n}} - C_1 > X_1,$$

or if $\frac{r_0 C_0}{1 - (1+r_0)^{-n}} > C_1,$

where C_1 is the investment in period 1.

j^{th} period, r_j the rate of return on C_j, and let the return per period on C_j be a constant k_j, with $k = \Sigma k_j$ being the total return on the whole investment. If the number of periods were indefinitely large, and if investment occurred only in the first m periods, the equation relating costs, returns, and internal rates would have the strikingly simple form of[6]

$$C = \sum_{0}^{m-1} C_j = \frac{k}{\bar{r}}, \quad (25)$$

where

$$\bar{r} = \sum_{0}^{m-1} w_j r_j, \quad w_j = \frac{C_j}{C},$$

and

$$\sum_{0}^{m-1} w_j = 1. \quad (26)$$

Total cost, defined simply as the sum of costs during each period, would equal the capitalized value of returns, the rate of capitalization being a weighted average of the rates of return on the individual investments. Any sequence of internal rates or investment costs is permitted, no matter what the pattern of rises and declines, or the form of investments, be they a college education, an apprenticeship, ballet lessons, or a medical examination. Different investment programs would have the same ultimate effect on earnings whenever the average rate of return and the sum of investment costs were the same.[7]

---

[6] A proof is straightforward. An investment in period j would yield a return of the amount $k_j = r_j C_j$ in each succeeding period if the number of periods were infinite and the return were the same in each. Since the total return is the sum of individual returns,

$$k = \sum_{0}^{m-1} k_j = \sum_{0}^{m-1} r_j C_j = C \sum_{0}^{m-1} \frac{r_j C_j}{C} = \bar{r}C.$$

I am indebted to Helen Raffel for important suggestions which led to this simple proof.

[7] Note that the rate of return equating the present values of net earnings in X and Y is not necessarily equal to $\bar{r}$, for it would weight the rates of return on earlier investments more heavily than $\bar{r}$ does. For example, if rates were higher on investments in earlier than in later periods, the over-all rate

Equation (25) could be given an interesting interpretation if all rates of return were the same. The term k/r would then be the value at the beginning of the mth period of all succeeding net earning differentials between X and Y discounted at the internal rate, r.[8] Total costs would equal the value also at the beginning of the mth period—which is the end of the investment period—of the first m differentials between X and Y.[9] The value of the first m differentials between X and Y must equal the value of all succeeding differentials between Y and

---

would be greater than r, and vice versa if rates were higher in later periods. Sample calculations indicate, however, that the difference between the over-all rate and $\bar{r}$ tends to be small as long as the investment period was not very long and the systematic difference between internal rates not very great.

[8] That is,

$$\sum_{j=m}^{\infty}(Y_j - X_j)(1+r)^{m-1-j}$$
$$= k \sum_{m}^{\infty}(1+r)^{m-1-j} = \frac{k}{r}.$$

[9] Since, by definition,

$$X_0 - Y_0 = C_0, \quad X_1 - Y_1 = C_1 - rC_0,$$

and more generally

$$X_j - Y_j = C_j - r\sum_{k=0}^{j-1} C_k, \quad 0 \leq j < m,$$

then

$$\sum_{j=0}^{m-1}(X_j - Y_j)(1+r)^{m-1-j}$$
$$= \sum_{j=0}^{m-1}\left(C_j - r\sum_{0}^{j-1} C_k\right)(1+r)^{m-1-j}$$
$$= \sum_{0}^{m-1} C_j \{(1+r)^{m-1-j} - r[1 + (1+r) + \ldots + (1+r)^{m-2-j}]\}$$
$$= \sum_{0}^{m-1} C_j = C.$$

The analytical difference between the naive definition of costs advanced earlier and one in terms of foregone earnings is that the former measures total costs by the value of earning differentials at the beginning of the investment period and the latter by the value at the end of the period. Therefore, $C' = C(1+r)^{1-m}$, which follows from eq. (24) when $n = \infty$.

X, since r would be the rate of return equating the present values in X and Y.

The internal rate of return and the amount invested in each of the first m periods could be estimated from the net earnings streams in X and Y alone if the rate of return were the same on all investments. For the internal rate r could be determined from the condition that the present value of net earnings must be the same in X and Y, and the amount invested in each period seriatim from the relations[10]

$$C_0 = X_0 - Y_0,$$
$$C_1 = X_1 - Y_1 + rC_0$$
$$C_j = X_j - Y_j + r \sum_{k=0}^{j-1} C_k, 0 \leq j \leq m-1.\text{[11]} \quad (27)$$

Thus costs and the rate of return can be estimated from information on net earnings. This is fortunate since the return on human capital is never empirically separated from other earnings and the cost of such capital is only sometimes and incompletely separated.

The investment period of education can be measured by years of schooling, but the periods of on-the-job training, of the search for information, and of other investments are not readily available. Happily, one need not know the investment period to estimate

---

[10] If the rate of return were not the same on all investments there would be $2m$ unknowns—C_0, ... C_{m-1}, and r_0, ... r_{m-1}—and only $m+1$ equations—the m cost definitions and the equation

$$k = \sum_{0}^{m-1} r_i C_i.$$

An additional $m-1$ relation would be required to determine the $2m$ unknowns. The condition $r_0 = r_1 = \ldots = r_{m-1}$ is only one form these $m-1$ relations can take; another is that costs decrease at certain known rates. If the latter were assumed, all the r_i could be determined from the earnings data.

[11] In econometric terminology this set of equations form a "causal chain" because of the natural time ordering provided by the aging process. Consequently, there is no identification or "simultaneity" problem.

costs and returns, since all three can be simultaneously estimated from information on net earnings. If activity X were known to have no investment (a zero investment period), the amount invested in Y during any period would be defined by

$$C_j = X_j - Y_j + r \sum_{0}^{j-1} C_k, \text{ all } j, \quad (28)$$

and total costs by

$$C = \sum_{0}^{\infty} C_j. \quad (29)$$

The internal rate could be determined in the usual way from the equality between present values in X and Y, costs in each period from equation (28), and total costs from equation (29).

The definition of costs presented here simply extends to all periods the definition advanced earlier for the investment period.[12] The rationale for the general definition is the same: investment occurs in Y whenever

---

[12] Therefore, since the value of the first m earning differentials has been shown to equal

$$\sum_{0}^{m-1} C_j$$

at period m (see footnote 9), total costs could be estimated from the value of all differentials at the end of the earning period. That is,

$$C = \sum_{0}^{\infty} C_j = \sum_{0}^{\infty} (X_j - Y_j) \infty^{-1-j}.$$

Thus the value of all differentials would equal zero at the beginning of the earning period—by definition of the internal rate—and C at the end. The apparent paradox results from the infinite horizon, as can be seen from the following equation relating the value of the first f differentials at the beginning of the gth period to costs:

$$V(f, g) = \sum_{j=0}^{f-1} (X_j - Y_j)(1+r)^{g-1-j}$$
$$= \sum_{j=0}^{f-1} C_j (1+r)^{g-f}.$$

When $f = \infty$ and $g = 0$, $V = 0$, but whenever $f = g$,

$$V = \sum_{0}^{f-1} C_j.$$

In particular, if $f = g = \infty$, $V = C$.

earnings there are below the sum of those in X and the income accruing on prior investments. If costs were found to be greater than zero before some period m and equal to zero thereafter, the first m periods would be the empirically derived investment period. But costs and returns can be estimated from equation (28) even when there is no simple investment period.

A common objection to an earlier draft of this paper was that the general and rather formal definition of costs advanced here is all right when applied to on-the-job training, schooling, and other recognized investments, but goes too far by also including as investment costs many effects that should be treated otherwise.

Thus, so the protest might run, learning would automatically lead to a convex and relatively steep earnings profile not because of any associated investment in education or training, but because the well known "learning curve" is usually convex and rather steep. Since the method presented here, however, depends only on the shape of age-earnings profiles, the effect of learning would be considered an effect of investment in human capital. I accept the argument fully; indeed, I believe that it points up the power rather than the weakness of my analysis and the implied concept of human capital.

To see this requires a fuller analysis of the effect of learning. Assume that Z permits learning and that another activity X does not and has a flat earnings profile: Z might have the profile labeled TT . . . [in Figure 12.1 of this text] and X that labeled UU. If TT were everywhere above UU—i.e., earnings in Z were greater than those in X at each age—there would be a clear incentive for some persons to leave X and enter Z. The result would be a lowering of TT and raising of UU; generally the process would continue until TT was no longer everywhere above UU, as in Figure 12.1. Earnings would now be lower in Z than in X at younger ages and higher only later on, and workers would have to decide whether the later higher earnings compensated for the lower initial earnings.

They presumably would decide by comparing the present value of earnings in Z and X, or, what is equivalent, by comparing the rate of return that equates these present values with rates that could be obtained elsewhere. They would choose Z if the present value were greater there, or if the equalizing rate were greater than those elsewhere. Therefore, they would choose Z only if the rate of return on their learning were sufficiently great, i.e., only if the returns from learning—the higher earnings later on—offset the costs of learning—the lower earnings initially. Thus choosing between activities "with a future" and "dead-end" activities involves exactly the same considerations as choosing between continuing one's education and entering the labor force—whether returns in the form of higher subsequent earnings sufficiently offset costs in the form of lower initial ones. Although learning cannot be avoided once in activities like Z, it can be avoided beforehand because workers can enter activities like X that provide little or no learning. They or society would choose learning only if it were a sufficiently good investment in the same way that they or society would choose on-the-job training if it were sufficiently profitable.

Consequently, the conclusion must be that learning is a way to invest in human capital that is formally no different from education, on-the-job training, or other recognized investments. So it is a virtue rather than a defect of our formulation of costs and returns that learning is treated symmetrically with other investments. And there is no conflict between interpretations of the shape of earning profiles based on learning theory[13] and those based on investment in human capital because the former is a special case of the latter. Of course, the fact

[13] See, for example, J. Mincer, "Investment in Human Capital and Personal Income Distribution," *Journal of Political Economy,* August 1958, pp. 287–288.

that the physical and psychological factors associated with learning theory[14] are capable of producing rather steep concave profiles, like TT and even $T'T'$ in Figure 12.1, should make one hesitate in relating them to education and other conventional investments. The converse is also true, however: the fact that many investments in human capital in a market economy would produce "the learning curve" should make one hesitate in relating it to the various factors associated with learning theory.

Another frequent criticism is that many on-the-job investments are really free in that earnings are not reduced at any age. Although this would be formally consistent with my analysis since the rate of return need only be considered infinite (in Figure 12.1, TT would be nowhere below UU), I suspect that a closer examination of the alleged "facts" would usually reveal a much more conventional situation. For example, if abler employees were put through executive training programs, as is probable, they might earn no less than employees outside the programs but they might earn less than if they had not been in training.[15] Again, the earnings of employees receiving specific training may not be reduced for the reasons presented in Reading 12. Finally, one must have a very poor opinion of the ability of firms to look out for their own interests to believe that infinite rates of return are of great importance.

So much in defense of the approach. To estimate costs empirically still requires a priori knowledge that nothing is invested in activity X. Without such knowledge, only the *difference* between the amounts invested in any two activities with known net earning streams could be estimated from the definitions in equation (28). Were this done for all available streams, the investment in any activity beyond that in the activity with the smallest investment could be determined.[16] The observed minimum investment would not be zero, however, if the rate of return on some initial investment were sufficiently high to attract everyone. A relevant question is, therefore: can the shape of the stream in an activity with zero investment be specified a priori so that the total investment in any activity can be determined?

The statement "nothing is invested in an activity" only means that nothing was invested after the age when information on earnings first became available; investment can have occurred before that age. If, for example, the data begin at age eighteen, some investment in schooling, health, or information surely must have occurred at younger ages. The earning stream of persons who do not invest after age eighteen would have to be considered, at least in part, as a return on the investment before eighteen. Indeed, in the developmental approach to child-rearing, most if not all of these earnings would be so considered.

The earning stream in an activity with no investment beyond the initial age (activity X) would be flat if the developmental approach were followed and earnings were said to result entirely from earlier investment.[17] The incorporation of learning into the concept of investment in human capital also suggests that earnings profiles would be flat were there no (additional) investment. Finally, the empirical evidence, for what it is worth, suggests that earnings profiles in unskilled occupations are quite flat. If the earnings profile in X were flat, the unobserved investment could easily be determined

---

[14] See, e.g., R. Bush and F. Mosteller, *Stochastic Models for Learning*, New York, 1955.

[15] Some indirect evidence is cited by J. Mincer "On-the-Job Training: Costs, Returns, and Some Implications," *Investment in Human Beings*, NBER Special Conference 15, supplement to *Journal of Political Economy*, October 1962, p. 53 [Reading 15, p. 201, in this text—Eds.].

[16] The technique has been applied and developed further by Mincer (*ibid.*).

[17] If C measured the cost of investment before the initial age and r its rate of return, $k = rC$ would measure the return per period. If earnings were attributed entirely to this investment, $X_i = k = rC$, where X_i represents earnings at the ith period past the initial age.

in the usual way once an assumption were made about its rate of return.

The assumption that lifetimes are infinite, although descriptively unrealistic, often yields results that are a close approximation to the truth. For example, I show later that the average rate of return on college education in the United States would be only slightly raised if people remained in the labor force indefinitely. A finite earning period has, however, a greater effect on the rate of return of investments made at later ages, say, after forty; indeed, it helps explain why schooling and other investments are primarily made at younger ages.

An analysis of finite earning streams can be approached in two ways. One simply applies the concepts developed for infinite streams and says there is disinvestment in human capital when net earnings are above the amount that could be maintained indefinitely. Investment at younger ages would give way to disinvestment at older ages until no human capital remained at death (or retirement). This approach has several important applications and is used in parts of the study. An alternative that is more useful for some purposes lets the earning period itself influence the definitions of accrued income and cost. The income resulting from an investment during period j would be defined as

$$k_j = \frac{r_j C_j}{1 - (1 + r_j)^{j-n}}, \quad (30)$$

where $n + 1$ is the earning period, and the amount invested during j would be defined by

$$C_j = X_j - Y_j + \sum_{k=0}^{k=j-1} \frac{r_k C_k}{1 - (1 + r_k)^{k-n}}. \quad (31)$$

2. The Incentive to Invest

Number of Periods

Economists have long believed that the incentive to expand and improve physical resources depends on the rate of return expected. They have been very reluctant, however, to interpret improvements in the effectiveness and amount of human resources in the same way, namely, as systematic responses or "investments" resulting in good part from the returns expected. In this section and the next one, I try to show that an investment approach to human resources is a powerful and simple tool capable of explaining a wide range of phenomena, including much that has been either ignored or given *ad hoc* interpretations. The discussion covers many topics, starting with the lifespan of activities and ending with a theory of the distribution of earnings.

An increase in the lifespan of an activity would, other things the same, increase the rate of return on the investment made in any period. The influence of lifespan on the rate of return and thus on the incentive to invest is important and takes many forms, a few of which will now be discussed.

The number of periods is clearly affected by mortality and morbidity rates; the lower they are, the longer is the expected lifespan and the larger is the fraction of a lifetime that can be spent at any activity. The major secular decline of these rates in the United States and elsewhere probably increased the rates of return on investment in human capital,[18] thereby encouraging such investment.[19] This conclusion is independent of whether the secular improvement in health

[18] I say *probably* because rates of return are adversely affected (via the effects on marginal productivity) by the increase in labor force that would result from a decline in death and sickness. If the adverse effect were sufficiently great, their decline would reduce rates of return on human capital. I am indebted to my wife for emphasizing this point.

[19] The relation between investment in training and length of life is apparently even found in the training of animals, as evidenced by this statement from a book I read to my children: "Working elephants go through a long period of schooling. Training requires about ten years and costs nearly five thousand dollars. In view of the animal's long life of usefulness [they usually live more than sixty years], this is not considered too great an investment" (M. H. Wilson, *Animals of the World*, New York, 1960).

itself resulted from investment; if so, the secular increase in rates of return would be part of the return to the investment in health.

A relatively large fraction of younger persons are in school or on-the-job training, change jobs and locations, and add to their knowledge of economic, political, and social opportunities. The main explanation may not be that the young are relatively more interested in learning, able to absorb new ideas, less tied down by family responsibilities, more easily supported by parents, or more flexible about changing their routine and place of living. One need not rely only on life-cycle effects on capabilities, responsibilities, or attitudes as soon as one recognizes that schooling, training, mobility, and the like are ways to invest in human capital and that younger people have a greater incentive to invest because they can collect the return over more years. Indeed, there would be a greater incentive even if age had no effect on capabilities, responsibilities, and attitudes.

The ability to collect returns over more years would give young persons a much greater incentive to invest even if the internal rate of return did not decline much with age. The internal rate can be seriously misleading here, as the following example indicates. If $100 invested at any age yielded $10 a year additional income forever, the rate of return would be 10 per cent at every age, and there would be no special incentive to invest at younger ages if only the rate of return were taken into account. Consider, however, a cohort of persons aged eighteen deciding when to invest. If the rate of return elsewhere were 5 per cent and if they invested immediately, the present value of the gain would be $100. If they waited five years, the present value of the gain, i.e., as of age eighteen, would only be about $78, or 22 per cent less; if they waited ten years, the present value of the gain would be under $50, or less than half. Accordingly, a considerable incentive would exist for everyone to invest immediately rather than waiting. In less extreme examples some persons might wait until older ages, but the number investing would tend to decline rapidly with age even if the rate of return did not.[20]

Although the unification of these different kinds of behavior by the investment approach is important evidence in its favor, other evidence is needed. A powerful test can be developed along the following lines.[21] Suppose that investment in human capital raised earnings for p periods only, where p varied between 0 and n. The size of p would be affected by many factors, including the rate of obsolescence since the more rapidly an investment became obsolete the smaller p would be. The advantage in being young would be less the smaller p was, since the effect of age on the rate of return would be positively related to p. For example, if p equaled two years, the rate would be the same at all ages except the two nearest the "retirement" age. If the investment approach were correct, the difference between the amount invested at different ages would be positively correlated with p, which is not surprising since an expenditure with a small p would be less of an "investment" than one with a large p, and arguments based on

[20] One clear application of these considerations can be found in studies of migration, where some writers have rejected the importance of the period of returns because migration rates decline strongly with age, at least initially, while rates of return (or some equivalent) decline slowly (see the otherwise fine paper by L. Sjaastad, "The Costs and Returns of Human Migration," *Investment in Human Beings*, pp. 89–90 [Reading 18, p. 253, in this text—Eds.]. My analysis suggests, however, that persons with a clear gain from migration have a strong incentive to migrate early and not wait even a few years. Since the persons remaining presumably have either no incentive or little incentive to migrate, it is not surprising that their migration rates should be much lower than that of all persons.

[21] This test was suggested by George Stigler's discussion of the effect of different autocorrelation patterns on the incentive to invest in information (see "The Economics of Information," *Journal of Political Economy*, June 1961, and "Information in the Labor Market" in *Investment in Human Beings*, pp. 94–105 [Reading 16, p. 233, in this text—Eds.]).

an investment framework would be less applicable. None of the life-cycle arguments seem to imply any correlation with p, so this provides a powerful test of the importance of the investment approach.

The time spent in any one activity is determined not only by age, mortality, and morbidity but also by the amount of switching between activities. Women spend less time in the labor force than men and, therefore, have less incentive to invest in market skills; tourists spend little time in any one area and have less incentive than residents of the area to invest in knowledge of specific consumption opportunities;[22] temporary migrants to urban areas have less incentive to invest in urban skills than permanent residents; and, as a final example, draftees have less incentive than professional soldiers to invest in purely military skills.

Women, tourists, and the like have to find investments that increase productivity in several activities. A woman wants her investment to be useful both as a housewife and as a participant in the labor force, or a frequent traveler wants to be knowledgeable in many environments. Such investments would be less readily available than more specialized ones—after all, an investment increasing productivity in two activities also increases it in either one alone, extreme complementarity aside, while the converse does not hold; specialists, therefore, have greater incentive to invest in themselves than others do.

Specialization in an activity would be discouraged if the market were very limited; thus the incentive to specialize and to invest in oneself would increase as the extent of the market increased. Workers would be more skilled the larger the market, not only because "practice makes perfect," which is so often stressed in discussions of the division of labor,[23] but also because a larger market would *induce* a greater investment in skills.[24] Put differently, the usual analysis of the division of labor stresses that efficiency, and thus wage rates, would be greater the larger the market, and ignores the potential earnings period in any activity, while mine stresses that this period, and thus the incentive to *become* more "efficient," would be directly related to market size. Surprisingly little attention has been paid to the latter, that is, to the influence of market size on the incentive to invest in skills.

Wage Differentials and Secular Changes

According to equation (30), the internal rate of return depends on the ratio of the return per unit of time to investment costs. A change in the return and costs by the same percentage would not change the internal rate, while a greater percentage change in the return would change the internal rate in the same direction. The return is measured by the absolute income gain, or by the absolute income difference between persons differing only in the amount of their investment. Note that absolute, not relative, income differences determine the return and the internal rate.

Occupational and educational wage differentials are sometimes measured by relative, sometimes by absolute, wage differences,[25] although no one has adequately

---

[22] This example is from Stigler, "The Economics of Information," *Journal of Political Economy*, June 1961.

[23] See, for example, A. Marshall, *Principles of Economics*, New York, 1949, Bk. IV, Chap. ix.

[24] If "practice makes perfect" means that age-earnings profiles slope upward, then according to my approach it must be treated along with other kinds of learning as a way of investing in human capital. The above distinction between the effect of an increase in the market on practice and on the incentive to invest would then simply be that the incentive to invest in human capital is increased even aside from the effect of practice on earnings.

[25] See A. M. Ross and W. Goldner, "Forces Affecting the Interindustry Wage Structure," *Quarterly Journal of Economics*, May 1950; P. H. Bell, "Cyclical Variations and Trend in Occupational Wage Differentials in American Industry since 1914," *Review of Economics and Statistics*, November 1951; F. Meyers and R. L. Bowlby, "The Interindustry Wage Structure and Productivity," *Industrial and Labor Relations Review*, October

discussed their relative merits. Since marginal productivity analysis relates the derived demand for any class of workers to the ratio of their wages to those of other inputs,[26] wage ratios are more appropriate in understanding forces determining demand. They are not, however, the best measure of forces determining supply, for the return on investment in skills and other knowledge is determined by absolute wage differences. Therefore neither wage ratios nor wage differences are uniformly the best measure, ratios being more appropriate in demand studies and differences in supply studies.

The importance of distinguishing between wage ratios and differences, and the confusion resulting from the practice of using ratios to measure supply as well as demand forces, can be illustrated by considering the effects of technological progress. If progress were uniform in all industries and neutral with respect to all factors, and if there were constant costs, initially all wages would rise by the same proportion and the prices of all goods, including the output of industries supplying the investment in human capital,[27] would be unchanged. Since wage ratios would be unchanged, firms would have no incentive initially to alter their factor proportions. Wage differences, on the other hand, would rise at the same rate as wages, and since investment costs would be unchanged, there would be an incentive to invest more in human capital, and thus to increase the relative supply of skilled persons. The increased supply would in turn reduce the rate of increase of wage differences and produce an absolute narrowing of wage ratios.

In the United States during much of the last eighty years, a narrowing of wage ratios has gone hand in hand with an increasing relative supply of skill, an association that is usually said to result from the effect of an autonomous increase in the supply of skills—brought about by the spread of free education or the rise in incomes—on the return to skill, as measured by wage ratios. An alternative interpretation suggested by the analysis here is that the spread of education and the increased investment in other kinds of human capital were in large part *induced* by technological progress (and perhaps other changes) through the effect on the rate of return, as measured by wage differences and costs. Clearly a secular decline in wage ratios would not be inconsistent with a secular increase in real wage differences if average wages were rising, and, indeed, one important body of data on wages shows a decline in ratios and an even stronger rise in differences.[28]

The interpretation based on autonomous supply shifts has been favored partly because a decline in wage ratios has erroneously been taken as evidence of a decline in the return to skill. While a decision ultimately can be based only on a detailed reexamination of the evidence,[29] the induced

---

1953; G. Stigler and D. Blank, *The Demand and Supply of Scientific Personnel*, New York, NBER, 1957, Table 11; P. Keat, "Long-Run Changes in Occupational Wage Structure, 1900–1956," *Journal of Political Economy*, December 1960.

[26] Thus the elasticity of substitution is usually defined as the percentage change in the ratio of quantities employed per 1 per cent change in the ratio of wages.

[27] Some persons have argued that only direct investment costs would be unchanged, indirect costs or foregone earnings rising along with wages. Neutral progress implies, however, the same increase in the productivity of a student's time as in his teacher's time or in the use of raw materials, so even foregone earnings would not change.

[28] Keat's data for 1906 and 1953 in the United States show both an average annual decline of 0.8 per cent in the coefficient of variation of wages and an average annual rise of 1.2 per cent in the real standard deviation. The decline in the coefficient of variation was shown in his study (*ibid.*); I computed the change in the real standard deviation from data made available to me by Keat.

[29] For those believing that the qualitative evidence overwhelmingly indicates a continuous secular decline in rates of return on human capital, I reproduce Adam Smith's statement on earnings in some professions. "The lottery of the law, therefore, is very far from being a perfectly fair lottery; and that, as well as many other liberal and honourable professions, is, in point of pecuniary gain, evidently under-recompensed" (*The Wealth of Nations*, Modern Library edition, New York, 1937,

approach can be made more plausible by considering trends in physical capital. Economists have been aware that the rate of return on capital could be rising or at least not falling while the ratio of the "rental" price of capital to wages was falling. Consequently, although the rental price of capital declined relative to wages over time, the large secular increase in the amount of physical capital per man-hour is not usually considered autonomous, but rather induced by technological and other developments that, at least temporarily, raised the return. A common explanation based on the effects of economic progress may, then, account for the increase in both human and physical capital.[30]

Risk and Liquidity

An informed, rational person would invest only if the expected rate of return were greater than the sum of the interest rate on riskless assets and the liquidity and risk premiums associated with the investment. Not much need be said about the "pure" interest rate, but a few words are in order on risk and liquidity. Since human capital is a very illiquid asset—it cannot be sold and is rather poor collateral on loans—a positive liquidity premium, perhaps a sizable one, would be associated with such capital.

The actual return on human capital varies around the expected return because of uncertainty about several factors. There has always been considerable uncertainty about the length of life, one important determinant of the return. People are also uncertain about their ability, especially younger persons who do most of the investing. In addition, there is uncertainty about the return to a person of given age and ability because of numerous events that are not predictable. The long time required to collect the return on an investment in human capital reduces the knowledge available, for knowledge required is about the environment when the return is to be received, and the longer the average period between investment and return, the less such knowledge is available.

Informed observation as well as calculations I have made suggest that there is much uncertainty about the return to human capital.[31] The response to uncertainty is determined by its amount and nature and by tastes or attitudes. Many have argued that attitudes of investors in human capital are very different from those of investors in physical capital because the former tend to be younger,[32] and young persons are supposed to be especially prone to overestimate their ability and chance of good fortune.[33] Were this view correct, a human investment which promised a large return to exceptionally able or lucky persons would be more attractive than a similar physical investment. However, a "life-cycle" explanation of attitudes toward risk may be no more valid or necessary than life-cycle explanations of why investors in human capital are relatively

---

p. 106). Since economists tend to believe that law and most other liberal professions are now overcompensated relative to nonprofessional work "in point of pecuniary gain," the return to professional work could not have declined continuously if Smith's observations were accurate.

[30] Some quantitative evidence for the United States is discussed in Chapter VI, section 2.

[31] For example, Marshall said: "Not much less than a generation elapses between the choice by parents of a skilled trade for one of their children, and his reaping the full results of their choice. And meanwhile the character of the trade may have been almost revolutionized by changes on which some probably threw long shadows before them, but others were such as could not have been foreseen even by the shrewdest persons and those best acquainted with the circumstances of the trade" and "the circumstances by which the earnings are determined are less capable of being foreseen [than those for machinery]" (*Principles of Economics*, p. 571). . . .

[32] Note that our argument above implied that investors in human capital would be younger.

[33] Smith said: "The contempt of risk and the presumptuous hope of success, are in no period of life more active than at the age at which young people choose their professions" (*Wealth of Nations*, p. 109). Marshall said that "young men of an adventurous disposition are more attracted by the prospects of a great success than they are deterred by the fear of failure" (*Principles of Economics*, p. 554).

young (discussed above). Indeed, an alternative explanation of reactions to large gains has already appeared.[34]

Capital Markets and Knowledge

If investment decisions responded only to earning prospects, adjusted for risk and liquidity, the adjusted marginal rate of return would be the same on all investments. The rate of return on education, training, migration, health, and other human capital is supposed to be higher than on nonhuman capital, however, because of financing difficulties and inadequate knowledge of opportunities. These will now be discussed briefly.

Economists have long emphasized that it is difficult to borrow funds to invest in human capital because such capital cannot be offered as collateral, and courts have frowned on contracts which even indirectly suggest involuntary servitude. This argument has been explicitly used to explain the "apparent" underinvestment in education and training and also, although somewhat less explicitly, underinvestment in health, migration, and other human capital. The importance attached to capital market difficulties can be determined not only from the discussions of investment but also from the discussions of consumption. Young persons would consume relatively little, productivity and wages might be related, and some other consumption patterns would follow only if it were difficult to capitalize future earning power. Indeed, unless capital limitations applied to consumption as well as investment, the latter could be indirectly financed with "consumption" loans.[35]

Some other implications of capital market difficulties can also be mentioned:

1. Since large expenditures would be more difficult to finance, investment in, say, a college education would be more affected than in, say, short-term migration.
2. Internal financing would be common, and consequently wealthier families would tend to invest more than poorer ones.
3. Since employees' specific skills are part of the intangible assets or good will of firms and can be offered as collateral along with tangible assets, capital would be more readily available for specific than for general investments.
4. Some persons have argued that opportunity costs (foregone earnings) are more readily financed than direct costs because they require only to do "without," while the latter require outlays. Although superficially plausible, this view can easily be shown to be wrong: opportunity and direct costs can be financed equally readily, given the state of the capital market. If total investment costs were $800, potential earnings $1,000, and if all costs were foregone earnings, investors would have $200 of earnings to spend; if all were direct costs, they would initially have $1,000 to spend, but just $200 would remain after paying "tuition," so their *net* position would be exactly the same as before. The example can be readily generalized and the obvious inference is that indirect and direct investment costs are equivalent in imperfect as well as perfect capital markets.

While it is undeniably difficult to use the capital market to finance investments in human capital, there is some reason to doubt whether otherwise equivalent investments in physical capital can be financed much more easily. Consider an eighteen-year-old who wants to invest a given amount in equipment for a firm he is starting rather

---

[34] See M. Friedman and L. J. Savage, "The Utility Analysis of Choices Involving Risks," reprinted in *Readings in Price Theory*, G. J. Stigler and K. Boulding, eds., Chicago, 1952.

[35] A person with an income of X and investment costs of Y ($Y < X$) could either use X for consumption and receive an *investment loan* of Y, or use $X - Y$ for consumption, Y for investment, and receive a *consumption loan* of Y. He ends up with the same consumption and investment in both cases, the only difference being in the names attached to the loans.

than in a college education. What is his chance of borrowing the whole amount at a "moderate" interest rate? Very slight, I believe, since he would be untried and have a high debt-equity ratio; moreover, the collateral provided by his equipment would probably be very imperfect. He, too, would either have to borrow at high interest rates or self-finance. Although the difficulties of financing investments in human capital have usually been related to special properties of human capital, in large measure they also seem to beset comparable investments in physical capital.

A recurring theme is that young persons are especially prone to be ignorant of their abilities and of the investment opportunities available. If so, investors in human capital, being younger, would be less aware of opportunities and thus more likely to err than investors in tangible capital. I suggested earlier that investors in human capital are younger partly because of the cost in postponing their investment to older ages. The desire to acquire additional knowledge about the return and about alternatives provides an incentive to postpone any risky investment, but since an investment in human capital is more costly to postpone, it would be made earlier and presumably with less knowledge than comparable nonhuman investments. Therefore, investors in human capital may not have less knowledge *because* of their age; rather both might be a *joint* product of the incentive not to delay investing.

The eighteen-year-old in our example who could not finance a purchase of machinery might, without too much cost, postpone the investment for a number of years until his reputation and equity were sufficient to provide the "personal" collateral required to borrow funds. Financing may prove a more formidable obstacle to investors in human capital because they cannot postpone their investment so readily. Perhaps this accounts for the tendency of economists to stress capital market imperfections when discussing investments in human capital.

3. Some Effects of Human Capital

Examples

Differences in earnings among persons, areas, or time periods are usually said to result from differences in physical capital, technological knowledge, ability, or institutions (such as unionization or socialized production). The previous discussion indicates, however, that investment in human capital also has an important effect on observed earnings because earnings tend to be net of investment costs and gross of investment returns. Indeed, an appreciation of the direct and indirect importance of human capital appears to resolve many otherwise puzzling empirical findings about earnings. Consider the following examples:

1. Almost all studies show that age-earnings profiles tend to be steeper among more skilled and educated persons. I argued earlier (Reading 12, section 1) that on-the-job training would steepen age-earnings profiles, and the analysis of section 1 of this chapter generalizes the argument to all human capital. For since observed earnings are gross of returns and net of costs, investment in human capital at younger ages would reduce observed earnings then and raise them at older ages, thus steepening the age-earnings profile.[36] Likewise, investment in human

[36] According to eq. (28) earnings at age j can be approximated by

$$Y_j = X_j + \sum_{k=0}^{k=j-1} r_k C_k - C_j,$$

where X_j are earnings at j of persons who have not invested in themselves, C_k is the investment at age k, and r_k is its rate of return. The rate of increase in earnings would be at least as steep in Y as in X at each age and not only from "younger" to "older" ages if and only if

$$\frac{\Delta Y_j}{\Delta_j} \geqq \frac{\Delta X_j}{\Delta_j},$$

or

$$r_j C_j \geqq \frac{\Delta C_j}{\Delta_j}.$$

This condition is usually satisfied since $r_j C_j \geqq 0$ and the amount invested tends to decline with age.

capital would make the profile more concave.[37]

2. In recent years students of international trade theory have been somewhat shaken by findings that the United States, said to have a relative scarcity of labor and an abundance of capital, apparently exports relatively labor-intensive commodities and imports relatively capital-intensive commodities. For example, one study found that export industries pay higher wages than import-competing ones.[38]

An interpretation consistent with the Ohlin-Heckscher emphasis on the relative abundance of different factors argues that the United States has an even more (relatively) abundant supply of human than of physical capital. An increase in human capital would, however, show up as an apparent increase in labor intensity since earnings are gross of the return on such capital. Thus export industries might pay higher wages than import-competing ones primarily because they employ more skilled or healthier workers.[39]

3. Several recent studies have tried to estimate empirically the elasticity of substitution between capital and labor. Usually a ratio of the input of physical capital (or output) to the input of labor is regressed on the wage rate in different areas or time periods, the regression coefficient being an estimate of the elasticity of substitution.[40] Countries, states, or time periods that have relatively high wages and inputs of physical capital also tend to have much human capital. Just as a correlation between wages, physical capital, and human capital seems to obscure the relationship between relative factor supplies and commodity prices, so it obscures the relationship between relative factor supplies and factor prices. For if wages were high primarily because of human capital, a regression of the relative amount of physical capital on wages could give a seriously biased picture of the effect on wages of factor proportions.[41]

4. A secular increase in average earnings has usually been said to result from increases in technological knowledge and physical capital per earner. The average earner, in effect, is supposed to benefit indirectly from activities by entrepreneurs, investors, and

---

[37] Following the notation of the previous footnote, Y would be more concave than X if and only if
$$\Delta\left(\frac{\Delta Y_j}{\Delta j}\right) - \Delta\left(\frac{\Delta X_j}{\Delta j}\right)$$
$$= \Delta\left(\frac{r_j C_j}{\Delta j}\right) - \Delta\left(\frac{\Delta C_j}{\Delta j}\right) < 0.$$
The first term on the right is certain to be negative, at least eventually, because both r_j and C_j would eventually decline, while the second term would be positive because C_j would eventually decline at a decreasing rate. Consequently, the inequality would tend to hold and the earnings profile in Y would be more concave than that in X.

[38] See I. Kravis, "Wages and Foreign Trade," *Review of Economics and Statistics*, February 1956.

[39] This kind of interpretation has been put forward by many writers; see, for example, the discussion in W. Leontief, "Factor Proportions and the Structure of American Trade: Further Theoretical and Empirical Analysis," *Review of Economics and Statistics*, November 1956.

[40] Interstate estimates for several industries can be found in J. Minasian, "Elasticities of Substitution and Constant-Output Demand Curves for Labor," *Journal of Political Economy*, June 1961, pp. 261–270; intercountry estimates in Kenneth Arrow, Hollis B. Chenery, Bagicha Minhas, and Robert M. Solow, "Capital-Labor Substitution and Economic Efficiency," *Review of Economics and Statistics*, August 1961; as yet unpublished studies by Philip Nelson and Robert Solow contain both interstate and time-series estimates.

[41] Minasian's argument (in his article cited above, p. 264) that interstate variations in skill level necessarily bias his estimates toward unity is actually correct only if skill is a perfect substitute for "labor." (In correspondence Minasian stated that he intended to make this condition explicit.) If, on the other hand, human and physical capital were perfect substitutes, I have shown (in an unpublished memorandum) that the estimates would always have a downward bias, regardless of the true substitution between labor and capital. Perhaps the most reasonable assumption would be that physical capital is more complementary with human capital than with labor; I have not, however, been able generally to determine the direction of bias in this case.

D. O'Neill is currently finishing a dissertation at Columbia University in which estimates of human capital are explicitly incorporated into the cross-sectional regressions.

others. Another explanation put forward in recent years argues that earnings can rise because of direct investment in earners.[42] Instead of only benefiting from activities by others, the average earner is made a prime mover of development through the investment in himself.[43]

Ability and the Distribution of Earnings

An emphasis on human capital not only helps explain differences in earnings over time and among areas but also among persons or families within an area. This application will be discussed in greater detail than the others because a link is provided between earnings, ability, and the incentive to invest in human capital.

Economists have long been aware that conventional measures of ability—intelligence tests or aptitude scores, school grades, and personality tests—while undoubtedly relevant at times, do not reliably measure the talents required to succeed in the economic sphere. The latter consists of particular kinds of personality, persistence, and intelligence. Accordingly, some writers have gone to the opposite extreme and argued that the only relevant way to measure economic talent is by results, or by earnings themselves.[44] Persons with higher earnings would simply have more ability than others, and a skewed distribution of earnings would imply a skewed distribution of abilities. This approach goes too far, however, in the opposite direction. The main reason for relating ability to earning is to distinguish its effects from differences in education, training, health, and other such factors, and a definition equating ability and earnings *ipso facto* precludes such a distinction. Nevertheless, results are very relevant and should not be ignored.

A compromise might be reached through defining ability by earnings only when several variables have been held constant. Since the public is very concerned about separating ability from education, on-the-job training, health, and other human capital, the amount invested in such capital would have to be held constant. Although a full analysis would also hold discrimination, nepotism, luck, and several other factors constant, a reasonable first approximation would say that if two persons have the same investment in human capital, the one who earns more is demonstrating greater economic talent.

Since observed earnings are gross of the return on human capital, they are affected by changes in the amount and rate of return. Indeed, it has been shown that, after the investment period, earnings (Y) can be simply approximated by

$$Y = X + rC, \qquad (32)$$

where C measures total investment costs, r the average rate of return, and X earnings when there is no investment in human capital. If the distribution of X is ignored for now, Y would depend only on r when C was held constant, so "ability" would be measured by the average rate of return on human capital.[45]

In most capital markets the amount invested is not the same for everyone nor

---

[42] The major figure here is T. W. Schultz. Of his many articles, see especially "Education and Economic Growth" in *Social Forces Influencing American Education*, Sixtieth Yearbook of the National Society for the Study of Education, Chicago, 1961, Part II, Chap. 3.

[43] One caveat is called for, however. Since observed earnings are not only gross of the return from investments in human capital but also are net of some costs, an increased investment in human capital would both raise and reduce earnings. Although average earnings would tend to increase as long as the rate of return was positive, the increase would be less than if the cost of human capital, like that of physical capital, was not deducted from national income.

[44] Let me state again that the word "earnings" stands for real earnings, or the sum of monetary earnings and the monetary equivalent of psychic earnings.

[45] Since r is a function of C, Y would indirectly as well as directly depend on C, and therefore the distribution of ability would depend on the amount of human capital. Some persons might rank high in earnings and thus high in ability if everyone were unskilled, and quite low if education and other training were widespread.

rigidly fixed for any given person, but depends in part on the rate of return. Persons receiving a high marginal rate of return would have an incentive to invest more than others.[46] Since marginal and average rates are presumably positively correlated[47] and since ability is measured by the average rate, one can say that abler persons would invest more than others. The end result would be a positive correlation between ability and the investment in human capital,[48] a correlation with several important implications.

One is that the tendency for abler persons to migrate, continue their education,[49] and generally invest more in themselves can be explained without recourse to an assumption that noneconomic forces or demand conditions favor them at higher investment levels. A second implication is that the separation of "nature from nurture" or ability from education and other environmental factors is apt to be difficult, for high earnings would tend to signify both more ability and a better environment. Thus the earnings differential between college and high-school graduates does not measure the effect of college alone since college graduates are abler and would earn more even without the additional education. Or reliable estimates of the income elasticity of demand for children have been difficult to obtain because higher-income families also invest more in contraceptive knowledge.[50]

The main implication, however, is in personal income distribution. At least ever since the time of Pigou economists have tried to reconcile the strong skewness in the distribution of earnings and other income with a presumed symmetrical distribution of abilities.[51] Pigou's main suggestion—that property income is not symmetrically distributed—does not directly help explain the skewness in earnings. Subsequent attempts have largely concentrated on developing *ad hoc* random and other probabilistic mechanisms that have little relation to the mainstream of economic thought.[52] The approach presented here, however, offers an explanation that is not only consistent with economic analysis but actually relies on one of its fundamental tenets, namely, that the amount invested is a function of the rate of return expected. In conjunction with the effect of human capital on earnings, this tenet can explain several well-known properties of earnings distributions.

By definition, the distribution of earnings would be exactly the same as the distribution of ability if everyone invested the same amount in human capital; in particular, if ability were symmetrically distributed, earnings would also be. Equation (32) shows that the distribution of earnings would be exactly the same as the distribution of investment if all persons were equally able; again, if investment were symmetrically distributed,

---

[46] In addition, they would find it easier to invest if the marginal return and the resources of parents and other relatives were positively correlated.

[47] According to a well-known formula,

$$r_m = r_a \left(1 + \frac{1}{e_a}\right),$$

where r_m is the marginal rate of return, r_a the average rate, and e_a the elasticity of the average rate with respect to the amount invested. The rates r_m and r_a would be positively correlated unless r_a and $1/e_a$ were sufficiently negatively correlated.

[48] This kind of argument is not new; Marshall argued that business ability and the ownership of physical capital would be positively correlated: "[economic] forces . . . bring about the result that there is a far more close correspondence between the ability of business men and the size of the businesses which they own than at first sight would appear probable" (*Principles of Economics*, p. 312).

[49] The first is frequently alleged (see, for example, *ibid.*, p. 199). Evidence on the second is discussed in Chapter IV, section 2.

[50] See my "An Economic Analysis of Fertility" in *Demographic and Economic Change in Developed Countries*, Special Conference 11, Princeton for NBER, 1960.

[51] See A. C. Pigou, *The Economics of Welfare*, 4th ed., London, 1950, Part IV, Chap. ii.

[52] A sophisticated example can be found in B. Mandelbrot, "The Pareto-Lévy Law and the Distribution of Income," *International Economic Review*, May 1960. In a recent paper, however, Mandelbrot has brought in maximizing behavior (see "Paretian Distributions and Income Maximization," *Quarterly Journal of Economics*, February 1962).

earnings would also be.[53] If ability and investment both varied, earnings would tend to be skewed even when ability and investment were not, but the skewness would be small as long as the amount invested were statistically independent of ability.[54]

It has been shown, however, that abler persons would tend to invest more than others, so ability and investment would be positively correlated, perhaps quite strongly. Now the product of two symmetrical distributions is more positively skewed the higher the positive correlation between them, and might be quite skewed.[55] The economic incentive given abler persons to invest relatively large amounts in themselves does seem capable, therefore, of reconciling a strong positive skewness in earnings with a presumed symmetrical distribution of abilities.

Variations in X help explain an important difference among skill categories in the degree of skewness. The smaller the fraction of total earnings resulting from investment in human capital—the smaller rC relative to X—the more the distribution of earnings would be dominated by the distribution of X. Higher-skill categories have a greater average investment in human capital and thus presumably a larger rC relative to X. The distribution of "unskilled ability," X, would, therefore, tend to dominate the distribution of earnings in relatively unskilled categories while the distribution of a product of ability and the amount invested, rC, would dominate in skilled categories. Hence if abilities were symmetrically distributed, earnings would tend to be more symmetrically distributed among the unskilled than among the skilled.[56]

Equation (32) holds only when investment costs are small, which tends to be true at later ages, say, after age 35. Net earnings at earlier ages would be given by

$$Y_j = X_j + \sum_{0}^{j-1} r_i C_i + (-C_j), \quad (33)$$

where j refers to the current year and i to previous years, C_i measures the investment cost of age i, C_j current costs, and r_i the rate of return on C_j. The distribution of $-C_j$

---

[53] Jacob Mincer ("Investment in Human Capital and Personal Income Distribution," *Journal of Political Economy*, August 1958) concluded that a symmetrical distribution of investment in education implies a skewed distribution of earnings because he defines educational investment by school years rather than costs. If Mincer is followed in assuming that everyone was equally able, that schooling was the only investment, and that the cost of the nth year of schooling equaled the earnings of persons with $n-1$ years of schooling, then, say, a normal distribution of schooling can be shown to imply a log-normal distribution of school costs and thus a log-normal distribution of earnings.

The difference between the earnings of persons with $n-1$ and n years of schooling would be $k_n = Y_n - Y_{n-1} = r_n C_n$. Since r_n is assumed to equal r for all n, and $C_n = Y_{n-1}$, this equation becomes $Y_n = (1+r) Y_{n-1}$, and therefore

$C_1 = Y_0$
$C_2 = Y_1 = Y_0 (1+r)$
$C_3 = Y_2 = Y_1 (1+r) = Y_0 (1+r)^2$
$C_n = Y_{n-1} = \ldots = Y_0 (1+r)^{n-1}$,

or the cost of each additional year of schooling increases at a constant *rate*. Since total costs have the same distribution as $(1+r)^n$, a symmetrical, say, a normal, distribution of school years, n, implies a log-normal distribution of costs and hence by eq. (32) a log-normal distribution of earnings. I am indebted to Mincer for a helpful discussion of the comparison and especially for the stimulation provided by his pioneering work. Incidentally, his article and the dissertation on which it is based cover a much broader area than has been indicated here.

[54] For example, C. C. Craig has shown that the product of two independent normal distributions is only slightly skewed (see his "On the Frequency Function of XY," *Annals of Mathematical Statistics*, March 1936, p. 3).

[55] Craig (*ibid.*, pp. 9–10) showed that the product of two normal distributions would be more positively skewed the higher the positive correlation between them, and that the skewness would be considerable with high correlations.

[56] As noted earlier, X does not really represent earnings when there is no investment in human capital, but only earnings when there is no investment after the initial age (be it 14, 25, or 6). Indeed, the developmental approach to child-rearing argues that earnings would be close to zero if there were no investment at all in human capital. The distribution of X, therefore, would be at least partly determined by the distribution of investment before the initial age, and if it and ability were positively correlated, X might be positively skewed, even though ability was not.

would be an important determinant of the distribution of Y_j since investment is large at these ages. Hence the analysis would predict a smaller (positive) skewness at younger than at older ages partly because X would be more important relative to $\Sigma r_i C_i$ at younger ages and partly because the presumed negative correlation between $-C_j$ and $\sum_{0}^{j-1} r_i C_i$ would counteract the positive correlation between r_i and C_i.

A simple analysis of the incentive to invest in human capital seems capable of explaining, therefore, not only why the over-all distribution of earnings is more skewed than the distribution of abilities, but also why earnings are more skewed among older and skilled persons than among younger and less skilled ones. The renewed interest in investment in human capital may provide the means of bringing the theory of personal income distribution back into economics.

14
Investment in Human Capital:
A Comment

R. S. Eckaus

I. Introduction

The theoretical analysis of investment in human capital that recently appeared in this *Journal* performs a useful service by raising many relevant issues and in suggesting relationships.[1] Without wishing to ascribe to the author's results a greater degree of definitiveness than he himself claims, it seemed to this reader that certain of them were put forward with more certainty than is warranted. In general I do not want to question the logical validity of those results. Rather, it is their generality, whether they provide reasonably accurate descriptions of reality and good predictions, that I shall mainly discuss.

The analytic exemplar of the article is the discussion of on-the-job training, and it deserves to be the starting point of any criticism. From there this comment will pass briefly to some of the other issues raised.

II. Who Bears the Cost of On-the-Job Training When There Are Perfect Markets?

On-the-job training is, for nearly all of Becker's analysis, quite distinct from the production processes of a firm in the sense that inputs into training are never, to any extent, inputs into production. The decision to train or not train is, therefore, one that can be isolated and based solely on the costs and returns associated with the training procedure. In this case, according to Becker, if one makes the customary assumptions associated with perfect markets, the individual worker will bear the burden of whatever training makes a *general* contribution to his productivity.

This conclusion is certainly correct under the assumptions. Becker's reasoning on this point occurs at several places in his article.

Reprinted from the *Journal of Political Economy* (October 1963) by permission of The University of Chicago Press. Copyright, 1963, pp. 501–504.

[1] Gary S. Becker, "Investment in Human Capital: A Theoretical Analysis," *Journal of Political Economy*, LXX, Supplement (October, 1962), 9–49. Page numbers given in text in parentheses refer to this article.

197

The following quotation is intended to represent it:

> Income maximizing firms in competitive labor markets would not pay the cost of general training and would pay trained persons the market wage. If, however, training costs were paid, many persons would seek training, few would quit during the training period, and labor costs would be relatively high. Firms that did not pay trained persons the market wage have difficulty satisfying their skill requirements and would also tend to be less profitable than other firms. Firms that both paid for training and less than the market wage for trained persons would have the worst of both worlds, for they would attract too many trainees and too few trained persons [p. 16].

A slight amplification of the argument may help demonstrate the dependence of the conclusions on the particular assumptions. The complete separability of training and production costs and the perfect mobility of labor make firms into nothing more than private schools for general training. Because of competition and free mobility workers would never accept less than their marginal product. As a result, firms could never possibly afford to "invest" in any training that makes a general contribution to labor productivity because the full increment of any addition to their productivity would always be captured by workers. On the other hand, because training costs are separate and identifiable, firms can always collect the exact costs of the training offered.

According to Becker, since workers have permanent title to themselves, they face no special risks in perfect markets in investing in their own general training in order to increase their own productivity. The role of the firm in labor training under his assumptions is one of supplying information on costs and returns and of doing training. The production activities of firms are no more than sources of information. Workers would base their demand for general training on its properly discounted costs and returns. Firms would supply general training on the basis of the profitability of training activities only. The production levels and relative input proportions of the firm would, in turn, adjust to the decisions taken in the training "market."

Specific training is defined by Becker as training whose marginal productivity is higher in the firm giving the training than in other firms. The conditions of perfect markets are violated, at least on the employer side, since the training firms stands in a unique relation to its trainees. Otherwise, the assumptions of perfect markets are maintained.

"Special training" as defined by Becker would not improve the worker's productivity in other firms. As a result the firm giving such training would not face competition by other firms for the added skills of the workers who are made more capable by having had such training. Thus, no market mechanism would operate to give the worker the full benefits of special training.

The firm investing in special training would be aware, however, that if a worker left its employment it would lose its investment. How would the firm giving this type of training protect the capital created? Becker's answer to this is that the firm will always find it better to pay somewhat higher wages to eliminate labor mobility rather than to equate discounted returns and costs on investment in specific training taking into account the risks of losing workers (p. 20). Yet, if the firm wants to create some degree of labor immobility by paying higher wages, then it must regard such payments, as well as the costs of special labor training, as if they were similar to investments in physical capital with, perhaps, more than ordinary risks of losing their investment. Then the amount of the increment in wages that the firm would pay in order to confer immobility would be determined by a calculation of the returns to such a risky investment.

Suppose now that on-the-job training is an "unavoidable" joint product with the firm's regular output, that is, that neither the marginal nor average costs of production and training are completely separable. Becker mentions this case without, I believe, developing its implications (p. 20). Under these conditions the previous conclusions require some revision.

When goods, education, and other outputs are produced jointly in "fixed" proportions[2] then the marginal costs of each cannot be defined. Only the familiar equilibrium conditions for the firm must be met: that the marginal costs of both together must equal the sum of the prices of each. For each good, of course, the total quantity supplied must equal the total demanded. The costs of general training under these conditions need not be fully shifted to workers. It is, in fact, impossible to know exactly what these costs are. The firm produces; workers become better trained by example, by practice, and by maturing in a job situation. The amount that the firm will be able to extract from workers in compensation for the training is not determined by training costs. On the one hand, the firm cannot pay the worker less than his marginal productivity in goods production in any other line or the worker will make the move that his general training makes possible. On the other hand, the firm cannot avoid giving the training. The level of wages will, in turn, depend on the overall demand for labor and its supply, which will reflect the opportunities created by the training as well as opportunities in other sectors.[3]

Turning to special training as defined by Becker, if it were created in a process of joint production, the conclusions drawn above for the non-joint product case would still hold. There is no identifiable set of training costs, and there is no way for the firm to pass any part of the burden of total costs to the worker by paying less than the wages of untrained workers in alternative employment as long as there are perfect labor markets.

There are, no doubt, many instances of firms establishing facilities for training workers that are completely independent of their production facilities. However, this probably constitutes a small proportion of all on-the-job training. Apprenticeship programs, for example, are not entirely or even mainly in this category. The relatively informal, unorganized type of vocational training through casual instruction and as a joint product with actual work experience is, I believe, much more significant.

III. On-the-Job Training in Less Than Perfect Labor Markets

Let us now put aside the assumptions of perfect factor markets. Certainly it has often been argued that achievement of the results of perfect markets does not require that every participant conform to the assumptions. It does require, at least, a mechanism that rewards and punishes as if the assumptions were valid. The extent to which such a mechanism exists and operates will remain a matter of judgment. It may, however, assist in that judgment if some of the imperfections and their consequences are reviewed briefly to provide contrast with Becker's conclusions. Becker's conclusions that workers bear the cost of "general" on-the-job training and firms the cost of "specific" on-the-job training have the appeal of concreteness. Yet these conclusions, based on Becker's assumptions of perfect markets and the complete separation of production costs and training costs, must be abandoned as soon as the assumptions are dropped.

Becker does refer to market "difficulties" (p. 31), but apparently he thinks that for practical purposes they do not vitiate his analysis. Yet if, for example, there is some degree of labor immobility, that is, not perfect, free, and frictionless response to wage differentials, his conclusion that firms will never bear the cost of the on-the-job general

---

[2] "Fixity" here may imply no more than some limit to the variability of the proportions of the joint output.

[3] Of course, when general training is produced in variable proportions with output, no firm would undertake any marginal expense for training for which it was not reimbursed, just as in the non-joint production case.

training which he defines no longer holds. Under "perfect" conditions firms never would bear this cost because they could never collect any returns. But, if there is some degree of immobility, firms can collect part of the extra product training creates and therefore can consider such general training as if it were an investment in fixed capital. If, at prevailing wages, workers with the desired training do not present themselves in the numbers desired by the firm, based on its production plans, a firm may undertake to give and pay the costs of general training. In these circumstances they could rely on labor immobility to provide them with the necessary return on their investment. On the other hand labor immobility would reduce the need for firms to pay premiums above alternative wages in order to keep "specially trained" workers.

The lack of knowledge of alternatives which characterizes job markets must be recognized and the role of union bargaining in setting wages and conditions of labor. These too would interfere with Becker's conclusions on the incidence of on-the-job training costs.

Becker argues that the difficulties of financing education are similar to those for financing "comparable" investments in physical capital, reasoning, for example, that an eighteen-year-old would have just as much trouble financing physical capital as education (p. 42). Presumably the point of the story is that there is no more need to worry about imperfections in "human" capital markets than in physical capital markets. But an argument based on such an example cannot be taken seriously unless Becker wants also to propose that eighteen-year-olds undertake as significant a part of investment in physical capital as in education.

Apart from money incomes there are social status features associated with particular occupations and their training. Workers may be willing to bear all or part of the costs of specific training or refuse to bear the costs of general training, or vice versa, depending on the status aspects.

It is true that Becker recognized that there are market imperfections and obstacles to the working of the price system that impair the arguments based on perfect markets. However, he seems to regard these as only minor qualifications to the main conclusions. External economies in on-the-job training that arise from the inability of firms to collect the full benefits of such training are, for example, brushed away by Becker in his original argument (p. 21) and never brought back by his qualifications. However, if training is an unavoidable joint product with goods production, or if firms, because of various imperfections, bear part of the cost of that training that is not "joint," the price system will not necessarily fully reflect relative skill resource scarcities and costs of training.

IV. Conclusion

Economic analysis applied to labor and training can be an extremely powerful tool, as Becker shows in many interesting speculations about the sources of various labor and labor market phenomenon. He demonstrates, for example, the effects of differential amounts of education and training in creating a personal income distribution more skewed than the distribution of abilities. Other conclusions, however, depend so strictly on the assumptions of perfect factor markets that the arguments, however ingenious, must be suspect. For example, differentials in occupational wage streams would, in perfect markets, reflect the differences in "human investment." In actuality relative differences may measure primarily the significant market imperfections among occupations.

Extension of the assumptions of perfect markets for goods to areas such as education raises the danger of creating an analysis that caricatures reality. The ghost of "economic man" walks again when Becker argues that individual decisions on "outside" investments, as in better diets, health, and congenial households, are made by comparison of their productivity with the productivity of investment in education.

15
On-the-Job Training:
Costs, Returns, and
Some Implications[1]

Jacob Mincer

Introduction

In the context of the economist's concern with education as a process of investment in manpower, it is important to be reminded that formal school instruction is neither an exclusive nor a sufficient method of training the labor force. Graduation from some level of schooling does not signify the completion of a training process. It is usually the end of a more general and preparatory stage, and the beginning of a more specialized and often prolonged process of acquisition of occupational skill, after entry into the labor force. This second stage, training on the job, ranges from formally organized activities such as apprenticeships and other training programs[2] to the informal processes of learning from experience. Indeed, historically, skills have been acquired mainly by experience on the job. The vast schooling system and the delayed entry into the labor force are distinctly modern phenomena.

As history suggests, it is useful to view

Reprinted from the *Journal of Political Economy* (Supplement, October, 1962) by permission of The University of Chicago Press. Copyright, 1962, pp. 50–79.

[1] This work was stimulated and made possible by Gary Becker's fundamental theoretical analysis of investment in human capital. H. G. Lewis contributed very thoughtful and useful comments on the first version of the paper. I am also indebted for helpful comments to T. W. Schultz, G. H. Moore, G. P. Shultz, Z. Griliches, and H. Gilman. Dave O'Neill provided highly competent research assistance. Financial support by the Carnegie Corporation of New York is gratefully acknowledged.

[2] A good sample of a growing literature on the subject includes P. H. Douglas, *American Apprenticeship and Industrial Education* (New York: Columbia University Press, 1921); United States Department of Labor, Bureau of Apprenticeship and Training, *Apprenticeships Past and Present* (Washington, 1955); *Apprentice Training* (Washington, 1956); and *Employee Training in New Jersey Industry* (Washington, 1960); National Manpower Council, *A Policy for Skilled Manpower* (New York: Columbia University Press, 1954) and *Improving the Work Skills of the Nation* (New York: Columbia University Press, 1955); H. F. Clark, and H. S. Sloan, *Classrooms in the Factories* (Rutherford, N.J.: Fairleigh Dickinson College, 1958); O. N. Serbein, *Educational Activities of Business* (Washington: American Council on Education, 1961).

the two broad classes of training not only as a sequence of stages but also as alternatives or substitutes. In many cases, the same degree of occupational skill can be achieved by "shortening" formal schooling and "lengthening" on-the-job training or by the reverse. The degree of substitutability between the two will, of course, vary among jobs and over time with changes in technology.

When training is viewed as a process of capital formation in people, three major empirical questions may be raised for economic analysis. (1) How large is the allocation of resources to the training process? (2) What is the rate of return on this form of investment? (3) How useful is knowledge about such investments in explaining particular features of labor-force behavior?

Recently flourishing research in these areas provides some tentative answers.[3] T. W. Schultz estimated the amount and growth of resources devoted by the economy to formal education. G. S. Becker estimated the rate of return to training at higher levels of education. In his National Bureau of Economic Research study, now in progress, Becker outlines the capital-theoretical approach to investment in people and shows it to be a tool of great analytical power and of extensive empirical relevance.

My first task in this paper is to estimate the amount of investment in on-the-job training. The estimates are indirect, and the concept of on-the-job training rather broad, but I am hopeful that results are at least suggestive of the orders of magnitude involved. The estimates and a discussion of their limitations are given in the first section of the paper. In the second section I attempt to estimate rates of return on some particular forms of on-the-job training, such as apprenticeships and medical specialization. The results are then compared with the rates of return on investment which includes both components: formal education and on-the-job training. In consequence, some tentative inferences are formulated about the separate components. In the final section of the paper I consider some preliminary empirical implications of my results. In particular, differentials in on-the-job training are related to income and employment differentials among population subgroups, classified by levels of education, occupation, sex, and race. The observed behavior patterns seem largely consistent with the investment hypothesis underlying this study, though it was not possible in this preliminary empirical exploration to control for all other important factors at play.

I. Estimates of Costs of On-the-Job Training

For the purpose of this paper, the term "training" denotes investment in acquisition of skill or in improvement of worker productivity. The concept, therefore, includes schooling and training obtained on the job. The latter, under this definition, is a much broader concept than what is conveyed by the common usage of the word "on-the-job training." It includes formal and informal training programs in a job situation, as well as what is called "learning from experience."

The method of estimating the volume of investment in on-the-job training, which is described in this section, treats "learning from experience" as an investment in the same sense as are the more obvious forms of on-the-job training, such as, say, apprenticeship programs. Put in simple terms, an individual takes a job with an initially lower pay than he could otherwise get because he knows that he will benefit from the experience gained in the job taken.[4] In this sense,

---

[3] G. S. Becker, "Investment in People" (unpublished manuscript, National Bureau of Economic Research, 1961), and his "Underinvestment in College Education?" *American Economic Review, Papers and Proceedings*, May, 1960; T. W. Schultz, "Capital Formation in Education," *Journal of Political Economy*, December, 1960, and his "Investment in Human Capital," *American Economic Review*, March, 1961.

[4] This proposition is sometimes questioned on the basis of casual observation. Greater learning from experience is characteristic of workers with greater motivation and ability, and their earnings at the

the opportunity to learn from experience involves an investment cost which is captured in the estimation method.

While data are much more scarce and the arithmetic is more arduous, calculation of on-the-job training costs is guided by the same theoretical principles[5] as the calculation of schooling costs. Costs of schooling consist of direct outlays (private tuition and public support), and of indirect, "invisible" opportunity costs, such as foregone earnings of students resulting from the necessary reduction of their labor-force activities while at school. Once the direct outlays are known, it is possible to infer the costs of an increment of schooling from comparative data on earnings of two sets of individuals: students, and people similar to them with respect to previous educational attainment, age, sex, ability, except that they are "economically active" in the labor force and do not engage in additional schooling. In empirical work these conditions are approximated as well as data permit.

According to the available calculations,[6] foregone earnings constitute over half of total costs of schooling and about 75 per cent of the costs borne by students. Foregone earnings bulk even more in the costs borne by trainees on the job. Indeed, nowadays it is difficult to think of any important direct payments by trainees, though in the past it was not uncommon for apprentices to pay their masters for the training. This does not mean, however, that no direct outlays are incurred in the training of workers on the job. Firms do spend sizable sums to finance apprenticeships and other training programs: equipment must be purchased and instructors paid. These sums presumably appear in accounts of firms as costs of training workers, though such data are rarely available.

Should all or a part of *firm outlays* be added to the sum of *foregone earnings of workers* to arrive at a total figure of costs of on-the-job training, indirect and direct? The answer is no, if *all* of the firm outlays are currently charged to the worker in the form of a reduction in wages. In this case the worker buys training services from the firm. The cost of the purchase is simply part of his foregone earnings—the other part being the difference between the actual marginal product of the trainee and the larger amount he could produce if he did not engage in training. Adding firm outlays in this case would constitute double counting.

It is likely, however, that some fraction of firm outlays is not charged currently to the workers but recouped by the firm at a later date.[7] The part of firm outlays which is not matched by current reductions in wages of trainees should be added to foregone earnings of workers. Unfortunately, it is impossible to estimate how large a fraction of firm outlays are costs borne by the firm. Worse yet, data on costs of training (whether borne by firms or workers) are not only scarce but, in principle, highly unreliable. Such items as loss of production by experienced workers who are helping the trainees or wear and tear of equipment do not show up in any entry as direct costs of training. Rather, they are likely to be hidden in the wage and depreciation costs. Even if all costs of training were borne by firms, so that they would also pay all the foregone

---

early stages of the career may in some cases be as high or higher than those of other workers. But such finding that people with greater ability have higher productivity than others at any given stage of experience does not negate the existence of investment in on-the-job training, though it may bias the estimation of its magnitude.

[5] The conceptual and mathematical framework are developed and stated in Becker's "Investment in Human Capital: A Theoretical Analysis," in this Supplement.

[6] See references in n. 3.

[7] Under competitive conditions, all of the firm's costs will be charged to the worker if the training increases his future productivity in other firms just as much as in the firm in which he is training. Some fraction of costs will not be charged to the worker if the training contains elements of specificity, that is, if it increases the worker's future productivity in the firm more than in other firms. For a full exposition see Becker, "Investment in Human Capital . . . ," *op. cit.*

earnings of workers, only a fraction of costs would be revealed by accounting data. I conclude that an attempt to gauge costs of on-the-job training in the economy by accounting data of firms, even if they were made available, would lead to severe underestimates.

On the other hand, working with earnings data of workers to estimate their foregone earnings also leads to an underestimate, to the extent that some training costs are borne by firms. The calculation reported below is an estimate of foregone earnings of workers, using Census income data rather than firm accounting data. At least, in terms of population coverage, this is a complete calculation of what probably is the more important component of on-the-job training costs. The alternative procedure, of using firm data, is practically ruled out because of the meager supply of information, aside from the serious conceptual inadequacies. However, some attempt is made to supplement the estimates obtained from workers' income data with fragmentary estimates of firm costs.

A direct computation of foregone earnings of workers engaged in on-the-job training would be possible if data were available on their earnings during and after the period of training, and on earnings of a comparison group of workers who have the same amount of formal schooling and are otherwise similar to the trainees, but do not receive any on-the-job training. Presumably, the latter would have a flatter age-earnings profile than the former. That is, trainees would initially receive lower earnings than those not training, the difference representing costs of training. At a later age, earnings of trainees would rise above earnings of the untrained, the difference constituting a return on the investment. Unfortunately, it is impossible to classify workers empirically into such comparison groups.[8] Given the group, say, of all male college graduates, there is no readily available statistic which would provide information on differential amounts of on-the-job training received by subgroups, and no income data are provided by such subclassifications. Even the fragmentary information on apprenticeships does not satisfy these requirements.

Fortunately, an alternative procedure based on Becker's theoretical analysis of investment in people[9] permits utilization of the comprehensive income data available in the United States Censuses. The procedure consists of a comparison of two average income streams of workers differing by levels of schooling, such as male college graduates and high-school graduates.

Taking this comparison as an example, the procedure involves year-by-year estimation of training costs which a high-school

---

were college-educated males who started on their first full-time job approximately twelve years before the survey date. The correlation between initial earnings of these individuals with their current earnings was used to test the existence of investment in on-the-job training by the predicted effects on age-earnings profiles:

Consider Y_t, the earnings of any individual at time t, as consisting of four additive components: $\overline{Y}_t$, average earnings of the group; a_t, an ability component of the individual; c_t, the investment component (a cost if negative, return if positive); and u_t, a random component.

$$Y_t = \overline{Y}_t + a_t + c_t + u_t.$$

For simplicity assume that the components are not correlated with one another, and u is not correlated over time. Since $\overline{Y}_t$ is the same for all individuals in the group, the covariance between earnings in the first and the twelfth year is:

Cov (Y_1, Y_{12}) = Cov $(a + c + u_1, a_{12}$
$+ c_{12} + u_{12})$ = Cov (a_1, a_{12}) + Cov (c_1, c_{12}).

The correlation was found to be very close to zero. Since the covariance of the ability factor is surely positive (and roughly equal to the variance of the ability component of earnings), the second covariance must be negative and equally sizable. That is, the larger (more negative) the initially foregone earnings (c_1), the larger (more positive) the return twelve years later (c_{12}).

[8] One interesting exception is the information obtained from an analysis of a sample of more than four hundred heads of households from the Consumer Union Panel, taken in 1959. The respondents

[9] Becker, "Investment in Human Capital . . . ," op. cit.

graduate must incur in order to acquire a college education and the additional amount of training on the job which is, on the average, characteristic of college graduates. Such estimates are obtained on the assumption that the rate of return is the same on each year's investment whether at school or on the job.[10] In any given year j after high-school graduation, those who go on to, or have graduated from, college would have earnings (Y_j) which equal the earnings of high-school graduates (X_j) plus the income earned on differential investment in training made since graduation from high school, *provided no further investment in training was incurred by them during the year* j. Costs of (incremental) training in year j are, therefore, measured by the difference between Y_j and X_j augmented by the (foregone) return on the previous (incremental) costs.

The procedure and the basic data utilized in it are shown in detail in the Appendix. The first step in the procedure is to compute the rate of return (r) on the investment in training by which the two groups differ. This is done by equating the sum of discounted earnings differences to zero, after direct schooling outlays are netted out of earnings.

Once the rate of return is obtained, the comparison of net earnings streams Y_j and X_j permits the following step-by-step calculation of training costs: let $j = 1$ denote the first year of additional training. Then training costs in year 1 are $C_1 = X_1 - Y_1$, the observed income differential. In year 2 the costs are $C_2 = (X_2 + ra_1C_1) - Y_2$, the observed income differential, augmented by the (foregone) return on previous costs.[11]

Proceeding sequentially, training costs in any year j are

$$C_j = X_j + (r \sum_{i=1}^{j-1} a_i C_i) - Y_j. \quad (1)$$

$$a_i = \frac{1}{1 - (1/1+r)^{n-i}},$$

a is a correction factor for finite life,[12] n is the length of the working life.

Figures in Table 15.1 were computed in this fashion and cumulated over the working life. They constitute estimates of training costs: these are schooling costs before entry into the labor force and opportunity costs of on-the-job training afterward. The cumulation of annual costs over the working life stops at about fifteen to twenty years after entry into the labor force, since the computed training costs decline with age after labor-force entry and become negligible, fluctuating around zero, around age forty (see cols. [4], [5], and [6] in Appendix Tables 15.9–15.16). The decline of training with age is consistent with a priori expectations about investment behavior; younger people have a greater incentive to invest in themselves than older ones, because they can collect the returns for a longer time.[13]

---

[10] This assumption is later questioned. However, the fragmentary evidence in Sec. II below suggests that the assumption of equal rates is not unreasonable, when rates are computed on the sum of private and public costs of training.

[11] After a year of additional training, the income alternatives of the trainee are better than those indicated by the age profile X_j, which assumes no additional training.

[12] The correction factor a is not a sufficient correction for the effective length of the working life. Use of this factor alone assumes that all of a given cohort survive to a given age and have a 100 per cent labor-force participation rate (after schooling) to this age. A complete correction should take into account mortality rates and the fraction of a cohort which is out of the labor force at each age. Adjustments for mortality and for labor-force participation were not incorporated in the estimating procedure. Neither have any significant effects on age-income profiles of males before the age of fifty. The effects on income *differentials* are small. According to Becker's work the mortality adjustment results in a small reduction of the rate of return, if the same mortality table is used for all education groups. The correction factor was used in the initial set of calculations, but discarded in the final revision, as it turned out to be negligible. Leaving out all these "survival" factors results in a small overstatement of costs, as is discussed later in the text.

[13] Becker, "Investment in Human Capital . . . ," *op. cit.*

TABLE 15.1 LIFETIME INVESTMENT IN TRAINING PER CAPITA AT SCHOOL AND ON-THE-JOB, UNITED STATES MALES, 1939, 1949, 1958, BY LEVEL OF SCHOOLING (IN THOUSANDS)

Educational Level	Current Dollars						1954 Dollars*					
	Marginal Cost			Total Cost			Marginal Cost			Total Cost		
	School (1)	On-the-Job (2)	Sum (3)	School (4)	On-the-Job (5)	Sum (6)	School (1)	On-the-Job (2)	Sum (3)	School (4)	On-the-Job (5)	Sum (6)
1939:												
College	4.9	3.5	8.4	7.7	7.9	15.6	9.4	6.7	16.2	14.7	15.2	29.9
High school	2.0	2.4	4.4	2.8	4.4	7.2	3.9	4.6	8.5	5.2	8.5	13.7
Elementary school	.8	2.0	2.8	.8	2.0	2.8	1.3	3.9	5.2	1.3	3.9	5.2
1949:												
College	10.2	15.7	25.9	15.9	24.3	40.2	11.5	17.7	29.3	18.0	27.4	45.4
High school	4.1	4.7	8.8	5.7	8.6	14.2	4.6	5.3	9.9	6.4	9.7	16.0
Elementary school	1.6	3.9	5.5	1.6	3.9	5.5	1.8	4.4	6.2	1.8	4.4	6.2
1958:												
College	16.4	22.5	38.9	26.0	30.7	56.7	15.3	21.2	36.5	24.1	28.8	52.9
High school	7.1	2.9	10.0	9.5	8.2	17.7	6.6	2.7	9.3	8.8	7.6	16.4
Elementary school	2.4	5.3	7.7	2.4	5.3	7.7	2.2	4.9	7.1	2.2	4.9	7.1

Source: Appendix [Tables 15.9–15.15].
* Deflated by the Bureau of Labor Statistics' Consumer Price Index.

The age-earnings profiles which are the basic data used in deriving estimates of training costs are presented in Appendix Tables 15.10–15.12. These are before tax incomes of United States males (wage and salary in 1939, income in 1949 and in 1958), classified by age and education, and adjusted to approximate the relevant concepts. The adjustments involve netting out direct school costs and corrections for part-time employment of students during the period of school attendance. For these purposes, and in order to separate school and on-the-job training costs, the assumption was made that people with none up to eight years of schooling enter the labor force at age fourteen and have no foregone earnings while at school; high-school graduates enter the labor force at age eighteen, and their foregone earnings during high-school attendance are obtainable by comparison with incomes of elementary-school graduates of the same age; college students graduate at ages twenty-two to twenty-three, and estimates of relevant income differentials are constructed in a similar way.

For each date and education group, year-by-year estimates of marginal costs of training were calculated by equation (1). An illustrative calculation is shown in Appendix Table 15.12. Detailed annual figures are shown in Tables 15.13–15.15, columns (1), (2), and (3). The annual estimates of marginal costs are then cumulated horizontally in columns (4), (5), and (6) of Tables 15.13–15.15, to obtain annual total costs of schooling and of on-the-job training. Summing the figures in each column yields, separately, lifetime total costs of schooling and of on-the-job training typical of groups with given levels of schooling per person. The results are presented in Table 15.1.

In reading this table it is important to distinguish between the "marginal" and "total" figures. The cost of attending high school, shown as marginal costs of high-school education, do not measure the total costs of schooling of the individual up to and including high school. For this purpose the costs of high-school attendance must be added to the costs of elementary-school attendance. Similarly, the costs of on-the-job training of a high-school graduate as obtained by equation (1) are *additional* costs over and above the costs of on-the-job training incurred by elementary-school graduates. These marginal costs (col. [2] in Table 15.1) are first differences of the total costs of on-the-job training for graduates of any particular level of schooling, shown in column (5) of Table 15.1.

The estimates of on-the-job training costs in Table 15.1 are per capita magnitudes approximating the sum of resources the average male of a given educational level may be expected to invest in training on the job during his working life. Estimates of the aggregate investment by male workers in the economy during a given year are shown in Table 15.2. They are obtained by multiplying the year-by-year costs of training, as shown in Tables 15.13–15.15 (cols. [4], [5], and [6]), by the number of workers[14] (student enrolment during the period of schooling) in the corresponding age and educational groups (cols. [7], [8], and [9]). The cross-products are then summed to obtain aggregate costs corresponding to the total cost classifications in Table 15.1, columns (3), (4), and (5).

In contrast to Table 15.1, Table 15.2 represents actual opportunity costs in the economy, not expectations of individuals. The relative sizes of the two components of training costs, formal and on the job, are also different in the two tables. This is because the aggregative estimates in Table 15.2 depend on the age distribution of workers with given levels of educational attainment. Secular trends in population size and in educational attainments affect the relevant age distributions in a way which makes the aggregative on-the-job training costs somewhat smaller in relation to school costs than is true on the per capita basis.

Before proceeding to discussion and interpretation of the findings one must raise questions about their validity and reliability. A number of possible sources of bias are easily identified. First, the estimates of per capita training costs (Table 15.1) are based on cross-section income profiles. They, therefore, may approximate expectations of an average male of a given educational level, provided the differences between his earnings and earnings of males at the next lower educational level will change year after year in the future, precisely the way they do change in the cross-sectional comparison from one cohort to the next, one year older. If secular trends are expected to tilt both income streams upward by the same percentage, the returns (income differentials at a later stage of life) are likely to increase somewhat, with income differentials at an early stage largely unaffected. On this assumption, the procedure involves a small underestimate of the rate of return since differentials later in life are heavily discounted. In turn, this implies an understatement of costs, to the extent that costs are, in part, a positive function of the discount rate (eq. [1]).

Another bias is introduced by using the cross-sectional patterns as approximations for the true earnings streams. This is the misreporting of years of schooling by Census respondents. According to Denison, the older the group in an education class, the larger the fraction of persons reporting a level of education higher than the one they reported at the previous Census.[15] This

---

[14] To obtain estimates of investments by all workers, those with "some elementary schooling," "some high school," and "some college" have to be included in the calculation. It was assumed that their investment costs are halfway between investment costs of graduates at neighboring educational levels. See notes to Appendix Tables A5–A7.

[15] E. F. Denison, "A Note on Education, Economic Growth, and Gaps in Information," in this Supplement.

TABLE 15.2 AGGREGATE ANNUAL INVESTMENT IN TRAINING AT SCHOOL AND ON-THE-JOB, UNITED STATES MALES, 1939, 1949, 1958, BY LEVEL OF SCHOOLING (IN $ BILLIONS)

Educational Level	1939			1949			1958		
	School	Job	Total	School	Job	Total	School	Job	Total
	Current Dollars								
College	1.1	1.0	2.1	3.8	4.3	8.1	8.7	8.7	17.4
High School	1.8	1.4	3.2	3.4	3.8	7.2	8.4	3.8	12.2
Elementary	.9	.6	1.5	2.1	.9	3.0	4.5	1.0	5.5
All levels	3.8	3.0	6.8	9.3	9.0	18.3	21.6	13.5	35.1
	1954 Dollars								
College	2.1	1.9	4.0	4.3	4.7	9.0	8.1	8.1	16.2
High school	3.5	2.7	6.2	3.8	4.2	8.0	7.8	3.5	11.3
Elementary	1.9	1.1	2.8	2.4	1.0	3.4	4.2	.9	5.1
All levels	7.3	5.7	13.0	10.5	9.9	20.4	20.1	12.5	32.6

Source: Appendix [Tables 15.9–15.15].

means that observed cross-sectional age-income profiles are biased downward at older ages in all educational groups except the lowest. The failure to tilt the income streams upward leads, as before, to an understatement of costs, mainly at the upper levels of education.

For another reason, costs were underestimated also at the lower levels of education. I compared the earnings stream of elementary-school graduates with that of persons with one to four years of schooling rather than with persons with zero schooling. The group with no schooling is small, and its composition so different from that of the other groups (it is heavily weighted with farm workers, single persons, and non-whites) that its age-earnings profile could not serve as a bench mark. To the extent that persons with zero to four years of schooling undergo some on-the-job training, which is undoubtedly true, the costs of such training have been omitted from my estimates.

An opposite bias is imparted by omission of the survival factors, as mentioned previously (n. 12). Lack of adjustment for mortality, for example, means that earnings differentials at later ages are overstated. Costs are therefore *overestimated,* because the rate of return is overestimated, though by a small amount.

The 1949 and 1958 income figures include property income in addition to labor income, and this too tends to widen differentials between profiles noticeably at later ages. This is because of a positive correlation of property income with age and with education. The result is a slight overestimate of costs by an overestimate of the rate of return.

A more serious question is posed by the assumption that differences in income streams of the groups compared are attributable to differences in training. Such an assumption disregards other factors which may affect shapes and levels of age profiles. Biases will arise if these other factors are not independent of the classificatory criteria: for example, the higher the years of schooling and the higher the age, the lower the fraction of males who are non-white. Farmers and farm laborers are disproportionately distributed in the low years of schooling and low age classes. Restriction of estimates to non-farm whites (as in 1939) avoids the distortions, but such data were not available for all the periods. It is clear, however, that, even in data which are quite homogeneous by Census criteria, certain selective or restrictive factors are not neutral with respect to the educational classification: people who undertake more training are likely to have higher intelligence quotients, higher parental income and education, more motivation and information.

The extent to which earnings of more trained persons exceed earnings of less trained persons is, therefore, an *overestimate* of the return on training. Part of the observed return is a return to these "ability" factors. But, for the same reasons, the observed data are likely to underestimate the costs incurred: if more capable high-school students enter college, their foregone earnings are probably underestimated by the observed earnings of the less capable high-school graduates who did not go on to college. It is difficult to say, a priori, how large such biases may be. But, if a correction for the "ability" factor involves a decrease in return and a simultaneous increase in cost via income differentials, it is clear that the relative decline in the rate of return must be larger than the relative increase in costs.[16] According to Becker an adjustment for class standing of high-school graduates brings the rate of return down by about 15 per cent. If costs are underestimated, this figure measures the maximum amount of bias, when the dimension of ability which is measured by class standing is taken into account. Other factors may account for more.

Once again, the bias need not be in one direction. To the extent that the restrictive factors under discussion affect returns (earnings differentials after the training period) *without* affecting income differentials during the training period, the rate of return *and* costs are overestimated. This is because costs, as we computed them, are in part a positive function of the rate of return.

Possibly the largest source of downward bias in the estimation of costs was already mentioned: the omission of costs of training which are borne by firms. These costs do not show up in the income data at all. As a simple example, take the case of a firm which pays half the costs of training, the other half being paid by the worker. Later on, the firm captures half of the returns. Rates of return are not affected, and foregone earnings of workers are cut in half.

It is not possible to arrive at an over-all notion of the direction of bias without knowing more about the magnitudes of each possible error. But, if there is some reason to believe that totals are underestimated, there are reasons to believe that the distortion is weaker when it comes to relative sizes of subtotals in the classifications of Tables 15.1 and 15.2. If ability factors bias costs in the comparison of college and high school, they have similar effects in the high school and elementary school.

The striking finding in Table 15.1 is that the opportunity costs of on-the-job training per male are almost without exception somewhat higher than costs of a comparable increment of schooling. But while per capita amounts of formal schooling (as measured by costs in constant dollars) grew between 1939 and 1958 at all levels, the corresponding quantities of on-the-job training per capita grew mainly at the higher educational levels.

On an aggregative basis (Table 15.2) on-the-job training costs were a little smaller than schooling costs in 1939 and grew at a slower rate than the former. Formal education expenditures grew rapidly at all levels during the 1939–58 period. On-the-job training expenditures grew just as fast as schooling at the highest educational level, increased before 1949 and decreased afterward at the high-school level, and continuously declined at the elementary-school level. The per capita figures (Table 15.1) indicate, however, that the decline in aggregate on-the-job training for the elementary-school class was not a result of a decline in costs per head but a decline in the number

---

[16] The rate of return is a ratio of returns to costs. $r = k/c$. If only c were increased, with k left the same, the relative (per cent) decrease in r would equal the relative increase in c. But, since k is decreased, the relative decrease in r is stronger than the relative increase in c.

of heads. Similarly, the increase in on-the-job costs in the aggregate for the college class also consisted mainly in an increase in the number of heads rather than in training costs per head, particularly in the second decade.

One feature of the findings in Table 15.1 is worthy of closer attention: on-the-job training is a larger quantity the higher the level of education. This is not a truism as in the case of schooling, where the marginal quantities of schooling are positive by definition. There is nothing in the calculation of on-the-job training costs that would make the marginal quantities necessarily positive. In other words, the positive association between school training and on-the-job training is not definitional; it is an empirical inference from the observed income data. More training seems to involve more of both forms of training, though not in any fixed proportion. This is reasonable: school education is a prerequisite, a basis on which to build the further, more specialized training.

Some independent evidence on this positive association is provided by recent Department of Labor estimates of amounts of school and on-the-job training, both measured in school-grade equivalents, required for the acquisition of occupational skill in four thousand detailed occupations.[17] From the four thousand occupations listed in the publication, a sample of 158 occupations was selected on the basis of comparability with the 1950 Census occupational breakdown. The two measures of school and on-the-job training requirements given in rank form, were correlated with coefficient +.86.

The positive association between schooling and on-the-job training helps in understanding trends. It suggests that an expansion of education is likely to bring about an expansion of on-the-job training, a development indicated in Tables 15.1 and 15.2. To the extent that an expansion of education is induced by a decrease in its price relative to the price of on-the-job training, some substitution will take place, and education may grow at the expense of on-the-job training. Such factors, among others, may underlie the slower growth of on-the-job training than of schooling. More precisely, the data suggest slow or no growth of on-the-job training at the lower educational levels and pronounced growth at upper educational levels. This finding supports popular impressions about the changing levels of on-the-job training: a shift from apprenticeships to technicians, scientific personnel, and executive development programs. Such shifts may, in the aggregate, reflect the upward trend in supplies of labor with high levels of educational attainment and possibly some substitution phenomena at the lower levels. The questions about trends are very intriguing, but the data do not lend themselves to more than conjectures.

Turning to bodies of data other than the comprehensive income statistics, I tried to exploit them, though not very intensively, for two purposes: (1) to provide some empirical checks on the reliability of estimates based on foregone incomes of workers, (2) to form some guesses about firm costs or outlays.

1. On the basis of the BLS publication on skill requirements for 4,000 occupations, Eckaus estimated the average number of college-equivalent years of on-the-job training imbedded in the labor force (including females).[18] The estimate was 1.66 and 1.72 for 1939 and 1949, respectively. But these are average quantities for the whole age distribution, figures representing a stock. We are interested in the flow of current investment in on-the-job training, and this is incurred mainly by the younger age groups.

[17] United States Department of Labor, Bureau of Employment Security, United States Employment Service, *Estimates of Worker Trait Requirements for 4,000 Jobs as Defined in the Dictionary of Occupational Titles* (Washington, 1956).

[18] R. S. Eckaus, "Education and Economic Growth," in *Economics of Higher Education*, ed. Selma J. Mushkin (Washington: United States Department of Health, Education, and Welfare [forthcoming]), Tables 1 and 2. College equivalence is implied in United States Department of Labor, Bureau of Employment Security, United States Employment Service, *op. cit.*, p. 111.

TABLE 15.3 GI BILL EXPENDITURES, BY LEVEL AND TYPE OF TRAINING, 1945–55

Level of Training	No. of Veterans (Millions) (1)	GI Bill Expenditures		All Males, Aggregates for 1949	
		$ Billions (2)	Per cent (3)	$ Billions (4)	Per cent (5)
College	2.2	5.5	38.1	4.5	40.8
High school	1.4	2.2	15.3	3.3	30.0
Trade school	2.1	3.3	23.1		
On the job	2.1	3.5	24.5	3.2	29.2
Total	7.8	14.5	100.0	11.0	100.0

Source: Cols. (1) and (2), President's Commission on Veterans' Pensions, *Readjustment Benefits, Staff Report* (No. IX, Part B [Washington: Government Printing Office, September 12, 1956]), pp. 22–24, 30–32.

These groups have higher education levels than the labor force as a whole and are, therefore, likely to invest more also in on-the-job training. In 1949 the age group 18–29 had a median schooling of 12 years compared to a labor force median of 10 years. The discrepancy between means was even greater. Since the investment in on-the-job training is higher at higher educational levels, an upward adjustment is required. Using the ratio of medians to revise Eckaus' estimates upward, roughly in proportion, yields 1.99 and 2.06 years for 1939 and 1949 respectively.

In terms of equivalent college costs per year, 2.06 years of training would cost about $6,000 per member of the labor force in 1950, according to Table 15.1. The average female invests in on-the-job training about one-tenth as much as the average male,[19] and the number of females was slightly over a third of the total labor force in the age group 18–29. Hence, the implicit cost (C) on-the-job training incurred per male in 1949 is:

$$\$5,200 = \tfrac{2}{3} C + \tfrac{1}{30} C$$
$$C = \$7,500.$$

This compares with our estimates of $8,600 costs of on-the-job training of male high-school graduates (Table 15.1, col. [5]), the modal group in the population. A similar calculation for 1939 yields about $3,600 to be compared with our estimate $4,400. Elements of subjectivity in the BLS-derived figures make the comparison difficult, but the fact that the two sets of estimates are not very far apart is encouraging.

Another piece of supplementary evidence is provided by data on the distribution of federal expenditures on the GI Bill for 1945–55. The expenditures and their distribution are given in Table 15.3. In columns (3) and (5) we compare the percentage distributions of expenditures: costs of college training of veterans during the ten-year period are compared with costs of college of all males in 1949; a similar comparison of veterans' costs is made with marginal costs of high school, and with total costs of on-the-job training of high-school graduates. The distributions (col. [3] and col. [5]) look reasonably comparable. The greater selectivity of veterans toward college and vocational training (trade schools and on the job) in comparison to all males is understandable in view of differences in age and in educational backgrounds already acquired.

2. Several recent surveys of training activities in firms have shown that such functions are carried by many firms.[20] Of course, only formally arranged programs

[19] See Part III below.

[20] Clark and Sloan, *op. cit.*, Serbein, *op. cit.*, and the 1960 New Jersey Survey of the Bureau of Apprenticeships and Training.

are described in such surveys. Unfortunately, questions about costs are seldom raised in these surveys. Undoubtedly, it would be difficult to interpret the financial data, even if they were forthcoming. In only one of the recent studies were such questions asked, with these results:

Although questions were asked concerning total expenditures for in-company education, few firms replied—Perhaps the chief reason was that often the books of the firm were not kept in a manner that would make it easy to separate educational costs from other costs. Other reasons centered around questions of allocation and items to be considered as costs— The data reported are not comparable, since some of the figures include salaries and some exclude them. It is not certain that the figures reported include all in-company programs. In one case it was specifically stated that the figure reported was for one program.[21]

If the scant financial replies shown in this survey are blown up to an aggregate, the result is an estimate below $1 billion for 1957, undoubtedly a severe underestimate of even those current firm outlays which are easily identifiable. Smaller case studies indicate that firm expenditures on formal training programs must be much larger: estimates range from $85 for an operative in training[22] to over $10,000 for an executive training program.[23] According to the recent comprehensive survey of New Jersey industries made by the Bureau of Apprenticeship and Training,[24] the proportion of workers participating in formal training programs in 1959 was about 5 per cent. Of these 20 per cent enrolled in management development programs, 10 per cent in apprenticeships, 10 per cent in technical (semiprofessional) training, 12 per cent in sales training, and the rest in short programs of operative training, orientation, safety, etc. Applying almost any vaguely reasonable dollar figures—from $85 per operative to a conservative $2,000 per executive trainee per annum, and projecting to the aggregate labor force in recent years, yields an estimate of $2–$3 billion. But this, of course, misses all costs incurred in informal training, which is the typical situation: only 16.2 per cent of firms in New Jersey had *formal* training programs.

One estimate which takes into account "invisible" costs of firms, including costs in informal training processes, can be obtained using figures shown in a recent study of California firms by the American Management Association.[25] In this study estimates were made of costs of labor turnover to the firm. The concept of replacement cost includes hiring costs such as advertising, recruitment, interviews, and separation costs; on-the-job training costs are defined more comprehensively as "the expense brought about by sub-standard production of new employees while learning their job assignments and becoming adjusted to their work environment; the dollar value of time spent by supervisors and others employees who assist in breaking in new employees on their job assignment, and costs of organized training programs."[26] These training costs per worker replacement were estimated at about $230. If hiring and separation costs are included the figure doubles. Multiplying these costs of a replacement by the total number of replacements in industry in 1958[27] yields an estimate of $7 billion. Inclusion of hiring and separation costs raises the estimate to $14 billion. The assumption that all of these costs are borne by the firms is, of course, highly questionable. How much is shifted back to the trainee in the form of a wage reduction is not known. At the same time, a large part of the opportunity cost of workers—the difference between what they did produce while in training and what they

---

[21] Serbein, *op. cit.*, pp. 9–10.
[22] "Training Manpower," *Fortune*, July, 1951.
[23] Clark and Sloan, *op. cit.*, p. 3.
[24] See references cited in n. 2.

[25] Merchants and Manufacturers Association, *Labor Turnover: Causes, Costs and Methods of Control* (New York, February, 1959).
[26] *Ibid.*
[27] About thirty million, using the observed average monthly replacement rate of 4 per cent.

could produce if they did not train—is also missed in these figures.

All these heroic attempts to estimate firm costs add up to an uncomfortable range of uncertainty when it comes to answering the question: how much of firm costs should be added to the estimates of foregone incomes of workers? It is possible that billions of dollars are involved, but it is not clear how many.

Besides firm costs, two more items must be added to our estimates in Table 15.2 to get total costs of on-the-job training in the economy: training costs incurred by women and training expenditures in the Armed Forces. The latter are estimated at $1.6 billion[28] in 1959, and the former at $1.4 billion[29] in 1958. According to Table 15.2, aggregate opportunity costs of male workers were about $13.5 billion in 1958. Addition of the two items brings the figure up to $16.5 billion, more than half of the aggregate costs of schooling (males and females) in 1956.[30] The addition of possibly several billion dollars of costs borne by firms narrows the difference but may not close it. Since most of the on-the-job training costs are incurred by and spent on male workers, it is probably correct to say that, in the male half of the world, on-the-job training—measured in dollar costs—is as important as formal schooling.

II. Estimates of Rates of Return

An estimate of rates of return to on-the-job training is both desirable and difficult to obtain. The rate of return computed by equating the present values of net earnings of two education groups should not be in-

[28] Includes military schools and graining programs but excludes basic training and depreciation of equipment (estimated by R. C. Blitz in "The Nations Educational Outlay," in Mushkin (ed.), *Economics of Higher Education*).
[29] Based on 1949 estimates for female college graduates (see Part III, below).
[30] According to Schultz, the total cost of schooling was $28.7 billion in 1956 ("Investment in Human Capital," *op. cit.*).

terpreted as a rate of return on schooling costs. The computed rate is some average of rates of return to schooling and to on-the-job training. The hybrid rate depends on the weights (costs) of the two training components and on the rates on each component.[31] If the rate on one component is known, the other can be approximated in a residual fashion. What is immediately important, the larger the difference between the rates of return on investment in schooling and in on-the-job training, the less accurate are the cost estimates in the preceding section, as well as the various recent estimates of rates of return on (school) education. If the rate of return on schooling exceeds the rate on on-the-job training, the estimates are on the low side.

It is not obvious, on a priori grounds, whether the money rate of return to on-the-job training is likely to be smaller or larger than the rate on formal education. It could be argued that non-pecuniary, "consumption" elements may be a more important part of the real return to formal education then to on-the-job training. If so, and if this were the only difference, the money rate of return on schooling would appear smaller than the rate to on-the-job training. Larger public subsidies to formal education would also have this effect, if returns are computed on total costs (private and public). These arguments are based on an assumption of equality of the real (pecuniary and non-pecuniary) private rate of return in both training sectors.

One could argue, however, that larger impediments to a flow of investment into formal education make for higher rates of return to schooling than to on-the-job training. Income constraints are less severe in the latter case as costs are more spread out over time. Perhaps more important is that this investment is undertaken at a later age and in the context of a concrete, existing

[31] It also depends on timing. The chronologically earlier component receives greater weight (see Becker, "Investment in Human Capital . . . ," *op. cit.*).

work situation: there is much less uncertainty about future prospects, about one's own abilities and motivations, etc. These circumstances tend to produce a lower *real* rate of return to on-the-job training and may well reduce the *money* rate on it to a lower level than the money rate on formal education.

There are no comprehensive data comparable to the Census classifications by formal education level from which to compute rates to on-the-job training. The rates shown in Table 15.4 were estimated for a few selected skills for which tolerably good data are available. These refer to apprenticeship training in the several industries in which they are concentrated. All estimates are for 1949.

The rates of return on apprenticeship training were computed in three different ways providing a range of estimates, from the highest values in column (1) to the lowest in column (3) of Table 15.4. However, the lowest values (col. [3]) are conceptually the soundest. The computations involve equating to zero the present value of differentials between earnings of workers who served an apprenticeship and earnings of their assumed alternative occupational groups. During the period of training the apprentice receives an average wage W_a, after which he becomes a journeyman receiving an average wage W_m. A suitable alternative occupation,[32] where almost no training is involved, is the operative, and his average wage is W_o. The annual wage differential $d = W_a - W_o$ is negative during the training period and positive afterward, $k = W_m - W_o$ assumed constant for the rest of the working life. Under these assumptions, and disregarding a negligible correction for the finiteness of working life, the rate of return (r) is easily obtained from:[33]

$$(1 + r)^n = 1 + \frac{k}{d}, \qquad (2)$$

where n is the number of years of training, or length of the apprenticeship.

Estimates in column (1) of Table 15.4 are based on comparisons of earnings of apprentices, journeymen, and operatives *in the same industries*. While operatives and corresponding craftsmen had the same median schooling, the apprentices had two to three more years of schooling than the other two groups in 1949. Thus k, the difference between earnings of journeymen and operatives, is computed correctly, holding formal schooling the same. But foregone earnings of apprentices are underestimated: having more schooling than the operatives with whom they are compared, the apprentices could earn more in alternative jobs. With returns correct and costs underestimated, figures in column (1) are too high.

In column (2) this defect is corrected to a large extent. In the calculation, k is the same as before, but d was computed from

TABLE 15.4 RATES OF RETURN ON APPRENTICESHIP TRAINING, SELECTED TRADES, 1949

	Assumptions about Alternative Income Streams		
Trades	Operatives in Same Industries	Operatives with Highest Schooling	Assuming a 10 Per Cent Return on Additional Schooling
	(1)	(2)	(3)
Metal	16.4	10.4	9.5
Printing	16.0	12.6	9.0
Building	18.3	11.3	9.7

Source: Table 15.16.

[32] This occupation is more appropriate as an alternative, in terms of educational background, than laborers. Clerical work is an alternative, but it probably contains more on-the-job training than operative jobs, which involve at most a few months of training.

[33] Calculated from

$$d \cdot \sum_{i=1}^{n} \frac{1}{(1+r)^i} = k \cdot \sum_{j=n+1}^{\infty} \frac{1}{(1+r)^i}.$$

The assumption of infinite life creates a negligible error.

a comparison of wages of apprentices with wages of operatives whose schooling levels are closer to levels of apprentices, regardless of industry attachment. As Table 15.16 shows, however, median schooling of these operatives is still about a year less than of apprentices, so rates may still be overestimated.

In column (3) the same k is used again, but the opportunity cost is computed by adding to d (as computed in col. [1]) a return on additional years of (high-school) education[34] by which apprentices exceed the operatives with whom they are compared in column (1). This brings the rates down to the levels shown in column (3).

The estimates probably suffer from several biases. Operatives have some on-the-job training, but so do craftsmen after completion of apprenticeships. If the additional training of the latter exceeds that of the former, the rates of return on apprenticeships are overestimated. On the other hand, abstraction from secular rates of growth, as in the general case,[35] may have the opposite effect. It is also possible that the union restrictions on entry to apprenticeships resulted in higher returns in the several fields selected in Table 15.4 than in other kinds of on-the-job training.[36]

For a comparison with another high level of skill, I computed rates of return on medical specialization, comparing incomes of residents and specialists (after residency) with incomes of general practitioners. The computation utilizes age-income profiles of independent medical specialists, starting with an initial period of residency, with the income profile of independent general practitioners, starting with the first year in practice. Estimates of income in money

[34] A 10 per cent rate was used. Higher rates would lower the figures in col. (3) even more.
[35] See Part I, above.
[36] However, according to a recent study by H. G. Lewis, the impact of unionism on wage differentials was very small in the 1945–50 period ("Union Effects on Relative Wages," in *Aspects of Labor Economics* [National Bureau of Economic Research Conference, 1960 (New York, 1960)]).

and kind of residents were obtained from American Medical Association sources;[37] earnings from 1950 Census sources.[38] The calculation on before-tax incomes showed a return of 12.7 per cent. A rough adjustment for taxes brought the rate down to 11.3 per cent. It is difficult to judge whether this is high or low in comparison with apprenticeships.[39]

Table 15.5 compares estimated rates of return on apprenticeships and on training at the college level.

Generalizing boldly, a comparison of columns (1) and (2) suggests that money rates of return (before tax) on *total costs* (public and private) are similar for school and on-the-job training. Figures in column (1) are weighted averages of returns on the two sectors; similarity of average and component means that rates on each component are alike. It does appear, however, that private rates of return are lower for the selected instances of on-the-job training than for

[37] *Journal of the American Medical Association*, September 22, 1956, pp. 277 ff., and October 10, 1959, pp. 665 ff.
[38] "Income of Physicians," *Survey of Current Business*, July, 1951.
[39] The 1950 rate of return to medical specialization may have been above equilibrium. The proportion of specialists among physicians was less than half in 1950 and increased to about two-thirds by 1960 (according to *Medical Economics*, 1961). If this was a supply shift in response to a high level of demand, the rate of return on specialization should be less today than in 1950. Data from medical sources (*Physicians Earnings and Expenses*, published by *Medical Economics*, 1961) indicate that in 1959 the money income differential between specialists and general practitioners is no larger than it was in 1949, despite the fact that the average incomes of specialists rose over 60 per cent during the period, residencies lengthened somewhat, and opportunity costs clearly increased. If the data are reliable, it would seem that rates of return today are a few percentage points lower than in 1949. Incidentally, estimates of rates of return on specialization in medicine have little bearing on the question of alleged monopoly returns in medicine. Whatever the barriers to entry into medicine, once a medical degree was obtained, institutional obstacles to specialization are weak.

TABLE 15.5 RETURNS TO "EDUCATION" AND TO ON-THE-JOB TRAINING, 1950

	Per Cent	
	College Level* (1)	On-the-Job Training† (2)
Total costs	11	9.0–12.7
Private costs before tax	14	
Private costs after tax	13	8.5–11.3

* Source: G. S. Becker, "Underinvestment in College Education?" op. cit.
† Range based on column 2 and 3 of Table 15.4, and on return to medical specialization.

total training at college levels. If the selected instances can be generalized, the rate of return on college education per se is somewhat underestimated by the figures in column (1). Apparently, the greater ease of investing in on-the-job training outweighs the possibly greater consumption elements in college education. Another intriguing implication is that the apparent, but not clearly documented, stability over time in the rates of return to training (both in school and on the job) may conceal a decline in the rate of return to formal education, given that investment in education seems to have grown faster than in on-the-job training, at least at the lower levels.

These conclusions are hazardous. The rates are not adjusted for ability factors. If there is a greater selectivity (based on ability) for admission into college, differences between adjusted rates in the two sectors may disappear, or reverse. But this is not at all obvious. More detailed data and intensive research are needed.

III. On-the-Job Training as a Factor in Income and Employment Behavior

In the first section of this paper, the economic theory of investment in people was used to bring the very elusive process of on-the-job training under the measuring rod of money. In this section the theory will be used to produce additional measurements and to explain, in part, certain well-known but not well-understood patterns of income and employment in population subgroups. The empirical analyses sketched below are no more than preliminary, but perhaps they are sufficiently indicative.

A calculation of (marginal) on-the-job training costs per capita for female college graduates in 1949 provided two estimates: (a) $830, (b) $2,160. The comparable figure for males was $15,700 (Table 15.1, col. [2]). The calculation is the same as the one underlying Table 15.1. It is based on a comparison of net earnings of college and high-school graduates, given in Table 15.17. Estimate (a) is based on earnings data adjusted for (multiplied by) labor-force rates of women in the various age groups (Table 15.17, cols. [3] and [4]); estimate (b) is based on the unadjusted earnings (Table 15.17, cols. [1] and [2]). The adjustment for participation rates assumes that the return on investment in training of women (at college and on the job) is obtainable only in the labor market. If it is believed that this investment in training results also in the same amount of productivity increase in the "home industry," earnings should not be adjusted by labor-force rates. This certainly cannot be assumed of investments on the job, but may be true of schooling. The estimate (b) based on unadjusted earnings is, of course, larger. Both assumptions are extreme, and, in principle, provide limits for a correct estimate.[40]

While formal education costs are not much smaller for females than for males, investments in on-the-job training are very small, about one-tenth (taking a middle figure between the two estimates) of the amounts invested by males. The figures may

[40] Empirical evidence on labor-force behavior of married women is more consistent with the first than with the second assumption (see my "Labor Force Participation of Married Women," in *Aspects of Labor Economics, op. cit.*).

not be highly reliable, but their smallness is quite reasonable, in the light of investment theory: the average female expects to spend less than half her working life in the labor force. In particular, she has a high probability of dropping out of the work force for prolonged periods of child-rearing soon after, and possibly during, the training period. It is clear that returns on prolonged on-the-job training would be small. Hence pecuniary incentives to invest in on-the-job training leading to higher levels of skill are weak. And even when a girl plans on a career, that is, expects to be permanently attached to the labor force, the opportunity for investing in on-the-job training is likely to be limited. So long as there are some elements of specificity in any training programs or promotional schemes of the firm, the employer will prefer men to women trainees, even if the latter profess occupational ambitions. This also implies that to the extent that women do obtain specific training they bear a larger fraction of the total costs of such training than men and, therefore, that the difference between on-the-job training costs (including those borne by employees) for women and those for men is even larger than is suggested by our estimate.

Some direct evidence on scant female participation in on-the-job training is provided in a recent international survey.[41] In all countries surveyed, apprenticeships are shorter for women than for men. They are half the length of male apprenticeships in the United States in bookbinding and in the garment industry, where women concentrate. In other industries, numbers of women apprentices are negligible, perhaps because of physical requirements but not because of any legal obstacles. It is interesting to find that, in contrast to other countries, applications for apprenticeships by women were quite numerous in the early postwar years in Germany and Austria. By 1949 in these countries, the number of skilled women in trades previously considered male was quite pronounced and increasing. Because of the war-caused imbalance in the sex ratio in the young age groups, unfavorable marriage prospects of young females clearly increased worker and employer expectations of their more permanent attachment to the labor force. Larger investment in on-the-job training became economical to both parties. Aside from patriotism, such motivations may play a role in the increased labor-force rates and job-training of women during wars in all countries. And the willingness of employers to train women as well as men is enhanced by governmental subsidies of the training function.

Returning to our estimates: the small amounts of investment in on-the-job training by females were derived from female age-income profiles. This procedure is, of course, equivalent to a hypothesis which emphasizes the lack of on-the-job training as the factor responsible for both the observed flatness of females' age-income profiles and the small differential between observed incomes of women of different levels of formal education.

A recent detailed study of income differentials between males and females shows that wage rates approach equality when the detailed job specification is identical for both sexes.[42] The rougher the occupational classification, the bigger the wage differentials at the higher skill levels. Lack of on-the-job training fits these phenomena quite well.

These same phenomena, however, are possibly attributable to differential market discrimination against women appearing at the more skilled job levels and increasing with levels of skill. The calculation based on Table 15.13 indeed revealed a somewhat lower rate (about two percentage points) of return on total training of women than of men. The lower rate may reflect discrimina-

---

[41] "The Apprenticeships of Women and Girls," *International Labor Review*, October, 1955.

[42] H. Sanborn, "Male-Female Income Differentials" (unpublished doctoral dissertation, University of Chicago, 1959).

TABLE 15.6 COSTS PER NON-WHITE MALE OF SCHOOL AND ON-THE-JOB TRAINING, 1949 (IN $ THOUSANDS)

Educational Level	Marginal Costs		Total Costs		Total Costs of All United States Males	
	School	On the Job	School	On the Job	School	On the Job
College	8.05	3.98	13.20	7.87	15.9	24.3
High school	3.92	0.46	5.15	3.89	5.7	8.6
Elementary school	1.23	3.43	1.23	3.43	1.6	3.9

Source: Table 15.18 and Table 15.1.

tion. Another explanation which is consistent with the investment hypothesis[43] is that, in view of the expected smaller rate of participation in the labor market, education of women is more strongly focused on the "consumption" sphere, and returns are in larger part non-pecuniary than for males. Hence the apparently smaller money rate of return.

In Table 15.6 a 1949 comparison of training costs of Negro and white males indicates much smaller investments in on-the-job training by Negroes, though the investments are not negligible. The investment in on-the-job training is also smaller in relation to investment in formal schooling, suggesting a lesser access to on-the-job training than to formal education. Again, fragmentary direct evidence abounds on the small proportions of Negroes in apprenticeships and other training programs.

Conversely, the smaller amounts of on-the-job training received by Negroes than by whites is an interpretation of income differentials: the relative flatness of their age-income profiles and the smaller differentials in earnings by education (even when the latter are standardized in terms of cost). The lesser on-the-job training relative to school training of Negroes is an element in their occupational distribution. It creates an even lower skill concentration in the occupational distribution than would be predicted by the educational distribution. As in the sex comparison this results in a statistical finding that the ratio of non-white to white incomes declines with increasing level of formal education.[44]

It has long been observed that at lower levels of skill and education workers are affected by a stronger incidence of unemployment than those at higher occupational and educational levels. The reasons for this phenomenon have never been clarified.

In his analysis of investment in people, Becker points out that, for a given demand situation, turnover and unemployment rates are likely to be milder under conditions of specific on-the-job training than elsewhere. Specific training is defined as an investment which increases the worker's marginal product in the firm in which he is trained more than elsewhere. According to this theory marginal products of specifically trained workers exceed their wages, but the latter are higher than in alternative employments.[45] Hence employers have more incentive to retain such workers, and these have more incentive to remain with the firm. The differential behavior is implicit both for cross-sectional observations and for cyclical changes. In a recent study, a similar hypoth-

[43] Yet another explanation, suggested by Becker ("Underinvestment in College Education?" *op. cit.*) is that the personal money returns shown above understate the money returns which actually accrue to women as family members. According to this argument family income differentials are the relevant measures.

[44] See M. Zeman, "A Quantitative Analysis of White–Non-white Income Differentials in the United States" (unpublished doctoral dissertation, University of Chicago, 1955).

[45] Becker, "Investment in People," *op. cit.*

esis was elaborated and put to an empirical test by Walter Oi.[46] Oi related the severity of cyclical changes (1929–33) in employment to levels of wages in a particular industry and found an inverse correlation between the two. He also correlated average wages by industry with turnover rates for a number of industries at a given time. Here again the (partial) correlation was negative. Oi interprets his results as favorable evidence for the investment hypothesis, on the assumption that wage levels (by occupation and industry) are a proxy for amounts of specific training.

This is a bold assumption. Even if cross-sectional wage differentials (by occupation and industry) represented returns to training only, these conceptually reflect returns to two forms of training: school training which is "general," and on-the-job training which may be "general" or "specific." It is not easy to see why the total return should be particularly strongly correlated with what is probably the smallest component: that part of on-the-job training which is specific. Oi did not attempt to segregate the explanatory factors into "general" and "specific" components of training because his data did not permit standardizations by education or by age. Without such standardizations the results are ambiguous. The wage rate reflects schooling as well as on-the-job training: a higher rate will prevail with very little on-the-job training but sufficiently more school training. This might obscure the relation which is tested. Conversely, the lack of control for age makes for a spurious correlation between the wage rate and turnover. Larger proportions of younger people in an industry, or occupation, mean both more turnover and lower wages.

In an attempt to get a stronger test of the investment hypothesis and more insight into factors affecting turnover and unemployment, I ran a multiple regression relating a hybrid unemployment and turnover variable to average full-time incomes in 1949 of males in eighty-seven detailed occupations, standardizing by educational level, age, and industrial distribution. The dependent variable (y) is the proportion of wage and salary workers who worked fifty to fifty-two weeks in 1949. This variable reflects both differential turnover and unemployment incidence among the groups, so it is well suited for the purpose.[47] The independent variables are full-time mean incomes in the occupations (X_1), median years of schooling (X_2), proportion of workers less than twenty-five years old (X_3), and (X_4) proportion of workers employed in durable-goods manufacturing and in construction.

The rationale for the choice of independent variables is as follows: according to the investment hypothesis, the turnover plus unemployment variable Y is a positive function of specific training costs, part of which are borne by workers, part by firms. Unfortunately, there are no data or readily available proxies for specific costs. I shall assume that such costs are positively related to the total of on-the-job training. This is a much weaker assumption than that of a positive correlation of specific training costs with wage rates.

Consider now the average wage X_1 in an occupation. This wage will tend to be higher, the higher is the average education X_2 and the greater the amount of on-the-job training in the occupation. For given values of X_2, larger X_1 will therefore tend to reflect more on-the-job training. Thus the sign of the partial regression coefficient of X_1 is expected to be positive. Conversely, for given occupational wage levels X_1, the higher the schooling X_2, the less on-the-job training in the occupation. Unless formal schooling itself has an effect on turnover and unemployment, the sign at X_2 should be negative.

---

[46] "Labor as a Quasi-fixed Factor of Production" (unpublished doctoral dissertation, University of Chicago, 1961).

[47] The variable is also affected by seasonality. The obvious cases where seasonality is strong had fewer than 50 per cent of workers employed year-round. To avoid arbitrariness, all occupations (more than twenty) with $y < 50$ per cent were excluded from the analysis.

The two additional variables used in the regression, age, X_3 and industrial composition, X_4, standardize for factors other than training. Among persons less than twenty-five years of age there is more job and labor-force mobility than among older people, even when the other variables are held constant. X_4 crudely standardizes for effects of short-run demand fluctuations by industry.

Using these variables, the following regression was obtained (all variables are measured as deviations from their means; standard errors of regression coefficients are in parentheses):

$$y = 2.08X_1 + 1.86X_2 - 2.29X_3 - .74X_4$$
$$(1.04) \quad (.46) \quad (.68) \quad (.21)$$

$$R^2 = .65 \ .$$

All variables are statistically significant. All signs, except that for X_2, conform to expectations. In particular, the positive effect of X_1 is consistent with the investment hypothesis.

Even if formal education per se had no effect on employment stability, the effects of on-the-job training (reflected in the coefficient at X_1) would explain the previously described systematic patterns of unemployment rates of workers classified by educational levels. As we have seen in Table 15.1, more on-the-job training is received by workers at higher educational levels.

However, in terms of the investment hypothesis, which emphasizes specific training in this context, the positive sign at X_2 is puzzling. Could it possibly reverse if the analysis were expanded to include such variables as urbanization, unionization, race, marital status? Such an expansion, if feasible, would be desirable. I experimented with inclusion of two easily accessible variables: X_5, percentage of males older than fifty-five, and X_6, percentage of non-whites in an occupation. Neither was statistically significant. Their inclusion did not increase the correlation coefficient, nor did it affect the coefficient of X_2. The inclusion of the racial variable X_6, however, lowered the coefficient of X_1 and weakened its reliability.

Is stability of employment affected by training, regardless of whether it is general or specific, acquired at school or on the job? One could argue, to be monistic, that educational levels are more strongly correlated with specific training than is on-the-job training. For example, the employer may be using information on educational attainment as an index of capability or suitability for selection to specific on-the-job training. If so, the coefficient of education (at X_2) "catches" more of the effects of specific training than does the coefficient at X_1. However, there may be good reasons for the behavior of X_2 other than the investment hypothesis, and it remains an open question for some

TABLE 15.7 NEGRO-WHITE UNEMPLOYMENT DIFFERENTIALS,* BY AGE AND EDUCATION, UNITED STATES MALES, CIVILIAN LABOR FORCE, 1950

Years of Schooling	Age					Total
	25–29	30–34	35–44	45–54	55–64	
0	0.9	.8	−1.1	.3	.6	−.2
1–4	0.0	.2	.3	.3	.6	.3
5–7	.6	1.4	1.5	1.3	1.3	1.8
8	4.4	3.1	3.3	2.3	2.8	3.5
9–11	5.8	3.5	4.4	3.3	2.5	4.7
12	5.6	4.7	4.0	2.8	3.9	4.4
13–15	4.8	4.9	4.0	.4	3.8	3.8
16 or more	0.0	3.0	.9	.8	1.7	1.2

* Negro minus white unemployment rate.
Source: *U.S. Census of Population, 1950, Special Reports, Education*: Table 9.

TABLE 15.8 MALE-FEMALE UNEMPLOYMENT DIFFERENTIALS,* BY AGE AND EDUCATION, CIVILIAN LABOR FORCE, 1950

Years of Schooling	Age				
	25–29	30–34	35–44	45–54	55–64
0	2.6	−1.4	.3	−.4	−1.5
1–4	2.5	2.2	1.4	.4	−1.4
5–7	.5	1.2	.3	.1	−.4
8	.3	1.0	.3	−.1	−.5
9–11	.8	.7	.5	.2	.3
12	−.1	.7	.1	−.3	−.6
13–15	−.6	.2	.1	−.4	−.6
16 or more	−.8	.7	.1	−.2	−.6

* Female minus male unemployment rate.
Source: *U.S. Census of Population, 1950, Special Reports, Education,* Table 9.

significant exploration of unemployment phenomena.

Another way of discerning the effects of on-the-job training on employment stability is to compare population groups with the same amount of formal education but differing in on-the-job training. Comparisons by race and sex should serve the purpose. As we have seen (in this section and Table 15.1) the amounts invested in on-the-job training differ substantially among the groups compared within the same educational levels. It also appears that differences in amounts of on-the-job training increase with increasing educational level in both race and sex comparisons. If on-the-job training were a major factor in explaining differentials in employment stability, the investment hypothesis would predict higher unemployment rates for Negroes than for whites at each educational level and an increasing differential in rates the higher the educational level. A similar prediction would apply to the female-male comparison.

Data shown in Table 15.7 are differences between unemployment rates of Negro and white males classified by age and education in 1950. Negro unemployment rates are higher in almost all classifications; the difference is negligible at the lowest educational levels and, generally, increases with education. The differentials remain positive, but decrease at the highest educational level.

Similar patterns have been observed by Harry Gilman for an occupational breakdown of the Negro and white male labor force, both for cross-sectional differences and cyclical changes.[48] In the occupational breakdown, the differentials increase with skill level in the "blue-collar" groups; differentials remain positive but the increase is halted in the "white-collar" groups. Additional factors, such as differential industrial attachments of "blue-collar" and "white-collar" groups are likely to be responsible for some of the deviations from the theoretical predictions. A multivariate analysis is clearly desirable. But, by and large, even the gross comparisons suggest that the investment hypothesis is relevant in explaining differences in unemployment incidence of Negro and white labor.[49]

Comparison of unemployment rates of males and females, classified by education, show only small, apparently random, differences (Table 15.8). The levels are similar and decline with increasing education in both groups. Does this mean that formal

[48] "Discrimination and the White–Non-white Unemployment Differentials" (doctoral dissertation, University of Chicago).
[49] The turnover regression analysis described before is also suggestive: once the levels of education and of on-the-job training were taken into account, the racial factor did not seem to have any discernible effects on turnover plus unemployment.

education affects unemployment rates and on-the-job training does not? This would be, prima facie, inconsistent with the other findings. A multivariate analysis is needed in which the net effect of the training factor could be isolated, in order to resolve this puzzle.[50]

Summary

The empirical exploration described in this paper was designed to achieve several purposes: (1) to estimate the amount of resources invested in on-the-job training as distinguished from investments in the formal educational system, (2) to estimate rates of return on such investments, (3) to investigate the relevance of these investments to certain well-known but not well-understood patterns of income and employment behavior of population groups.

Since the research was exploratory rather than intensive, the conclusions reached are very tentative. Briefly stated: (1) Investment in on-the-job training is a very large component of total investment in education in the United States economy. Measured in terms of costs, it is as important as formal education for the male labor force and amounts to more than a half of total (male and female) expenditures on school education. Aggregate and per capita investments in on-the-job training have been increasing since 1939, though at a slower rate than investments in formal education. It seems, however, that on-the-job training has grown at a much faster rate at higher skill levels than at lower ones.

(2) The rate of return on selected investments in on-the-job training, such as apprenticeships and medical specialization, was not different from the rate of return on total costs of college education, both unadjusted for ability factors. However, the private return, that is, the return on private costs seems to be higher in formal education than in on-the-job training. These findings raise questions about possible downward biases in the calculated rates of return to education.

(3) The last section of the paper is a preliminary analysis of differential income and employment patterns of population groups, classified by education, occupation, sex, and race. The analyses are incomplete, but they suggest that new empirical knowledge about forms and amounts of investments in people can lead to a significant increase in our understanding of such major areas of economic behavior as income distribution, unemployment incidence, and labor mobility.

Empirical ventures into unexplored territory are hazardous. The margins of error are difficult to assess, and they are likely to be large. At least the findings should provoke further research. The need for more, better, and different data is evident. I hope that some guides for future research do emerge from this preliminary work.

---

[50] The prevalence of women in cyclically insensitive jobs (clerical, government, teaching, and nursing) is an obviously plausible explanation.

Appendix to Reading 15

TABLE 15.9 NET AVERAGE WAGE AND SALARY INCOMES,* BY YEARS OF SCHOOLING AND AGE, WHITE URBAN MALES, UNITED STATES, 1939 (IN DOLLARS)

Age	Years of Schooling			
	16 or more	12	7–8	1–4
Less than 14†	−850	−850	−850	−340
14–15‡	−115	−115	281	258
16–17‡	−103	−103	352	315
18–19‡	−452	481	443	373
20–21‡	−400	755	579	431
22–24	1,028	947	750	503
25–29	1,661	1,244	959	648
30–34	2,395	1,606	1,179	802
35–44	3,147	2,073	1,434	916
45–54	3,483	2,286	1,570	1,018
55–64	3,147	2,105	1,439	950

* All income data are before tax.
† This now shows total rather than annual costs of elementary school per student.
‡ Gross earnings of high-school and of college students were assumed to be one quarter of earnings of elementary-school graduates and of high-school graduates, respectively.
Source: Wage and Salary Incomes: Unpublished National Bureau of Economic Research materials of G. S. Becker, based on 1940 Population Census. Direct costs per student were derived from Tables 3, 5, and 6 in T. W. Schultz, "Capital Formation by Education," *Journal of Political Economy,* December, 1960, and from *Biennial Survey of Education in the United States, 1939–40.*

TABLE 15.10 NET AVERAGE INCOMES,* BY YEARS OF SCHOOLING AND AGE, UNITED STATES MALES, 1949 (IN DOLLARS)

	Years of Schooling			
Age	16+	12	8	1–3
Less than 14†	−1,576	−1,576	−1,576	−394
14–17‡	−205	−205	676	670
18–19‡	−910	1,071	1,079	720
20–21‡	−753	1,745	1,523	952
22–24	2,284	2,356	1,929	1,192
25–29	3,441	2,975	2,341	1,474
30–34	4,846	3,576	2,680	1,667
35–44	7,085	4,055	3,029	1,814
45–54	8,116	4,689	3,247	1,990
55–64	7,655	4,548	3,010	1,892

* See n. * in Table 15.9. Here income includes property income.
† See n. † in Table 15.9.
‡ See n. ‡ in Table 15.9.
Source: Income data derived from *1950 Census of Population,* Ser. P-E, No. 5B, *Education,* Tables 12 and 13 (also H. P. Miller, "Income in Relation to Education," *American Economic Review,* December, 1960, Table 1. Direct costs per student derived from T. W. Schultz, *op. cit.,* and *Biennial Survey of Education, 1948–50.*

TABLE 15.11 NET AVERAGE INCOMES,* BY YEARS OF SCHOOLING AND AGE, UNITED STATES MALES, 1958 (IN DOLLARS)

	Years of Schooling			
Age	16+	12	8	0–4
Less than 14†	−2,400	−2,400	−2,400	−600
14–17‡	−224	−224	1,208	1,080
18–21‡	−682	2,800	1,910	1,532
22–24	3,663	3,537	2,520	1,931
25–29	5,723	4,381	3,223	2,387
30–34	7,889	5,182	3,848	2,757
35–44	10,106	6,007	4,403	3,023
45–54	11,214	6,295	4,337	3,008
55–64	10,966	6,110	3,960	2,956

* See n. * in Table 15.10.
† See n. † in Table 15.9.
‡ See n. ‡ in Table 15.9.
Source: Income data derived from the March, 1959, *Current Population Survey,* and Miller, *op. cit.* Direct costs per student derived from *Statistical Abstract of the United States, 1960.*

TABLE 15.12 ILLUSTRATIVE CALCULATION OF ANNUAL INCREMENTAL COSTS OF INVESTMENT IN SCHOOLING AND IN ON-THE-JOB TRAINING, MALE COLLEGE GRADUATES, 1939 ($r = 11.0$ PER CENT)*

Age	Net Earnings of High School Graduates†	Net Earnings of College Graduates†	Differentials in Earnings ([1] − [2])	Returns on Last Year's Cost ($r \cdot C_{j-i}$)	Return on All Previous Costs ($j-1$ $r \cdot \Sigma C_k$ $k = 18$)	Cost‡ at Age j ([3] + [5])
	(1)	(2)	(3)	(4)	(5)	(6)
18	409	−468	877	—	—	877
19	563	−437	1,000	96	96	1,096
20	717	−407	1,124	121	217	1,341
21	793	−391	1,184	148	365	1,549
22	870	870	0	170	535	535
23	947	1,028	−81	59	594	513
24	1,021	1,186	−165	56	650	485
25	1,095	1,344	−249	53	703	454
26	1,169	1,502	−333	50	753	420
27	1,244	1,661	−417	46	799	382
28	1,316	1,807	−491	42	841	350
29	1,388	1,954	−566	39	880	314
30	1,460	2,101	−641	35	915	274
31	1,533	2,248	−715	30	945	230
32	1,606	2,395	−789	25	970	181
33	1,668	2,495	−827	20	990	163
34	1,730	2,595	−865	18	1,008	143
35	1,792	2,695	−903	16	1,024	121
36	1,854	2,795	−941	13	1,037	96
37	1,916	2,895	−979	10	1,047	68
38	1,978	2,995	−1,017	7	1,054	37
39	2,041	3,096	−1,055	4	1,058	3

* Obtained by equating to zero the present value of col. (3) (continued to age 65).
† Age-earnings profiles from Table 15.9, interpolated within age groups.
‡ School cost for ages 18–21; on-the-job training cost thereafter.

TABLE 15.13* ESTIMATED COST OF SCHOOLING AND OF ON-THE-JOB TRAINING, BY AGE AND LEVEL OF EDUCATION, UNITED STATES MALES, 1939

Age	Marginal Costs ($)			Total Costs ($)			"Employment" (Thousands)		
	Elementary School ($r=20.9$)	High School ($r=12.5$)	College ($r=11.0$)	Elementary School ([4] = [1])	High School ([1] + [2])	College ([1] + [2] + [3])	Elementary School	High School	College
	(1)	(2)	(3)	(4)	(5)	(6)	(7)	(8)	(9)
14	<u>510</u>	0	0	510	510	510	—	—	—
14	85	388	0	85	388	388	105.7	—	—
15	98	455	0	98	455	455	105.7	—	—
16	110	545	0	110	545	545	193.2	—	—
17	125	<u>643</u>	0	125	<u>643</u>	643	193.2	—	—
18	142	254	877	142	396	877	246.1	283.1	—
19	133	200	1,096	133	333	1,096	246.1	283.1	—
20	122	139	1,341	122	261	1,341	288.7	349.6	—
21	108	148	<u>1,549</u>	108	256	<u>1,549</u>	288.7	349.6	—
22	92	158	535	92	250	785	322.8	377.9	164.3
23	71	170	513	71	241	754	322.8	377.9	156.7
24	70	169	485	70	239	724	322.8	377.9	149.9
25	69	168	454	69	237	691	368.7	331.2	131.1
26	67	167	420	67	234	654	368.7	331.2	129.1
27	65	166	382	65	231	613	368.7	331.2	127.4
28	65	159	350	65	224	574	368.7	331.2	127.1
29	66	151	314	66	217	531	368.7	331.2	128.8
30	67	142	274	67	209	483	375.7	256.4	119.7
31	68	131	230	68	199	429	375.7	256.4	112.6
32	69	118	181	69	187	368	375.7	256.4	108.6
33	64	105	163	64	169	332	375.7	256.4	104.7
34	58	90	143	58	148	291	375.7	256.4	101.2
35	51	73	121	51	124	245	360.4	167.1	90.0
36	42	54	96	42	96	192	360.4	167.1	67.2
37	31	37	68	31	67	135	360.4	167.1	67.2
38	18	14	37	18	32	69	360.4	167.1	67.2
39	4	—	3	4	4	7	360.4	167.1	67.2
	Total cost of on-the-job training			2,000	4,400	7,900			

* Cols. (1), (2), (3) obtained by the method represented by eq. (1) in the text and illustrated in Table 15.12. Schooling costs are above the broken lines; on-the-job costs below it. r is the internal rate of return on the marginal costs. Columns terminate at ages when costs become zero. Thereafter they turn negative and positive for several runs; but they are small, and their sum is negligible.

Cols. (4), (5), (6) are horizontally cumulated costs for each year of training, separately for schooling (above the broken line), and for training on the job (below the broken line). Vertical sums (rounded) of training costs in cols. (4), (5), (6) are shown in the bottom row. These are entered in col. (5) of text Table 15.1. Figures in col. (2) of text Table 15.1 are first differences of figures in col. (5), not vertical sums of cols. (1, 2, 3) in Tables 15.13–15.15.

Col. (7) includes male workers with eight years of education, plus half the workers with less than eight years and half the workers with more than eight and less than twelve years of schooling.

Col. (8) includes workers who have high-school education, plus half of the "some high-school" and of "some college" groups.

Col. (9) includes workers who have college education or more, plus half of the "some college" group.

In principle, the employment figures (cols. [7], [8], [9]) are supposed to represent numbers of workers of a given educational category by numbers of years elapsed since completion of schooling, and not by age. Clearly, all college students do not graduate at age twenty-two. Very few graduate at an earlier age, but large proportions do at later ages. The number of college graduates aged twenty-two, therefore, severely underestimates the number of persons who are in their first year after college gradu-

TABLE 15.14* ESTIMATED COSTS OF SCHOOLING AND OF ON-THE-JOB TRAINING, BY AGE AND LEVEL OF EDUCATION, UNITED STATES MALES, 1949

Age	Marginal Costs ($)			Total Costs ($)			"Employment" (Thousands)		
	Elementary School ($r = 22.2$)	High School ($r = 11.8$)	College ($r = 10.6$)	Elementary School	High School	College	Elementary School	High School	College
	(1)	(2)	(3)	(4)	(5)	(6)	(7)	(8)	(9)
14	1,182	0	0	1,182	1,182	1,182	—	—	—
14	375	777	0	375	777	777	98.3	—	—
15	382	939	0	382	939	939	98.3	—	—
16	377	1,121	0	377	1,121	1,121	184.1	—	—
17	401	1,309	0	401	1,309	1,309	184.1	—	—
18	316	544	1,881	316	860	1,881	233.1	425.5	—
19	263	538	2,268	263	801	2,268	233.1	425.5	—
20	231	441	2,778	231	672	2,778	244.7	415.7	—
21	202	383	3,304	202	585	3,304	244.7	415.7	—
22	157	363	1,143	157	520	1,663	285.1	443.7	342.0
23	125	329	1,273	125	454	1,727	285.1	443.7	266.7
24	130	315	1,329	130	445	1,774	285.1	443.7	204.7
25	129	307	1,335	129	436	1,771	303.5	476.8	118.3
26	123	293	1,311	123	416	1,727	303.5	476.8	114.6
27	108	268	1,294	108	376	1,670	303.5	476.8	112.0
28	114	264	1,267	114	378	1,640	303.5	476.8	138.6
29	104	255	1,260	104	359	1,619	303.5	476.8	169.7
30	102	225	1,252	102	327	1,579	329.5	442.1	169.2
31	94	196	1,218	94	290	1,508	329.5	442.1	173.1
32	76	148	1,150	76	224	1,374	329.5	442.1	164.2
33	45	161	1,075	45	206	1,281	329.5	442.1	157.8
34	30	154	1,008	30	184	1,192	329.5	442.1	150.1
35	16	167	884	16	183	1,067	379.3	387.5	139.5
36	—	151	763	—	151	914	—	387.5	125.8
37	—	143	599	—	143	742	—	387.5	125.8
38	—	149	432	—	149	581	—	387.5	125.8
39	—	156	228	—	156	384	—	387.5	125.8
40	—	129	47	—	129	176	—	267.5	115.8
41	—	89	17	—	89	106	—	267.5	115.8
42	—	65	—	—	65	65	—	267.5	115.8
43	—	17	—	—	17	17	—	267.5	115.8
Total cost of on-the-job training				3,902	8,600	24,300			

* See notes to Table 15.13.

ation. The bias in numbers of workers, of course, reverses at later ages. However, since higher costs of on-the-job training decline with age, aggregate costs (Table 15.2) would be underestimated. This bias is roughly corrected at the college level (col. [9]) by the use of graduation rather than employment data. No such correction was made at the lower levels. Graduation at the lower levels cannot be equated with labor-force participation, and the problem of bias is less acute anyway: age dispersion at graduation and cost figures are much smaller.

Source: Cols. (7), (8), (9) *1940 Census of Population, Education,* Tables 75, 76, *1950 Census of Population,* G-E, No. 5B, *Education,* Table 9. Bureau of Labor Statistics, *Special Labor Force Reports,* No. 1, February, 1960, Table D; United States Department of Health, Education, and Welfare, *Earned Degrees Conferred by Higher Educational Institutions, 1948–58; Biennial Survey of Education,* before 1948.

TABLE 15.15* ESTIMATED COSTS OF SCHOOLING AND OF ON-THE-JOB TRAINING, BY AGE AND LEVEL OF EDUCATION, UNITED STATES MALES, 1958

Age	Marginal Costs ($)			Total Costs ($)			"Employment" (Thousands)		
	Elementary School ($r = 19.3$)	High School ($r = 15.1$)	College ($r = 11.5$)	Elementary School	High School	College	Elementary School	High School	College
	(1)	(2)	(3)	(4)	(5)	(6)	(7)	(8)	(9)
14	1,800	0	0	1,800	1,800	1,800	—	—	—
14	296	1,266	0	296	1,266	1,266	65.8	—	—
15	314	1,538	0	314	1,538	1,538	65.8	—	—
16	303	1,917	0	303	1,917	1,917	73.8	—	—
17	300	2,338	0	300	2,338	2,338	73.8	—	—
18	297	225	3,246	297	522	3,246	191.5	361.4	—
19	293	224	3,776	293	517	3,776	191.5	361.4	—
20	289	223	4,368	289	512	4,368	182.4	432.3	—
21	284	222	5,027	284	506	5,027	182.4	432.3	—
22	278	220	2,090	278	498	2,588	182.4	432.3	385.7
23	271	217	2,001	271	488	2,489	182.4	432.3	360.0
24	262	214	1,902	262	476	2,378	182.4	432.3	335.3
25	251	211	1,891	251	462	2,353	254.5	502.1	285.4
26	237	208	1,880	237	445	2,325	254.5	502.1	289.0
27	221	204	1,660	221	425	2,085	254.5	502.1	304.4
28	202	200	1,528	202	402	1,930	254.5	502.1	332.7
29	180	195	1,367	180	375	1,752	254.5	502.1	387.3
30	161	189	1,197	161	350	1,547	254.5	502.1	392.2
31	153	183	1,149	153	336	1,485	254.5	502.1	359.5
32	144	175	1,096	144	319	1,415	254.5	502.1	264.2
33	133	165	1,037	133	298	1,335	254.5	502.1	192.2
34	120	154	971	120	274	1,245	254.5	502.1	125.9
35	104	141	898	104	245	1,143	323.5	501.6	117.1
36	85	126	815	85	211	1,026	323.5	501.6	114.0
37	63	109	719	63	172	991	323.5	501.6	140.6
38	37	89	616	37	126	742	323.5	501.6	171.7
39	6	67	501	6	73	574	323.5	501.6	175.6
40	—	43	423	—	43	466	—	501.6	165.0
41	—	16	339	—	16	355	—	501.6	165.0
42	—	—	245	—	—	246	—	—	165.0
43	—	—	144	—	—	144	—	—	165.0
44	—	—	27	—	—	27	—	—	165.0
Total cost of on-the-job training				5,300	8,200	30,700			

* See notes to Table 15.13.

TABLE 15.16 AVERAGE WAGE AND SALARY INCOME AND MEDIAN YEARS OF SCHOOLING OF APPRENTICES, OPERATIVES, AND JOURNEYMEN IN THREE INDUSTRY GROUPS, 1949

	Metal Trades (4 Years)*		Printing and Publishing (5.5 Years)*		Construction (3.8 Years)*	
	Schooling	Wage	Schooling	Wage	Schooling	Wage
Apprentices	12.2	$2,480	12.2	$2,525	11.8	$2,576
Operatives (in same industry)	9.0	3,015	10.4	3,239	8.8	2,937
With more schooling†	11.3	3,286	11.3	3,500	11.3	3,208
Assuming a 10 per cent return on schooling‡	—	3,415	—	3,540	—	3,340
Journeymen	9.5	3,534	10.9	4,138	8.9	3,216

* Average length of apprenticeship.
† In industries where they are found.
‡ This return is added to the wage figure in second row. k = row 5 minus row 2; d_1 = row 2 minus row 1; d_2 = row 3 minus row 1; d_3 = row 4 minus row 1.
Source: *U.S. Census of Population, 1950: Special Reports, Occupational Characteristics,* Tables 10 and 23.

TABLE 15.17 NET AVERAGE INCOMES OF FEMALES WITH AND WITHOUT ADJUSTMENT FOR LABOR-FORCE PARTICIPATION RATES, BY LEVEL OF EDUCATION AND AGE, 1949 (IN DOLLARS)

	Unadjusted		Adjusted*	
Age	High School (1)	College (2)	High School (3)	College (4)
18–19	970	−786	970	−786
20–21	1,468	−706	1,468	−706
22–24	1,614	1,900	734	1,313
25–29	1,635	2,120	520	939
30–34	1,674	2,293	532	1,016
35–44	1,859	2,600	662	1,277
45–54	2,062	2,907	767	1,608
55–64	1,968	2,974	559	1,448

* Observed average incomes multiplied by labor-force rates after age twenty-two. Rates from Gertrude Bancroft, *The American Labor Force* (New York: John Wiley & Son, 1958), Table D, p. 62.
Source: *U.S. Census of Population, 1950, Special Reports, Education,* Tables 10 and 12.

TABLE 15.18 MEAN INCOMES OF NON-WHITE MALES, BY AGE AND EDUCATION LEVEL, UNITED STATES, 1950 (IN DOLLARS)

Age	Education			
	No Schooling	Elementary School	High School	College or More
18–19	570	809	809	—
20–21	808	1,177	1,349	—
22–24	997	1,520	1,783	1,555
25–29	1,109	1,747	2,137	2,121
30–34	1,187	1,916	2,374	2,950
35–44	1,300	2,008	2,453	3,437
45–54	1,254	2,068	2,419	3,639
55–64	1,108	1,921	2,238	3,246

Source: Computed from distributions given in *U.S. Census of Population, 1950,* Vol. IV, *Special Reports, Education,* Table 12.

PART V
INFORMATION

The competitive theory of the labor market predicts that the equilibrium wage rate for a given occupation in a given area should be uniform across firms for workers of a given quality, but wage surveys persistently indicate the existence of a dispersion of rates for a given job in a given market. In theory, the equilibrium wage is attained as workers obtain information on the dispersion of wages and move from relatively low- to relatively high-wage jobs, but labor market studies consistently find that workers neither possess extensive knowledge of alternative pecuniary and nonpecuniary conditions of employment nor develop that knowledge by systematic job search activities.[1] These observations have led some labor market analysts to conclude that (1) there is inadequate information for the efficient operation of the labor market and therefore (2) the competitive model of the labor market is of dubious validity.

George J. Stigler's article connects wage dispersion to incomplete knowledge, and shows that the presence of either is not necessarily inconsistent with labor market efficiency. Building on an analysis developed earlier to explain price dispersion in the product market,[2] Stigler generates an explanation of wage dispersion by dropping the assumption of perfect knowledge and noting that information has a cost, particularly the opportunity cost of a worker's time. From this observation it is a short but important step to the determination of the optimal duration of search for an income maximizing employee. Since the search for information will be of limited duration because of the costs incurred, all wage offers will not be identified, and some wage dispersion will result.[3]

Although Stigler's theory is of considerable usefulness, some of its implications appear to be contradicted by the findings of several local

---

[1] For a survey of these studies, see Herbert S. Parnes, "The Labor Force and Labor Markets," in Herbert G. Heneman, Jr., et al., eds., *Employment Relations Research* (New York: Harper & Row, Publishers, 1960), pp. 1–42.

[2] George J. Stigler, "The Economics of Information," *Journal of Political Economy*, vol. 69 (June 1961), pp. 213–225.

[3] Stigler, in Reading 16, implicitly provides the basis of a theory of frictional unemployment, for the optimal duration of search may be interpreted as the average duration of frictional unemployment. Contemporary theoretical research on unemployment and the microeconomic foundations of aggregate wage behavior generally use this theory of information as a point of departure. Examples of this approach may be found in Melvin W. Reder, "The Theory of Frictional Unemployment," *Economica*, February 1969; and Armen Alchian, "Information Costs, Pricing, and Resource Unemployment," *Western Economic Journal*, vol. 7, no. 2 (June 1969), pp. 109–28.

labor market studies completed during the post–World War II period. Normally, young workers would be expected to search longer, because the expected income gain from job search increases with the prospective length of employment, and one would predict the widespread use of dealers in information, such as employment services, to reduce the cost of search. Neither of these predictions has been substantiated, but Stigler's article contains a rich vein of hypotheses which deserve to be tested in a rigorous manner.

Drawing on evidence produced by the most recent labor market study, Albert Rees describes the patterns of information search observed in the Chicago area and notes that the search is confined to the identification of additional wage offers only when there is negligible quality variance among alternative jobs. (Quality on both sides of the labor market is assumed constant throughout most of Stigler's analysis.) However, when the quality variation among jobs is substantial, search activity focuses on developing additional information on the nonpecuniary elements of a job. This type of information is most easily acquired personally and cannot be conveyed effectively by dealers in information. The importance of quality variance may account for the apparent contradictions between some of Stigler's hypotheses and the findings of postwar studies of the blue-collar labor market. However, Rees does present some evidence for white-collar occupations which is consistent with some of the hypotheses developed by Stigler. Further evidence on search behavior can be found in the final report of the Chicago labor market study.[4]

These two articles introduce one major qualification to the traditional competitive theory of the labor market, in which information is implicitly considered a free good. When information is not free, the existence of some wage dispersion within a market does not imply a welfare loss in the economic sense. At this time, however, there is no clear evidence for or against the proposition that observed patterns of wage dispersion are the result of the operation of an efficient market with a high cost of search. Evaluation of this proposition must await more sophisticated empirical tests.

Nevertheless, one provisional test of the extent and influence of labor market information is to evaluate the patterns of labor mobility and wage differentials found in empirical investigations. In Parts VI and VII we examine the ability of the competitive model to predict the behavior of labor mobility and wage differentials.

[4] Albert Rees and George P. Shultz, *Workers and Wages in an Urban Labor Market* (Chicago: University of Chicago Press, 1970).

16
Information in the Labor Market

George J. Stigler[1]

The young person entering the labor market for the first time has an immense number of potential employers, scarce as they may seem the first day. If he is an unskilled or a semi-skilled worker, the number of potential employers is strictly in the millions. Even if he has a specialized training, the number of potential employers will be in the thousands: the young Ph.D. in economics, for example, has scores of colleges and universities, dozens of governmental agencies, hundreds of business firms, and the Ford Foundation as potential employers. As the worker becomes older the number of potential employers may shrink more often than it grows, but the number will seldom fall to even a thousand.

Reprinted from the *Journal of Political Economy* (Supplement, October 1962) by permission of The University of Chicago Press. Copyright, 1962, pp. 94–105.
[1] I am deeply indebted to Claire Friedland for the statistical work in this paper. H. Gregg Lewis made very helpful comments on an earlier version.

No worker, unless his degree of specialization is pathological, will ever be able to become informed on the prospective earnings which would be obtained from every one of these potential employers at any given time, let alone keep this information up to date. He faces the problem of how to acquire information on wage rates, stability of employment, conditions of employment, and other determinants of job choice, and how to keep this information current. I shall concentrate attention on the determination of wage rates.

1. The Dispersion of Wage Rates

Even with strict homogeneity of commodities, we usually find some dispersion in the prices which are offered by sellers or buyers. Only if either buyers have complete knowledge of all sellers' offers, or all sellers have complete knowledge of all buyers' offers, will there be a single price. Complete knowledge, however, is seldom possessed,

233

simply because it costs more to learn of alternative prices than (at the margin) this information yields.[2]

The labor markets display the same characteristics, but their analysis is much complicated by the lack of homogeneity of the workers (and, to a much lesser extent, of non-wage conditions of employment). In order to form some estimate of the nature of the "pure" dispersion of wages due to imperfect knowledge, we shall begin with a very special class of college graduates.

A tolerably pure estimate of the dispersion of wage offers to homogeneous labor is provided by the contemporary offers to the same person. For forty-four graduates of the Graduate School of Business at the University of Chicago who received 144 offers (in 1960 and 1961) from corporations, the standard deviation of monthly rates was $43. The mean offer was $540.7, so the coefficient of variation was 7.9 per cent.[3]

Since this job market was completely localized in one office, and there is considerable intercommunication among the national companies whose representatives solicit prospective employees (and among prospective employees), this appears to be a conservative estimate of the gross dispersion for given quality. The fact that each student on average solicited only 2.25 offers works in the same direction. The differences in the attractiveness of non-wage elements of the various jobs, however, are impossible to discover.[4] On balance it appears that the true dispersion is substantially underestimated, and later evidence suggests that it may be much larger in less organized markets.

Unfortunately, distributions of offers to given individuals are not available for any large occupational group or any extended geographical market. One must deal with offers (or wage rates paid) by individual employers or groups of employers, and the dispersion of such offers may be either larger or smaller than the true distribution we desire. The dispersion of distributions of company average offers will be larger insofar as they reflect differences in quality of workers (or of jobs),[5] or cover several labor markets; the dispersion will be smaller insofar as intracompany dispersion is eliminated. In our sample of business graduates, the standard deviation of the average offers of companies is $40, compared with that of $43 for given students. Although no unique relationship between these dispersions can be assumed, we can and will assume that for similar labor markets they are reasonably well correlated.

The dispersion of wage offers in the small Chicago sample is approximately equal to that of the national sample of wage offers made each year by Frank Endicott.[6]. The coefficients of variation of groups other than engineers range from 6.4 per cent to 9.1 per cent (Table 16.1); the corresponding figure for our sample was 7.3 per cent.

If the expected period of employment exceeds one year (as it does), the worker must also make an estimate of future wage differences among employers. Endicott's data permit an estimate of the correlation of suc-

---

[2] The argument is elaborated in my "The Economics of Information," *Journal of Political Economy*, June 1961.

[3] There was no systematic or significant difference in the standard deviations for those who received 2, 3, 4, or 5 or more offers:

No. of Offers	No. of Students	Standard Deviation
2	17	$46
3	13	35
4	7	49
5 or more	7	43

The basic data were made available by courtesy of David Huntington of the Placement Bureau of the Graduate School of Business.

[4] The extent to which initial wage rates are reliable indexes of subsequent wage rates is investigated below.

[5] The variance of offers, within a given specialty, is usually much larger between than "within" individuals who have received multiple offers.

[6] We are indebted to Endicott for permission to examine the company reports for three years.

Information in the Labor Market 235

TABLE 16.1 MONTHLY HIRING RATES OF LARGE CORPORATIONS FOR COLLEGE GRADUATES, 1958–60

Occupation	No. of Companies	1958	1959	1960
1. Mean Salaries				
Engineers	66	$472	$493	$515
Accountants	40	421	435	457
Salesmen	29	410	426	447
General business	41	403	416	431
2. Coefficient of Variation (Per Cent)				
Engineers	66	4.04	4.22	4.26
Accountants	40	6.45	6.93	6.42
Salesmen	29	8.78	8.18	9.11
General business	41	8.60	8.96	8.64

Source: Endicott Survey worksheets. All companies here included reported in each of the three years.

TABLE 16.2 CORRELATION COEFFICIENTS OF SALARY RATES IN 1958, 1959, AND 1960 FOR COLLEGE GRADUATES

Occupation	No. of Companies	Correlation Coefficient		
		1958 and 1959	1959 and 1960	1958 and 1960
Engineers	66	.660	.761	.577
Accountants	40	.723	.872	.720
Sales	29	.849	.885	.871
General business	41	.853	.891	.873

Source: Same as Table 16.1.

cessive annual rates (Table 16.2). The correlations are high, and—what is more surprising—two of the four cases show no tendency to diminish when the time period is lengthened to two years. If the correlations were to remain high for long periods, the differences in wages would presumably reflect compensating differences in the nonwage terms of employment. But the normal pattern surely is one of declining correlation coefficients as the period is lengthened, if only as a Galton regression phenomenon.

Differences in initial wage rates would also be offset by different rates of increase in wages, so the present values of different jobs could still be equal. Endicott's survey for 1960 reported the average salary paid to college graduates after one year of service, and these salaries may be compared with those paid initially. The relationship for accountants was

$$W_2 = 24.71 + 1.039 W_1, \qquad (N = 67),$$
$$(.062)$$

where W_2 was the wage in 1960 and W_1 the wage in 1959; the relationship is close ($r = .900$). So far as these data go, they suggest that initial wage rates are a good predictor of wage rates in the following year.

These fragments illustrate rather than prove the existence of substantial dispersion in hiring rates for homogeneous labor. This dispersion cannot be measured precisely, but is of the order of magnitude of 5–10 per cent even in so well organized a market as that of college graduates at a single university.

II. The Problem of Information

A worker will search for wage offers (and an employer will search for wage demands) until the expected marginal return equals the marginal cost of search. Under what conditions will this search eliminate all dispersion of wage rates for homogeneous labor?

The conditions are severe. It is not sufficient for demand and supply to have been stable indefinitely long, and hence "the" equilibrium wage not to have changed for an indefinitely long period, in order to eliminate all dispersion. If workers were to change employment (perhaps because of improving skills) or employers were to change identity (because of the turnover of firms), it still would not pay to search enough to eliminate all dispersion. But if these changes were infrequent—say, once every three years or more—the dispersion of wage rates would be fairly small, although not negligible.[7] Changes in jobs due to changes in workers' tastes and abilities and employers' identities therefore set some minimum on the dispersion of wage rates. If the market has appreciable geographical extent, transportation costs of workers (and plants) add to this minimum dispersion.

The fluctuations of supply-and-demand conditions add a new source of dispersion. The information of the worker (and employer) now becomes obsolete with time: there will be changes in the level of wages and in the relative wage rates of different employers (and workers) which call for additional search. The more rapidly "the" equilibrium wage rate changes, the smaller the returns from search and hence the smaller the amount of search that will be undertaken—and the larger the resulting wage dispersion.

The subsequent analysis is devoted to an application of this approach to the costs and returns from search for various types of workers. The unavailability of a temporal sequence of closely spaced wage distributions makes it impossible to explore the effects of rates of change of equilibrium prices on the amount of dispersion.

The Returns from Search by Workers

We shall begin our analysis of the returns from search by forming some estimate of the magnitude of the return as a function of the amount of search. To this end, let us assume that the wage offers by all possible employers are normally distributed.[8] Then the expected maximum wage offer (w_m) a man will encounter in n searches is approximately[9]

$$w_m = .65 n^{.37} \sigma_w + \bar{w},$$

and the marginal wage rate increase from one additional search is

$$\frac{\partial w_n}{\partial n} = \frac{.24 \sigma_w}{n^{.63}}.$$

If $\sigma_w = \bar{w}/10$, the marginal wage rate gain from additional search is:

Search (n)	Marginal Wage Rate Gain
5	.0087 $\bar{w}$
10	.0056 $\bar{w}$
15	.0044 $\bar{w}$
20	.0036 $\bar{w}$

If the annual wage rate is $6,000, the marginal wage rate gain is therefore of the order of $20 to $50 in this range of search.

If the structure of employer wage offers

---

[7] With a rectangular wage offer distribution between 0 and 1, the average maximum wage encountered in n searches is $n/(n+1)$, so the expected marginal wage rate gain from $(n+1)$ searches is

$$\frac{n+1}{n+2} - \frac{n}{n+1} = \frac{1}{(n+1)(n+2)},$$

which, multiplied by the expected duration of employment, is the marginal income gain from search. If employment is expected to last m days, and the cost of search is k days, the amount of search will be given by

$$\frac{m}{(n+1)(n+2)} = \frac{kn}{n+1},$$

or n is approximately $\sqrt{m/k}$, or (say) 25 with three years of expected employment, and $k = 1$. The coefficient of variation of wages is

$$\sqrt{\frac{n}{(n+1)^2(n+2)} \cdot \frac{n+1}{n}}$$

$$= \frac{1}{\sqrt{n(n+2)}} = \sqrt{\frac{k}{m}},$$

which would be 4 per cent in our example. This argument is an adaptation of that in "The Economics of Information," op. cit., p. 215.

[8] The Chicago student wage offers are consistent with this assumption, and it seems intuitively more plausible than the rectangular distribution which was used (for algebraic convenience) in "The Economics of Information" and in n. 7.

[9] The expression is simply an approximation (for $3 < n < 20$) to the mean maximum observation from a normal population in random samples of size n; the precise values are given in W. J. Dixon and F. J. Massey, Introduction to Statistical Analysis (New York, 1957), p. 407.

were permanently fixed, and if the worker lived forever, the marginal income gain from additional search would be simply the capitalized value of the marginal *wage-rate* gain. If the structure were permanent and the duration of employment t_o years, the marginal *income* gain would be the value of the corresponding annuity, namely,

$$\frac{\partial w_n}{\partial n} \frac{(1+i)^{t_o} - 1}{i(1+i)^{t_o}}.$$

In this extreme case of a permanent wage structure, the order of magnitude of the marginal income gain from search is illustrated by the following table, where $\sigma_w = \overline{w}/10$ and $i = 6$ per cent.

Prospective Years of Employment	Amount of Search	
	5 Employers	15 Employers
3	.023 $\overline{w}$	.032 $\overline{w}$
5	.037 $\overline{w}$	.018 $\overline{w}$
10	.064 $\overline{w}$	.032 $\overline{w}$

For the $6,000 salary level, these marginal income gains run from $66 (fifteen employers, three years) to $384 (five employers, ten years).

But these gains are exaggerated because there is not a perfect correlation between the wage offers of employers in successive time periods. The employers themselves do not know wage offers sufficiently well to preserve a perfect correlation, even if they mysteriously wished it, and the appearance of new employers adds a further reason for continued search by the worker.

When the correlation of successive wage offers is positive but less than unity it will still pay the worker to search more intensively in the earlier periods because this search will have some value in subsequent periods. In a simple two-period model, the details of which are given in the appendix, the increased search in the first period due to correlation of wage rates will increase the expected maximum wage offer in the proportion $br^2/(1-b)$, or approximately $r^2/2$. If $r = .5$, the amount of search in period 1 will be increased by 20 per cent, with roughly a 12 per cent increase in salary.

It would be possible to analyze a variety of phenomena in the light of the correlation of successive wage offers. For example, the higher the correlation, the longer the expected tenure of a worker with a company, and therefore the lower the quit rate. Unfortunately there are no published data, so far as I know, which allow calculation of the correlations, although of course these data dwell in the worksheets of numerous wage surveys.

As a poor substitute, one can examine the average wage rates (measured by earnings per worker) on a geographical basis. The average earnings per worker in a state will be an index of wage rates in the given industry, and it will be a better index the more similar the occupational and wage structures of the industry in various states. A sample of such calculations is reported in Table 16.3.

Several features of these geographical patterns are noteworthy. The dispersion of earnings among states is much smaller in the recent period, and the decline occurred in twenty-one of twenty-five industries. The inference is that the national market has become more perfect, and the inference is commended by the fact that costs of movement have fallen substantially relative to wage rates over the period. The correlation coefficients reveal a slight decline on average, although they are based upon a seven-year interval in the later period (including a year of turbulent demobilization) as against a five-year interval in the earlier period.[10] The comparison timidly suggests that the difference in earnings increasingly represents differences in the quality of labor rather than in its compensation.

The most direct implication of the formal analysis is that the gains from search are

---

[10] The industries are also more homogeneous in the later period, and this serves to increase the correlation coefficients.

TABLE 16.3 CHARACTERISTICS OF AVERAGE EARNINGS IN SELECTED MANUFACTURING INDUSTRIES, 1904–9 AND 1947–54 (IDENTICAL STATES)

Industry	No. of States	Correlation Coefficients		Average Coefficient of Variation (Per Cent)	
		1904 and 1909	1947 and 1954	1904 and 1909	1947 and 1954
Non-ferrous foundries	8	.895	.663	15.3	8.7
Motor vehicles and equipment	9	.349	.106	8.9	4.9
Structural clay products	23	.982	.938	29.4	19.3
Ship and boat building	9	.894	.703	17.6	10.6
Rubber products	8	.270	.672	8.1	6.4
Musical instruments and parts	7	.953	.460	25.7	8.7
Confectionery products	17	.819	.876	15.3	17.8
Beer and ale	12	.921	.834	15.4	10.8
Mattresses and bedsprings	9	.830	.906	22.0	22.9
Furniture and fixtures, excluding mattresses and bedsprings	33	.941	.912	26.2	17.0
Fertilizers	13	.905	.952	20.4	20.4
Meat products	29	.728	.922	18.5	15.8
Flour and meal	14	.935	.530	21.8	12.0
Bakery products	20	.952	.918	18.2	12.6
Bottled soft drinks	15	.954	.874	20.1	18.4
Manufactured ice	21	.926	.854	22.8	25.5
Woolen and worsted fabrics	8	.987	.844	17.6	8.7
Knitting mills	17	.955	.774	23.5	11.2
Paperboard containers	18	.906	.926	17.1	14.0
Printing and publishing	47	.912	.906	21.3	11.8
Drugs and medicines	13	.725	.924	16.2	14.0
Soap and related products	10	.950	.681	14.8	12.0
Paints and allied products	15	.742	.870	18.4	11.2
Leather tanning and finishing	9	.968	.906	19.0	13.8
Footwear (except rubber)	12	.932	.703	13.1	9.2
Average		.853	.786	18.7	13.5

larger the longer the prospective period of employment. When search is more extensive, however, the dispersion of maximum wage rates will be smaller—the lowest wage offers will more often be rejected for known better offers.[11] So the realized dispersion of wage rates should be smaller the longer the prospective period of employment. Several tests of this implication can be made.

Women generally expect to stay in the labor force a shorter period than men do, so among homogeneous groups of men and women we should expect that the latter have larger dispersions. The occupational wage surveys do reveal this expected difference.[12] The major difficulty in making extensive tests of this prediction is that the tabulated

[11] Or, more precisely, the distribution of maximum offers has a variance that decreases as the number of searches increases.

[12] For example, hourly earnings of shipping packers in manufacturing in Chicago have the following characteristics:

	1952	1957
Males:		
Interquartile range	23.4¢	43.8¢
Median rate	144.2	182.0
Interquartile ratio (per cent)	16.2	24.1
Females:		
Interquartile range	28.4¢	45.8¢
Median rate	109.8	175.7
Interquartile ratio (per cent)	25.9	26.1

Source: Bureau of Labor Statistics, Bulls. 1105 and 1202–15.
With normally distributed variates, the interquartile ratio is 1.35 times the coefficient of variation.

Census data on earnings (in 1940 and 1950) do not allow the removal of the effects of age (men have a much wider dispersion of ages) and of race (Negro women are a larger fraction of the female labor force than Negro men are of the male labor force).[13]

Similar comparisons can be made of younger and older workers. The coefficient of variation increases with age for engineers (see Table 16.4). The coefficient of variation of 1949 earnings of plumbers and pipefitters was 40.8 per cent; that of apprentices was 32.9 per cent.[14] The dispersion of salaries of college teachers is larger the higher the rank (and age) of the teacher.[15] A more

TABLE 16.4 MONTHLY ENGINEERING EARNINGS, BY AGE, 1929

Age	Mean Monthly Earnings	Standard Deviation	Coefficient of Variation (Per Cent)
23	161.0	85.1*	52.9*
24–25	189.5	58.2	30.7
26–27	230.1	86.4	37.6
28–31	282.8	117.5	41.6
32–35	349.9	175.7	50.2
36–39	400.0	221.6	55.4
40–47	464.1	294.5	63.5
48–55	510.0	346.0	67.8
56–63	544.3	399.8	73.4
64 or more	487.6	356.3	73.1

Source: A. Fraser, Jr., "Employment and Earnings in the Engineering Profession, 1929 to 1934," Bureau of Labor Statistics, Bull. No. 682, 233, Table 2.
* This class appears to be heterogeneous: two of the respondents had salaries 20 standard deviations above the mean.

---

[13] A moderately extensive analysis was made of dispersions of income in 1949 in large cities for selected occupations, and an analysis was made of earnings in 1939 for waiters and waitresses. The 1949 data showed larger dispersions for women than for men; the 1939 data for the one occupation showed the opposite. The heterogeneity of age and race (and in 1940 the inclusion of self-employed workers) are such that I believe the results are wholly inconclusive. For the same reason, the consistently smaller *average* wages of women (which are predicted by the theory) are not supporting evidence.

[14] On the other hand, the coefficients of variation for machinists and tool makers (30.1 per cent) and apprentices (29.7 per cent) were essentially identical. These are all United States data, influenced by extent of part-time work (which was much higher among apprentices than among machinists).

[15] The interquartile ratios $[(Q_3 - Q_1)/Q_2]$ of academic salaries in 1959–60 were:

Rank	Per Cent	
	Men	Women
Professor	33.0	31.8
Associate professor	23.3	26.2
Assistant professor	19.7	24.2
Instructor	19.3	21.7

These calculations are based upon National Education Association, Higher Education Series, Research Report, 1960–R3. See also my *Trends in Employment in the Service Industries* (New York: National Bureau of Economic Research, 1956), p. 128.

The smaller dispersion of salaries of women professors is found in every type of college and university reported. Women make up less than one-twelfth of the full professors and more than

---

powerful test would be provided by a comparison of wages of students in summer employment with young men of the same age who had permanently left school.

Our original estimate of the coefficient of variation of earnings in section 1 was of the order of 10 per cent. The differences cited above—for example, 60 per cent versus 30 per cent for engineers of fifty-five and twenty-five years of age—might suggest a much larger estimate of the effects of ignorance. These gross dispersions are due to at least three different components, however, only the first two of which involve information:

i. The dispersion of earnings of engineers increases with age because younger engineers make more extensive search than older engineers.
ii. The difference in ability of engineers becomes better known as they become

---

twice as large a fraction even of associate professors. The roles of ability and discrimination in producing this reversal of the basic pattern would be interesting to know.

older (and have worked longer for a given employer).[16]

iii. The older engineers have made different amounts of "on-the-job" investment in training, which serves to increase their dispersion of abilities, a phenomenon discussed in Professor Mincer's paper.

The disentanglement of the second and third components of dispersion is especially difficult. We reach again the conclusion that the differences in quality of workers cast a deep shadow over all measures of pure dispersion due to differences in knowledge (or, for that matter, due to other forms of investment).

The effect of the absolute level of earnings, which may also enter into the determination of the gain from search, will be considered in the next section.

The Costs of Search

The larger the cost of search the less search will be undertaken by a worker at a given level of dispersion of employers' wage offers. These costs will vary systematically with various characteristics of occupations.

When prospective employers of a worker are readily identified—which is partly associated with how specialized a worker is—search for a job is more economical: one does not have to waste inquiries on wholly irrelevant possibilities. We should therefore expect the dispersion of actual wage rates to be less the more easily the employers are identified.

This prediction is supported by several analyses of earnings in the twenty metropolitan areas in 1950. Domestic servants have higher coefficients of variations than laundry operatives in nineteen of twenty areas (with means of 75.2 per cent and 54.0 per cent, respectively). The confirmation is less emphatic in the comparison of taxi drivers with truck drivers (the former have lower coefficients of variations in thirteen of twenty regions, but the means are virtually identical: 44.2 per cent and 45.7 per cent).[17]

The costs of search are also lower the higher the probability that a given, identified employer is taking on men. This would argue that in periods of expanding employment the dispersion of wages will be smaller. But unemployment among a class of workers also works in the opposite direction to reduce the cost of search. Within local markets the costs of search is primarily a cost in time, to be valued (at least approximately) by the mean wage rate, as a measure of the leisure value of time. But for the unemployed worker, this alternative cost of leisure is negligible. In the search in other labor markets, however, both transportation costs and foregone earnings must be incurred.[18]

The effects of the level of earnings on the amount of search are equally difficult to disentangle. If the absolute dispersion (σ_w) is proportional to the mean wage, the mean wage affects costs and returns from search proportionately, and there is no effect on the amount of search. On the other hand, it appears to have been the regular practice for employment agencies to charge a fee that is a higher percentage of larger initial salaries—the fee is progressive.[19] The simplest explanation would be that the expected duration of employment is greater the higher the initial wage rate. On the whole, this kind of evidence seems much more persuasive than that based on interoccupational comparisons.

The search for information may take forms other than direct solicitation: newspaper advertisements, employment agencies,

---

[16] This increased dispersion in earnings due to better recognition of differences in ability (the search for information on the quality of workers) is of course to be reckoned as a reduction in the dispersion of earnings of homogeneous workers.

[17] These Census data are moderately more persuasive than those rejected earlier because differences due to race, part-time work, and age are smaller.

[18] Hence the mean wage rates for given work should vary more among establishments in an extensive area than within a single labor market.

[19] P. H. Douglas and A. Director, *The Problem of Unemployment* (1931), p. 267.

employer search, and the myriad forms of pooling information by workers. Some require little expenditure of time and—if used alone—would lead us to expect that the dispersion of wage rates should be equal in absolute terms (standard deviations, not coefficients of variation) for workers at different wage levels. Such information, however, is incomplete and limited, and if more is needed solicitation is eventually resorted to. The marginal cost of search may rise as search increases.

The private employment agencies offer a fertile field for investigation from this viewpoint. Their *raison d'être* is information, and they should have specialized in the occupations in which information is most difficult for the employer or worker to obtain. Their fees, indeed, would provide a direct estimate of the marginal cost of information in these occupations.

III. The Employers' Search

There is direct search by employers wholly comparable to that of workers, in certain industries. College teaching is an obvious example: the employer canvasses graduate schools, professional journals, and the like for potential employees and invites them in to be looked over. This kind of direct solicitation is most probable when the workers are highly specialized, of course.

The main reason for workers undertaking the burden of solicitation is that it is cheaper for them than for employers. When an employer has numerous employees the probability that a given employer needs additional workers is much greater than the probability that a given worker will accept a job offer. The identification problem is usually also less for a worker than for an employer—the fraction of wasted search will be much smaller for a steelworker than for a steel company. But where the number of employees per employer approaches unity (domestic service, vice-presidents in charge of marketing), the employer usually takes on some or all of the task of search.

The employers' search involves more than the identification of potential workers: they must be "processed" to a degree set by the personnel practices, and there are training costs (including low productivity) for a time. Walter Oi estimates that the initial hiring and training cost per worker was (in 1951) about $382 for International Harvester, the cost rising rapidly with the level of skill.[20]

One way to reduce hiring costs is to pay higher relative wages. Not only is the quit rate of existing workers reduced by high wages, but on average, more obviously high-quality workers will accept offers. Wage rates and skilled search for substitutes for the employer: the more efficiently he detects workers of superior quality the less he need pay for such quality.

The small company has distinct advantages in the hiring process, so far as judging the quality of workers is concerned. The employer can directly observe the performance of the new worker and need not resort to expensive and uncertain rating practices to estimate the workers' performance. It is well known that wage rates are less in small plants than in large, and the difference reflects at least in part (and perhaps in whole) the lower costs to the small-scale employer of judging quality. A similar result obtains with respect to dispersion of wages: a sample of such data is given in Table 16.5. Men should in general enter smaller companies the greater their ability.

These last remarks represent in a sense a contradiction to the main argument of this paper. For previously I have accepted wage dispersion as a measure of ignorance but now take it as a measure of ability (less dispersion implies greater ignorance). The contradiction is only superficial because the problem of information on quality has been replacing that of information on price, and heterogeneity of quality has replaced homogeneity. Yet this shift poses again the central difficulty with which we began: the

[20] "Labor as a Quasi-Fixed Factor of Production" (unpublished Ph.D. dissertation, University of Chicago, 1961).

TABLE 16.5 COEFFICIENTS OF VARIATION OF HOURLY WAGE RATES OF MALE EMPLOYEES IN SELECTED MANUFACTURING INDUSTRIES BY CLASS OF WORKER

Industry and Employer	No. of Plants	Coefficient of Variation (Per Cent)		
		Skilled	Semiskilled	Unskilled
Radios:				
Two largest companies	2	12.8	16.7	13.8
Other companies	22	24.6	24.9	20.9
Soap:				
Large companies	13	15.1	16.8	17.2
Other companies	59	25.6	24.5	23.3
Explosives:				
Three largest companies	28	16.2	14.1	15.8
Other companies	23	19.8	17.4	19.5
Meatpacking:				
Four largest companies	59	—	20.4	—
Small companies	182	—	28.1	—

Source: *Hourly Earnings of Employees in Large and Small Enterprises* ("Temporary National Economic Committee Monograph," No. 14, 1948), pp. 21, 54, 59, 66, 70. The same pattern holds without exception for female employees. The meatpacking data refer to the northern wage district, and to all employees.

entanglement of quality and price variation in labor markets.

IV. Information as Capital

The information a man possesses on the labor market is capital: it was produced at the cost of search, and it yields a higher wage rate than on average would be received in its absence.

From the viewpoint of the individual worker, the capital value of his knowledge can be calculated by the usual method of valuing an asset; that is, discounting its future revenue. In section 1, above, we gave the marginal income gain from search as

$$\frac{\partial w_n}{\partial n} \frac{(1+i)^{t_o} - 1}{i(1+i)^{t_o}}.$$

that is, the marginal wage-rate gain times the present value of an annuity of duration t_o. The total income gained is the integral of this expression over the range of search, or

$$(w_m - \bar{w}) \frac{(1+i)^{t_o} - 1}{i(1+i)^{t_o}}.$$

This formula, as we observed, is an overestimate to the extent that future wage rates paid by various employers are not perfectly correlated with present wage rates. Conversely, if the duration of work with one employer is t_o, there will be some value to the knowledge presently acquired, in the search for alternative employments after t_o. This offset will be larger the larger the correlation of wage offers over time.

The duration of given jobs varies systematically with age and skill. Gladys Palmer's study suggested an average duration of a job of about three years for men between the ages of twenty-five and thirty-four, rising to six years for men over sixty-five.[21] The turnover of jobs is higher among unskilled workers than among skilled workers. If the worker has a prospective job duration of three years, and the coefficient of variation of wage offers is 10 per cent, the capital value of his knowledge, by the above formula (with $i = .06$), would be

.32 $\bar{w}$ if 5 wage offers are found,
.47 $\bar{w}$ if 15 wage offers are found.

[21] *Labor Mobility in Six Cities* (New York, 1954), p. 53. The durations are biased downward for the younger men because not all were in the labor force for an entire decade.

If such numbers are applied to the entire labor force, one gets an aggregate of private capital in laborer's information on the order of $100 billion.

The employer has a corresponding capital value of information: it is equal to the present value of the savings in wage rates for given quality of workers (or the superior quality of workers at given wage rates). The larger the amount of search by workers, the less will be the opportunity (or the greater the cost) for the employer to achieve a given saving in wage rates. The division of the investment in information between employers and workers will be determined by institutional characteristics of the market: where it is more economical for one party to acquire the information, the other party will make relatively small investments.

From the social viewpoint, the return from investment in information consists in a more efficient allocation of the labor force: the better informed the labor market, the closer each worker's (marginal) product is to its maximum at any given time. From this viewpoint, the function of information is to prevent less efficient employers from obtaining labor, and inefficient workers from obtaining the better jobs. In a regime of ignorance, Enrico Fermi would have been a gardener, Von Neumann a checkout clerk at a drugstore.

The social capital is not necessarily equal to the sum of the private capitals. If most workers search intensively, employers who offer low wage rates will be unable to fill their jobs and will be forced either to close down or to raise wage rates—so if I enter the labor market and do not search, I nevertheless profit from others' knowledge of the market. This effect arises because of the existence of the economies of scale.

The amounts and kinds of information needed for the efficient allocation of labor, whether judged from the viewpoint of the laborer, the employer, or the community, extend far beyond the determination of wage rates. The kinds and amounts of skill men should acquire pose parallel informational problems, and so too do the non-monetary conditions of employment. The traditional literature has not done these problems justice. It is doubtful that justice would be more closely approached by making exaggerated claims of the importance of the problem of information. There is no exaggeration however, in the suggestion that the analysis of the precise problems of information and of the methods an economy uses to deal with them appears to be a highly rewarding area for future research.

Appendix to Reading 16

Let n_1 and n_2 be the search in the two periods, λ the average cost of search. Then the "profit" of a worker from search, neglecting interest, is

$$\pi = w_1 + w_2 - \lambda(n_1 + n_2),$$

where

$$w_1 = an_1{}^b,$$
$$w_2 = a(n_2 + r^2n_1)^b.$$

For a maximum,

$$\frac{\partial \pi}{\partial n_1} = abn_1{}^{b-1} \qquad (1)$$
$$+ ab(n_2 + r^2n_1)^{b-1}r^2 - \lambda = 0.$$

$$\frac{\partial \pi}{\partial n_2} = ab(n_2 + r^2n_1)^{b-1} - \lambda = 0. \quad (2)$$

Equating values of λ,

$$n_2 = n_1\{(1 - r^2)^{1/(1-b)} - r^2\}. \quad (3)$$

It follows from (3) that $n_2 = n_1$ when $r = 0$. It can be shown that if $r = 1$, $n_2 = 0$,[22] and

---

[22] If r approaches unity, equations (1) and (2) yield

$$\frac{ab}{n_1{}^{1-b}} = 0,$$

$$n_1 = \left(\frac{\lambda}{2ab}\right)^{1/(b-1)}.$$

Search in period 1 makes a marginal wage contribution of

$$\frac{\partial w_2}{\partial n_1} = ab(n_2 + r^2n_1)^{b-1}r^2$$

in period 2. The optimum amount of search in period 1, from equations (1) and (2), is

$$n_1 = \left(\frac{\lambda}{ab}\right)^{1/(b-1)}(1 - r^2)^{1/(b-1)}. \quad (4)$$

The wage rate in period 1 with a correlation of r exceeds that with no correlation in the proportion

$$\frac{a(\lambda/ab)^{b/(b-1)}(1 - r^2)^{b/(b-1)} - a(\lambda/ab)^{b/(b-1)}}{a(\lambda/ab)^{b/(b-1)}},$$

or by $(1 - r^2)^{b/(b-1)} - 1$, or approximately by $br^2/(1 - b)$.

---

or n_1 becomes infinite, and by equation (2),

$$n_2 + r^2n_1 = \left(\frac{\lambda}{ab}\right)^{1/(b-1)}$$

so n_2/n_1 approaches $-r^2$ as n_1 approaches infinity. Since n_2 has a minimum of zero, n_1 is fixed by (1) at the expression in the text.

17
Information Networks in Labor Markets

Albert Rees

This paper is not concerned with the information about the labor market provided by labor statistics. Rather it deals with the information that participants in the market have about one another—with the ways in which job seekers find jobs and employers find employees. I shall draw heavily on a study of the Chicago labor market now in progress in which my associates are George P. Shultz, Joseph C. Ullman, David P. Taylor, and Mary Hamilton.[1] The focus of the paper is accordingly on local rather than national markets.

We may divide information networks in the labor market into two groups: formal and informal. The formal networks include the state employment services, private fee-charging employment agencies, newspaper advertisements, union hiring halls, and school or college placement bureaus. The informal sources include referrals from employees, other employers, and miscellaneous sources, and walk-ins or hiring at the gate.

The literature stresses the great importance of the informal channels, and our study of the Chicago labor market offers additional support for this emphasis. In the four white-collar occupations under study, informal sources account for about half of all hires; in the eight blue-collar occupations, informal sources account for more than four-fifths of all hires.

Economists have traditionally taken a dim view of informal networks of labor market information. The typical discussion of channels of employment begins with an analogy between the public employment service and stock or commodity exchanges. To be sure, various reasons are given why the analogy is imperfect and a "grain exchange for labor" cannot be established. But in the end, the disorganization of the labor

---

Reprinted with permission from the *American Economic Review*, May 1966, pp. 559–566, by permission of the publisher and author.

[1] I am indebted to these associates and to George J. Stigler and Arnold R. Weber for helpful comments on a draft of this paper. I am also indebted to the Ford Foundation for its generous support of this study.

market is deplored and suggestions are made for the improvement of the employment service.

For example, a recent textbook in labor economics starts a discussion of the effectiveness of the labor market by using the New York Stock Exchange as a model of efficiency. It notes that formal intermediaries in the labor market are not widely used, and concludes that "the worker who sets out to find employment very likely goes through a process of chasing down vague rumors or leads." "All too frequently," it adds, "the buyers and sellers, blindfolded by a lack of knowledge, simply grope about until they bump into each other."[2] I shall argue here that the analogies with commodity and security markets, even when qualified, are mischievous and misleading and that the effectiveness and advantages of informal networks of information have been too little appreciated.

The search for information in any market has both an extensive and an intensive margin. A buyer can search at the extensive margin by getting a quotation from one more seller. He can search at the intensive margin by getting additional information concerning an offer already received. Where the goods and services sold are highly standardized, the extensive margin is the more important; when there is great variation in quality, the intensive margin moves to the forefront. This point can be illustrated by considering the markets for new and used cars. Since there is relatively little variation in the quality of new cars of the same make and model and since the costs of variation are reduced by factory guarantees, the extensive margin of search is the important one. A rational buyer will get quotations from additional dealers until the probable reduction in price from one additional quotation is less than the cost of obtaining it.[3]

In used cars of the same make, model, and year much of the variation in asking prices reflects differences in the condition of the cars, and this calls for a substantial change in the strategy of the rational buyer. He will invest less in obtaining large numbers of offers and much more in examining each car. For example, he may have each car he seriously considers inspected by a mechanic. He may want information on the history of the car as a substitute for the direct assessment of condition and will pass up a used taxi in favor of the car owned by the proverbial little old lady who drives only to church. It will not be irrational for him to pay a relatively high price for a car owned by a friend if he has favorable information about his friend's habits as a car owner.

Organized commodity and security exchanges deal in highly standardized or perfectly uniform contracts, where the intensive margin of search is effectively eliminated. One is entirely indifferent as to whether one buys 100 shares of General Motors from a taxi company, a little old lady, or Alfred P. Sloan, though much search may enter into the decision to buy General Motors rather than some other security. Organized exchanges perform a highly effective job of widening the extensive margin of search and need to transmit only a few bits of information (the name of the contract, the quantity, and the price) to conclude a transaction. Labor markets lie as far from this pole as used car markets, and a grain exchange for labor is about as possible as a contract on the Chicago Board of Trade for 1960 Chevrolet sedans.

The large variance of wages within narrowly defined occupations in particular local markets affords some evidence of the variance in the quality of labor and in the attractiveness of jobs, though it has other sources as well. For example, in our sample of maintenance electricians in the Chicago area we found a range of hourly earnings in June, 1963, of from $1.75 to $4.75 an hour. Their formal educations ranged from less than four years of schooling to some college. They worked in places ranging from spot-

---

[2] Sanford Cohen, *Labor in the United States* (Charles E. Merrill, 1960), p. 351.
[3] See George J. Stigler, "The Economics of Information," *J.P.E.*, June, 1961.

less modern plants in pleasant suburbs to old loft buildings in central city slums.

Variation in the quality of applicants in many dimensions is one reason why employers invest so much in the selection of new employees. A second is that present seniority arrangements, both contractual and traditional, mean that in a large number of occupations an employee who survives the probationary period is likely to be with the firm for many years. The total of his wages over this period will run to tens of thousands of dollars. The hiring of an employee is a transaction analogous in size to the purchase of a car or even a house by a consumer and justifies substantial costs of search.

It is therefore not surprising to find employers using many different selection devices. An applicant for employment may be examined in several or in extreme cases all of the following ways: a written application for employment, an interview, paper and pencil tests, work sample tests, a medical examination, a check of credit standing, a check of school and employment references, and even police record checks. The problem facing the employer is not to get in touch with the largest possible number of potential applicants; rather it is to find a few applicants promising enough to be worth the investment of thorough investigation. This is particularly true since in general the buyer and not the seller in labor markets quotes the starting wage. The employer usually has little interest in discovering applicants willing to work at less than the prevailing rate; if he is covered by a union contract, he has none at all.

Many employer hiring standards can be viewed as devices to narrow the intensive field of search by reducing the number of applicants to manageable proportions. Within the narrowed field defined by hiring standards, extensive search can be conducted through the most appropriate channels. Thus we encounter such rules as the following: clerical workers must be high school graduates; material handlers must weigh at least 150 pounds; janitors must have lived a year in the metropolitan area; employees who use public transportation must not need to make more than two transfers. Each of these rules has some relevance to job performance, but lack of the qualities specified could be compensated for by the presence of others. Such rules are often relaxed if there is a shortage of applicants who can meet them. This flexibility is illustrated by a large Chicago area manufacturing establishment whose newspaper ads for blue-collar workers when the market is loose specify, "Must be high school graduate"; when the market tightens, this is replaced by, "Average piece rate earnings $3.19 an hour." In addition to formal hiring standards, employers have a still more flexible set of preferences among job applicants, such as the preference for married men for unskilled work because they are thought to have lower quit rates.

Most employers have a strong preference for using informal information networks, for a variety of reasons. Employee referrals—the most important informal channel—usually provide good screening for employers who are satisfied with their present workforce. Present employees tend to refer people like themselves, and they may feel that their own reputation is affected by the quality of the referrals. Informal sources also tend to provide applicants from the neighborhood in which the establishment is located; this is particularly important for female employees in reducing turnover, absenteeism, and tardiness resulting from transportation difficulties. Moreover, informal channels are usually costless to the employer, though we have found a few cases in which bonuses are paid for employee referrals that result in hires. Of course, some formal channels such as the state employment service are also costless. The few employers who deliberately avoid informal sources are either those who are seeking to upgrade their work force or those who have had bad experience with nepotism or cliques.

The informal sources also have important benefits to the applicant. He can obtain much more information from a friend who does the kind of work in which he is interested than from an ad in the paper or a counselor at an employment agency, and he places more trust in it. He can ask the counselor about the fairness of supervision in a factory, but he cannot often get an informed or reliable answer. If informal sources result in a placement in the applicant's home neighborhood, he minimizes transportation costs, both in time and in direct outlay. Finally, the presence of a friend in the plant may be an important "fringe benefit," making the job more attractive to the worker at no cost to the employer.

The fact that employers generally prefer informal sources does not mean they are always able to use them. As George Stigler has pointed out, high wages and high search costs are substitutes for an employer; low-wage employers are therefore forced to use high-cost information channels, such as newspaper advertising and private employment agencies.[4] This hypothesis receives strong support from the findings of Joseph C. Ullman, who has analyzed the Chicago market for two female clerical occupations: typists and keypunch operators. Ullman reports significant negative relationships between wages and the proportion of clerical workers hired through newspaper advertising and private agencies.[5]

The literature on formal information networks is uniformly hostile to private employment agencies. One of the leading scholars in the field, E. Wight Bakke, speaks of unemployed workers "falling into the clutches of exploiting fee-charging agencies, who took from ignorant people in desperate need of jobs a big toll from their pay for providing a very poor labor broker service."[6] Many employers also have little use for private agencies, or "flesh peddlers." Some complain of pirating—attempts by agencies to hire away people they have previously placed in order to earn another fee—and many complain of being pestered by phone calls from agency counselors. Some agencies do a poor screening job because of the high turnover of counselors. Since there are many agencies and there is vigorous competition among them, employers who complain about the practices of a particular agency often shift their business to a competing agency rather than turning to an alternative type of hiring channel.

Despite complaints from professors and employers, private agencies have been growing rapidly. Between 1943 and 1958 the number of private employment agencies in the United States increased from 2,200 to 3,900, their receipts tripled, and their payrolls quadrupled.[7] One is forced to at least grudging admiration of an industry that can thrive on selling at substantial fees a service that the government provides gratis.

In fact, our employer interviews reveal that many employers are well satisfied with private agencies. This is especially true in the clerical market, where Chicago employers typically pay agency fees of 60 or 72 percent of a month's salary. There is some tendency for the firms that use agencies extensively to be smaller than average, with fewer facilities in their own personnel departments, which suggests the presence within limits of economies of scale in hiring. The most satisfactory relationships are often with agencies that are specialized in terms of occupation, industry, or location, and involve dealings over a prolonged period with a particular counselor who knows the employer's needs.

The number of employers in our sample who make frequent use of the Illinois or Indiana Employment Services and are well satisfied with them is considerably smaller

[4] See George J. Stigler, "Information in the Labor Market," *J.P.E.*, Oct., 1962, Sup. [Reading 16 in this text—Eds.]

[5] Joseph C. Ullman, "Inter-firm Differences in the Cost of Search for White Collar Workers" (unpublished doctoral dissertation, Graduate School of Business, Univ. of Chicago, 1965).

[6] E. Wight Bakke, *A Positive Labor Market Policy* (Charles E. Merrill, 1960), p. 15.

[7] See Eaton Conant, "An Evaluation of Private Employment Agencies as Sources of Job Vacancy Data," in *The Measurement and Interpretation of Job Vacancies* (N.B.E.R., 1966).

than the number who report good results from private agencies. Private agencies placed from 10 to 32 percent of the workers in the four white-collar occupations we studied; the state employment services placed only from 1 to 3 percent. In the eight blue-collar occupations, private agencies were more important than the employment services in three and less important in three others; in no case were hires through the state employment services more than 4 percent of the total.

The highest level of satisfaction with the state employment services was reported by employers who deal with suburban offices rather than central city offices. In these cases they often mentioned regular contact with the same counselor as the key factor in good service.

We encountered some employers who object on principle to the government running an employment service, and several who avoid the employment service because, despite Fair Employment Practices Acts, they do not hire Negroes. However, such cases were clearly not the main sources of dissatisfaction or nonuse in our sample. The most frequent complaints against the employment service are slowness and poor screening. Some respondents gave specific examples, such as this one from a branch store of a large department store chain: "A year or so ago we placed an order with the Employment Service for a couple of high school graduates for openings in the credit department. We didn't care too much about experience, and would take trainees. They sent over forty applicants and about half weren't high school graduates. Most of the rest were overqualified and wouldn't accept the jobs. I finally hired a couple of people, but it just wasn't worth the effort to talk to them." Stories such as this suggest that the number of referrals is a very poor yardstick for evaluating an employment service—the number of placements is a better one, and the ratio of placements to referrals may be better still.

A manufacturing firm that has employed Negro blue-collar workers for many years stated that it does not use the employment service because "instead of trying to meet our qualifications, they just send over people who have trouble finding jobs, and they aren't the best people." Such employer reactions suggest the strong tension between the employer objective of getting the best for his money and the objectives of agencies that seek to promote social welfare by referring the workers whose needs are greatest. Unfortunately, referrals alone do not alleviate need—only placements do.

Chicago area employers use newspaper advertising extensively in recruiting white-collar workers (from 14 to 23 percent of all hires in four occupations) and to a smaller but still significant extent for blue-collar workers (1 to 13 percent of hires in eight occupations). In no occupation was the employment service more important than newspaper advertising. Many employers prefer neighborhood to metropolitan papers. In some cases this is again a device for racial screening, but more often it is intended to minimize transportation costs and thus to cut turnover and encourage attendance. Trade papers and foreign language papers are important in some industries, such as men's clothing.

The preceding discussion fails to suggest the rich variety of hiring channels in a metropolitan labor market. Referrals from unions are important in trucking and in the printing trades, as well as in construction, which was excluded from our sample. Referrals from one employer to another occur in cases of layoffs and plant shutdowns. Public utilities recruit clerical workers extensively from high schools; private vocational schools are important in the data processing occupations; and college recruiting is important for professional and managerial jobs. Some of the hiring channels we discovered do not fit any of the usual categories. One manufacturer hires truck drivers through a large trucking firm located across the street; another employer hires accountants through the public accounting firm that audits its books. A large distributor of furniture and home appliances hires warehousemen from moving and storage companies, whose slack season coincides with this employer's peak season. Such arrangements seem untidy in terms of the design of an orderly information network; yet they may nonetheless be highly effective.

In some cases matching an opening with an applicant requires search over a wide geographical area. Such cases arise largely for a few highly skilled crafts and for specialized managerial and professional jobs. The employer with a sudden need for a bassoon player, a deep sea diver, or a specialist in the chemistry of fluorine compounds might be willing to recruit from across the country or around the world. Such needs are served in part by the professional office network of the United States Employment Service and in part by the private executive recruiting or "head hunting" agencies. Search at long distances is also indicated when there are serious local imbalances between supply and demand. The employer will engage in long-distance search in cases of excess demand and the employee in cases of excess supply.

It is in such cases that direct communications networks connecting widely separated locations make the most sense. A highly sophisticated network would enable the university in New England with a vacancy for a mathematical economist to call the nearest professional office of the employment service, which through its link to a computer in Washington would discover in microseconds a well-trained mathematical economist on the Pacific Coast dissatisfied because he had been passed over for promotion. Yet even a system with such capabilities would have to struggle for users against the network of personal contacts built up within industries and professions. It is quite possible that the department chairman in New England would prefer, even in making his initial list of prospects, to phone or write to one or two senior mathematical economists whose judgment he has learned to trust.

For the major portion of the market, the crucial characteristic of an effective formal information system is not the length or the number of interconnections between geographical locations or the number of applications and openings that can be brought together at one place. Rather, it is the richness and reliability of the information carried over each link. The crucial component of such a system will not in our life-times be built by I.B.M. or Western Electric. It is the experienced employment service counselor who is a good judge of applicants and of their records and who knows thoroughly and respects the requirements of a small number of employers he has served for a long time. This in turn implies a compensation system in which such skill and experience are well rewarded.

PART VI
LABOR MOBILITY

In the introduction to Part V we traced the controversy concerning the extent of information in the labor market. A similar controversy exists concerning labor mobility. Mobility plays a crucial role in the competitive model of the labor market because workers must move to the most attractive jobs in order to increase their own incomes, to eliminate wage differentials unwarranted by productivity differences, and to maximize the total welfare of the economy.

The generally accepted view of labor mobility as of 1960 was captured by Herbert S. Parnes. He found "evidence of a substantial amount of mobility in the United States . . . . considerably greater than in most European countries."[1] Some of the patterns of mobility could be explained by characteristics of workers, such as age, sex, race, and occupations, but "the most significant point to be made about all of the factors . . . is that even their combined influence seems to account for only a small proportion of the total variation in mobility among individuals."[2] More damaging to the competitive model were some of Parnes's generalizations. "In the first place, there is mounting evidence that most voluntary separations by manual workers are made before the worker has 'lined up' a new job. This in itself seems significant, because it means that only a minority of voluntary separations occur because the worker has been 'attracted into' a better job. Secondly, wages appear to be the dominant factor in explaining only a minority of voluntary job changes."[3] Parnes's ultimate conclusion was that "all of the empirical studies of labor markets make it abundantly clear that there are wide departures between the actual labor market behavior of both workers and employers and the assumptions on which the traditional theory of wage determination and labor allocation is based."[4]

Two studies of labor mobility which have appeared since Parnes's survey are reprinted here. Larry A. Sjaastad has formulated human migration, a form of labor mobility, in terms of the human capital approach, which treats migration as an investment increasing the productivity of human resources. He catalogs the money and non-money costs and returns of this form of investment and suggests some tests which might be made with this approach to mobility. His em-

---

[1] Herbert S. Parnes, "The Labor Force and Labor Markets," in Herbert G. Heneman, Jr., et al., eds., *Employment Relations Research* (New York: Harper & Row, Publishers, 1960), p. 19.
[2] *Ibid.*, p. 24.
[3] *Ibid.*, p. 28.
[4] *Ibid.*, p. 33.

pirical work suggests that the gains from migration are high compared to the likely cost, and he "is strongly tempted to appeal to market imperfections such as the lack of information to explain the apparently high distance cost of migration. Unfortunately, no simple way has been devised for testing that hypothesis."[5]

John E. Parker and John F. Burton, Jr., examine whether or not the amount of voluntary mobility in the U.S. manufacturing sector has been changing through time, after adjustments are made for the economic conditions which might be expected to influence mobility. If it were found for given labor market conditions that the amount of labor mobility has been declining through time, one might expect this decline to impede the operation of the labor market. Parker and Burton's results suggest that mobility has declined from the 1930s and 1940s (through 1948) to the rest of the postwar period, but most significantly, perhaps, they find no decline in labor mobility since 1949.

Labor market theory may be viewed as a chain of causation, running from information (for example, wage differentials have widened) to mobility (for example, workers move to the higher-wage jobs) to certain patterns of resource allocation (for example, disequilibrium wage differentials are removed). We concluded earlier that there is an unresolved controversy concerning the adequacy of labor market information, and a similar conclusion seems appropriate for labor mobility. Some patterns of labor mobility are consistent with labor market theory, but other patterns are not. Whether these deficiencies are seriously damaging to labor market theory can be resolved ultimately only by examining the last step in the chain. In Part VII we turn to the task of deciding whether the predictions of labor market theory for the behavior of wage differentials are confirmed by empirical studies.

[5] Larry A. Sjaastad, "The Costs and Returns of Human Migration," *Journal of Political Economy,* vol. 70 (Supplement: October 1962), p. 84 [Reading 18 in this text—Eds.].

18
The Costs and Returns of Human Migration[1]

Larry A. Sjaastad

Migration research has dealt mainly with the forces which affect migration and how strongly they have affected it, but little has been done to determine the influence of migration as an equilibrating mechanism in a changing economy. The movements of migrants clearly are in the appropriate direction, but we do not know whether the numbers are sufficient to be efficient in correcting income disparities as they emerge.[2]

Reprinted from the *Journal of Political Economy* (Supplement, October 1962) by permission of The University of Chicago Press. Copyright, 1962, pp. 80–93.

[1] I wish to acknowledge discussion and comments on an earlier draft by Anthony M. Tang and John C. Hause. In addition, I am indebted to T. W. Schultz for extensive comments and aid in revision. Remaining errors and omissions are, of course, my sole responsibility.

[2] A substantial number of highly creditable studies on the nature and strength of the forces affecting human migration have been completed; the earliest of these was published more than seventy-five years ago (see E. G. Ravenstein, "The Laws of Migration," *Journal of the (Royal) Statistical Society,* Vol. XLVIII [June, 1885]). The main concern of

There is a strong presumption that they are not.

The central purpose of this paper is to develop the concepts and tools with which to attack the latter problem. I propose to identify some of the important costs and returns to migration—both public and private—and, to a limited extent, devise methods for estimating them. This treatment places migration in a resource allocation framework because it treats migration as a means in promoting efficient resource allocation and because migration is an activity which requires resources. Within this framework, my goal will be to determine the re-

economists has been with the response of individuals to economic opportunity at a distance. Harry Jerome's *Migration and Business Cycles* (New York: National Bureau of Economic Research, 1926) leaves little doubt that international migration is influenced by the business cycle, and more recent work indicates a parallel relation for internal migration. Moreover, recent statistical studies have revealed a relationship between internal migration and income differentials as well.

I. Migration: Too Much or Too Little?

Economists and others are generally dissatisfied with the past performance of migration in narrowing geographic income differentials in spite of the tremendous amount of internal migration taking place in the United States.[3] During the twelve months preceding the 1950 Census of Population, 5.6 per cent of the United States population moved to a different county and 2.6 per cent to a different state.[4] Accordingly, there were enough interstate migrants to replace the population of Delaware every month and even that of mighty New York within twenty-one months. Nevertheless, Delaware's per capita personal income continues to be two and one-half to three times that of Mississippi. How can these large income differences persist in the face of such massive movements?

Part of the answer lies in the fact that these movements are *gross* rather than *net* migration rates, and that the gross migration rate at the state level is typically several times the net rate. But this fact raises an even more perplexing problem: why is gross migration in one direction the best single indicator of the amount of backflow, as appears to be true? For example, the Census estimates that 62,500 persons migrated from Mississippi in the year preceding the 1950 count; but it also estimates that 51,900 migrated into the state during the same period.[5] If people insist upon migrating into the lowest income state in the union at such a rate, how are economists to rationalize their behavior—much less prescribe the remedy for their alleged sorry earnings? If we take the out-migration of 62,500 persons as evidence that Mississippi is a low earnings area, we must by the same token accept the 51,900 as counter evidence that it is indeed a good place to earn a living. The simple majority favors the out-migrants, but this majority is unimpressively small put alongside the income statistics. It is one thing to find lack of mobility the culprit that prevents spatial equalization of incomes; it is quite another to suggest that a lot of mobility in the wrong direction may be the cause!

These remarks, of course, beg the question. Mississippi's per capita income may have risen as much from the 51,900 influx as from the 62,500 outflow. Men are not created equal, nor would they be likely to stay so if they were. A 10 per cent in-migration of highly skilled persons (with few children) may improve Mississippi's per capita income more than a larger but less selective outflow. One can conceive of conditions which would cause incomes to rise faster the smaller is net migration.

How may one explain Mississippi's migration pattern (which, incidentally, is typical of that of most states)? The year 1949 was one of recession, which generates an increase in return migration. Moreover, Mississippi is homogeneous neither in occupations nor in industries. The out-migrants may have left declining industries and may not have been qualified for employment in the expanding ones. Or, some or all of the in-migrants may have been disillusioned out-migrants of previous years. There are also retirements. Retired persons may seek places where labor is cheap, whereas employed people are attracted to areas where it is dear; or people who are retiring return to communities in which they were reared and spent the earlier years of their lives.

Whatever may be the best hypothesis for this seemingly paradoxical behavior, three related points become clear: (1) Net migration is not necessarily a useful measure for testing the labor market's ability to

---

[3] On this point see George H. Borts, "The Equalization of Returns and Regional Economic Growth," *American Economic Review*, L, No. 3 (June, 1960), 319–47.
[4] United States Bureau of the Census, *1950 Population Census Report*, P-E, No. 4B (Washington: Government Printing Office, 1956), p. 13, Table 1.
[5] United States Bureau of the Census, *op. cit.*, p. 32, Table 8.

remove earnings differentials. (2) Disaggregation of both the migrant and parent population by at least age and occupation may be required to conform (or deny) the alleged failure of migration to achieve a reasonably equal income distribution over space. (3) The "perverse" behavior of gross migration is consistent with observed income differentials being generated by occupational as well as geographic immobility. Let me add that the somewhat paradoxical relation between gross in- and out-migration may be substantially an aggregation problem, as I have argued elsewhere.[6]

II. Differences in Earnings

Migration poses two broad and distinct questions for the economist. The first, and the one which has received the major attention, concerns the direction and magnitude of the response of migrants to labor earnings differentials over space. The second question pertains to the connection between migration and those earnings, that is, how effective is migration in equalizing inter-regional earnings of comparable labor? The latter question has received much less attention than the former. It is also the more difficult of the two.

Most studies concerned about the first question have focused upon *net* migration to or from various geographic areas or between pairs of such areas. Most of them have found a relationship between income or earnings and migration, and usually in the expected direction (that is, high earnings are associated with net *in*-migration, low earnings with net *out*-migration). The qualifications, however, are numerous; and the observed relationship is usually quite small and weak. My study of interstate migration, for example, shows that over the 1940–50 decade, an increase in per capita labor earnings of $100 (1947–49 dollars) induces net in-migration or retards net out-migration by only 4 or at most 5 per cent of the population aged fifteen to twenty-four years at the end of the decade.[7] The percentage was lower for other ages and hence lower for the total population. This modest response of net migration to earnings differentials implies that per capita earnings must be low indeed for net out-migration to overcome natural increase and effect a local population reduction. My study indicates that during the 1940's the earnings level in a particular state would need to be roughly one-half the national average in order for migration from that state to offset completely the natural increase, thus leaving a static population.

But as was suggested earlier, net migration alone is not the only mechanism for removing earnings differentials; one should also consider gross migration. Presumably, net migration is required only from those industries (or occupations) with locally depressed wage rates. If low earnings characterize all or most industries in a particular area, net out-migration is required; and it should bring about an increase in the wage rate relative to the case without out-migration. If some industries in the area, however, are paying higher wages than elsewhere, and the workers leaving the low-wage industries are unqualified and cannot easily become qualified for employment in the high-wage industries, in-migration should also occur. But this diversification among high- and low-wage industries is almost certain to *weaken* the expected relation between average earnings levels and net migration, although there remains a strong presumption that low average earnings will induce net out-migration.

Occupational composition can account for some, but not all of the differences in earnings among states. The results of Frank Hanna's admirable study show that: (1) the low income states are dominated by occupations with relatively low earnings at the national level, and (2) the earnings within

---

[6] See my "Migration in the Upper Midwest" in "Four Papers on Methodology" (an unpublished manuscript of the Upper Midwest Economic Study, University of Minnesota).

[7] Larry A. Sjaastad, "Income and Migration in the United States" (unpublished Ph.D. dissertation, University of Chicago, 1961), p. 38.

particular occupations in low-income states tend to be lower than the national average.[8] Opposite relationships characterize the high-income states. Hanna's study, together with the observed relation between income and net migration, supports the hypothesis that migration does constitute a response to *spatial* earnings differentials; moreover, this evidence is consistent with the hypothesis that migration is a search for opportunities in *higher-paying occupations*. Both hypotheses are reassuring to the economist.

Although the studies of net migration to date partially reveal the functioning of the labor market, they tell us little more than the fact that net migration is in the "right" direction. The estimated response magnitude of net migration to gaps in earnings is of little value in gauging the effectiveness of migration as an equilibrator. There are, however, several alternative approaches. One simple approach is to compare rates of (gross) migration with changes in earnings over time. Numerous compositional corrections would be necessary, and this approach would still have to answer the difficult question of how much equalization of earnings should be brought about by a given amount of migration. Moreover, it is possible that the impact of migration can be offset by further changes in the economic forces which originally generated the earnings differentials.

A better alternative, at least analytically, is to cast the problem strictly as one of resource allocation. To do this, we treat migration as an *investment increasing the productivity of human resources,* an investment which has costs and which also renders returns.

Treating migration as an investment removes one of the difficulties inherent to the first approach; there exists a ready-made criterion to test the effectiveness of migration in reducing earnings differentials over space. That criterion is, of course, the rate of return on resources allocated to migration. The difficulty of the method is that it is necessary to identify and measure the costs as well as the returns to migration; its credit is the possibility of meaningful comparisons between migration and alternative methods of promoting better resource allocation.[9]

III. The Private Costs of Migration

The private costs can be broken down into money and non-money costs. The former include the out-of-pocket expenses of movement, while the latter include foregone earnings and the "psychic" costs of changing one's environment. Each of these is treated in turn below.

1. The Money Costs

There are no data to my knowledge on the expenses incurred by migrants in the course of moving. Although these data could be collected only from the migrants themselves, these costs could, no doubt, be estimated reasonably well for given distances (and number of dependents, if one treats migration of families). Such estimates have been made, but I suspect they are quite conservative.[10] Nevertheless, since the money costs one ought to include are only the *increase* in expenditure for food, lodging, transportation (for both migrants and their belongings), etc., necessitated by migration,

---

[8] Frank A. Hanna, *State Income Differentials, 1919–1954,* (Durham, N.C.: Duke University Press, 1959), p. 128.

[9] Obviously, complete or perfect spatial equalization of earnings is ruled out (other than by chance) so long as migration involves costs to the migrant.
[10] James G. Maddox, for example, estimates "that many farm people can travel as far as five hundred miles from their home, take ten days to find non-farm jobs, and wait a week for their first paycheck after they start work with a nest egg of no more than $100 per person" ("Private and Social Costs of Movement of People out of Agriculture," *American Economic Review*, L [May, 1960], p. 393). Note that this is an estimate of capital requirements as opposed to money costs, since Maddox does not take account of what it would cost to live without migrating.

the order of magnitude of these costs is surely sufficiently small that it cannot account for the large earnings differentials encountered in the data (even after taking into account foregone earnings). Moreover, the results of my study of internal migration in the United States, 1949–50, suggest that the marginal costs associated with additional distance are considerably higher than could be attributed to the costs considered in Maddox's estimate. The migration variable was defined as the number of (net) migrants going from state i to state j as a fraction of all (net) migrants from state i. Regression coefficients obtained indicate that the attractiveness of a given destination was unaffected by a 10 per cent gain in annual per capita labor earnings *and* a simultaneous 16 per cent increase in distance.[11] At the mean of the income and distance variables these percentages imply that the typical migrant would be indifferent between two destinations, one of which was 146 miles more distant than the other, if the average annual labor earnings were $106 (1947–49 dollars) higher in the more distant one.[12] Marginal costs per mile of migration would have to be high indeed to reconcile this negative effect of distance with the present value of the earnings differential even at very high discount rates, particularly since the persons involved are already migrants and only their allocation over space is in question. Moreover, this result cannot stem from migrants moving in a series of short jumps. That explanation would be plausible if the allocation of gross migrants were being studied; in the case under question, however, the variable is net migration. One is strongly tempted to appeal to market imperfections such as the lack of information to explain the apparently high distance cost of migration. Unfortunately, no simple way has been devised for testing that hypothesis—although attempts have been made.[13] Even so, the migration-impeding effects of uncertainty remain to be measured.

2. The Non-Money Costs

The non-money considerations involved in migration are surely significant, probably far more so than the money costs. The first non-money costs to consider are opportunity costs—the earnings foregone while traveling, searching for, and learning a new job.[14] Part of these foregone earnings will be a function of the distance of migration. In addition the time required to find a new job is presumably affected by the level of unemployment. Clearly one should be able to estimate these components. The costs of learning a new job (on-the-job training) are treated in detail by Mincer in another paper in this Supplement. As Mincer demonstates, these costs are subject to measurement. Since they are reflected by reduced earnings, these costs are to be taken into account by choosing the appropriate expected earnings stream (after migration) for comparison with the expected stream had the migrant not moved.[15]

[11] Sjaastad, "Income and Migration in the United States," p. 63.

[12] These estimates are partial regression coefficients and since an occupational mix variable was also present, it is assumed that the occupational mix is either constant or changes such that average earnings of the labor force remain constant if each member earns the national average within his occupation. The occupational mix correction is that devised by Hanna and called "rate constant earnings" (*op. cit.*, chap. v).

[13] In particular, see Philip Nelson, "A Study in the Geographic Mobility of Labor" (unpublished Ph.D. dissertation, Columbia University, 1957).

[14] One could include in opportunity costs the entire earnings stream the migrant is expected to earn had he not migrated, and then include in returns the expected earnings stream after migration. The alternative followed in this paper is to look only at the increment to costs and earnings associated with migration.

[15] Risk and uncertainty "costs" can be treated in a fashion similar to on-the-job training costs; that is, by an appropriate increase in the rate of discount for the increment to expected future earnings created by migration. Moreover, the adjustment in the discount rate need not be made explicitly if internal rate of return calculations are made.

A second form of non-money costs must be considered. Since people are often genuinely reluctant to leave familiar surroundings, family, and friends, migration involves a "psychic" cost. It would be difficult to quantify these costs; moreover, if they were quantified, they should be treated quite differently from the costs previously considered. The costs treated above represent real resource costs; however, the psychic costs do not. Rather they are of the nature of lost consumer (or producer) surplus on the part of the migrant. Given the earnings levels at all other places, there is some minimum earning level at location i which will cause a given individual to be indifferent between migrating and remaining at i. For any higher earnings at i, he collects a surplus in the sense that part of his earnings could be taxed away and that taxation would not cause him to migrate. The maximum amount that could be taken away without inducing migration represents the value of the surplus. By perfect discrimination, it would be possible to take away the full amount of the surplus, but in doing so leave resource allocation unaffected (other than through distributive effects). Hence, the psychic costs of migration involve no resources for the economy and should not be included as part of the investment in migration.

Although the psychic costs involve no resource cost, they do affect resource allocation. Very likely, more migration would take place if psychic costs were zero for everyone. In addition, even if knowledge were perfect, psychic costs could explain the existence of earnings differentials larger than those implied by the money and opportunity costs of migration. However, these excessive differentials would not represent resource misallocation. The optimal allocation of resources must take tastes as given, and will differ accordingly if people prefer familiar over strange surroundings. Migration incentive transfers to compensate for these psychic costs would be as inappropriate as transfers to render people indifferent among occupations even though strong preferences may exist. To compensate for psychic costs would result in resources being used for migration to obtain earnings with a lower value than those received before. To draw upon an old example, because the public hangman earns a high income owing to his distasteful job, it does not necessarily follow that welfare would be improved with more hangmen!

Although we should not treat psychic costs as a component of the costs of migration, they pose a problem for the analysis of rate of return. To the extent that some part of existing earnings differentials represents tastes alone, the rate of return to resources allocated to migration is biased. One manner in which this problem can be partially circumvented is to consider only persons for whom the marginal psychic cost is zero. The allocation of actual migrants by distance migrated should be relatively free of the influence of psychic costs, although the percentage of all persons who become migrants is not. Using education as an analogy, this approach is similar to determining the rate of return on the nth year of schooling as compared to the rate on n years.

IV. The Private Returns to Migration

For any particular individual, the money returns to migration will consist of a positive or negative increment to his real earnings stream to be obtained by moving to another place. This increment will arise from a change in nominal earnings, a change in costs of employment, a change in prices, or a combination of these three. Money returns so defined are sufficiently general to encompass not only those returns stemming from earnings differentials between places, but also the returns accruing to the migrant in his capacity as a consumer. Both of these returns are net gains; increased efficiency in consumption is logically equivalent to increased efficiency in production. In addition, there will be a non-money component, again positive or negative, reflecting his preference for that place as compared to his former residence.[16] Finally, there is pure consumption. The pure consumption return should be regarded as the satisfaction or dissatisfaction the migrant receives in the course of his actual travel. This is analogous, again in the case of education, to the satisfaction the student experiences merely from being on campus, quite apart from the non-marketable satisfactions he may obtain over his life span as a result of his education.[17] The non-money returns will be examined first.

1. The Non-Money Returns

Earlier it was found that we can safely ignore psychic costs of migration since they involve no resource cost; likewise, we should ignore non-money returns arising from locational preferences to the extent that they represent consumption which has a zero cost of production. Some people, for example, may be indifferent between earnings at one level in Minnesota and a lower level in California owing to a preference for the latter's climate. If a large portion of the population showed this preference, California would have a locational advantage, and industry would migrate in that direction to enjoy the resultant lower labor costs. In a world of perfect competition and resource mobility no earnings differentials arising from these preferences would remain in final equilibrium; if discrimination were perfect, the existence of the preferences would be totally reflected in rents earned by factors (land) specific to the climate. Moreover, the pure rents so paid should not be treated as costs of employment since they arise from tastes for location rather than differences in productivity.

Even in a world of perfect competition and resource mobility there can be earnings differentials arising from variations in costs of employment (which must be offset by corresponding differentials in productivity). Larger cities typically reveal higher earnings within occupations than smaller cities. Costs of employment are higher in larger cities due to additional transportation, rent, etc., which are compensated by higher earnings. If one includes the former as a return to migration to the larger city, he should deduct the latter as additional cost of employment. Locational preferences pose a problem in estimating the return to migration to the extent that they can give rise to rents not to be counted as costs of employment; but additional costs arising from the superior productivity of a specific location are to be deducted. Although a distinction between those returns to migration which represent higher productivity and those which are merely consumption of zero cost goods is analytically useful for considering the returns to migration arising from increased efficiency, it is of no practical use. Final spatial equilibrium in the real world would permit variations in earnings (within occupations) resulting from non-labor resource immobility (particularly natural resources) and from lack of competition as well as from differentials in cost of employment and labor immobility. Moreover, since discrimination in the land market is not perfect, persons can and do receive windfalls by moving to a place of their preference. Private non-money returns to migration may very well exist and influence behavior; and they cannot be separated from those private returns reflecting higher pro-

---

[16] Preference for familiar versus strange surroundings are included in psychic cost and are excluded here. Preference at this point refers to such factors as climate, smog, and congestion. It is assumed that the individual's production and consumption occur at the same place; if that were not true, his preferences would be reflected in the amount of cost he is willing to bear to consume at one place and to be employed at another.

[17] The consumption-investment dichotomy I have in mind is based strictly upon the point in time at which the migrant actually receives the satisfactions. An outlay made to increase future productivity is usually called an investment; an outlay for immediate satisfaction is labeled consumption. Moreover, if a person uses some of his resources to increase future satisfactions, it should not matter whether or not the increase is reflected in future market transactions. From this point of view, there is no logical difference between a consumer or producer durable; I choose to call them both an investment.

ductivity alone. Even in a world of perfect competition, of resource mobility, and of discrimination according to preference it would not be feasible to classify costs of employment into the two categories outlined above. For practical purposes, the only alternative appears to be the unrealistic assumption that variation in tastes permits a spatial distribution of persons such that no rents arise from differences in amount and composition of natural amenities, and that this distribution does not seriously differ from the "optimal" distribution from the viewpoint of resource allocation.

2. The Money Returns

It is obviously not sufficient simply to compare labor earnings over space and assume that any observed differences arise from disequilibrium in the labor market. Hanna's study reveals that occupational composition explains a significant portion of earnings differentials among states.[18] Other variables such as age and sex affect earnings within an occupation.[19] However, assuming occupation, age, and sex to be the more important compositional variables affecting earnings, first estimates of the return to migration is the difference in earnings within occupations, ages, and sexes, and between all places. These estimates would almost surely be underestimates because they fail to take into account possible disequilibrium between as well as within occupations and because a change in occupation may necessitate migration. The more relevant alternatives for migrants may be *among* rather than *within* occupations. While one may be able to show that the Alabama farm laborer can improve his earnings on an Iowa farm, his prospective opportunities may be far more in an urban area and occupation.

If the return to migration can be increased by occupational upgrading, the problem in estimating the return becomes far more complex. In this context it is particularly useful to employ the human capital concept and to view migration, training, and experience as *investments in the human agent*. These investments, specific to the individual, are subject to depreciation and deterioration both in a physical and an economic sense. If market forces reduce the relative wages of a particular occupation, practitioners of that occupation suffer a capital loss and are faced with the alternatives of accepting the lower earnings or making additional investments in themselves to increase their earnings in a more favorable market. If the relative wages in an occupation are adversely affected locally, migration alone is sufficient; if the adverse effect is national, such as the earnings in agriculture, the entire occupational earnings structure is under stress and migration is feasible only if new skills are acquired by the migrant. Whether or not the additional investment is worthwhile depends crucially upon the age of the individual. Young persons will typically have made only a small investment in themselves through training for and experience in a specific occupation and a relatively large one through formal education; whereas a large portion of the investment in older persons presumably arises from skill and experience specific to a particular employment.[20] For the former group, obsolescence is a far smaller threat; moreover, their longer life expectancy increases the present value of the returns to additional investment relative to the older group.

Since the age-income relation within an occupation is at least partially due to the accumulated experience (on-the-job training), older persons entering a given occu-

---

[18] *Op. cit.*, p. 121.

[19] The value of leisure is also neglected when comparing earnings. If the individual labor supply function is not backward bending, smaller earnings will necessarily be accompanied by larger amounts of leisure time, which should not be valued at zero. Thus one should look at hours of work as well as earnings. There remains the problem of the value to impute to an hour's leisure. While an imputation probably cannot be accurately made, this omission should be borne in mind.

[20] In the United States, the difference in this intangible "portfolio" is exaggerated by the secular increase in levels of formal education attained.

pation even after minimal training are likely to receive lower earnings than persons of similar age but well experienced in that occupation. Hence, comparisons across occupational groups but within age groups lead to overestimates of the rate of return to migration alone. The return so estimated is to be attributed to *both* the migration investment and the investment in on-the-job training, as well as costs of pre-employment training. Estimates of the return to migration alone must be preceded by an explanation of the age-earnings relation so that earnings representing equal experience are compared.

If it is true that complementary investments are required to make migration feasible, particularly among the older migrants, one must be extremely careful in making broad comparisons of earnings and, upon finding significant differences over space, in concluding that voluntary migration is incapable of efficient allocation of labor resources. It is clearly possible that the migration mechanism could be working extremely well in the sense that the marginal return to additional migration is not "high," but that substantial differentials in earnings may persist. I strongly suspect, for example, that the lack of relevant alternatives for older farmers in non-farm occupations may go a long way in explaining why off-farm migration has not increased relative earnings in agriculture so that "comparable" factors receive comparable returns. The point is that factors are not really comparable, having had different occupational histories.

I have estimated net migration rates from rural areas in the upper Midwest which sharply reveal the age selectivity of net migration from agricultural areas.[21] These are presented in Table 18.1.[22] Although nearly half of the persons, aged 10–14 years in 1950, migrated from the rural areas during the 1950–60 decade, less than one in ten of the persons 20 years of age and over in 1950, migrated. Although one might plausibly argue that both money and non-money costs of migration increase with age, it seems doubtful that the increase in these costs as initial age rises from 15–19 to 20–24 can be sufficient to reduce the out-migration rate from over 30 per cent to less than 10 per cent. If increases in costs reduce rural out-migration as age increases, the same cost increases should be borne by all migrants. Table 18.1 also presents gross migration in

TABLE 18.1 1950–60 NET OUT-MIGRATION FROM RURAL AREAS, UPPER MIDWEST, AS A PER CENT OF 1950 POPULATION, AND GROSS MIGRATION RATES, UNITED STATES, 1949

1950 Age	Upper Midwest Per Cent Out-Migration Rate	United States Per Cent Gross Migration*
0–4	13.7	7.0†
5–9	25.1	5.0
10–14	44.5	4.0‡
15–19	30.6	6.9§
20–24	9.1	11.3
25–29	10.4	9.4
30–34	10.7	6.7
35–39	9.8 ⎱	4.7
40–44	8.6 ⎰	
45–49	9.2 ⎱	
50–54	7.5 ⎸	
55–59	9.4 ⎥	3.0
60–64	8.8 ⎰	
65+	1.8	2.6

* Source: Bureau of the Census, *1950 Population Census Report,* P-E, No. 4D, Tables 1 and 2.
† Aged 1–4 in 1950.
‡ Aged 10–13 in 1950.
§ Aged 14–19 in 1950.

[21] The upper Midwest includes the following states and parts of states: Montana, North and South Dakota, Minnesota, northwestern Wisconsin, and Upper Michigan. The migration rates are estimated by the census-survival rate method using 1950–60 census-survival rates developed by the author in connection with his research on the Upper Midwest Economic Study.

[22] Since these migration estimates are from rural areas only, the problem of the difference between net and gross migration is less serious than suggested earlier. The rural areas of a given region are likely to be quite homogeneous, so only a small amount of cross-migration is anticipated.

1949 for the United States as a per cent of parent population. The age-migration pattern there is quite different. However, the data are not comparable since the age range for 1950–60 upper Midwest migrants differs, for example, 0 to 4 in 1950 is from 0 through 14 over the decade. The data are reorganized in Table 18.2 for identical age groups, and the pattern is similar. Although the migration rate falls 70 per cent in the upper Midwest as one goes from age ranges 15–29 to 20–34, it remains constant for the United States. Although not conclusive, the evidence for the United States strongly suggests that little of the decline in migration rates as age increases can be explained by associated increases in the money or nonmoney costs of migration.

As age increases, of course, there is a shortening of the time period over which the migrant expects to recapture these costs; but again it seems unlikely that this effect can so sharply reduce the migration rate. If retirement comes at age 65 to 70, the group aged 15 to 19 in 1950 will have about 45 years, on the average over the decade, remaining in the labor force—as compared with 40 years for those initially aged 20 to 24. At a discount rate of 10 per cent, the present value of an additional dollar per year for the former group is $9.89; for the latter group it is $9.82, a mere 7 cents less. The dispersion in cost of migration would have to be fantastically small if a reduction in present value of returns by less than 1 per cent (owing to the shortening of the amortization period) would reduce the migration rate by 70 per cent. Neither increasing costs of migration nor reduction in the amortization period alone can explain the age-migration relation observed in the upper Midwest.[23]

However, if substantial additional costs of retraining for a new occupation must be borne by these rural out-migrants, the age-migration pattern displayed in Table 18.2 becomes more comprehensible. The majority of the rural out-migrants from the upper Midwest will necessarily be changing occupations. Clearly they come from agricultural occupations but are entering urban occupations. New skills must be acquired. Only a smaller portion of the gross United States migrants, however, need to change occupations; much of this mobility can be merely geographic and not occupational. For the latter group, the total costs to the individual for migration and acquiring new skills can be much smaller than for the former.

The sharp reduction in rural out-migration at relatively early ages and its near constancy thereafter suggests that (a) the investment in skills in rural occupations is

TABLE 18.2 COMPARISON OF RURAL OUT-MIGRATION, UPPER MIDWEST, WITH GROSS MIGRATION RATES, UNITED STATES

Age Range	Average of Range	Upper Midwest Per Cent Out-Migration Rate	United States Per Cent Gross Migration
0–14	7.5	13.7	5.5*
5–19	12.5	25.1	5.4
10–24	17.5	44.5	7.6
15–29	22.5	30.6	9.1†
20–34	27.5	9.1	9.1
25–44	35.0	10.5	6.5
35–44	40.0	10.0‡	4.7
45–64	55.0	8.4	3.0
65+	—	1.8	2.6

* Aged 0–13.
† Aged 14–29.
‡ Approximate.

[23] Suppose that the distribution of costs, as well as the present value, of returns to migration for all potential migrants is normal, mean C and PV, respectively; variance S^2 and zero, respectively, and that costs and returns are independent. For the 15–19 age group, $C = C_1$, $S^2 = S_1^2$, $PV = PV_1$; for 20–24, $C = C_2$, $S^2 = S_2^2$, $PV = PV_2$; assume a discount rate less than 10 per cent so that $PV_2 = 0.99 PV_1$. For 30.6 per cent of the persons aged 15–19, $PV_1 \geqq$ cost; for 9.1 per cent of those aged 20–24, $PV_2 \geqq$ cost. At the margins, $PV_1 = C_1 - .5S_1$; $PV_2 = C_2 - 1.3S_2$. Let $C_1 = C_2 = C$; $S_1 = S_2 = S$; then $S/C = 0.0135$. The implied coefficient of variation is a mere 1.35 per cent. More reasonable coefficients of variation for both costs and present values are possible if there exists a strong positive correlation between these two variables. Some positive correlation is expected.

concentrated in early years, and (*b*) consequently, the rural age-earning relation should rise sharply as returns to this investment are realized. Both of these propositions can be tested by the analysis developed in Mincer's paper. Moreover, this hypothesis implies that the degree of disequilibrium may differ among age groups—being largest for the young and less for the older persons. Differences in earnings could, of course, become larger for the older persons; but this is not inconsistent with efficient resource allocation. These older people may have suffered a capital loss, and their remaining lifetime is too short to justify large additional investments in themselves. To the extent that the above characterization is true, such disparaties in earnings become a question of social policy rather than one of resource allocation.[24]

If, as I suggest, interoccupational earning differences may be the more relevant ones in dealing with migration, but if there is as yet no way of making sense out of these differences in terms of actual incentives offered migrants of different ages, some alternative approach to estimating the rate of return on migration is necessary. Fruitful lines of attack may be to focus upon migrants only or to make comparisons between migrants and non-migrants of similar age.[25] Conceptually, there is no problem in determining whether and by how much a migrant's earnings are altered by his move. Cross-classified data concerning vital characteristics of migrants such as age, occupation, earnings before and after migration, etc., are a prerequisite to a thorough study of return to migration along these lines. Fortunately, substantial data of this sort will be available in the 1960 *Population Census Special Reports* and will cover a five-year period; the negative transitory effect of migration upon the earnings of migrants should largely disappear. As far as I know there will be no earnings data for migrants before migration, but cross-classification may permit use of earnings of comparable non-migrants as a substitute.[26]

V. Private Versus Social Costs and Returns

Does the migrant bear all the costs of migration and receive the total reward for his activity? The obvious answer is probably not. Migration will typically involve costs (and rewards) to non-migrants as well as migrants; the relative prices seen by the migrants are likely to be at variances with transformation rates for the economy as a whole. Divergences between social costs and returns arising from externalities pose knotty analytical problems; those arising from market imperfections and institutional factors are somewhat easier to examine and are my main concern here. The cases considered are illustrative rather than exhaustive; con-

---

[24] For a bold approach to the social policy question posed by persons "locked-in" their historic occupations, see T. W. Schultz, "A Policy To Redistribute Losses from Economic Progress" (prepared for a labor mobility conference, Iowa State University, November, 1960) (mimeographed). In this paper Schultz argues that since the losses to individuals from economic progress are much more narrowly distributed than are the gains, a case can be made for redistributing those losses over a larger group.

[25] By focusing upon migrants only it would be possible to eliminate the effects of differences in psychic costs, as was mentioned above.

[26] If a study of the returns to migration were carried out along these lines, one additional factor must be considered. I have assumed that migration is mainly in response to differences in earnings over space. In the case of off-farm migration, however, rising unemployment in the non-farm sector has been observed to attenuate sharply the outflow from agriculture even though we may assume earnings differentials (for employed persons) to remain relatively stable. If unemployment is high, the probability of the off-farm migrant obtaining a job at a given level of earnings is reduced, perhaps much more than rates of unemployment would indicate, owing to seniority rules and the like. Observed earnings differentials must be further discounted for the risk of unemployment and the appropriate discount rate may be very high, as imperfections in the capital market may prevent potential migrants from assuming this risk during periods of moderate to heavy unemployment. The logical choice in this circumstance is to defer the move until more favorable labor market conditions prevail.

sequently, the omissions may be the more important.[27]

The above discussion of private costs and returns places voluntary migration in the general framework of a competitive economy satisfying the minimal requirements permitting an "optimum" allocation of resources. Among other features, wages must be freely determined and there must be no barriers to the free movement of labor and other inputs among industries or across space.[28] Even if wages are freely determined and equal marginal product, differences in the relation between wages and, for example, retained earnings in different areas will cause private returns to differ from social returns. Consider the case of local differences in the degree of progression in income taxation; migration redistributes resources in a fashion to equate earnings over space *subject to the taxation structure,* a process which may indeed be detrimental to resource allocation.

Divergence between private and social costs of migration can also occur when the charges for services collectively provided (such as schools) are based upon the per capita cost rather than the actual marginal cost of providing those services to migrants. However, capital losses imposed by migrants upon the privately held fixed assets of non-migrants in an area experiencing a population decline generally cannot be admitted as an excess of social over private cost. These losses involve no resource cost; persons presumably will not migrate until their productivity elsewhere is sufficiently high to compensate for rent differentials.

Another source of an excess of social over private returns to migration arises from a failure of migrants to consider the returns to their progeny from the resulting change in the latter's (initial) location. By assuming the current change in market conditions to continue indefinitely into the future, a crude first approximation of this excess is possible. Suppose the migrant includes as private return the additional earnings obtained by himself and his immediate family but excludes any return to unborn children. The rate of interest, compounded instantaneously, is assumed to be 10 per cent per year; and the rate of population increase at 1.5 per cent per year. If his first as-yet-unborn child enters the labor market in twenty years, and if earnings differentials are and remain the same for all occupations (since there is no certainty that the migrant's progeny will enter his occupation), each dollar of his (uniform) earnings stream for a forty-five year participation in the labor force has a present value of $9.90. The present value of a permanent income stream of $1.00 beginning in twenty years and growing at the rate of 1.5 per cent per year (due to natural population increase) is about $1.62. The first figure is the present value of the return to the migrant aged twenty years of each dollar of earnings differential; the second is the present value of the return to the stream of unborn children he will generate.[29] If the migrant neglects the

---

[27] This section draws heavily upon the comments of Anthony M. Tang on an earlier draft.

[28] We must also require that product prices also be freely determined and barriers to free trade nonexistent.

[29] The present value of the income stream of the migrant of $1.00 per year is computed as

$$\int_0^{45} e^{-rt}\, dt = 9.90$$

when $r = 0.10$. It is assumed that the migrant's children will realize an equal gain per year, and that the first child will not enter the labor force until twenty years in the future, their number growing continuously at 1.5 per cent per year thereafter. The present value of one income stream of $1.00 per year but which grows in number at 1.5 per cent per year and which will not begin for twenty years is

$$\int_0^\infty \frac{(e^{nt})e^{-rt}}{(e^{20r})}dt,$$

which reduces to

$$\left[\left(\frac{1}{e^{20r}}\right)\frac{1}{(n-r)e^{-(r-n)t}}\right]_0^\infty.$$

If r is greater than n, the expression is finite and equal to 1.62 for $r = 0.10$ and $n = 0.015$.

latter completely, the social return to migration will be 16.4 per cent in excess of the private return; if the private rate of return is in fact 10 per cent, the additional social rate of return will be 1.164 per cent. For older migrants the excess of the social return over the private will approach zero (they are less likely to have more children); and for younger migrants the social rate also approaches the private rate because a longer period will elapse before their children enter the labor market. For all migrants the excess of the social over the private rate of return is less than the estimate made above.

VI. Concluding Comments

My effort in this paper has been to place human migration in an investment context and in so doing to formulate testable hypotheses germane to observed migration behavior. My main conclusion remains that migration cannot be viewed in isolation; complementary investments in the human agent are probably as important or more important than the migration process itself. As I have indicated, cognizance of, and attention to, these additional investments offer a promising clue to observed immobility in the face of large differentials in *current* earnings. In addition, only the estimation of the direct as well as associated costs of migration together with returns can reveal the extent of resource misallocation created by the frequently alleged barriers to mobility.

Costs and returns to migration have been consistently viewed in a real resource sense. Our tools of analysis are applicable only when costs and returns are so restricted; measures of psychic cost of migration, for example, are hard to come by. As I have suggested at various points, indeed the very need for these measures can often be circumvented.

Although my discussion provides only a sketchy framework for further empirical study of migration, the following additional conclusions are relevant to empirical undertakings. (1) Gross rather than net migration is a more relevant concept for studying the returns to migration as well as the impact of migration upon earnings differentials. (2) Migration rates are not an appropriate measure for estimating the effect of migration. (3) Age is significant as a variable influencing migration and must be considered in interpreting earnings differentials over space and among occupations. (4) The relation between private and social costs of, and returns to, migration at best depends upon market structure, resource mobility in general, and revenue policies of state and local governments.

19
Voluntary Labor Mobility in the U.S. Manufacturing Sector

John E. Parker • John F. Burton, Jr.

This paper is concerned with the secular behavior of voluntary labor mobility in the U.S. manufacturing sector. The topic has been largely dormant since the 1958 investigation by Arthur Ross, whose general conclusion was that: "All in all, little evidence can be found for the proposition that labor resources have become immobilized and a new industrial feudalism has been created because men can no longer afford to quit their jobs."[1] A reexamination of Ross's conclusion is important because of the crucial role that labor mobility plays in shaping the performance of the economy.

I. A Theoretical Framework

The statistic which best measures voluntary labor mobility is the quit rate, which is the number of quits per month for each 100 employees. Quits "are terminations of employment initiated by employees for any reason except retirement, transfer to another establishment of the same firm, or service in the Armed Forces."[2]

Bearing in mind the definition of the quit rate, one can postulate a model:[3]

$$QR = f(I, O, P, X), \qquad (1)$$

where QR is the quit rate, I is a set of variables which measure the incentives for workers to quit, O is a set of variables which measure the cyclical or short-run variations in the opportunities for workers to move, P is a set of variables which measure factors subject to control by public policy that in-

---

Reprinted by permission from Industrial Relations Research Association, *Proceedings of the Twentieth Annual Winter Meeting*, Gerald G. Somers, ed., (1968), pp. 61–70.
[1] Arthur M. Ross, "Do We Have a New Industrial Feudalism?" *American Economic Review*, Vol. 48 (Dec. 1958), p. 918.

[2] U.S. Bureau of Labor Statistics, *Measurement of Labor Turnover* (June 1966), p. 2.
[3] Because we are currently engaged in research on several facets of voluntary labor mobility, including a study of 1960 interindustry variations in the quit rate, we have attempted to develop a general model which can explain both secular and cross section behavior of the quit rate.

fluence voluntary mobility, and X is a set of variables which measure all other factors that influence the quit rate.

Interindustry wage differentials are an example of I, those variables which measure the incentives for workers to quit because of the comparisons they make of the attributes of their own firm and other firms. Labor market theory assumes that a worker will quit his job if he feels that an alternative job offers a net advantage. The most obvious inducement to a worker that would cause him to quit his job is a higher paying job elsewhere, assuming that the nonwage aspects of the two jobs are equivalent. One might expect, therefore, that the volume of quits would increase as interindustry wage differentials increase because the widening differentials would cause an increasing volume of turnover in the low wage industries.[4]

It can be argued that an increase in interindustry wage differentials will not necessarily lead to an increase in voluntary mobility. Even when there are no pecuniary incentives for workers to leave their firms, there is a normal level of voluntary turnover because employees become disillusioned with their jobs, exchange acrimonious words with their foremen, or because of innumerable other reasons associated with the vagaries of being human. If the interindustry wage differentials now widen, it can be argued that the increase in quits in the low wage industries will be offset by a decrease in the normal amount of quits in the high wage industries. On a priori grounds, however, it seems more likely that widening wage differentials will provide a net increase in mobility because much of the normal turnover is largely insensitive to pecuniary considerations and therefore the increase in quits in low wage industries will not be matched by an equivalent decline of quits in the high wage industries.

Geographical and interfirm (but intra-industry) wage differentials also belong to the set of I variables because workers receiving high wages along these dimensions should also have less incentive to quit than workers receiving low wages. There are other I variables in addition to wage differentials. An example is an industry attribute such as seasonality, which will probably be unattractive to workers.

The variables discussed above measure the incentives for workers to quit and move to superior jobs. The volume of voluntary mobility also depends on the workers' opportunities to move to these jobs. The opportunity variables, labeled O variables, measure cyclical or short-run variations in the state of the labor market. The variables which seem to be the most appropriate measures of O are the unemployment rate and the accession rate. We believe that workers are less likely to quit when they perceive that the labor market they would enter is slack, and we believe that the O variables are the most likely indicators of employees' attitudes.[5]

The third set of variables, P, includes those factors which might be regulated by public control for the purpose of influencing the amount of voluntary mobility in the economy.[6] Examples are the extent of unionism, an institution which many have argued has a restrictive impact on mobility, or the extent of the information-disseminating ac-

[4] The response of increased quits to widening wage differentials assumes that the widened differentials represent short-run deviations from the long-run equilibrium wage structure.

[5] Theoretically, a worker should be able to move to a superior job for which he is qualified even if the work force for that job is not being expanded —the envious worker need only offer his services at a lower rate than the going wage for the job and he will displace a previous employee. In practice, workers seldom behave in this manner and only attempt to move to superior employers when these employers are actually seeking workers.

[6] More precisely, the P category includes those variables that influence the quit rate which are subject to direct control but which do not fall in the I or O categories of variables. Thus, even though the unemployment rate is affected by public policy, it is classified as an O variable because it is used to measure cyclical variations in the state of the labor market.

tivities of the employment service, a factor which should increase mobility.

The final set of variables is X, which includes those factors that may influence the quit rate but that do not fall into the previous categories of variables. The primary significance of this category is that it includes factors influencing the amount of mobility that are not subject to public control. For example, the amount of voluntary mobility may vary through time because of variations in the proportions of certain sectors of the labor force which have distinctive mobility traits. If skilled workers are less prone to quit and skilled workers constitute a larger proportion of the work force now than 30 years ago, then *ceteris paribus* the quit rate should be decreasing through time. Despite such a trend, few would suggest that skilled workers should be barred from the labor force in order to increase the quit rate. Other X factors include sex composition and age distribution of the economy's labor force.[7]

Assuming that all the variables that affect the quit rate can be assigned to one of the categories I, O, P, or X, and assuming that the primary goal of voluntary mobility is an efficient allocation of resources, the model can be used to prescribe desirable relationships between the quit rate and the variables of the different categories. It is hoped that increased incentives to mobility, as measured by the I variables, would lead to a higher quit rate because presumably this mobility pattern will lead to the desired allocation of labor. The appropriate relationship between the quit rate and variations in the O variables would be less mobility when labor market conditions are adverse, since this relationship indicates that workers both learn about and respond to changing labor market conditions.

The desired relationship between the P variables and the quit rate is that an increase in the strength of the P program or institution, such as unionism, would not reduce the quit rate, because presumably this reduction would interfere with the most efficient allocation of resources. Finally, we are generally indifferent to changes through time in the amount of voluntary mobility associated with variations in the X variables because these variables merely measure the demographic characteristics of the labor force and are not subject to public control.

Again assuming that the quit rate is solely influenced by variables in the categories I, O, P, and X, there are statistical tests which can be used to determine if the amount of voluntary mobility has been declining through time and to determine whether any such decline in mobility is undesirable. Let a time series analysis be made of the equation:

$$QR = f(I, O, T), \qquad (2)$$

where QR, I, and O retain their previous meanings and T measures time. If the coefficient for T is negative and significant, the result is consistent with the proposition that, after adjusting for the incentives and opportunities for voluntary mobility, voluntary mobility is declining through time. While this result is disquieting, a complete evaluation of the time trend of labor mobility requires a statistical examination of the full model:

$$QR = f(I, O, X, P, T). \qquad (3)$$

If T is no longer significant in equation (3), an examination of the coefficients for the X and P variables may enable a determination to be made of the causes of the decline in voluntary mobility. If, for example, the coefficients for the X variables are significant while the coefficients for the P variables are not significant, then one could conclude that the decline in mobility through

---

[7] It is necessary to distinguish between the average age of the labor force, which is largely beyond the influence of direct public control, and the average age of the workers employed in the manufacturing sector, which might be influenced by public regulation of seniority systems and pension plans.

time was not a matter of concern for public policy. On the other hand, if the P variables have been increasing through time and the coefficients for the P variables are negative and significant, then there is cause for concern. If T is still negative and significant in equation (3), a failure to include all relevant independent variables would not appear to be an inappropriate conclusion. A variety of other combinations of results for the tests for equations (2) and (3) is possible, but the discussion of the implications of any particular set of results will only be included as necessary in the subsequent sections.

II. A Time Series Analysis

This section first describes the actual variables used to represent the categories of the model. Then statistical results are presented for the 1930–66 period and for two subperiods: 1943–66 and 1949–66.

Variables Used in the Analysis

Incentive Variables. Included in our regressions are two incentive variables. The first is a measure of interindustry wage differentials within the manufacturing sector: we expect that the quit rate will increase as differentials within manufacturing widen. The second I variable is a measure of the manufacturing-all economy wage differential. As manufacturing wages increase relative to wages in the rest of the economy, the quit rate in the manufacturing sector should decline since manufacturing jobs become relatively more attractive and consequently incentives for intersectoral transfers diminish.

Opportunity Variables. We also have two variables which measure the opportunity characteristics of the labor market. The first is the civilian unemployment rate. The hypothesis supporting its use is that a high rate of unemployment indicates to an employed worker that there are few jobs to which he can directly transfer and also that there is a high risk of unemployment if he quits his job and enters the labor market in search of a new job.

The accession rate is also used as an opportunity variable. Accessions are additions to the work force, and the accession rate is a monthly measure of the number of additions per one hundred employees. The primary justification for the use of the accession rate as an opportunity variable is that workers are more likely to quit their present jobs if other employers are hiring.

Public Policy Variables. Union membership as a percentage of the nonagricultural labor force is used as a P variable. This formulation does not make an assessment of the importance of union mobility-inhibiting policies, such as the encouragement of seniority systems, as these have changed through time. Nonetheless, it is the best measure available of this aspect of factor market structure. Most commentators assume that unions have reduced mobility.

Other Variables. For the variables in the X category—those not subject to control by public policy—we have used nonproduction workers as a percent of total employees in the manufacturing sector. The percentage of all employees who are nonproduction workers probably should be negatively correlated with the quit rate because previous studies have revealed a general inverse relationship between mobility and socioeconomic rank. However, this relationship is partially due to involuntary turnover in lower occupations and since the present study concentrates on voluntary turnover, the normal relationship between skill and mobility may be absent.

The final variable is time, which is included in order to determine if there has been a change in the relationship between the independent and dependent variables during recent decades. Based on Ross's work, we have distinguished three subperiods

TABLE 19.1 DETERMINANTS OF THE 1930–66 VARIATIONS IN THE QUIT RATE

	Equations[a]			
	A	B*	C	D
Constant	6.7805	3.7206	6.8741	4.1728
Intra-Manufacturing Wage Dispersion	−1.9569 (1.1100)		−1.9121 (1.0630)	
Manufacturing—All Economy Wage Differential	−2.4469 (2.9467)[2]		−2.6296 (2.4218)[1]	
Log Unemployment Rate	−1.6523 (13.854)[2]	−1.5121 (11.196)[2]	−1.6515 (13.628)[2]	−1.5772 (12.638)[2]
Accession Rate	0.4082 (8.9304)[2]	0.3563 (7.3933)[2]	0.4120 (8.4775)[2]	0.3495 (7.8693)[2]
War Time Dummy	−0.1249 (0.4596)	0.2275 (0.8353)	−0.1609 (0.5239)	0.2933 (1.1220)
Postwar Time Dummy	−1.2911 (6.5840)[2]	−1.0422 (4.9718)[2]	−1.3229 (5.7012)[2]	−0.9713 (5.0117)[2]
Unionization			0.0029 (0.2673)	−0.0124 (1.4140)
Adjusted Coefficient of Determination	.9813	.9773	.9807	.9780
First Order Serial Correlation Coefficient	−0.0013	0.2322	0.0152	0.0959
Durbin-Watson Statistic	1.9895	1.5088	1.9597	1.7997

[1] Significant at the .05 level. (*t*-values in parentheses)
[2] Significant at the .01 level.
[a] The results for each regression display the first order serial correlation coefficient calculated from the original data. When the absolute value exceeded .1, the data were transformed to take account of autocorrelated disturbances. Transformed regressions are indicated by an asterisk: the results for each of these regressions include the regression coefficients, *t*-values, adjusted coefficient of determination, and the Durbin-Watson statistic found after transformation for first order serial correlation. For details on the transformation process, see Hodson Thornber, "Manual for (B34T, 8 Mar 66): A Stepwise Regression Program," Technical Report No. 6603 (1966), Center for Mathematical Studies in Business and Economics, University of Chicago.

within the 1930–66 period: the 1930–41 prewar period, the war and adjustment period of 1942–48,[8] and the 1949–66 postwar period. In Tables 19.1 and 19.2, the periods are distinguished by the use of dummy variables. In Table 19.3, time is entered as a linear variable (with a value of 1 for 1949) to determine if there has been a change in the functional relationship within the period.

[8] The years 1946, 1947, and 1948 are included since they still give evidence of abnormally high quit rates of the war and early postwar years. Ross, *op. cit.*, p. 908, argued ". . . that quit rates in wartime and immediate postwar periods are affected by short-run changes in the propensity . . . to move." The Korean War did not have such an impact. *Ibid.*, p. 905, footnote 2.

Statistical Results

Tables 19.1–19.3 presents the results for various time periods for the model developed in Section I, as well as for a modified version which excludes the incentive variables from the analysis on the assumption that the available incentive variables may provide an inaccurate measurement of wage differentials.

1930–1966. Equations A and B, which correspond to equation (2), indicate that there is no difference between the prewar and war periods in the ability of the *I* and *O* variables to explain the level of the quit rate, but that the postwar predictions of the quit

TABLE 19.2 DETERMINANTS OF THE 1943–66 VARIATIONS IN THE QUIT RATE

	Equations[a]			
	A*	B	C*	D
Constant	2.8489	2.2704	6.3396	0.9340
Intra-Manufacturing Wage Dispersion	−1.1312 (0.7172)		5.7192 (2.3817)[1]	
Manufacturing—All Economy Wage Differential	−0.6471 (0.6459)		−4.4477 (3.5300)[2]	
Log Unemployment Rate	−1.2553 (7.7073)[2]	−1.2403 (9.8935)[2]	−1.2600 (9.9245)[2]	−1.2029 (9.6539)[2]
Accession Rate	0.6116 (11.530)[2]	0.5587 (11.253)[2]	0.5101 (9.9540)[2]	0.5743 (10.339)[2]
Postwar Time Dummy	−0.8193 (6.7303)[2]	−0.8945 (6.2313)[2]	−0.6201 (5.7772)[2]	−0.8404 (5.8377)[2]
Unionization			0.0369 (2.3507)[1]	0.0336 (1.5038)
Nonproduction Employees			−0.0866 (3.0444)[2]	0.0041 (0.2243)
Adjusted Coefficient of Determination	.9946	.9910	.9969	.9915
First Order Serial Correlation Coefficient	−0.2162	−0.0998	−0.2902	0.0122
Durbin-Watson Statistic	2.2320	2.0304	2.3922	1.7729

Footnotes: See Table 19.1.

rate are systematically too high. The size of the postwar time dummy suggests that after adjusting for the influence of the I and O variables, the quit rate is about one unit lower in the 1949–66 period than it was in the 1930–41 and 1942–48 periods. Since the average value of the quit rate for the entire 1930–66 period was only 2.2865, the decline in mobility indicated by Table 19.1 is far from trivial.

Equations C and D of Table 19.1 correspond to equation (3). There is no evidence that unions have caused the decline in voluntary mobility since 1930. Unfortunately, as revealed by the continued significance of the postwar time dummy in equations C and D, we were unable to determine what did cause the decline.

1943–1966. Table 19.2 begins with 1943 because of the change that year in the definition of the quit rate. The inclusion in the quit rate of information for nonproduction workers as well as for production workers—the only group previously covered by the statistic—enables us to use an additional independent variable, namely the percentage of all employees who are nonproduction workers. The addition of this variable does not materially affect our results.

Equations A and B of Table 19.2 again reveal that the I and O variables consistently overpredict the amount of voluntary mobility in the postwar period. The coefficient for the postwar time dummy is about .8, compared to the 1943–66 average of 2.6958 for the quit rate.

Equations C and D attempt to isolate the causes of the decline in mobility since 1943. The statistically most favorable results are in Equation C, which suggests that increased union strength is associated with a higher quit rate and that an increasing proportion of nonproduction workers is associated with less mobility. But even though every I, O, X, and P variable in our arsenal is significant

TABLE 19.3 DETERMINANTS OF THE 1949–66 VARIATIONS IN THE QUIT RATE

	Equations[a]			
	A*	B	C*	D*
Constant	4.5877	1.5123	2.6391	3.0831
Intra-Manufacturing Wage Dispersion	−13.832 (2.4228)[1]		−11.686 (1.5333)	
Manufacturing—All Economy Wage Differential	−0.5095 (0.2179)		0.3081 (0.1035)	
Log Unemployment Rate	−1.2077 (6.9254)[2]	−1.1802 (7.0816)[2]	−0.9993 (4.4322)[2]	−1.0610 (6.3570)[2]
Accession Rate	0.4671 (7.5890)[2]	0.5247 (7.1433)[2]	0.5173 (5.1774)[2]	0.4641 (4.9195)[2]
Time	0.0370 (1.1913)	−0.0088 (1.3784)	0.0804 (1.8619)	0.0572 (2.1011)
Unionization			0.0373 (0.9487)	0.0162 (0.4668)
Nonproduction Employees			−0.0623 (0.9293)	−0.1156 (2.8933)[1]
Adjusted Coefficient of Determination	.9828	.9525	.9832	.9830
First Order Serial Correlation Coefficient	−0.1999	0.0572	−0.2017	−0.2087
Durbin-Watson Statistic	1.7808	1.4274	1.8262	1.9141

Footnotes: See Table 19.1.

in equation C, the negative coefficient for the postwar time dummy remains highly significant. In short, we cannot locate the cause of the apparent decline in voluntary labor mobility which has occurred since 1943.

1949–1966. Table 19.3 presents our attempt to determine if there has been a continuing decline in voluntary mobility within the postwar period. Given the limited number of observations, the adjusted coefficients of determination are reasonably high, but fewer variables have significant coefficients. The O variables—unemployment and the accession rate—remain highly significant, but the only significant I variable has a perverse sign. There is weak evidence that an increased proportion of nonproduction workers is associated with a lower quit rate. Of central importance, there is no statistically significant evidence of a trend within the postwar period toward greater or less voluntary mobility.

III. Conclusions

One conclusion is that, after adjusting for the incentives and opportunities for voluntary mobility, there has been a substantial decline in voluntary mobility from the prewar and the war periods to the postwar period, although there is no evidence of a continuing decline within the postwar period. As indicated in the discussion of equation (2), this finding may be disquieting, but a meaningful evaluation of the time trend in voluntary mobility requires a consideration of the impact of the X and P variables.

Unfortunately, the use of the test specified in equation (3) does not enable us to reach a normative conclusion about the decline in mobility. Unionization (at least as we have measured it) does not explain any decline in mobility, and the increasing proportion of nonproduction workers only provides a partial explanation of the decline.

We have thus found an apparent decline in voluntary mobility in the U.S. manufacturing sector over the past several decades, but we have not found the reason. Part of the explanation may be due to the impact of variables which we are unable to include in this analysis, and we are currently working on other approaches to this topic which may enable us to identify better the determinants of voluntary mobility. For the moment, however, our research has only carried us to the point where we are certain the comforting conclusion reached by Arthur Ross that there is "little evidence" of "a new industrial feudalism" must be thoroughly reexamined.

PART VII
WAGE DIFFERENTIALS

Wage differentials have long been a topic of interest to economists. Indeed, the most significant test of a model of the labor market is its ability to predict the magnitudes and movements in the wage differentials actually observed in the labor market. Furthermore, the existence and behavior of these differentials provide the clearest indication of the efficiency of the labor market, discrimination by race and sex, and the distribution of income. Although much remains to be learned in these areas, significant progress has been made in recent years, in part because of more systematic and sophisticated application of economic theory, better data files, improved statistical techniques, and a diminished ideological dimension in the discussions. The readings we include are representative of recent studies of wage differentials by industry, occupation, geographical area, race, and union membership.

VII A. Interindustry Wage Differentials

The implications of the competitive theory for interindustry and occupational wage differentials are discussed in Reading 20 by Melvin W. Reder, who argues that there are theoretical reasons, notably variations in the relative costs of search and hire, for expecting the wage differentials between skill groups and between new and old employees to vary with the tightness of the labor market. The articles on specific training in Part IV[1] and information in Part V, as well as Reder's earlier work on occupational wage differentials,[2] are directly related to these issues. Reder examines the theory and evidence concerning the expected short- and long-run association among interindustry wage differentials, profits, growth rates, and productivity changes; and he concludes that the competitive model provides reasonably reliable explanations of long-term variations in interindustry and skill differentials, but that the theory does not as reliably predict short-term variations.

The OECD study reaches the same conclusions on the short-run behavior of interindustry wage differentials. And in this study, the finding that short-term changes in wages and employment across industries are uncorrelated is interpreted as evidence that wage differentials do not perform an allocative function among industries in the short run. However, it is not clear that a low simple correlation

---

[1] See also Walter Oi, "Labor as a Quasi-Fixed Factor," *Journal of Political Economy*, vol. 70 (December 1962), pp. 538–555.
[2] Melvin W. Reder, "The Theory of Occupational Wage Differentials," *American Economic Review*, vol. 45 (December 1955), pp. 833–852.

between changes in employment and changes in wage rates by industry in the short run is inconsistent with competitive behavior in the labor market. More complicated models must be tested before the connection between labor market efficiency and short-run changes in wages and employment can be interpreted with confidence. Moreover, changes in average wage rates by industry may provide only a crude index of changing total compensation. Reder notes that from the point of view of both the employer and the employee variations in the quality of jobs and the labor force amount to changes in real wages when average pecuniary compensation remains constant. Notwithstanding these difficulties, the OECD study provides a more skeptical assessment of the efficiency of the labor market and offers measures of empirical relationships among wages, employment, concentration, and profits which cannot be dismissed without further analysis simply because they may be inconsistent with a competitive theory of the labor market.

Reading 22, by Leonard W. Weiss, provides a more detailed empirical investigation of the association between interindustry wage differentials and employer concentration in the product market. Weiss finds that concentrated industries obtain higher-quality workers and that when interindustry quality variations are held constant, the simple correlation between wages and concentration disappears. Why concentrated industries hire workers of higher quality than more competitive industries remains an intriguing and unanswered question. Weiss's results on the effects of unions can be read profitably with the selections in Section VII E.

VII B. Occupational Wage Differentials

Since the time of Adam Smith, economists have argued that other things being equal, workers will move in the direction of higher net pecuniary returns, and Reading 1, by Milton Friedman, spells out the theoretical considerations in this argument. In this section we include two empirical examinations of the response of individual career choices to occupational wage differentials. Bruce W. Wilkinson's study compares present values of lifetime earnings among different occupations, and also compares earnings for different levels of education within these occupations. Wilkinson finds there are differences in discounted returns for varying levels of education within occupations, but that the differences among occupations are much greater. He also finds the change in the number of students entering teaching as compared to engineering is positively associated with the change in relative discounted incomes over the period 1957–1962.

Although considerable economic research has tested the predictions of the theory of occupational choice, very few studies have investigated the dynamics of career choice. Reading 24, from Richard Freeman's forthcoming book, is one of the more ambitious attempts to investigate the latter question. Freeman develops a cobweb model to relate the incomes of engineers to the flow of college students into engineering programs and finds that students respond rapidly to changing income prospects. While one might argue that Freeman's use of changes in initial salaries may not be a good index of changing lifetime income patterns, more appropriate income information is not available.

VII C. Geographical Wage Differentials

Two essentially descriptive articles are included on geographical wage differentials. First, Lee Benham, Alex Maurizi, and Melvin W. Reder study the geographical wage differentials and mobility of physicians and dentists. These two professions differ in the extent of their barriers to geographical mobility: physicians are relatively free to move among states, while dentists are more constrained by state licensing regulations. The geographical market for physicians appears to be working well in the sense that physicians respond readily to regional shifts in demand. This finding has implications for policies which attempt to increase the supply of physicians in rural or other "shortage" areas, since it suggests that offering fellowships or building medical schools in a given area will not result in much of a net increase in the area's supply of physicians. The barriers to interstate movement of dentists discussed in this study are only one example of widespread restrictions on mobility of workers, professional and otherwise. The consequences of these restrictions are reflected in the geographical variation in incomes of dentists, their geographical distribution, and presumably the prices of their services.

In Reading 26, Victor Fuchs investigates the extent to which wage differentials between the South and the rest of the country are due to "quality" differences in the labor force, and estimates that approximately two-thirds of the difference can be accounted for by such characteristics as education, city size, and race, independent of the regional effect.

VII D. Racial Wage Differentials

The general problem of racial discrimination is manifested in many forms in the labor market. The substantial white-nonwhite annual income differences can be partially explained by racial differences in educational attainment, on-the-job training (see Reading 15 by Jacob Mincer, in Part IV), labor force participation (see Reading 7, also by Mincer, in Part III), and unemployment,[3] but each of these factors may be the result of some form of discrimination. The remaining differences between white and nonwhite incomes is presumably due to a racial wage differential for workers of equal equality. The magnitude of this differential provides a measure of the "taste" of employers and employees for racial discrimination.[4]

---

[3] For a study of racial unemployment differences, see Harry Gilman, "Economic Discrimination and Unemployment," *American Economic Review,* vol. 55 (December 1965), pp. 1077–1096.

[4] For an elaboration of this treatment of discrimination, see Gary S. Becker, *The Economics of Discrimination* (Chicago: University of Chicago Press, 1957).

David Taylor's study investigates racial wage differentials in two unskilled occupations in Chicago in 1963. After standardizing for differences in education, seniority, experience, and commuting distance, Taylor finds that nonwhites are paid a lower hourly wage than whites.

VII E. Union Impact on Wage Differentials

Can unions secure a wage advantage for their members? If so what are the economic repercussions on unorganized sectors of the economy? These questions have been the source of persistent interest and debate among labor economists, and the selections in this section summarize the present theoretical and empirical answers.

In the absence of a well-developed theory of union economic strength, Milton Friedman began the theoretical debate reflected in these pages with the application to labor unions of Alfred Marshall's laws of derived demand for factors of production. This analysis led Friedman to conclude that craft unions may raise the relative wages of their members because they possess essential skills and comprise a small fraction of total production costs, but industrial unions are powerless in this sense.[5] In his response, Lloyd Ulman restates Friedman's argument and extends the derived demand analysis to indicate a number of characteristics of institutional behavior which would tend to increase the power of industrial unions relative to craft unions. Ulman also considers the potential impact of union wage behavior on unorganized sectors and on the general level of wages.

A considerable body of empirical research on the question of the impact of unions on wage differentials has been undertaken since the Ulman article. The landmark among these studies is H. Gregg Lewis's *Unions and Relative Wages in the United States*.[6] In the excerpts included here, Lewis reviews the concepts and methods used in investigating the relative wage impact of unions, summarizes earlier studies, and in Table 29.2 presents his conclusions about the effect of unionism. He finds that the union-nonunion differential has varied considerably over time, ranging from 0–5 per cent in 1945–1949 to more than 25 per cent in 1931–1933. He also concludes that "the impact of unionism on relative wage inequality among all workers has been small—under 6 per cent. The direction of the effect, on presently available evidence, is ambiguous."

Reading 30, by Harold M. Levinson, examines several hypotheses concerning the relation between union relative wage impact and product market structure. In the debate over this issue, some economists have argued that unions will have more power in concentrated industries, where the existence of monopoly rents permits greater discretion

---

[5] Milton Friedman, "Some Comments on the Significance of Labor Unions for Economic Policy," in David McCord Wright, ed., *The Impact of the Union* (New York: Harcourt, Brace & World, Inc., 1951), p. 204.

[6] (Chicago: University of Chicago Press, 1963). For a careful review of this book, see Melvin W. Reder, "Unions and Wages: the Problems of Measurement," *Journal of Political Economy*, vol. 73 (April 1965), pp. 188–196.

in meeting union wage demands. Moreover, unions in concentrated industries generally do not have to contend with new employers entering the market and undercutting union wages. Others have noted that employers in concentrated industries have greater resources to resist union demands and that powerful unions are organized in several competitive industries. Levinson argues that unions are able to maintain jurisdictional control in some competitive industries such as construction and trucking where spatial limitations on the market reduce the costs of organizing the work force. He predicts that unions will be stronger in these industries because employers' resistance will be weaker.

Since 1945, a number of wage "rounds" have occurred in which the package of wage and fringe benefit increases obtained in one key industry are emulated in subsequent negotiations in other sectors. Albert Rees and Mary T. Hamilton, in Reading 31, study the extent of these patterns by assessing the impact of unions on interindustry wage dispersion. Rees and Hamilton argue that if these rounds of absolute wage increases are truly widespread, a narrowing of the relative interindustry wage dispersion should be observed. After reviewing the actual behavior of wage dispersion, they conclude that interindustry pattern-following was more important in the immediate postwar period than in recent years.

We now have a large body of careful research on the impact of labor unions on wage differentials and resource allocation but remain relatively ignorant of the professional groups who possess comparable powers. Considering that over half of total employment in the United States is now in the service sector, an extension of analysis into this area appears desirable.

The readings in Part VII do not explicitly consider the magnitude of the aggregate change in economic welfare resulting from activities of unions. In the final reading in this part, Albert Rees discusses the effects on resource allocation of direct union restrictions as well as the union influence on the interindustry and intraindustry wage structure. Drawing on data from Lewis's study, Rees estimates the general order of magnitude of these effects and argues that direct restrictions (e.g., featherbedding and superfluous training requirements) result in the most serious resource misallocations.

• • •

We believe that the proper test of a theory is its predictive ability. Using this test, how valuable is the competitive theory of the labor market, as extended and translated into testable hypotheses?

For some topics, such as occupational choice and long-run movements in interindustry wage differentials, the competitive model provides predictions which are generally verified. For other topics, however, such as short-run movements in interindustry wage differentials, the predictions of the competitive model are often unsupported or are contradicted by the empirical evidence. To be sure, more refined studies may yet provide strong support for the usefulness of the theory for topics where its record is so far sullied.[7] And, to be sure, if wishes were horses, beggars would ride. In the meantime, beggars walk and—for a range of topics—competitive theory is not always reliable.

What explains the deficiencies of competitive labor market theory for certain problems? One possibility relates to the "chain of causation" running from information to mobility to changes in the wage structure. In Parts V and VI, concerned with information and labor mobility respectively, we noted several controversies. For example, some argue that information in the labor market is used inefficiently, while others argue that efficient utilization patterns exist. In both the information and mobility introductions, we argued that a resolution of the controversy was impossible by just examining that topic, and that ultimately the seriousness of any deficiencies could only be resolved by examining the behavior of wage differentials. Now that we have examined these differentials and found their behavior to be inconsistent with the predictions of the competitive model for some important topics, we are prepared to offer a retrospective judgment that the deficiencies in information utilization and mobility are significant in the short run.

[7] More refined studies incorporating recent research on labor market information, costs of employment, turnover, and on-the-job training appear to be fruitful approaches to some of the unexplained phenomena.

A. INTERINDUSTRY WAGE DIFFERENTIALS

20
Wage Differentials:
Theory and Measurement

Melvin W. Reder

This paper reports an investigation of certain aspects of wage differentials. The array of earnings of individuals from work may be arranged in many ways: in this paper we consider only two arrangements, by skill (or occupation) and by industry. In analyzing the behavior of wage differentials, it is difficult to avoid drastic simplification in their measurement; we frequently treat the number of workers at each level of skill and in each industry as though it were a quantity, and either their mean or their median wage as though it were a price.

The violence this does to a very complicated set of facts is obvious. Though some of the appropriate warnings are given where needed, others are not; therefore it may be helpful if, at the outset, a few precautionary remarks are made.

1. As usually measured, wages exclude the pecuniary value of fringe benefits. This may well distort interindustry or interoccupational wage comparisons for the postwar period. However, an appropriate set of corrections is not at hand, and, willy-nilly, we have written as though we believed fringe benefits were distributed more or less proportionately to wages. This could affect some of our results; all we can do is hope that the necessary amendments would not prove catastrophic.

2. When we speak of the wage level of an occupation or an industry, we refer indifferently (unless otherwise specified) to straight-time average hourly earnings; average hourly earnings, including overtime premiums; mean or median weekly or annual earnings. These various concepts of earnings do not vary proportionally from one industry or occupation

Reprinted from *Aspects of Labor Economics*, (New York: National Bureau of Economic Research, 1962), pp. 257–299. Copyright © 1962 by National Bureau of Economic Research. All Rights Reserved.
NOTE. This paper is part of a longer study on wage differentials, which has been financed by a grant from the Ford Foundation to the Economics Department of Stanford University.

to another, and we must take care not to make statements, based on data referring to one concept of earnings, as though they were necessarily applicable to data pertaining to other concepts.
3. We indicate whole frequency distributions of industrial or occupational wage payments by a single measure of central tendency, a mean or a median. This leaves completely unexplored the effect of industry or occupation on other characteristics of earnings distributions.
4. Finally, in treating the mean or median of an industry's or occupation's earnings distribution as an indicator of the price of a particular kind of labor, we abstract from all variations in hiring requirements —labor "quality" as judged by the employer, and all variations in job attractiveness as judged by the worker. However, these variations reflect an important aspect of labor-market behavior.

Certainly we attempt to take these various factors into account at places where they are especially pertinent. But there are places, particularly in the section on industrial differentials, where paucity of data and the usages of an existing literature lead us to speak of "average wages" in an industry as though it were much more closely related to the "price of a factor of production" than it actually is. Obviously, in individual cases where the consequences of abstraction are known, they are taken into account. However, there are many cases where these consequences are not known and we proceed to apply economic theory without, each time, mentioning all the necessary reservations. For this one can only point to the need for reasonable brevity, and explain in advance.

Occupational Wage Structure

Since J. S. Mill invented the concept of noncompeting groups, if not before, economic theorists have tended to explain occupational differences in wages by differences in costs of training or other obstacles to supply. But this explanation is, at most, supposed to account only for long-run differences. In the short run, as usually defined, the number of persons in one occupation is assumed to be virtually fixed, and earnings are therefore presumed to be affected by recent changes in labor demand and wage rigidities, as well as by supply influences. It will therefore be convenient to separate the long- and short-run aspects of the matter and discuss them separately, though giving their interrelation due attention.

In discussing occupational or skill differentials, we adopt a particular, though customary, definition of the wage recipients whom we designate as skilled and unskilled. Here, the skilled workers are usually some sort of manual craftsmen, e.g., carpenters, millwrights, electricians, etc., while the unskilled are laborers, sweepers, watchmen, and the like. The record of the wages paid in the specific occupations chosen suffer from the usual limitations of samples and, in addition, the occupations used to represent skilled and unskilled workers are themselves samples of skilled and unskilled occupations generally. The existence and relative increase of intermediate grades of skill create problems of demarcating skilled from unskilled occupations. One study, Keat's, measures skill differentials by the coefficient of variation of the ratio of the wage rates in 141 specific occupations to the average hourly earnings in all manufacturing; this largely overcomes the aforementioned difficulties except for those resulting from the limitations of manufacturing as a sample of the whole economy.

We measure the skill differential as the *percentage* difference between the hourly earnings of workers designated as skilled and those designated as unskilled. This is not the only possible measure that could be used; an alternative would be to measure the *absolute* differential—the dollar amount of the differential. We have chosen to measure the differential in percentage terms because we are primarily interested in the skill differential as one indicator of the relative economic well-being of two groups of earners. Though neither the absolute, the percentage, nor any one-dimensional measure of the earnings differential will be completely satisfactory for the purpose, we believe that changes in the percentage differential far more closely approximate that by which economists and others judge relative economic well-being than changes in the absolute differential do.

In an unpublished study, Gary S. Becker (properly) argues that the percentage differential is not always relevant in analyzing resource allocation. He contends that it is appropriate when we are attempting to explain variations in relative demand for skilled and unskilled workers. But if we should be interested in explaining variations in the resources devoted to investment in "human capital"—to education and training—as compared with those devoted to other uses, then it is the absolute difference that is relevant. This is because the percentage return on a given dollar investment in human capital is identified with the skill differential.

This view implies that if the dollar (i.e., absolute) skill differential between occupations A and B declined from t_0 to t_1, but in proportion with a decline in the difference in training costs, the skill differential (as measured) would be unchanged. However, we would still be interested, from a "welfare-distribution" point of view, in the differential earnings of the *persons* engaged in these occupations as well as in the return on the differential (dollar) investments they embody. Since we have, *inter alia,* this welfare-distributive interest, we concentrate upon the behavior of percentage differentials.

Now let us turn to a consideration of the long-run characteristics of the wage structure.

Secular Behavior of the Occupational Wage Structure

Most writers, including the present one, have contended that occupational relative (i.e., percentage) wage differentials, on an hourly basis (hereafter called the "skill margin"), have shown a secular tendency to diminish.[1] One important reason for this belief is empirical; the available evidence has seemed to support this view.[2] But, as we shall see, the facts do not tell a completely unambiguous story. If they did, we should expect to find that close substitutes of unskilled *urban*[3] workers would also have experienced a relative increase in hourly earnings—and some have not done so. For example, we should expect that the hourly wages of farm workers, who are closer substitutes for urban unskilled and semiskilled

---

[1] M. W. Reder, "The Theory of Occupational Wage Differentials," *American Economic Review*, Dec. 1955, pp. 833–852, especially n. 1, contains a fairly extensive bibliography of the literature before that date. The more important contributions since then are L. G. Reynolds and C. H. Taft, *The Evolution of Wage Structure*, New Haven, 1956; *Economic Survey of Europe in 1955*, United Nations, 1956, pp. 153–157; M. Rothbaum, "National Wage-structure Comparisons," *New Concepts in Wage Determination*, G. W. Taylor and F. C. Pierson, eds., New York, 1957, pp. 299–327; *The Theory of Wage Determination*, J. T. Dunlop, ed., London, 1957, especially the papers of Clark Kerr and Lloyd Reynolds; R. Perlman, "Forces Widening Occupational Wage Differentials," *Review of Economics and Statistics*, May 1958, pp. 107–115; W. Yanowitch, "Trends in Soviet Occupational Wage Differentials," *Industrial and Labor Relations Review*, Jan. 1960, pp. 166–191; William Goldner, "Labor Market Factors and Skill Differentials in Wage Rates," *Proceedings of the Industrial Relations Research Association*, 1957, pp. 207–216; and an unpublished doctoral dissertation by P. G. Keat, "Changes in Occupational Wage Structure, 1900–1956," at the University of Chicago, 1959. An article by Keat, "Long-run Changes in Occupational Wage Structure, 1900–1956," *Journal of Political Economy*, Dec. 1960, pp. 584–600, is based on his thesis.

[2] The best data summaries are in Reynolds and Taft, *The Evolution*, pp. 32–38; 59–63; 92–96; 108–128; 213–218; 240–242; 269–275; 293–298; and 319–327; and in Keat, "Changes in Occupational." Perlman, "Forces Widening," also contains some useful discussion of the data.

[3] The data on skill differentials refer almost exclusively to urban workers.

than for urban skilled workers,[4] would rise relative to skilled earnings, but it is not clear that they have done so. The data in Table 20.1 clearly imply that in 1956 the ratio of their earnings to average hourly earnings in manufacturing was well below what it was in 1929, which was less than it had been in 1914. However, these data are not beyond challenge: H. G. Lewis has shown me some unpublished computations of average hourly compensation in agriculture and manufacturing which show that with the ratio, $\frac{\text{AVERAGE HOURLY EARNINGS IN AGRICULTURE}}{\text{AVERAGE HOURLY EARNINGS IN MANUFACTURING}}$, put equal to 100 in 1929, its value stood at 118 in 1956; i.e., contrary to the implication of Table 20.1, agricultural hourly compensation rose relatively to manufacturing. Fortunately, for the purposes of this paper, it is not necessary to choose between the two sets of estimates or even attempt to reconcile them.[5] But despite their differences, both series reveal a marked decline (about 20 per cent) in the above ratio during the 1950's, when the skill margin was about constant. This implies either that rural and urban labor markets are somewhat insulated from one another or that their interrelation is subject to a prolonged lag. In either event, there arises the possibility that the observed behavior of skill differentials in part of the economy may be a misleading guide to what has happened in other parts.

Laundry workers, like farm workers, are far better substitutes for unskilled than for skilled workers. And, in the absence of a competing series, we shall assert that their hourly earnings have declined relative to those in manufacturing from 1929 to 1957. Hence, if the trend toward reduced skill differentials is genuine, it is necessary to explain the growing gap between hourly earnings in manufacturing and in laundries, as well as the questionable relation between agricultural and manufacturing earnings.

One explanation of the growing wage disadvantage of the laundry workers is that, in terms of employment, laundering is a declining industry. From 1947 through 1958, employment in this industry fell 14 per cent (from 365,000 to 313,000). Thus it might be possible to rationalize the behavior of laundry wages as that of a declining industry in which some older workers are trapped but from which the more mobile are escaping; such an explanation is

---

[4] Since one critic has challenged this assertion, we submit the following data from the 1950 Census: Among employed persons (both sexes) who resided in urban or rural nonfarm locations in March 1950 and were employed in nonfarm occupations, but had resided on farms in 1949, 55.8 per cent were occupationally classified as operatives and kindred workers; laborers except farm and mine or service workers—these are what are usually considered unskilled or semiskilled jobs. Classified as craftsmen, foremen, etc.—i.e., as skilled manual workers—were 13.8 per cent. For all other employed persons, the corresponding percentages were 40.3 per cent in the various unskilled and semiskilled categories, and 15.7 per cent in the craftsmen, etc., group (data from *1950 Population Census*, Special Report P-E, No. 4C, *Population Mobility—Farm-Nonfarm Movers*, Table 3, p. 4C–14). In other words, recent rural-urban migrants were more prone to be employed as unskilled or semiskilled manual workers, and less likely to be employed as skilled—at least in 1950 —than the remainder of the labor force.

[5] The main source of difference between Lewis's data and those cited in Table 20.1 is in the figures on agricultural earnings. The series in Table 20.1 is derived directly from the Department of Agriculture surveys, while Lewis's compensation data come from the Department of Commerce and from some unpublished hours-per-year data supplied by John Kendrick. The disagreement between the two sets of data lies mainly in their trends in hourly agricultural compensation: in Lewis's series the average rate of increase between 1929 and 1956 is about 1½ times as great as in that of Table 1. However, both series show (1) an appreciable (over 30 per cent) decline in the ratio of average hourly compensation in agriculture to that in industry during the early 1930's; (2) a very sharp rise in this same ratio during World War II; and (3) a sharp fall in this ratio from 1950–51 through (at least) 1957.

In fairness to Lewis, it should be noted that he does *not* claim his series to be superior to that in Table 20.1; he merely believes that, on available information, there is not an adequate base for choosing.

TABLE 20.1 AVERAGE GROSS HOURLY EARNINGS IN MANUFACTURING, LAUNDRIES, AND AGRICULTURE, SELECTED DATES, 1929–58

	All Manufacturing	Index	Laundries	Index	Agriculture	Index
1929	$0.566	100	n.a.		$0.241	100
1934	0.532	94	$0.378	100	0.152	63
1939	0.633	112	0.422	112	0.166	69
1940	0.661	117	0.429	113	0.169	70
1941	0.729	129	0.444	117	0.206	86
1945	1.023	181	0.648	172	0.472	196
1948	1.350	239	0.817	216	0.588	241
1955	1.88	332	1.01	267	0.675	280
1956	1.98	350	1.05	268	0.705	292
1957	2.07	366	1.09	277	0.728	302
1958	2.13	376	1.13	299	0.757	314
1959	2.22	392	1.17	310	0.798	331
1960	2.29	405	1.22	323	0.818	339

Source: Department of Labor and Department of Agriculture.

an entirely conventional application of short-run equilibrium analysis. No doubt there is validity in this explanation, but it is hard to believe that it is the whole story. For, in the postwar period, employment opportunities have usually been adequate to permit the escape of most workers into low-skilled jobs in manufacturing. A further explanatory factor that we believe should be taken into account is the probable relaxation of hiring standards to accept increasingly less eligible workers,[6] and some related phenomena to be discussed.

The declining industry hypothesis—i.e., relative declines in hourly earnings in an industry result from an uncompleted adjustment to a reduction in employment—could also be applied to explain the behavior of agricultural earnings, if such earnings have shown a relative decline. But, once again, the opportunities for interindustry mobility have raised a question as to whether there has been a differential change in hiring standards as between agriculture and the rest of the economy.

[6] It is difficult to test this surmise on census data since the Census Bureau does not publish detailed characteristics of laundry workers separately, but combines them with those of persons employed in cleaning and dyeing establishments. However, the matter can surely be investigated further.

It might seem that the declining industry hypothesis, with a slight modification, could account for the relative wage behavior in both agriculture and laundries. That is, the conventional short-run analysis of a declining industry's relative wages implies that they will fall because some workers cannot or will not shift industries, though when they retire they will not be replaced. As the immobile workers disproportionately represent the older segment of the industry's labor force, it is to be expected that in the short run there will be a decline in the quality of the labor force as well as in employment; this will appear as a change in hiring standards.

The main factors which this analysis leaves out of account are such "institutional" ones as the differential effect of minimum wage laws, trade union pressure, curbs on child labor, etc. Clearly, minimum wage laws affect far larger segments of manufacturing than of either laundering or agriculture. Consequently, the relative decline of hourly earnings in the latter two industries may simply indicate the fact that market forces were free to set low wages in many of these industries' local markets but were prevented from doing so in manufacturing.

In other words, the usual measures of skill margins refer to differences in hourly earnings of different occupational groups in a large section of the economy, but do not reflect events in another part which is of some importance. The available statistics refer to urban areas and are collected disproportionately from large firms which are fairly long-lived; conversely, they underrepresent firms with the opposite characteristics. This creates the possibility that divergent movements in the "premium for skill" in these two parts of the economy may render data from either sector a misleading guide to skill margins in the economy as a whole.

Did this possibility materialize in the United States and elsewhere during the past twenty-five to fifty years? In our judgment, the answer is probably not. The compression of differentials in annual earnings since 1929, noted by Kuznets, Goldsmith, and others, would imply that this distribution behaved as though there had been a contraction in the margin for skill. Moreover, from 1939 to 1949 (at least), the dispersion of the medians of annual earnings of (full-year) wage and salary workers in different occupations declined during that period; this would suggest the same conclusion, though for a shorter period.[7]

There is further evidence, though of a different kind, which also suggests that there was secular shrinkage in the skill margin. It will not be seriously disputed that persons engaged in what are normally called skilled occupations generally have a higher level of education (more years of schooling) than those in unskilled trades. It will also be agreed that, whatever the causal pattern, variations in years of school attendance are associated with variations in occupational levels. Clearly, in the past fifty years, if not longer, there has been a marked cumulative increase in the median number of years of school completed by members of the American labor force. This would, *ceteris paribus,* have the effect of increasing the fraction of the labor force able to hold skilled jobs.

Since the fraction of the labor force in skilled employment has increased secularly,[8] it is tempting to relate this fact and the decline in the skill margin by a conventional application of price theory.

This argument is as follows: there has been a secular increase in the relative supply of skilled as compared with unskilled workers which has led—because of a failure of relative demand for skilled workers to increase as much (at relevant ratios of skilled to unskilled wage rates)—to a decline in the skill differentials. The relative increase in the number of skilled workers is thus consistent with the above theory and with a decline in the skill margin; therefore it would seem to provide an additional reason for believing that the skill margin really has declined secularly.

But this argument is not free from difficulty: it is possible that the secular increase in the relative number of skilled workers is due mainly to changes in relative demand rather than supply. We do not have any independent measure of changes in relative demands for skilled and unskilled workers, and we cannot deny that the spreading of education may have been partly a response to relative changes in labor demand.[9] If this possibility is accepted as an "important" cause of the relative increase in the number of skilled workers, we cannot buttress the finding of a declining skill margin by the behavior of the relative numbers of skilled and unskilled workers.

However, we are inclined to deny that there have been important changes in rela-

---

[7] H. P. Miller, *Income of the American People,* New York, Wiley, 1955, Chap. 9, especially pp. 120–21 and Table 67.

[8] From 1900 to 1950, craftsmen, foremen and kindred workers (roughly, skilled manual workers) increased from 10.5 per cent to 14.2 per cent of the labor force. Operatives, etc. (the semiskilled) increased even more (in percentage terms) during that period, but laborers, both farm and nonfarm (the urban unskilled and their substitutes) decreased sharply (see D. J. Bogue, *The Population of the United States,* Glencoe, Illinois, 1959, Table 17.1, p. 475).

[9] This possibility is indicated very clearly in G. S. Becker's . . . "Human Capital." [New York: National Bureau of Economic Research, 1964. Chap-

tive demand for the following reasons: (1) below the college level—and it is with this range that we are concerned—increased schooling has been due in good part to laws compelling school attendance; (2) a substantial role in the relative decline of unskilled labor has been the sharp reduction in child labor (under legal pressure) and, in the United States, the reduction in immigration. Both of these developments tended to reduce the relative supply of the unskilled at the same time that they raised the median years of schooling of the labor force. (3) Of the increase in private expenditure for education that has occurred, the major explanatory factor has been the increased income (of parents); i.e., private educational expenditure *below the college level* has been viewed as a consumer luxury good rather than as a producer good. (4) Those ambitious persons who respond to the lure of higher incomes by increasing their training— at least in the United States—have not gone into skilled manual work but into business or the professions. Consequently, their effect on the supply of skilled labor would have been small.

While we believe that these assertions can be supported with empirical evidence (1 and 2 easily, 3 with a little effort, and 4 with considerable effort), for the present consider them merely as assertions. If all were true, they could not prove that changes in relative demand had no part, or even a smaller part than changes in relative supply, in narrowing the margin for skill. All they are intended to do is indicate the evidence that could be marshalled in support of the claim that sup-

---

ters II and III appear in the present volume as Readings 12 and 13—Eds.] For the purpose of our paper, delayed (supply) response to an initial skill differential in excess of the (long-run) equilibrium level would yield the same price-quantity behavior as a shift in the supply function with instantaneous adjustments; i.e., the relative quantity of the skilled will increase and their differential wage advantage will shrink. Hence, we shall not bother to distinguish this from a downward shift in the long-run supply function.

ply factors are adequate to explain the secular decline in the skill differential. But it cannot be denied that an adequate alternative explanation stressing demand factors might yet be offered.

The explanation of a secular decline in the skill margin offered here would strongly suggest that the decline will continue. However, not everyone agrees: one recent writer[10] has argued that because of the possibility of relaxing hiring standards, it is likely that in the future skill differentials will be widening rather than narrowing. That is, employers will relax hiring standards for the unskilled more than for the skilled, thereby causing a widening of the skill margin. Moreover, as he contends, it is possible that technical progress will have the effect of increasing the ratio, $\frac{\text{DEMAND FOR SKILLED WORKERS}}{\text{DEMAND FOR UNSKILLED WORKERS}}$, more than broadened educational opportunities will increase the ratio, $\frac{\text{SUPPLY OF SKILLED WORKERS}}{\text{SUPPLY OF UNSKILLED WORKERS}}$, at a given set of relative wages.[11] This possibility could manifest itself by drawing an increasing fraction of full-time adult male earners toward skilled trades, with their places being taken (in part) by "the transient, the very young, the very old, and the physically, mentally and socially handicapped."

However, this "labor reserve" has always been available and, moreover, was in the past bolstered by elements no longer available, e.g., children and immigrants. Perlman offers no reason to suppose that the net result of these various factors should be a different secular trend in the skill margin than has existed hitherto. Nevertheless, it is possible that technical progress in transportation (e.g., the automobile) and in household appliances has shifted downward the supply schedule of the typical housewife's

---

[10] R. Perlman, "Forces Widening Occupational Wage Differentials," *Review of Economics and Statistics*, May 1958, pp. 107–115.
[11] This statement, and the one following, is my interpretation of Perlman's argument on p. 113.

labor services.¹² In considering this possibility, it is necessary to recognize that many housewives, wishing employment at going wage rates, have often been frustrated by employer hiring requirements or legal restraints on hiring, or both.¹³ Relaxation of either of these restraints clearly may lower unskilled wage rates relative to others.¹⁴

Another possibility is that with rising family incomes it is possible that secondary earners will tend to substitute lower-paying, but pleasanter, jobs for jobs with the reverse characteristics. This would, *ceteris paribus,* reduce the wage rates on what have traditionally been considered pleasant jobs, and raise them on jobs traditionally considered unpleasant. If we assume unskilled manual labor to be "unpleasant," and white-collar jobs to be "pleasant," this would imply a decline in the relative earnings of white-collar to manual jobs. It seems likely that something of this sort has happened over the last half-century.¹⁵

In short, it is possible that the concomitants of economic progress will, as Douglas once surmised, transform the occupational wage structure so that the jobs at the bottom will be comparatively pleasant and their low remuneration a "compensating" differential. Whether this comes to pass will depend more upon employer hiring standards concerning part-time workers, especially married women, etc., and upon legal and customary restraints upon hourly wages, than upon the relative costs of educating such workers.

In other words, the secular behavior of skill differentials reflects not only variations in relative costs of "producing" skilled and unskilled workers, but also the restraints upon the labor market imposed by legal action (e.g., minimum wage laws, restrictions on child labor, etc.) and the variations in relative labor supply of skilled and unskilled labor services consequent upon rising real incomes. The operation of these latter factors *could* alter the trend in skill differentials and make it widen in the future; however, in our judgment there is no reason for thinking that these forces will be more powerful in the future than they have been heretofore.

So far in our discussion we have deliberately ignored the alleged influence of inflation on the skill differential. One writer (Perlman) contends that "our inflation-conscious public, government, and monetary authorities will exert every effort to stabilize prices, thus removing the strongest force in narrowing the differential—inflation."¹⁶ Let us put aside the prognostication about the future of the price level and concentrate on the analytical issue—the relation of wage structure and inflation. Perlman's contention is that unskilled workers "need" larger percentage increases in hourly wages than skilled and, therefore, exert "more urgent upward pressure on wages."¹⁷

This argument is not peculiar to any one author,¹⁸ but despite its currency, we find

---

¹² The secular rise in the fraction of the female population in the labor force is, of course, no evidence for or against this possibility; at least part of this rise has been simply a movement along a given supply function in response to increased demand; on this point the reader should see . . . Jacob Mincer, ["Labor Force Participation of Married Women," in A Conference of the Universities—National Bureau Committee for Economic Research, *Aspects of Labor Economics* (Princeton: Princeton University Press, 1962)].

¹³ For example, minimum wage laws, laws against industrial homework, etc.

¹⁴ I have discussed this point elsewhere: "Theory of Occupational Wage Differentials," pp. 838–840.

¹⁵ Cf. K. M. McCaffree, "The Earnings Differential Between White Collar and Manual Occupations," *Review of Economics and Statistics,* Feb. 1953, pp. 20–30, especially pp. 20–21; also P. H. Douglas, *Real Wages in the United States, 1890–1926,* Boston, Houghton Mifflin, 1930, pp. 367–368.

¹⁶ Perlman, "Forces Widening," p. 115.

¹⁷ This is a dubious contention for periods of full employment which frequently coexist with inflation. For with full employment, families whose principal earner has deficient wages can remedy the deficit by supplying secondary earners. That is, since unemployment hits the unskilled more than the skilled, full employment benefits them proportionately more.

¹⁸ For example, it is also expressed by Knowles and Robertson, "Differences between the Wages of Skilled and Unskilled Workers, 1880–1950," *Bulletin of the Oxford Institute of Statistics,* Apr. 1951, pp. 109–127.

it simply implausible. Our objection to the argument does not refer to its use as an ad hoc explanation of events in a specific (short-run) situation; in such applications, one must judge it as best one can, case by case. The following remarks are directed solely to its use as an explanation of a secular trend in wage differentials.

As we have argued elsewhere, there is, in nearly every community, a minimum real hourly wage below which the hiring of labor services is not permitted.[19] The minimum is closely related to unskilled wage rates (but not to skilled rates) and variations in it may therefore have a marked—and possibly permanent—effect on skill differentials. The argument we are considering goes further: it alleges (in effect) that this minimum is subject to a money illusion; i.e., the relative value of the minimum rises with the price level in such a way that the greater the secular rise of the latter, the greater the secular decline in the skill margin. Testing this contention would not be difficult if we were free to assume that both the skilled and the unskilled labor markets were in equilibrium. However, the existence of a minimum real wage has frequently caused unemployment of the unskilled; this is one of the strongest arguments to support the hypothesis of a minimum real wage. This makes the hypothesis of labor market equilibrium doubtful, which, in turn, puts the above-mentioned money-illusion thesis beyond reach of simple tests.[20] For the present, one is free to accept it if he chooses; but there is no reason for doing so.

The Pattern of Short-Run Fluctuations in Skill Margins

It is generally agreed that in the short run skill margins change relatively little during "normal" periods, but contract sharply during periods of over-full employment. It is also possible that they widen during major depressions, though this is not clear.[21] We have attempted elsewhere to account for the sharp reduction in skill margins during the two World Wars when there was excess demand for all types of labor.[22] What is not accounted for is why the sharp narrowing of occupational wage rates that has occurred during war periods has been only partially reversed subsequently.

If we grant that there is a secular decline in the skill margin, and that little or no decline occurs in "normal" periods, it is a matter of arithmetic that wartime declines must exceed postwar increases. The analytical question is why a trend that presumably reflects more or less steady changes in supply should manifest itself in short violent movements followed by long periods of comparative quiescence. There may be many possible explanations of this phenomenon; let us consider two.

The first of these is as follows: the relative supply of skilled and unskilled workers is only indirectly affected by the educational attainment of the labor force. Having more schooling does not automatically fit a man for a more skilled job; it merely increases his ability to absorb the specific training that qualifies him for such a job. To obtain this training it is necessary to serve an apprenticeship, attend a trade school, or get it on the job. In some cases (e.g., where training must come through a union-influenced apprentice program), availability of training may be limited by the current employment

---

[19] Reder, "Theory of Occupational," pp. 839–840.
[20] What is needed, as a minimum, are data measuring excess demand or unemployment for skilled and unskilled workers, separately, under conditions of secular inflation; i.e., we need long-time series or at least a few observations well separated in time.

[21] Keat ("Changes in Occupational," Chapter II) finds evidence of this in both the 1920–21 and 1929–32 depressions. P. W. Bell ("Cyclical Variations and Trends in Occupational Wage Differentials in American Industry since 1914," *Review of Economics and Statistics*, Nov. 1951, pp. 329–337), however, found a widening of the differential only in the 1920–21 contraction. Knowles and Robertson ("Differences Between the Wages," especially p. 111) found that skill differentials did not widen in Great Britain during 1929–32, though they did in the early 1920's.
[22] Reder, "Theory of Occupational," pp. 840–845.

situation. In others, workers seem uninterested in taking advantage of training programs unless they are connected with the imminent prospect of promotion or unless they involve on-the-job training. This lack of interest largely reflects the apparent reluctance (or inability) of employers to accept inexperienced or partially skilled workers merely in order to reduce the wage premium on skilled jobs. According to this piece of speculation, in "normal" times, supply and demand for skilled workers is kept more or less in balance at current skill margins by the various obstacles (and discouragements) to acquiring requisite skill.

To elaborate a bit: Much of the difference between a highly competent skilled worker and one less competent lies in the greater range of tasks that the more competent worker can perform. Assuming, realistically, that labor turnover involves expense,[23] the differential advantage of the more competent skilled worker to his employer will become greater the more varied are the tasks that the firm's output pattern imposes on him. Conversely, long runs of one particular product minimize variation in a skilled worker's productive role, and hence in his differential advantage.

During a war period, huge orders create the possibility of producing long runs of one particular product. This makes it possible to keep partially trained workers continuously occupied at a narrow range of tasks; consequently, it may—though it need not—absolutely reduce the demand for the broadly trained. Put differently, the elasticity of substitution between partially (narrowly) and fully (broadly) skilled workers is increased. Furthermore, in wartime the premium on speed of delivery makes it more profitable than normally to hire workers whose limited skills compel them to be idle—"unproductive"—for part of the time spent on the job. The relatively short and simple training needed to learn one or a few specific skills further encourages training and use of partially skilled workers.[24]

In short, in a war period, there is a relative shift in labor demand from more to less broadly skilled workers, with the less broadly skilled tending to acquire the titles but only part of the functions of those more fully trained. The effect is (1) to increase the supply of workers able to fill jobs with skilled titles and (2) to curb the increase in demand for workers with specific high-level skills. While (1) acts as a brake upon wage increases to those holding jobs with skilled titles,[25] (2) curbs wage increases to those who have broad skills.

After the war, labor demand reverts, more or less, to its prewar composition in response to the relative decline in large orders which require long runs and permit the use of limited skill workers. However, the partial training acquired during the war reduces the prime cost of becoming fully trained, as compared with starting from scratch. Furthermore, many of the workers promoted during the war display such industry and aptitude that they are offered continued employment on skilled jobs if only they acquire the full range of skills needed for peacetime employment; sometimes employers will even defray the training costs involved. The effect of a job promise, combined with successful experience, is greatly to reduce the uncertainty of getting employment which is a real, though nonpecuniary, cost of training. Thus, the relative supply of skilled workers is increased, which tends to prevent a return to the prewar skill margin.

A second explanation is suggested by the behavior of "experience differentials." By experience differentials I refer to the wage differentials that are associated with length of service in a given firm or organization. There is a very extensive overlap of skill and experience; in many cases skill, and the reward thereof, is simply a by-product of

---

[23] The importance of this point is brought home by an unpublished doctoral dissertation of W. Y. Oi of the University of Chicago.

[24] This statement implies that firms become short-run monopsonists with regard to fully trained workers, but not with regard to the partially trained (see fuller discussion below).

[25] Which is what the data reflect.

long experience in a particular line of work, and is acquired more or less by osmosis. Often, when an employer specifies that he wants an "experienced" worker, what he means is that he wants a relatively skilled one, and considers successful experience as an indication of skill. Consequently, it is not surprising that skill and experience should be confused, both in practical and theoretical discourse.

For reasons that will become apparent, we believe that the wages of unskilled or inexperienced workers or both are apt to be more sensitive to the state of the labor market than those of workers with the reverse characteristics. In support of this proposition, let us consider a rather rare type of data: the behavior of earnings data classified by years of experience of the earner. Such data are quite rare: one of the few good sources is the data for engineers presented by Blank and Stigler.[26] These data are the monthly salaries of engineers, classified by years of experience, for selected years in the period from 1894 to 1953; they reveal a pronounced upward trend in the ratio (1) of the salaries of starting engineers[27] to those of experienced engineers and (2) of the salaries of less experienced engineers to those of more experienced. What is more to our present purpose, these ratios rose especially rapidly in periods when the overall demand for engineers rose with unusual speed but then subsequently declined, contrary to trend, when the demand for engineers declined. For example: during World Wars I and II and during the Korean episode (periods of sharp increase in demand) the salaries of inexperienced engineers rose markedly relative to those of engineers with more experience.[28] And, in each case, soon after the demand for engineering service slackened, the salaries of inexperienced en-

---

[26] D. M. Blank and G. J. Stigler, *The Demand and Supply of Scientific Personnel*, New York, National Bureau of Economic Research, 1957; see Appendix Tables A-3 (p. 117), A-9 (pp. 133–134), A-14 and A-15 (pp. 140–141).

Since this section was written, an excellent study by Robert Evans, Jr. ("Worker Quality and Wage Dispersion: An Analysis of a Clerical Labor Market in Boston," *Proc. Industrial Relations Research Association*, Dec. 1961, pp. 246–259) has appeared. In his paper, Evans presents strong evidence of experience differentials among Boston stenographers (see pp. 250–251).

[27] That is, those with less than one year of experience. Years of experience refers to years elapsed since start of first professional job, though in some cases this is estimated (imperfectly) by the difference between an engineer's age and the median age at which graduate engineers receive their first degree. Thus defined, experience is not length of experience with one firm as the argument requires; however, it is likely to be strongly correlated with it.

[28] As Blank and Stigler summarize the data for the World War I period, "the increase in earnings at the starting level and at one and two years experience ranged between 61 and 80 per cent between 1914–1916 and 1919–1921, while the increase for engineering graduates with 10, 15 and 20 years experience ranged between zero and 20 per cent" (*The Demand and Supply*, pp. 124–125, and Table A-5).

For the World War II period, the data in Table A-8 (p. 130 of Blank and Stigler) show that the median salary for engineers with less than 1 year of experience rose by 80 per cent between 1939 and 1946, but rose by only 58 per cent (during the same period) for those with 9–11 years of experience and by only 27 per cent for those with 30–34 years experience. (Tables A-10 and A-11, pp. 135–136, show that a similar relation existed within each field of engineering.)

During the Korean War, average monthly salaries for engineers of varying levels of experience behaved as indicated in the following table, which shows the annual percentage changes in average monthly salaries of research engineers and scientists with B.S. degrees, by years of experience, 1948–55. The relevant pairs of years are 1951–52 and 1952–53.

	Percentage Changes, by Years of Experience				
	0	1	9	10	11
1948–49	−3.2	−0.3	2.8	1.1	0.9
1949–50	1.8	1.7	2.0	3.5	3.2
1950–51	6.9	5.0	7.6	6.7	6.9
1951–52	11.3	12.7	8.2	9.4	8.1
1952–53	6.8	6.7	3.8	4.0	4.4
1953–54	3.7	5.5	1.6	2.1	3.4
1954–55	7.2	5.0	16.6	8.9	8.0

Source: National Survey of Professional Scientific Salaries, Los Alamos Scientific Laboratory of the University of California, 1949 through 1955. Each set of percentages derived from data collected in a single survey, to avoid the effects of changes in coverage. Taken from Blank and Stigler, Table A-15, p. 141.

gineers underwent a relative decline.[29] Furthermore, during the depressed 1930's (1929–39), the salaries of inexperienced engineers declined relative to those with more experience.[30]

It is possible that this argument rests upon a statistical mirage. That is, the tendency for the experience differential among engineers to diminish in periods of sharp increase in demand might be due mainly to the fact that in such periods demand is concentrated on certain newly developed specialties (e.g., in the early 1950's, the strong demand was for electronic engineers, aeronautical engineers, and so forth) in which there is literally no stock of experienced practitioners. If so, the relative increase in wages of the inexperienced has occurred only because the pressure of increased demand has been greatest in those specialties where the number of experienced engineers was extremely small relative to demand. If this were the whole story, we would expect that there would be no tendency for the experience differential, within given categories of engineers (especially those little affected by temporary "shortages"), to contract. However, the available data are inconsistent with this surmise; during World War II, at least, the "margin for experience" contracted in each of the five specialties for which data are available.[31]

Therefore, for the present we shall assume that the behavior of the experience differ-

---

[29] In the post-World War I period, from 1919 to 1924, the median monthly starting salary for engineers rose by 14 per cent, while that of engineers with 9–11 years experience rose by one-third (Table A-6, Blank and Stigler, *The Demand and Supply*, p. 126).

Data for the post-World War II period are given in the table in footnote 28. These data show that in each of the pairs of years between 1948 and 1951 (with the exception of new graduates as compared with those of 10 and 11 years experience in 1950–51) the salaries of engineers with zero or one year of experience declined relative to those with 9, 10, or 11 years of experience. In the post-Korean period, 1953–54 and 1954–55, the wages of the engineers with zero and one year of experience declined relative to those with 9 or more years. This decline does not appear in 1953–54, but it is marked in 1954–55 and also in the two-year period 1953–55.

[30] Between 1929 and 1932, the median salary of engineers with less than one year's experience declined relatively more than that of all engineers; salaries for those with one year's experience fell 26.5 per cent as compared to 18.7 per cent for all engineers. For the decade 1929–39, the median for beginning engineers declined 14.1 per cent; for all engineers the decline was 4.2 per cent.

From 1932 to 1934 the median salary of new engineers declined less than for all engineers (Blank and Stigler, *The Demand and Supply*, Table A-8, p. 130). This accompanied a marked decline in the ratio of the interquartile difference to the median from .43 to .35 for engineers with less than 1 year of experience, while the corresponding ratio for those with 9–11 years of experience was virtually unchanged (.45 in 1932 and .44 in 1934) and increased from .72 to .75 for those with 30–34 years of experience (Blank and Stigler, Table A-3, p. 117). I would suggest that this reflects the upward pressure upon very low wages that stemmed from the National Industrial Recovery Act and related phenomena; this interpretation is supported by the fact that, between 1932 and 1934, the lowest quartile of salaries for engineers with less than 1 year of experience rose from $89 to $91 per month, while the median fell from $111 to $110 and the highest quartile fell from $137 to $129. For experienced engineers, all quartiles fell from 1932 to 1934.

[31] Blank and Stigler, *The Demand and Supply*, p. 136.

Despite these facts, there may be a connection between the sharp rise in demand for certain specialties, and the contraction in the experience differential. Consider: the sharp rise in the entrance rates for certain types of engineers may have led to a switch to those specialties by students—which could occur within two years—thereby decreasing the relative supply of graduates in other fields and (*ceteris paribus*) causing a rise in their entrance rate. Whether such a shift took place during (say) the Korean episode is not easy to determine: the data on percentage of engineering degrees awarded in various fields reveal a suspicious tendency for the percentage in "other" to rise from 1950 to 1953. (Cf. Blank and Stigler, Tables C-5, C-6, C-7, and C-8, pp. 160–165. "Other" is other than civil, mechanical, electrical, chemical and mining; specifically it includes aeronautical and electronic engineers.) However, it is obvious that a more detailed analysis is necessary to see if the data will bear this interpretation; but even if they do, it is far from clear that this "mirage argument" provides a complete explanation of the behavior of the experience differential.

ential is not entirely due to a statistical mirage and, in part, reflects other factors. One of these may be that the relative demand for inexperienced (as against experienced) engineers increases when total demand for engineers increases, and vice versa.

One possible explanation of why it is more profitable, given the initial difference in salaries, to train and promote inexperienced engineers to senior positions than to recruit experienced engineers *in a tight labor market,* but that it is more profitable to do the reverse in other kinds of markets, is as follows.

In a normal labor market, the individual firm can hire both experienced and inexperienced engineers in the quantities it desires from the unemployed resulting from normal labor turnover. But in a tight labor market, experienced engineers cannot be hired from the ranks of the unemployed, but must be bid away from their current employers. (The reverse is true of newly graduated and, by definition, inexperienced engineers.) There are two reasons why this is more costly than hiring comparable engineers who are currently unemployed: (1) it is time-consuming to find an appropriately skilled and experienced engineer who is currently employed and "pirate" him and (2) it is costly to induce him to leave a situation where he has known and favorable prospects for advancement, good personal relations, etc. and, where done, it is usually at a substantial increase over his current salary. Both of these factors make the *marginal cost* of hiring *additional* experienced engineers rise substantially when the labor market tightens, but do not affect the wage rate that must be paid to those experienced engineers already hired, provided no new ones are added. And they do not apply to new engineering graduates. Hence, the marginal cost of recruiting experienced engineers rises relative to that of hiring inexperienced ones, even though their relative wage rates remain unchanged.[32]

This tends to reduce the demand for additional experienced engineers (relative to that for inexperienced) at given relative wage rates, thereby (given the supply functions) driving up the relative wages of the inexperienced.[33]

Conversely, when the market for engineers loosens, it becomes easier for an employer who needs an experienced engineer to find one currently looking for a job so that the marginal cost of hiring him is no greater than the wage paid those already employed. Thus, when the over-all demand for engineers falls, the marginal cost of hiring an experienced one falls relatively (to that of hiring an inexperienced one), if relative wage rates are unchanged; therefore there is a tendency for the relative demand for and wages of the inexperienced to decline.

This explanation applies directly to the case of engineers. Superficially, at least, it also seems consistent with the behavior of teachers' salaries. And we believe it is applicable to a wide variety of labor market situations. Indeed, whenever a firm has an incentive to prefer previously hired workers to new ones—either because of a desire to minimize the costs of labor turnover or because it has made an investment in training its workers—it will try to keep its present employees from desiring to leave. Since it

---

[32] That is, in a tight labor market, the supply curve of experienced engineers to a firm develops a discontinuity at the quantity currently hired. However, this discontinuity disappears—or is greatly reduced—in a "normal" or "loose" market; this is a species of monopsonistic behavior.

[33] One would expect that the (few) experienced engineers who do get onto the labor market when it is tight would receive higher wages than those who do not. Perhaps they do, but two contrary possibilities must be considered: (1) that the experienced engineers appearing on the market may be an inferior sample of the relevant population and (2) that, because of the market situation, employers have made such *short-run* arrangements that they cannot effectively use additional experienced men. Furthermore, it is notoriously difficult to discriminate in favor of newcomers without creating grave discontent among old employees. The need to extend the "recruitment price" to those already hired may be a serious deterrent to recruiting experienced personnel; this is typical of monopsony.

does not have a parallel incentive for the newly hired, it may follow the market for that group, but maintain a given wage rate for each job among the more experienced.[34] This will generate a pattern of fluctuations in experienced differentials in response to labor demand similar to that which students have observed. Given the association between skill and experience, which is implied by the practice of promotion from within, the skill differential is likely to move with the experience differential.

Interindustry Differentials

Long Run[35]

Most discussions of interindustry wage differentials proceed without much explicit consideration of economic theory. The literature abounds in ad hoc hypotheses, some of which are consistent with neoclassical price theory but many of which are not. However, these various hypotheses are usually treated as being equally plausible, a priori; consistency with the implications of price theory has counted for very little in appraising the merits of a theory. Our attitude is somewhat different; we believe that if a theory is inconsistent with the implications of price theory it is cause for concern, and that an explanation is in order. Consequently it will be helpful if we begin our discussion by spelling out what is implied by price theory for interindustrial differentials.

In the long run, under competitive conditions,[36] any industry will pay the same price for a given grade of labor as any other industry hiring in the same location. This remark must be qualified for differences in the nonpecuniary attractions of different industries and locations, but let us abstract from these at first. Therefore, in the long run, real wage differentials among industries will reflect differences in the skill mix. Money wage differences among locations, for given skill, should be no greater than can be rationalized by differences in living costs.

This means that there should be no association of industry wage levels either with the amount of labor employed or with the amount of capital employed (total or per worker) except insofar as either of these quantities is correlated with the skill mix. This absence of association between industry wage level and quantity of labor utilized is an important distinguishing characteristic between long- and short-run situations. In the short run, the greater the increase in employment over the recent past, the more likely is an industry to encounter rising wages because of short-run inelasticities of labor supply; hence the theory implies a positive association of increase in labor quantity used and wage increase in short periods, but not in long periods. Moreover, it seems reasonable to suppose that it will be more likely that skilled labor will become relatively scarce[37] to an expanding industry than nonskilled. Therefore, in the short run, skill differentials should be positively associated with changes in employment.[38]

That is, we interpret price theory as saying that in the long run each industry's wage level will, *ceteris paribus,* vary in the same direction as its skill and locational mix (see

---

[34] To do this a firm need not juggle its starting rate continuously. It will suffice simply to have two or more similar entering job titles with different rates, and hire for the job title consistent with the current market rate.

[35] In this section, the distinction between long and short run is drawn very sharply. The theoretical basis of the distinction is the usual Marshallian one. In practice, we interpret a period as long, for the purpose in hand, if shifting the initial or terminal date to any other year in the same reference cycle would not alter the argument. Specifically, we regard 1899–1953 or 1909–53 or even 1929–53 as "long periods," but not 1929–38. . . .

[36] We shall assume, except when the contrary is specifically stated, that competitive conditions exist.

[37] That is, it will take longer to train workers with skills peculiar to the industry than unspecialized workers and hence, for a time, their elasticity of supply will be less.

[38] This is analogous to Clark Kerr's contention that, "The lesser the degree and the greater the rate of industrialization, the wider will be the occupational differentials and the greater the premiums for skill." (See "Wage Relationships—The Comparative Impact of Market and Power Forces," in *The Theory of Wage Determination* [cited in footnote 1], p. 187, especially no. ·2.)

below) and, in particular, will not be related to changes in the quantities of labor or capital employed. Now if *ceteris* were exactly *paribus*, and our sample were large enough, the correlation coefficient (among industries) between long-run changes in wage levels and those in (any) factor quantity would be exactly zero. But our samples are limited and ceteris is never exactly paribus; hence the theory will be considered "not inconsistent with the evidence" if the above mentioned correlation coefficients are approximately zero. Inconsistency with the evidence will emerge if ceteris is insufficiently paribus in the sense that forces affecting long-run relative wage changes are significantly correlated with long-run relative changes in factor quantities.[39]

Now, how do these inferences square with available evidence? One body of evidence is presented by Fabricant[40] in a study of average growth rates of real hourly wages, labor employed, and capital utilized in 33 industries from 1899 to 1953.[41] Let us suppose that in a period of 54 years the long-run forces that affect the relative levels of industries' wages make changes sufficiently large to permit us to treat differences between 1899 and 1953 as reflecting mainly these forces and, only to a minor degree, random and short-run forces.[42] That is, the differences between 1899 and 1953 are assumed to be explicable on the hypothesis that they are, save for random disturbances, positions of comparative statics. If so, there should be no association between either the relative growth in the quantity of labor utilized, or the relative growth in the stock of capital employed in a given industry, and the relative growth in wages (measured by average hourly earnings) in that industry. The rank correlation coefficients between (a) wages and labor employed and (b) wages and tangible capital owned,[43] with each industry taken as a single observation, are $+.21$ between wages and labor quantity and $+.29$ between wages and capital quantity. The standard error of the rank correlation coefficient with 33 observations is .17, and hence neither coefficient is statistically significant at the 5 per cent level.[44]

These findings are compatible with the

---

[39] Now a word about the nonpecuniary attraction of different industries. It is hard to believe—though imaginable—that industries *as such* have differing degrees of nonpecuniary attractiveness to labor force members. Most of the apparent nonpecuniary differences among industries would seem to boil down to differences in the relative attractiveness of different locations and of the specific jobs offered. For example, we submit that a job as bookkeeper in the New York office of a coal mining firm is no less attractive than a similar job in the same location in an electronics firm. However, coal mining will offer proportionately more jobs in mining towns, and underground, than (say) electronics manufacturing and therefore might well face a higher *pecuniary* supply price for its labor.

It would not be correct, conceptually, to identify unskilled jobs with unattractive ones, but historically there has been a strong positive association. In general, as industries have shifted away from unskilled labor they have also improved working conditions and reduced nonpecuniary disutilities. And since it is obviously very difficult to measure or indicate the relative nonpecuniary attractiveness of different industries, we have assumed that the *rank* of the various industries with respect to nonpecuniary utilities varies with the percentage of its workers employed in unskilled jobs. Clearly, this is a rough approximation which must later be improved upon.

[40] S. Fabricant, *Basic Facts on Productivity Change*, New York, NBER, Occasional Paper 63, 1959, especially pp. 29–37.

[41] These data are represented in extended form in J. W. Kendrick, *Productivity Trends in the United States*, Princeton for NBER, 1961.

[42] See Methodological Appendix [in *Aspects of Labor Economics*].

[43] Perforce, we use the Kendrick-Fabricant definitions of labor, capital, and output. The data used are contained in Table B, pp. 46–47, of Fabricant, *Basic Facts*. "Wages," "labor," and "capital" mean here percentage change in each of these variables between 1899 and 1953.

[44] It might be contended that, because we have two coefficients differing from zero, and with the same sign, the two coefficients together differ significantly from zero (to which theory implies they are both equal). However, output, capital, and labor are all highly correlated so that we cannot suppose the two coefficients to be independent, and combining the tests is therefore extremely difficult.

competitive hypothesis.[45] Indeed, the fact that both of the correlation coefficients are positive, as well as small, is what might be expected because of the tendency for rapidly growing industries to locate (as of 1953) in relatively high-wage urban centers. There is, moreover, further evidence that is also favorable to the competitive hypothesis.

(1) Contrary to much of the recent literature, there was only a slight correlation between productivity[46] and average hourly labor compensation among 33 industry groups during the period 1899–1953. The rank correlation during that period was $+.24$ (insignificant at the 5 per cent level); in various shorter periods the coefficient was appreciably higher.[47] Confirming this is the fact that during 1899–1947, among 80 manufacturing industries, the rank correlation coefficient between output per man-hour and average hourly labor compensation was 0.26—not quite significant at 5 per cent; during individual decades of that period, the coefficient was invariably higher than this.[48]

It would be possible to hide behind the insignificance of the above coefficients and say that the competitive hypothesis is not disconfirmed. However, it seems more plausible to suppose that the two coefficients (noted above) together indicate the operation of some rather weak force systematically correlating average hourly labor compensation and productivity. One explanation of this that would not be incompatible with the competitive hypothesis is that there is a tendency for industries with a greater than average increase in productivity to experience a greater than average "improvement" in skill mix[49] and, therefore, to have a greater than average increase in hourly labor compensation. Though not directly testable, this explanation seems to have considerable plausibility. Another possibility consistent with the competitive hypothesis is that increases in productivity are weakly associated with a tendency toward urbanization and higher wages. Last, but not least, in the short run a positive correlation between relative wages and employment is to be expected (see below). This coefficient may approach zero in the long run, but it may remain positive and finite for a very long time—long enough to generate (at least) some of the positive coefficients reported in this section.[50] Obviously, failing empirical tests of these and rival hypotheses, there is room for doubt and debate.

(2) Another finding consistent with the competitive hypothesis is that the ratio of capital compensation per unit of capital service is only slightly correlated with changes in average hourly labor compensation among 33 industries in the period 1929–

---

[45] By "competitive hypothesis," I mean the hypothesis that prices and quantities behave as though they were in long-run equilibrium under conditions of pure competition. When we speak of the short-run competitive hypothesis we mean the same hypothesis except for the modifications introduced by the substitution of Marshallian short-run equilibrium for long run.

[46] "Productivity" is total productivity as defined by Kendrick; i.e., output per unit of input of both labor and capital. However, output per unit of labor input is highly correlated with total productivity (rank correlation coefficient among 33 industry groups is $+0.94$) and, as Kendrick says, "Thus analysis of productivity change based on output-per-manhour measures should give results comparable to analyses based on total factor productivity" (p. 155). Therefore, we shall consider Kendrick's results, where "total productivity" is interchangeable with man-hour productivity.

The competitive hypothesis implies that there will be no correlation *in the long run* between (average) productivity and wages. That is, industries in which average productivity grows relatively to others will show an increasing ratio of average to marginal (labor) productivity because all industries must pay the same for given grades of labor *in the long run*. This, of course, is not true in the short run.

[47] Kendrick, *Productivity Trends*, Table 55, p. 198.

[48] *Ibid.*

[49] That is, a greater than average increase in the percentage of high-earning and presumably skilled workers employed. "Skill mix" is defined more precisely below.

[50] This possibility is discussed in more detail in the appendix. The point was raised in discussion by both M. J. Bailey and H. G. Lewis.

53; the rank correlation coefficient was only $+.12$.[51] The competitive hypothesis implies that this coefficient be zero. Though the coefficient is insignificant at the 5 per cent level, we are inclined to take its positive sign seriously and rationalize it as follows: in industries with a higher than average rate of increase in productivity, there is a slight tendency for both labor and capital "quality" to increase more than the average.[52] A further finding that tends to support this conclusion is the very slight positive correlation ($+.05$) between (1) factor compensation (of both labor and capital) per unit of input, and (2) productivity among 33 industries in 1899–1953.

Contrasted with these slight positive correlations is the very substantial negative rank correlation coefficient, during 1899–1953, between unit prices of output and factor productivity, $-.55$, which is significant at 5 per cent.[53] The sign of this coefficient is what the competitive hypothesis would lead one to expect. Combined with the other findings cited it bears out the view that, as between industries, the relative gains of factor productivity are passed on to buyers and none accrue to the factors employed.

(3) Still a third finding that bears upon the competitive hypothesis is the behavior of the interindustrial wage structure itself. We have seen that there has been a secular decline in skill differentials in the economy as a whole. What has been said of skill differentials also applies to geographical differentials.

We also know that the ranking of industries with respect to their level of earnings per worker is quite stable over long periods of time. That is, the rank correlation of an industry's position in the industrial wage hierarchy in one year (or period) with another very distant in time is "quite high." For example, Cullen[54] found a rank correlation coefficient of $+.66$ for 76 manufacturing industries between ranks of per-worker annual earnings in 1899 and 1950. In Kendrick's data, the rank correlation between average hourly earnings in 1899–1909 and 1948–53 was $+.46$.[55] Slichter found a coefficient of rank correlation of $+.7289$ between the average hourly earnings of male unskilled labor among 20 manufacturing industries in 1923 and 1946.[56]

Because of the secular decline in skill margins and in regional differentials, the competitive hypothesis implies that there would have been a secular decrease in interindustry relative wage dispersion if the skills and geographical mix had remained more or less unchanged.[57] The evidence that there has been a secular decrease in interindustry relative wage dispersion is far from conclusive; and Cullen's scepticism of this evidence as proof of secularly[58] reduced dispersion seems fully warranted.[59] It is possible that

---

[51] Kendrick, *Productivity Trends*, Table 55.

[52] By "capital quality," I refer to the intangible (and unmeasured) inputs that add to the nonlabor income of an enterprise, but are not included in its measured capital stock. Included in these would be entrepreneurial skill and investment in research and development. In this connection, Kendrick reports (Ch. VI, p. 183) a rank correlation coefficient of $+.68$ between research and development expenditures, as a per cent of sales in 1953, and the average annual rate of change in total factor productivity in 1948–53.

[53] Kendrick, *Productivity Trends*, Table 57.

[54] D. E. Cullen, "The Inter-industry Wage Structure, 1899–1950," *American Economic Review*, June 1956, pp. 353–69, especially Table II, p. 359.

[55] Kendrick, *Productivity Trends*, computed from Table 54.

[56] S. H. Slichter, "Notes on the Structure of Wages," *Review of Economics and Statistics*, Feb. 1950, pp. 80–91, especially p. 88 and Table 7.

[57] Kerr ("Wage Relationships," pp. 189–191) argues this very strongly, though without indicating the crucial role of the competitive hypothesis.

[58] The very marked and undisputed declines since the late 1930's are irrelevant for long-run analysis, as it seems clear that at that time these differentials were abnormally large.

[59] Cullen, "The Inter-industry Wage Structure," p. 361. Further evidence to the same general effect is provided by correlating the percentage wage change between 1899 and 1953 (from Kendrick's data) with the index of "richness of skill mix" by industry, in 1950 (see n. 63). If the relative richness of skill mix of the various industries had been unchanged over time, the percentage wage in-

further investigation will show that dispersion has indeed been reduced. But if it does not, certain more or less alternative inferences may be drawn: (1) despite the general decline in skill margins, the relative wage premiums that must be paid by industries that are expanding their labor forces rapidly were as great in the late 1940's as at the turn of the century;[60] (2) there was an increasing dispersion in the "richness" of industrial skill mixes[61] which offset the reduced skill margins; (3) there were offsetting interindustry changes in skill mixes, locational mixes, etc.; and (4) the competitive hypothesis is wrong. These inferences are not mutually exclusive, and they could all be true to a degree; however, none of the first three has yet been tested, though it is far from impossible to do so.

We have already presented some evidence which tends to reject (4); i.e., which tends to support the competitive hypothesis. And there is some further evidence to the same effect: both Cullen and Woytinsky find evidence of diminishing secular dispersion of interindustrial earning among the particular industries that happened to be at the upper and lower extremes of the distribution in a particular year.[62] This means that, although the over-all interindustry dispersion among a collection of industries may not have diminished appreciably over time, the spread among the group of industries that happened

---

crease should have been the smaller, the richer the skill mix, because of the secular decline in skill margins. However, the rank correlation coefficient was only −.086 (between richness of skill mix in 1950 and percentage change in wages between 1899 and 1953). The sign is in accord with the hypothesis of no change in relative skill mix, but far too small to be taken seriously.

[60] That is, the industries that are "very high" wage payers in any given year include a disproportionate number of those expanding rapidly, and therefore trying to increase their total labor force; the converse applies to those industries that are "very low" wage payers. Industries at either end of the rankings include a disproportionate fraction of those in temporary disequilibrium. Naturally, those industries need not be the same ones in 1899 and 1950.

[61] By "richness of the skill mix," I refer to the relative numbers of skilled, semi-skilled, and unskilled workers employed. An industry's skill mix is richer, the greater the fraction of the first, and the smaller the fraction of the last in the work force.

We can measure the richness of the skill mix of different industries in 1950 from the statistics of *Occupation by Industry* which, so far as we are aware, has not been published for any other Census. The measure of the richness of an industry's skill mix is defined as the following weighted average:

$$R_i = \frac{\sum_{j=1}^{n} a_{ji} W_j}{E_i} \text{ (males)} + \frac{\sum_{j=1}^{n} a_{ji} W_j}{E_i} \text{ (females)}$$

This weighted average refers to the i th industry; W_j is the median annual earnings of persons in the j occupation throughout the economy; a_{ji} is the number of persons of given sex employed in the i th industry, and the i th occupation; and E_i is the number of persons employed in the i th industry. R_i is a weighted average of the nationwide median occupational earnings of the employees in the i th industry with the fraction of the i th industry employment in the various age-sex classes serving as weights.

Sex, as well as occupation, is treated as a determinant of skill mix because women, even in the same occupational category and industry, tend to be paid less than men (for whatever reason). It would have been better to have corrected our weights for degree of unemployment, but we were unable to do so. The richness of skill mix in 1950 was rank correlated with median industrial annual earnings in 1949 by a coefficient of +.613.

[62] Cullen ("Inter-industry Wage," Table III, p. 361) found a reduction between 1899 and 1947–50 of 8–12 per cent in the difference between the median annual earnings in industries in the upper and lower quartiles of the distribution of 84 manufacturing industries, in 1899. W. S. Woytinsky (*Employment and Wages in the United States*, New York, Twentieth Century Fund, 1953, Chap. 39, pp. 460–462 and 507–509) found a tendency for low-wage industries in 1929 to have climbed relatively to high-wage industries by 1950.

Cullen (pp. 364–365) notes that most of the narrowing in dispersion in his data occurred before 1921. This, of course, would suggest that the short-run disturbances had been washed out before that date. This interpretation of Cullen's findings is different from (and possibly inconsistent with) his own.

to be paying very high and very low wages in a given base year (e.g., 1899 or 1929) diminished. In other words, the particular industries that are toward the high and low extremes in the interindustrial earnings hierarchy in a given year tended to regress toward the mean with the passage of time.

This is what the competitive hypothesis implies will happen; for, in any given year, part of the interindustry dispersion of wages is due to disequilibrium of industries expanding and contracting employment more than the average, and this source of interindustry wage dispersion is reduced over time by the operation of the price system. The competitive hypothesis implies nothing concerning the long-term trend in interindustrial wage dispersion among a particular group of industries as a whole, except that it should depend solely upon variations in skill and locational differentials and random disturbances.

One further hypothesis, not strictly of a long-run variety, should be mentioned. The rise of an economy from a less- to a more-full utilization of its labor force (including its reserves) may cause a reduction in interindustry differentials, as happened when the economy emerged from the depression of the 1930's to the full employment of the 1940's.[63] Such behavior would follow from the narrowing of skill differentials during such periods. Whether this limited experience can be generalized to a proposition relating level of employment, or growth rate in labor demand, to the interindustry dispersion of wage rates is not clear. However, it is a possibility.

Several other hypotheses concerning the long-run equilibrium industrial structure of wage rates have been advanced by Slichter:[64]

(1) "The average hourly earnings of male unskilled labor (U) tend to be high where the average hourly earnings of male semi-skilled and skilled labor (S) are high." Slichter found, in 1939, a rank correlation coefficient of $+.7098$ (among 20 manufacturing industries) between U and S. If this correlation is interpreted as resulting from a tendency for industries using relatively expensive types of skilled labor also to use expensive types of nonskilled, then it is compatible with the competitive hypothesis. Slichter accepts this interpretation in part,[65] but also contends that the correlation is partly due to company wage policy, which presumably is independent of market forces; on this point, see below. It should be noted that it is also possible that Slichter's observation reflects short-period and not long-period forces; i.e., expanding industries are more likely than others to encounter increasing supply prices (as a function of rate of increase of employment) for all kinds of labor.[66]

(2) "The hourly earnings of male common labor (M) have some (not pronounced) tendency to be low where the percentage of women (W) among wage earners is high." The coefficient of rank correlation between M and W in 1939 (for 19 manufacturing industries) was $+.4491$, and in 1929, $+.5224$.[67] This, as Slichter (in effect) argues, may well reflect the operation of the competitive mechanism; i.e., women

---

[63] This has been stressed in two studies of English data: P. Haddy and N. A. Tolles, "British and American Changes in Inter-industry Wage Structure under Full Employment," *Review of Economics and Statistics*, Nov. 1957, pp. 408–414; and P. Haddy and M. E. Currell, British Inter-Industrial Earnings Differentials, 1924–1955," *Economic Journal*, Mar. 1958, pp. 104–111. This tendency also appears in Cullen's data ("Interindustry Wage") for World War II; however, it does not appear during World War I.

[64] Slichter, "Notes on the Structure of Wages." Slichter does not distinguish carefully between long- and short-run relations; consequently, the interpretation placed on his findings is entirely our own.

[65] *Ibid.*, p. 84.

[66] This possibility would seem less likely in 1939, to which Slichter's data refer, than in the 1920's, 1940's, or 1950's. It is also possible that the correlation reflects the common effect of locational factors.

[67] Industries are ranked in inverse order of male common labor earnings.

are hired mainly in low-wage industries and men, in order to compete with them, must accept less than the average male wage. That is, the correlation is presumed to reflect competition for similar jobs, and not osmosis. If this explanation is correct, then the industries where women are most highly concentrated should be those in which the unfavored (by the market) males, e.g., Negroes, are also concentrated; and this seems to be the case.[68]

(3) Slichter also found substantial rank correlation between net income after taxes, as a percentage of sales, π, and average hourly earnings both of unskilled and of skilled and semiskilled workers.[69] Slichter interpreted π as an index of profitability. Accepting this interpretation, we could easily rationalize the observed rank correlations as short-period phenomena resulting from the short-run association between increased labor demand and profitability. However, Slichter, like many other writers, contends that this phenomenon "reinforces the view that wages, within a considerable range, reflect managerial discretion, and that where managements are barely breaking even, they tend to keep wages down."[70] This interpretation is incompatible with the competitive hypothesis.

We believe that the importance of this possibility can easily be exaggerated. Nonetheless, the field work on our study of interfirm wage differentials has confirmed the oft-expressed view that large and profitable firms will often ignore local labor market situations by over-paying on certain jobs in certain areas in order to avoid undesired intercompany differentials. Such firms also manifest a desire to be toward the top of any labor market in which they hire, both for reasons of prestige and quality selection.

To be sure, there is a tendency for out-of-line wages to be corrected "as soon as the opportunity presents itself," but it is also true that large firms are more dilatory about correcting overpayment (e.g., red circle rates) than correcting underpayment. This, together with a preference for selective recruitment policies, creates an upward bias in wage level relative to the market as of any given moment. Thus, we would be inclined to agree that large and profitable firms do tend to pay more at any one time than could be explained by the competitive hypothesis. However, this cannot explain *movements* in relative wages; at most, it can explain relative wage levels as of a given moment.

These remarks pertain directly to individual firms, and not to entire industries. Their relation to the industrial wage structure results from the fact that in some industries the percentage of workers employed in large firms is greater than in others. Industries concentrating relatively large fractions of their labor forces in large firms should tend to exhibit relatively high concentration ratios;[71] hence there might well be an association between high concentration ratios and high wages at a *given moment of time*.

However, this is no reason to suppose there would be an association between *changes* in relative industrial wage levels over time and the index of concentration as of a given moment, as some writers have argued.[72] These writers contend that the index of concentration is a rough (inverse) indicator of

---

[68] The rank correlation coefficient between percentage of women and percentage of Negroes (among males) employed (from 1950 Census data) for 14 industries was +.386; when finance and agriculture are excluded, the coefficient is raised to +.662. However, the osmosis hypothesis requires further investigation.

[69] Slichter, "Notes on the Structure of Wages," p. 88.

[70] *Ibid.*, see also p. 90.

[71] As measured by (say) the percentage of the industry's employment concentrated in the four or eight largest firms.

[72] For example, H. M. Levinson, "Post-war Movement in Prices and Wages in Manufacturing Industries," *Study Paper No. 4,* Joint Economic Committee, Congress of the United States, 1960, pp. 2–5 and 21; also J. W. Garbarino, "A Theory of Inter-industry Wage Structure," *Quarterly Journal of Economics,* May 1950, pp. 282–305, especially pp. 299–300.

the relative degree of competitiveness of an industry;[73] and that noncompetitive industries tend to raise wages more than others. But, since it is not alleged that the indexes of concentration for different industries have changed during the relevant time period, it cannot be permanent differences in industry structure that are responsible for differential wage behavior; it must be differential *changes* in industry behavior. That is, what must be explained are differential changes in the willingness or ability or both of highly concentrated industries (relative to others) to grant wage increases; to our knowledge this has never been attempted. It should also be noted that to relate *levels* of concentration with *increases* (in favor of concentrated industries) in wages implies a secular increase in wage dispersion which is grossly inconsistent with known facts.

Because the hypothesis that interindustrial differences in degree of monopoly are an important factor in explaining the interindustrial differences in wage behavior has had wide currency, and is obviously a rival to the competitive hypothesis, we have attempted one rather simple test of it. We have taken Nutter's data on the relative extent of monopoly in 1899 and 1937 by major industry groups,[74] and correlated the change in the rankings between those dates with the change in the rankings of wages paid by those groups.[75] The correlation coefficient of these rank changes was —.05, indicating a slight (negligible) tendency for a decrease in monopoly to accompany an increase in wages—inconsistent with the hypothesis.[76]

(4) Slichter alleges a strong inverse association between hourly earnings of unskilled labor and the ratio of payrolls to sales. He explains this by saying: "Managements naturally are more concerned about the rates which they pay for labor when payrolls are large in relation to the receipts of the enterprise than when payrolls are small."[77] One (slightly astonishing) implication of this is that vertical disintegration, per se, leads to high wages. But leaving this aside, let us concede that, in the absence of competition, a low ratio does make it easier for a benevolent employer or an aggressive union to raise wages than otherwise. However, before accepting this as an important determinant of industrial wage differences, we would urge consideration of the following alternative: high ratios of payrolls to sales are more likely to be found in industries that specialize in fabricating operations, and are associated with low wages because the likelihood of such specialization is greater where the fabrication can be performed by low-wage labor.

But at the very most, the above relation obtains only at a given instant. It provides no warrant for a long-run interpretation of Dunlop's contention that "wage and salary rates would be expected to increase most . . . where labor costs are a small percentage of total costs."[78] So far as we are aware

---

[73] This is highly debatable but, for the sake of argument, let us concede it.

[74] G. W. Nutter, *The Extent of Enterprise Monopoly in the United States, 1899–1939*, University of Chicago Press, 1951, Tables 10 and 11.

[75] The wage figures were obtained as follows: 1953 (annual average) hourly wages were extrapolated back to 1899 by means of Kendrick's data, and ranks were obtained; these were compared with the ranks of median annual earnings per worker in 1939 as reported in the 1940 Census (see H. P. Miller, "Changes in the Industrial Wage Distribution of Wages in the United States, 1939–1949," *An Appraisal of the 1950 Census Income Data*, Studies in Income and Wealth, Vol. 23, Princeton for NBER, 1958, Table B-2). It is assumed that the 1937 and 1939 rankings would be virtually the same.

[76] David Schwartzman ("Monopoly and Wages," *Canadian Journal of Economics and Political Science*, Aug. 1960, pp. 428–38) reaches a similar conclusion on the basis of comparing United States and Canadian industries with varying concentration ratios.

[77] Slichter, "Notes on the Structure of Wages," p. 87.

[78] J. T. Dunlop, "Productivity and the Wage Structure," *Income, Employment and Public Policy, Essays in Honor of A. H. Hansen*," New York, Norton, 1948, p. 360. In fairness to Dunlop, it should be noted that he has not indicated whether he intended this relationship as long or short run. The short-run version is discussed below.

this contention has never been substantiated *for the long run.*

(5) One determinant of an industry's place in the interindustry wage hierarchy at a given moment is the relative richness of its skill mix. For 1950, we ranked industries by richness of skill mix and correlated this with rank in the interindustry wage hierarchy; the rank correlation coefficient was +.612.[79] This cross-sectional relationship reflects departures from long-run equilibrium, crudeness of industrial classifications, etc. Nonetheless it indicates a substantial degree of relation between the two sets of rankings.

Short Run

Let us begin our discussion of the short-run behavior of the interindustry wage structure by considering the relation of its variations to those in employment. The competitive hypothesis explains such variations as due to wages rising in industries where employment is expanding because of short-run inelasticities of labor supply, and falling in industries where employment is shrinking because of labor immobility. In the short run, *differential* changes in skill mix are assumed to be uncorrelated with differential changes in employment.[80]

There has been a number of studies of the relation of variations in the interindustry wage structure to changes in employment. Unfortunately, not all of their findings are mutually consistent. For example, Garbarino[81] found a rank correlation coefficient of +.48 between percentage changes in hourly earnings and employment (for 34 manufacturing industries) in 1923–40; Ross and Goldner found that in three of four periods studied there was a strong positive association of percentage increases in hourly earnings and percentage increases in employment.[82] Ostry found that in Canada there had been an appreciable correlation between percentage changes in hourly earnings and in employment; among 36 industries, the correlation coefficient in 1945–49 was +.44; in 1949–56 it was +.53, and for 1945–56, +.56.[83]

Moreover, Hansen and Rehn, in a study of wage differentials from 1947 to 1954 among eight industries in Sweden,[84] found substantial interindustry correlation between wage drift[85] and excess demand[86] for labor, which is consistent with the hypothesis that short-run wage differentials result mainly from differing rates of increase in labor demand. They found virtually no correlation of wage drift with gains in average man-hour productivity, but were unable to use Swedish profit data for interindustry analyses.

But the data do not all point to one conclusion: Slichter found among 20 industries, during 1923–39, a coefficient of rank correlation (between percentage changes in

---

[79] This coefficient was computed from an analysis of 14 major industry groups.
[80] See Appendix [in *Aspects of Labor Economics*].
[81] Garbarino, "Theory of Inter-industry Wage Structure," p. 304.
[82] A. M. Ross and W. Goldner, "Forces Affecting the Inter-industry Wage Structure," *Quarterly Journal of Economics*, May 1950, pp. 254–281, especially Table VI, and pp. 272–276. The four periods studied were 1933–38, 1938–42, 1942–46, and 1933–46; the deviant period was the wartime interval 1942–46. The authors present no correlations but merely place industries into four quartiles in accordance with the percentage increase in employment.
F. C. Pierson (*Community Wage Patterns*, University of California Press, 1953, Chap. VI) also finds a positive rank correlation between average hourly earnings and employment for manufacturing industries among several cities between 1929 and 1939, but not during the war period, 1940–48.
[83] S. W. Ostry, "Inter-industry Earnings Differentials in Canada, 1945–1956," *Industrial and Labor Relations Review*, Apr. 1959, pp. 335–352, especially pp. 341–343.
[84] B. Hansen and Gosta Rehn, "On Wage-Drift: A Problem of Money-Wage Dynamics," *Twenty-five Economic Essays in Honour of Erik Lindahl*, Stockholm, 1956, pp. 87–133, especially pp. 105–106 and 128–133.
[85] That is, wage increase in excess of what was implied in collective bargaining agreements.
[86] That is, unfilled vacancies minus unemployment.

hourly earnings and percentage changes in employment) of only +.2812.[87] Eisemann found that in 1939–47, percentage increases in manufacturing wages were negatively correlated with percentage increases in employment; however, the absolute increase in average hourly earnings was positively correlated with percentage increases in employment.[88] Levinson[89] has found that in 4 of the 11 year-to-year changes between 1947 and 1958 there was a negative correlation among 19 manufacturing industries between percentage changes in straight-time hourly earnings and percentage changes in production worker employment. He also found a negative partial correlation coefficient between this pair of variables for 1947–53 and a negligible positive one (+.0046) for 1953–58.[90]

Bowen[91] computed correlation coefficients between percentage changes in average hourly earnings, w, and percentage changes in employment, e, during six subperiods of the interval 1947–59. These various coefficients reflect the association between w and e among 20 two-digit manufacturing industries. Bowen computed both simple and partial correlation coefficients. The partial coefficients between w and e held constant some or all of the following: (1) average level of profits in the industry; (2) the concentration ratio (in 1954); and (3) the percentage of the production workers unionized (in 1958). All possible first and second order partial correlation coefficients between w and e (holding constant the other variables, both singly and in pairs) are presented. The coefficients show a positive correlation between w and e in the three subperiods when unemployment was relatively low,[92] and this relation is generally stronger in the partial than in the simple coefficients. In the three subperiods in which unemployment was relatively high, the coefficients showed a different pattern: in two of these three subperiods the simple coefficients were negative; in one of them all of the partials were negative; and in another, half of them were negative.

Thus Bowen's findings (on this point) tend to support the competitive hypothesis for periods of "low unemployment," but not for those of higher unemployment. That the relation between w and e should be stronger in periods of low unemployment is in the spirit of the competitive hypothesis (though not its letter);[93] i.e., in periods of low unemployment, short-run elasticities of labor supply to industries are likely to be smaller, and differential increases in employment therefore more likely to produce differential

---

[87] Slichter ("Notes on the Structure of Wages," p. 90) argues very explicitly that the relation between hourly earnings and profits is due to wage policy and not labor-market pressure. He found a small *negative* coefficient of rank correlation between changes in employment and changes in average hourly earnings in 1923–39 for *unskilled* workers (as contrasted to the positive coefficient for all workers). Somehow, this argument is not very impressive. (1) As argued above, one would expect the supply of unskilled workers to a given industry to be more elastic in the short run than that of semiskilled and skilled. (2) Slichter's period is almost identical with that of Garbarino ("Theory of Inter-industry Wage Structure"), who found evidence of a stronger relationship than Slichter, and with better data.

[88] Doris M. Eisemann, "Inter-Industry Wage Changes, 1939–1947," *Review of Economics and Statistics*, Nov. 1956, p. 446.

[89] Levinson, "Post-war Movements," Table 1, p. 3.

[90] *Ibid.*, Table 2, p. 4. A. H. Conrad ("The Share of Wages and Salaries in Manufacturing Incomes, 1947–1956," *Study Paper No. 9*, Joint Economic Committee of Congress, Washington, 1959) obtained similar results on *Census of Manufactures* data for all 61 three-digit industries, for the period 1949–56.

[91] W. G. Bowen, *The Wage-Price Issue: A Theoretical Analysis*, Princeton University Press, 1960, pp. 59–66 and Table E-1, pp. 134–135.

[92] The subperiods of low unemployment are characterized by an unemployment percentage (of the civilian labor force) that was "generally below 4.3." The subperiods of high unemployment are those where the unemployment percentage was always above 4.3. Bowen, pp. 24–29.

[93] The letter of the competitive hypothesis makes no provision for unemployment as a variable in supply or demand functions.

wage changes. But if Bowen's findings are accepted, then the competitive hypothesis is uninformative, if not invalid, as an explanation of short-run wage movements in the presence of "appreciable"[94] unemployment.

In short, the evidence does not give unqualified support to the view that short-run variations in labor demand are a major cause of variation in straight-time hourly earnings. Some of the contrary evidence can be "explained away." The adverse findings of Ross and Goldner for 1942–46 and of Eisemann for 1939–47 may well be due to the fact that the war industries which expanded most rapidly were the very ones where dilution of the skill mix was greatest. However, it is harder to explain away the findings of Levinson, Conrad, and especially Bowen. Let us now turn to alternative explanations.

Profits, Concentration, and Related Variables

Levinson suggests that relative industry wage levels have varied either with (industry levels of) current profits or with profits lagged one year.[95] He measures profits as return on stockholders' equity both before or after taxes. This alleged relation is not, of itself, inconsistent with the competitive hypothesis, for the level of current profits would be expected to be associated with recent increases in employment. However, Levinson computes partial correlation coefficients between percentage wage changes, w, and percentage increases in employment, e (average profit level, P, constant), for 1947–53 and 1953–58 and also between w and P (e constant) for the same interval. In 1947–53, the coefficient between w and e was negative, while that between w and P was positive; in 1953–58, the latter coefficient substantially exceeded the former though both were positive.[96]

These findings were similar to those of Bowen, who finds a consistent positive correlation (among 20 manufacturing industries) between percentage change in average hourly earnings and percentage change in average level of profits.[97] This positive relation is found in the simple correlation coefficients in all of Bowen's subperiods; it is also found among the partial coefficients (save for three small negative ones).

What are we to make of these findings? Barring some unperceived differential change in hiring requirements (among industries), we would seem driven to accept Slichter's judgment that "wages, within a considerable range, reflect managerial discretion, that where managements can easily pay high wages they tend to do so, and that where managements are barely breaking even, they tend to keep wages down."[98] This judgment is, of course, incompatible with the competitive hypothesis for the short run.

It is important to distinguish sharply between levels and movements. It is entirely in keeping with the competitive hypothesis that more profitable firms should find it advantageous to demand superior personnel, and pay more to get it. This is essentially what Slichter, Reynolds, and others have contended. What is more difficult to accept is the finding that differences in profit levels also explain *movements* in interindustry differentials.

For certain periods, the *level* of current profits may well be related to the *change* in wage rates. One such period seems to have been 1947–58, and perhaps there have been others. But unless we are to infer a secular trend toward increasing wage dis-

---

[94] Using Bowen's 4.3 per cent as a criterion for distinguishing years of appreciable unemployment from others, 33 of the first 58 years of this century were years of "appreciable unemployment." Even if we exclude the 11 years, 1930–40, 22 out of 47 years showed appreciable unemployment. (These figures are Stanley Lebergott's as quoted by Bowen in Appendix A, pp. 99–101.)
[95] Levinson, "Post-war Movement," pp. 2–7.
[96] Levinson, "Post-war Movement," Table 2, p. 4.
[97] Bowen, *Wage-Price Issue*, pp. 67–69 and 134–135.
[98] Slichter, "Notes on the Structure of Wages," p. 88.

persion in favor of the high-profit industries—a trend no one has alleged and which would be inconsistent with the available evidence—we are left with the problem of explaining why the profit-wage relation is so intermittent. To say that the relation may well hold for one period but not for another is merely to state the facts. The problem of theory is to indicate the differential characteristics of the periods when it does hold and those when it does not. Let us consider a possible explanation.

Despite the evidence he presents on the association of wage change and profit level, Bowen distrusts differentials in profit levels as an explanatory factor of differential in wage changes among industries.[99] He does so mainly because he feels that the partial correlations in the 1954 and 1958 recessions were very small, and that the dominant factor in the simple correlation was the high intercorrelation among wage changes, concentration ratios, and degree of unionization.

Because of the behavior of the partial correlation coefficients Bowen (rightly) rejects the possibility of a consistent *ceteris paribus* relation between wage changes and either concentration or unionization, taken separately. However, he contends that when we consider the combined effect of concentration and unionization (which are strongly intercorrelated in his sample), we find a stable relationship.[100] In discussing this, Bowen abandons correlation analysis and instead divides his industries into two groups: a "market power" sector (consisting of industries that are both highly concentrated and highly unionized) and a "competitive" sector in which the industries have the reverse characteristics. He argues that, with one exception,[101] the percentage change in average hourly earnings was greater in the market-power sector in all of the subperiods between 1947 and 1959. Although recognizing that the average level of profits was generally higher in the market-power sector, he says "that the importance of profits in this picture ought not to be exaggerated."[102] He also rejects the possibility that different rates of growth in employment are a differentiating characteristic of the two sectors.[103]

Bowen does not allege that what he has observed is part of a secular trend, but neither does he attempt to indicate what special characteristics of the period, 1947–59, are responsible for the unusual behavior observed, or why such behavior cannot persist indefinitely.[104] However, one possible explanation seems to be fairly obvious: the market power sector contains a relatively large number of firms that respond to market stimuli rather slowly as compared with firms in the competitive sector. This relative sluggishness reflects the fact that *investment* decisions are expensive; can be made only infrequently and cannot easily be reversed. This would seem to be most characteristic of those sectors of the economy where "productive capacity" per unit of output is relatively expensive and long lived. Firms with these characteristics typically produce durable goods and are disproportionately found in Bowen's market-power sector. Investment and output decisions in these firms respond not so much to current profits, as in the competitive sector, but to (moving) averages of current and past sales and profits which serve (along with other indicators) as a guide to the future.

[99] Bowen, *Wage-Price Issue*, p. 68.
[100] *Ibid.*, pp. 74–81.
[101] The period January 1949–October 1950.
[102] Bowen, *Wage-Price Issue*, p. 78.
[103] Whatever the validity of this contention, it is not consistent with his own data. From Table 13, p. 77, we can compute (putting initial employment in Jan. 1947 = 100) that employment in June 1959 was 102.5 in the market-power sector but only 97.7 in the competitive sector.
[104] Bowen does offer an explanation, in spirit similar to what follows, of wage behavior in the 1954 and 1958 recessions (pp. 82–84). However, he does not recognize that if there is growth in differentials in recessions, there must be either (1) contraction of the differentials in periods of high employment or (2) a secular trend (in the differentials).

On this view, the wage behavior described by Bowen is explained thus: at the end of World War II both sectors were confronted with situations of strong demand and high profits. The competitive sector acted to eliminate its excess demand faster than the market-power sector where long gestation periods of capital goods combined with a cautious outlook to hold back the investment program. This made the market-power sector's period of high profits, full capacity operation, and "strength" in product prices last longer than the competitive sector's period did. This, in turn, facilitated the payment of relative increases in earnings (in the market-power sector) during most of the 1950's.

If this explanation is correct, the growth of excess capacity and price weakness in the market-power sector during the late 1950's will soon end its relative wage gains, if it has not already done so. Also, if true, there should have been similar periods to the 1950's in the past—e.g., in the 1920's, as an aftermath of World War I. This particular hypothesis implies the same response pattern of wage changes to current profits or to current labor market conditions in Bowen's two sectors; it requires (1) that the two sectors both start from initial positions of excess product demand; (2) that the response mechanism of the market-power sector to excess product demand be slower, so that it takes a longer period to reach equilibrium; and (3) that relative wages in the competitive sector be high enough to obviate the need for short-run adjustments under pressure of a growing relative labor scarcity. It is quite possible that the wage adjustment mechanism in the market-power sector is also more sluggish; the differential incidence of long-term contracts with automatic deferred wage increases would suggest this.

We also suspect that, in the above explanation, the role of product prices is crucial. That is, when firms believe that cost increases can be passed on to buyers, they are more inclined to grant wage increases than when the reverse is the case. This is consistent with some findings of Dunlop on the relation of changes in wages and product prices,[105] which should be investigated further and brought up to date, especially the interrelation among changes in wages, product prices, and profits.

But if there is anything to the idea that there are two important sectors of the economy in which the ratio of *current* wages to the *current* marginal productivity of labor[106] behaves differently, it is incompatible with the competitive hypothesis as an explanation of wage behavior in the short run. This is because shifts in the ratio of current wages to current marginal productivity of labor can always be expressed as changes in the elasticities of (imagined) supply of factor or demand for product curves or both, whose alleged shifts are the staple of noncompetitive explanations of relative wage and price behavior. Such short-run shifts are simply the obverse side of a pattern of delayed response to market stimuli; it may also be true that a pattern of delayed response— especially in adding to productive capacity —requires some restriction upon entry and a substantial degree of concentration. Failure of either of these conditions to obtain may make it impossible for any one firm to hold off on expansion because of its inability to keep communicating with—or even to keep track of—all its potential rivals. The reader will understand that this is to

---

[105] J. T. Dunlop, *Wage Determination under Trade Unions,* 2nd ed. New York, Kelley, 1950, Chap. VII. Dunlop found a strong positive association (among industries) between declines in wage rates and product prices during the recessions of 1929–32 and 1937–38, and presents substantial evidence to support this observation for the two depressions in question. However, Levinson ("Post-war Movement," p. 15) found that from 1947 through 1951–52 "price changes were unrelated to changes in gross hourly earnings—after that point, however, the correlation became very much stronger."

[106] That is the value of the marginal physical product as reflected in the output records for the *same* accounting period to which the wages are imputed. The reason for this rather narrow view of the competitive hypothesis is indicated in the Appendix.

suggest an hypothesis; testing it is another and far more difficult matter.

There are a number of other ad hoc short-period hypotheses concerning the behavior of industry wage levels. For example, it has been suggested that changes in industry wage levels tend to be more closely related in absolute than in percentage terms. While more careful writers have usually agreed that neither percentage nor absolute measures of changing differentials was ideal, the argument is that, because of union or governmental pressure, or both, industries tend to obtain equal absolute wage increases rather than equal percentage hikes.[107] This argument has been widely discussed in recent years, and appears to have had considerable validity for the period 1933–45, when interindustry (like other) differentials were narrowing. However, for the periods since 1947, the hypothesis does not seem so plausible.[108] It is worth noting that this hypothesis implies, contrary to the competitive hypothesis, that in the short run relative wage levels are altered by variations in supply determinants (union and government policies) rather than by variations in demand determinants.

To argue that movements in relative wage levels are strongly correlated with levels of relative profits or changes in relative product prices is not to contradict the competitive hypothesis, per se. For both of the aforementioned independent variables may be correlated with variations in the levels of employment and reflect only the influence of this variable on relative wage levels. Moreover, industries with high current profits might well be industries in process of an unusually marked tendency to be hiring workers to operate new processes or to work in newly developing high-wage areas, or both. Either or both of these tendencies could create (upward) labor market pressure on wage rates despite a tendency for over-all employment to decline. None of the studies to which reference has been made has attempted to control against these possibilities.

Productivity

Some writers have found that the increase in average hourly earnings was greater in industries where the increase in physical production per man-hour was greater; e.g., Dunlop[109] and Garbarino.[110] Barring a correlation of skill mix and/or location with productivity, such a relationship is incompatible with the competitive hypothesis in the long run; whether it is compatible in the short run depends upon whether increases in man-hour productivity are positively correlated with increases in employment via correlation with the *value* of labor's marginal physical product.

The alleged factual relation between man-hour productivity and wages has itself been disputed by Levinson,[111] Meyers and Bowlby,[112] and Perlman.[113] These authors, especially the last, rightly stress the importance of product price movements in determining the relative average value productivity of labor in different industries. Despite the dispute about whether the various correlation coefficients are significant, and which periods should be studied, it seems that the coefficients are usually positive,[114] which suggests the existence of a positive short-run association, but one which is disturbed by

---

[107] A very large number of writers have argued in this fashion. One of the earliest was A. M. Ross, *Trade Union Wage Policy*, University of California Press, 1948, Chap. VI.

[108] For example, Levinson's data would not seem consistent with it.

[109] Dunlop, "Productivity and the Wage Structure."

[110] Garbarino, "Theory of Inter-industry Wage Structure," pp. 298–300.

[111] "Post-war Movement," Table 1, p. 3.

[112] F. Meyers and R. L. Bowlby, "The Inter-industry Wage Structure and Productivity," *Industrial and Labor Relations Review*, Oct. 1953, pp. 93–102.

[113] R. Perlman, "Value Productivity and the Inter-industry Wage Structure," *Industrial and Labor Relations Review*, Oct. 1956, pp. 26–39.

[114] But not always: Meyers and Bowlby turned up some negative coefficients ("Inter-industry Wage Structure," p. 98) and so did Levinson.

extraneous factors whose intensity varies from one period to another.

How one is to interpret this association is another matter. Garbarino found that in Dunlop's data (where the correlation between increases in man-hour productivity and wages was strong), the coefficient of rank correlation between increases in employment and in man-hour productivity was only $+.08$.[115] Obviously this militates against the short-run competitive hypothesis that there is a positive association between changes in hourly earnings and changes in man-hour productivity, because of an empirical association of the latter with rising output and employment. Another possible explanation, of pertinence in the long run as well as the short, is that industries in which man-hour productivity increases most are those in which the skill mix is likely to improve most. Yet another possible explanation of this phenomenon posits the existence of a link between wage increases and rises in productivity via profits and ability to pay, à la Slichter, Levinson, et al. But there is no good reason, either in theory or fact, for accepting any of these hypotheses.[116]

Unions

Our discussion of interindustry wage differentials has obviously left out unions; the omission is intentional. The main reason for exclusion is the failure of previous research to obtain very satisfactory results in relating them either to the levels or movements in interindustry wage differentials. The well-known conclusion of Douglas and of Ross and Goldner[117] that new unionism is associated with differential percentage wage gains to an industry, but long-established unionism is not, was about as far as anyone had been able to go before the work reported on by H. G. Lewis in this volume. We shall not attempt to appraise this work here but only note its relevance to our discussion.

One possibility of detecting the influence of unionism is to analyze the association among industries between wage changes and profit levels, holding employment changes constant. If unionism is effective in making wages higher than they would have been in its absence, this should be reflected in a forced sharing of profits[118] which should be, in the short run, over and above the influence of labor market conditions. That is, the positive partial association between wage changes and profit levels should increase with the strength of unionism—however measured. Of course, the influence of extraneous factors such as changes in skill and locational mix must be somehow taken into account.

Conclusion

This paper's point of departure is that relative wage levels, both by skill and industry, behave more or less as though they were market prices reflecting predominantly the interplay of changing tastes, techniques, and resources—the competitive hypothesis.

---

[115] "Theory of Inter-industry Wage Structure," p. 285.

[116] In a recent paper, L. Johansen ("A Note on the Theory of Inter-industrial Wage Differentials," *Review of Economic Studies*, Feb. 1958, pp. 109–113) concludes that "we may expect not changes in wage differentials, but wage differentials themselves to be correlated with the changes in productivity." This result, however, refers only to differentials that reflect labor market disequilibrium; i.e., his results depend on labor market disequilibrium embodied in his equation (4) on p. 110. For the short run, his conclusion is identical in empirical content with the conventional Marshallian one, where productivity is reflected in a parameter of the industry labor demand fraction.

[117] P. H. Douglas, *Real Wages in the United States*, p. 564; Ross and Goldner, "Forces Affecting," p. 267.

[118] To test our hypothesis, it is necessary that unions be not "too strong"; i.e., unions must compel relatively more profitable firms to *share* their "excess profits" with wage earners (but not obliterate them), so that there are still greater than average profits to be observed. It is conceivable—though not likely—that unions could be so effective in raising wages that all potential supernormal profits were transferred to wages, completely obscuring the hypothesized relation.

The implications of this hypothesis, however, are not so simple as they might seem because tastes, techniques, and resources interact in peculiar and complicated ways. Moreover, the basic hypothesis has required amendment to allow for the effect of changes in minimum wage laws, etc., for secular rural-urban migration, and for the gradual broadening of educational opportunities.

The competitive hypothesis is at its best, both in explaining skill margins and interindustry differentials, when it is used to explain variations over long periods of time. It can hardly be said to be firmly established as an explanation of wage phenomena even for long periods; but it has at least survived (reasonably well) the tests to which it has so far been put.

For the short run the competitive hypothesis does not appear very reliable. There are a number of findings concerning interindustry differentials which simply are not consistent with its short-run implication that relative industry wage rates vary in the same direction as relative changes in employment, in any given short-time interval. We are not without alternative short-run hypotheses; but these either break down during one time interval or another, or still are in a primitive state of formulation and testing.

In this paper we have discussed only skill and industrial differentials. No attempt has been made to analyze interfirm, interplant, and interregional differentials which, incidentally, may be associated with skill or industry differentials. However, this task will be attempted in the near future.

21
The Relation of Differential Wage Movements and the Redistribution of Labour Among Industries

Organization for Economic Co-operation and Development

The number of studies which exist on this subject is far from negligible. Most of them have approached it in what appears to be the most direct way, that is by making statistical assessments of the strength of the relationship appearing between changes in relative earnings and changes in relative employment. But while this relation is clearly of central importance to any understanding of the mechanisms involved, it cannot be seen in isolation. An attempt has been made in the preceding chapters to set the background to the present one by putting the alternative motivations of different types of labour flow into perspective.

Comparison of the results obtained in different studies covering different countries and periods of time brings out a remarkable similarity in the factual results obtained. A positive association appears between changes in relative earnings and relative employment more frequently than a negative one; but where the coefficients are high enough to make the observed association statistically significant, they rarely suggest that the relationship is a strong one. Moreover, the sign of the relationship frequently changes, depending on the time period in question or the particular series chosen, which, for the same country, differ with respect to coverage, unit of observation or source of data.

To the concordance of the factual results there corresponds a remarkable degree of divergence in the interpretation of these results. This is indicative of the extreme difficulty of the subject. As it is essential to our mandate, the Secretariat has, at our request, carried out a more detailed and comprehensive analysis, which is described below. The data cover a wider range of countries, earnings classifications and periods of variable length than it has hitherto been possible to consider in the scope of a single piece of

Reprinted from *Wages and Labour Mobility* (Paris: Organization for Economic Co-operation and Development, July 1965), pp. 85–118, by permission of the publisher.

research. A full list of the countries and series studied will be found in Table 21.1. As will be seen, they confirm the factual findings of the earlier studies, but leave the problem of interpretation very open.

The Limits of the Analysis

Considerable use has been made of correlation analysis, and to this extent the results are not merely open to alternative interpretation, but in some cases are not relevant to certain of the most important aspects of the question under examination. Some of these difficulties are inherent in all correlation analysis, i.e. whether an observed association is merely a joint response by the variables under study to some outside influences which operate on both, or whether it is in fact a causal relationship and if so, what is the direction of causality. This is particularly important in the study of the allocative role of wages. To the extent that the analysis does indicate an association between earnings and employment changes, this is consistent with the view that wages are fulfilling an allocative role, i.e. that wage *changes* are operating to redistribute labour as a direct response to changes in demand for labour. But it is also consistent with the view that when demand rises in a given sector, employment will increase as a result of the newly available job vacancies at the same time as conditions are created which encourage unions to demand, and employers to grant, above-average wage increases, i.e. that the existence of job vacancies suffices to induce manpower to come forward at the *current* wage.

Further difficulties of interpretation arise from the composite nature of most series on both employment and earnings. One difficulty is that the coverages of the series are often different.[1] What is more serious is that each series itself is an aggregate within which many relevant movements of its components may be hidden, or cancelled out against each other while the behaviour of the aggregate becomes dominated by some irrelevant feature that the components have in common. A particular occupation in an industry, for example, may show a marked association between changes in employment and earnings, but changes of many kinds are at the same time occurring in other occupations of the same industry, and in particular, there may be substantial changes in relative numbers in occupations, firms and regions providing different levels of earnings. The resultant movements of average-earnings show the joint outcome of many factors besides those we are trying to isolate. Although it has been possible in some cases to study the relationship in successively finer breakdowns of the same population, the data are always subject to some degree of aggregation, and therefore liable to some distortion from these "extraneous" influences.

But there are also difficulties even where the series for employment and earnings are for a single homogeneous group. They correspond to those met in attempts to derive supply and demand functions from time series of quantity and price. If shifts in supply have been greater, the relationship to appear will be predominantly between quantity and demand price. Thus in the labour market, higher employment may be associated with a lower relative wage because of an increase in the numbers seeking that kind of work. But there is reason to believe that in the countries and periods we have studied, the shifts in supply have been generally smaller than those in demand. The labour markets studied have mostly (but not all and not always) experienced conditions ranging

---

[1] e.g. total male employment in Great Britain and earnings of adult males in the United Kingdom; total employment, and hourly earnings of wage employees in France.... The absence of comparability between the industrial and occupational breakdowns adopted in different countries makes generalisation of conclusions a hazardous affair, and points up the need for still further progress in the international systematisation of concepts and nomenclatures.

TABLE 21.1 SUMMARY LISTING OF EARNINGS, EMPLOYMENT AND RELATED SERIES STUDIED[1]

Classification	Period Studied	Employment Series		Earnings Series		Related Series	
		Code	Description	Code	Description	Code	Description
USA							
1. 10 Sectors	1948 to 1961	02240	Full and Part-time employees	02140	Annual Compensation	02360	Profits
2. 61 Manufacturing Industries	1951 to 1961	02200	Production Workers	02100	Hourly Earnings		
3. 21 Manufacturing Industries	1948 to 1961	02200	Production Workers	02100	Hourly Earnings	02307	Concentration
						02350	Profit rates
						02326	Index of Production
4. 21 Manufacturing Industries	1948 to 1960	02220	Full and Part-time production workers	02120	Annual Earnings	02360	Profits
						02380	Ratio of labour cost to sales
5. 21 Manufacturing Industries	1948 to 1960	02230	Full and Part-time non-production workers	02130	Annual Earnings	02360	Profits
						02380	Ratio of labour cost to sales
6. 21 Manufacturing Industries	1948 to 1961	02240	Full and Part-time employees	02140	Annual Compensation	02360	Profits
						02380	Ratio of labour cost to sales
7. 31 Industries (21 Manufacturing)	1948 to 1961	02200	Production Workers	02100	Hourly Earnings		
8. 60 Industries (21 Manufacturing)	1948 to 1961	02240	Full and Part-time employees	02140	Annual Compensation	02360	Profits
9. 10 non-manufacturing industries (and total manufacturing)	1948 to 1961	02200	Production Workers	02100	Hourly Earnings		
		02240	Full and Part-time employees	02140	Annual Compensation		
10. 36 Service Industries	1948 to 1961					02360	Profits
11. 51 States	1947 to 1961	02250	All employees in Manufacturing	02150	Annual Earnings		

CANADA

#	Category	Period	Code 1	Description 1	Code 2	Description 2	Code 3	Description 3	Code 4	Description 4
12.	10 Sectors	1950 to 1961	01240	Index of total employment	01140	Weekly Earnings				
13.	17 Manufacturing Industries	1949 to 1960	01200	Male Wage Earners	01100	Hourly Earnings	01307	Concentration		
					01110	Weekly Earnings	01360	Profits		
							01326	Index of Production		
							01380	Ratio of labour cost to sales		
14.	17 Manufacturing Industries	1949 to 1960	01205	Male Salaried employees	01105	Weekly Earnings				
15.	17 Manufacturing Industries	1950 to 1961	01240	Index of total employment	01140	Weekly Earnings				
16.	53 Manufacturing Industries	1950 to 1960	01240	Index of total employment	01140	Weekly Earnings				
17.	38 Industries (17 Manufacturing)	1950 to 1961	01240	Index of total employment	01140	Weekly Earnings				
18.	21 Service Industries	1950 to 1961	01240	Index of total employment	01140	Weekly Earnings				
19.	17 Manufacturing Industries	1951–54–57 and 1959–60	01206	Male office and clerical	01106	Weekly Earnings				
20.	17 Manufacturing Industries	1951–54–57 and 1959–60	01207	Male managerial and professional employees	01107	Weekly Earnings				
21.	10 Provinces	1949 to 1959	01250	All employees in Manufacturing	01150	Annual Earnings				
22.	16 Manufacturing Industries (Montreal)	1949 to 1960	01280	Male wage earners	01180	Hourly Earnings	01307	Concentration		
					01181	Weekly Earnings	01326	Index of Production		
23.	16 Manufacturing Industries (Montreal)	1949 to 1960	01285	Male Salaried employees	01185	Weekly Earnings				
24.	13 Manufacturing Industries (Toronto)	1949 to 1960	01290	Male Wage Earners	01190	Hourly Earnings	01307	Concentration		
					01191	Weekly Earnings	01326	Index of Production		
25.	13 Manufacturing Industries (Toronto)	1949 to 1960	01295	Male Salaried employees	01195	Weekly Earnings				

TABLE 21.1 SUMMARY LISTING OF EARNINGS, EMPLOYMENT AND RELATED SERIES STUDIED[1] (*continued*)

Classification	Period Studied	Employment Series Code	Employment Series Description	Earnings Series Code	Earnings Series Description	Related Series Code	Related Series Description
GERMANY							
26. 27 Industries (26 Manufacturing)	1950 to 1960	16200	Wage Earners	16100	Hourly Earnings		
27. 32 Industries (29 Manufacturing)	1957 to 1962	16240	Male Wage Earners	16140	Hourly Earnings	16307	Concentration
				16141	Index of standard Hourly Earnings	16380	Ratio of labour cost to sales
28. 32 Industries (29 Manufacturing)	1957 to 1962	16210	Male Wage Earners, skill group 1 (highest skill group)	16110	Hourly Earnings	16307	Concentration
						16380	Ratio of labour cost to sales
29. 32 Industries (29 Manufacturing)	1957 to 1962	16220	Male Wage Earners, skill group 2	16120	Hourly Earnings	16307	Concentration
						16380	Ratio of labour cost to sales
30. 32 Industries (29 Manufacturing)	1957 to 1962	16230	Male Wage Earners, skill group 3	16130	Hourly Earnings	16307	Concentration
						16380	Ratio of labour cost to sales
31. 9 Regions	1957 to 1962	16210	Male Wage Earners, skill group 1	16110	Hourly Earnings	16308	Concentration
				16111	Standard[2] hourly earnings		
32. 9 Regions	1957 to 1962	16220	Male Wage Earners, skill group 2	16120	Hourly Earnings	16308	Concentration
				16121	Standard[2] hourly earnings		
33. 9 Regions	1957 to 1962	16230	Male Wage Earners, skill group 3	16130	Hourly Earnings	16308	Concentration
				16131	Standard[2] hourly earnings		
UNITED KINGDOM							
34. 109 Manufacturing Industries	1949 to 1958	28240	Male employees	28100	Hourly Earnings of male wage-earners	28307	Concentration

#	Industries	Period	Code	Category	Code	Variable	Code	Variable
35.	13 Manufacturing Industries	1949 to 1959	28240	Male employees	28100	Hourly Earnings of male wage-earners	28360	Profits
							28326	Index of Production
36.	17 Industries (14 Manufacturing)	1949 to 1959	28240	Male employees	28100	Hourly Earnings of male wage-earners		

FRANCE

#	Industries	Period	Code	Category	Code	Variable	Code	Variable
37.	20 Industries (15 Manufacturing)	1946 to 1962	15240	Index of total employment	15100	Index of hourly earnings of hourly paid workers	15360	Profits
							15300	Index of activity
38.	25 Industries (14 Manufacturing)	1955 to 1960	15220	Male Wage Earners	15120	Annual Earnings		
39.	89 Departments	1955 to 1960	15250	Male employees	15150	Annual Earnings	15307	Concentration

SWEDEN

#	Industries	Period	Code	Category	Code	Variable	Code	Variable
40.	10 Manufacturing Industries	1952 to 1960	25220	Wage-earners	25120	Annual Earnings	25307	Concentration
							25380	Ratio of labour cost to sales
41.	88 Manufacturing Industries	1952 to 1960	25220	Wage-earners	25120	Annual Earnings	25307	Concentration
							25380	Ratio of labour cost to sales
42.	10 Manufacturing Industries	1952 to 1960	25230	Salaried employees	25130	Annual Earnings	25307	Concentration
							25380	Ratio of labour cost to sales
43.	88 Manufacturing Industries	1952 to 1960	25230	Salaried employees	25130	Annual Earnings	25307	Concentration
							25380	Ratio of labour cost to sales
44.	11 Industries (10 Manufacturing)	1954 to 1959	25200	Male wage-earners	25100	Hourly Earnings	25360	Profits
45.	30 Manufacturing Industries	1952 to 1961			25100	Hourly earnings of male wage-earners		

TABLE 21.1 SUMMARY LISTING OF EARNINGS, EMPLOYMENT AND RELATED SERIES STUDIED[1] (continued)

Classification	Period Studied	Employment Series		Earnings Series		Related Series	
		Code	Description	Code	Description	Code	Description
Norway							
46. 20 Manufacturing Industries	1950 to 1959	22200	Male wage-earners	22120	Annual Earnings	22326 22380	Index of Production Ratio of labour cost to sales
47. 20 Manufacturing Industries	1950 to 1959	22230	Salaried employees	22130	Annual Earnings	22326 22380	Index of Production Ratio of labour cost to sales
48. 25 Industries (20 Manufacturing)	1955 to 1959	22200	Male wage-earners	22100	Hourly Earnings		
Belgium							
49. 11 Sectors	1949, 1955 and 1962	11200	Male wage-earners	11100	Daily Earnings		
50. 23 Manufacturing Industries	1945, 1955 and 1962	11200	Male wage-earners	11100	Daily Earnings		
Netherlands							
51. 20 Manufacturing Industries	1954 and 1960	21220	Male semi-skilled workers	21120 21121	Hourly Earnings Weekly Earnings		
52. 20 Manufacturing	1954 and 1960	21230	Male unskilled workers	21130 21131	Hourly Earnings Weekly Earnings		

[1] For full description of the coverage of these series, see Annex I [of *Wages and Labour Mobility*]. The earnings series in principle include overtime payments, but other earnings supplements are included to varying degrees. When not otherwise specified, earnings data relate to the same labour force as the employment figures.
[2] Adjusted for differences in industrial composition of employment.

from equilibrium to excess demand. Insofar as changes in production patterns and technology have generated changes in the amount and structure of the aggregate volume of labour required, and may be judged to have been of more significance than autonomous changes in the supply of labour arising from labour force growth, changes in qualifications and education etc., one may really be measuring the extent to which employment tends to move in the direction of higher relative earnings offered by employers with vacancies to fill. In other words, on *a priori* reasoning —and given, as we believe to have been the case, a reasonable degree of imperfection in labour markets enabling both differential earnings movements and the employment response to them to be identified—one would be led to expect a predominantly positive correlation, and that the measurements made are meaningful.

It must nevertheless be borne in mind that many factors tend to obscure the positive relationship between changes in earnings and employment which one might expect to observe if earnings were merely a price serving to determine the distribution of labour between activities. Damping down, or even reversal of the relationship can follow from differential supply elasticities. Thus, two industries, confronted with the same increased demand for their production (in terms of labour needs) may have varying success in acquiring new workers. In one case, little or no change in earnings may be needed to obtain a substantial increase in employment —the industry may be well placed to attract or intercept the appropriate recruitment stream. In the other case, wages may be forced up with relatively little increase in employment, e.g. if the grades of labour demanded were in short supply and took a long time to train. The result of this, by itself, would be a negative correlation between employment and earnings. Similarly, there is the case in which too rapid increases in earnings, given product market conditions, may oblige employers to cut back production and therefore employment, or alternatively to invest in labour-saving equipment—again with a reduction in employment. In certain circumstances, mechanisation may reduce the number employed while making possible a marked rise in the relative pay of those retained in employment. Where such relationships hold, correlation analysis will throw up apparently "perverse" results.

Timing is another factor which must be taken into account. In essence, correlation analysis consists of testing whether certain relationships which it seems reasonable to consider as possibly of practical significance are in fact so. Insofar as the central relation under study is that between earnings and employment changes, it may be that if the market mechanism were working really efficiently, earnings differentials would open just long enough to attract the required inflow of labour and then might close again, i.e. one would not necessarily expect to find any association. In fact, the evidence reviewed in previous chapters suggests that the labour market is far from perfect, so that perhaps not too much weight need be given to this point. But in the same order of thought, it is relevant to enquire whether barriers to mobility may not make for a lagged response by labour to differential earnings possibilities. In the analysis done, an attempt has been made to test for lagged reactions, but there is the difficulty that such relationships may differ as between different types of labour market, and within any one market may not be the same at different times.

Further criticism relates to the choice of earnings as the measure of the price of labour. It is by no means certain that changes in relative earnings alone accurately reflect changes in the overall attractiveness of entry into a given industry, occupation or region. Some differences in industries' average earnings arise from the occupational composition of their employment, and some may be offset, in part or in total, by differences in fringe benefits or in non-pecuniary working conditions. But even allowing for this, differences in wage ranking frequently appear to reflect genuine wage differences for similar types of labour in different industries.² This is a field in which statistics are notably deficient, and it has only been possible to assemble data on total labour costs per worker in a limited number of cases.³ In general, the figures used are as close as possible to total earnings so as best to measure the incentive effect of wage changes. This also has its disadvantages. For example, up to a certain point, expanding demand for labour can result in an increase in overtime working without any change in numbers employed—a specific illustration of the general point that observed *changes in employment* are not synonymous with changes in the *demand for labour*.⁴ Where the time periods compared relate to different phases of the trade cycle, the overtime element will promote a bias towards a diminution of the correlation which would otherwise be observed, since there is a margin within which a relative earnings gain from premium rates is not accompanied by any increase in numbers employed.⁵

There is also scope for discussion whether the use of absolute or percentage changes in earnings is more appropriate for study of the significance of the wage allocative process. These two measures occasionally yield quite different results in correlation with other factors. If industries high in the earnings ranking implement wage increases which are below-average in percentage terms, this may still imply an expansion of absolute differentials, particularly in periods of rapid wage rise. If these industries are losing employment relative to the low wage sector, a positive relation appears between percentage earnings changes and employment changes, but if they are gaining, the positive relation will appear to be between absolute earnings changes and employment changes. It is therefore possible to "prove" a positive association by referring to one or the other type of measure whereas in fact all that exists is a statistical relationship between the two measures.⁶ Further, if the high wage sector is experiencing greater percentage increases of earnings, and its relative employment is expanding (contracting) a positive (negative) association between percentage wage increases and employment movements will be noted, but the numerical value of the measure of association of absolute changes and employment changes will be greater. A number of check calculations were made to test the possible importance of these relationships. In a limited number of cases there were quite substantial differences pointing up the importance for analyses of individual cases of going beyond the correlation coefficient to the underlying phenomena. But taking the results as a whole, there is a close degree of

---

² The evidence cited in support of this in various parts of this chapter is supported by the fact that in practise examples of firms and industries with reputations as "good payers" are far from rare. An experimental check calculation suggests that "good payers" are also good earners. Profits as a percentage of equity capital are positively correlated with an industry's earning level each year for United States manufacturing industry 1948/1961, the majority of the coefficients being at or above the 5 per cent significance level.
³ Efforts are being made to improve the position. In particular, mention should be made of a meeting of experts convened by ILO (7th–16th Sept., 1964) to define total labour costs and recommend an internationally comparable classification. It is hoped that the conclusions reached will in due time be reflected in national statistical practises.
⁴ The appropriate employment measure in this case would be man-hours; but data on this are rarely available. In a check calculation for France, the results derived from use of employment indices differed little from those derived using activity (man-hour) indices.
⁵ See John T. Dunlop, *Wage Determination under Trade Unions*, N.Y., 1950, pp. 19–27 and J. E. Maher "Union and Non-Union Wage Differentials," *American Economic Review*, June 1956, for a more detailed discussion of the pitfalls involved in using average earnings as a measure of labour reward.
⁶ See for example S. Ostry "Interindustry Earnings Differentials in Canada, 1945–56," *Industrial and Labour Relations Review*, Vol. 12, No. 3, April 1959. (This author uses both types of measures simultaneously), and A. M. Ross and W. Goldner, "Forces affecting the Inter-industry Wage Structure," *Quarterly Journal of Economics*, May, 1950.

concordance, and certainly the general conclusions reached below would have been in no way modified if absolute rather than percentage differentials had been used. In the present examination, there were two main reasons for concentrating on percentage relationships. Some of the earnings data were available in index form only, and comparability of the measures for different countries would have been defective. Further, so far as motivation is concerned, the inducement potential of a given wage difference will vary according to the percentage of income which it represents.

Finally, it is necessary to allow for the influence of the existing earnings structure on employment movements. In those cases in which employment has tended to grow most rapidly in high-wage industries,[7] there may be a presumption that such industries, by virtue of their place in the earnings hierarchy may have less need to increase their relative earnings than would otherwise have been the case. This suggests that in measuring employment change/earnings change relationships, there may be a need to allow for the influence on employment shifts of an industry's position in the wage structure. Accordingly, in addition to direct measures of the relationship, partial correlation coefficients have been calculated to assess what the degree of association would have been in the absence of any earnings level effect. Comparison of the two sets of coefficients indicates that the relationships are much the same in either case. If anything, the partial coefficients suggest a lower degree of association between relative earnings and employment changes when the influence of the earnings structure is held constant.

As already stated, the results concord well with those obtained in other independent studies in which the same line of approach has been adopted. Further, rather similar relationships have been observed in the different types of labour market studied, but there are important differences between them in (*a*) the amount of data available from which to draw general conclusions, (*b*) the forces at work, (*c*) implications for policy; and certain markets are therefore considered separately.

Changes in Earnings and Employment as Between Economic Sectors

At the level of broad economic sectors, there have been two major types of employment flow presenting very different features:

a) In all countries, labour has moved out of agriculture—in the direction of higher wages.
b) Outside agriculture, the tendency has been for employment in low wage sectors (e.g. certain services, particularly in the more industrialised countries) to expand more rapidly than employment elsewhere —i.e. much of the movement has been in the direction of lower wages.

When employment flows are considered in relation to changes in earnings, data for North America show in general no association between changes in relative earnings and contemporary changes in relative employment; although it should be borne in mind that these economies have on the whole been underemployed through the period. There is, however, some evidence of what appears to be a lagged response of earnings to employment movements in certain sectors. In the USA, the services sector ranked seventh out of eight in respect of its rate of wage *change* over the period 1948–1957,[8] but second in 1957–1960, whereas its share of total employment had been climbing steadily throughout the whole 12-year period. In the opposite direction, the employment trend in

---

[7] It may be noted in passing that the coefficient of correlation between earnings levels and changes in employment is a useful indicator of the direction of labour flows; a negative coefficient indicates a more rapid rise of employment in low-wage industries.

[8] Data relate to total employment and annual wages and salaries per employee.

mining was steeply downward throughout the entire period 1948–1960, but this sector's wage-change ranking, after climbing from 4 (1948–1953) to 1 (in 1953–1957) only declined (to 8) in the last three years of the period, when for the first time its wage and salary increases fell below the average for the entire non-agricultural sector. However, the strength of this relationship is not over-impressive. One would expect these trends to be associated with some compression of the sectoral earnings structure, to the extent that earnings rose more rapidly in the low-wage sectors (in which the employment gain occurred). In fact, no such tendency existed during the period reviewed: the coefficient of variation for wages and salaries per employee rose slightly during these years (see Table 3 [of *Wages and Labour Mobility*]).

In common with the United States, employment in Canada has been rising most rapidly in low-wage sectors. The data contain a much stronger indication that earnings changes have tended to *follow* changes in employment. A positive association is observed throughout the entire period when employment change is related to wage change in the following year.[9] Further, there is no consistent relation between employment and earnings changes in the same year, and the relationship between earnings changes and employment changes in the following year is uniformly of negative sign. On this particular point, see also pages 325–326.

It is of interest to compare earnings and employment developments in total manufacturing in the United States with those in other sectors, the (rather miscellaneous) service sector in particular. Over the period 1948 to 1960–1961, manufacturing employment rose *less* rapidly than in other sectors, while per-worker compensation rose *more rapidly*. Two reasons for this are to be found within the manufacturing sector itself. One consists of the increasing demand for professional, technical, and other white-collar employees, which, both in the United States and Canada, has been associated with rising salaries within manufacturing.[10] Another consists in the operation of collective bargaining, which has affected wage movements not only in the labour markets where "key wage bargains" were negotiated but in others as well.[11] Duesenberry has concluded on this point that wage movements in manufacturing have reflected the influence of collective bargaining[12] whereas increases in service wages reflected more the influence of excess demand for labour in sectors in which trade union organisation was weak.

At the same time, the period after 1957 in the United States was one of generally low levels of aggregate demand, and there is some likelihood that generally high levels of recorded unemployment had a degree of underemployment as a counterpart, reflected in part by an increase in numbers employed in service trades. The continued growth of service employment after 1957 may have represented an increase in the supply of as well as the demand for labour; and to this extent it is correspondingly likely that the lagged response of service earnings to employment

---

[9] All year-to-year correlation coefficients are positive, four of them significantly so, with a further three on the threshold of significance.

[10] and, from Canadian data, in all other sectors as well.

[11] For a discussion on United States collective bargaining developments see G. Seltzer, "Pattern Bargaining and the United Steel Workers," *Journal of Political Economy*, August 1951, pp. 319–331; H. M. Levinson, "Pattern Bargaining: A Case Study of the Automobile Workers," *Quarterly Journal of Economics*, May 1960, pp. 269–317; J. E. Maher, "The Wage Pattern in the United States, 1946–1957," *Industrial and Labour Relations Review*, October 1961, pp. 3–20; O. Eckstein and T. Wilson, "The Determination of Money Wages in American Industry," *Quarterly Journal of Economics*, August 1962, pp. 379–414.

[12] J. Duesenberry, "Underlying factors in the Postwar Inflation," in American Assembly, *Wages, Prices, Profits and Productivity*, New York: (Columbia University Press, 1959), Ch. 3. His conclusion cannot be extended to Canada, where nationwide spread of industries is the exception rather than the rule, and the majority of "patterns," where they can be discerned, go no further than regional boundaries.

growth is more apparent than real. On the other hand, the lagged relationship between earnings and employment movements in the mining sector appears to reflect an attempt by the parties to collective bargaining to maintain or improve relative earnings despite falling employment; and this attempt was successful for quite some time.

A number of influences thus appear to have been operative in the determination of earnings levels, illustrating the need in relevant cases to go behind the correlations to the underlying phenomena. The main point suggested by the data is that large employment shifts could and did take place without any concurrent same-direction movement of relative earnings. It is not possible to say whether or not the "wrong" differential may have made for some inefficiency in the reallocation process by hindering the employment shifts from taking place as rapidly as they might otherwise have done. But it is relevant that employment falls were registered in high-income branches, which, at least for a time, continued to implement above average increases in compensation, while many of the employment gains were made by low-paying activities in which compensation rose less than average, at least until 1957.

Employment/Earnings Relationships Between Industries

The data mainly cover manufacturing but material has also been available to make a parallel study of the relation between relative changes in earnings and employment for non-manufacturing industries, usually in the services sector, for a number of countries. In general, the results can be summarised as follows:

i) In most countries, there has been an association, occasionally quite strong, between movements in relative earnings and in employment, at the level of broad (2-digit) industry groupings within manufacturing.

ii) There is little or no association for non-manufacturing 2-digit industry groupings.

iii) There is little or no association when a finer manufacturing breakdown is studied.

2-Digit Industries

When the data for production workers in general or for total employment are examined at 2-digit industry level, there is a marked contrast between the results for manufacturing industries and the corresponding results for industries outside manufacturing. Within manufacturing, the long time series for the United States[13] (1948–1961), the United Kingdom (1949–1959), Canada (1949–1961), Norway (1950–1959) and France (1946–1962) all show a marked excess of positive over negative relations between employment and earnings changes, a relationship which holds whether the data are studied in 1, 3, or 5-year spans. In general, the association is weak, although there are individual years or spans when a high relationship is observed.

Over all countries, the number of 2-digit manufacturing industries studied varies from 14 to 25, so that the significance value[14] of the correlation coefficient varies from .53 to .40. Less than 20 per cent of the individual relationships studied exceed this value, i.e. for four-fifths of the relationships examined, statistical analysis indicates that in each case the observed co-variation of relative earnings and relative employment changes could have arisen by chance. The broad statements made in the text are justified only because they are based on observation of a large number of coefficients. For the remaining relationships, the correlation coefficients, although statistically significant, are not usually high enough to suggest more than a faint degree

---

[13] Similar results are obtained whether gross hourly or annual earnings are studied.

[14] In line with established practise, the "5 per cent level" is used as an indicator of whether an observed relationship is statistically significant or not.

of association in practice. For example, a correlation coefficient of 0.5 (a value which is observed only rarely) indicates that as much as 75 per cent of the changes in relative employment do not appear to have been associated with changes in relative earnings.[15] At the same time, taking the entire population of industry correlation coefficients it is striking that positive relationships outnumber negative ones by a factor of about 5 to 2, and there are periods within individual countries when a positive relation is observed for as many as 7 or 9 successive years.[16]

The material available for study of non-manufacturing industries at approximately 2-digit level is rather more restricted. For the United States, there is some consistency of sign when earnings and employment changes are related over 1-year periods for 10 non-agricultural industries and manufacturing total, but the relationship is not statistically significant and it is not apparent when considered in terms of longer spans; while for 36 service industries there is no systematic relationship at all. The same is true for 21 Canadian tertiary industries (although here there are some signs of a positive relationship between earnings changes and employment changes in the following year), and for Belgian non-manufacturing industries (one 13-year, and two 6- and 7-year subperiods). However, the Belgian data are at a very aggregate level by comparison with those studied for the USA and Canada.

3-Digit Industries, Manufacturing

When more detailed manufacturing groups are studied, the relationship noted at 2-digit level becomes greatly attenuated or disappears entirely. The data refer to 61 United States, 53 Canadian and 109 British 3-digit manufacturing industries over roughly the 1950 decade. The United States results indicate a dissolution of the positive 2-digit level relationships. There are still more signs of a relationship in the United Kingdom and Canadian data, but it just barely crosses the significance level and in practical terms its effect is negligible.[17] Comparison of the results for the three countries is made in Table 21.2 for 1-year spans.

Data for 88 Swedish 3-digit manufacturing industries exhibit a predominantly negative association whether considered over 1-year, 3-year or 5-year spans. Due to the classification adopted in Swedish national statistics, these results cannot be compared with the relationship at 2-digit level but when these industries are analysed in 10 very aggregate groupings, there is a higher proportion of positive signs, although negative signs are still far from being rare, i.e. what was an indeterminate relationship at aggregate level focuses into a predominantly negative relationship (with some statistically significant values) at 3-digit level.[18]

A marked weakening of the relationship when passing from broader to more finely detailed industrial groups was first observed

---

[15] The square of the correlation coefficient indicates what percentage of the movement in one variable is associated with changes in the other. However, as the coefficient itself is only "accurate" to within the range given by plus or minus twice its standard error, it would be more correct to say that in each individual case the percentage explanation was between ... and ... For example, and very roughly, with a correlation coefficient of 0.5 and a standard error of 0.2, the true value of the coefficient may be anywhere between 0.1 and 0.9, and the degree of explanation between 1 per cent and 81 per cent.

[16] It is uncertain that use of the 5 per cent level is appropriate for study of sets of relationships. If the degree of accuracy required is lowered so that statements regarding significance of relationships are true only half of the time (50 per cent level), the data can still be summarised as being characterised by a predominantly positive association if positive and significant relationships outnumber all others by more than 2 to 1.

[17] Since the number of observations increases, the standard error of the 3-digit estimates is considerably lower, i.e. the coefficients are a relatively safer estimate of the actual degree of relationship.

[18] Series 25120 (wage earners) and 25130 (salaried employees). The phenomenon is particularly marked in respect of the latter.

TABLE 21.2 CORRELATION COEFFICIENTS: RELATIVE CHANGES IN EARNINGS AND EMPLOYMENT IN MANUFACTURING IN THE UNITED KINGDOM, THE UNITED STATES AND CANADA

Period	United Kingdom—Wage Earners			US Production Workers					Canada—All Employees			
	17 2-Digit* Industries	109 3-Digit Manufacturing Industries		20 2-Digit Manufacturing Industries		61 3-Digit† Manufacturing Industries		17 2-Digit Manufacturing Industries		53 3-Digit Manufacturing Industries	
		Simple	Partial‡	Simple	Partial‡	Simple	Partial‡	Simple	Partial‡	Simple	Partial‡
1948-49	—	—	—	.04	.05	—	—	—	—	—	—
1949-50	.31	.35	.36	−.32	−.33	—	—	—	—	—	—
1950-51	.25	.08	.05	.52	.51	.29	.26	.12	−.49	(.24)	.09
1951-52	.68	.47	.46	.20	.15	.14	.07	.26	.14	(.26)	.23
1952-53	.44	.25	.26	.26	.09	.27	.32	.38	.37	.28	.27
1953-54	.36	.13	.13	.44	.55	.20	.12	.66	.59	.48	.48
1954-55	.53	.24	.22	.53	.53	−.05	.06	.29	.22	.30	.27
1955-56	.57	.28	.26	−.13	−.03	.35	.25	.64	.47	.20	.08
1956-57	.40	.34	.34	.27	.07	−.09	.21	.59	.54	.25	.23
1957-58	.70	−.11	.02	−.37	−.11	−.18	−.21	.02	.00	.10	.11
1958-59	.24	—	—	−.03	.09	.14	.15	−.16	−.08	.14	.13
1959-60	—	—	—	.00	.03	.14	.15	.42	.37	.09	.07
1960-61	—	—	—	.02	.16	.21	.26	−.12	−.32	−.19	−.16

* Includes 3 non-manufacturing industries.
† Does not exhaust the manufacturing sector.
‡ Holding the influence of the earnings structure constant.
NOTE. Underlined coefficients are significant at the 5 per cent level. Bracketed figures are not comparable with the others. They were taken into account in the analysis only where it was possible to estimate the approximate effect of this lack of comparability. . . .

by Reddaway[19] who studied changes in earnings and employment of male workers in British 2- and 3-digit industries over the period 1951–1956. Our results, which relate to three countries over periods of length ranging from 1 to 12 years, and appear to be confirmed by the results for a fourth country, suggest that this effect is a quite general one. Reddaway analysed the underlying relation as follows:

... if one follows the idea that wage bargains are largely determined by "social" and "conventional" considerations, it is not difficult to understand why 3-digit industries tend to have much the same wage increase, despite differences in their character and their fortune. In some cases there is really only a single bargain covering an entire 2-digit industry[20] or virtually all of it (e.g. engineering). In others, it is regarded as almost axiomatic that the wage increases should be made closely similar to those in some broadly related industry (which will commonly be in the same 2-digit group. . . .)

Reddaway's explanation is particularly relevant to British wage-setting. Bargains at 2-digit level contain some element of "customary relativities," but also reflect the specific economic experience of the branch as a whole, i.e. the (rather small) differences in settlement levels correspond to differences in rates of expansion and relative prosperity. At 3-digit level, customary relativities are of predominant importance; the change of earnings is to a large extent given so far as the individual industry is concerned. In the United States, the operation of key bargaining would tend to produce a similar although perhaps weaker effect.

An alternative, or rather, complementary explanation is that 3-digit industries within a branch are affected at a given time in roughly the same way by movements of demand, so that their prosperity tends to be affected in the same direction. When these industries are aggregated into 2-digit units the impact of relative differences in prosperity on both earnings and employment appears more clearly.

An explanation from another field may help to clarify the statistical phenomenon involved. When schoolchildren are studied individually, there may appear to be only slight relationship between their ability in languages and in mathematics. But when the same children are grouped by school (i.e. at 2-digit level), the superiority of certain schools results in their pupils showing above-average aptitude in both subjects, and some relationship will appear between ability in mathematics and ability in languages. The essential point is that this relationship reflects the difference between schools rather than any fundamental relationship between ability in one and the other subject. In the same way, the association observed at 2-digit industry level will tend to reflect the prosperity (or labour market) characteristics of 2-digit industries, rather than any employment/earnings relationship at 3-digit level. The latter data therefore appear to give a more valid picture of the actual degree of association which has obtained; and the data in Table 21.2 suggest that in practice this has been faint. Reddaway's conclusion for the United Kingdom therefore appears to be of fairly general validity:

It seems fairly clear that, where the wage change was much the same, e.g. within 2-digit industries, the pattern of the labour force could nevertheless be greatly changed, hence it also seems plausible that substantial changes could have occurred as between different 2-digit groups, even if the wage change had in fact been much the same there also.

The results up to this point relate to earnings and employment relationships as measured directly. While in general they show some, if not very marked, statistical association, it is relevant to enquire if the nature of

---

[19] W. B. Reddaway, "Wage Flexibility and the Distribution of Labour," *Lloyds Bank Review*, Oct. 1959.

[20] In the author's words, "the whole of an Order." The citation has been slightly paraphrased to render the terminology consonant with that used in the present report.

the relationship is not rather different in practice to that assessed using same-period changes in the two variables chosen. A number of alternative forms of employment/earnings relationships are discussed below. These are respectively (a) the importance of fringe benefits as an alternative to earnings as an inducement to labour redistribution, (b) the possibility of a lagged relationship between earnings changes and changes in employment, (c) the possibility that a stronger relationship between these two variables may be observed at certain phases of the economic cycle.

Fringe Benefits

In recent years, fringe benefits have come to account for an ever-growing share of wage costs, and in certain countries and labour markets, employers have attempted to use improvements in non-wage conditions of employment as a means of attracting employment of the desired quantity or quality. However, in some countries scope for competition in this field is relatively limited; the majority of fringes are represented by payments of different kinds made by the public authorities, and legal provisions govern unemployment benefits, medical plans, working hours, holiday length, etc. In countries where governmental participation or control is less extensive, e.g. in the United States, initiatives concerning fringe benefits taken by an industry or union have usually though not invariably[21] been followed elsewhere, and differentiation in respect of non-wage benefit changes may at times be hardly more marked than for earnings changes.[22] While the coverage of the data is very limited (material on fringes, or wage payments including fringes was available for the United States, Canada and the Netherlands), it suggests that if fringe benefits had been taken into account, industries' relative positions would not have been greatly altered. The conclusions to be drawn from the direct study of earnings/employment relationships thus do not appear to be subject to any significant modification.

A Lagged Response of Employment to Differential Earnings Changes

A lagged response of employment to earnings changes might be expected for several reasons. In a theoretically perfect market, adjustment to increased demand for labour will be instantaneous.[23] But labour markets are far from perfect; workers get different pay for the same job in different industries and regions, and indeed within the same industry; housing problems, local ties, seniority privileges and other factors prevent people from moving quickly and frequently. Nor, as has been pointed out, can rational behaviour always be assumed. All these factors lead to a blurred and delayed response to available job opportunities.

The length of such lags will vary depending on the character of the labour market, the educational system, training facilities, the efficiency of employment exchanges etc. and may therefore vary among occupations or industries within a country as well as between countries. In order to test the possibility that the working out of the allocative function may take considerable time before the employment response focuses into a wage-motivated distribution, industry earnings changes were correlated with employment changes in the following year.[24] The results suggest the absence of any relationship. Positive and negative associations are

---

[21] For example, in the United States, certain fringe benefits, in particular supplemental unemployment benefits, have been implemented in only a limited number of industries.

[22] In France the rapidity with which the grant of a fourth week's holiday by the State-owned Renault car factory was followed by similar arrangements in other collective bargains attests the difficulty of maintaining a significant advantage in respect of fringes.

[23] Under classical static analysis, the wage structure shifts only marginally to induce the required (marginal) employment change; an equilibrium position obtains throughout.

[24] Occupational data, which would have provided a complementary test of lag relationships, were not available for this purpose.

about equally frequent, only a very few reach the significance limit, and many of these are negative. Owing to the nature of the data, it was not possible to test for a lag shorter than one year. It may also be noted that if a lagged reaction carries the employment response over a period boundary, the annual data will not fully reflect the relationship, although it may appear when comparison is made over a longer period. The figures, however, show no tendency for the association measured over a longer period to be greater than the average indicated by study of one year spans within the period.

A Lagged Response of Earnings to Changes in Employment

It was noted at page 320 that as between main economic sectors in North America, there has been some tendency for earnings trends to follow employment movements after a greater or lesser interval. This could be interpreted as being consistent with a lagged impact of labour or product market developments on collective bargaining arrangements. For example, assuming that expanding industries are well placed to fill their labour requirements at going rates (whether because they are already high in the earnings structure, or more simply because the availability of vacancies enables them to increase their interception of recruitment streams), their continued prosperity may induce labour to claim, or employers to grant, above-average wage increases at some later time. In the reverse direction, the exercise of market power by unions or employers has in certain cases enabled above-average wage increases to be implemented for a while even with falling employment levels, but relative earnings have subsequently declined as continuously unfavourable labour or product market conditions have at length exhausted any room for manoeuvre.

It may also be observed here that a rise in relative pay lagged behind a rise in relative employment may serve a useful allocational purpose. An expanding industry—even if its average wage is at excess-supply level—may find it more economical to reduce quit rates than to increase its hiring by an equivalent amount. Theoretically it would carry this to the point where the marginal saving in indirect employment costs (personnel department, etc.) equals the increase in direct wage costs involved in reducing the quit rate. Again, if an industry runs out of supplies of recruits at some stage in the process of expanding employment and then raises wages in an attempt to attract some labour, this will appear statistically as a lag of wage increase behind employment increase.

However, at 2-digit level, the study of lagged associations suggests that this has been a relatively insignificant influence by comparison with other factors entering into earnings and employment relationships. The association between employment changes and earnings changes in the subsequent period was examined at this level for five countries (Canada, France, Germany, UK, and USA). The results, given in Annex I, [of *Ways and Labour Mobility*] do not suggest any systematic effect of this type.

Variations in the Relationships between Changes in Earnings and Employment

It is fairly widely held that during periods of significant unemployment, workers, if they move at all, move to where jobs are available; wage differentials play a decidedly secondary rôle. In fact, few attempts have been made to test whether, when labour markets are tight, there is a greater tendency for manpower to move towards those industries or sectors in which faster earnings increases have been or are taking place. In one of the rare studies dealing with this question, Bowen states:

there is a pronounced cyclical difference in the relationship between inter-industry changes in employment and inter-industry changes in wages. During periods of generally low unemployment, wages have shown a tendency to go up most rapidly in industries characterised by relatively favourable employment trends. That is, industries in which employment has either gone up at a more rapid rate, or fallen at a slower rate than employment in the "average" industry have tended to raise wages faster than industries in the opposite circumstances. This pattern does not show up, however, in the recession periods.[25]

Examination of the material available for different countries does not fully confirm that a strengthening of the earnings/employment relationship takes place with falling unemployment levels. In the first place, making broad inter-country comparisons, there is in general no tendency for the value of the correlation coefficients observed at similar levels of industry detail to vary in line with country unemployment rankings over the period taken as a whole. This is true whether comparison is made for economic sectors or at 2-digit industry level. At 3-digit level, the data for British manufacturing exhibit a statistically significant relationship rather more consistently than do the United States figures. On the other hand, a rather stronger association is noted for Canada (where percentage unemployment has been higher than in the USA since 1952) than for the United Kingdom, while the data for Sweden, a country which has long had a high degree of full employment, in general display a negative association between changes in relative earnings and changes in employment.

An alternative line of approach has been to examine the intensity of the earnings/employment relationship within individual countries[26] in relation to: (*a*) unemployment levels during a given period; (*b*) changes in unemployment over the period; (*c*) both taken together. Taking the whole range of countries and breakdowns studied, the first two columns of Table 21.3 suggest that the higher employment/earnings relationships tend to be observed rather more frequently in periods of low unemployment than in periods of high unemployment, and in both Canada and the United States there is some tendency for a greater concentration of significant positive coefficients in periods of low unemployment than at other times. This is quite marked for some Canadian series, and may be of some significance for our analysis given the high degree of flexibility present in the Canadian labour market, where collective bargaining, and therefore wage setting, are decentralised. However, negative coefficients are by no means rare at such times,[27] and in general the average level of association observed is weak, i.e. under conditions of very low unemployment, one should not necessarily expect that wages will tend to go up most rapidly in industries characterised by relatively favourable employment trends. The use of partial earnings/employment correlation coefficients does not change this picture; nor does any tendency to a greater concentration of high (or low) correlations appear when changes in unemployment during the years studied are taken into account. A similar comparison of unemployment levels in the years in which the highest and lowest correlations are observed gives similar results (Table 21.3, last two columns). Average unemployment levels are lower where the correlations are higher, but in most countries (Canada appears to be an important exception) there is little practical difference between these unemployment levels and the average unemployment levels corresponding to the periods in which the lowest (i.e. least positive or more negative) coefficients are registered.

It would have been preferable to study

---

[25] W. G. Bowen, "Wage Behaviour in the Postwar Period," *Industrial Relations Section*, Princeton University, 1960.

[26] Before and after allowing for the influence on the relationship of base year earnings, and where data were available, profits.

[27] This can readily be seen by consulting the individual correlation coefficients presented in Annex 1. It may also be noted that for the war and postwar period characterised by tight labour markets in the USA, D. Eisemann ("Inter-industry wage changes, 1939–1947, *Review of Economics and Statistics*, Nov. 1956, p. 445) found a significant and *negative* correlation between earnings and employment changes.

TABLE 21.3 THE EMPLOYMENT/EARNINGS CHANGE RELATION IN PERIODS OF HIGH AND LOW UNEMPLOYMENT

Country	Series*	Period	Industries Examined		Average of Correlation Coefficients Observed over the Three† Single Years		Average Level of Unemployment over the Three† Years	
			Total	of which Manuf.	with Lowest Unemployment Level	with Highest Unemployment Level	in which Relationship Strongest	in which Relationship Weakest
USA	02240/02140	1948–61	10³	1	.18	−.22	3.7	5.9
USA	02200/02100	1951–61	61	61	.23	.07	3.5	5.2
USA	02200/02100	1948–61	20	20	.30	.06	4.6	4.9
USA	02220/02120	1948–60	21	21	.30	.21	4.6	5.2
USA	02230/02130	1948–60	21	21	.14	.02	3.9	4.4
USA	02240/02140	1948–61	21	21	.28	.29	4.6	4.8
USA	02200/02100	1948–61	31	21	.11	−.02	5.1	4.8
USA	02240/02140	1948–61	60	21	.21	.17	4.2	4.7
USA	02240/02140	1948–61	36§	0	.18	−.04	4.1	4.7
Canada	01240/01140	1950–61	10‡	1	.26	−.05	3.6	4.6
Canada	01200/01100	1949–60	17	17	.30	−.01	3.5	5.5
Canada	01205/01105	1949–60	17	17	.08	−.43	4.2	4.9
Canada	01240/01140	1950–61	7	17	.43	.05	3.5	6.1
Canada	01240/01140	1950–61	53	53	<u>.34</u>	.01	3.4	5.8
Canada	01240/01140	1950–61	38	17	.04	−.28	3.6	4.3
Canada	01240/01140	1950–61	21§	0	.21	−.32	3.3	5.5
Germany	16200/16100	1950–60	27	26	.22	.15	3.7	3.9
Germany	16240/16140	1957–62	29	28	.33‡	.37‡	1.7‡	2.3‡
Germany	16210/16110	1957–62	32	29	.32‡	−.01‡	0.8‡	2.3‡
Germany	16220/16120	1957–62	32	29	.30‡	.01‡	0.8‡	2.3‡
Germany	16230/16130	1957–62	32	29	<u>.45</u>‡	.25‡	0.8‡	2.3‡
UK	28240/28100	1949–58	109	109	<u>.36</u>	.24	1.0	1.2
UK	28240/28100	1949–59	13	13	<u>.55</u>	.34	1.0	1.2
UK	28240/28100	1949–59	17	14	<u>.55</u>	.35	0.9	1.4
France	15240/15100	1954–62	20	15	.27	.10	1.1	1.4
Norway	22200/22120	1950–59	20	20	.05	.12	1.1	0.8
Norway	22230/22130	1950–59	20	20	−.17	−.20	0.9	0.9

* For series identification see Table 21.1.
† Over two years only for these figures.
‡ Sectoral breakdown.
§ Service industries.

NOTE.
a) This table is based on a comparison of bivariate correlation coefficients between changes in earnings and in employment (calculated over 1-year spans), with average levels of unemployment rates. In the analysis, similar comparisons were made adding, where available, correlation coefficients allowing for the influence of base-year earnings and/or changes in profits, and changes in the level of unemployment.
b) Underlined figures represent averages which exceed the level at which individual correlation coefficients are significant. Non-underlined figures include some individual coefficients which were statistically significant.

Sources: Correlation coefficients: Annex I.
Unemployment rates: Manpower statistics 1950–62 (OECD), Employment and Earnings (BLS).

TABLE 21.4 AVERAGE WAGE AND EMPLOYMENT CHANGES OF UPPER AND LOWER QUARTILE GROUPS IN 24 UNITED STATES MANUFACTURING INDUSTRIES

Production Workers.

	1948–60	1948–53	1948–57	1953–60	1957–60
Per Cent Change in Earnings*					
Lower employment quartile	67	27	50	28	11
Whole distribution	70	31	53	30	11
Upper employment quartile	75	32	56	33	11
Per Cent Change in Employment*					
Lower earnings quartile	−13	4	−7	−10	−6
Whole distribution	4	7	4	−7	−4
Upper earnings quartile	5	10	10	4	−5

* The industries in the upper or lower employment quartiles are not the same as the industries in the upper or lower quartiles when the ordering is according to rate of earnings change.
Source: Employment and Earnings (BLS).

this question in terms of sharply defined cyclical periods, but the nature of the data did not enable this to be done. On the whole, the appropriate conclusion to draw from the data examined appears to be that there is a rather weak tendency for a higher relationship to be noted between earnings and employment changes when unemployment levels are relatively low. But there are many exceptions, and in neither type of period does a very high association appear.

Taken as a whole, then, the results of a direct correlation analysis show no close and consistent relationship between changes in relative earnings and changes in relative employment either in the short or in the long-term. Nevertheless, the data do exhibit a tendency for what might be called a "limiting condition" to exist. While the general weakness of the year-to-year relationships confirms the impression to be gained by direct study of industries' experience, namely that differential wage movements can take place without any marked short-term tendency for employment movements to correspond with them, there appears to be a certain stage beyond which progressive deterioration of an industry's earnings position will be observed to be accompanied by relative declines in employment. This point is put as follows by Phelps Brown and Browne in their study of earnings and employment in United Kingdom manufacturing over the decade from 1948:

within a wide range, the rate of (employment) growth of an industry seems to have imposed no particular requirements on the relative earnings it offered but outside that range it did. Yet even here it seems to have acted according to no continuous relation, by which the greater the expansion the higher the required rise in earnings, but only as a blanket negative—industries that are to expand by more than 30 per cent in a decade must not let their relative earnings fall; the forces that make industries contract by more than 5 per cent in a decade will seldom let their relative earnings rise.[28]

A similar relationship appears to exist for the United States, although it is not very strong. Comparison is made for 1948–1960 and selected subperiods of the mean and quartile earnings and employment increase in twenty-four manufacturing industries. (Table 21.4). The increases shown by the upper quartiles are higher, and those shown by the lower quartiles lower than the corresponding mean increases for the entire sample, except possibly for 1957–1960. The

[28] E. H. Phelps Brown and M. H. Browne, "Earnings in Industries of the United Kingdom, 1948–59," *The Economic Journal*, Sept. 1962.

latter is a period of high unemployment in which there is some indication of a negative relation between employment changes and the original level of earnings.[29]

Influences on the Wage Structure

As noted at the outset, correlation analysis does not in itself identify causality. The association observed between changes in relative earnings and the deployment of labour at the level of broad industry groups might be interpreted as an example of wages performing their allocative function or of a prosperous and expanding industry being able to put higher wage increases into operation although these are not necessary to attract or retain labour.

Extension of the use of correlation techniques enables the examination to be carried further by comparing the relative strength of the employment change/earnings change association observed when other variables are related to earnings changes. The material presented below suggests that certain product market variables are at least as highly correlated with changes in relative earnings as are changes in relative employment. To the extent that some of them are correlated with each other as well as with both earnings and employment, the nature of the causal relationships is still open to alternative interpretations; but at the very least the evidence that product market developments are relevant to changes in earnings is suggestive. In addition, further results obtained when variables representing the structural or competitive characteristics of an industry are related to earnings suggest that there are other factors whose influence in promoting differential rates of earnings increase, although often overshadowed by the impact of market developments (labour or product), is quite pervasive.

[29] See detailed results in Annex 1. Series 02100 (3b) lists a bivariate correlation coefficient of −0.44 which is just significant at the 5 per cent level.

Profits

Data on profits by industry exist in various forms for the United States, France and Canada, Sweden and the United Kingdom.[30] Except for the United States, only absolute figures relating to a limited number of industries are available. For all five countries the correlation between per cent changes in profits and relative changes in earnings in the same period was analysed. In addition, for the first four countries listed, the change in profits was correlated with the change in earnings in the subsequent period. The lagged relationship is weak and unsystematic, but for the same-period correlations, there is a majority of positive relationships. Rather stronger relationships are found for the United States than for other countries through to 1957 but not subsequently.[31] The lower relationship in the later years is to be expected: wage movements at this time reflected the impact of long-term contracts relating to important groups of the labour force covering roughly the years 1957–1959, and arranged during the previous period of high activity. It may also be noted that the Canadian relationships between profits and earnings changes appear to improve in the recession years after 1957, at the same time as there is some evidence of a decline in the strength of the association between earnings and employment changes.

The United States is the only country for which data on profit rates[32] were available (manufacturing industries only). A marked positive association appears between profitability and changes in relative earnings through the entire period from 1948. This association is observed whether profit rates

[30] Usually enterprise statistics; the earnings and employment data used are typically establishment statistics.
[31] The profit change/earnings change relationship in the United States is observed for all distributions studied (production workers, total employment) except at sector level (all employment) where it is less clear, and non-production workers in manufacturing (at least over one-year spans).
[32] Profits as a percentage of stockholders equity.

in the preceding year or in the same year are used as an explanatory variable. With one exception (1955–56), the same-year coefficients are all positive, six of them significant at the 5 per cent level. The lagged relationship is slightly less strong.

A selection of the results obtained is given in Table 21.5. Those for the United States correspond closely with those obtained in independent American studies. The report of the Joint Economic Committee of Congress found that within nineteen manufacturing industries, the most important factors related to wage changes after 1951 were the level of profits and the degree of competition in the product market (no significant relationship was found between changes in hourly earnings and employment).[33] Bowen found that for six subperiods between January 1947 and June 1959, profits had a more consistent relationship with wage changes than employment, concentration or unionisation, although in each interval studied one of these variables had a higher correlation coefficient.[34] Eckstein and Wilson also emphasise the importance of profits as a determinant of changes in the wage structure. They suggest that unemployment is the strategic variable influencing the balance of bargaining power in wage negotiations, while the profit rate both affects bargaining power and reflects the long run structural characteristics, such as degree of monopoly, of the product market. They find that these two "standard variables" account for the bulk of wage changes in the United States manufacturing, once the institutional characteristics of the wage determination process—collective bargaining in wage rounds, the existence of a "key" group of related heavy industries —are taken into consideration.[35]

It may be remarked here that Lipsey and Steuer, studying 10 branches of United Kingdom industry found profits "on the whole unsatisfactory as an explanatory variable of wage changes" for the period 1949–1958.[36] This is of course true, industry by industry, for wage developments throughout the period were strongly influenced by inter-bargain spread of arrangements made by wage-round leaders.[37] However, when a rather different question is taken up, namely whether the differentiation that did occur (which was smaller in the United Kingdom than in most other countries studied) was in line with relative profits experience, the data in Table 21.5 appear to support this hypothesis.

The strength of the relationship between changes in earnings and profits brings out the difficulty of drawing conclusions directly from employment/earnings relationships concerning the importance of wage changes per se in the allocation of labour. In an attempt to throw further light on this issue, relative changes in total output (measured by the index of industrial production) were correlated with changes in relative employment. The vast majority of the coefficients were positive, significant and high (Table 21.6), and they did not change very greatly when recalculated as partial correlation coefficients with the influence of changes in earnings held constant. Other relationships observed were an association between profits

---

[33] United States Congress, *JEC Staff Report on Employment, Growth and Price Levels*, 1959, pp. 130–158, based largely on the analysis by H. M. Levinson: "Postwar Movement of Prices and Wages in Manufacturing Industry," *Joint Economic Committee Study of Employment, Growth and Price Levels*, Study Paper No. 21, Jan. 1960.

[34] W. G. Bowen, "Inter-industry Variations in the Unemployment Wage Relationship," *Wage Behaviour in the Postwar Period*, 1960.

[35] O. Eckstein and T. A. Wilson, "The Determination of Money Wages in American Industry," *Quarterly Journal of Economics*, Aug. 1962. The data used refer to a very limited number of observations.

[36] R. G. Lipsey and M. D. Steuer, "The Relation between Profits and Wage Rates," *Economica*, May 1961. Their analysis is based on time series for each industry.

[37] For a detailed analysis of influences affecting wage-bargaining in the United Kingdom, see *The Problem of Rising Prices*, OEEC, Paris 1961, pp. 419–450.

TABLE 21.5 THE RELATION BETWEEN RELATIVE CHANGES IN PROFITS AND IN EARNINGS

a) 1-Year Spans

	48/9	49/50	50/1	51/2	52/3	53/4	54/5	55/6	56/7	57/8	58/9	59/60
USA*: 21 manuf. indust. of which	.64	.16	.77	.14	.65	.56	.25	.46	.39	(−.16)	(−.21)	—
Production workers	(.74)	(.15)	.68	.38	.43	.58	.36	.44	.37	(.26)	(.33)	—
Non-production workers	.65	.03	−.35	−.38	.26	−.11	−.11	.52	.19	(−.44)	(.07)	—
42 industries (incl. 21 manuf.)	.43	.19	.22	.19	.28	.22	(.20)	(.33)	(.21)	(−.14)	(−.14)	—
8 main economic sectors	.56	.31	−.01	.62	.07	.12	.35	.16	−.34	.32	−.01	—
France†: 17 industries (incl. 13 manufacturing)	—	—	.39	.46	−.15	−.04	(.51)	(−.30)	(.16)	(.23)	(.46)	—
Canada‡: 13 manuf. industries	—	—	—	—	—	.40	−.47	.44	(.03)	(.17)	.54	.53
UK‡: 13 manuf. indust.	—	.05	.53	.57	.41	.26	.42	.16	.72	.38	.11	—
Sweden‡: 30 manuf. indust.	—	—	—	—	−.04	.11	.14	−.03	.09	.39	.14	−.19
USA†: 19 manufacturing industries												
a) profit rate and changes in earnings	.19	.17	.28	.60	.49	.59	.52	−.21	.52	.66	.22	.43
b) changes in earnings and profits	.48	−.24	.36	−.23	.01	.58	−.25	.17	.44	−.09	−.10	.29
c) profit changes holding influence of profit rates constant	.55	−.18	.36	.35	.20	.51	.15	.05	.32	.19	.09	.18

b) *3-Year Spans*

	48/51	49/52	50/53	51/54	52/55	53/56	54/57	55/58	56/59	57/60
*USA**: 21 manufacturing industries, of which	.71	.32	.76	.51	.61	−.10	.07	(.38)	−.10	—
Production workers	(.84)	(.54)	.67	.50	.60	.07	.25	(.46)	−.11	—
Non-production workers	.49	.14	.16	.31	.11	−.26	−.32	(.18)	−.07	—
42 industries (incl. 21 manufacturing)	.17	.04	.33	.58	(.42)	(−.06)	(−.07)	(.09)	(−.28)	—
8 main economic sectors	.43	.19	.00	.81	.73	−.21	−.34	−.15	.35	—
France†: 17 industries (incl. 13 manufacturing)	—	—	−.05	.45	(−.20)	(.49)	(.23)	(.29)	(.31)	—
Canada‡: 13 manuf. industries	—	—	—	—	—	−.22	(.08)	.24	−.14	(.08)
UK‡: 13 manuf. industries	—	.25	.50	.56	.15	.55	.57	.60	.22	.14
Sweden‡: 30 manuf. industries	—	—	—	—	−.25	.03	.26	−.07	.05	.14
USA†: 19 manufacturing industries										
a) profit rates and changes in earnings	.21	.26	.45	.65	.62	.60	.55	.36	.63	.67
b) changes in earnings and profits	.74	.51	.51	−.03	−.07	−.27	−.28	.37	−.40	−.30
c) profit changes holding influence of profit rates constant	.73	.60	.59	.55	.27	.31	.11	.62	−.06	−.13

* Average annual earnings of relevant group.
† Average hourly earnings of all wage earners.
‡ Average hourly earnings of male wage-earners.

NOTE. Underlined coefficients are significant at the 5 per cent level. Bracketed figures are not comparable with the others. They were taken into account in the analysis only where it was possible to estimate the approximate effect of this lack of comparability. The problems met are discussed in the introduction to Annex I [of *Wage and Labour Mobility*].
Source: Annex I [of *Wage and Labour Mobility*].

334   Wage Differentials

TABLE 21.6 THE RELATIONSHIP BETWEEN CHANGES IN EMPLOYMENT AND IN THE INDEX OF PRODUCTION
(a) DIRECTLY CALCULATED,
(b) HOLDING CONSTANT THE INFLUENCE OF CHANGES IN EARNINGS

First Year of Span	United States		Canada		United Kingdom		Norway			
							Male Wage-Earners		Salaried Employees	
	(a)	(b)	(a)	(b)	(a)	(b)	(a)	(b)	(a)	(b)
1-year spans										
1948	.83	.83	—	—	—	—	—	—	—	—
1949	.86	.86	.32	.28	.62	.68	—	—	—	—
1950	.83	.78	.52	.52	.72	.65	(.75)	(.75)	(.43)	(.41)
1951	.89	.89	.43	.44	.76	.60	(.63)	(.44)	(.54)	(.61)
1952	.91	.90	.64	.76	.86	.85	(.29)	(.39)	(−.08)	(−.08)
1953	.71	.71	.70	.72	.75	.77	.62	.62	.53	.70
1954	.81	.73	.60	.61	.84	.65	.49	.64	.36	.51
1955	.71	.84	.18	−.01	.74	.67	.57	.57	−.09	.07
1956	.68	.65	.83	.85	.71	.70	.45	.45	.67	.74
1957	.92	.91	.79	.78	.79	.54	.27	.25	.12	.10
1958	(.74)	(.74)	.46	.48	−.02	.03	.58	.57	−.10	−.08
3-year spans										
1948	.79	.77	—	—	—	—	—	—	—	—
1949	.90	.88	.45	.48	.84	.83	—	—	—	—
1950	.94	.93	.73	.72	.88	.86	(.65)	(.66)	(.41)	(.61)
1951	.74	.74	.61	.57	.88	.85	(.46)	(.39)	(.43)	(.42)
1952	.69	.65	.50	.43	.82	.82	(.40)	(.58)	(.79)	(.77)
1953	.60	.59	.67	.61	.93	.87	.77	.75	.70	.70
1954	.70	.71	.53	.47	.91	.75	.76	.74	.64	.71
1955	—	—	.79	.79	.86	.65	.47	.47	.24	.55
1956	(.60)	(.53)	.81	.80	.69	.50	.39	.38	.26	.32
1957	(.59)	(.55)	—	—	—	—	—	—	—	—
1958	(.38)	(.45)	—	—	—	—	—	—	—	—

United States: 20 Manufacturing industries; production workers' employment (ref. 02200). *Canada:* 17 Manufacturing industries, male wage-earners' employment (ref. 01200). *United Kingdom:* 13 Manufacturing industries; total employment (ref. 28240). *Norway:* 20 Manufacturing industries; (ref. 22200-22230).

NOTE. Underlined coefficients are significant at the 5 per cent level. Bracketed figures are not comparable with the others. They were taken into account in the analysis only where it was possible to estimate the approximate effect of this lack of comparability. The problems met are discussed in the introduction to Annex I.
Source: Annex I.

change and employment change, almost always positive and occasionally quite strong, and (not surprisingly in view of the other relationships) output changes were usually positively related to changes in earnings, although the relationship was usually far weaker than that between changes in profits and in earnings.

The general picture suggested by this set of relationships, and in particular the failure of the association between output and employment to weaken considerably after abstraction of the effect of changes in earnings is consistent with the "prosperity thesis" that wage structure developments reflect industries' ability to pay, while their employment requirements are dictated by events in the product market. Stating this in another way, the separate influences of output and productivity developments on employment, and of profit developments on earnings, result in same-direction movements of the two variables, so that although one should normally expect an association between earnings and employment changes, it may be no more than a similar response by both variables to factors which operate to move them in the same direction.

In fact, because of the inter-relationships between the different variables one can safely say only that the direct relationship between earnings and employment changes does not itself clarify the precise importance of differential wage movements. Estimates can, however, be made of what this relationship would be in the absence of any impact on earnings and employment of influences operating on either or both. The "prosperity thesis" suggests the particular importance of profits in this context. Partial correlation coefficients measuring the employment/earnings relationship when the influence of changes in profits is held constant are presented in Table 21.7.

It can be seen from this table that there is a general tendency, particularly marked in the case of the USA but rather less evident in the Canadian data, for lower estimates of the employment/earnings relationship to be observed as one passes from the direct to the partial coefficients. This suggests that employment and wage changes both reflect profits developments and that when this influence is eliminated, the earnings/employment relationship becomes rather more tenuous. This is consistent with, but does not prove, the "prosperity thesis." It is quite feasible to argue that increasing production implies increasing profits and employment, and that the additional labour would not have been forthcoming unless the higher relative earnings made possible by favourable profit trends had been put into effect.

Since profits and employment do tend to move together, it is clear that the observed profits/earnings association will facilitate redistribution of labour in the required directions. A complementary approach is to test the extent to which relative profits and earnings increases occur simultaneously in the absence of differential employment experience as between industries.[38] When this calculation is made (Table 21.8), different results are derived for different countries. For the United States, Canada and France, the initial relationship between profits and earnings changes is seen to be subject to only a slight downward modification. On the other hand, for the limited number of UK industries in the sample studied, there is an important fall in the level of the correlation coefficients, greater than the fall registered by the earnings/employment coefficients when the influence of profit changes is held constant. Insofar as some causal significance can be read into the data, there is some evidence in favour of, and some evidence against the hypothesis that changes in earnings are more closely related to profits trends than to employment requirements. Whereas for the first three countries, profits appear relevant to the differentiation that would have occurred in the absence of employment changes, the UK figures suggest that any influence in this direction was minor, in particular by comparison with the apparent influence of employment change. But it should be borne in mind that earnings have differentiated to a much lower extent in the United Kingdom than in any other of the countries studied; bargaining cohesiveness, much more than either profitability or employment requirements, has been the major influence on the development of relative earnings.

In general, a purely mechanistic interpretation of these relationships may be deceptive. Increasing profits and earnings can be associated with declining employment as a result of technological change,[39] and where normal outward mobility is insufficient to

---

[38] i.e. holding the influence of changes in employment constant.

[39] Increasing labour costs may also induce employers to adopt capital-intensive production methods to protect rather than to improve their profits position.

TABLE 21.7 THE RELATIONSHIP BETWEEN RELATIVE CHANGES IN EMPLOYMENT AND EARNINGS
a) DIRECTLY CALCULATED *b*) HOLDING CONSTANT THE INFLUENCE OF CHANGES IN PROFITS

First Year of Period	United States: 21 Manuf. Industries Production Workers Annual Earnings				Canada: 13 Manuf. Industries Production Workers Hourly Earnings				France: 17 Industries; All Employees Hourly Earnings of Wage Earners				United Kingdom: 13 Manuf. Industries; Total Male Employment; Hourly Earnings of Male Wage-Earners			
	Over 1-Year Spans		Over 3-Year Spans		Over 1-Year Spans		Over 3-Year Spans		Over 1-Year Spans		Over 3-Year Spans		Over 1-Year Spans		Over 3-Year Spans	
	(a)	(b)	(a)	(b)	(a)	(b)	(a)	(b)	(a)	(b)	(a)	(b)	(a)	(b)	(a)	(b)
1948	(.43)	(.17)	.44	(−.28)	—	—	—	—	—	—	—	—	—	—	—	—
1949	(.07)	(.03)	(.42)	(.02)	—	—	—	—	—	—	—	—	.00	−.05	—	—
1950	.76	.69	.58	.21	—	—	—	—	.32	.22	.19	.26	.43	.22	.23	.06
1951	−.01	−.22	.19	−.27	—	—	—	—	.31	.04	.04	.20	.73	.56	.51	.32
1952	.32	.27	.40	.27	—	—	—	—	.30	.30	—	—	.26	.00	.50	.22
1953	.59	.50	.24	.24	.35	.13	.30	.24	−.31	−.31	(−.18)	(−.14)	.38	.29	.45	.43
1954	.56	.48	.05	(.05)	.23	.36	(.47)	(.47)	(−.26)	(−.42)	(−.22)	(−.34)	.84	.81	.71	.57
1955	.29	−.09	.31	(.00)	.56	.70	.03	.02	(.11)	(.05)	(.22)	(.24)	.62	.69	.85	.79
1956	.26	.11	−.35	(−.34)	(.69)	(.73)	.20	.24	(.25)	(.39)	(.16)	(.14)	.30	.15	.85	.76
1957	.11	(−.04)	−.26	—	(−.01)	(−.09)	(−.12)	(.10)	(.18)	(.05)	(.22)	(.22)	.72	.66	.59	.58
1958	−.01	(.28)	—	—	−.46	−.34	—	—	(.47)	(.36)	—	—	.39	.38	—	—
1959	−.30	—	—	—	.02	−.23	—	—	—	—	—	—	—	—	—	—

NOTE. Underlined coefficients are significant at the 5 per cent level. Bracketed figures are not comparable with the others. They were taken into account in the analysis only where it was possible to estimate the approximate effect of this lack of comparability. The problems met are discussed in the introduction to Annex I [of *Wage and Labour Mobility*].
Source: Annex I [of *Wage and Labour Mobility*].

TABLE 21.8 THE RELATIONSHIP BETWEEN RELATIVE CHANGES IN PROFITS AND EARNINGS
a) DIRECTLY CALCULATED   *b*) HOLDING CONSTANT THE INFLUENCE OF CHANGES IN EMPLOYMENT

1st Year of Period	United States: Production Workers 21 Manuf. Industries Annual Earnings				Canada: Production Workers 13 Manuf. Industries Hourly Earnings				France: All Employees; 17 Industries Hourly Earnings of Wage Earners				United Kingdom: All Employees 13 Manuf. Industries Hourly Earnings of Male Wage Earners			
	Over 1-Year Spans		Over 3-Year Spans		Over 1-Year Spans		Over 3-Year Spans		Over 1-Year Spans		Over 3-Year Spans		Over 1-Year Spans		Over 3-Year Spans	
	(a)	(b)	(a)	(b)	(a)	(b)	(a)	(b)	(a)	(b)	(a)	(b)	(a)	(b)	(a)	(b)
1948	(.74)	(.68)	(.84)	(.82)	—	—	—	—	—	—	—	—	—	—	—	—
1949	(.15)	(.14)	(.54)	(.37)	—	—	—	—	—	—	—	—	.05	.07	.25	.12
1950	.68	.58	.67	(.45)	—	—	—	—	.39	.32	—	—	.53	.40	.50	.30
1951	.38	.43	.50	.53	—	—	—	—	.46	.36	−.05	−.19	.57	.05	.56	.36
1952	.43	.40	.60	.54	—	—	—	—	−.15	−.15	.45	.29	.41	.33	.15	.07
1953	.58	.48	.07	−.08	.40	.24	—	—	−.04	−.04	(−.20)	(−.17)	.26	.02	.55	.24
1954	.36	.13	.25	(.25)	−.47	−.53	−.22	−.13	(.51)	(.59)	(.49)	(.54)	.42	.22	.57	.33
1955	.44	.36	(.46)	(.36)	.44	.64	(.08)	(−.06)	(−.30)	(−.29)	(.23)	(.24)	.16	−.41	.60	−.01
1956	.37	.29	−.11	(−.06)	(.03)	(−.31)	.24	.24	(.16)	(.34)	(.29)	(.28)	.72	.70	.22	.18
1957	(.26)	(.24)	—	—	(.17)	(.19)	−.14	−.18	(.23)	(.14)	(.31)	(.31)	.38	−.05	—	—
1958	(.33)	(.42)	—	—	.54	.45	(.08)	(.04)	(.46)	(.35)	—	—	.11	.00	—	—
1959	—	—	—	—	.53	.56	—	—	—	—	—	—	—	—	—	—

NOTE. Underlined coefficients are significant at the 5 per cent level. Bracketed figures are not comparable with the others. They were taken into account in the analysis only where it was possible to estimate the approximate effect of this lack of comparability. The problems met are discussed in the introduction to Annex I [of *Wage and Labour Mobility*].
Source: Annex I [of Wage and Labour Mobility].

reduce the labour force to the extent necessary, industries in this position can resort to employee discharges. Insofar as this option is available, an accurate measure of the employment/earnings relationship can be computed only after omitting from the analysis those industries in which rising profits and earnings coincide with relative employment declines. But this automatically implies a high inter-correlation of earnings, profits and employment for the branches left in the analysis, and leaves completely open the question whether the earnings increases were necessary for, or merely happened at the same time as, increasing employment.

Productivity

The data examined by us indicate no significant tendency for above-average productivity gains[40] to be associated with more rapid earnings increase, although due weight must be given to the possibility that the apparent absence of any relationship may be accounted for by the very great difficulties of measuring changes in productivity adequately. These findings are in line with those of the majority of earlier studies.[41] Exceptionally, both Dunlop[42] and Garbarino[43] find a statistically significant (rank) correlation between productivity and wage change over the 1920–1940 period in the United States; Dunlop suggests that the highest productivity gains are to be expected early in an industry's life when output is expanding rapidly, and attributes above-average wage increases not only to ability to pay but also to these industries' need to attract an expanding work force. But Myers and Bowlby[44] point out that these two authors omit industries considered as "abnormal" from their analysis, and argue that if abnormalities occur frequently enough to affect the results substantially they should not be disregarded. On the basis of full industry lists, they suggest that there was some cyclical relationship between productivity and earnings changes up to about 1933, with recovery-induced productivity gains permitting differentiation of wage increases during the upward phase of cycles, but that thereafter, changes in the institutional framework (unionisation, governmental wage setting) introduced determinants of inter-industry wage change other than productivity.

Gross Value Productivity

Productivity increases may lead to relative or even absolute price declines rather than rising wages, and demand factors working through price and profit changes may

---

[40] Measured conventionally as real output per unit of labour input. The drawbacks and conceptual difficulties attending these measurements need not be enlarged on here.

[41] D. M. Eisemann, Inter-industry Wage Changes, 1939–47, *Review of Economics and Statistics*, Nov. 1956; H. M. Levinson, "Postwar Movement of Prices and Wages in Manufacturing Industries," op. cit.; D. G. Brown, "Expected Ability to Pay and Inter-industry Wage Structure in Manufacturing," *Industrial and Labour Relations Review*, Oct. 1962. The last author finds an apparent relationship between value added per manhour and earnings change, which disappears when other explanatory variables are taken into consideration. Bombach, ("Quantitative und monetäre Aspekte des Wirtschaftswachstums," *Verein für Sozialpolitik*, Gesellschaft für Wirtschafts-und Sozialwissenschaft, Baden-Baden, 1958), points out that wages have not always or necessarily increased in industries with the highest growth of individual productivity, adding that if there were any continuing relationship between productivity and individual wages, this would rapidly lead to an absurd earnings structure. See also E. H. Phelps Brown and M. H. Browne, "Earnings in Industries of the United Kingdom, 1948–1959," *Economic Journal*, Sept. 1962; C. H. Feinstein "Income and Expenditure in the 1950's," *London and Cambridge Economic Bulletin*, December 1960; W. E. G. Salter, *Productivity and Technical Change* (1950), Chapter XII; S. Fabricant, *Employment in Manufacturing* 1899–1939 (National Bureau of Economic Research, 1942); F. Myers and R. L. Bowlby, "The Inter-industry Wage Structure and Productivity," Industrial and Labour Relations Review, Vol. 7, October 1953; J. W. Kendrick, *Productivity Trends in the United States* (1961), p. 198.

[42] J. T. Dunlop, *Income, Employment and Wage Policy*, 1948.

[43] J. W. Garbarino, *op. cit.*

[44] F. Myers and R. L. Bowlby, *op. cit.*

raise wages without comparable productivity changes. Physical productivity is therefore not necessarily the best indicator of the value of a worker's productive effort; Perlman[45] suggests that gross value productivity per worker (which allows for relative changes in output price) is a superior explanatory variable. This author finds rank correlation coefficients of 0.68 and 0.58 between sales per manhour and average hourly earnings in 20 United States manufacturing industries for the periods 1939–1947 and 1947–1953 respectively. On the other hand, in a Secretariat calculation for 86 United Kingdom industries for the period 1948–1954, no relation between changes in gross output at current prices per worker and earnings was found.[46]

Structural Variables

A useful distinction can be drawn between those variables which, while operative on the wage structure are also inter-correlated among themselves, and those which are not. The latter are mainly structural variables representing technical or market characteristics of different industries; and some of them appear to be related to changes in the wage structure independently of differential product market and profits experience. One such variable is the ratio of labour to total costs, which can be considered as a combined indicator of both willingness and ability to pay. Data on the ratio of labour costs to sales proceeds have been related to relative earnings changes for Canada, Germany, the United States, Sweden and Norway. In all but one country (Norway) there is a marked preponderance of negative signs, suggesting that employers are the more ready to accord above-average wage increases the smaller the share of wages in their costs, and that this is true of earnings both of salaried employees and wage-receivers. The relationship is a weak but rather systematic one and constitutes more of a background condition than an operative influence; it is overshadowed by the association between the various market variables and earnings changes in particular periods. Further, it is not possible in general to say whether its influence will be in the same or the opposite direction to that of the market variables; industries with low labour cost ratios may or may not be those in which profits, production and employment are rising more rapidly. In a calculation for United States and Canadian production workers to abstract the apparent influence of profits changes on earnings, the inverse relationship of labour cost ratio and changes in earnings was found to subsist, and—particularly where the data are considered over three-year spans—to be of some strength in certain periods. A selection of the results is given in Table 21.9.

Concentration[47]

A number of studies stress the importance of the degree of concentration of an industry as a factor making for above average rates of wage increase. Reasons for suggesting

---

[45] R. Perlman, "Value Productivity and the Inter-industry Wage Structure," *Industrial and Labour Relations Review*, October 1956.

[46] Coefficient of correlation: 0.05. Curiously enough, there is a statistical relationship between an industry's earnings *level* in 1948 and the increase in gross output per worker at current prices in the following six years. (Coefficient of correlation: 0.41).

[47] The concentration measures used in the analysis were based on employment, not on turnover, and are calculated as the percent of total employment in the industry accounted for by units employing more than x persons (x variable according to country, according to data availability), except for the USA and UK, where the concentration measure is the percentage of the industry's employment accounted for by the three (US) or four (UK) largest companies (USA) or business units (UK). Use of establishment data (Canada, Germany; the scope of the French data is uncertain) imports a degree of measurement of size-of-establishment characteristics rather than of concentration of ownership: the same enterprise may, of course, control several establishments. The consistency of the results for the different countries, however suggests that there is a close correlation between an industry's establishment size characteristics and the extent to which its ownership is concentrated into a greater or lesser number of enterprises.

340   Wage Differentials

TABLE 21.9 THE ASSOCIATION BETWEEN THE RATIO OF LABOUR COST TO SALES PROCEEDS* AND DIFFERENTIAL MOVEMENTS IN EARNINGS (MEASURED OVER 3-YEAR SPANS)

First Year of Span	Sweden†	Norway‡	Germany§	Canada‖	United States#	Influence of Profits Change Held Constant	
						United States#	Canada‖
a) Wage-Earners							
1948	—	—	—	—	(.00)	(−.12)	—
1949	—	—	—	—	(.03)	(−.31)	—
1950	—	(−.16)	—	—	.08	.19	—
1951	—	(.34)	—	—	−.18	−.29	—
1952	−.19	(.36)	—	—	−.32	−.31	—
1953	−.38	.41	—	−.06	−.61	−.65	−.06
1954	−.19	−.06	—	(−.56)	−.52	−.50	(−.56)
1955	.29	.34	—	−.62	(−.40)	(−.36)	−.76
1956	.28	.04	—	−.52	−.53	−.59	−.56
1957	−.04	—	−.24	(−.63)	—	—	(−.70)
1958	—	—	−.40	—	—	—	—
1959	—	—	−.26	—	—	—	—
b) Salaried or Non-production Employees							
1948	—	—	—	—	.02	−.05	—
1949	—	—	—	—	.16	.11	—
1950	—	—	—	—	−.05	−.04	—
1951	—	—	—	—	−.28	−.34	—
1952	−.15	(.13)	—	—	−.11	−.10	—
1953	−.05	(.56)	—	—	.21	.29	—
1954	−.11	(.21)	—	—	−.09	−.16	—
1955	.15	.49	—	—	(−.07)	(−.04)	—
1956	.07	.10	—	—	−.02	−.04	—
1957	.06	.08	—	—	—	—	—
1958	—	.29	—	—	—	—	—
1959	—	—	—	—	—	—	—

* *Sweden:* Sales value of firms employing 5 or more persons. *Norway:* Gross value of production of firms employing 6 or more persons. *Germany:* Turnover of firms with more than 10 employees. *Canada:* Gross value of production. *US:* Corporative Sales.
† Annual earnings; 88 manufacturing industries.
‡ Annual earnings (male wage-earners, both sexes for salaried employees); 20 manufacturing industries.
§ Hourly earnings of male workers, 28 manufacturing industries and one non-manufacturing.
‖ Hourly earnings of male wage-earners, 13 manufacturing industries.
Annual earnings, 21 manufacturing industries.
NOTE. Bracketed figures are not comparable with the others. They were taken into account in the analysis only where it was possible to estimate the approximate effect of this lack of comparability. The problems met are discussed in the introduction to Annex I [of *Wage and Labour Mobility*]. Underlined figures are significant at the 5 per cent level.

that this is an economically significant relationship are:

i) the possibility of the exercise of monopolistic power by concentrated industries and the probability that firms which are potential entrants to large scale industries would have to pay union wage scales;[48]

[48] J. R. Meyer, "Wage Price, and National Income Relationships in the Light of Recent Findings on the Behaviour of Large Business Corporations" in Bradley (ed.), *The Public Stake in Union Power*, Charlottesville, University of Virginia

ii) the probability that union coverage or bargaining power will cover a greater part of the industry;

iii) technological and economic factors which operate in such a way that the industries best placed to agree high wage increases are also most likely to be highly concentrated.

Most of the studies on this question deal with the United States.[49] Our own analysis of the period 1948–1961 confirms their findings of a marked association between the degree of concentration and the relative rate of production worker wage advance there.[50] In the United Kingdom, the relationship was in the same direction as for the United States, but is weak, and of limited practical significance.[51] Extension to other countries suggests rather different conclusions. For Germany, there has been a marked tendency for less concentrated industries to experience relative earnings gains. In France, Sweden and Canada, workers in more concentrated industries have done neither better nor worse than in less concentrated ones.

When the American and British data are examined more closely, it is found that the earnings structures in both countries widened over the period studied. This suggests that in both cases the concentration/wage change relationship may to some extent merely be a reflection of the greater earnings differentials, i.e. the forces which made for opening of the wage structure tended to divide up among industries in line with their degree of concentration. No conclusive answer can be given, but it is reasonable to attribute the deterioration of the earnings position in industries such as textiles and apparel as much to their unhappy profits and employment experience as to their low concentration. This would explain a significant amount of the apparent relationship between high concentration and relative wage gains, although it would be wrong to deny that the exercise of market power in specific instances has enabled some concentrated industries to implement wage increases which were higher than they otherwise would have been. However, it is by no means certain that this fact outweighs the influence of product market conditions, which happened to be least favourable to the least concentrated branches.

By contrast, there is in all six countries a positive association between an industry's concentration and its wage *level,* and for Germany, France and Canada, the association is quite strong. This could be thought to reflect a tendency for concentrated industries to use proportionately greater quantities of relatively skilled labour. But the German evidence indicates that this is not so: an almost identical association is observed when industry wage levels for skilled, semi-skilled or unskilled groups of workers are related to the degree of concentration. Further, the Canadian and Swedish data suggest that both wage earners and salaried employees, when considered separately, earn more in concentrated industries. Concentrated industries, it would seem, pay *better;*[52] but they do not necessarily advance their earnings more rapidly,

---

1959, pp. 274–275. See also M. Segal, "The Relation between Union Wage Impact and Market Structure," *Quarterly Journal of Economics,* Feb. 1963, pp. 96–114.

[49] See, for example, D. G. Brown, "Expected Ability to pay and Inter-industry Wage Structure in Manufacturing," *Industrial and Labour Relations Review,* October 1962; H. M. Levinson, "Postwar Movement of Prices and Wages in Manufacturing Industries," *op. cit.*; W. G. Bowen, "Inter-industry Variations in the Unemployment Wage Relationship," *op. cit.*; J. W. Garbarino, "A Theory of Inter-industry Wage Structure Variation," *Quarterly Journal of Economics,* May, 1950.

[50] The *average* level of the correlation coefficients over 3-year spans is as high as 0.52.

[51] For the period 1948–54, the concentration/earnings change correlation coefficient for 79 industries is 0.15. For 1948–59 it is 0.34 and for 1954–1958, 0.28. The last two values are significant at the 5 per cent level, but they imply that at most 12 per cent of the differential movement of earnings is related to the degree of concentration.

[52] Concentrated industries also tend to be more highly capitalised, so that productivity per worker is likely to be higher. On the other hand, as has already been noted (page 338) productivity *changes* are not a very good direct explanatory variable of *changes* in the wage structure.

although they must have done so at some time in the past.

Interpretative Implications

Taken in combination, the product market and structural variables examined provide grounds for suggesting that some movements of the earnings structure result from influences other than employers' relative labour requirements. But the high interrelation of the majority of the explanatory variables makes it difficult to assess the relative importance of product and labour market influences on the development of relative earnings. Thus the data are at all times open to two alternative explanations. The first is that product market influences have operated to generate changes in relative earnings in the same direction as those which would have been observed had earnings been discharging an allocative function in the redistribution of labour; it would be reasonable to add that to the extent that this is true, the observed movements of the earnings structure have in general been such as to facilitate the required labour flows. The alternative is that the allocation of labour has been predominantly determined by changes in relative earnings. Corresponding movements of the product market variables would still be expected in this case, since a priori it is likely that the strongest employment gains will be registered in the most prosperous industries, i.e. those which are expanding production, profits, or both relatively more rapidly. While it is difficult to carry the analysis any further than this, two main conclusions can nevertheless be drawn from the material presented in this chapter:

a) There appears to be some association between changes in relative earnings and changes in relative employment. On the whole it is weak; but there is some evidence that a "limiting condition" exists, in the sense that exceptionally marked declines in employment tend to be associated with a deterioration of position in the earnings structure.

b) Other influences, acting jointly or independently, have been more important than relative labour requirements in determining the way earnings have moved.

Summary

The findings of the present chapter are summarised below. Before presenting them, the difficulties of interpretation discussed at the beginning of the chapter may be recalled. In particular, it will be borne in mind that the absence of any statistical relationship between changes in earnings and employment is consistent with the frictionless operation of labour markets. The Group, however, does not incline to this view. Employment markets are sufficiently rigid for the demand for labour, as expressed in the form of higher wage offers, and the employment response to these offers, to be observed in the statistics. Even then, the meaningfulness of the results of the analysis is affected both by the technical properties of the methods applied and the ability of the data to represent the phenomena which they are intended to measure. The findings set forth below have been arrived at taking into consideration as far as possible these limitations of the materials.

1. When manufacturing industries are studied at 2-digit level, some association is observed between changes in the net numbers of blue-collar workers employed and changes in their relative earnings. In general it is rather weak, but in Britain and Canada and the USA up to about 1957, there have been periods for which a quite strong relationship is observed.
2. In general no relationship with change in earnings is observed for interindustry movement of white collar workers in manufacturing, or for blue or white collar worker movements between non-manufacturing industries.
3. For the majority of the groups studied there is some evidence that a higher association between changes in earnings and employment may be observed under full

employment. But exceptions are by no means infrequent.

4. The blue collar relationship observed in manufacturing becomes attenuated when the same industries are studied at 3-digit level of detail (Canada, USA, UK and possibly Sweden). This suggests that what is being measured at 2-digit level is the effect of forces which affect the prosperity, and therefore the employment and earnings, of branches of industry considered as units. With wage spread being propagated through institutional arrangements and customary relativities, individual 3-digit industries have in general had to accept the prevailing rate of wage-change in their branch as a datum. The low correlation observed at this level indicates that they were able to expand or contract their employment as conditions dictated in the absence of any notable differential movements of earnings.

5. Other variables than labour requirements have been important in determining the way earnings have moved in recent years, and taken in conjunction, their influence has been predominant. In particular, confirmation of the prosperity effect can be inferred from the fact that profit rates and changes in profits appear to exercise considerable influence on the development of relative earnings. When the relationship between changes in earnings and in employment is recalculated on the assumption that no changes in profits took place, the degree of association is found to be still weaker. It is also noteworthy that the relationship between production changes and changes in employment is almost unaltered when recalculated on the assumption that no changes in relative earnings occurred.

6. Among the other variables making for higher (or lower) rates of wage advance are employment experience in a previous period, the degree of concentration, the rate of production growth, all of which are found to be important at certain times for certain employment groups, but not systematically. The ratio of labour costs to total costs appears to be an important background factor, but in individual cases its influence tends to be obscured by movements reflecting the impact of other variables. It was also found that concentrated industries tend to have a higher wage *level*.

7. Overall, changing wage differentials appear to play a very small role in inter-industry movements of labour. Industries have in general been able to expand their employment as necessary by increasing their interception of new entrants, the unemployed, and employed jobseekers. But there are circumstances in which differential wage changes may be of importance:

   1. Declining relative earnings appear to operate as an incentive to job-leaving (although the observed lag in earnings in those industries in which employment declined most rapidly seems to be mainly a reflection on both earnings and employment of these industries' lack of prosperity);

   2. An expanding industry which is poorly placed to intercept a recruitment stream because it is in a remote region or stands low in the earnings structure may find it necessary to implement an above-average wage increase for some or all grades of the labour required.

22
Concentration and Labor Earnings

Leonard W. Weiss[1]

There have been periodic suggestions in the literature that concentrated industries may tend to pay exceptional wages [3] [6] [8] [10] [14] [16] [17].* If such a hypothesis could be given convincing support, it would have important implications for the evaluation of industrial performance. It would mean that the sum of monopoly rents would exceed greatly those identified in examinations of corporate profits. The resulting misallocation of resources would be understated even more seriously since the welfare loss due to monopoly pricing increases as the square of the margin between price and the opportunity cost of factors employed [7].

It has proved difficult to test for monopoly rents accruing to labor in concentrated industries because of the large number of variables pertinent to wage determination, many of which are correlated with industry structure. A number of studies have attempted to circumvent this difficulty by investigating wage changes [6] [8], but these really tested the distinct hypothesis that concentrated industries continuously increase wages relative to unconcentrated industries. Another investigator attempted to test the "monopoly wage" hypothesis by comparing the ratios of Canadian to U. S. wages in industries that were concentrated in Canada but not in the United States with other industries that were unconcentrated in both countries. His whole argument ultimately depended on nine mostly minor industries [13]. Altogether, it is doubtful whether many have been convinced by the evidence to date of either the presence or absence of monopoly rents in the wage payments of concentrated industries.

Reprinted from the *American Economic Review,* (March 1966), pp. 96–117, by permission of the publisher and author.
* Editors' Note: References in square brackets are listed at the end of the reading.
[1] This paper was prepared under a grant from the Graduate School of the University of Wisconsin. Computations were partially financed by the Social Systems Research Institute and by the National Science Foundation. Comments by Glen Cain, Hirschel Kasper, H. Gregg Lewis, and Gerald Somers were very helpful in the preparation of the study.

This paper attempts a new, direct test of the "monopoly wage" hypothesis using the 1/1000 sample of the 1960 Census of Population. The paper is divided into five parts. The first briefly reviews possible hypotheses. Part II describes the data; Part III presents the detailed results of multiple regression studies for semiskilled labor; and Part IV summarizes similar results for a number of other occupation groups. Part V presents some conclusions.

I. The Hypothesis

The notion that monopoly on product markets leads to high payments for hired factors does not arise automatically from the concept of a profit-maximizing firm. Indeed, simple theory might suggest low rather than high wages in concentrated industries since output restriction would carry with it a restriction of employment. It is quite possible to find plausible arguments to support the opposite hypothesis, however. The profit-maximization assumption need not yield equally good predictions in all areas. Pecuniary profit motives might well be weaker in wage policy than in other business decisions. While high profits won by technical advance or effective market forecasts often enjoy general approval, high profits attained by paying meager wages almost certainly will win censure for the entrepreneur. A relatively profitable firm might well pay above-average wages to avoid such opprobrium, i.e., firms with exceptional profits might choose to use part of their earnings to buy public approval. This might be particularly true of firms with monopoly power because of their vulnerability to a bad press.

Even on the assumption of unequivocal profit-maximization, a high-wage policy might be plausible. Industries with high profits, whether due to monopoly or other causes, might attract trade unionism since they offer large prizes to the successful organizer. High wages might then result from the unionization of profitable industries or from managerial attempts to forestall such organization. Less-profitable industries might pay lower wages because the threat of organization might be less and/or because the firm might be less willing to pay to keep the union weak.

The increase in costs associated with a high-wage policy would probably not be as great as the increase in hourly wage rates in any event, since low wages would tend to result in high turnover, poor discipline, and poor-quality labor. A large, profitable firm which did pay high wages to buy public favor and/or to limit union power would have to pay less per "productivity unit" than per man-hour for its purchase.

In a perfectly competitive labor market an employer paying a high annual wage would get correspondingly superior workers. High earnings would not imply monopoly rents since laborers would still earn the values of their alternative products. While the tendency for labor quality to be related to earnings has long been recognized, some economists have doubted that it could fully account for interindustry wage differences. For instance, Sumner Slichter argued that if employers actually believed that higher wages brought them proportionately higher quality labor, the employers under the greatest competitive pressure would pay high rather than low wage rates [15, p. 90].

This paper tries to test two hypotheses: (1) that concentrated industries pay high annual rates for labor of particular "occupations"; and (2) that these high earnings are more than can be accounted for by the personal characteristics of the labor employed. Most previous studies have been limited by the data to the first hypothesis. The 1/1000 Census tape makes it possible to test both.

Since concentration and unionization are closely related, they must both be considered. The effect of unionism with varying degrees of product market monopoly may be complex. In unconcentrated industries, strong union power might yield high wages, but in concentrated industries, where wages may already be high, unions may not add much. For one thing, if high wages in unorganized but concentrated industries result from the threat of unionism, then concentration and unionization would represent the same force. If this is true, the combined effects of concentration and unionization would be less than the sum of the effects of the two taken separately. In addition, unions seem likely to have greater bargaining power where they are the source of monopoly power on product markets—e.g., coal or construction—than where market power would exist without them—e.g., automobiles or steel [11, p. 138].

On the basis of these arguments, this study uses the model:

$$Y = b_0 + b_1 CR + b_2 U + b_3 U \cdot CR \qquad (1)$$

where Y is annual earnings, CR is the concentration ratio, and U is the extent of collective bargaining coverage, to test for the existence of "monopoly wages" in concentrated and/or unionized industries.[2] The above argument suggests positive signs for b_1 and b_2 and a negative sign for b_3. The monopoly-wage hypothesis would be supported in some form if b_1 were positive and large relative to b_3. It would also be supported if b_1 and b_3 were both positive or, even if b_1 were negative, if b_3 were large and positive. The monopoly-wage hypothesis would have to be rejected if b_1 and b_3 were both negative or if either b_1 or b_3 were negative and large relative to the other.[3]

Concentration and/or unionization may be proxies for other industry characteristics. These other variables must also be introduced.

[2] This model had been formulated before the author saw the similar results of H. G. Lewis, [9, pp. 161, 178].
[3] Since the partial derivative of Y with respect to CR is $\partial Y / \partial CR = b_1 + b_3 U$, the net effect of CR on Y will change sign when $U = -b_1/b_3$. If this number falls between 0 and +100 (the range of U as it will be measured here), the monopoly-wage hypothesis will be confirmed over only a portion of the feasible range of U. It will be confirmed over the higher values of U where b_3 is positive and the lower values of U where b_3 is negative. By similar reasoning, the effect of unionization on earnings would change sign where $CR = -b_2/b_3$.

1. One might expect industries with rapidly increasing employment to show higher earnings than others, on the assumption that relative changes in employment opportunities are not perfectly foreseen by workers and that the short-run supply of labor in particular industries is not perfectly elastic. In effect, we assume that an increase in employment in any one industry represents an increase in demand rather than supply. This appears reasonable when large groups of workers employable in many different industries are involved.
2. There may be some justification for distinguishing durable- from nondurable-goods industries. The former are less stable over the cycle and would yield higher earnings in boom years to offset long periods of unemployment. In addition, there is a tradition that durable-goods industries require heavier work presumably implying better pay.
3. It is commonly supposed that large employers pay high wages. At first glance one might expect large employers to be associated with monopsony power, but this need not be so because they tend to be located in large labor markets. Many of the arguments for the monopoly-wage hypothesis can also be used to argue for high earnings in large shops.
4. Some argue that the over-all labor force characteristics affect industry wage rates paid [15]. E.g., earnings of a male worker would be lower in an industry with a large proportion of female workers than in one where most workers were male. This might occur if personnel policies or collective bargaining agreements apply the terms appropriate to the main core of the work force to all workers in a shop. Again, if all firms in an industry must meet one another's product prices, they may be forced by competition into similar wage policies. E.g., a firm in the North may pay low wages if a large proportion of its competitors are in the South. The

five labor force characteristics for which this sort of argument seems most plausible are the percentages of the labor force that are (a) male, (b) skilled, (c) white, (d) in the South, and (e) of nonurban residence.

Finally, there are many personal characteristics important in the determination of labor earnings. There seem to be good reasons to expect that a person's age, race, region, urban or rural residence, mobility, education, intelligence, health, strength, manual dexterity, and appearance will affect his potential earnings in alternative employments, and therefore the minimum payments that his employer must make to get his services. Since the purpose of this paper is to determine the extent of monopoly rents included in labor earnings, it is important to introduce these personal variables. Even if earnings were high in concentrated or heavily unionized industries, workers would not be earning monopoly rents if their exceptional incomes could be wholly accounted for by exceptional personal attributes.

II. The Data

The dependent variable throughout this study is the private wage and salary income in 1959 reported by individuals in the 1/1000 sample of the 1960 Census (see [4]). The populations used consist of all persons of specified occupation and sex employed for more than 13 weeks during 1959 and reporting their main employment in April, 1960 in (a) mining, construction, or manufacturing, or in (b) mining, construction, manufacturing, transportation, communications, or public utilities.[4] The regulated industries were excluded from population (a) because concentration and unionization seemed likely to have different effects on wages with and without regulation. When population (b) was used, a dummy variable was introduced with a value of one when the industry involved was regulated. Agriculture, distribution, and services were excluded from the study because the large numbers self-employed and, at least in agriculture, the large amounts of nonwage income made it difficult to compare earnings with other industries.

The year 1959 is an adequate, though not perfect, year for our purposes. It falls at the end of a long, stable prosperity, so adjustments to the open inflation of the 1940's should be largely complete. There is evidence that neither monopoly nor union power was fully exploited during the 1940's and that they were re-exerted during the 1950's [1] [3] [5] [8] [9, p. 193] [19]. If there were monopoly-wage advantages, therefore, they were more likely to show up in 1959 than in earlier years. On the other hand, 1959 annual earnings are affected by the unemployment remaining after the 1958 recession and, in certain industries, by the long 1959 steel strike. The effect of unemployment is at least partially corrected by including the numbers of weeks worked in 1959 as variables.

Some fuzziness is introduced because characteristics are reported as of April, 1960, while earnings refer to 1959. Most personal characteristics (e.g., sex or education) remain stable from one year to the next, but in some cases incomes are reported for persons with different 1959 industries, occupations, or residences from those used. The most serious error of this sort is probably in the number of hours worked. These refer to "last week" (usually in March or April, 1960) and can differ sharply from the average weekly hours in 1959.

Each individual is assigned the characteristics of the industry that he reported. For instance, everyone employed in the shoe industry is assigned the shoe industry's indexes of concentration, unionization, growth, plant size, durability, and labor force characteristics as well as his own personal characteris-

---

[4] Persons employed in industry 249, not specified metal industries, 326, not specified food industries, 459, not specified manufacturing, and 579, not specified utilities, were excluded.

tics. The five labor force variables are derived from the 1/1000 sample itself, and the employment-growth variable is the 1960 industry employment divided by the 1950 industry employment, both taken from Censuses of Population. Industry definitions involve no problems for these six variables.[5] However, the indexes of concentration, unionization, and employer size are based on weighted averages of the component three- and four-digit industry figures using employment reported in the 1960 *Annual Survey of Manufactures* or *Employment and Earnings* as weights.

Two concentration indexes are used. The simplest is just a weighted average of 1958 four-firm concentration ratios by four-digit product class. These are imperfect indexes of market power because of the varying regional character of the markets for some commodities and the varying extent of noncompeting subproducts for others. A second concentration index identified hereafter as CCR (corrected concentration ratio) is also computed using weighted averages of five-digit concentration ratios for noncompeting subproducts and an arbitrary scaling-up of national concentration ratios in industries with clearly regional or local markets.[6] These corrections are far from perfect, but the values of CCR should measure market power on a more nearly uniform basis in interindustry comparisons than those of the uncorrected average concentration ratios.[7]

The employer-size index is the percentage of employees in establishments with 250 or more employees in 1958. Establishments are used instead of firms because (1) employer size seems to be mainly a matter of his impact on local labor markets which depends on the size of his plants rather than his whole firm; (2) establishments are more accurately assigned to industries than firms are; and (3) because plant-size data are available for more industries than are firm-size data. The cut-off size of 250 employees is selected as a point by which impersonal employment relationships are likely to have developed. A further reason for using establishments rather than firms and for using 250 rather than a larger number of employees is to reduce the colinearity between the concentration and plant-size variables. There is undoubtedly some effect of employer bigness that cannot be distinguished from market concentration, but the measure used here does separate out important elements of employer size.

The existing measures of union power by industry are incomplete and often conflicting. Special estimates were developed for this study based on a wide range of sources. The BLS *Industry Wage Surveys* were taken as the basic source where available, and estimates based on other materials were adjusted to the concepts used in those Surveys.[8] Conceptually, union power in an industry is measured by the percentage of employees in establishments where more than half of the production workers are covered by collective bargaining agreements. The collective-bargaining-coverage approach does not distinguish between plants organized by locals of national unions and those organized by independent locals, nor between plants where all production workers are union members and those with collective bargaining agreements covering many nonunion members. Moreover, all employees in an industry are assigned the same collective-bargaining-coverage index regardless of whether or not they are themselves covered. There may be a tendency for our index to overstate unionism in industries with many small firms [9, pp. 273–75 and correspondence with

---

[5] In industry 347, "Textile Dyeing and Finishing, Except Wool and Knit Goods," the population Census figure is wildly different from the Annual Survey of Manufacturers figures for the same years. In that case a special figure derived from the Annual Survey of Manufacturers was used.

[6] The procedures used were approximately those used in [18].

[7] The corrections used are described in more detail in an appendix available on request from the writer, Economics Department, University of Wisconsin, Madison, Wisconsin 53706.

[8] The sources and techniques used are described in an appendix available from the writer on request (see n. 6).

Lewis], though the employer-size variable should pick up much of the effect of unionism missed for this reason.

An industry-wide measure of unionism seems appropriate in industries selling on national markets. Earnings at nonunion plants in highly unionized industries would tend to be high owing to the threat of unionism, and earnings at organized plants in industries where unions are weak would tend to be low because of competitive pressures. In localized industries, however, the *national* extent of collective bargaining coverage is, in effect, a weighted average of local-contract-coverage percentages. Such an average may be a poor union power variable if unionization varies greatly from locality to locality. Happily, the majority of observations in our study are in industries selling on national markets.

Regressions are computed for (a) unregulated industries and (b) regulated and unregulated industries together for the following four broad Census occupation and sex classes:

301–370 Clerical and Kindred Workers (Females only)
401–545 Craftsmen, Foremen, and Kindred Workers (Males only)
601–775 Operatives and Kindred Workers (Males only)
960–985 Laborers Except Farm and Mine (Males only)

In addition, regressions are computed for the unregulated industries only for the following, more narrow Census occupation-sex classes:

074 Draftsmen (Males only)
085 Mechanical Engineers (Males only)
290 Managers, Officials, and Proprietors, N.E.C. (Males only)
360 Typists (Females only)
465 Machinists (Males only)
715 Truck and Tractor Drivers (Males only)
775 Operatives and Kindred Workers, N.E.C. (Males only)
775 Operatives and Kindred Workers, N.E.C. (Females only)
834 Janitors and Sextons (Males only)
985 Laborers, N.E.C. (Males only)

Most other detailed occupations are specific to particular industries. Indeed, even this list contains several lopsided samples: 42 per cent of the "Laborers, N.E.C." and 30 per cent of the "Truck and Tractor Drivers" are in industry 196 "Construction"; 34 per cent of the machinists, 21 per cent of the mechanical engineers, and 18 per cent of the draftsmen are in industry 258 "Miscellaneous Machinery," and 22 per cent of the female operatives are in industry 359 "Apparel and Accessories." The distribution of the four broad occupation classes among industries is closer to the distribution of the entire work force, but here the diversity of included occupations may introduce a great deal of unexplained variability. These problems are both near a minimum in the case of occupation class 601–775 "Operatives and Kindred Workers." In view of the relative ease with which new semiskilled trades can be learned, it seems more appropriate to treat operatives as a homogeneous group of workers than to treat craftsmen or clerical workers that way. Occupation class 601–775 also avoids the overweighting of construction that occurs in the case of "laborers" (960–985). Moreover, the estimates of unionism which refer to percentages of production workers seem to apply more accurately to operatives than to other occupations. The unregulated industries probably provide the more useful sample for our purposes because concentration has a clearer meaning there, since our estimates of the unionism variable are more solid there, and because 47 per cent of the "operatives" in the regulated industries are in the rather special group "Truck and Tractor Drivers." Male operatives in unregulated industries are used in Part III of the paper to illustrate the statistical analysis used. Results for other populations are summarized in tabular form in Part IV.

350   Wage Differentials

TABLE 22.1 REGRESSION AND CORRELATION COEFFICIENTS RELATING 1959 WAGE AND SALARY INCOME TO CONCENTRATION AND UNIONIZATION FOR MALE OPERATIVES AND KINDRED WORKERS IN UNREGULATED INDUSTRIES (OCCUPATIONS 601–775 IN INDUSTRIES 126–438)

	N = 5187				
Mean Wage and Salary Income	Regression Coefficients				R^2 (Degrees of Freedom; Corrected)
	b_0 (Constant)	b_1 (CR or CCR)	b_2 (U)	b_3 ($U \cdot CR$ or $U \cdot CCR$)	
Using CR:					
4419	3872 (62.51)	16.70 (1.664)			.0189
	3248 (110.2)	11.04 (1.851)	11.75 (1.712)		.0275
	2691 (246.9)	31.90 (8.468)	19.26 (3.434)	−.2659 (.1053)	.0285
Using CCR:					
4419	3358 (84.34)	26.53 (1.967)			.0337
	3039 (112.8)	21.40 (2.304)	7.606 (1.790)		.0369
	1936 (280.5)	53.47 (7.811)	23.74 (4.159)	−.4426 (.1030)	.0401

III. Regression Results for Semiskilled Males

Regression coefficients relating total 1959 private wage and salary earnings to concentration and unionization for male operatives in unregulated industries are shown in Table 22.1. Two sets of coefficients are shown, one using uncorrected average concentration ratios (CR) and the other using corrected average concentration ratios (CCR). The second set of regressions seems most reliable on a priori grounds. Although the adjustments are rough, CCR surely comes closer to measuring market power on a basis comparable among industries than the uncorrected index. All of the regression coefficients are statistically significant and have the initially expected signs. The effect of concentration is unequivocally positive. The marginal effect of unionization is positive if CR is less than 72 or if CCR is less than 54.

The apparent effect of unionization and concentration are computed in Table 22.2 for two illustrative values of CCR and U.

TABLE 22.2 ESTIMATED VALUES OF Y FOR CERTAIN VALUES OF CCR AND U

		Value of U	
		50	90
Value of CCR	20	3750	4345
	60	5003	4891

The particular values of *CCR* and *U* are selected as "high" and "low" values in each case. Values of *CCR* are below 20 for only 9 per cent of the male operatives in unregulated industries and above 60 for only 8 per cent. Values of *U* are below 50 and 17 per cent of these observations and above 90 for 14 per cent. Unionization seems to raise annual earnings by about 16 per cent when concentration is low, but to have no effect when *CCR* is high. Concentration seems to raise earnings by about 33 per cent when unions are weak, but by only 13 per cent when they are strong. Disregarding other variables, the monopoly rents included in labor income could be very large.

When other industry characteristics are introduced as additional variables, the effects of *CCR* and *U* on *Y* are reduced. The equation becomes:

$$Y = 1751 \quad + 20.13 CCR + 10.15 U$$
$$(349.7) \quad (9.259) \quad\quad (4.845)$$
$$-.08907 U \cdot CCR + 5.494 G$$
$$(.1268) \quad\quad\quad (.9169)$$
$$+ 4.253 L - 401.8 D + 7.372 M \quad (2)$$
$$(1.929) \quad (83.47) \quad (2.694)$$
$$+ 5.997 Sk$$
$$(3.278) \quad\quad R^2 = .0491$$

where *G* is 1960 employment/1950 employment, *L* is the percentage of employees in establishments with 250 or more employees, *D* is a dummy with a value of 1 if the product is durable, *M* is the percentage of the labor force that is male, and *Sk* is the percentage of production workers who are skilled (the number in occupations 401–545 as a percentage of the number in occupations 401– 985). All of these industry characteristics have significant effects on earnings except for the interaction term ($U \cdot CCR$) and the percentage skilled (*Sk*). All have the expected signs except durability. Taken by itself, durability is positively related to earnings, but it becomes negative when other industry variables are introduced. This is partly due to the relatively depressed conditions and the steel strike of 1959. Although the coefficients of *CCR* and *U* are both reduced, they remain statistically significant. Earnings now rise with either *CCR* or *U* over the entire observed range. Values of *Y* computed from this new equation are shown in Table 22.3 for the same illustrative values of *CCR* and *U* that were used in Table 22.2, assigning mean values to *G, L, M,* and *Sk* and zero to *D*. Taking other industry variables into account, unionization seems to add about 9 per cent to annual earnings when concentration is low and 4 per cent when it is high. Concentration adds 16 per cent to earnings when unions are weak, but 11 per cent when they are strong.

Thirty-one personal characteristics and three more industry characteristics are next added to form a third regression. The new industry characteristics are the white, rural, and Southern shares of the labor force. The sex and skill composition of the labor force are pure industry characteristics because only semiskilled males are in our population, but the white, rural, and Southern shares of the labor force include elements of personal as well as industry characteristics until the corresponding personal characteristics are introduced.

TABLE 22.3 VALUES OF *Y* IN NONDURABLE-GOODS INDUSTRIES USING CERTAIN VALUES OF *CCR* AND *U* AND MEAN VALUES FOR OTHER INDUSTRY CHARACTERISTICS

		Value of *U*	
		50	90
Value of *CCR*	20	4215	4576
	60	4869	5061

The third equation with descriptions of the new variables used is listed below:

$$Y = -156.2 + .2930 CCR + 6.167 U + .06872 U \cdot CCR$$
$$(623.9) \quad (8.195) \quad\quad (4.293) \quad\quad (.1110)$$
$$+ .6150 G + 2.622 L - 211.5 D + 6.192 M + 5.309 Sk \text{ plus} \quad (3)$$
$$(.8668) \quad (1.930) \quad\;\; (86.43) \quad (2.683) \quad\;\; (3.368)$$

1.952	Percentage of industry employees white with other than Spanish surnames (Variable 9)
(6.075)	
$-$3.937	Percentage of industry employees with residence outside SMSA's or urbanized areas (Variable 10)
(3.375)	
6.276	Percentage of industry employees in the South (Variable 11)
(2.957)	
$-$247.8	Dummy with a value of one if residence in the South (Variable 12)
(77.54)	
$-$483.6	Dummy with a value of one if residence outside SMSA or urbanized areas (Variable 13)
(70.54)	
$-$668.1	Dummy with a value of one if nonwhite, non-Negro, or if white with Spanish surname (Variable 14)
(185.80)	
$-$681.3	Dummy with a value of one if Negro (Variable 15)
(93.10)	
342.2	Dummy with a value of one if North Central residence (Variable 16)
(67.13)	
633.6	Dummy with a value of one if Western residence (Variable 17)
(96.53)	
$-$83.00	Dummy with a value of one if residence in a SMSA of less than 250,000 population (Variable 18)
(85.75)	
141.60	Age (Variable 19)
(13.19)	
$-$1.410	Age squared (Variable 20)
(.1609)	
$-$438.3	Dummy with a value of one if less than five years of schooling (Variable 21)
(146.2)	
$-$300.6	Dummy with a value of one if five to seven years of schooling (Variable 22)
(100.0)	
$-$285.5	Dummy with a value of one if eight to eleven years of schooling (Variable 23)
(68.57)	
165.0	Dummy with a value of one if one to three years of college (Variable 24)
(141.10)	
$-$65.02	Dummy with a value of one if presently in school (Variable 25)
(183.40)	
$-$1134.	Dummy with a value of one if not the principle source of support of the family (Variable 26)
(83.97)	
291.9	Family size (in numbers of persons) (Variable 27)
(46.22)	
$-$23.12	Family size squared (Variable 28)
(4.463)	
56.21	Dummy with a value of one if moved since 1955 from an urban county in the same or contiguous state (Variable 29)
(117.70)	
$-$441.5	Dummy with a value of one if moved since 1955 from an urban

(145.9)	county in another state that is not contiguous to present state of residence (Variable 30)
−223.4 (69.83)	Dummy with a value of one if moved since 1955 from a non-SMSA residence (Variable 31)
243.10 (70.32)	Dummy with a value of one if native born with at least one foreign born parent (Variable 32)
−392.2 (107.6)	Dummy with a value of one if worked 15–29 hours "last week" (usually in the first half of April, 1960) (Variable 33)
−214.0 (134.3)	Dummy with a value of one if worked 30–34 hours "last week" (Variable 34)
−35.10 (130.5)	Dummy with a value of one if worked 35–39 hours "last week" (Variable 35)
131.0 (70.27)	Dummy with a value of one if worked 41–48 hours "last week" (Variable 36)
349.8 (101.8)	Dummy with a value of one if worked 49–59 hours "last week" (Variable 37)
250.1 (133.6)	Dummy with a value of one if worked 60 or more (Variable 38)
−2095. (120.7)	Dummy with a value of one if worked 14–26 weeks in 1959 (Variable 39)
−1501. (91.62)	Dummy with a value of one if worked 27–39 weeks in 1959 (Variable 40)
−768.4 (80.15)	Dummy with a value of one if worked 40–47 weeks in 1959 (Variable 41)
−93.80 (95.34)	Dummy with a value of one if worked 48–50 weeks in 1959 (Variable 42)

$R^2 = .3421$

A large proportion of the personal characteristics are significantly related to Y, and many that are not have the expected signs and roughly the expected values (e.g., the time- and weeks-worked variables number 34, 35, 36, 38, and 42). A few of the coefficients have unexpected signs. One wonders why migration from distant cities should have a negative effect on earnings or why second-generation Americans should do better than those who are native-born of native parents. Perhaps the first reflects lack of seniority or incomplete knowledge of employment opportunities and the second is a partial proxy for prolonged urban residence. A more serious problem is that the line of causation between earnings and personal characteristics may be obscured. The positive effect of mobility from nearby urban residences may mean that more mobile persons have better opportunities or it may mean that the better paid more often moved to the suburbs during 1955–60. Again, the low earnings of persons who are not the main sources of support in their families may reflect a lower productivity of part-time workers, but a worker with very low earnings is apt to fall into this category almost by definition. However, when this regression was repeated with variables 26, 29, 30, and 32 excluded, the signs and statistical significance of the coefficients for the industry variables did not change.

Once the personal characteristics are introduced, the coefficients relating Y to U and CCR drop to nonsignificance. Table 22.4 shows estimated values of Y with the same values of CCR and U used in Tables 22.2 and 22.3, assigning zero to all dummy variables and mean values to all others. In other words, Table 22.4 illustrates the effects of concentration and unionization on the earn-

TABLE 22.4 COMPUTED VALUES OF Y WITH GIVEN VALUES OF CCR AND U ASSUMING ZERO VALUES FOR ALL DUMMY VARIABLES AND MEAN VALUES FOR ALL OTHER VARIABLES

		Values of U	
		50	90
Value of CCR	20	5165	5488
	60	5314	5747

ings of urban, white males with high school diplomas living in the Northeast who worked 51–52 weeks in 1959 and 40 hours in a nondurable-goods industry "last week" (April, 1960) and had mean values for age, family size, and the various industry characteristics. Concentration increases the earnings of such workers by only 3 to 5 per cent, and unionization increases their earnings by 6–8 per cent. When the same regression is run without the interaction variable ($U \cdot CCR$), a 40 point increase in U increases Y by 8 per cent and a 40 point increase in CCR increases Y by 5 per cent. The coefficient for U becomes highly significant ($t = 5.0$) when $U \cdot CCR$ is dropped, but the coefficient for CCR is barely so ($t = 2.1$). The implication seems to be that firms in concentrated industries do pay their employees more, but that they get higher "quality" labor in the bargain. The incomes won by unions for their members more clearly exceed what those workers would earn in their best alternative employments.

Most other industry characteristics drop to nonsignificance when personal characteristics are introduced, and two of the remaining significant coefficients have unexpected signs.[9] This is partly due to measurement errors. While concentration and important elements of union power are correctly measured on an industry-wide basis, employer size should ideally be measured on a personal basis, and employment growth on a SMSA-industry basis. However, the decline in the effect of industry characteristics as personal characteristics are introduced is consistent with labor market theory. Employers who, for any reasons, are in special positions which lead them to pay exceptional wages might be expected to get exceptional labor in the bargain.

The number of weeks and hours worked is understandably among the most important of personal characteristics in determining earnings. Leaving out all other personal characteristics, the equation becomes:

$$Y = 2736 + \text{variables 33–42}$$
$$(324.3)$$
$$+ 9.162 CCR + 8.961 U$$
$$(8.420) \quad\quad (4.411)$$
$$+ .04811 U \cdot CCR + 2.167 G \quad\quad (4)$$
$$(.1154) \quad\quad\quad (.8403)$$
$$+ 2.619 L - 261.6 D + 7.222 M$$
$$(1.771) \quad (76.23) \quad (2.567)$$
$$+ 8.551 Sk$$
$$(2.973) \quad\quad R^2 = .2203$$

The time variables reduce the effect of concentration, growth, employer size, and durability by about half compared with the equation (2) where only industry characteristics were used. The effects of unionization and the sex composition of the industrial labor force are roughly unchanged. The effects of concentration and unionization on earnings as other variables are introduced are summarized in Table 22.5. The time variables

---

[9] Perhaps the time and weeks worked as reported in the Census do not identify the full effect of 1959 unemployment on earnings in durable-goods industries, or it may be that the often-observed high earnings in durables are due wholly to the unionization, concentration, employer size, or skill and sex mix in those industries. Another regression using average hourly earnings (from *Employment and Earnings*) also yielded a significant negative effect of durability when other industry variables were considered.

TABLE 22.5 PERCENTAGE INCREASES IN ANNUAL EARNINGS WITH INDICATED INCREASES IN *CCR* AND *U* TAKING DIFFERENT VARIABLES INTO ACCOUNT

	Effect of Increase in CCR from 20 to 60		Effect of Increase in U from 50 to 90	
	if U is 50	if U is 90	if CCR is 20	if CCR is 60
Using Only *CCR* and *U*	3.4%	12.6%	15.9%	−2.2%
Using Other Industry Characteristics	15.5	10.6	8.6	3.9
Using Industry and Time Variables	10.0	10.7	8.6	9.3
Using Industry, Time, and Other Personal Variables	2.9	4.7	6.3	8.1

reduce the effect of concentration sharply but enhance the effect of unionization, if anything.[10]

Concentration has less effect on the price of labor than on total earnings. This implies that, even if the earnings of labor in concentrated industries do contain an element of monopoly rent, the allocative effect is small. High earnings due to more time worked do not mean misallocation of resources, as high wage rates uncompensated by superior "quality" of labor might. The effect of unionization on earnings, on the other hand, seems to operate through wage rates rather than time worked, implying that resource misallocation would occur to the extent that high earnings in unionized industries do not simply reflect personal characteristics.

Time variables are in part proxies for other personal variables. Table 22.6 shows the distribution of various personal and industry characteristics by the number of weeks worked in 1959. The persons with short periods of employment were younger, more poorly educated, more likely to be currently in school, more likely to live in the South or in rural areas, and the more likely to have recently moved from a rural residence or from a distant SMSA. They were particularly likely to work short hours and to be a secondary source of family income. They were employed more often in slowly growing industries with small plants. In other words, short-time employment was not distributed randomly. It was most noticeable among the less-desirable employees, and as a result, the effect of time variables on earnings is at least partially due to the "quality" of labor involved.

IV. Regression Results for Other Occupation-Sex Groups

The results spelled out in detail for male operatives in manufacturing, construction, and mining in Part III are similar to those found for some but not all of the other populations studied.[11] The coefficient for *CCR*

---

[10] The results of this analysis hold in spite of several possible revisions in the sample or the model. The effects of *CCR* and *U* are both significantly positive when taken by themselves or with an interaction term whether we (1) eliminate apprentices (occupations 601–630) from the sample; (2) eliminate construction and mining (industries 126–196) from the sample; and/or (3) use estimated average hourly earnings as the dependent variable. The introduction of industry characteristics weakens but usually does not remove the effect of *CCR* on earnings. The introduction of only a few personal characteristics (age, race, and Southern and rural residences) does eliminate the effect of concentration in most cases. On the other hand, these revisions enhance the effect of *U* even when all the personal characteristics in equation (4) are included. Coefficients for these alternative samples and income variables are shown in the appendix available from the author.

[11] Coefficients for *CCR*, *U*, and *U · CCR* for all occupations and industries studied are included in the statistical appendix which is available on request.

TABLE 22.6 CHARACTERISTICS OF MALE OPERATIVES AND KINDRED WORKERS BY NUMBER OF WEEKS WORKED IN 1959

Characteristic	Number of Weeks Worked in 1959									
	14–26 Weeks		27–39 Weeks		40–47 Weeks		48–50 Weeks		51–52 Weeks	
	No.	%	No.	%	No.	%	No.	%	No.	%
Southern Residence	89	29	135	27	159	25	107	27	835	25
Rural Residence	81	27	145	28	150	23	94	23	642	19
Negro	35	12	50	10	65	10	94	14	265	8
Moved from Distant SMSA since 1955	17	6	23	5	25	4	13	3	90	3
Moved from Non-SMSA since 1955	73	24	110	22	142	22	97	23	636	19
1–5 Yrs. of School	36	12	41	8	49	8	37	9	204	6
6–8 Yrs. of School	58	19	98	19	160	25	79	19	594	18
9–11 Yrs. of School	117	39	247	48	278	43	189	46	1560	47
12 Yrs. of School	63	21	100	20	130	20	94	23	812	24
Currently in School	35	12	22	4	13	2	2	—	43	1
Less Than 30 Hours Worked Last Week (April 1960)	111	37	104	20	65	10	35	8	65	2
Not Chief Income Recipient in Family	140	46	114	22	86	13	39	9	286	9
Employed in a Durable-Goods Industry	178	59	374	73	446	69	262	63	1911	58
Total Observations	301	100	510	100	642	100	415	100	3315	100
	Mean Values									
Age	34.5		37.4		39.1		39.2		39.8	
Family Size	3.9		3.9		3.9		3.8		3.9	
U	68		74		71		68		68	
CCR	38		40		41		39		40	
L	51		56		55		56		57	
G	117		114		117		123		130	

alone is always positive and almost always significantly so when no other variables are used. It remains positive in all cases except typists and retains its significance in most cases when U is introduced.

Table 22.7 summarizes the effects of concentration and unionization on Y when only $CCR, U, U \cdot CCR$ are used. The great majority of cases are consistent with the monopoly-wage hypothesis. The effects of CCR and U on Y are statistically significant for most male production workers. The only occupations that are unequivocally inconsistent with the monopoly-wage hypothesis are clerical workers when regulated industries are included,[12] and typists. In addition, female clerical workers in unregulated industries, female operatives, and draftsmen, all have substantial numbers of observations in ranges where CCR and U have negative marginal effects, and managers have a substantial number of observations in a range where U has a negative marginal effect. None of the coefficients that result in these equivocal cases is statistically significant.

The introduction of industry and personal characteristics changes the findings sharply

[12] This result is dominated by the large number of telephone operators included in female clerical workers in regulated industries.

Concentration and Labor Earnings 357

TABLE 22.7 OCCUPATIONS CLASSIFIED BY MARGINAL EFFECT OF *CCR* AND *U* ON *Y* DISREGARDING OTHER VARIABLES

	Range of U Where CCR Has Positive Marginal Effect on Y	Range of CCR Where U Has Positive Marginal Effect on Y
Cases that support the "monopoly wage" hypothesis:		
b_3 positive		
401–545, Craftsmen, Unregulated Industries	0–100*	0–100†
960–985, Laborers, Unregulated Industries	0–100	0–100†
301–370, Clerical, Unregulated Industries, Female	30–100	31–100
715, Truckdrivers	0–100	0–100
074, Draftsmen	32–100	34–100
775, Operatives, N.E.C., Female	47–100	18–100
b_3 negative		
601–775, Operatives, Unregulated Industries, Male	0–100*	0– 54†
601–775, Operatives, Regulated and Unregulated Industries, Male	0–100*	0–100†
401–545, Craftsmen, Regulated and Unregulated Industries	0–100*	0– 98†
960–985, Laborers, Regulated and Unregulated Industries	0–100*	0–100†
775, Operatives, N.E.C., Male	0– 92*	0– 67†
465, Machinists	0–100	0– 50
834, Janitors	0– 88	0– 82
985, Laborers, N.E.C.	0–100*	0– 81†
085, Mechanical Engineers	0–100	0–100
290, Managers	0–100	0– 42
Cases that conflict with the "monopoly wage" hypothesis:		
b_3 positive		
301–370, Clerical Workers, Regulated and Unregulated Industries, Female	66–100	12–100
360, Typists	78–100	0–100

* Coefficient of *CCR* more than twice its standard error.
† Coefficient of *U* more than twice its standard error.

once more.[13] Table 22.8 classifies occupations by their degree of support for the "monopoly wage" hypothesis when all these other variables are used. Concentration now has a negative marginal effect on earnings over some range for most occupations, and the over-all effect of concentration is negative in as many cases as it is positive. The effect of unionism is more consistently positive. The positive effect of concentration and unionization on earnings seems to hold up best in the case of "craftsmen," perhaps because of greater power of the union there.

[13] The same personal characteristics were used for each occupation as for operatives and kindred workers except that two more education dummies (for 4 years of college and 5 or more years of college) were introduced in the cases of "mechanical engineers" and "managers, officials, and proprietors, N.E.C."

358   Wage Differentials

TABLE 22.8 CLASSIFICATION OF OCCUPATIONS BY DIRECTION OF EFFECT OF CONCENTRATION ON EARNINGS WITH OTHER INDUSTRY AND PERSONAL VARIABLES TAKEN INTO ACCOUNT

	Range of U Where CCR has Positive Marginal Effect on Y	Range of CCR Where U has Positive Marginal Effect on Y
Cases that support the "monopoly wage" hypothesis		
b_3 positive:		
601–775, Operatives, Unregulated Industries, Male	0–100	0–100
401–545, Craftsmen, Unregulated Industries, Male	49–100*	0–100†
985, Laborers, N.E.C.	49–100	0–100
775, Female Operatives, N.E.C.	0–100	0–100
b_3 negative:		
401–454, Craftsmen, Regulated and Unregulated Industries, Male	0– 79*	0–100†
775, Male Operatives, N.E.C.	0– 76	0–100†
074, Draftsmen	0–100	0–100
465, Machinists, Unregulated Industries	0–100	—
Cases that conflict with "monopoly wage" hypothesis		
b_3 positive:		
601–775, Operatives, Regulated and Unregulated, Male	—*(neg)	0–100†
960–985, Laborers, Unregulated, Male	66–100	18–100
960–985, Laborers, Regulated and Unregulated, Male	93–100*(neg)	0–100
300–370, Clerical, Unregulated Industries, Female	58–100	45–100
300–370, Clerical, Regulated and Unregulated, Female	63–100*(neg)	43–100†(neg)
360, Typists, Unregulated Industries	65–100	0–100
b_3 negative:		
085, Mechanical Engineers, Unregulated Industries	—	—
290, Managers, Unregulated Industries	0– 10	0– 31
715, Truck and Tractor Drivers, Unregulated Industries	0– 1	0–100

* Coefficient of CCR is more than twice its standard error; "neg" if significant coefficient has negative sign.
† Coefficient of U is more than twice its standard error; "neg" if significant coefficient has negative sign.

One intriguing result is the *negative* effect of concentration and unionization on the incomes of female clerical workers. Their earnings are increased if both CCR and U are high, but concentrated nonunion industries or unconcentrated, unionized industries seem to pay low clerical incomes. The high CCR-low U industries are mainly rapidly growing "high brow" industries (drugs, professional equipment and supplies, office, computing and accounting machines, photographic equipment and supplies, and at the borderline, miscellaneous chemicals). A possible explanation is that these industries must (and can) pay high wages to keep their production workers from organizing, but they face little such threat with their female clerical workers. The high U-low CCR industries are such fields as construction, trucking, coal mining, and beverages. Unions in such industries often organize the major occupations involved on an interfirm basis. They may not be much concerned with the pay scale of clerical help outside their membership. Indeed, to the extent that they secure high wages for the male production workers they represent, they may actually depress the demand for and, therefore, the price of complementary services such as those of female clerical workers. These suggested reasons for the apparent "exploitation" of clerical help in certain industries is blatant after-the-fact reasoning. We make no claim to have tested this "exploitation" hypothesis as we have the monopoly-wage hypothesis.

V. Conclusions

This paper examined two forms of the monopoly-wage hypothesis: (1) that concentrated industries pay high incomes for given occupations, and (2) that these incomes exceed the alternative costs of the labor involved. The first hypothesis holds up well, as it has in previous studies. The relationship is strongest for male production workers where the threat of unionization is undoubtedly greatest. Moreover, the interaction between concentration and unionism most commonly has a negative effect for such workers. Both results give support to the notion that it is unionism or the threat of unionism that produces high wages in concentrated industries.

The second hypothesis should apparently be rejected. Once personal characteristics are introduced, the relationship between concentration and earnings is no longer significant and is negative about as often as it is positive. The monopolistic industries do get superior "quality" for the incomes they offer. Moreover, a substantial portion of the relationship between the earnings of labor in concentrated industries and their quality is due to a relationship of both variables with the number of weeks worked. The laborers in concentrated industries seem to receive no more for their services than they might in alternative employments for persons with similar personal characteristics. Their earnings contain little or no monopoly rent.

This does not necessarily imply that no misallocation results from high-wage payments in concentrated industries. Labor "quality" in this study includes such personal characteristics as race, which may be quite irrelevant to the objectively evaluated productivity of the laborer involved. It has been suggested that firms with monopoly power use part of their "profits" to hire congenial or socially acceptable employees [2], an option not available to employers subject to more stringent competitive pressures. If so, the earnings of labor in monopolistic industries may still exceed its marginal-revenue product, even though they apparently approximate the value of its alternative product.

The conclusion with respect to the effect of unionism on labor earnings is more equivocal than the results for concentration. The relationship between unionism and earnings does not decline greatly when personal characteristics are introduced for nonregulated industries. Unions that organize their entire jurisdictions seemed to raise earnings by 8 to 15 per cent for craftsmen[14] and 6 to 8 per cent for operatives, compared with poorly organized industries. The relationship between unionism and earnings is often nonsignificant after personal characteristics are introduced, but this may well be the result of measurement errors. U was certainly the most difficult variable to estimate in this study. It has been claimed that the BLS Industry Wage Surveys overstate the extent of contract coverage because small employers are underrepresented. If this is correct, some of the effect of differing de-

[14] Editors' Note: This paragraph was changed from the original at the author's request. See page 115 of the original article and *American Economic Review*, Vol. 58 (March 1968), pp. 174–184.

grees of unionization may actually be included in the coefficients for the establishment-size variable instead of the coefficients for the establishment-size variable instead of the coefficient for U. Finally, the only effect of unionism accounted for in this paper is its industry-wide impact. Differences within an industry between persons covered by collective bargaining contracts and those not covered had to be ignored. All of these considerations seem to point toward an understatement of the effect of unionism on earnings.

A possible case of misallocation due to the effects of concentration and unionism on earnings is the particularly low income of female clerical workers in concentrated *or* unionized industries (but not in concentrated *and* unionized industries). Some sort of "monopsonistic exploitation" hypothesis may apply here. Little can be claimed for this hypothesis, however, since, unlike the monopoly- and union-wage hypotheses, it was not developed in advance of the empirical study.

The effects of most industry characteristics are nonsignificant and often of unexpected signs after personal characteristics are introduced. In general, employers who for any reason pay high salaries receive "superior" labor in the bargain. The general picture is one of fairly efficiently working labor markets, even where substantial monopoly may exist.

All of the conclusions of this paper are necessarily tentative because the indexes of concentration used are imperfect, because industry definitions are arbitrary, because weights used in combining markets to match Census industries are arbitrary, and because the Census places some persons in the wrong industries. It might be argued that the nonsignificance of concentration as a factor in income determination once personal variables are introduced is due merely to measurement errors. On the other hand, the significant results before personal characteristics are introduced suggest that much of the effect of monopoly power has in fact been identified, and that at least this identified portion is almost entirely accounted for by personal characteristics. Moreover, a great number of personal characteristics could not be adequately measured, either. Such obviously pertinent variables as health, intelligence, appearance, strength, manual dexterity, sobriety, and responsibility could only be approximated by distant proxies such as age, sex, education, and family status if they were included at all. If the high-wage employers were as successful at hiring and retaining intelligent and responsible persons as they were in hiring educated ones, it would seem as likely that the residual effects of concentration are exaggerated in this study as that they have been missed.

References

1. M. ADELMAN, "Steel, Administered Prices, and Oligopolistic Inflation," *Quart. Jour. Econ.*, Feb. 1961, 75, 16–40.
2. A. A. ALCHIAN AND R. A. KESSEL, "Competition, Monopoly, and the Pursuit of Money," in *Aspects of Labor Economics*, Princeton 1960, pp. 70–81.
3. W. G. BOWEN, *Wage Behavior in the Postwar Period: An Empirical Analysis*. Princeton 1960.
4. BUREAU OF THE CENSUS, *U.S. Censuses of Population and Housing: 1960 1/1000 and 1/10,000, Two National Samples of the Population of the United States* (Processed).
5. O. ECKSTEIN AND G. FROMM, "Steel and the Postwar Inflation," Joint Economic Committee, *Study of Income, Employment, and Prices*, Study Paper No. 2, Washington 1959.
6. J. W. GARBARINO, "A Theory of Inter-Industry Wage Variation," *Quart. Jour. Econ.*, May 1950, 64, 299–305.
7. A. C. HARBERGER, "Monopoly and Resource Allocation," *Am. Econ. Rev., Proc.*, May 1954, 44, 77–87.
8. H. M. LEVINSON, "Postwar Movements in Prices and Wages in Manufacturing Industries," Joint Economic Committee,

Study of Income, Employment, and Prices, Study Paper No. 21, Washington 1960.
9. H. G. LEWIS, *Unionism and Relative Wages in the United States*. Chicago 1963.
10. M. REDER, "Wage Differentials, Theory and Measurement," in *Aspects of Labor Economics*, Princeton 1962, pp. 285–86 [Reading 20, pp. 281–309, in this text—Eds.].
11. A. REES, "Union Wage Gains and Enterprise Monopoly," in *Essays in Industrial Relations Research*, Institute of Labor and Industrial Relations, University of Michigan-Wayne State University 1961, pp. 125–39.
12. A. M. ROSS AND W. GOLDNER, "Forces Affecting the Inter-Industry Wage Structure," *Quart. Jour. Econ.*, May 1950, *64*, 254–81.
13. D. SCHWARTZMAN, "Monopoly and Wages," *Can. Jour. Econ.*, Aug. 1960, *25*, 428–38.
14. M. SEGAL, "The Relation Between Union Wage Impact and Market Structure," *Quart. Jour. Econ.*, Feb. 1964, *78*, 96–114.
15. S. H. SLICHTER, "Notes on the Structure of Wages," *Rev. Econ. Stat.*, Feb. 1950, *32*, 80–91.
16. G. STIGLER, "The Statistics of Monopoly and Merger," *Jour. Pol. Econ.*, Feb. 1956, 33–40.
17. L. W. WEISS, *Economics and American Industry*, New York 1961, pp. 506–7.
18. ———, "Average Concentration Ratios and Industry Performance," *Jour. Ind. Econ.*, July 1963, *11*, 240–41.
19. ———, "Business Pricing Policies and Inflation Reconsidered," *Jour. Pol. Econ.*, April 1966.

B. OCCUPATIONAL WAGE DIFFERENTIALS

23
Present Values of Lifetime Earnings for Different Occupations

Bruce W. Wilkinson[1]

In recent years there have been a number of attempts to use social rates-of-return to determine what has been the contribution of education to economic growth and what share of a nation's resources should in the future be devoted to education (see Schultz, 1963, and Hunt, 1964). The approach has been severely—and I believe correctly—criticized (Vaizey, 1958; Eckaus, 1964; and Wilkinson, 1965).

However, we should not be in haste to discard completely the use of rates-of-return or present discounted values in our analysis of economic-educational problems. *Private* rates-of-return or present discounted values as yet have not received the attention they deserve.[2] The purposes of this paper are, in fact, to examine discounted returns for several specific occupations and for various levels of educational attainment within these occupations and to review the meaning and significance of our observations.

Of particular interest is the suggestion that individuals may be responding to differences in expected net lifetime earnings, discounted at some common external rate, when selecting their occupations and when deciding upon the amount of education to acquire before entering an occupation. We find, for example, that discounted returns to various levels of education within jobs are roughly the same—which may mean that an equalization process has been occurring. We also find that the rising discounted returns to teachers relative to engineers may

---

Reprinted from the *Journal of Political Economy*, Vol. 74 (December 1966) by permission of The University of Chicago Press. Copyright, 1966, pp. 556–572.

[1] I am indebted to Professors Mary Jean Bowman, Richard S. Eckaus, Franklin M. Fisher, Harry G. Johnson, and Charles P. Kindleberger for valuable comments on earlier drafts of this paper. The deficiencies that remain, however, are entirely my own responsibiltiy.

[2] I do not claim originality for the suggestion that private present-value calculations may be important. Walsh (1935), Friedman and Kuznets (1954, pp. 84–87), and Blank and Stigler (1957, pp. 79–83) all employed such calculations in their analyses.

be at least partly responsible for the increasing enrolments in colleges of education relative to engineering colleges.

Wide variations in returns to given amounts of education still exist, however. These variations suggest the importance of such factors as diversity in ability, on-the-job and off-the-job training, market imperfections such as the lack of knowledge of opportunities, and tradition-based wage-salary scales; but they do not necessarily refute the hypothesis that individuals may be implicitly considering disparities in present values of lifetime incomes when choosing among occupations or when selecting the amount of education to obtain prior to entering an occupation. These arguments as well as one or two other items of interest will be developed in the subsequent discussion.

In the following section I shall briefly indicate why I use present discounted values in my subsequent calculations rather than rates-of-return. In Section II, I review the nature of the earnings data employed in most of the subsequent discussion. Section III is devoted to an examination of net present values of lifetime earnings for broad levels of education and, more important, for particular occupations and levels of education within these occupations. The final section considers variations in the relation between expected discounted returns for the two occupations of teacher and engineer over time and the apparent effect of these variations on enrolments in the college courses prescribed for these vocations.

I. Present Values

The superiority of the present-value rule over rates-of-return calculations has been demonstrated in other papers (see esp. Hirshliefer, 1958, and Feldstein and Flemming, 1964), so I need not enter into a detailed discussion of the reasons for my choice of this rule. It is worth mentioning, however, two or three advantages of the present-value approach that are of particular interest in this analysis.

First, if the rate-of-return approach is employed, then—where the *net* stream of revenues (after subtracting the one stream from the other) changes sign more than once—there can be as many rates-of-return as there are changes in sign of the revenue stream. The rate may also be imaginary under these circumstances. The possibility of more than one reversal in sign of the net revenues may be remote when one is dealing with two physical capital investments. But an examination of incomes of persons with varying amounts of education in different occupations indicates a number of cases where additional reversals do occur. The use of discounted values therefore precludes the complications that these changes may present.

Moreover, even if one and only one real solution were possible when there are a number of projects to be considered, it is much easier to calculate the present value of each project than it is to subtract one income stream from another and compute rates-of-return for *every* possible comparison of projects.[3]

Hansen (1963, pp. 137–40) apparently disregards these advantages of the present-value technique over the rate-of-return approach when he argues that the rate-of-return technique is superior. While he rightly criticizes Houthakker for not considering school and university costs of education when discounting, this is not a substantive criticism of the present-value technique itself. Only the mechanics of application are involved. Moreover, Hansen assumes that earnings foregone for persons with a grade 8 or less are zero. Since there is normally no tuition charge for such schooling and incidental costs are negligible, his procedure implies that rates-of-return on these levels of schooling are infinitely large; hence, the results have little meaning. If present values are used, this difficulty does not arise.

---

[3] Moreover, if, as in the present study, several discount rates are employed, *crude* rates-of-return can easily be imputed from the present-value calculations if desired. I do this at one or two junctures in the subsequent analysis.

364 Wage Differentials

TABLE 23.1 AVERAGE ANNUAL WAGE AND SALARY EARNINGS, AGE AND YEARS OF SCHOOLING COMPLETED, MALES, CANADA, 1961

Age	Years of Schooling Completed				
	Grade 5 to the End of Elementary	High School One to Two	High School Four	Some University	University Degree
15–19	$1,135	$1,193	$1,205	$ 722	—
20–24	2,195	2,654	2,943	2,007	$3,008
25–34	3,125	3,781	4,454	4,750	5,923
35–44	3,436	4,165	5,188	5,968	7,927
45–54	3,452	4,205	5,395	6,075	8,336
55–64	3,352	4,058	5,096	5,686	8,066
65–over	2,489	2,972	3,710	4,128	5,981

Source: Canada, Dominion Bureau of Statistics, 1963.

II. The Data

The basic earnings data for *all* occupations in Canada are presented in Table 23.1. They include all males who either had a job or looked for work during the week prior to the 1961 Canadian Census, minus those who never worked and those self-employed or receiving no income, such as unpaid family workers. Certain aspects of these figures warrant discussion.

1. The exclusion of self-employed workers, particularly professionals, may cause returns to higher education to be underestimated.

2. The Census category "university degree" does not permit us to distinguish between persons with a three-year degree beyond Grade 12 and those with two degrees or graduate training entailing as much as twenty or more years of schooling. I have assumed sixteen years of schooling for this group—which probably *underestimates* average training time and thus *overstates* returns to a university degree. Such overstatement may offset to a large extent, if not completely, any tendency for returns to university people to be understated because of neglecting self-employed professional people.

3. In the first, second, and fourth education categories shown, the earnings data refer to averages of more than one year's schooling. For the grouping "Grade 5 to the end of elementary school," Grade 8 is assumed; for "high school, one to two years," Grade 10; and for "some university," two years beyond Grade 12. The effect of my assumptions will be to underestimate the returns from Grade 8 and Grade 10 education (or, conversely, cause a relative overestimate of the returns to higher education), because the figures used include earnings of individuals with less education. The assumption that "some university" equals fourteen years of schooling should not, however, be far amiss. It implies that students drop out after their first or second year in a university depending upon whether they live in the provinces that require thirteen or only twelve years of schooling, respectively, before they may enter a university.[4]

4. The wage-salary figures cover earnings during the previous twelve months of all those who either possessed a job or looked for work during the week prior to the Census. The figures, therefore, already reflect unemployment rates without a special adjustment being required. That is, the earnings of many of those who worked only

[4] About one-half of the ten provinces require thirteen years schooling prior to university entrance. No detailed dropout data is available, but the Dominion Bureau of Statistics estimates that most students who leave university do so during or after their first two years.

a part of the year will be included in the average figures, thus lowering them. Only people who have dropped out of the labor force entirely because of repeated failure to obtain work are omitted. Paucity of information on such people makes adjustment for it impossible.

5. Even if the figures for all educational levels reflect unemployment, the earnings may be too low for persons with some university in the fifteen to nineteen or twenty to twenty-four age cohorts. For example, annual average earnings of students *still attending university,* from summer and part-time employment during the academic year, were $725 (Canada, Dominion Bureau of Statistics, Education Division, 1963; Wilkinson, 1964, Appendix VI, Table A). This is a little *more* than the earnings for persons aged fifteen to nineteen with some university shown in Table 23.1. One might at first think the low Census earnings for these recent university dropouts compared to earnings of high school graduates in the same age cohorts, as well as to earnings of earlier university dropouts (who are now in the age twenty-five and over groups), may reflect some recent, basic worsening in society's attitude toward, and hence in the pay offered to, such persons. However, the same type of phenomenon can be observed in the calculations for the United States in 1949 by Hansen (1963, Table 1, p. 130), so I do not consider this a likely explanation. Nor would it be correct to suggest that unemployment is especially serious for such persons. Unpublished data from the Dominion Bureau of Statistics indicates that unemployment rates are considerably lower for this group than for similar-aged persons with less education. It is conceivable that part of the explanation is that university dropouts adopt careers involving much general on-the-job training, which would reduce their initial net earnings.

Also, there is some evidence, at least for the United States, that the average ability of college dropouts is the same as, or a little lower than, the ability of high school graduates with no college; in addition, the ability range, both up and down, is less for the college dropout than for the man with four years high school (see, for example, Becker, 1964, Table 4, p. 80). If these facts hold true for Canada, too, the low earnings of recent university dropouts aged fifteen to twenty-four relative to high school graduates in the same age groups may be partially traceable to the lower ability or to the greater range of ability among university dropouts. If one wishes to use this argument, however, one must also hypothesize that after age twenty-four, when the income of the college dropout begins to exceed that of the high school graduate, the extra education or on-the-job training of the college dropout is more than sufficient to compensate for any lack of ability he may have relative to the high school graduate.

The most plausible explanation relates to the fact that the university academic year terminates at the end of April, whereas the Census was conducted May 31. Consequently, in many cases the Census would have recorded the summer and part-time earnings during the previous twelve months of continuing students who were either working or looking for work in the week prior to enumeration and who had worked before —thus lowering the average yearly income figures for the relevant age-education cohorts as well as the estimated net returns from some university education.[5] An upward adjustment has thus been made for those with some university in the fifteen to nineteen and

[5] Hansen (1963) ignores this fact in his analysis and concludes that the rate-of-return to some college education is extremely low. Yet, in the introduction to the data on which he bases his calculations, it states, "For men of college age, the relationship between income and education in less distinct than for men with other levels of education, possibly as a consequence of the fact that a large proportion of those in this age group who are enrolled in school have only part-time employment and therefore have relatively small earnings" (U.S. Department of Commerce, 1953, p. 11)

twenty to twenty-four age cohorts by considering their earnings as equal to the earnings of persons with four years of high school.[6]

6. The basic earnings data provide no indication of the extent to which the higher incomes of some of the people with additional education are due to their extra education or to such influences as parents' education, wealth, and positions; ability and motivation; and variations in the amounts of on-the-job and off-the-job training possessed by these people.

Since the above figures cover only wages and salaries and exclude other income such as interest or rents, a major portion (although not all) of the income that might result from family wealth and inheritance may already be eliminated.[7]

The significance of ability as a factor in determining whether a person finishes a particular level of schooling, and therefore the returns to different academic attainments, has been examined in several studies. Results have varied. Becker (1965, pp. 79–88 and 124–27) estimated that the rate-of-return on a college education for 1939 and 1949 in the United States would be reduced about 12 per cent by adjustments for ability and that for a high school education the return would be lowered somewhat more. Employing some of the same data Becker used, Denison (1964, pp. 86–100) found support for his original assumption that about 60 per cent of the crude percentage differential in earnings between levels of formal schooling was a result of education. Hunt (1964) considered a number of other factors in addition to ability, only to find returns to education rising or remaining roughly the same rather than *falling* as one would expect would occur when the effects of these other income determinants were excluded.

These results suggest that ability may have some importance but that the extent of its influence is still much in doubt. I shall make no fresh effort to isolate its effects. But I shall have more to say about its influence as well as the influence of several other factors when I come to discuss the implications of the observed similarities and differences in present discounted returns for different levels of education within and between occupations.

7. Finally, the data cover incomes at the Census date for persons of each age group at a given education level, not the actual lifetime earnings of these persons. I shall assume that these cross-section figures provide a reasonable approximation of the lifetime earnings that may be expected by an individual entering the labor force with a specified amount of education.[8]

The private costs of obtaining education consist of earnings foregone, tuition and incidental costs of schooling (dues, books, and transportation to school other than of a local nature), less summer and part-time earnings.

For university students, the average tuition in 1961 was $400, while incidental costs were about $150—making a total of $550. However, summer and part-time earnings averaged $725 (Canada, Dominion Bureau of Statistics, Education Division, 1963; Wilkinson, 1964, Appendix VI, Table A). Thus,

---

[6] The average earnings of those aged twenty to twenty-four with a university degree may also be understated to some extent because a number of these persons will have just graduated in May. Consequently, their income over the previous twelve months will include only earnings in May plus income from part-time work during the academic year or from employment the previous summer. I have not made any attempt to adjust for this possibility, but one should keep it in mind when interpreting the results.

[7] For an interesting study of the monetary value of parents' education for childrens' earnings, see Swift and Weisbrod (1965).

[8] Becker (1965, p. 73) adjusted his cross-section data for the secular growth in earnings per capita by assuming two annual rates of growth in the differential between college and high school earnings: 0.0125 and 0.02. Since these rates are, of necessity, largely speculative, there seemed little value in adopting this technique for the present study.

on balance, these items yielded a *net return* to the university student.

Information is not available on incidental high school costs or summer and part-time earnings of high school students, so it will be assumed that they are equal. In any event, the sums involved would not be large and would be unlikely to affect materially the results which are rounded to the closest thousand dollars.

Earnings foregone need not be subtracted explicitly. Since I shall be discounting all earnings to age fourteen (the age when young people are presumed to have completed Grade 8), the opportunity costs of those remaining in school are already considered; their incomes from regular (not summer and part-time) employment are set at zero, while those persons of the same age already in the labor force are receiving positive income.[9]

Three discount rates are employed—5, 8, and 10 per cent—to reflect three possible rates of time preference that individuals may have as well as different investment opportunities that may be open to them. For example, 5 per cent is roughly the rate on long-term Government of Canada bonds; 8 per cent is close to the estimated *average* rate-of-return (defined as the ratio of after-tax profits to capital) for U.S. manufacturing industries (Stigler, 1963, Table 10). Personal rates of time preference for some young people may be even higher than the 10 per cent figure used. As the study by Ginzberg, Ginsberg, Axelrod, and Jerma (1963, p. 134) has pointed out, "Money assumes so central a position in the scheme of values [of young people] as to overshadow education."[10] Thus, the rates employed can only be considered approximations.

In making the present-value calculations, both earnings and cost figures were reduced to account for mortality.[11] To arrive at net earnings *after* income tax, average tax payments in 1961 for each income group were subtracted from income adjusted for mortality.[12] Retirement age was assumed to be 65; even if it were a few years beyond this age, the lengthy discount period on earnings received after sixty-five would mean that the configuration of total present-value figures would be little affected.[13]

III. Discounted Returns for Different Levels of Education and Various Occupations

In Table 23.2, net present values of lifetime earnings for different levels of general education are presented.

At a 5 per cent discount rate, additional education yields greater present values in every case, although between four years high school and some university the difference is small relative to the disparity among other consecutive levels of education. At 8 and 10 per cent, dollar variations in discounted net earnings among levels of schooling are, as one would expect, considerably smaller than at 5 per cent, and from four years high

---

[9] Space limitations prohibit a fuller discussion of the point; see Wilkinson (1964, pp. 238–40).

[10] If the interest rates charged on personal loans are any indication of what individuals' rates of time preference are, a much higher discount rate may be realistic in some cases; for example, studies by the U.S. Federal Reserve System (1957, pp. 50–60) show that the charges for personal loans range from 12 per cent to 28 per cent.

[11] The Canadian Life Table for 1965 was employed to compute the number of survivors at each age assuming there were 100,000 persons at age fourteen. Canada, Dominion Bureau of Statistics, Health and Welfare Division (1963, p. 228). To arrive at expected earnings for a person at a particular age, the observed income at that age was multiplied by the number of estimated survivors taken as a percentage of 100,000.

[12] Average tax rates used were for 1960 (paid in 1961) as shown in Canada, Dominion Bureau of Statistics, Handbook and Library Division 1962 Table 17, p. 1040). As will be seen below, present values *before* income tax were also computed for a number of individual occupations.

[13] For example, the discounted returns at age fourteen of the difference between earnings of someone aged sixty-six with Grades 5–8 and someone of the same age with a university degree is only about $275 using a 5 per cent discount rate, $64 at 8 per cent, and less than $20 at 10 per cent.

TABLE 23.2 PRIVATE NET PRESENT VALUES, AFTER INCOME TAX, AT AGE FOURTEEN, FOR DIFFERENT LEVELS OF EDUCATION, ALL OCCUPATIONS, MALES, 1961

Level of Education	Present Discounted Values (Thousands of Dollars)		
	At 5 Per Cent	At 8 Per Cent	At 10 Per Cent
No high school	$42.7	$26.3	$20.2
Some high school (two years)	49.0	29.3	22.1
Four years high school	56.1	33.3	23.7
Some university (two years)	58.2	32.7	23.4
University degree (four years)	68.8	36.7	25.4

school to some university there is even a slight decline.

Not only absolute dollar inequalities but also relative inequalities in discounted returns diminish as the interest rate rises. For example, the returns to a university degree are only 25.7 per cent greater than the net returns to no high school when the 10 per cent discount rate is employed, whereas they are 61.9 per cent greater at the 5 per cent rate.

It is evident, then, that if a sufficiently high discount rate were used, the discounted returns to a university education would be no greater than returns on an elementary school background. Knowing this, it is tempting to hypothesize that individuals who achieve only the lower levels of education have discount rates considerably higher than 10 per cent (probably reflecting high marginal rates of time preference), so that for them the net present values of earnings from such education are equal to the present value of earnings from a university training.[14] There is no doubt an element of truth in

this idea (particularly, as I shall indicate below, with respect to the implied conjecture that individuals are responding to divergences in present value of lifetime earnings, discounted at some specific external rate, in their choice of which level of schooling to obtain). But the grouping together of all occupations tends to exclude a number of other phenomena that warrant consideration and tends to oversimplify the problem of interpreting the observed variations in discounted returns to different levels of education.

Consider, then, net present values for various amounts of schooling within several specific occupational categories. The same source of data was used as for Table 23.2, and the qualifications offered earlier with respect to the data again apply. Table 23.3 shows net returns, at age fourteen, after income tax, for six occupations and for three levels of education within each occupation.[15]

[14] This statement contains the implicit assumption that *marginal* returns on education would be at least roughly similar to the average returns calculated from the Census figures. Obviously, the marginal returns govern, not the average.

[15] See Table 23.5 for returns to the same occupations and educational levels calculated *before* income tax deductions. When we consider the possibility of individuals responding to differences in discounted returns in choosing the amounts and types of education to obtain, there is some evidence to suggest that the return before income tax is the more relevant measure; see Grubel and Edwards (1964). These authors concluded from a survey of the reasons students have for entering particular occupations that income tax was not an important consideration. However, as a comparison of the tables for returns before and after income tax will indicate, there is little difference between the two methods of computation in the resulting pattern of returns. (In fact, only for carpenters with four years high school at 8 per cent discount rate, draftsmen with four years high school at 5 per cent, and technicians with a university degree at 5 per cent is there *any* variation in the pattern.) Consequently, our discussion would not be altered significantly regardless of which table we use.

It should also be noted that we are interested in considering only net private returns to people from various levels and types of education, not social returns. If social returns were our concern, earnings before tax would definitely have to be used, and we would then have to include all public expenditure for formal education and eliminate tuition fees to arrive at the unduplicated total of social costs of education.

TABLE 23.3 PRIVATE NET PRESENT VALUES, AFTER INCOME TAX, AT AGE FOURTEEN, FOR DIFFERENT LEVELS OF EDUCATION, SELECTED OCCUPATIONS, MALES, 1961

Occupation and Level of Education	Present Discounted Values (Thousands of Dollars)		
	At 5 Per Cent	At 8 Per Cent	At 10 Per Cent
Laborers:			
No high school	$33.3	$20.8	$16.1
Some high school	36.2	22.7	16.9
Four years high school	36.4	21.7	16.2
Carpenters:			
No high school	41.1	26.1	20.5
Some high school	42.7	26.4	20.3
Four years high school	44.3	25.1	19.9
Compositors and typesetters:			
No high school	57.6	35.4	27.2
Some high school	60.1	36.3	27.5
Four years high school	57.2	33.4	24.7
Draftsmen:			
No high school	59.3	36.5	28.2
Some high school	60.5	36.6	27.8
Four years high school	57.2	34.9	25.8
Science and engineering technicians:			
Four years high school	60.8	35.9	26.7
Some university	56.8	32.3	23.4
University degree	56.7	30.8	21.6
Engineers:			
Four years high school	72.5	41.6	30.6
Some university	71.8	40.1	28.7
University degree	76.5	40.8	28.3

First, let us examine returns *within* occupations. At any one discount rate there exists a rough similarity of discounted net earnings for persons with varying amounts of education. In only two instances are inequalities in returns between any two levels of education, within one occupation, at a given rate of discount, greater than 10 per cent. Both of these exceptions occur with respect to science and engineering technicians at the 10 per cent external rate. In three other instances, differences in returns to varying education levels seem particularly small at all three discount rates: between laborers with some high school and four years high school, between carpenters with no high school and some high school, and between draftsmen with no high school and some high school.

These crude similarities in discounted returns within occupations at any one external rate may be accounted for in two ways.[16] First of all, we know that, if two income streams lie close together through most of their range, then, at discount rates such as those used in this study, the present values of the two streams, at any single rate, will be quite similar.[17] Second, if one or more of the external rates employed are very close to the internal rate-of-return (which equates to zero the differences in net revenue streams between two levels of schooling), then the discrepancies in the present-value figures at these external rates will be small.

Consider these two possible "explanations" for the case of laborers. The present value of four years high school is greater than some high school at 5 per cent but less than some high school at 8 per cent. Obviously, then, the internal rate between four years high school and some high school for

[16] Several comments by Mary Jean Bowman were very helpful at this juncture.
[17] At lower external rates, the present values of the two streams being compared will show a considerably greater dollar discrepancy than any discrepancy we observe in Table 23.3. But even in these cases the *relative* divergence in the present values of the two streams will not be unlike the relative differences in Table 23.3. As an illustration, consider the divergence in net discounted lifetime earnings of laborers with no high school and laborers with some high school, when a zero external rate is used. The discrepancy in "discounted" returns (which in this case would equal the algebraic sum of the divergencies between the two streams through their range) is about $9,500. Although in absolute terms this amount perhaps seems large, in relative terms the figure is still slightly less than 10 per cent of the total value of the lifetime earnings of laborers with no high school.

laborers lies somewhere between these two external rates and is apparently much closer to the lower one. The similarity in present values between the two levels of schooling at 5 and 8 per cent, especially at 5 per cent, may therefore be attributed in part to these external rates not being far from the internal rate. Also, the original earnings data suggest that some of the correspondence in present values at these two rates may be attributed to the closeness of the income streams for persons with these two amounts of schooling. The rough agreement of returns at the 10 per cent rate would have to be "explained" primarily by the closeness of income streams rather than because of this rate of discount being near the internal rate.

Similar discussions might be developed for comparisons between the other education levels in the laboring group and between education categories in other occupations as well, although varying degrees of emphasis would have to be placed on the two ways of accounting for the crude conformities of present values.[18]

Up to this juncture I have said nothing about the forces that may cause the income streams for varying amounts of schooling, within occupations, to be alike. This is not the place to enter into a detailed discussion of the many determinants of income similarities (or differentials) within occupations, but two broad statements might be made. First, it is clear that the similarities in returns to diverse amounts of schooling may be due in part to employers making only minor distinctions in the pay given to workers within occupations who have different amounts of education. Second, adjustments on the supply side by workers themselves may cause income streams for varying amounts of education to be close through their entire range.

Let me elaborate somewhat on this second statement. Suppose young people who are planning to become carpenters decide on the amount of education to obtain according to which level of schooling appears to offer the highest present value of lifetime earnings, discounted at some common rate such as 8 per cent. If, then, the returns, discounted at 8 per cent, to carpenters with some high school are greater than returns to carpenters with no high school, we should expect more of the young people entering carpentry to acquire some high school rather than entering the occupation with only public school education. That is, the supply curve of carpenters with some high school would shift to the right—thus competing down wages or salaries for this group and hence net returns.[19]

If 8 per cent were the common external rate that all individuals were using in evaluating diverse investments in education, then, in general, the effect of this type of behavior by people (ignoring other complications for a moment) would be that returns at the margin, for different amounts of schooling, within occupations, would be equalized. Moreover, this process would tend to cause

[18] In a like manner, we might "explain" the closeness of discounted returns to people of all occupations with four years high school and some university that was evident in Table 23.2. First, we may observe from Table 23.1 that the income streams for persons in these two educational levels are generally closer together than are the streams of any two other levels of schooling. (Remember, also, that before discounting I adjusted upward the incomes of those in the fifteen to nineteen and twenty to twenty-four age cohorts with some university to equal the incomes of those with four years high school in these age groups. Hence, the two streams would be even closer together than Table 23.1 indicates.) In addition, the 5 and 8 per cent external rates are quite close to the internal rate on the investment in some university as compared to four years high school. This internal rate lies somewhere between 5 and 8 per cent. (This is apparent from the fact that at the 5 per cent discount rate some university has a higher present value than four years high school, whereas at the 8 per cent rate four years high school gives the greatest discounted returns.) In contrast, the internal rate between any two other amounts of schooling lies somewhere above 10 per cent.

[19] It is beyond my purpose in this paper to develop the detailed characteristics of the supply curve or the adjustment mechanism. It is sufficient to note that the supply curve would be a function of net lifetime earnings discounted at the 8 per cent external rate, not of current income.

the income streams for the different levels of schooling within an occupation to be close to one another. Hence, at other rates of discount, such as the 5 and 10 per cent rates used in Table 23.3, there would be crude similarities in discounted returns—as we in fact observe to be the case.[20]

[20] Several assumptions are implicit in the above discussion. First, I have assumed that employers do pay different wages or salaries to workers according to the educational attainment of the workers. If employers made *no* distinction and paid all workers in an occupation the same amount regardless of their schooling, then automatically the individual with the least education in any one job would have the highest expected net present value of lifetime earnings—at whatever positive discount rate was chosen—simply because his costs of schooling would be less, yet his expected returns would be the same as for those with more education. In addition, under these circumstances, movements of persons within an occupation from one education category to another (assuming no change in the total number of persons in that occupation) would have no effect upon discounted returns to a given amount of education. Second, I have assumed that employers' demand curves for each education level are less than perfectly elastic. If perfect elasticity prevailed, then of course changes in the supply of workers with a particular amount of education would have no effect upon the values of discounted earnings to different amounts of schooling. Third, I am again assuming that the marginal returns on education would be roughly comparable to the average returns presented in this paper.

Note also that the analysis has been phrased entirely in terms of the response of young people deciding whether to continue school or enter the labor force for the first time. A more complete discussion would entail consideration of the possible response of differences in returns, discounted at the assumed 8 per cent interest rate, of older persons already in the labor force. Present values associated with diverse levels of education would differ from those shown in Table 23.3 depending upon the age of the worker and whether he resolves to obtain more education by enrolling in night classes or correspondence courses (in which case the major cost item—earnings foregone—would be zero) or by quitting work to do so. The response of older workers to differences in returns discounted at the 8 per cent rate is likely, however, to be less complete simply because learning new material becomes more difficult as one grows older and because a man with family commitments may lack the time and/or financial resources to obtain additional education.

There are, of course, a number of influences that would normally prevent perfect adjustment from occurring. Individuals may lack knowledge of opportunities for persons with varying amounts of education (see Stigler, 1962). In addition, because the decisions whether to leave school are highly individualistic, there will undoubtedly be some overshooting or undershooting in the numbers entering each education category. Moreover, the changing demands of the marketplace will lead to differences in returns at any point in time. In some cases, lack of funds may prevent persons from obtaining more education. Consequently, the observed discrepancies in the earnings from diverse amounts of education within occupations, discounted at 8 per cent, could conceivably be attributed to these complicating factors.

It is perhaps worth emphasizing at this juncture that the foregoing analysis is highly speculative. One can say no more than that the observed results are not incompatible with the hypothesis that individuals may be choosing between more and less education before entering a particular job by a technique of implicitly discounting expected lifetime earnings at some common external rate, such as the 8 per cent figure used above. Certainly, the data do not prove this hypothesis.[21]

[21] There is one shred of evidence, however, that suggests that, if people are using some common rate of discount in choosing between education levels, this rate is probably less than 10 per cent. Hence, the 8 per cent figure I used in the above discussion may not be far wrong. Consider the following argument. If individuals were using some external rate *in excess of* 10 per cent, then, if adjustment were complete and we applied a lower rate (such as 10 per cent) to the stream of returns for each level of education within an occupation, we should expect to find discounted returns to persons with the most education within an occupation to be greater than the discounted returns to those with less education. (This should occur because the effect of using a rate lower than the one that equalizes present values at the margin is to assign a greater weight to the larger returns which the higher level of schooling yields once the individual finishes his education.) However, it does not occur in any occupation except for laborers with some high school compared with

Another interesting observation about returns to different amounts of education *within* occupations is that it is by no means always true that additional education, even for a single job, will result in higher discounted earnings, as Miller (1964, pp. 141–48) states is the case. For example, four years high school is not a worthwhile investment for either laborers or carpenters if their discount rates are either 8 or 10 per cent. With respect to compositors and typesetters, four years high school is not profitable even at a 5 per cent rate of discount. A similar pattern prevails for draftsmen, although even some high school is not profitable if the discount rate is 10 per cent. For technicians, neither a university degree nor some university is a good investment; returns are highest at each discount rate for people with four years high school. For engineers, a university degree is clearly worthwhile if the discount rate is 5 per cent, but not if it is 8 or 10 per cent.

Of course, in some cases (engineers, for example) a certain level of general education is becoming almost a necessity—like a union card—so that individuals may have to achieve this level if they intend to enter that occupation. Moreover, the formal school system may be a much quicker way of achieving a particular level of skill than other methods of training. But still this does not deny that additional formal education may not yield higher discounted values from the individual's viewpoint.

So far we have considered only returns to various amounts of education within occupations. When we compare discounted earnings for given levels of formal education for *different* occupations, we find significant variations in several cases. At each discount rate, for instance, discounted earnings from four years high school for an engineer are about double what a laborer with this education receives. Even carpenters receive several thousand dollars more than laborers with identical amounts of formal schooling.

These wide discrepancies existing among net present values in different occupations seem to suggest that, even if people are responding to discrepancies in expected future earnings for diverse amounts of education *within* occupations, discounted at some rate such as 8 per cent, they certainly are not doing so in choosing between occupations. If they were, *and if no other influences were involved,* then there should have been movements of workers from the lower-paying occupations to the higher paying ones, raising wages (and hence discounted returns) in the former and competing down wages (and hence discounted returns) in the latter. However, there are a number of other influences involved, so that our static comparison of returns among occupations neither "proves" nor "disproves" the idea that individuals may be behaving as though they are looking at net anticipated earnings streams, discounted at 8 per cent, when selecting their occupation. Let us examine a number of these factors.

The very nature of the occupations listed in Table 23.3 suggests that inequalities in the amounts of on-the-job training or off-the-job training such as may be obtained from technical schools, correspondence courses, evening courses, or private study may be important in accounting for the observed disparities in discounted returns. That is, the higher returns of carpenters, for example, compared to laborers with the

---

laborers having no high school, and compositors in the same two education categories. In contrast, if the common external rate that people are using is *less than* 10 per cent, then, if adjustment were complete and we applied a 10 per cent discount rate to the lifetime earnings of two education levels within an occupation, we should expect to find the lower level of schooling to have a higher discounted value than the higher amount of schooling—simply because the higher rate reduces the weight assigned to the higher incomes received by those with more schooling in their later working years. This is, in fact, what occurs between each consecutive pair of levels of education for four of the occupations (engineers, technicians, draftsmen, and carpenters), and in the other two occupations (laborers and compositors) between workers with some high school and workers with four years high school. I am indebted to Professor Harry Johnson for a comment which suggested this line of argument.

same level of general schooling may reflect additional training that carpenters receive outside the formal school system. And the still greater returns of engineers with Grade 12 compared to carpenters with Grade 12 may reflect the greater amounts of on- and off-the-job training engineers obtain.

This seems to contradict the finding of Mincer (1962, p. 59) that the workers with more formal schooling are also the ones who obtain the most additional training. The amount of training appears to depend more upon the occupation one enters than on the level of education one achieves. However, Mincer's conclusion is broadly correct in that workers in the occupations with the higher discounted returns do, on the average, possess more formal schooling than do workers in the jobs with low discounted earnings.[22] Hence, if we look at just the *average* education levels in each occupation, it holds true that greater on- and off-the-job training is associated with greater amounts of formal schooling (assuming the amount of this training is accurately reflected by the differences in returns).

It is clear that something more must be introduced at this juncture if we are to explain why even those with less than the average amount of education in a particular occupation receive more training than persons with identical formal schooling in other occupations. The suggestion is that variations in ability are important. The 4 per cent of all recorded engineers with only Grade 12 may have been more intelligent than laborers with Grade 12 and, hence, were able to learn more from twelve years in school than were those who are now laborers. Or their greater ability (which might well be interpreted broadly to include such traits as ambition and perseverance as well) may show itself by enabling them to absorb on-the-job or off-the-job training and providing the motivation for them to do so.

There is as yet no satisfactory way to separate the effect of ability from that of general education and training or to determine the extent to which ability differences control the amount of self-study or on-the-job training one undertakes.[23] We have to be content with the weak statement that ability inequalities may be largely responsible for the wide differences in returns to given levels of education either directly or through their influence on the amount of training men receive after leaving school.[24]

Several other factors may account in part for the observed discrepancies in returns to given levels of education among occupations. First, when unemployment rates are high, as they were in 1960–61, it is well known that those in the lower-skill-cohorts generally experience unemployment rates

---

[22] To illustrate, for both the engineering and laboring jobs those with Grade 12 comprised only 4 per cent of the total men in each job. But 72 per cent of the engineers had a university degree, whereas 51 per cent of the laborers possessed only five to eight years schooling.

[23] See my earlier discussion of attempts to isolate the effects of ability. Becker (1962, pp. 30–37; 1964, pp. 37–48) has devised a method of estimating the total costs of on-the-job training, and Mincer (1962) used this approach to compute training costs in the United States for 1939, 1949, and 1958. But the technique requires the assumption that the rate-of-return on such training is the same as the rate on the additional formal schooling possessed by the individual involved. Consequently, although Mincer's attempt at estimating such costs is interesting, the assumption upon which it is based clearly leaves the results open to much question. Off-the-job-training costs would be even more difficult to estimate. However, if it is correct that the most important cost item for on-the-job training is earnings foregone, then off-the-job training (with no foregone earnings) would involve next to zero costs, and hence the returns to such training would likely be much higher than returns to training on the job.

[24] It should be noted, however, that if ability differences are important this does not mean that the higher returns in some jobs reflect a *shortage* of potentially able persons. Rather, it may suggest a lack of persons with their abilities fully developed. Studies by Dael Wolfe and others indicate that even in a society like United States, where a higher proportion of young people attend university than anywhere else in the world, there still appears to be a significant reserve of potential intellectual talent that might be developed, given the appropriate environment; see Halsey (1961, esp. pp. 49–65 and 137–75).

much higher than the average rates. The lower net discounted returns in the lower-skill-groups, therefore, undoubtedly reflect to some extent the higher unemployment of these groups.[25]

Second, lack of knowledge regarding opportunities in those occupations with the higher discounted returns may have reduced the flow of young people into them and thereby prevented the wage-salary levels in these occupations from being competed down. Perhaps tradition-based wage-salary scales and variations in the bargaining power of the different occupational groups may also account for some inequalities of returns.

Some might also wish to argue that for the majority of the labor force there are non-pecuniary disadvantages associated with the higher-paying occupations that are compensated for by the additional earnings. This seems questionable—at least for the jobs under review here. Where the discounted returns are highest, working conditions on the whole are normally more agreeable. Moreover, there is some empirical evidence to suggest that even workers in occupations where net discounted returns are low would prefer those jobs where returns were higher.[26] The concept of "compensating differences" consequently does not appear to be an appropriate explanation of the variations in present values from a given level of education in the jobs in Table 23.3.

In summary, discounted values of earnings from diverse amounts of education within occupations appear to be relatively small at all three discount rates employed. The smallness of the differences indicates that one or more of these external rates are close to the internal rate-of-return and/or that the income streams are similar through their range. The similarity of income streams may be due in part to adjustments therein resulting from individuals employing some common rate of discount, such as 8 per cent, and deciding upon the amount of education to obtain according to the present value of the income streams associated with the different amounts of education. The greater inequalities in returns among occupations suggest that variations in ability, on- and off-the-job training, knowledge regarding opportunities in the jobs with larger returns, unemployment rates for persons of different skill levels, and perhaps variations in bargaining power or tradition-based wage-salary scales are important in determining these returns. Also, the data indicate that additional education, even within occupations, does not always pay.

IV. Changes in Discounted Returns to Teachers and Engineers in Relation to Changes in College Enrolments

So far, in discussing the possibility that individuals may be considering present values of lifetime earnings, discounted at some common external rate, when selecting their occupation and education level, I have used only data for one point of time. A thorough test of the significance of this possibility would involve relating total changes in the numbers in various occupations, and education levels within occupations (excluding changes due to death and retirement), to changes over time in present values of earnings, discounted at the "appropriate" external rate, for these occupations and education levels. While the paucity of data makes a detailed study of this type impossi-

---

[25] A related possibility, although one difficult to verify precisely, is that demand conditions may have been changing so rapidly in favor of the jobs requiring higher levels of skill that the supplies of such workers lagged behind. Hence, returns to such persons would rise.

[26] In a study by Canada, Department of Labour, workers from five occupations—electronic technicians, draftsmen, sheet-metal workers, tool- and die-makers, and floor-molders—were asked to rank these occupations as well as professional engineering, punch-press operation, and office work in terms of preference for themselves, prestige, and occupation desired for their sons. The career of professional engineer almost invariably was ranked first on all three factors; electronic technicians followed, with drafting third. Sheet-metal work and tool- and die-making generally were next, while punch-press work, floor-molding, and office work were regarded as unattractive. Another more extensive study that produced similar results is that by Blishen (1958).

ble, there is some information available that permits rough calculations to be made for two professions—teaching and engineering.

Thus, in Table 23.4 I show present values of lifetime incomes at 5, 8, and 10 per cent rates of discount, for 1957 (the first year for which annual engineering earnings are available) and 1961, along with university enrolments in these two faculties for both years. The method of calculation is the same as for Tables 23.2 and 23.3, except that discounting has been done to age seventeen —when the decision on which faculty to enter at university must generally be made— rather than to age fourteen.

Accompanying the sizable increase in teachers' discounted earnings between 1957 and 1961 (17 per cent at a 5 per cent rate of discount and 19.7 per cent at both the 8 and 10 per cent discount rates—in constant 1957 dollars) was a 133 per cent expansion of the enrolment in education. In contrast, there was a rise of only about 4 to 5 per cent in discounted returns for engineers and a meager 3.8 per cent increase in enrolment. An alternative way to make this comparison is to say that, while discounted returns to teachers rose from about 65 per cent of engineers' earnings in 1957 to 72 per cent in 1961, university enrolment in education rose from 24 per cent to 54 per cent of engineering enrolment.

Part of the increased enrolment in education may be due to the following: (1) the increasing numbers of women attending university frequently favor education, (2) teacher-training has been shifted from teachers' colleges to the university campus and such colleges have been incorporated in education faculties, and (3) the increasing numbers of students attending university may choose education because it is easier to finance than engineering: a person can take one or two years of training, then commence teaching and obtain the balance of his university education at summer school or by correspondence courses designed for this purpose.

But even if we assume that *three-quarters* of the increased enrolment of students in

TABLE 23.4 PRESENT DISCOUNTED VALUES OF LIFETIME INCOMES, AT AGE SEVENTEEN, AND UNIVERSITY ENROLMENTS, TEACHERS AND ENGINEERS, 1957 AND 1961*

	Enrolment (N)	Thousands of Current Dollars			Thousands of Constant 1957 Dollars		
		At 5 Per Cent	At 8 Per Cent	At 10 Per Cent	At 5 Per Cent	At 8 Per Cent	At 10 Per Cent
			Teachers				
1957–58	3,406	$67.5	$40.7	$30.9	$67.5	$40.7	$30.9
1961–62	7,941	84.1	51.6	39.2	79.3	48.7	37.0
Increase	4,535	$16.6	$10.9	$ 8.3	$11.8	$ 8.0	$ 6.1
Percentage Increase	133.1	24.6	26.8	26.9	17.5	19.7	19.7
			Engineers				
1957–58	14,096	$106.5	$64.3	$48.3	$106.5	$64.3	$48.3
1961–62	14,611	117.6	71.1	53.6	110.9	67.1	50.6
Increase	535	$ 11.1	$ 6.8	$ 5.3	$ 4.4	$ 2.8	$ 2.3
Percentage Increase	3.8	10.4	10.6	10.9	4.1	4.3	4.7

* Since the cost-revenue statistics on teachers excluded Ontario and Quebec, the enrolment data have been adjusted to omit these two provinces as well. Enrolments for teachers are for the education faculty alone; no attempt has been made to estimate the numbers of arts and science students who also plan to enter the teaching profession.
Source: Wilkinson (1964, Appendix VI, Tables H–K).

TABLE 23.5 PRIVATE NET PRESENT VALUES, BEFORE INCOME TAX, AT AGE FOURTEEN, FOR SELECTED OCCUPATIONS, AT DIFFERENT LEVELS OF EDUCATION, MALES, 1961

Occupation and Level of Education	Present Discounted Values (Thousands of Dollars)		
	At 5 Per Cent	At 8 Per Cent	At 10 Per Cent
Laborers:			
No high school	$35.0	$21.7	$16.8
Some high school	38.2	23.4	17.8
Four years high school	38.6	22.9	17.1
Carpenters:			
No high school	43.3	27.5	21.5
Some high school	45.3	27.9	21.4
Four years high school	47.2	28.2	21.1
Compositors and typesetters:			
No high school	62.6	37.7	28.9
Some high school	64.6	38.9	29.0
Four years high school	61.8	36.0	26.5
Draftsmen:			
No high school	63.4	39.0	30.0
Some high school	65.0	39.1	29.8
Four years high school	64.6	37.6	27.7
Science and engineering technicians:			
Four years high school	65.9	38.8	28.8
Some university	61.4	34.9	25.3
University degree	61.7	33.5	23.5
Engineers:			
Four years high school	79.5	45.6	33.3
Some university	79.2	44.1	31.5
University degree	85.6	45.5	31.4

education is a result of these influences, there would still be a 33 per cent increase in enrolment in education associated with about 19 per cent real rise in net discounted lifetime earnings. The data suggest, in a crude way, that the net present value of lifetime income in diverse occupations, although undoubtedly calculated only roughly or implicitly (at some external rate people deem appropriate), may be important in persons' occupational selections.

It is not important whether present values of net earnings for different occupations (or even levels of education within occupations) are ever precisely equalized at some particular interest rate. Influences such as ability differences, on- and off-the-job training, market imperfections, and rapid changes in demand for various types of workers would generally prevent complete equalization from occurring. Of much greater significance is the *tendency* for individuals to move into jobs or educational levels where, according to the discount rate they are using, the net present values of earnings are the largest.

Much more work must be done to either confirm or refute the conjectures outlined in the foregoing analysis. If they prove to be correct, a number of significant implications for labor market policy and educational policy will follow therefrom. But to discuss these here would be outside the scope of this paper.

References

Becker, G. "Investment in Human Capital: A Theoretical Analysis," *J.P.E.*, LXX, Suppl. (October, 1962), 9–49.

———. *Human Capital. A Theoretical and Empirical Analysis with Special Reference to Education.* New York: National Bureau of Economic Research, 1964.

Blank, D. M., and Stigler, G. J. *The Demand and Supply of Scientific Personnel.* New York: National Bureau of Economic Research, 1957.

Blishen, B. H. "The Construction and Use of an Occupational Class Scale," *Canadian J. Econ. and Polit. Sci.*, XXIV (November, 1958), 519–531.

Canada, Department of Labour, Economics and Research Branch. *Acquisition of Skills.* Ottawa: Queen's Printer, 1960.

Canada, Dominion Bureau of Statistics, Census Division. Unpublished data from 1961 Census of Canada. Ottawa: Dominion Bureau of Statistics, 1963.

Canada, Dominion Bureau of Statistics, Education Division. *University Student Expenditure and Income in Canada, 1961–62,* Part II: *Canadian Undergraduate Students.* Ottawa: Queen's Printer, 1963.

Canada, Dominion Bureau of Statistics, Handbook and Library Division. *Canada Year Book 1962.* Ottawa: Queen's Printer, 1962.

Canada, Dominion Bureau of Statistics, Health and Welfare Division. *Vital Statistics, 1961.* Ottawa: Queen's Printer, 1963.

Denison, E. F. "Measuring the Contribution of Education (and the Residual) to Economic Growth: Appendix," *The Residual Factor and Economic Growth.* Paris: Organization for Economic Cooperation and Development, Study Group in the Economics of Education, 1964.

Eckaus, R. S. "Investment Criteria for Education and Training," *Rev. Econ. and Statis.,* XLVI (May, 1964), 181–90.

Feldstein, M. S., and Flemming, J. S. "The Problems of Time-Stream Evaluation: Present Value Versus Internal Rate of Return Values," *Bull. Econ. and Statis.,* XXVI (1964), 79–85.

Friedman, M., and Kuznets, S. *Income from Independent Professional Practice.* New York: National Bureau of Economic Research, 1954.

Ginzberg, E., Ginsburg, S. W., Axelrod, S., and Herma, J. L. *Occupational Choice: An Approach to a General Theory.* New York: Columbia Univ. Press, 1963.

Grubel, H. G., and Edwards, D. R. "Personal Income Taxation and Choice of Professions," *Q.J.E.,* LXXVIII (February, 1964), 158–63.

Halsey, A. H. (ed.). *Ability and Educational Opportunity.* Paris: Organization for Economic Cooperation and Development, 1961.

Hansen, Lee, "Total and Private Returns to Investment in Schooling," *J.P.E.,* LXXI (April, 1963), 128–40.

Hirshleifer, J. "On the Theory of the Optimal Investment Decision," *J.P.E.,* LXVI (August, 1958), 329–352.

Hunt, S. J. *Income Determinants for College Graduates and the Return to Education Investment.* New Haven, Conn.: Yale Univ. Economic Growth Center, 1964.

Miller, Herman. *Rich Man, Poor Man.* New York: Thomas Y. Crowell Co., 1964.

Mincer, Jacob. "On-the-Job Training: Costs, Returns, and Some Implications," *J.P.E.,* LXX, Suppl. (October, 1962), 50–79 [Reading 15 in this text—Eds.].

Schultz, T. W. *The Economic Value of Education.* New York: Columbia Univ. Press, 1963.

Stigler, G. J. "Information in the Labor Market," *J.P.E.,* LXX, Suppl. (October, 1962), 94–105 [Reading 16 in this text —Eds.].

———. *Capital and Rates of Return in Manufacturing Industries.* Princeton, N.J.: National Bureau of Economic Research, 1963.

Swift, W. J., and Weisbrod, B. A. "On the Monetary Value of Education's Intergeneration Effects," *J.P.E.,* LXXIII (December, 1965), 643–49.

U.S. Department of Commerce, Bureau of the Census. *1950 United States Census of Population, Special Report.* "Education." (P.E. No. 5-B.) Washington: Government Printing Office, 1953.

U.S. Federal Reserve System, Board of Governors. *Consumer Installment Credit,* Vol. I, Part I: "Growth and Import." Washington: Government Printing Office, 1957.

Vaizey, John. *The Economics of Education.* London: Allen & Unwin, 1958.

Walsh, J. R. "Capital Concept Applied to Man," *Q.J.E.,* XLIX (February, 1935), 255–85.

Wilkinson, B. W. "Some Economic Aspects of Education in Canada." Ph.D. dissertation, Mass. Inst. of Tech., 1964.

———. *Studies in the Economics of Education.* (Department of Labour, Economics and Research Branch, Occasional Paper No. 4.) Ottawa: Queen's Printer, 1965.

24
Training Lags and the Cobweb Pattern in Engineering

Richard B. Freeman

1. The Time Structure of Supply Response

"The supply of labor in a trade in any generation tends to conform," observed Marshall, "to its earnings not in that but in the preceding generation."[1] There are two reasons for this: (1) the years of training and education required for specialized work and (2) the time needed to learn about and adjust to new conditions. Delays of the former kind, *training lags*, operate on the supply side only and give the market for high-level manpower a *recursive* structure, with supply ordinarily lagging demand.[2] Delays of the second type, or *information-decision* lags, affect both suppliers and employers.

Training Lags

The training lag for most high-level jobs is set by the period of production in the university system and, for institutional technical reasons, is well specified by the educational process. Bachelor's training, for example, usually takes four years, with the sciences and engineering requiring the entire period in the major, and social sciences or humanities just two years. Professional training in law, medicine, or business also have definite periods of production, ranging from two to four years. Only in the doctorate program, where many students spend more than four or five years, is there noticeable variation in the length of training.

© Copyright 1971 by the President and Fellows of Harvard College. From Richard B. Freeman, *The Market for College-Trained Manpower* (Cambridge, Mass.: Harvard University Press, 1971).

[1] A. Marshall, *Principles of Economics* (New York: Macmillan, 1920), p. 571.

[2] This assumes that the information-decision lag in demand is equal or less than that in supply. A priori, equality seems to be the most realistic assumption. The only plausible argument for different-sized lags is that suppliers respond to wages that already reflect employer responsiveness. However, as long as suppliers react to nonwage information as well as to wages, there need be no difference in the lag pattern. There is, at any rate, no indication that the supply response is so rapid as to balance the training lag.

Under some circumstances the lead time needed to train specialists exceeds the college delay. College students, after all, must have appropriate high school preparation before they undertake a college major.[3] However, because the educational system is shaped like a pyramid, with the bulk of students at lower levels of training, most adjustments in supply do *not* require changes in precollege training. Even in the sciences the number of students with strong high school training far exceeds the number in college programs. For example, if just an additional 1 percent of the high school students taking math in their senior year shifted into the college major, the output of B.S.s in mathematics would increase by *one-third*.[4] Thus, the college delay is an appropriate measure of the lag between the decision to supply specialized labor and actual supply.

The pipeline of production in the university system also facilitates adjustment with a minimum lead time. In fields with cumulative rigorous training—engineering, premedicine, science—many freshmen or sophomores with indefinite career plans enroll to preserve the *option* of choosing the specialties. If the decisions of these students to continue in a program are influenced by market incentive, the number of graduates can be altered without changing the number of enrollees. Similar adjustments in the behavior of graduate students "with all but the dissertation" permit flexibility in doctorate production. Thus, for limited periods of time the "effective training lag" may be shorter than the period of formal study. The steeper the pyramid of training, the more flexible are decisions to change majors and the shorter the adjustment delay.

Information-Decision Lags

Information-decision lags are complex phenomena whose extent is difficult to determine a priori. It seems reasonable, however, that they will be greater the greater the *random variation* of wages or employment in a market, the greater the *economic resources* committed by a decision, and the greater the *nonprofit* motive of enterprises. In the first case, variability confuses permanent developments with transitory ones, making it wise to wait for additional facts before reacting to change. In the second instance, the dollar value of resources affects the time devoted to search by increasing the payoff in obtaining correct information.[5] And finally, the absence of clear economic signals and goals probably makes nonprofit enterprises slower to respond to market developments than profit-maximizing firms.

Short-Run Adjustments

In addition to changes in the supply of new entrants there are several other mechanisms by which the labor market adjusts to new conditions. These relatively short-run mechanisms allow for greater flexibility and smaller lags in the market than are depicted in models of career choice. Some of the principal short-run mechanisms are

1. Alterations in hours worked: this mechanism is especially important in professions where teaching is frequent, since university faculty have summers free and spend relatively few hours in the classroom.
2. Alterations in labor participation: retirement decisions and the work decisions of marginally committed women offer a way of expanding or contracting the work force in the short run.
3. Allocation of time: by a shift in the amount of time devoted to different work activities, such as research, teaching, or

---

[3] The need for precollege training of scientists and engineers is stressed in A. Alchian, K. Arrow, and W. Capron. *An Economic Analysis of the Market for Scientists and Engineers* (Rand: Santa Monica, 1958), pp. 85–86.

[4] In 1961–1962, 572,000 students took mathematics courses in their senior year of high school. First degrees in mathematics in 1964 were awarded to 19,000 people.

[5] See G. Stigler, "The Economics of Information," *Journal of Political Economy*, Vol. 69 (June 1961), pp. 213–225.

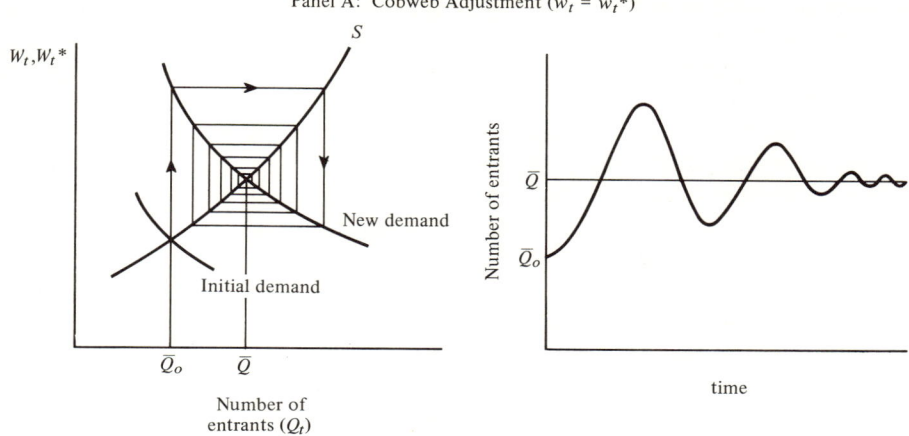

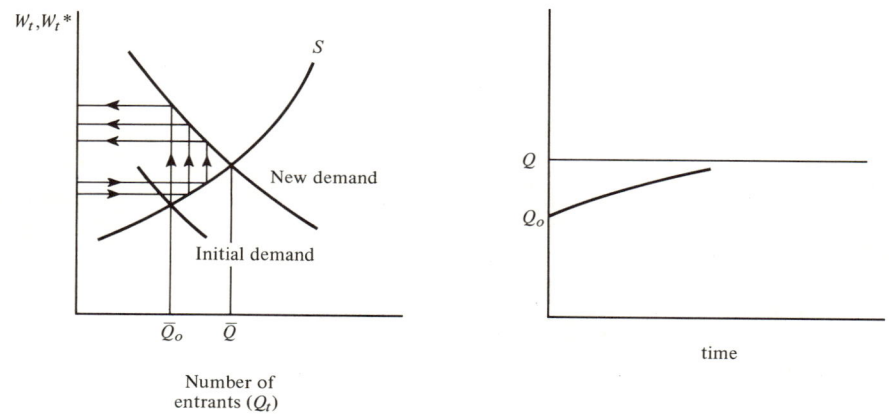

FIGURE 24.1 Adjustment of New Entrants

administration, the man-hours in specific activities may be increased or decreased.
4. Occupational mobility: mobility may occur among related specialties (physiology and zoology, for example) or between managerial and professional work.
5. Alteration of job context: by adding or subtracting tasks, employers can change the skills required for a job to make best use of the available work force.
6. Training older workers: since older workers often pick up additional skills, on-the-job training or retraining may upgrade the work force more quickly than training the young.
7. Substitution among skill classes or between labor and capital: the degree to which this adjustment mechanism can be used depends on technical production possibilities.

Equilibrium Conditions and Disequilibrium Adjustment

Labor market equilibrium occurs when the stock of workers remains fixed over time,[6] for example, when the flow of new entrants equals the outflow from deprecia-

---

[6] Equilibrium can also be defined as *steady-state* growth, in which all variables increase at a proportionate rate. There is no conceptual advantage to this formulation.

tion. When this condition is satisfied, expected and actual wages are equal in all time periods, so that no cohort has the incentive to change supply.

The model generates two adjustment paths to equilibrium: a *cobweb* path, in which variables oscillate toward equilibrium, and an *incomplete adjustment* path, in which they approach equilibrium but fail to attain it for several periods of time. Figure 24.1 depicts the paths in the market for new entrants: Figure 24.1(a) is the usual cobweb diagram, in which an initial shift in demand raises wages, leading to additional entrants and an ensuing reduction in wages; over time, wages and the number of entrants move toward the $(\bar{E}, \bar{W})$ point; Figure 24.1(b) shows incomplete adjustment, with the increased wage having a modest impact on expectations and supply and with disequilibrium continuing for several periods.

2. The Cobweb Model in B.S. Engineering

The cobweb variant of the basic labor market model can be used to explain postwar developments in the largest scientific profession, engineering. Engineers prepare for work through formal college programs leading to a degree or through a combination of on-the-job training and nondegree courses in technical institutes, junior colleges, and correspondence or special schools. The college-trained specialists constitute over half the profession, earn 15 to 30 percent more than nondegree engineers of the same age, and account for about 60 percent of the engineering wage bill. Nondegree specialists also prepare for work by *formal study* in educational institutions. The majority spend one to three years taking academic courses, supplemented with considerable on-the-job training and work experience.

The cobweb model used to explain developments in the engineering market is specified in equations (1)–(3) below. To reduce problems of multicollinearity, the equations are in first (logarithmic) difference form.

Supply of freshman engineers:

$$\Delta \ln ENR_t = a_0 \Delta \ln FRSH_t \\ + a_1 \Delta \ln ESAL_t - a_2 \Delta \ln PSAL_t \\ + a_3 \Delta \ln VET_t \\ - a_4 \ln(ENR/FRSH)_{t-1}. \quad (1)$$

Supply of graduates:

$$\Delta \ln GRD_{t+4} = b_0 \Delta \ln ENR_t \\ + b_1 \Delta \ln(ESAL_{t+2} + ESAL_{t+1}) \\ - b_2 \Delta \ln(PSAL_{t+2} + PSAL_{t+1}) \\ + b_3 \Delta \ln CVET_{t+4} \\ - b_4 \ln(ENR/FRSH_t). \quad (2)$$

Salary determination:

$$\Delta \ln ESAL_t = -c_0 \Delta \ln GRD_t \\ + c_1 \Delta \ln RD_t + c_2 \Delta \ln DUR_t \quad (3)$$

where

ENR_t = number of first-year enrollments in B.S. engineering programs throughout the United States.

$FRSH_t$ = number of male freshmen enrolling in four year educational institutions.

$ESAL_t$ = starting salaries of B.S. engineers.

$PSAL_t$ = annual earnings of professional workers.

GRD_t = number of engineers graduating with B.S. degrees.

$(ENR/FRSH)_t$ = proportion of the freshman class enrolled in engineering.

VET_t = number of veterans enrolled as freshmen.

$CVET_t$ = number of veterans enrolled as sophomores or upperclassmen.

RD_t = annual expenditure for research and development.

DUR_t = output in durable goods industries.

The endogenous variables are *ENR, GRD,* and *ESAL.*

The Supply Relations

The model contains two supply equations, one determining the number of freshmen enrolling in the major, the other the number of enrollees graduating four years later. For empirical convenience, the theory of occupational choice is simplified in both cases. First, the incentive of engineering is measured by starting salaries, not by discounted lifetime incomes. As long as age-earning curves are relatively stable over time this simplification causes no problem, for with stable curves initial salaries are good indicators of lifetime opportunities. In support of the overall validity of the assumption, a recent study of engineers found that "large differentials in the starting salaries of different specialties play a major role in maintaining the long-term rank order of salaries associated with specialties."[7] Second, alternatives to engineering are represented by annual male professional earnings—a plausible but crude measure of the opportunities facing potential engineers. This measure is dictated by the absence of annual salary statistics for college men, a major gap in manpower information. Third, the lag structure in both supply equations is simple: in equation (1) only current salaries affect the initial enrollment decision (that is, expected income equals current income, $W_t^* = W_t$); in equation (2), salaries prevailing during the student's freshman-sophomore years taken together influence the decision to complete the program. The former specification is relaxed in empirical calculations. The latter is justified by the fact that most field switching occurs prior to the junior year.[8]

The remaining supply variables specify the population of prospective engineers. In equation (1), the number of male freshmen is chosen as the relevant population of first-year engineering students because almost all American engineers are male.[9] If the model is properly specified, the coefficient in this term will be unity in regression calculations. The next variable, the number of veterans enrolled in college, is designed to test a hypothesis advanced by the Committee for the Analysis of Engineering Enrollment that the pattern of demobilization is the main cause of fluctuations in enrollment. Demobilization is important because of an alleged special propensity of veterans for the engineering major.[10] The last variable in equation (1), the proportion of freshmen in engineering in the preceding year, is expected to reduce the rate of growth. There are three reasons for this: first, large classes reduce future job opportunities and thus deter some from engineering; second, the capacity of engineering schools may be strained by substantial enrollment; third, supply elasticity is expected to decline as an increasingly large fraction of a cohort choose a field.

In equation (2), the population variables are the number of initial enrollees in engineering, and the number of veterans with premilitary college training,[11] and the percentage of freshmen choosing engineering. The number of veterans is introduced to catch the distorted enrollment-graduation sequence of students who interrupt college for military service. The percentage of freshman choosing the field is expected to reduce the rate of graduation because large classes

---

[7] Albert Shapero, "Government R and D Contracting," in *Factors in the Transfer of Technology*, ed. W. H. Gruber and D. G. Marquis (Cambridge: MIT Press, 1969), p. 198.

[8] Note that specifying equal coefficients on freshman and sophomore salaries has the desirable effect of reducing the terms to changes in salaries over a two-year period (that is, $\ln[ESAL_{t+2}] - \ln[ESAL_{t+3}]$).

[9] This specification ignores the possibility that some potential engineering students decide against college when they reject engineering.

[10] The "veterans" hypothesis is developed in the report of the Committee for the Analysis of Engineering Enrollment, American Society for Engineering Education, *Factors Influencing Engineering Enrollment* (Washington: ASEE, 1965).

[11] According to the Veterans Administration, a large number of veterans in college have previous experience in institutions of higher education. In the 1948–1966 period, one in four enrolled veterans reported one-to-three years of premilitary college training.

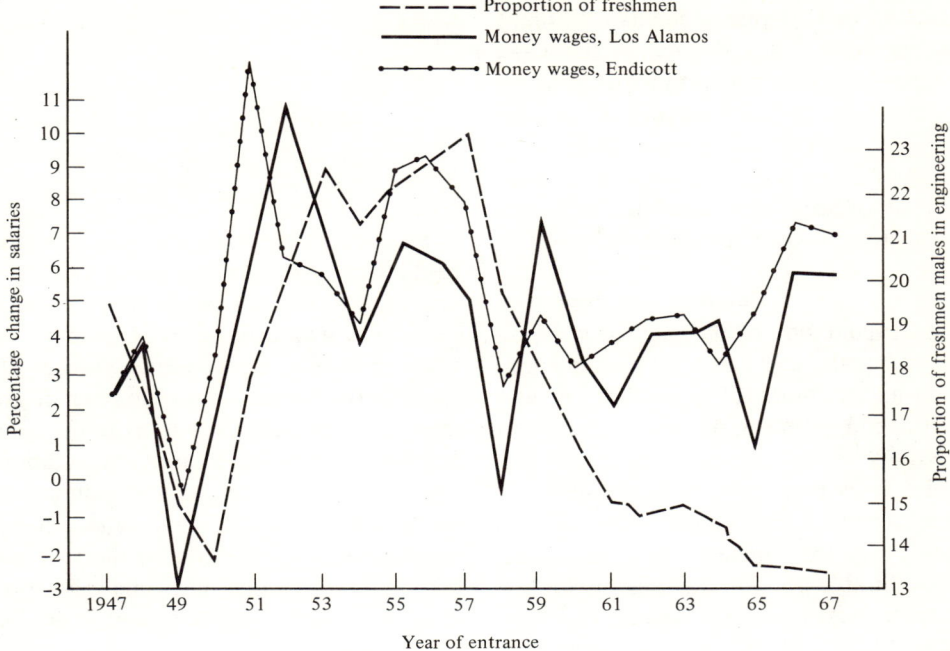

FIGURE 24.2 Proportion of Freshmen in Engineering and Changes in Engineering Salaries, 1947–1967

are likely to contain many less qualified persons.

The supply behavior to be explained by the equations is depicted in Figures 24.2 and 24.3. Figure 24.2 shows that the fraction of male freshmen choosing engineering varied greatly in postwar years, jumping from 14 percent in 1950, for example, to 24 percent in 1957 and back to 14 percent five years later. Underlying the fluctuations is enormous variability in the rate of growth of engineering enrollment, which has a coefficient of variation of 13.2 compared to a coefficient of just 2.1 for the rate of change of all male freshmen. Figure 24.2 also indicates that changes in the fraction of freshmen in engineering are closely related to changes in engineering starting salaries, suggesting an economic explanation of the fluctuations. Correlation analysis provides further evidence of economic behavior, revealing an extremely close connection between *changes* in enrollment and *changes* in engineering starting salaries. ($r = 0.71$, where the 1 percent significance level is 0.55).[12]

Figure 24.3 shows a similar variability in

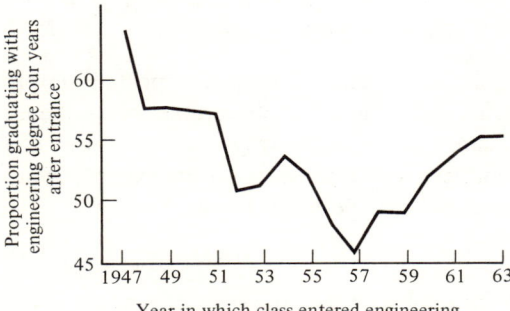

FIGURE 24.3 Proportion of Engineering Freshmen Graduating Four Years Later, 1947–1963

[12] The correlation here is greater than that between changes in enrollment and changes in the size of the student population ($r = 0.59$), indicating a larger effect for economic than for demographic factors in determining the number of future engineers.

the fraction of first-year students eventually graduating with a B.S. degree. In this case, the proportion of a class completing a degree program ranges from 65 percent of the men entering in 1947 to 45 percent of those in the class of 1957. The attrition rate in engineering is clearly not constant, as often assumed in manpower projections.

Demand for Engineers

The demand side of the market is represented in equation (3) as a relation between salaries and number of graduates, R & D spending, and output in durable manufacturing. Salary is the appropriate dependent variable since the number of graduates is predetermined by past supply decisions. The R & D activity of engineers and the importance of durable goods industries in employment motivates these explanatory variables.

Equation (3) suffers from one weakness. By relating salaries to current period variables only, it implicitly assumes that the market is cleared in every recruitment period. In a market that is not a continuous bourse with perfect information or recontracting this is an unrealistic assumption. To allow for a slower adjustment of salaries to market conditions, the equation is modified by a two-step procedure.

First, salaries are assumed to depend on the *initial salary* plans of firms as well as on the current state of the market. According to the Endicott survey of engineer employing firms, many large enterprises plan their salary offers in the winter preceding the spring recruitment period,[13] presumably on the basis of expected market conditions. The observed market salary is thus a weighted average of initial plans and the market-clearing, or equilibrium, salary, with the weight dependent on the speed with which firms adjust to unexpected conditions:

$$\ln ESAL = (1-w)\ln ESAL^p \\ + w\ln ESAL^e \quad (4)$$

[13] See any of the reports by F. S. Endicott on salaries entitled *Trends in the Employment of College and University Graduates* (Evanston: Northwestern University, 1949–69).

where

$ESAL$ = actual salary
$ESAL^p$ = planned salary
$ESAL^e$ = equilibrium salary
w = adjustment coefficient $(0 \leq w \leq 1)$.

Second, planned salaries are assumed to result from the intersection of the demand curve and an *expected supply function*. Firms are aware of their demand for engineers but may misconstrue future supply because of changes in the number of graduates and demand elsewhere in the market. Whenever firms have faulty expectations of the supply of engineers, their planned salary will deviate from the equilibrium set by the intersection of demand with the true supply schedule. Equations (5) and (6) present the postulated planned and equilibrium salary equations:

$$\ln ESAL^p = -c_o\ln GRD^p \\ + \text{Demand shift variables} \quad (5)$$

where

GRD^p = planned or expected supply,

and

$$\ln ESAL^e = -c_o\ln GRD \\ + \text{Demand shift variables.} \quad (6)$$

Substituting (5) and (6) into equation (4) yields a relation for actual salaries

$$\ln ESAL \\ = -wc_o\ln GRD - (1-w)c_o\ln GRD^p \\ + \text{Demand shift variables.} \quad (7)$$

To complete the model, expected supply must be related to observable phenomena. There are several ways to do this. The simplest is to assume that firms expect supply to equal last period's supply:

$$GRD_t^p = GRD_{t-1}. \quad (8)$$

Figure 24.4 depicts the operation of the market in this case. Figure 24.4(a) shows the adjustment of a firm to an exogenous increase in demand. The firm plans its salary offer on the basis of the new demand curve and the previous (that is, expected) supply

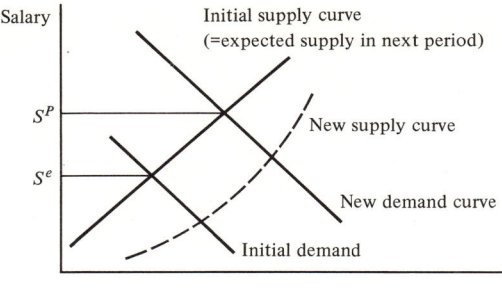

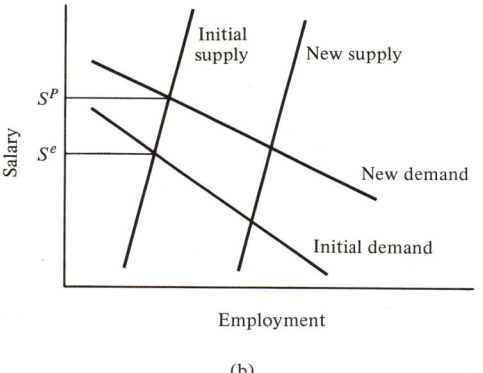

FIGURE 24.4 Lagged Adjustment of Salaries to Shifts in Supply When Firms Expect Supply to Equal Last Period's

schedule, leading to planned salaries in excess of equilibrium and actual salaries between the two extremes. In Figure 24.4(b) adjustment in the entire market is illustrated. Since aggregate supply is predetermined, the actual salary-employment point lies to the right of the demand curve, producing a surplus of engineers.

A more complex theory of expected supply allows firms to extrapolate past changes into the future:

$$\ln GRD_{t-1}^p = \ln GRD_{t-1} \\ + \ln(GRD_{t-1}/GRD_{t-2}) \\ = 2(\ln GRD_{t-1}) - \ln GRD_{t-2}. \quad (9)$$

Finally, if firms take account of past errors in expected supply, we obtain a third approximation to the formation of salary plans:

$$\ln GRD_t^p = 2(\ln GRD_{t-1}) \\ - \ln GRD_{t-2} \\ + c\ln(GRD_{t-1}/GRD_{t-2}^p) \quad (10)$$

or substituting and simplifying

$$\ln GRD_t^p = (2+c)\ln GRD_{t+1} \\ - (1+2c)\ln GRD_{t-2} \\ - c\ln GRD_{t-1}$$

where $c =$ correction coefficient.

When equations (8), (9), or (10) are entered into the salary equation, the result is a testable relation between salaries and current and lagged supply. The coefficients on the lagged supply terms are linear transformations of the structural parameter. Overidentification permits an internal check on the consistency of the postulated structure.

Empirical evidence regarding the salary determination process is presented in Table 24.1. The significant correlation of salaries with R & D spending and durable goods output and between salaries and current and *lagged* numbers of graduates suggest that the modified salary equation is a reasonable representation of market phenomena. The absence of lags between demand-shift variables and salaries supports the hypothesis that lagged salary determination is due primarily to slow adjustment to unexpected supply conditions.

3. Supply of B.S. Engineers

Since the cobweb model is recursive, the supply equations are estimated by ordinary least squares. Two series of engineering salaries are used—one from the Endicott placement survey and the other from the Los Alamos Scientific Laboratory.[14] Differences

---

[14] The Los Alamos data are contained in Los Alamos Scientific Laboratory, *National Survey of Professional and Scientific Salaries* (Los Alamos, N. M.: Los Alamos Scientific Laboratory, 1948–68), passim. The Endicott data, published since 1949, are from Endicott, *passim*.

TABLE 24.1 CORRELATION EVIDENCE OF THE LAGGED EFFECT OF THE NUMBER OF ENGINEERING GRADUATES ON STARTING SALARIES

(*a*) THE CORRELATION OF THE LOG CHANGE IN ENGINEERING STARTING SALARIES WITH THE NUMBER OF B.S. GRADUATES SEEKING WORK, 1949–1967

Log Change in the Number of Graduates	Simple Correlation Coefficient	Correlation Coefficient with Changes in R&D Spending Held Fixed
Current period	−.642	−.732
Lagged one period	−.646	−.690
Lagged two periods	−.348	−.279
Lagged three periods	−.026	.144

(*b*) THE CORRELATION OF THE LOG CHANGE IN ENGINEERING STARTING SALARIES WITH CHANGES IN THE DEMAND FOR ENGINEERS, 1949–1967

Log Change of	Simple Correlation Coefficient	Correlation Coefficient with Changes in Number of Graduates Held Fixed
R&D spending	.481	.625
R&D spending, lagged one period	.123	.265
Output in durable manufacturing	.525	.513
Output in durable manufacturing lagged one period	.067	−.010

The level of significance for the simple correlation coefficients are 1%, 0.590; 5%, 0.468.
For the multiple correlations, the levels of significance are 1%, 0.606; 5%, 0.482.
Note: This table uses the starting salaries of the Los Alamos survey; analogous results are obtained with use of the Endicott survey data.

in the salaries reported in the surveys due to the sample and period covered were relatively minor and do not substantially affect the statistical findings.

The Enrollment Decision

Estimates of the enrollment equation contained in Table 24.2 provide strong evidence of economically rational supply behavior on the part of freshmen considering engineering. First, the postulated structure explains most of the variation in enrollment in a sensible way, with independent variables obtaining coefficients with appropriate signs and, in most cases, high statistical significance. The overall ability of the equation to explain the fluctuations described earlier is illustrated graphically in Figure 24.5. Second, the chief explanatory variable is engineering starting salaries, which by itself accounts for over half the variance in $\Delta \ln ENR$. Most of the salary effect occurs in a single time interval, the remainder within a year (regression 2 in Table 24.2). The estimated elasticity of supply is quite substantial, on the order of 2½ to 3.[15] The alternative income variable, on the other hand, performs less satisfactorily, probably because professional earnings are only a crude indicator of nonengineering work opportunities. Experimentation with other measures of alternatives yield similar results.[16]

[15] This finding is supported by additional experiments with Koyck lags.
[16] In preliminary calculations, one highly significant cross-relation was uncovered. Starting salaries for chemists had a well-defined negative impact on engineering enrollment. Given the relative size of engineering and chemistry, however, and the crudity of the chemist salary series, this finding was omitted in the final calculations.

TABLE 24.2 SUPPLY OF FIRST YEAR STUDENTS TO ENGINEERING, 1948–1967

Equation Number	Regression coefficients and t-statistics								
	Constant	$\Delta\ln FRSH$	$\Delta\ln ESAL$	$\Delta\ln PROF$	$\Delta\ln VET$	$\Delta\ln SHR_{-1}$	$\Delta\ln ESAL_{-1}$	R^2	d.w.
	(with Los Alamos salary series)								
1	−.11 (3.67)	.76 (3.80)	2.70 (5.19)	−.47 (1.47)				.75	1.64
2	−.72 (3.43)	.70 (3.68)	2.48 (5.90)	.42 (1.62)	.17 (1.89)	−.35 (2.69)	1.30 (2.50)	.87	1.26
	(with Endicott salary series)								
3	−.16 (5.33)	.92 (6.57)	2.86 (7.15)	−.31 (1.41)	.20 (3.36)			.89	1.61
4	−.36 (3.27)	.96 (6.40)	2.86 (6.98)	−.28 (1.23)	.22 (3.69)	−.16 (3.20)	.19 (.69)	.93	1.68

The levels of significance for the *t*-statistics are 1%: 2.95, 3.06, 2.98; 5%: 2.13, 2.18, 2.15 for the three equations respectively.
Supply Regressions: The dependent variable is $\Delta\ln ENR$, the log change of enrollment of freshmen in engineering.

The remaining variables are accorded proper signs and significance. Male freshmen have the proportional impact on enrollment required of a well-specified model: in some equations its coefficient is nearly one, in others a standard deviation away. The enrollment of veterans increases the number of first-year engineering students, but with a coefficient small enough to decisively reject the demobilization explanation of postwar developments.[17] Finally, the lagged fraction of freshmen in engineering has the expected negative impact on the growth of enrollment.

Noneconometric evidence corroborates the regression findings of responsive supply behavior in the engineering market. First, survey results show that students have the information about starting salaries, life-cycle earnings, and relative incomes needed for rational supply behavior. Engineering majors, in particular, report sensible income expectations and accurate knowledge of job opportunities—which is perhaps not surprising in view of the publicity given the profession and the large number of engineers in the United States. Second, a study of California high school seniors shows that students respond to perceptions of salaries in an economically rational way. The vast majority (80 percent) of male seniors rating engineering first in income relative to other college-level careers express the intention of entering the field. By contrast, just one-fourth of those ranking engineering low in salary plan on engineering careers.[18] Third, another survey has found engineering majors to be exceptionally vocationally oriented and thus presumably responsive to economic incentives.[19]

---

[17] Because of the absence of a series on veterans in freshman programs, I estimated *VET* in two ways: by the total number of enrolled veterans and by the number of "original" entrants into college (of whom perhaps one-half are freshmen). The results reported given the "best fit" variable in order to provide the maximum measure of the veterans' effect. Even so, it is obvious that only a small fraction of the variation in engineering enrollment can be attributed to demobilization of the military.

[18] D. R. Coombe, *High School Seniors and the Engineering Career* (San Jose: San Jose State College, February, 1966), p. 17.

[19] To be precise, 49 percent of all males cite vocational reasons as the primary reason for selecting an undergraduate major compared to 66 percent of engineering students. National Science Foundation, *Two Years after the College Degree* (Washington: U.S. Government Printing Office, 1963), p. 228.

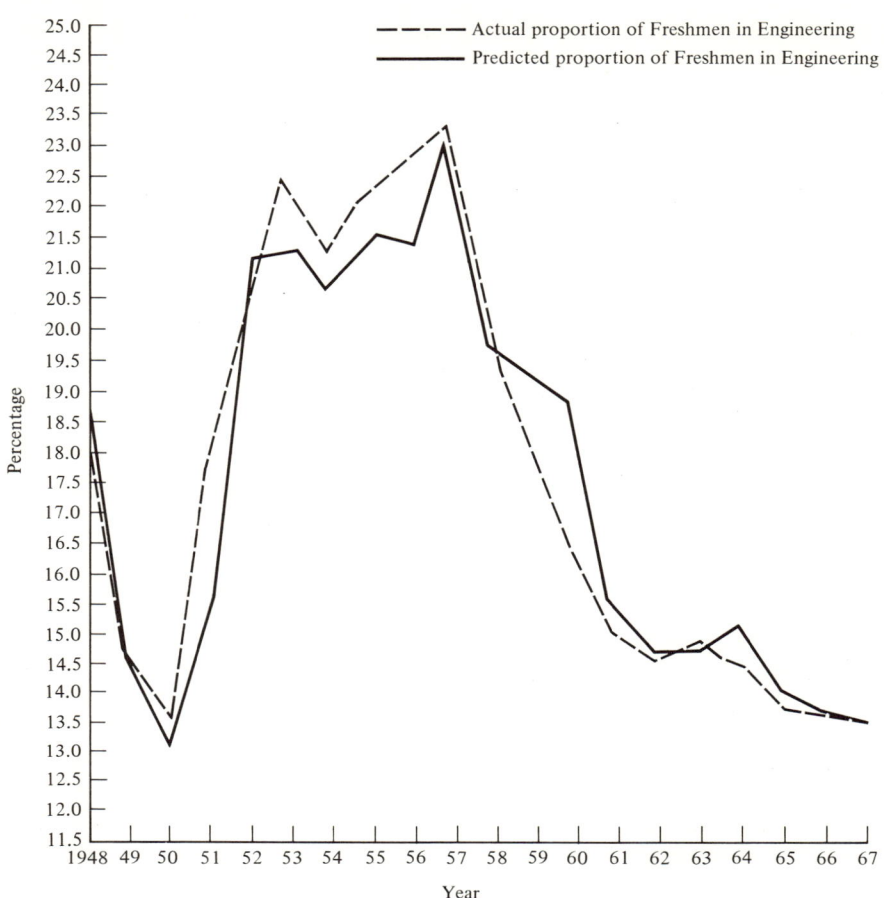

FIGURE 24.5 The Percentage of Freshmen in Engineering Compared to the Proportion Predicted by the Cobweb Supply Equation, 1948–1967

The Completion Decision

Regression estimates of equation (2), which deals with the decision to complete an engineering program, indicate that responsive supply behavior is not limited to the initial selection of a major. Salaries during the freshman-sophomore years have, according to the calculations in Table 24.3, a unit-elastic impact on the number of graduates (regressions (2)–(4) in Table 24.3). The elasticity is below that for the initial supply decision because of the cost of switching fields after several years of study.

The estimated role of the other variables of equation (2) supports the general validity of the model. Necessarily, most of the variation in the number of graduates is attributable to the number of freshman engineers four years earlier (regression (1) in Table 24.3). The proportion of freshmen in a class also has a significant effect on graduates, reducing the rate of completion, while the number of veterans has the opposite effect (regression (3) in Table 24.3). Finally, professional earnings are insignificantly related to the supply of graduates, though with the appropriate negative sign (regression (4) in Table 24.3).

4. Demand for B.S. Engineers

Salary determination equations for actual and planned salaries were estimated under several specifications of the formation of expected supply. Planned salaries are meas-

TABLE 24.3 SUPPLY OF ENGINEERING GRADUATES, 1951–1967

Equation Number	Regression coefficients and t-statistics						
	$\Delta \ln FRSH_{t-4}$	$\Delta(\ln ESAL_{t-2} + \ln ESAL_{t-3})$	$\Delta \ln CVET$	$(ENR/FRSH)$	$\Delta(\ln PROF_{t-2} + \ln PROF_{t-3})$	R^2	d.w.
(1)	.72 (5.60)	.56 (1.22)				.794	1.5
(2)	.40 (3.53)	.85 (2.77)	.0087 (4.14)			.920	1.5
(3)	.51 (4.31)	.97 (3.41)	.0088 (4.52)	−.28 (1.86)		.940	2.20
(4)	.45 (4.27)	1.29 (3.36)	.0079 (4.51)	−.29 (1.84)	−.005 (.009)	.948	1.88

The levels of significance for the *t*-statistics are 1%: 2.98, 3.01, 3.06, 3.11; 5%: 2.15, 2.16, 2.18, 2.20 for the four equations respectively.
Note: To close the model, the dependent variable in these calculations is the log change in the number of graduates seeking work. Regressions with the total number of graduates yield similar results. The computations in the table are based on the data from the Los Alamos survey. Results of equations of the Endicott placement data depict a similar picture of supply responsiveness.
Supply Regressions: The dependent variable is $\Delta \ln GRD$, the log change in number of engineering graduates seeking work.

ured by the plans of firms in the winter prior to recruitment as reported in the Endicott survey, actual salaries by June starting salaries in the Los Alamos survey.

Actual Salary Determination

Table 24.4 summarizes the results of a multiple regression analysis of starting salaries for the period 1948–1967. Overall, the regressions support the salary equation of the cobweb model, explaining most of the variation in the log-change of salaries by shifts in demand (because of R & D and durable goods spending) and movements along the demand curve (because of the changing number of graduates seeking work). With the simplest specification of salary determination—that of immediate market clearing—the current number of graduates has a pronounced negative effect on salaries and an estimated flexibility of one-tenth (regression (1) in Table 24.4). Serial correlation of the errors suggests, however, that the equation is not correctly specified.

Addition of lagged supply variables to improve the specification leads to better statistical results. Under the assumption that expected supply equals the last period's, the R^2 increases and serial correlation diminishes (regression (2) in Table 24.4). In this case the lagged and current number of graduates obtain roughly equal coefficients, indicating an adjustment coefficient of one-half. The flexibility of salaries remains on the order of one-tenth. With the addition of graduates lagged two periods to represent extrapolation of supply, there is a further improvement in the statistical fit and decrease in serial correlation (regression (3) in Table 24.4). More important, the size and sign of the estimated coefficients support the extrapolation hypothesis: the double-lagged term has a positive coefficient approximately half that on the graduates lagged one period. The drop in significance of current supply suggests slow adjustment to new conditions. The final regression (4) describes salary determination with a correction for errors in expectations. Again, the statistical results are improved and coefficients receive the appropriate size and sign.

TABLE 24.4 THE DETERMINATION OF CHANGES IN ENGINEERING STARTING SALARIES, 1948–1967

Equation Number	\	Regression coefficients and t-statistics							
	Constant	$\Delta \ln RD$	$\Delta \ln DUR$	$\Delta \ln GRD$	$\Delta \ln GRD_{t-1}$	$\Delta \ln GRD_{t-2}$	$\Delta \ln GRD_{t-3}$	R^2	d.w.
(1)	.001	.323 (3.97)	.102 (3.31)	−.095 (4.44)				.805	3.27
(2)	.005	.302 (4.17)	.107 (3.92)	−.051 (1.83)	−.047 (2.15)			8.60	3.03
(3)	−.003	.356 (7.23)	.101 (5.56)	−.002 (0.08)	−.149 (5.20)	.075 (4.11)		.945	2.53
(4)	.000	.335 (7.41)	.116 (6.49)	−.026 (1.07)	−.150 (5.91)	.116 (4.43)	−.043 (1.99)	.961	2.30

Note: The levels of significance for the t-statistics are 1%: 2.98, 3.01, 3.06, 3.11; 5%: 2.15, 2.16, 2.18, 2.20, for the four equations respectively.
Salary equations: The dependent variable is $\Delta \ln ESAL$, the log change in the starting salary of B.S. engineers, as reported in the Los Alamos survey.

Solving the first three coefficients for the structural parameters yields the following estimates:

$a = 0.09$ (flexibility of salaries).
$w = 0.70$ (speed of adjustment).
$c = 0.45$ (correction coefficient).

According to the model, the coefficient on the number of graduates lagged three periods should equal the product of these parameters ($a\,w\,c$). In fact, the coefficient is −.03, which is within a standard deviation of the estimate (−.04).

While measurement and specification error make any single regression finding highly tentative, it seems safe to conclude from this exercise that salaries respond to changes in supply with a lag. Certainly, the market does not clear in a single recruitment period.

Planned Salary Determination

Analysis of the factors determining planned salaries provides further support for the lagged salary model. Planned salaries are, as predicted in the model, affected by demand at the time plans are formulated and by past supply conditions. Supply in the period to which salaries refer, on the other hand, has no effect on plans. In the case of simple extrapolation of past changes in supply, for example, we obtain the following statistically "good" explanation of planned salaries:

$\Delta \ln(ESAL)^p = -.096 + .253 \Delta \ln RD$
$ (5.02)$
$+ .306 \Delta \ln DUR - .125 \ln GRD_{-1}$
$ (3.93) (5.35)$
$+ .096 \Delta \ln GRD_{-2} - .051 \Delta \ln GRD_{-3}.$
$ (3.15) \phantom{\Delta \ln GRD_{-2} - .051} (2.71)$
$R^2 = .869$
d.w. = 2.32

An additional test of the planned salary process is possible for the period since 1953, when the Endicott survey began gathering actual as well as planned salary figures. In this test the difference between planned and previous salaries is regressed on changes in demand and lagged changes in supply, under the hypothesis that firms react to current demand, and through expectations, past supply.

$\ln(ESAL)_t^p - \ln(ESAL)_{t-1}$
$= 0.017 + 0.115 \Delta \ln RD$
$ (1.78) (1.62)$
$+ 0.050 \Delta \ln DUR - 0.142 \Delta \ln GRD_{t-1}.$
$ (1.57) (2.84)$
$R^2 = .63$
d.w. = 1.99

Both equations support the postulated structure and present a picture of salary determination consistent with that of the actual salary regressions. Traditional market forces —shifts in supply and demand—explain changes in engineering starting salaries, though with a lag because of sluggish adjustment to unexpected supply conditions.

5. The Cobweb Mechanism

The stability of the cobweb structure and the time required to attain equilibrium after an exogenous disturbance can be determined from the estimated supply and demand parameters. In the first case, it is evident that the cobweb fluctuations generated by the model are extremely stable. The product of the supply and salary coefficients is on the order of 0.30, fulfilling the usual criterion for stability that the product be less than unity. Stability is enhanced, moreover, by the negative impact of a large entering class on ensuing growth and on the fraction of enrollees earning a degree four years later. It is also apparent that the market restores equilibrium rapidly when faced with sudden disturbances. A one-period rise in salaries by 10 percent followed by a return to the previous level will, for example, increase the number of freshmen by 30 percent and the number of graduates by, at most, 20 percent. Since the salary coefficient is about one-tenth, the disturbance results in salaries just 2 percent below equilibrium four years later. Approximately 80 percent of the disturbance is eliminated in a single training period. Allowance for more complex supply and salary behavior does not change the picture of a rapid return to equilibrium. Barring extraordinary or recurrent disturbances, the market for engineers will be close to the equilibrium salary and number of entrants.

A Job Opportunities Interpretation

By substituting the salary equation (3) into the enrollment equation (2), the entire cobweb system can be summarized with a single equation relating enrollment to endogenous non-salary and exogenous variables. In the case of a simple nonlagged salary function, this yields:

$$\Delta \ln ENR_t = a_o \Delta \ln FRSH_t \\ - a_1 c_o \Delta \ln GRD_t + a_1 c_1 \Delta \ln RD_t \\ + a_1 c_2 \Delta \ln DUR_t - a_2 \Delta \ln PSAL_t \\ + a_3 \Delta \ln VET_t. \quad (11)$$

Conceptually this "cobweb equation" shows that a large graduating class reduces enrollment in a given year, and graduates four years later and thus causes an increase in enrollment at that time.

The elimination of engineering salaries from the model (and the possible analogous elimination of alternative salaries) suggests a "nonprice" interpretation of the cobweb mechanism. Specifically, equation (11) may be regarded as a relation between supply and job opportunities, where opportunities depend, reasonably enough, on the number of graduates seeking work relative to demand. According to this theory, students respond to labor market incentives like job vacancies, existence of attractive openings, and other measures of opportunity as well as, or instead of, to "pure" salary incentive.

Statistically, the estimates of the cobweb equation presented in Table 24.5 show that it explains enrollment in the 1948–1967 period as accurately as the supply equations of section 3. The coefficient of determination is sizable, variables are significant, and the number of current graduates has an especially significant effect on enrollment, as required by the model. By itself, the change in graduates is extraordinarily well correlated with the change in freshman enrollment in the same year ($r = -.801$). The cobweb dynamics posited at the onset of the chapter thus are strongly confirmed in these calculations.

Shortages and Surpluses

Recurring public concern over shortages or surpluses of engineering manpower is partially explicable by the cobweb structure of the market. First, cobweb fluctuations in the number of graduates—which in postwar years ranged from increases of 50 percent to decreases of 50 percent within the span of three years—would seem to be sufficient cause for concern over shortages or sur-

TABLE 24.5 "COBWEB EQUATION" FOR SUPPLY OF FIRST-YEAR STUDENTS TO ENGINEERING, 1948–1967

Equation Number	Constant	$\Delta \ln FRSH$	$\Delta \ln GRD$	$\Delta \ln RD$	$\Delta \ln DUR$	$\Delta \ln SHR$	R^2	d.w.
(1)	−0.70 (2.52)	0.57 (3.08)	−0.50 (5.72)	0.60 (2.68)	0.14 (1.25)		0.862	1.57
(2)	0.014 (0.80)	0.64 (4.59)	−0.47 (5.29)	0.77 (3.56)	0.29 (2.37)	−0.23 (2.69)	0.902	2.17

($\Delta \ln ENR$ is the dependent variable)

pluses, especially if cyclic phenomena are misinterpreted as trends. Second, the lagged adjustment of salaries, which produces job vacancies when supply is less than anticipated and surpluses when it is greater, is likely to exacerbate the impact of fluctuations on firms. These phenomena would seem to explain the uproar over shortages in the mid-1950s when the number of graduates fell from its 1951 peak.[20]

[20] This explanation of market disequilibrium and shortage is similar, though not identical, to the Arrow-Capron "dynamic shortage." In the present model, disequilibrium is due to lagged response of salaries to changes in supply rather than to changes in demand (cf. K. Arrow and W. M. Capron, "Dynamic Shortages and Price Rises: The Engineer-Scientist Case," *Quarterly Journal of Economics* [1959], pp. 292–308).

Summary

The principal findings of this chapter are

1. The supply of college students to B.S. engineering responds to economic incentive, with freshmen and undergraduate majors taking account of labor market conditions in their career plans.
2. The incentive in the market may be represented by salaries or employment opportunities.
3. Starting salaries are determined by classical labor market forces—shifts in supply and demand—with a lag due to slow adjustment to changed supply.
4. The market for engineers is well described by the cobweb variant of the basic labor market model, with stable highly dampened fluctuations.

C. GEOGRAPHICAL WAGE DIFFERENTIALS

25
Migration, Location
and Remuneration
of Medical Personnel:
Physicians and Dentists[1]

Lee Benham • Alex Maurizi • Melvin W. Reder

For many years there has been deep concern as to whether a shortage of doctors exists either nationally or in particular localities. This study investigates how well the distribution of the national stocks of medics (the generic term used here to refer to physicians and dentists) among areas corresponds to the distribution of population, and what influence is exerted by other variables such as effective demand for medical service, barriers to migration, and the locational preferences of medics.

The "unit" of area in this study is the state; this is mainly because of availability of data. However, differences of size among the states, as well as in the relative populations of rural and urban areas and in the distribution of the urban population among large and small cities, seriously affect the observations. To remedy the resulting distortions as fully as possible, one of the authors is now analyzing the determinants of physician location among counties with results to be presented in a subsequent paper. However, many more variables for longer periods of time can be analyzed for states as a whole than for smaller sub-divisions.[2]

The substance of our findings is contained in the regressions presented in the various tables. In considering them, the reader should bear in mind the following points: (1) We have analyzed a number of distinct types of medics: All Physicians, Self-employed Physicians and Dentists. Where our findings apply to all types we make

Reprinted from *The Review of Economics and Statistics*, Vol. 50 (August 1968), pp. 332–347, by permission of the publisher.
* Editors' Note: References in square brackets are listed at the end of the reading.
[1] This work was supported by a grant from the Ford Foundation.

[2] G. V. Rimlinger and H. B. Steele have analyzed the locational determinants of physicians at the regional level. "An Economic Interpretation of the Spatial Distribution of Physicians in the U.S.," *Southern Economic Journal*, July 1963, pp. 1–12, and "Income Opportunities and Physician Location Trends in the United States," *Western Economic Journal*, Spring 1965, pp. 182–194.

generic statements. (2) To avoid discursiveness we discuss only those coefficients believed indicative of pervasive long-run forces affecting the allocation of medics. (3) In section I, the discussion is purely descriptive, i.e., the regression coefficients reflect observed associations but are not estimates of the structural parameters of a particular model. They do, however, have theoretical relevance. Some estimates of demand and supply functions are discussed in section II. (4) The years studied are 1930, 1940, 1950 and 1960, or for some variables, years close to them. Lack of data for a sufficient number of years makes satisfactory time series analysis impossible. Section III summarizes our findings, and comments briefly upon their empirical implications.

Our dictionary of variables is as follows:

$X_1^{(i)}$—Number of medics in the ith state.
$X_2^{(i)}$—Population of the ith state.
$X_3^{(i)}$—(Total) personal income of the ith state.
$X_4^{(i)}$—Volume of training facilities (number of places in medical classes) in ith state.
$X_5^{(i)}$—Barriers to entry (percentage of applicants for licensure who fail examinations) in ith state.
$X_6^{(i)}$—Population in ith state living in urban areas of more than 2,500 persons.
$X_7^{(i)}$—Average income of medics in ith state.

Except where there is danger of confusion we shall hereafter abandon the superscript. Variables with an asterisk, e.g., X^*_1, represent per capita magnitudes, i.e., $X^*_1 \equiv X_1/X_2$. A variable with a single prime, e.g., X'_1, represents the initial level of a variable in a time interval; a double prime, e.g., X''_1, represents the terminal level of a variable in the interval, and $\Delta X_1 = X''_1 - X'_1$.

The equations discussed in section I are:

$$X_1 = f_1(X_2, X^*_3, X_4, X_5) \quad (1)$$
$$X^*_1 = f_{1a}(X^*_3, X^*_4, X_5, X^*_6) \quad (1a)$$
$$\Delta X_1 = f_2(\Delta X_2, \Delta X^*_3, \Delta X_4, \Delta X_5,$$
$$\quad X'_1, X'_2, X^{*'}_3, X'_4, X'_5) \quad (2)$$
$$\Delta X^*_1 = f_{2a}(\Delta^*_2, \Delta X^*_3, \Delta X^*_4, \Delta X_5,$$
$$\quad \Delta X^*_6; X^{*'}_1, X^{*'}_3, X^{*'}_4, X'_5 \, X^{*'}_6) \quad (2a)$$
$$\Delta X^*_1 = f_3(X^{*'}_1, X'_7, \Delta X_7) \quad (3)$$
$$X_7 = f_4(X^*_1, X^*_3, X^*_4, X_5, X^*_6) \quad (4)$$
$$\Delta X_7 = f_5(X^{*'}_1, \Delta X^*_1, X'_7) \quad (5)$$

The regression coefficients found by fitting these equations to the data are presented in tables 25.1 to 25.5. (25.1), (25.1a) and (25.4), in which all variables refer to the same year, are cross sections and will be so designated; (25.2), (25.2a), (25.3) and (25.5) are inter-temporal in that they reflect changes between pairs of years.

I

1) Table 25.1 shows that in every year studied the major determinant of the number of medics in a state is its population. Moreover, as can be seen in table 25.2, change in population is the major determinant of the change in the number of medics in a state between all years except 1930–1940. This is not due to spurious correlation of a "part with a whole"; medics are not an appreciable part of a state's population, nor is the change in the number of medics an appreciable part of the change in the population of a state.

It has been suggested that a similar finding might be obtained for any occupation where demand is strongly related to the number of persons to be served, e.g., in most service industries. Though this may be so, it is not deducible from a priori considerations. If the statement that X_1 depends mainly on X_2 and ΔX_1 mainly on ΔX_2 is true, it suggests that market forces are extremely powerful in directing the flow of medics among states despite obstacles to interstate movement. That is, the high t values of the coefficients of X_2 in the regressions in table 25.1, and of ΔX_2 in table 25.2,[3] are consistent with the hypothesis that medics seeking to maximize their individual satisfaction (which depends upon pecuniary

[3] The percentages of total variance in X_1 and ΔX_1 explained by X_2 and ΔX_2, respectively, as indicated by the squared zero order correlations between "All Physicians" and population are above 0.8 in all regressions utilized except that for 1930–1940.

income and various aspects of "professional satisfaction") so allocate themselves that, in effect, interstate migrants (roughly) bring their own medics to care for them. This occurs despite well-known obstacles to mobility discussed below. It is to be emphasized that this statement applies to Self-employed Physicians and to Dentists as well as to All Physicians.

2) The predominance of the population variable suggests that medics are more responsive in their locational choices to the size of the population to be served than to its per capita income.[4]

These results are part of a complex of forces which cannot be completely disentangled because of multicollinearity. For what it is worth, our interpretation of the results in tables 25.1 and 25.2 is that the cross-sectional relationship between X_1 and X^*_3 reflects an association existing before 1930 but which has not held between the *increments in* X_1 *and* X^*_3 since 1930. However it is possible that since 1930, increments in X_1 have been positively correlated with the 1930 level of X^*_3.

3) The response of medics to the pull of demand forces (reflected in X_2 and X^*_3) was made despite the existence of institutional impediments to interstate mobility. We attempt to measure the strength of these impediments by X_5, which reflects the difficulty of securing a license to practice. As an indicator of this difficulty, X_5 is very imperfect; making the licensure examination difficult is only one way of impeding entry to practice in a given state. A state may also restrict entry to a profession by requiring citizenship or a minimum period of residence prior to licensure or by refusing reciprocity to licensees of other states, i.e., by requiring persons licensed in other states to pass an examination or otherwise qualify before being admitted to practice. Also, a high failure rate may be associated with greater or less difficulty for entry depending upon the number of times an applicant may retake the examination and the period he must wait in order to make another attempt.

For physicians, the regression coefficients of X_1 and X_5 are consistently positive, suggesting that higher failure percentages are a concomitant (perhaps a result) of a state being relatively attractive to physicians, or to physicians with an atypically high propensity to fail. That is, relatively attractive states may impose higher than average barriers to entry, but the barriers are not set high enough to obliterate the positive association indicated by the regression coefficients.

There is good reason to suppose that the barriers to *interstate migration* of physicians have a smaller impact on relative supply than those affecting dentists. The reason is that there are extensive provisions for reciprocity (reciprocal licensing) among states with regard to physicians; i.e., it is relatively easy for *American-trained physicians* licensed in one state to secure a license to practise in most others. However, there is substantially less reciprocity in dentistry, so that members of this profession have more difficulty in relocating in response to market forces than physicians.[5]

Despite widespread interstate reciprocity in licensing physicians, there is substantial

---

[4] In general, the elasticity of the number of medics with respect to per capita income is greater for dentists than physicians, presumably reflecting the greater income elasticity of demand for dental care.

[5] In both dentistry and medicine, the written examination is only one part of the licensure requirement; there usually is a clinical examination also. For those states which accept the National Board Examinations (in either dentistry or medicine) it is not necessary to retake the written part if one wishes to move to another state. However, it is necessary to retake the clinical portion, unless a reciprocity or endorsement agreement has been established between the state one is leaving and the state one is entering. The existence of such reciprocity arrangements is much more widespread in medicine than in dentistry. For data on reciprocity among states regarding physicians, see the annual State Board Number of *The Journal of the American Medical Association*. For analogous information concerning dentists, see *Facts About States for the Dentist Seeking a Location*, published annually by the American Dental Association, Chicago, Illinois.

TABLE 25.1 CROSS-SECTIONAL REGRESSIONS OF NUMBER OF MEDICS ON SELECTED EXPLANATORY VARIABLES IN SELECTED YEARS (48 STATES AND DISTRICT OF COLUMBIA)

X_1	Year	Constant	Coefficient, t Ratio and Elasticity at Mean of				$R^2(c)$
			X_2	X^*_3	X_4	X_5	
All Physicians	1930	−1355.23	1.23 (17.70) .99	1.64 (3.89) .33	.75 (2.28) .10	12.96 (1.40) .01	.98
All Physicians	1940	−2175.24	1.34 (10.91) 1.06	2.29 (2.75) .37	1.03 (1.77) .13	43.43 (2.33) .07	.95
All Physicians	1950	−2959.81	1.33 (11.44) 1.03	1.35 (2.41) .48	1.02 (1.78) .13	70.97 (4.13) .10	.95
All Physicians	1960	−3204.83	1.25 (12.01) .97	1.05 (2.02) .47	1.36 (2.52) .18	41.84 (2.24) .07	.95
Self-employed Physicians	1950	−1912.64	.93 (13.73) 1.11	.89 (2.70) .49	.33 (1.01) .07	38.77 (3.88) .09	.96
Self-employed Physicians	1960	−2000.10	.89 (14.32) 1.07	.64 (2.05) .44	.44 (1.37) .09	23.06 (2.06) .06	.96
Self-employed General Practitioners	1950	−682.34	.48 (15.57) .98	.30 (2.06) .29	.36 (2.38) .12	18.40 (4.08) .07	.97
Self-employed General Practitioners	1960	−535.68	.39 (13.76) .86	.13 (.93) .17	.63 (4.24) .23	12.70 (2.45) .06	.97
Self-employed Specialists	1950	−1230.29	.45 (10.78) 1.28	.58 (2.85) .76	−.02 (.11) −.01	20.36 (3.27) .11	.93
Self-employed Specialists	1960	−1464.42	.49 (11.85) 1.33	.50 (2.41) .78	−.19 (.88) −.08	10.35 (1.38) .06	.93
Dentists	1930	−1202.22	.58 (13.56) 1.01	1.59 (5.16) .69	.62 (2.16) .11	1.66 (.39) .02	.95
Dentists	1940	−1099.71	.57 (11.05) 1.07	1.68 (4.07) .65	.88 (1.51) .10	−4.64 (.77) −.05	.94
Dentists	1950	−2046.29	.67 (13.10) 1.34	1.30 (4.06) 1.20	−.71 (1.41) −.11	−8.38 (1.11) −.09	.92
Dentists	1960	−2219.63	.58 (13.12) 1.25	1.03 (3.94) 1.28	−.71 (1.37) −.11	−12.02 (1.68) −.10	.93
Self-employed Dentists	1950	−1800.26	.58 (13.22) 1.33	1.16 (4.17) 1.21	−.61 (1.41) −.11	−8.06 (1.23) −.10	.92
Self-employed Dentists	1960	−2088.22	.53 (13.27) 1.25	.97 (4.09) 1.31	−.63 (1.34) −.11	−11.75 (1.80) −.11	.93

TABLE 25.1a CROSS-SECTIONAL REGRESSIONS OF PER CAPITA NUMBER OF MEDICS ON SELECTED EXPLANATORY VARIABLES IN SELECTED YEARS (48 STATES AND DISTRICT OF COLUMBIA)

Year	Constant	Coefficient, t Ratio and Elasticity at Mean of				$R^2(c)$
		X^*_3	X^*_4	X^*_6	X_5	
All Physicians—X^*_1						
1930	66.98	.07 (3.67) .39	.69 (8.13) .10	−.01 (.05) −.00	−.01 (.03) −.00	.79
1940	35.60	.08 (6.12) .41	.91 (8.40) .12	.37 (2.36) .15	.31 (1.40) .02	.90
1950	14.73	.05 (4.91) .60	.76 (6.06) .11	.29 (1.29) .13	.83 (3.62) .04	.80
1960	27.97	.04 (3.72) .66	.85 (5.31) .12	−.23 (.80) −.11	.77 (2.31) .05	.62
Self-employed Physicians—X^*_1						
1950	20.05	.03 (4.39) .54	.17 (2.05) .04	.17 (1.14) .11	.55 (3.57) .04	.70
1960	25.48	.03 (3.63) .69	.23 (2.08) .05	−.17 (.85) −.13	.51 (2.36) .05	.45
All Dentists—X^*_1						
1930	14.01	.04 (2.39) .46	.81 (4.20) .12	.14 (.74) .12	.14 (1.11) .04	.65
1940	17.32	.05 (2.76) .53	.31 (1.07) .03	.19 (1.09) .19	−.31 (2.16) −.10	.53
1950	−2.27	.03 (5.29) .99	.06 (.47) .01	.16 (1.31) .19	−.37 (3.74) −.13	.65
1960	−2.22	.02 (5.77) 1.18	−.002 (.02) .00	.03 (.27) −.04	−.28 (2.91) −.09	.47
Self-employed Dentists—X^*_1						
1960	−4.38	.02 (6.04) 1.24	−.03 (.29) −.01	−.01 (.14) −.02	−.28 (3.18) −.10	.51

interstate variation in the percentage of applicants failing examinations, and the relative "propensity to fail" shows great stability among the states from one decade to the next.[6] This is principally due to the concentration of failures among graduates of foreign medical schools. Applicants trained abroad tend to seek licensure in particular states, i.e., those having large cosmopolitan cities,

---

[6] Among states, the correlation coefficient between percentage of applicants for medical licensure failing in 1940 and 1950 was +0.90; between 1940 and 1960, it was +0.83; between 1950 and 1960, +0.85.

TABLE 25.2 REGRESSIONS OF CHANGE IN NUMBER OF MEDICS ON SELECTED EXPLANATORY VARIABLES (48 STATES AND DISTRICT OF COLUMBIA)

Coefficient, t Ratio and Elasticity at Mean of

Years	Constant	X'_1	X'_2	$X^{*'}_3$	X'_4	X'_5	ΔX_2	ΔX^*_3	ΔX_4	ΔX_5	$R^2(c)$
					All Physicians—ΔX_1						
1930–40	−559.56	.46 (2.69) 6.18	−.34 (1.63) −3.57	.68 (1.18) 1.81	−.64 (1.65) −1.21	12.83 (1.31) .20	.19 (.35) .14	.07 (.03) −.02	.08 (.06) −.00	−6.27 (1.05) −.16	.62
1940–50	678.44	.26 (7.67) 1.57	−.37 (6.82) −1.78	−.23 (.87) −.23	.11 (.83) .09	8.89 (2.10) .09	1.42 (19.26) .97	−.64 (2.05) −.99	.43 (1.17) .06	−2.09 (.35) −.00	.96
1950–60	261.93	.03 (.63) .18	−.07 (.87) −.32	−.25 (.97) −.49	−.06 (.24) −.04	−7.34 (.96) −.06	1.43 (11.23) 1.09	.30 (.40) .28	.13 (.18) .02	−2.45 (.34) −.00	.89
1930–60	−19.79	.90 (4.01) 1.88	−1.03 (3.72) −1.70	1.15 (1.08) .48	−.71 (1.32) −.21	11.45 (.78) −.03	.97 (8.87) .71	−.48 (.52) −.46	3.02 (3.87) .31	−8.80 (.61) −.03	.91
1930–50	−277.05	.85 (4.33) 3.40	−.82 (3.43) −2.60	.78 (1.05) .63	−.71 (1.64) −.41	22.23 (1.84) .11	.73 (3.71) .51	−.54 (.60) −.54	2.14 (2.29) .18	29.27 (1.58) .07	.86
1940–60	1507.69	.27 (3.10) .71	−.43 (3.21) −.90	.32 (.38) .14	.14 (.38) .05	4.73 (.44) .02	1.46 (18.41) 1.06	−1.02 (1.50) −1.24	.05 (.07) .00	−7.06 (.70) −.01	.94
					General Practitioners—ΔX_1						
1950–60	65.16	.03 (2.40) .56	−.01 (.61) −.19	−.04 (.78) −.32	−.12 (2.28) −.33	−4.19 (2.68) −.13	.22 (8.42) .67	.03 (.20) .11	.59 (4.11) .29	−1.86 (1.24) −.03	.92

Specialists—ΔX_1										
1950–60	380.94	−.02 (.25) −.14	−.07 (1.12) −.81	−.14 (.74) −.73	.16 (.89) .31	3.44 (.61) .07	.91 (9.63) 1.83	−.26 (.47) −.64	.85 (1.69) −.28	1.06 (.20) .00	.77
All Dentists—ΔX_1										
1930–40	−171.85	−.02 (.32) 1.72	.04 (1.49) −8.12	.08 (.62) −3.79	−.29 (1.64) 5.51	2.00 (1.09) −2.19	.12 (1.03) −1.53	−.16 (.33) −.92	−.32 (1.18) −2.25	1.91 (1.04) −.24	.07
1940–50	228.26	.19 (2.66) 2.89	.00 (.01) .01	.34 (1.43) 2.01	−.83 (3.11) −1.38	2.50 (.89) .43	.18 (2.61) .71	−.60 (1.95) −5.49	−.65 (1.93) −.63	.61 (.29) .01	.62
1950–60	155.94	−.02 (.46) −.21	−.03 (.61) −.53	−.13 (1.00) −1.16	−.00 (.04) −.01	.91 (.38) .09	.42 (8.18) 1.52	.06 (.20) .25	.43 (.91) .07	1.81 (.61) −.03	.75
1930–60	30.72	.02 (.15) .11	.11 (1.22) 1.18	.54 (1.18) 1.47	−1.21 (3.54) −1.28	2.41 (.47) .15	.33 (7.02) 1.53	−.36 (.83) −2.20	−.78 (1.91) −.08	4.58 (.88) −.01	.68
1930–50	−157.24	.13 (1.40) 2.38	.06 (.96) 1.89	.40 (1.44) 3.10	−1.14 (4.94) −3.51	−3.53 (.70) −.64	.24 (3.37) 1.64	−.23 (.66) −2.24	−.80 (2.50) .03	−3.43 (.89) .30	.57
1940–60	567.47	.14 (1.34) .83	.01 (.17) .14	.64 (1.50) 1.42	−1.09 (2.98) −.69	4.29 (1.06) .28	.33 (7.37) 1.24	−.69 (1.80) −4.23	−.56 (1.36) −.26	.43 (.08) −.00	.74
Self-employed Dentists—ΔX_1										
1950–60	112.82	.02 (.50) .17	−.02 (.53) −.34	−.11 (.91) −.79	−.01 (.04) −.00	1.45 (.63) .12	.40 (7.84) 1.08	.05 (.19) .18	.41 (.89) .05	1.66 (.58) −.02	.79

TABLE 25.2a REGRESSIONS OF CHANGE IN NUMBER OF MEDICS PER CAPITA ON SELECTED EXPLANATORY VARIABLES (48 STATES AND DISTRICT OF COLUMBIA)

Years	Constant	Coefficient, t Ratio and Elasticity at Mean of										
		$X^{*'}_1$	$X^{*'}_3$	$X^{*'}_4$	X'_5	$X^{*'}_6$	ΔX^*_2	ΔX^*_3	ΔX^*_4	ΔX_5	ΔX^*_6	$R^2(c)$

All Physicians—ΔX^*_1

1930–40	5.95	−.44 (6.00) 12.02	.05 (4.13) −6.78	.36 (2.61) −1.44	.23 (1.89) −.19	.21 (1.76) −2.23	.01 (.27) .12	−.23 (1.39) .42	.53 (1.97) .37	.02 (.23) −.03	.004 (.00) −.00	.71
1940–50	10.80	.04 (.39) 3.69	.0026 (.16) 1.08	−.09 (.69) −.99	.38 (2.31) 1.59	−.16 (1.33) −5.72	−.01 (.68) −5.42	−.05 (.56) −.58	.07 (.24) .09	.05 (.23) .00	−.31 (.93) −.80	.03
1950–60	21.98	.42 (3.02) 32.13	−.02 (1.49) −14.40	−.24 (1.43) −2.57	−.19 (.82) −.72	−.40 (2.22) −13.51	−.03 (1.28) −14.49	−.05 (.35) −.56	.27 (.59) .14	.04 (.19) .07	.18 (.51) .63	.17
1930–60	3.24	−.40 (1.76) 31.77	−.01 (.41) 7.08	.44 (1.60) −5.06	.84 (2.05) −2.03	−.02 (.07) .76	.03 (1.19) −30.61	.0096 (.13) −.32	.99 (1.44) .35	.62 (1.47) −1.84	−.48 (1.19) 3.00	.17
1930–50	17.34	−.49 (3.86) 19.12	.04 (2.03) −9.41	.32 (1.90) −1.89	.60 (2.78) −.73	.02 (.12) −.37	.0053 (.30) −1.34	−.04 (.49) .37	.61 (1.63) .27	.47 (1.38) −.30	−.62 (1.65) .91	.54
1940–60	29.53	.33 (1.33) 13.58	−.03 (.71) −5.83	−.13 (.43) −.71	.41 (1.14) .82	−.59 (2.20) −9.96	−.01 (.52) −6.89	.03 (.42) .48	−.09 (.22) −.08	.35 (1.00) .32	−.34 (.84) −1.03	.00

Self-employed Physicians—ΔX^*_1

| 1950–60 | 10.19 | .24
(1.44)
165.32 | −.0003
(.04)
−4.04 | .01
(.15)
2.30 | .03
(.20)
1.98 | −.34
(2.22)
−157.23 | −.01
(.78)
−102.40 | −.02
(.25)
−4.51 | .14
(.37)
1.03 | .13
(.66)
2.96 | .14
(.44)
6.41 | .00 |

General Practitioners—ΔX^*_1												
1950–60	11.69	.07 (.57) –1.99	.0055 (1.40) 4.71	.07 (1.41) .72	.05 (.72) –.21	.01 (.26) –.56	–.01 (1.46) 5.28	–.09 (1.79) 1.00	.22 (1.35) –.11	.13 (1.56) –.20	.17 (1.31) –.56	.38
Specialists—ΔX^*_1												
1950–60	–1.04	.0027 (.01) .05	.0080 (.94) 6.37	.12 (1.18) 1.13	.06 (.36) .22	–.33 (2.05) –9.78	.0079 (.36) 3.00	.07 (.65) .80	–.09 (.25) –.04	.04 (.22) .06	–.07 (.24) –.22	.00
All Dentists—ΔX^*_1												
1930–40	5.78	–.26 (5.07) 2.68	.0079 (1.17) –.95	–.12 (1.06) .20	–.0022 (.03) .01	.01 (.18) –.11	–.40 (4.48) .63	–.01 (1.22) –.23	.03 (.56) –.01	–.23 (1.29) –.16	–.24 (.86) .05	.66
1940–50	5.64	–.17 (2.58) 2.16	.01 (1.42) –1.71	–.15 (1.08) .17	–.06 (.70) .28	.05 (.90) –.73	–.08 (1.38) .34	–.0092 (2.07) 1.21	–.01 (.04) –.27	–.18 (.12) .98	.19 (.17) –1.07	.42
1950–60	5.67	–.15 (1.49) 5.16	.0046 (.71) –4.99	–.15 (1.75) .80	.10 (1.16) –1.27	–.12 (1.62) 5.07	–.09 (1.51) 1.36	.0014 (.16) –.75	–.02 (.31) .10	.20 (.50) –.02	.03 (.18) –.13	.29
1930–60	–0.21	–.56 (5.48) 2.92	.0098 (.62) –.59	–.28 (1.81) .22	–.18 (.88) .26	–.04 (.31) .22	–.03 (.70) .15	.01 (1.52) –2.19	–.15 (.88) –.01	–.11 (.68) –.01	–.0083 (.06) .01	.66
1930–50	5.44	–.42 (5.34) 2.51	.01 (1.08) –.77	–.22 (1.78) .20	.03 (.30) –.06	–.09 (.87) –.49	–.17 (3.57) .47	.0033 (.41) –.29	.03 (.37) .03	–.22 (1.70) –.03	–.04 (.28) .02	.66
1940–60	11.80	–.35 (3.30) 3.36	.02 (1.26) –2.42	–.30 (1.37) .26	–.04 (.25) .13	–.09 (.81) .88	–.04 (.89) .31	–.0029 (.27) .87	–.07 (.48) –.03	–.09 (.38) .05	.06 (.39) –.11	.45
Self-employed Dentists—ΔX^*_1												
1950–60	2.71	–.12 (1.21) –163.06	.0038 (.63) 176.36	–.09 (1.12) –20.11	.07 (.96) 41.13	–.10 (1.44) –175.84	–.05 (.97) –34.44	.0036 (.43) 78.97	–.01 (.25) –3.20	.23 (.64) 1.80	.06 (.40) 11.33	.13

where there are many persons who speak a foreign language. Substituting the variable, "percentage of applicants graduating from foreign medical schools," for X_5 in equation (1), leaves all coefficients substantially unchanged.[7]

Among dentists the results are quite different; in virtually all of the cross sections in table 25.1, the coefficients of X_5 were negative. This is consistent with the frequently heard allegation that entry restriction has been an important phenomenon in the interstate allocation of dentists. There have been strong hints from authoritative sources that *state* examinations for licensure to practise dentistry have been used to limit the number of dentists entering practise (within the state), especially by failing applicants trained outside of the state.[8] The charges of entry restriction stress that applicants trained out-of-state are failed more frequently than those trained within the state.[9] This suggests that the effect of entry restriction might be reflected more clearly in the failure rate of out-of-state applicants (or in the difference in failure rates between in-state and out-of-state applicants) than in the overall failure rate. Unfortunately, however, it was only for 1960 that we were able to obtain failure rates for in-state and out-of-state applicants separately.[10]

Turning to table 25.4, we find that the coefficients of X_5 clearly indicate that, whatever the mechanism that determines failure

---

[7] The bivariate correlation coefficient between percentage of state population that is foreign born (outside U.S.) and percentage of applicants failing examination for physician licensure was +0.58 in 1950 and +0.54 in 1960. Substituting percentage of foreign born, X_8, for percentage failing physician licensure examinations in the cross-sectional regressions left all substantive results unchanged.

It should be noted that since 1950, the relative importance of foreign-trained physicians has sharply increased, largely as Residents at hospitals. Availability of residencies has probably become, therefore, a more important determinant of the location of M.D.'s within the last decade than previously. Since United States-trained graduates are preferred to foreign-trained, for a number of reasons, availability of Residencies to the foreign trained increases both with the number offered and their *unattractiveness* to United States-trained applicants. Analysis of this interesting question is not essential to our main theme.

[8] For example, see B. S. Hollinshead et al., "The Survey of Dentistry," American Council on Education, Washington, D.C., 1961, pp. 390–402, especially tables 156–158. Hollinshead (pp. 391–392) reports that 35 per cent of the members of State Boards of Dental Examiners who responded to a questionnaire believed that State Boards place "arbitrary limitations on the number of dentists licensed each year" and another 35 per cent thought it was probably true.

In California, the requirement that candidates fill class 2, 3 and 4 cavities with gold foil during their "practical" examination has caused much complaint; in most other states only class 5 cavities are used in this test of practical skill. Out-of-state (non-California) schools rarely give the requisite training while in-state (California) schools are, willy-nilly, compelled to give it. Few, if any, other states have a similar requirement, and the need for it has been seriously challenged. The overall percentage of successful applicants in California was next to lowest (among all states for which data is available) in 1949 and lowest in 1960. The difference between in-state and out-of-state percentage of applicants passed was 63 per cent (98 per cent minus 35 per cent) in 1960. The difference is believed to be largely due to the gold foil requirement. The statements in this paragraph are based on those in "Dental Education and Manpower," *A Report of the Coordinating Council for Higher Education*, Number 1015, Sacramento and San Francisco, December 1964, chap. III, pp. 15–18.

[9] Hollinshead, op. cit., pp. 390–392.

[10] These data are confidential and cannot be presented in detail. However, they can be used in analyses of this type without violating any confidence. It is believed that comparable data for a number of other years are in the possession of the American Dental Association, but thus far we have been unable to obtain them. In 1960, the mean out-of-state failure rate was 19.7 per cent and the mean overall failure rate 14 per cent. The bivariate R^2 between the two failure rates was 0.62; since the out-of-state failure rate is a part of the overall, the R^2 between the in-state and out-of-state failure rates must be appreciably lower. Nevertheless, use of the out-of-state failure rate (for 1960) changed the coefficient of X_5 only slightly from what it was when overall failure rates were used. Therefore, tentatively, we conclude that the overall failure rate adequately reflects the effect of examination failures on the number of dentists per capita.

percentages, it is one that gives them a positive (partial) association with average dentist incomes. However, the meaning of this association is by no means obvious; the failure percentage for a given state reflects the policy ("tastes") of examiners concerning inter alia: (1) absolute levels of performance of applicants, (2) upper and lower bounds to institutionally acceptable failure rates in a given year, (3) the propriety and feasibility of discriminating between in-state and out-of-state applicants in granting licenses, (4) the importance assigned to the need of the state for more practitioners relative to the claim of established practitioners for higher incomes and freedom from overcrowding." Appraising the importance of these and yet other possible determinants of failure percentages requires more information than is presently available.

It should not be assumed that failure rates for a given state are constant. There is clear evidence that, at least as regards California, sharp year-to-year variations in the failure rate have occurred.[11] Ultimately, these variations may be explicable in terms of the above variables, but formulating a useable hypothesis including the appropriate lagged relations is not yet possible.[12]

4) It is widely believed that medics have strong locational preferences, preferring to be near hospitals and other medical facilities. Like other professionals, they desire to locate where cultural facilities (schools, theatres, etc.) are available. Also, they presumably exhibit a normal degree of inertia that, ceteris paribus, leads them to prefer to re-main where they were raised and/or educated. After some experimentation, we concluded that X_4 was as good a single measure of these nonpecuniary preferences as could be found.

The effect of X_4 (volume of training facilities) on the number of All Physicians, X_1, was consistently positive, though significant in only two years out of four (see table 25.1). On a per capita basis, the relation between X^*_1 and X^*_4 (table 25.1a) is generally much stronger than that between X_1 and X_4. Substantially the same statement applies to Self-employed Physicians, but for Dentists the coefficients of both X_4 and X^*_4 vary markedly from one year to another. Though the relation between number of physicians and volume of training facilities appears stronger on a per capita than on an absolute basis in the cross section, the case is uncertain when we study the relation between the changes in these variables. This can be seen by comparing the coefficients of ΔX_4 and ΔX^*_4 in tables 25.2 and 25.2a, especially for the longer intervals.

In view of the well-known dangers of spurious relations when correlating ratios, we shall not dwell on these results but merely report them. In essence, we interpret our results as uncertain evidence for the existence of a positive association of training facilities and number of physicians, but not dentists.

5) The reader will note the omission of X_6 from the regression explaining X_1. This is because, after some experimentation, we found that the intercorrelation of X_2, X_3, X_5 and X_6 is so strong as to prevent our obtaining reasonable estimates of their respective coefficients. As a result we deleted X_6; the result was to make the coefficients of X_2, X_3 and X_5 algebraically larger, and substantially so, than they were in the presence of X_6. This means that the effect of population size, per capita income and failure percentage on the number of Physicians in a state is partially due to the intercorrelation of degree of urbanization with these other three variables.

---

[11] See "Dental Education and Manpower," op. cit., p. 10, table B.

[12] In an interesting study, Mrs. A. S. Holen found that the interstate dispersion of state (average) incomes was appreciably greater for dentists than for physicians. She attributes this to differentially greater obstacles to interstate movement of dentists associated with the licensing mechanism; her findings and interpretations are clearly in keeping with our view. A. S. Holen, "Effects of Professional Licensing Arrangements on Interstate Labor Mobility and Resource Allocation," *Journal of Political Economy*, Oct. 1965, pp. 492–498.

In the per capita regressions (table 25.1a) we introduce X^*_6 explicitly since, with X_2 removed, X^*_6 no longer obscures the relations of the other variables with the measure of phyiscian quantity. However, except for 1940, the coefficient of X^*_6 is not significant. The R^2 statistics for regressions having X_1 as the dependent variable are appreciably higher than those involving X^*_1; this further indicates the importance of the population variable in determining number of physicians.

Turning to table 25.2a, we find that during none of the periods, either decades or longer, did the *change* in any of the independent variables affect ΔX^*_1 sufficiently to generate a coefficient whose t value consistently exceeded 2. In other words, *changes* in the independent variables in equation (2a) do not furnish a good explanation of *changes* in the per capita number of physicians among the states. This is confirmed by the low values of R^2 in all periods except 1930–1940 and 1930–1950.

The initial condition variables, however, did exert considerable influence on ΔX^*_1. This was especially the case in 1930–1940 when physicians (per capita) strongly tended to move (relatively) away from where they were initially most concentrated toward states of higher per capita incomes, greater urbanization, more training facilities per capita and higher failure rates. In every case, the coefficients for 1950–1960 had the opposite sign from 1930–1940, though in all but one the absolute size was smaller in the later period.[13] The strong relationships of the 1930–1940 decade persist into the 1930–1950 period but are countered by the oppositely directed movements of the 1950's with the result that the 1930–1960 relationships are weak.

It is striking that in the regressions involving ΔX^*_1, it is the initial condition of, rather than the change in, the independent variables that exerts the major influence. We interpret this to mean that, *on a per capita basis,* the locational response of physicians has been to "correct" initial disequilibrium rather than to adjust to changing equilibrium conditions. Thus, the truly important secular force working to alter the relative demand of states for physicians is population shift, which is reflected in the regressions explaining X_1.

If the population variable is omitted, the major relevant differences between states lie in factors reflected in variables that change relatively slowly, e.g., X^*_3, X^*_4, X_5, X^*_6, and in which differences in relative initial (and terminal) values are far greater than the differences in the relative changes therein. Hence the dominant effect is of adjustment to initial (and persisting) differences in the determining variables rather than to their relative changes.

6) Thus far, in discussing the spatial allocation of medics we have stressed such indirect determinants as population and per capita income and ignored the immediate one, practitioner income. One good reason for avoiding use of medic income as a variable is the poor quantity of its measurements, especially when medics are classified by states. However, some data are available which, such as they are, are used as a measure of X_7. Putting X_7 into either (1) or (1a) does not yield analytically meaningful results, as X_7 is, in principle, determined by all the other "independent" variables. (The proper relation of X_7 to the other variables is discussed in greater detail in section II.)

X_7 should have some relation to ΔX_1 or ΔX^*_1. Economic theory suggests that, assuming some initial disequilibrium, the relative movement of earners (medics) should be toward states where X_7 was initially high,

---

[13] Why the 1930's should have been an almost mirror opposite of the 1950's in this respect is not clear. One interesting fact is the very much higher multiple R for 1930–1940 than for any other decade, or for 1930–1960. This suggests that the regression is much better suited to describing the 1930's than later periods; this is consistent with the generally lower t values in 1950–1960 than in 1930–1940.

i.e., X'_7 and X^*_1 should be positively correlated. Also, if we suppose that initially high levels of X_7 are associated with initially low levels of $X^{*'}_1$, then ΔX^*_1 and $X^{*'}_1$ should be negatively correlated. Finally, if the process is essentially one of correcting short-period disequilibrium, it is to be expected that ΔX_1 and ΔX_7 should be negatively correlated, i.e., high initial values of X_7 should be reduced as the obverse of increases in low initial levels of X_1.

This hypothesis is tested by means of equation (3) whose coefficients are presented in table 25.3. ΔX^*_1 rather than ΔX_1 was used as the dependent variable, as it was found that X_2 dominated the regression involving ΔX_1, obscuring all other relationships.

From table 25.3 the following appear to hold: (1) ΔX^*_1 is negatively correlated with $X^{*'}_1$, i.e., movements tended to correct an initial disequilibrium due to "over-concentration" of physicians per capita, (2) ΔX^*_1 is positively correlated with initially high incomes, X'_7, though the coefficient was insignificant, and (3) ΔX^*_1 has a negative correlation with ΔX_7. Points (2) and (3) are compatible with the hypothesis that the period 1929–1949 was one during which physicians per capita were moving toward states where average physician income was initially high (in 1929), and that the process of movement tended to reduce relative physician incomes in the states where they were initially high; the evidence is not as strong as one could wish. However, the credibility of the hypothesis is enhanced by the results presented in table 25.5 and discussed in the next section.

In general, like physicians, the number of dentists per capita tended relatively to increase in states where their average income was initially high, and relatively to decline in those where the initial number of dentists per capita was high. Also, the direction of movement in dentist average income is inverse to that of dentists per capita. All this is what would be expected to occur between any two dates during which a price (dentist income) and quantity adjustment to initial disequilibrium was in process.

7) In tables 25.4 and 25.5 we present the results of our regressions of medic income as determined by equations (4) and (5). For both All Physicians and the Self-employed, the cross-sectional regressions generally yielded low R^2's. Per capita income, X^*_3, was positively associated with X_7. One possible explanation of the positive sign of the coefficients of X^*_3 is that they reflect differences in physician "quality" that might be supposed to have a positive correlation with X^*_3. Another possibility is that X^*_3 measures per capita *money* income and that consumer price differences, which are correlated with money incomes, cause real incomes to differ less among states than money incomes. Another important possibility is that a substantial *general level* of difficulty of entry, randomly distributed among the states (and therefore not reflected in X_5) inhibits migration and gives relatively high incomes and a protected market to physicians in states of high per capita income.

Turning to table 25.5, we find that relative changes in physician income tend to vary inversely with relative changes in the number of physicians per capita. This is what would occur if the allocation process were leading physicians away from states that initially had more than their equilibrium number of physicians per head, and paid them (on the average) less than their equilibrium wage, and leading them toward states initially in the reverse position.

The relatively low t values of the coefficients in equations (4) and (5) are to be expected on the following grounds: if the spatial allocation process of physicians worked frictionlessly, i.e., without lags, so that each observed position was one of long-run equilibrium (except for random errors) then the expected values of all coefficients in (5) would be zero. The evidence (in table 25.4) from the cross-sectional coefficients of X_7 on X^*_1 indicates the presence

TABLE 25.3 REGRESSIONS OF CHANGE IN NUMBER OF PHYSICIANS PER CAPITA ON SELECTED EXPLANATORY VARIABLES

ΔX^*_1	Years	Constant	Coefficient, t Ratio and Elasticity at Mean of			$R^2(c)$	Number of States
			$X^{*'}_1$	X'_7	ΔX_7		
All Physicians[a]	1930–40	−49.43	−.11 (1.19) 10.44	.0057 (1.23) −38.40	−.0021 (.64) −7.96	.10	18
All Physicians[b]	1940–50	.84	.04 (.62) 1.70	−.0025 (1.24) −4.22	.0016 (.62) 3.23	.00	21
Self-employed Physicians[c]	1950–60	1.89	−.08 (.93) −9.78	.0001 (.21) 3.58	.0003 (.66) 4.44	.00	43
Self-employed Physicians[d]	1950–60	−9.55	−.04 (.38) −2.08	.0017 (1.28) 13.74	−.0008 (1.19) −4.38	.02	34
All Physicians[e]	1930–60	51.80	−.21 (2.19)	.0012 (.50)	−.0017 (2.13)	.11	43
All Physicians[f]	1930–50	34.73	−.15 (2.21) 5.89	.0010 (.67) −2.88	−.0025 (3.27) 9.27	.20	49
Dentists[g]	1930–40	7.44	−.2010 (2.05) 2.37	.0004 (.08) −.29	.0005 (.08) .17	.03	11
Dentists[h]	1940–50	2.95	−.1045 (1.13) .99	.0021 (.78) −.89	−.0026 (3.48) 1.33	.47	16
Dentists[i]	1950–60	4.89	−.22 (4.38) 7.68	.0009 (1.16) −4.64	−.0003 (.65) 1.70	.25	49
Dentists[k]	1950–60	12.05	−.20 (4.17) 6.96	.001 (1.24) −4.92	−.0013 (1.89) 8.04	.29	47
Dentists[q]	1930–60	21.86	−.46 (8.66) 1.96	.0046 (2.72) −1.60	−.0029 (4.22) 2.27	.84	20
Dentists[t]	1930–50	11.59	−.28 (4.32) 1.53	.0006 (.30) −.28	−.0050 (3.46) .85	.63	20
Dentists[v]	1940–60	25.19	−.2273 (1.84) 1.13	.0024 (.75) −.53	−.0024 (2.41) 2.33	.37	17

[a] (Net income non-salaried physicians 1941) [2]* minus (Gross income physicians 1928) [1].
[b] (Net income all physicians 1949) [3] minus (Net income all physicians 1941) [2].
[c] (Gross income physicians in solo-practice 1960) [4] minus (Gross income physicians in independent practice 1949) [3].
[d] (Net income physicians in solo-practice 1963) [7] minus (Net income physicians in independent practice 1949) [3].
[e] (Gross income physicians in solo-practice 1960) [4] minus (Gross income physicians 1928) [1].
[f] (Gross income physicians in independent practice 1949) [3] minus (Gross income physicians 1928) [1].

of a moderate degree of short-run disequilibrium (friction) in each of the various initial years. What is indicated in table 25.5 is a moderate response of relative physician income to this situation.

This "moderate" response must be interpreted against the background of large interstate movements of physicians occurring in response to large interstate movements of population. Presumably these movements took place without generating any significant correlation between average physician incomes and either $X^{*'}_1$ or ΔX^{*}_1. In other words, the interstate mobility of physicians was sufficient to direct the movement of physicians in response to population shifts, so that the effect of differential growth rates in physician demand (among states) did not have a strong effect on differential changes in average physician income, provided a decade was allowed for adjustment.

The results for income of dentists are very much clearer than for income of physicians. In the cross sections, the t values for certain coefficients usually exceed 2 and the R^2's, are quite high. In general, high average income for dentists is partially correlated with high per capita income and a low number of dentists per capita. But the most interesting result, by far, is the consistently strong positive effect of the failure rate on average incomes. Clearly, differentially high failure rates have been associated with high average incomes for dentists. However, these findings have already been discussed.

II. Structural Relations

Our data make possible an exploratory attempt to estimate the parameters of a simple structural model that determines the location of medics. This attempt suffers both from the poor quality of the data, especially that referring to physician income, and also from inadequate specification resulting from theoretical difficulties.

The model with which we have experimented thus far is one with two equations, supply and demand. This can be written in arithmetic form as follows:

$$X_1 = a^{(D)} + b_{62}^{(D)}X_2 + b_{63}X^*_3 \\ + b_{67}^{(D)}X_7 + U_D \quad (6\text{–D})$$
$$X_1 = a^{(S)} + b_{62}^{(S)}X_2 + b_{64}X_4 \\ + b_{65}X_5 + b_{66}X_6 \\ + b_{67}^{(S)}X_7 + U_S \quad (6\text{–S})$$

X_1 is defined as before; b_{6i} is the coefficient of X_i in equation (6); where needed, the superscript (D) demand or (S) supply is attached to a symbol; $a^{(S)}$ and $a^{(D)}$ are constants. Our model consists of two equations (supply and demand) and six variables; two of the variables (X_1 and X_7) are endogenous and the others (X_2, X^*_3, X_4, X_5 and X_6) are exogenous. The coefficients in the equations have been estimated by two stage least squares. Both equations are identified; the supply equation is just identified (excluding only X^*_3), while the demand equation is over-identified.

As table 25.6 shows, the coefficients of the variables in the demand equation have the appropriate signs.

The rationale of the signs is simple; the services of medics are a superior good and hence the per capita demand for them increases with per capita income. Higher per capita demand, with a fixed number of medics per capita, would lead to higher average incomes of each medic. This would, in turn, lead to movement of medics from states where their average incomes were relatively low, to states where they were higher, thereby leading to equalization of net advantage of location with states having

---

g (Net income dentists 1937) [6] minus (Income dentists 1928) [5].
h (Income dentists 1948) [8] minus (Income dentists 1937) [6].
i (Net income all dentists 1958) [9] minus (Net income all dentists 1949) [11].
k (Net income all dentists 1961) [10] minus (Net income all dentists 1949) [11].
q (Net income all dentists 1961) [10] minus (Income dentists 1928) [5].
t (Net income all dentists 1949) [11] minus (Income dentists 1928) [5].
v (Net income all dentists 1961) [10] minus (Income dentists 1937) [6].
* Numbers in square brackets specify the number of the corresponding data source.

TABLE 25.4 CROSS-SECTIONAL REGRESSIONS OF MEDIC INCOME ON SELECTED EXPLANATORY VARIABLES IN SELECTED YEARS

Year	Constant	Coefficient, t Ratio and Elasticity at Mean of					$R^2(c)$	No. of States
		X^*_3	X^*_4	X^*_6	X_5	X^*_1		

Physicians Income—X_7

1928	9700	6.84	−.84	−18.63	−8.67	−10.20	.14	49
		(2.51)	(.05)	(.68)	(.29)	(.57)		
		.45	−.00	−.09	−.00	−.13		
1941	3843	9.26	10.61	−8.60	−46.97	−28.15	.45	21
		(2.53)	(.51)	(.31)	(2.00)	(1.38)		
		1.07	.04	−.09	−.07	−.70		
1949	11747	4.00	9.92	−24.99	−25.18	−52.05	.22	49
		(3.45)	(.79)	(1.13)	(1.01)	(2.42)		
		.46	.01	−.11	−.01	−.33		
1960	24763	7.13	−48.62	−74.55	−132.65	−43.97	.10	43
		(2.37)	(1.50)	(1.03)	(1.93)	(.93)		
		.50	−.03	−.15	−.04	−.12		
1963	18197	3.62	59.36	−17.42	−67.29	−61.77	.04	34
		(1.42)	(.93)	(.27)	(1.42)	(1.65)		
		.37	.05	−.05	−.03	−.24		

Dentists Income—X_7

1929	3365	5.86	11.00	−28.88	9.20	−21.82	.68	20
		(3.80)	(.56)	(1.64)	(1.19)	(2.50)		
		.81	.02	−.31	.03	−.27		
1937	2147	4.43	−20.32	−11.05	−7.49	−20.23	.64	17
		(2.27)	(2.02)	(.70)	(1.01)	(2.36)		
		1.05	−.06	−.25	−.04	−.45		
1948	3358	2.24	33.25	−83.84	61.99	18.43	.19	22
		(1.37)	(.80)	(2.31)	(2.70)	(.56)		
		.89	.05	−.80	.15	.16		
1949	4713	2.01	−15.21	−39.06	32.61	−13.65	.18	23
		(1.93)	(.62)	(1.78)	(2.36)	(.69)		
		.69	−.02	−.34	.08	−.11		
1958	10941	4.25	−18.69	−40.00	48.36	−103.55	.53	49
		(4.71)	(.90)	(2.06)	(3.48)	(3.80)		
		.62	−.00	−.16	.07	−.29		
1961	12496	1.18	−6.08	14.69	59.01	−36.96	.49	47
		(1.11)	(.35)	(.73)	(5.03)	(1.46)		
		.16	−.00	.05	.07	−.10		
1963	14026	3.67	−14.86	−63.91	38.27	−108.34	.06	32
		(1.33)	(.17)	(1.10)	(1.47)	(1.68)		
		.54	−.00	−.26	.05	−.32		

higher per capita incomes also having more medics per capita.

The negative sign of $b_{67}^{(D)}$ was expected on the following grounds: given per capita income and population, greater numbers of medics cause lower fees and/or smaller quantities of services sold per medic, leading to lower average income per medic.[14] This argument has two variants: (1) interstate differences in number of medics (X_1)

[14] In this sentence the direction of "causality" runs from dependent to independent variable, rather than the reverse. However, this does not upset the argument.

TABLE 25.5 REGRESSIONS OF CHANGE IN AVERAGE MEDIC INCOME ON SELECTED EXPLANATORY VARIABLES

ΔX_7	Years	Constant	Coefficient, t Ratio and Elasticity at Mean of			$R^2(c)$	No. of States
			ΔX^*_1	$X^*'_1$	X'_7		
Physicians income[a]	1930–40	2169	−13.53 (.64) −.00	.98 (.13) −.03	−.82 (2.53) 1.46	.29	18
Physicians income[b]	1940–50	8493	13.46 (.62) .01	−13.08 (2.59) −.28	−.18 (1.02) −.16	.35	21
Physicians income[c]	1950–60	12294	33.42 (.66) .00	−6.31 (.21) −.05	−.12 (.68) −.27	.00	43
Physicians income[d]	1950–60	15986	−54.65 (1.19) −.01	−29.16 (1.08) −.28	−.46 (1.35) −.70	.02	34
Physicians income[e]	1930–60	28306	−60.37 (2.13) −.00	−21.49 (1.12) −.13	−.54 (1.29) −.23	.08	43
Physicians income[f]	1930–50	14664	−76.88 (3.27) .02	−14.33 (1.15) −.15	−.19 (.76) −.15	.15	49
Dentists income[k]	1950–60	7388	−60.17 (1.89) .01	−7.85 (.62) −.04	.19 (1.09) .15	.01	47
Dentists income[q]	1930–60	8259	−180.71 (4.22) −4.23	−76.67 (3.06) −.42	.88 (1.94) .40	.43	20
Dentists income[t]	1930–50	2721	−85.79 (3.46) .50	−18.75 (1.61) −.60	−.15 (.57) −.41	.34	20

[a] (Net income non-salaried physicians 1941) [2]* minus (Gross income physicians 1928) [1].
[b] (Net income all physicians 1949) [3] minus (Net income all physicians 1941) [2].
[c] (Gross income physicians in solo-practice 1960) [4] minus (Gross income physicians in independent practice 1949) [3].
[d] (Net income physicians in solo-practice 1963) [7] minus (Net income physicians in independent practice 1949) [3].
[e] (Gross income physicians in solo-practice 1960) [4] minus (Gross income physicians 1928) [1].
[f] (Gross income physicians in independent practice 1949) [3] minus (Gross income physicians 1928) [1].
[k] (Net income all dentists 1961) [10] minus (Net income all dentists 1949) [11].
[q] (Net income all dentists 1961) [10] minus (Income dentists 1928) [5].
[t] (Net income all dentists 1949) [11] minus (Income dentists 1928) [5].
* Numbers in square brackets specify the number of the corresponding data source.

reflect only incomplete adjustments to previous shifts in demand because, in equilibrium, average pecuniary income of medics is the same in every state. If this is true, $b_{67}^{(D)}$ is an estimate of the slope of the short-run demand curve. (2) Interstate variations in average medic income reflect compensating differentials to offset nonpecuniary disadvantages. In this case $b_{67}^{(D)}$ pertains to a long-run demand curve and, at the margin, medics accept lower money income in order to obtain nonpecuniary advantages. Of course these two effects are not mutually exclusive; they may reinforce or offset one

TABLE 25.6 TWO-STAGE LEAST-SQUARES ESTIMATES OF SUPPLY AND DEMAND EQUATIONS OF SELF-EMPLOYED PHYSICIANS, 1950

X_1	Constant	X_2	X^*_3	X_4	X_5	X_6	X_7	No. of States	
Self-employed physicians 1950	2.08	1.04 (46.5)	.90 (9.5)				−.99 (3.4)	49	Demand
Self-employed physicians 1950	−13.31	.91 (16.7)		.000086 (.9)	.0109 (3.6)	.50 (3.4)	1.238 (1.5)	49	Supply

another. The estimates of $b_{67}{}^{(D)}$ include both effects, which blurs their interpretation.[15]

The rationale of the supply function is fairly obvious. The only doubtful variable is X_6, urbanism, which probably reflects demand as well as supply forces. However, we believe that most of the demand influence is captured by X^*_3 and hence we included X_6 in supply. The signs of the supply coefficients are very similar to those obtained by ordinary least squares; the signs of all coefficients in the supply equation are positive.

The most striking result of our two stage regressions is that the coefficient of medic income in the supply equation is positive and in the demand equation is negative. This result is what theoretical considerations would suggest, although the theoretical ambiguity noted in connection with the demand function arises on the supply side as well.

The fact that the signs of $b_{67}{}^{(S)}$ and $b_{67}{}^{(D)}$ are "correct" lends confidence to the specification of the model. If we were sufficiently confident of this specification, we could make "if—then" statements concerning the effect of varying the "policy variables," X_4 and X_5.

However, we have grave misgivings about the specification assumption that both (or either X_4 and X_5 are exogenous. The discussion concerning the decision rules of state licensure boards clearly suggests that failure percentages are likely to be affected by medic incomes and the quantity of medics per capita. The quantity of privately financed training facilities is surely affected by a state's previous (per capita) wealth which is positively correlated with its present per capita income. Publicly financed facilities are likely, in part, to be substitutes for private facilities (i.e., in the absence of private facilities, public facilities are "needed"), but state tax structure, per capita income, attitudes toward education (probably positively correlated with demand for medical care) and economies of scale, all affect the supply of training facilities.

In other words, there is a supply function of training facilities which involves some of the other exogenous variables in the model. A correct specification of this model requires a theory of public expenditure on which serious work is only just beginning. Therefore any statement about the effect of public policy changes on the supply of medics to a state must reflect a large measure of judgment in addition to econometric results.

III. Conclusions

Our findings suggest that, in large part, medics have displayed a tropism for higher incomes that has caused them to migrate with the effective demand for their services.

---

[15] The negative sign of $b_{67}{}^{(D)}$ and the positive one of b_{68} are similar to those obtained by M. Friedman and S. Kuznets in their pioneering work, *Income from Independent Professional Practice*, National Bureau of Economic Research, New York, 1945, pp. 161–173.

Effective demand for medic services within a state has depended mainly upon its population, and secondarily upon its per capita income. There has also been some overall tendency for a secular "correction" of an initial inequality (as of 1930) in the per capita number of medics among the states. This behavior has been superimposed on a locational preference pattern that causes medics to sacrifice pecuniary income for the amenities of an urban environment.

For dentists, though not for physicians, the locational adjustment to relative movements of population and per capita income has been impeded by the way in which state licensure requirements have been administered. This suggests that changes in the policies, and quite possibly in the manner of selecting members of state examining boards, would be in the public interest.

It also appears that the per capita number (in a given state) of physicians increases with the state's volume of training facilities. (This is not true of dentists.)[16] Despite the aforementioned specification difficulties, we suspect that increasing training facilties in a state would tend to increase its per capita number of physicians. However, there may be more economical ways by which a state can achieve the same result.

References

(Sources for Income Data)

[1] Leland, R. G., "Income from Medical Practice," *Journal of the American Medical Association*, 96 (May 16, 1931), 1683–1691.

[2] Denison, E. F., and A. Slater, "Income in Selected Professions: Part 4, Medical Service," *Survey of Current Business*, 23 (Oct. 1943), Department of Commerce, 16–20.

[3] Weinfeld, W., "Incomes of Physicians, 1929–49," *Survey of Current Business*, 31 (July 1951), U.S. Department of Commerce, 9–26.

[4] Internal Revenue Service, "U.S. Business Tax Returns, July 1960–June 1961," Washington, 1963, 52.

[5] Leven, M., *The Practise of Dentistry and Incomes of Dentists in Twenty States: 1929*, University of Chicago Press, Chicago, Illinois, 1932.

[6] Lasken, H., "Incomes of Dentists and Osteopathic Physicians," *Survey of Current Business*, 19 (April 1939), U.S. Department of Commerce, 7–13.

[7] Internal Revenue Service, "U.S. Business Tax Returns," May 1966.

[8] Weinfeld, W., "Income of Dentists, 1929–48," *Survey of Current Business*, 30 (Jan. 1950), U.S. Department of Commerce, 8–16.

[9] "The 1959 Survey of Dental Practice II. Income of Dentists by Location, Age and Other Factors," *Journal of the American Dental Association*, 60 (May 1960), 102/650–108/656.

[10] "The 1962 Survey of Dental Practice II. Income of Dentists by Location, Age and Other Factors," *Journal of the American Dental Association*, 66 (April 1963), 122/554–129/561.

(Sources of Data on Location of Medical Personnel and Census Income Data for Physicians and Dentists)

[11] Altenderfer, M. E., and M. Y. Pennell, *Health Manpower Source Book 5. Industry and Occupational Data from 1950 Census by State*, U.S. Department of Health, Education and Welfare, Washington, 1954.

[12] Prindle, R. A., and M. Y. Pennell, *Health Manpower Source Book 17. Industry and Occupational Data from 1960 Census by States*, U.S. Department of Health, Education and Welfare, Washington, D.C., 1963.

[13] *American Medical Directory*, 18th edition, American Medical Association, Chicago, 1950.

---

[16] In view of the earlier argument on the determinants of failure rates, it seems reasonable to suppose that an increased number of dentists trained in-state would be offset, at least in part, by a greater failure rate of would-be immigrants.

[14] American Medical Association, Department of Economic Research, *Distribution of Physicians in the United States by State, Region, District and County, 1959,* Chicago, 1962.
[15] "Changes in the Distribution of Dentists, 1956–1960," *Journal of the American Dental Association,* 63 (Nov. 1961), 137/715–142/720.
[16] Moen, B. D., American Dental Association, Bureau of Economic Research and Statistics, "Distribution of Dentists in the United States," *Journal of the American Dental Association,* 39 (Oct. 1949), 489–492.

(Sources on Population and Per Capita Income)

[17] U.S. Bureau of the Census, *Statistical Abstract of the United States, 1946* (67th edition), Washington, D.C., 1946.
[18] U.S. Bureau of the Census, *Statistical Abstract of the United States, 1963* (84th edition), Washington, D.C., 1963.
[19] "Medical Education in the United States," *Journal of the American Medical Association,* 95 (Aug. 16, 1930), 487–534.
[20] "Medical Education in the United States and Canada," *Journal of the American Medical Association,* 115 (Aug. 31, 1940), 685–784.
[21] Anderson, D. G., and A. Tipner, "Medical Education in the United States and Canada," *Journal of the American Medical Association,* 144 (Sept. 9, 1950), 109–181.
[22] Wiggins, W. S., G. R. Leymaster, A. N. Taylor, and A. Tipner, "Medical Education in the United States and Canada," *Journal of the American Medical Association,* 174 (Nov. 12, 1960), 1423–1526.
[23] Carnegie Foundation for Advancement of Teaching, Bulletin 19-20, 1926–1927.
[24] World Health Organization, *World Directory of Dental Schools,* Geneva, 1961.

(Sources for State Licensure Examination Results and Training Facilities)

[25] *Journal of the American Medical Association,* 94–95 (1930), passim.
[26] "State Board Number," *Journal of the American Medical Association,* 114 (Apr. 27, 1940), 1645–1655.
[27] "Medical Licensure Statistics for 1949," *Journal of the American Medical Association,* 143 (June 3, 1950), 462.
[28] "State Board Number," *Journal of the American Medical Association,* 173 (May 28, 1960), 387.
[29] "Medical Education," *Journal of the American Medical Association,* 95 (Aug. 16, 1930), 505.
[30] "Medical Education," *Journal of the American Medical Association,* 115 (Aug. 31, 1940), 696.
[31] "Medical Education," *Journal of the American Medical Association,* 144 (Sept. 9, 1950), 112–114.
[32] "Medical Education," *Journal of the American Medical Association,* 174 (Nov. 12, 1960), 1426–1427.
[33] Maurizi, A., *An Economic Analysis of the Dental Profession,* Ph.D. dissertation, Stanford University, 1967.
[34] Holen, A. S., *Effect of State Licensing Arrangements in Five Professions on Interstate Labor Mobility and Resource Allocation,* M.A. thesis, Columbia University, 1962.

26
Hourly Earnings Differentials by Region and Size of City[1]

Victor R. Fuchs

The existence of lower wages in the South than in the rest of the United States has been a subject of continuing practical and scientific interest. For businessmen, union leaders, and public officials, the regional wage differential has significant implications for policy purposes. Some economists have concentrated their research on explaining the differential. Others have found it to be of considerable value in testing economic theories and in deriving quantitative estimates of important economic relationships.

Thus, the fact that the price of labor relative to the price of capital differs between regions permits the estimation of production functions for individual industries and the calculation of elasticities of substitution between labor and capital.

Similarly, if it is true that the regional wage differential is significantly greater for unskilled than for skilled labor, it should be possible to use this information to gain insights concerning the elasticity of substitution of human capital for raw labor. Such insights would contribute to an understanding of interindustry differences in rates of change of output per man over time. In addition to its role in the estimation of production functions, the wage differential is important in the analysis of income distribution, population migration, and changes in the location of manufacturing.

Geographical Standardization

Standardization for geographical differences in industry or occupation mix is a

---

Reprinted from *Monthly Labor Review*, U.S. Department of Labor, January 1967, pp. 22–26.

[1] Editor's Note: This is an excerpt from an Occasional Paper published by the National Bureau of Economic Research as part of its study of productivity in the service industries undertaken with the assistance of a grant from the Ford Foundation. For ease in reading, signs to denote elisions have not been employed. Most of the conclusions are presented; the full paper should be consulted for additional evidence, bibliographical references, and details concerning data and methodology. [See Victor R. Fuchs, "Differentials in Hourly Earnings by Region and City Size, 1959," Occasional Paper 101 (New York: National Bureau of Economic Research, 1967).—Eds.]

useful way of getting at the question of geographical differences in labor quality, but it is deficient to the extent that there are labor quality differences within the same industry or occupation. An alternative approach to the problem would be to look at such labor quality proxies as color, age, sex, and education, since it is well known that there are significant wage differentials at the national level associated with each of these variables.

The purpose of this paper is to present new estimates of geographical wage differentials based on average hourly earnings of all nonagricultural persons as calculated from the *1960 Census of Population*. The availability of a 1/1,000 sample of the census on punched cards makes it possible to standardize simultaneously for color, age, sex, and education[2] and to investigate the relation between city size and wages along with the analysis of regional differentials.

The population studied included all persons who were employed in nonagricultural industries during the Census "reference" week (varying weeks in April) in 1960, and who had some earnings in 1959. The total number of persons covered in the sample was 56,247. Estimates of annual hours worked were obtained for each worker by multiplying the number of weeks worked in 1959 by the number of hours worked in the Census reference week in April 1960. Though the use of hours for a single week in a different year and inaccuracy in reporting of hours may produce considerable error for any single worker, no large or systematic error is present in comparisons of groups.

Annual hours and annual earnings were each aggregated across workers in each group. Average hourly earnings for each group in 1959 were estimated by dividing aggregate earnings by man-hours. These estimates are referred to as "actual" hourly earnings to distinguish them from "expected" earnings.

"Expected" earnings for each region or city size were obtained by multiplying, for each worker, the estimated number of hours worked in 1959 by the national hourly earnings rate for his particular color, age, sex, and education cell. (There are 168 such cells.) These earnings were then aggregated and divided by the aggregate man-hours to get "expected" hourly earnings. To the extent that labor quality is associated with color, age, sex, and education, differences in average "expected" earnings across regions and city size groups measure differences in labor quality; differences in the ratio of estimated actual earnings to "expected" earnings measure differences in wages, holding labor quality constant.[3]

It should be noted that the differentials studied in this paper are *relative* differentials; they are obtained by dividing "actual" by "expected" earnings. It is also possible to study *absolute* differentials by subtracting expected from actual earnings. Because our primary interest is how demand for labor responds to changing wage rates, the relative differentials appear to be more relevant. If one were primarily interested in questions concerning the supply of labor, absolute differentials would be used.

Regional Differentials

The regional differentials in average hourly earnings in dollars and in index-

---

[2] The computer program was written by Charlotte Boschan of the National Bureau of Economic Research with the assistance of a grant of computer time from International Business Machine Corp. Details concerning the program are available upon request to the author.

Certain data used were derived from punch cards furnished under a joint project sponsored by the U.S. Bureau of Census and the Population Council. Neither the Census Bureau nor the Population Council assumes any responsibility of the validity of any of the figures or interpretations of them, published herein, based on this material.

[3] Systematic differences in national hourly earnings rates by color, age, sex, and education suggest that these variables do, to some extent at least, measure labor quality. The white-nonwhite differences are probably due in part to market discrimination, but color is relevant to quality because of the likelihood that, at given levels of education, nonwhites have received poorer quality schooling and less on-the-job training than have whites.

TABLE 26.1   AVERAGE HOURLY EARNINGS, NONAGRICULTURAL EMPLOYED PERSONS, BY REGION, 1959

Item	South	Non-South	Northeast	North Central	West
	Dollars per hour				
Total	$2.12	$2.65	$2.62	$2.60	$2.76
White males	$2.54	$2.99	$2.97	$2.94	$3.09
White females	1.56	1.83	1.84	1.75	1.97
Nonwhite males	1.40	2.22	2.07	2.25	2.43
Nonwhite females	.92	1.50	1.55	1.40	1.56
	Index, South = 100				
Total	100	125	124	123	130
White males	100	118	117	116	122
White females	100	117	118	113	126
Nonwhite males	100	159	149	161	174
Nonwhite females	100	163	168	152	170

Source: *U.S. Censuses of Population and Housing: 1960 1/1,000 Sample.*

number form with the South equal to 100, are shown in table 26.1. The figures contain few surprises. Earnings are significantly lower in the South than in other regions; earnings in the West are slightly higher than in the Northeast or North Central divisions. The difference between the South and the rest of the country is much greater for nonwhites than for whites; within each color group, the differentials for males and for females appear to be about the same.

The following tabulation shows the extent to which regional earnings differences can be explained by differences in color, age, sex, and education.

Where the comparison is for a given color-sex group, the effect of differences in age and education is reflected in the "expected" earnings. Labor quality, as measured by these variables, appears to be somewhat lower in the South than in the rest of the country, and highest in the West. The regional difference is slightly greater for males than for females. In fact, white females in the South have slightly higher "expected" earnings than in the Northeast and North Central.

A significant regional wage differential remains after standardizing for color, age, sex, and education. (See table 26.2.) For all nonagricultural employed persons, the

"EXPECTED" AVERAGE HOURLY EARNINGS, BY REGION, 1959 (DOLLARS PER HOUR)

	South	Non-South	Northeast	North Central	West
Total	2.38	2.54	2.53	2.52	2.61
White males	2.82	2.89	2.90	2.85	2.95
White females	1.77	1.76	1.72	1.75	1.85
Nonwhite males	1.74	1.91	1.90	1.88	2.01
Nonwhite females	1.16	1.24	1.19	1.21	1.31

TABLE 26.2   RATIO OF ACTUAL TO "EXPECTED" HOURLY EARNINGS, BY REGION, 1959

Item	South	Non-South	Northeast	North Central	West
			Ratio		
Total	0.89	1.04	1.04	1.03	1.06
White males	.90	1.03	1.02	1.03	1.05
White females	.89	1.04	1.07	1.00	1.07
Nonwhite males	.80	1.16	1.09	1.20	1.21
Nonwhite females	.79	1.21	1.30	1.16	1.19
		Index of ratio, South = 100			
Total	100	117	117	116	119
White males	100	114	113	114	117
White females	100	117	120	112	120
Nonwhite males	100	145	136	150	151
Nonwhite females	100	153	165	147	151

differential between the South and the rest of the country is approximately 17 percent. It is much greater for nonwhites than for whites and is smallest for white males where the differential is of the order of 14 percent.

It is worth noting that the standardization procedure used here is not the only one available for studying this problem. It would be equally appropriate to standardize by using the actual earnings rates for each color, age, sex, and education cell in each region, weighted by the national distribution of man-hours. When the two standardization procedures yield markedly different results, interpretation is difficult. Fortunately, in this instance the two standardization procedures give similar results. For white males the difference in results is of the order of 1 percent. For nonwhite females it goes as high as 2 percent.

This section has shown that only a portion of the gross non-South/South wage differential is attributable to demographic differences in the labor force. It is sometimes argued that the remainder is largely attributable to differences in city size, rather than to a regional differential at given city sizes. The next section deals with the question of wage differentials associated with city size.

City-Size Differentials

A strong and consistent positive relation exists between earnings and city size. Average hourly earnings tend to rise with city size in every region and for every color-sex group. The rate of increase is sharpest in the South, and least pronounced in the Northeast and West. It is also sharper for nonwhites than for whites. Because the South has a relatively large proportion of nonwhites, a question arises whether the sharper city-size gradient is predominantly a regional or color phenomenon. The last four rows of table 26.3 show that only the regional difference is significant. Holding color constant, the city-size gradient is steeper in the South than in the non-South for both whites and nonwhites. Holding region constant, there is no evidence of a steeper gradient for nonwhites than for whites.

Little of the city-size wage differential can be explained by differences in color, age, sex, or education (table 26.4). There is a slight tendency for "expected" earnings in rural areas to be below average, but on the

TABLE 26.3 AVERAGE HOURLY EARNINGS, NONAGRICULTURAL EMPLOYED PERSONS, BY CITY SIZE, 1959

Item	Rural	Urban places		Standard Metropolitan Statistical Areas			
		Under 10,000	10,000– 99,999	Under 250,000	250,000– 499,999	500,000– 999,999	1,000,000 and more
				Dollars per hour			
Total	$2.00	$2.12	$2.23	$2.39	$2.43	$2.56	$2.84
South	$1.71	$1.82	$1.94	$2.15	$2.31	$2.34	$2.62
Non-South	2.22	2.30	2.39	2.54	2.50	2.67	2.87
Northeast	2.33	2.37	2.41	2.41	2.36	2.51	2.79
North Central	2.11	2.22	2.33	2.61	2.61	2.79	2.90
West	2.36	2.43	2.50	2.65	2.62	2.71	2.98
White males	2.24	2.43	2.61	2.78	2.77	2.96	3.29
White females	1.45	1.49	1.57	1.65	1.69	1.82	2.00
Nonwhite males	1.28	1.26	1.33	1.53	1.89	2.00	2.08
Nonwhite females	.83	.69	.91	.85	1.05	1.24	1.47
South:							
Whites	1.80	1.98	2.14	2.34	2.46	2.54	2.86
Nonwhites	1.06	.99	.99	1.13	1.28	1.37	1.54
Non-South:							
Whites	2.22	2.31	2.40	2.56	2.52	2.71	2.96
Nonwhites	1.80*	1.62	1.84	1.90	2.13	2.18	1.96

* Based on fewer than 50 observations.

whole the labor force "mix" is similar in all city-size categories.[4] Strictly speaking, similarity of expected earnings only proves that the "mix" is similar on average; there could be significant offsetting differences in the distributions by years of schooling or other variables. In fact, the distributions are quite similar, but there is a tendency for the larger cities in the non-South to have a greater than average share of workers in the lowest and the highest educational classes.

The sharp variation in actual earnings, combined with great similarity in "expected" earnings, means that the ratio of actual to "expected" varies greatly with city size. These ratios indicate that within each region there is a very considerable range of earnings, after standardizing for color, age, sex, and education. They also show that within each color-sex group, wages vary considerably by city size after standardizing for age and education.[5]

Regional Differential Adjusted

The South has a much larger share of its nonagricultural work force outside of Standard Metropolitan Statistical Areas and a much smaller share in SMSA's of 1 million and over than does the non-South. This fact, plus the existence of a significant wage differential across city sizes within regions, suggests the possibility that a substantial portion of the regional wage differential observed in table 26.2 is a reflection of the city-size effect.

[4] When the differences in "mix" are very small, the problem of choosing between alternative standardization procedure is unimportant.

[5] The city-size differential may be biased upward to the extent that some nonagricultural employed persons may have been employed in agriculture in 1959, and a disproportionate share of such persons may be in the areas outside SMSA's. The chances of this being an important source of bias seem very slight.

TABLE 26.4 "EXPECTED" AVERAGE HOURLY EARNINGS, BY CITY SIZE, 1959

Item	Rural	Urban places		Standard Metropolitan Statistical Areas			
		Under 10,000	10,000–99,999	Under 250,000	250,000–499,999	500,000–999,999	1,000,000 and more
		Dollars per hour					
Total	$2.41	$2.53	$2.48	$2.49	$2.50	$2.50	$2.53
South	$2.26	$2.39	$2.35	$2.41	$2.46	$2.43	$2.47
Non-South	2.53	2.62	2.55	2.54	2.52	2.54	2.54
Northeast	2.56	2.59	2.55	2.51	2.46	2.53	2.54
North Central	2.49	2.60	2.51	2.54	2.54	2.52	2.51
West	2.59	2.72	2.64	2.63	2.62	2.57	2.61
White males	2.70	2.89	2.86	2.86	2.85	2.91	2.95
White females	1.74	1.77	1.78	1.76	1.76	1.78	1.76
Nonwhite males	1.63	1.68	1.76	1.86	1.82	1.87	1.89
Nonwhite females	1.10	1.09	1.18	1.17	1.18	1.23	1.23
South:							
Whites	2.37	2.56	2.53	2.57	2.59	2.60	2.66
Nonwhites	1.44	1.45	1.49	1.55	1.55	1.56	1.61
Non-South:							
Whites	2.54	2.63	2.57	2.57	2.55	2.61	2.63
Nonwhites	1.67*	1.55	1.63	1.74	1.63	1.77	1.69

* Based on fewer than 50 observations.

One method of adjustment consists of taking the ratio of actual to expected in each city size in each region and weighting it by the share of that city size in national total man-hours.[6]

Whereas, after adjusting for color, age, sex, and education, the differential between the non-South and the South was of the order of 17 percent; it is about 9 percent after city size is also taken into account. City size does make some difference, but does not explain all of the regional differential. It makes the greatest difference in the Northeast, and the least in the North Central. The regional differential continues to be much greater for nonwhites than for whites.

It is also possible to recalculate the city-size differentials holding region constant. The effect of this adjustment proves to be relatively small. In general, hourly earnings in the largest urban areas are approximately 30 percent higher than in the rural areas and small towns, and approximately 15 percent higher than in the small Standard Metropolitan Statistical Areas.

Conclusions

The observed average hourly earnings in the non-South are about 25 percent higher than in the South. About one-third of this differential is attributable to regional differences in the labor force as measured by color, age, sex, and education; about one-third is related to regional differences in city size; and about one-third of the differential remains, after adjusting for labor force composition and city size.

These estimates cannot be precise, partly because of the limitations of the data, and partly because the standardization techniques are necessarily imperfect. Some experimentation with alternative standardizations produced similar results; these estimates

---

[6] The possibility of an alternative standardization procedure arises again and again, fortunately, the other procedure gives very similar results, except for nonwhites in the individual regions of the non-South.

therefore are probably reasonably good guides to the order of magnitude of the various factors that contribute to the regional wage differential.

For white males alone, the gross non-South/South differential is approximately 18 percent. Differences in education and age explain less than one-fourth of the differential; city-size differences explain more than one-third; and the regional differential, after adjusting for all these factors, is slightly more than one-third the gross differential. In the case of white females, education and age do not explain any of the 17 percent regional differential, but city size explains about one-half of it. For nonwhites, the gross differential is of the order of 60 percent. Differences in education and age explain about one-fourth of the differential for males, but only one-tenth for females. The reverse is true for city size, so that both nonwhite groups show the same net differential, approximately 35 percent.

An attempt to explain interindustry differentials in average hourly earnings through multiple regression analysis offers some confirmation of these findings. The percentage of employment in the South, the percentage of employment in large cities, "expected" hourly earnings, extent of unionization, and size of employer were used as explanatory variables. Taken alone, the regional variable is significantly related (inversely) to hourly earnings. The significance of the relationship is sharply reduced when account is taken of "expected" earnings and is further reduced when account is also taken of the percentage of employment in large cities. The remaining relation between earnings and percentage in the South is entirely explained by industry differences in extent of unionization.

One of the important conclusions of the paper is the findings of a substantial difference in hourly earnings across city size. Furthermore, these differences are relatively unaffected by standardization for labor force composition and regional mix. Standardized hourly earnings in the SMSA's of 1 million and over are typically 25 to 35 percent higher than in the areas outside SMSA's within the same region, and about 15 percent higher than in SMSA's of less than 1 million. The city-size gradient is steeper in the South than in the rest of the country. Multiple regression analysis across industries again tends to confirm these findings. Furthermore, the regression analysis rejects the hypotheses that the higher earnings in the large cities can be attributed to unionization or size of employer.

The non-South/South differential is found to be inversely related to skill level as measured by education, sex, and color. The fact that the regional differential varies with education within each color may help to shed new light on an old problem—the reason for the large regional wage variation for nonwhites compared with whites. This has usually been explained in terms of greater market discrimination against nonwhites in the South than in the non-South. But there is an alternative explanation. It may reflect, at least in part, the fact that nonwhites are disproportionately of low skill, both in the South and the non-South, and that the regional differential is greater, the lower the skill level, regardless of color. This hypothesis appears worthy of further study. An alternative way of interpreting the data would be to say that there is more economic segregation in the South than in the non-South. This depresses the price of nonwhite unskilled labor but raises the relative price of nonwhite skilled labor because of its relative scarcity.

The city-size differential in hourly earnings appears to be about the same at all levels of education. One possible explanation of this differential is differences in cost of living. Adequate data are not available for a thorough check of this hypothesis. Fragmentary information provided by the Bureau of Labor Statistics on the cost of living in different cities suggests some slight correlation between hourly earnings and prices,[7] but inter-

---

[7] See "City Workers Family Budget for October 1951," *Monthly Labor Review*, May 1952, pp. 520–522, and "The Interim City Workers Family Budget," *Monthly Labor Review*, August 1960, pp. 785–808.

city differences in cost of living appear to be small relative to differences in hourly earnings. However, it should be noted that conventional measures of cost of living do not include items like length of time needed to get to work which may vary systematically with city size.

One of the most promising hypotheses to explain the city-size differential is that it reflects differences in labor quality not captured by standardization for color, age, sex, and education. This might take the form of better quality schooling, more on-the-job training, selective in-migration to the big cities of more ambitious and hard working persons, or other forms. Another possible explanation is the existence of a disequilibrium in the supply of labor and capital. Surplus labor from agriculture may tend to move first to the small towns, and then later to the larger cities. Capital may be more readily available in the large cities. If there is disequilibrium, we should observe a tendency for labor to migrate from small to large cities, and for industry to move in the reverse direction.

Possible explanations of the city-size differential such as unmeasured labor quality, cost of living, and disequilibrium are not mutually exclusive. Since the differential to be explained is quite large, it is possible that all of them are valid and significant, with each explaining a part. Just as the regional differential has been put to good use in the testing of economic theories, it would appear that the large city-size differentials in hourly earnings revealed in this paper could provide a fruitful basis for considerable new economic analysis.

D. RACIAL WAGE DIFFERENTIALS

27

Discrimination and Occupational Wage Differences in the Market for Unskilled Labor

David P. Taylor[1]

The increasing concern in recent years about the economic status of minority groups, particularly Negroes, is reflected in the growing body of literature relating race to employment characteristics. These studies have drawn on a variety of data sources including aggregate census and U.S. Bureau of Labor Statistics data,[2] employer interviews,[3] and reports of fair employment practices commissions.[4] This study, in contrast, relies on disaggregated data from personnel records. As a result, we can examine an important part of the discrimination issue by comparing the background and current status of whites and Negroes in particular occupations across a range of companies.

Study Findings

If racial discrimination affects the operation of a labor market, Negroes will earn less than whites in an occupation if the two groups are of comparable quality. That is, if a given employer has specific worker quality requirements and he chooses to hire only whites for a particular class of work, he is

---

Reprinted from the *Industrial and Labor Relations Review*, Vol. 21, (April 1968), pp. 375–390. Copyright © 1968 by Cornell University. All rights reserved.

[1] [The author] wishes to thank Professors Albert Rees, George P. Shultz, Arnold R. Weber and Mary T. Hamilton for many helpful suggestions on both the form of the study and the content of earlier drafts.—Eds.

[2] Gary S. Becker, *The Economics of Discrimination* (Chicago, Ill.: University of Chicago Press, 1957); U. S. Department of Labor, "The Economic Situation of Negroes in the United States" (Washington: G.P.O., 1960), Bulletin S-3; and see Dawn Wachtel, *The Negro and Discrimination in Employment* (Ann Arbor, Mich.: The University of Michigan-Wayne State University, Institute of Labor and Industrial Relations, 1965), for an extensive bibliography.

[3] For example, Paul Norgren, et al., *Employing the Negro in American Industry* (New York: Industrial Relations Counselors, 1959); and Arron Antonovsky and Lewis Lorwin, eds., *Discrimination and Low Incomes* (New York: New York State Commission Against Discrimination, 1959).

[4] Paul Norgren and Samuel Hill, *Toward Fair Employment* (New York: Columbia University Press, 1964).

restricting the potential supply of workers to fill these jobs by refusing to consider those Negroes who meet his quality specifications. In the absence of other factors, he will be obliged to pay a higher wage than if he were to accept Negroes in his work force.[5] A secondary effect of this behavior will be to lower the wage rates that nondiscriminating employers need to pay.

A similar indication that racial discrimination affects a labor market is that when whites and Negroes are receiving the same wage rate, the Negroes will be of higher relative quality. Since some employers refuse to hire Negroes no matter what their qualifications are, nondiscriminators can acquire Negro employees of higher quality than white employees at a given wage.

Another result of discrimination is that Negroes will travel farther to work than whites. Because of the limitations on their job opportunities, Negroes will accept employment at distances from their homes that would be unacceptable to whites. This factor imposes two types of costs on the Negro worker. First, he is faced with larger out-of-pocket commuting expense. Second, there is the cost in travel time which could be spent either at wage earning or leisure activities.

In the absence of housing discrimination, a finding that Negroes travel farther to work than whites would be a clear indication of discrimination in employment. When housing discrimination is operative, however, it plays a part in relative differences in commuting distance. When a white finds a job which is far from his home, he may move closer; or employers may consciously locate their establishments away from Negro neighborhoods in white suburban areas. There is apparently no obvious way to disentangle housing and employment discrimination effects on commuting distance.

Briefly, we found that Chicago area employers were readily able to discriminate on racial grounds and in a limited number of cases did so despite state and federal laws and Presidential orders. Our regression analyses indicate that Negroes in two unskilled occupations receive substantially less pay than whites when characteristics such as age, education, seniority, prior work experience, and others are taken into account statistically. The wage difference in some cases is considerably greater than census data would suggest. Negroes consistently travel farther to their jobs than whites, and thus their relative wage is reduced further. Furthermore, even when characteristics of the employing establishment (industry group, employment size, location, etc.) are added to the regressions, a negative wage differential remains. The data presented below comprise a strong case that racial discrimination has a significant impact on the operation of the market for unskilled workers.

Data Collection

The total sample of the Chicago Labor Market Study (CLMS) consisted of eighty establishments in the Chicago-Northwestern Indiana Standard Consolidated Area.[6] Seventy-five of these establishments were chosen at random, and the other five constituted a pilot study.[7] A standardized research routine

---

[5] However some employers, as we will see below, apparently feel that if they introduce Negroes into their work force, their wage bill will increase because of the reluctance of current employees to work with Negroes.

[6] The Chicago-northwestern Illinois Standard Consolidated Area is composed of Cook, Lake, DuPage, McHenry, Will, and Kane Counties in Illinois and Lake and Porter Counties in Indiana. Hereafter it is referred to as the Standard Consolidated Area.

[7] The random sample was selected in the following way. A deck of punch cards, each representing an establishment, was secured from the Illinois State Employment Service. This deck was supplemented with cards for noncovered establishments and establishments in the Indiana portion of the Standard Consolidated Area. Establishments were then randomly selected from this listing in two employment size strata: over 1,000 employees and 250–999 employees. A similar procedure was used to develop a random sample of small (50–249 employees) establishments. Government employment and construction firms were excluded from the CLMS.

was carried out in each establishment.[8] Personal history, work experience, and wage information were collected from personnel records for each of the company's employees in the twelve occupations included in the study. The appropriate personnel officer was interviewed regarding the firm's wage policies, hiring standards, collective bargaining relationships, and recruitment sources.

Of the twelve occupations included in the CLMS,[9] only two unskilled male occupations are used in this study, material handler and janitor. A material handler is a worker who manually or with unpowered equipment moves merchandise and supplies into, around, or out of a building (e.g., a loading dock worker). The definition of a janitor is familiar and clear-cut.

Limiting a study of discrimination to unskilled workers rather than including semiskilled, skilled, clerical, or professional workers has four important advantages. First, there are significant numbers of unskilled Negro workers in the Chicago area. The same statement cannot be made about professional or skilled manual workers or, if government employment is excluded, about clerical workers, although this situation may be changing. Second, difficult questions about skill levels and job content are not as consequential as they are in multioccupational analyses of patterns of discrimination.

Third, the charge is frequently made that Negroes do not succeed in the job market because they are poorly equipped in terms of training, education, and familiarity with urban life. By limiting this study to the unskilled sector, these factors will be standardized to the extent that the data permit, i.e., unskilled Negroes will be compared with unskilled whites, thus isolating the effects of job discrimination irrespective of discrimination in education and other areas.

Finally, those researchers who have approached the problem of racial discrimination through the use of census and other aggregate data have usually found that the impact of discrimination is least felt in the unskilled areas relative to the skilled, managerial, and professional markets.[10] Mydral's findings were similar.[11] This proposition makes some sense. If an employer refuses to hire Negroes because he personally has a distaste for their racial characteristics, he will be more likely to implement his prejudice in the occupational areas of his establishment with which he comes into personal contact. Moreover, certain unskilled and service jobs, particularly the custodial occupations, have been traditionally regarded as "suitable" for Negroes. Ironically, some of these, as in private household work, involve close personal contact with whites. But in the industrial context, as Negroes begin inching their way up the occupational ladder, they pose a greater and greater threat to white employees. Employers concerned about morale and productivity of their current work force will certainly take this factor into account when making a decision about where, if at all, to employ Negroes. While this study makes interoccupational comparisons of the existence of racial discrimination in only a limited way, it points out the extent and effects of this discrimination in an occupational area which according to earlier studies is least responsive to discriminatory activities of employers.

Employment Policy Making

The employment officials interviewed in connection with the CLMS expressed a broad range of views on equal opportunity hiring. A small group thoroughly endorsed both the

---

[8] While the statistical analysis presented below is based on data from the seventy-five randomly selected firms, the following employer discussion is based on all eighty establishments.

[9] The twelve occupations were accountant, tabulating machine operator, key punch operator, clerk-typist, tool and die maker, maintenance electrician, truck driver, punch press operator, fork lift trucker, material handler, janitor, and janitress.

[10] Becker, op. cit., p. 114. Harry J. Gilman, "Discrimination and White-Nonwhite Unemployment Differentials" (Ph.D. dissertation, Department of Economics, University of Chicago, 1963), p. 16.

[11] Gunnar Myrdal, An American Dilemma (New York: Harper and Brothers, 1944), p. 303.

letter and the spirit of the Illinois Fair Employment Practices Act, while a few reported unequivocal violation. A much larger number were neither in clear-cut compliance nor outright violation of the statute. One striking aspect of employer responses to inquiries about racial hiring policies was their ability to explain their activity in economic terms, through either the labor market or the product market, no matter what these policies were.

The labor market factors included:

(1) *Morale of current employees.* One employer noted that a large proportion of his current employees were Polish and other Eastern Europeans. "Now, if we were to start hiring Negroes in here, these people would raise the roof, and we'd end up with a terrific morale problem. I really believe that integrating this plant would cost us money. I know it would."

In contrast, other firms found little resentment among current employees when Negroes were introduced into the plant. Some companies took the precaution of forewarning supervisors and foremen, but others did not on the ground that it should be considered a routine matter. One personnel man said he received a call from a foreman when he sent their first Negro worker to the production line. The foreman asked the personnel man if he realized that the worker was a Negro. He replied that he did and that a new company policy was being implemented. The personnel man reported that he had virtually no problems as a result of the change in policy.

(2) *Relationship between the firm and the community.* An employer whose firm was located in a white residential neighborhood said, "We have always tried to be a good neighbor, and we rely on this neighborhood to provide a supply of labor. So we will hold off on changing our policy on this as long as we can. It really isn't much of a problem as we have very few [Negro] applicants and, of course, all of them live quite a distance from here."

In a different setting, an employer did not hesitate to import Negro workers to a fairly remote suburban town. The personnel officer contacted the state employment office in another city and asked for applicants, knowing that some would be Negro. He was confident that the townspeople would cause very little trouble, since the plant was the largest employer in the area.

(3) *Perceived quality of Negro workers.* Some employers insist that Negro workers are of lower quality than the whites in their current work force. They cite aggregate education, work experience data, and crime statistics to support this claim. In contrast, one employer said, "Since we started hiring Negroes, we've found that we can get better quality people at the same wage rate. Their attendance record is better, and they have lower turnover."

(4) *Negroes never apply at the firm's employment office.* A shortage of Negro applicants can be either a legitimate or a hypocritical reason for failing to hire Negroes. Thus, one employer said he preferred personal referrals to want ads, because want ads generated so many Negro applicants. Another employer switched his advertising from the *Chicago Tribune* to *Cicero Life*, because he was getting too many Negroes from his ads in the *Tribune*. In 1960, the city of Cicero had four Negro residents in a total population of nearly 70,000.[12] Of course, some firms never get Negro applicants because of long-standing reputations for discrimination.

Product market factors also affect hiring policy:

(1) *Relations with the government.* If a firm, because of the nature of its product or service, has frequent and intimate dealings with the government, particularly the federal government, it is probably difficult for it to maintain a discriminatory hiring policy. This is especially true if the company

---

[12] Evelyn Kitagawa and Karl E. Taeuber, *Local Community Fact Book, Chicago Metropolitan Area, 1960* (Chicago, Ill.: University of Chicago, Chicago Community Inventory, 1963).

is in a regulated industry or as a contractor is frequently visited by government representatives. On the other hand, it was not clear that just any business relationship with the government was sufficient to affect hiring policies. A firm which sold a substantial amount of its regular production to the government was not overly concerned. "We have to make quarterly reports to the government, but we have a Chinese engineer, and some Mexicans here at the main plant, and some Negro janitors at our sales offices throughout the country. We lump them all together on the report, and it doesn't look too bad. I suppose if the government people come around to inspect the plant and find no Negroes, we'll be in hot water. But until then I guess we'll just go along as we have been." This interview obviously took place before the passage of Title VII of the Civil Rights Act.

(2) *Consumer product vulnerability.* Similarly, if a firm's product or service is utilized or consumed directly by the public, it is susceptible to Negro consumer boycotts.[13]

In any particular situation, a number of these factors will come into play, and it is difficult or impossible to tell a priori which will predominate. For example, if a firm is located in a white community but produces a consumer item in heavy use in the Negro market, the outcome is unpredictable without knowledge of the relative strength of the factors involved and the employer's attitude toward equal opportunity employment.

Race and Wage Rates

The discussion of discriminatory hiring activity provides a background for a consideration of numerical data collected from Chicago-area firms. Racial discrimination should have an impact on relative wages of whites and Negroes, but these differences can only be attributed to discrimination when nonrace characteristics of the individuals in the sample are taken into account. The CLMS data on 473 janitors and 550 material handlers permit us to make these comparisons using regression analysis.

Since we collected the raw data, we had wide latitude in determining the forms the variables would take. While our analysis had strong theoretical underpinnings, we also used a pragmatic approach in deciding which form to use and which variable to include. As a result, some of our variables are linear, some are nonlinear, and some are introduced as dummies, depending on the goodness of fit, as well as on basic theoretical considerations.[14] We include, in any particular regression, only those variables that lower the standard error of the regression equation, have the expected sign,[15] and do not affect the values of other variables in an unreasonable way.[16]

The dependent variable is measured in dollars per hour at work. The stated hourly wages have been adjusted to take into account differences in the number of holidays and the length of annual vacation. Thus, if two workers are receiving the same hourly wage but one has two additional holidays a year, his wage will be adjusted upward for the purpose of our analysis.[17] While we would have liked to make similar adjust-

---

[13] See Robert B. McKersie, "The Civil Rights Movement and Employment," *Industrial Relations,* Vol. 3, No. 3 (May 1964), pp. 6–7.

[14] The dummy variables were constructed by first using the finest breakout possible. On succeeding trials, the sub parts of the dummy with comparable coefficients were combined and this process was continued until the best fit was achieved.

[15] It would be unsatisfactory to include a variable with an incorrect sign to increase the $\bar{R}^2$. That is, if in one of our equations we found there was a strong negative correlation between wages and seniority contrary to all expectations, it would be incorrect to use the relationship to "explain" wage dispersion in that occupation.

[16] In those few cases where data on one variable (such as education or distance) were unavailable, we used the mean of the establishment if the value was known for five or more individuals in the establishment. Otherwise, the overall sample mean was used.

[17] See Albert Rees, *New Measures of Wage-Earner Compensation in Manufacturing, 1914–1957* (New York: National Bureau of Economic Research, 1960), Occasional Paper No. 75, p. 4.

ments for all differences in fringe benefits, and we collected detailed information on benefits from each of the firms we visited, we were not able to reduce these data to a meaningful dollars-per-hour figure.[18]

First we will review the independent variables, and the regressions will be discussed in turn.

Individual characteristics were broken down as follows.

Race and origin. The race and origin variables enter the regressions as dummies. There are separate dummy variables for nonwhites and for workers with Spanish surnames; all other whites form the base group.

Age. In order to reflect the relatively high earning potential of workers in the prime age groups, we used a quadratic form for the age variable. Age enters the regressions as both age and age squared.

Education. Education either enters as a linear variable—school years completed—or as a dummy reflecting completion of high school as a minimum.

Marital status. Since we collected individual characteristics from personnel records and had to rely primarily on application forms, this variable relates to marital status at date of hire, not at the time the wage data were collected. Those who were not known to be married at hire are assigned a 1, all others a 0. We would expect employers to prefer married applicants in these male occupations, because they probably believe married men are more responsible or at least less mobile.

Weight. In these manual occupations, it is an advantage to be husky, and two of the CLMS firms had specific physical hiring standards; others certainly applied these standards informally. It would be difficult to rationalize a linear form for this variable, and we have therefore constructed a dummy using 165 pounds as the cutoff.

Experience on previous jobs. While we believe that the unskilled jobs which are represented here require no formal training, employers may, nonetheless, prefer employees with previous work experience. Previous exposure to an industrial environment may improve a worker's performance, even in an unskilled occupation, for the first few weeks on the job. This variable enters the regressions in two forms, and the reasons for this are explored later. In some of the regressions, a worker is assigned a 1 if he has had previous work experience; while in others, those with a job in Chicago and those with a job outside Chicago are separated. In both cases, the base group is those who have never held a job.

Seniority. The seniority variable enters the regression as the natural log of years plus one with the present employer.[19] A linear form of the seniority variable was also tried, but it was considerably inferior to the curvilinear form. The shape of this function implies that length of service is not entirely an institutional factor. An employee's value to his employer (or his productivity) increases at a decreasing rate over time.[20]

Distance. In unskilled occupations we would expect the wage rate to be positively related to the distance traveled to a job, since a worker will probably make a tradeoff between wages and commuting time and expense. The distance variable enters the regressions either in a linear form or as a

---

[18] There is considerable evidence that wage rates and fringe benefits are positively related. Holding union membership and turnover costs constant, "(1) wage supplements generally vary positively with money earnings independently of any of the other factors considered, (2) variations in wage supplement expenditures can be explained largely in terms of variations in money earnings, . . ." Robert Rice, "Skill, Earnings, and the Growth of Wage Supplements," *American Economic Review*, Vol. 56, No. 2 (May 1966), p. 588.

[19] It was necessary to add one year to each employee's seniority in order to use the logarithmic form.

[20] Because long-service employees tend to have longer vacations, there is a built-in relationship between seniority and wage per hour at work, our dependent variable. The importance of this relationship was tested by running the regressions using hourly wage as the dependent variable, and there were only slight drops in the seniority coefficients. the t values remained above ten.

dummy with a 1 assigned to those who travel seventy-one blocks (8.75 miles) or more and a 0 to all others.

Establishment characteristics are as follows.

Industry. It is well recognized that wages within an occupation vary from industry to industry. Thus average hourly earnings of male janitors, porters, and cleaners in April 1963 ranged from $1.61 an hour in service industries to $2.22 an hour in public utilities.[21] Some of this variation may be attributed to differences in job requirements and working conditions among industries. A number of institutional factors undoubtedly also enter the analysis.

The industry variables enter as dummies with a base group of durable goods manufacturing.

Location. The regional variables are designed to pick up the effect of wage contours, which presumably reflect the existence of fairly discrete local labor markets within the Standard Consolidated Area.[22] The base for this set of dummies is the loop, the near north side, and the area extending west to Harlem Avenue. Region I is the area south of this (including Cicero, Clearing, and the near west side) and the Calumet section of Indiana. Region II includes the north side of Chicago and the far northern and western fringe areas of the Standard Consolidated Area.

Racial composition of neighborhoods. Because Negro employment in our sample is concentrated in the near north area and inner fringe, an alternative characteristic of the employer's location was considered for the Negro workers in the sample. The Negro population as a percentage of total population in the firm's specific neighborhood plus contiguous neighborhoods was computed for each firm.[23] This variable then enters as the percentage assigned to all individuals in the firm.

Establishment size. Some previous studies have found that wage rates are positively correlated with firm size.[24] One rationale for this is that workers prefer smaller plants in which there is greater social cohesiveness and more opportunity for advancement based on merit, since supervision is on a more direct basis. In addition, it can be argued that larger firms are forced to draw on a geographically larger labor pool and thus pay higher wages for workers of equal quality to offset their greater commuting costs. A third possibility is that size is acting as a proxy for some other characteristic of the firm such as profitability, which relates to wage levels through a nonclassical mechanism. Again we tried both linear and nonlinear forms of this variable and, generally, the nonlinear form works better. This is probably consistent with any of the explanations offered; e.g., there is a great difference between a firm with 75 employees and one with 1,075, but there may be very little difference between one with 9,000 employees and another with 10,000. As a result, the size variable enters as the log of employment rounded to the nearest 100 employees.

Two basic sets of regressions are presented below, one set for material handlers and one for janitors. These are further broken down into two classes, one which includes only individual characteristics (age, education, seniority, etc.) and one which adds to this factors peculiar to particular establishments (location, industry group, etc.). Regressions were run for both races together and then separately for whites and nonwhites.

Material Handler Regressions

Table 27.1 presents the material handler regressions, and Tables 27.2 and 27.3 provide additional analyses of the age and

---

[21] U. S. Bureau of Labor Statistics, *Occupational Wage Survey, Chicago, Illinois* (Washington: G.P.O., 1963), Bulletin No. 1345–65.

[22] See George Seltzer, "Pattern Bargaining and the United States Steel Workers," *Journal of Political Economy*, Vol. 59, No. 4 (August 1951), pp. 326–329, for a discussion of wage contours in Chicago-area steel fabricating plants.

[23] These data were calculated on the basis of work by Kitagawa and Taeuber, *op. cit.*

[24] Rees, *op. cit.*, p. 12.

TABLE 27.1 MATERIAL HANDLER REGRESSION EQUATIONS FOR THE ENTIRE SAMPLE AND FOR THE RACES SEPARATELY (t-VALUES IN PARENTHESES)

	All Material Handlers		Whites, Puerto Ricans, and Mexicans		Nonwhites	
	Coefficients Using Individual Characteristics Only	Coefficients Using Both Individual and Establishment Characteristics	Coefficients Using Individual Characteristics Only	Coefficients Using Both Individual and Establishment Characteristics	Coefficients Using Individual Characteristics Only	Coefficients Using Both Individual and Establishment Characteristics
Individual variables						
Nonwhite dummy	−.308	−.130	—	—	—	—
	(−9.68)	(−4.90)				
Puerto Rican and Mexican dummy	−.152	−.126	−.153	−.143	—	—
	(−2.10)	(−2.38)	(−2.17)	(−2.70)		
Age	.018	.011	.008	.006	.051	.037
Age squared	−.0003	−.0002	−.0002	−.0001	−.0006	−.0005
Seniority log*	.214	.188	.198	.169	.237	.222
	(11.79)	(14.07)	(9.72)	(11.01)	(6.05)	(7.83)
Weight dummy	.047	—	.033	—	.075	.059
	(1.75)		(1.06)		(1.40)	(1.47)
Education (linear)	.020	.019	.030	.023	—	—
	(3.34)	(4.35)	(4.44)	(4.50)		
Marital status	−.111	−.049	−.103	−.056	−.111	—
	(−3.65)	(−2.18)	(−3.00)	(−2.14)	(−1.71)	
Experience dummy	.144	.050	.131	.045	—	—
	(3.48)	(1.63)	(2.71)	(1.24)		

	(1)	(2)	(3)	(4)
Job Chicago dummy	—	—	—	.158 (2.78)
Distance to work	—	—	—	.003 (3.46)
Establishment variables				
Printing and chemical industry	—	.071 (2.49)	.106 (2.91)	—
Food, transportation, public utility, trade, and services	—	.411 (14.38)	.394 (13.42)	—
Textiles, apparel, and paper	—	−.459 (−13.74)	−.438 (−9.28)	—
Region II	—	−.235 (−8.34)	−.251 (−8.63)	—
Percent Negro population in neighborhood	—	—	—	−.004 (−2.47)
Constant term	1.658 (10.43)	1.825 (15.65)	1.798 (10.42)	1.926 (14.79)	1.351 (6.03)
R^2	.348	.655	.264	.594	.735
Standard error of YX	.313	.228	.303	.226	.221
N	550†		394		133
Number of establishments	39		36		19
Dependent variable				
Mean	2.408		2.482		2.200
Standard deviation	0.384		0.349		0.419

* Measured in the natural log of years.
† The subgroups do not total to the all total because in 23 cases race was not determined.

TABLE 27.2 AGE-EARNINGS FUNCTIONS FOR MATERIAL HANDLERS

	All	White	Non-white
Mean age	34.6	35.3	33.1
Results of Regressions Using Individual Variables Only			
t value of age-earnings function at age			
25	1.08	−0.28	2.67
35	−1.40	−2.19	1.48
50	−4.59	−3.72	−2.12
Value of one more year at age			
25	$ 0.003	$−0.001	$ 0.018
35	−0.003	−0.005	0.005
50	−0.012	−0.010	−0.014
Age of peak earnings	30.7	22.2	39.3
Results of Regressions Including Establishment Variables			
t value of age-earnings function at age			
25	1.23	0.33	2.74
35	−0.34	−0.74	1.55
50	−2.89	−2.08	−2.11
Value of one more year at age			
25	$ 0.003	$ 0.001	$ 0.013
35	−0.001	−0.001	0.003
50	−0.005	−0.004	−0.011
Age of peak earnings	33.6	29.3	39.1

seniority variables. The most striking result is the size of the nonwhite coefficient, about 31 cents per hour.[25] This amounts to over 12 percent of the overall mean—substantially more than would have been expected on the basis of census data. In 1959, the difference in mean wages of whites and nonwhites was between 5.5 and 6.5 percent of the overall mean for both Chicago "laborers, not elsewhere classified" and "laborers, n.e.c., manufacturing." Although the census presents annual rather than hourly data, the percentages of nonwhites and all workers who were employed between fifty and fifty-two weeks in 1959 were very similar.[26]

When the establishment characteristics enter the regression, the nonwhite coefficient drops from 31 to 13 cents per hour. This strongly suggests that the nonwhites are disproportionately employed in the low-wage establishments.

This conclusion does not apply in the case of those workers with Spanish surnames. Here the differential remains between 13 and 15 cents in both the individual and the individual-plus establishment regressions. It is probably not useful to speculate at length about the behavior of this variable, since the twenty Mexican and Puerto Rican workers make up less than 4 percent of the material handler sample. But the values the variable takes seem consistent with the view that discrimination against these workers is exercised by getting better quality for the same wage rather than through allocation to low-wage firms.

The weight variable drops out in both the combined and white regressions when establishment characteristics are added. This is reasonable if the establishment characteristics are picking up some variations in hiring standards among establishments. This variable does little in either of the Negro regressions, but it is kept in because it lowers the standard error slightly.

The performance of the experience dummies suggests that employers treat prior work experience differently when dealing with whites than with nonwhites. The dummy

---

[25] The samples of workers used in the regressions presented here are cluster samples, since observations were selected from a population of establishments, not workers. The t values reported, however, are for the number of workers in the sample. Hence, no statements have been made about statistical significance of the coefficients.

[26] *U.S. Census of Population, 1960, Illinois: Detailed Characteristics*, PC(1)15 DIll, Table 124. Almost identical percentages were obtained when comparing medians and means which had been computed from the distributions. Neither estimate, however, is precisely accurate.

TABLE 27.3 VALUE OF SENIORITY FOR MATERIAL HANDLERS

	All	White	Non-white
Mean seniority (years)	5.8	6.2	5.4
Results of Regressions Using Individual Variables Only			
Value of			
One year	$0.149	$0.137	$0.164
Five years	0.384	0.354	0.424
Ten years	0.514	0.474	0.568
One more year at five	0.033	0.030	0.037
One more year at ten	0.019	0.017	0.021
Results of Regressions Including Establishment Variables			
Value of			
One year	$0.130	$0.117	$0.154
Five years	0.337	0.303	0.398
Ten years	0.451	0.405	0.533
One more year at five	0.029	0.026	0.034
One more year at ten	0.016	0.015	0.019

variable which assigned a 1 to those who had had any previous work experience works best for the combined and white regressions. This was then divided into previous job in Chicago and previous job outside Chicago. This worked no better than the earlier try in the combined and white regressions; but in the case of nonwhites, we found that the job outside Chicago did absolutely nothing (the coefficient was virtually zero), while the job-in-Chicago variable had about a 16 cent coefficient with a *t* value of 2.78. (When the combined dummy—any previous job—was used in the nonwhite regression, it had a *t* value of 1.85.) Employers of nonwhites may be more interested in checking references, and this can be done conveniently only when the applicant has local work experience.

Employers also seem to consider education differently in the white and nonwhite cases. For both groups, the mean school years completed was 10.2 with a standard deviation of 2.5. The cents-per-hour variation is 3 cents per school year for the whites or 12 cents per hour for the difference between someone with eight years of schooling and a high school graduate. For the nonwhites, however, education does not contribute to the fit of the equation. There may be two factors operating to produce this result. First, employers could be considering whites but not Negroes as potentially promotable to more skilled jobs, and their educational level is thus of some significance. Second, employers may view the educational attainment of Negroes as irrelevant because of their feelings, justified or not, about the quality of nonwhite schools.

The age-wage relationship for whites and nonwhites lends further support to the proposition that the whites are considered promotable while the nonwhites are less likely to move up to more skilled jobs. The peak age for whites is about twenty-two and for nonwhites it is thirty-nine, despite the fact that the nonwhites are two years younger on the average. Thus, the promotable whites have left this unskilled occupation before they reach the age at which the nonwhite earnings are at a maximum.

Length of service on the present job was an important variable in all three equations, but distance traveled to work contributed to the fit of the regression only in the case of the nonwhites, where the coefficient amounted to .27 cents per block. This is 2.16 cents per hour for each mile traveled to work or a premium of about $1.73 a day for a commuting trip of ten miles. The linear form of this variable worked better than the log which we had originally thought made more sense. It may be, however, that because Negroes must rely heavily on public transportation, the economies of scale in commuting are negligible.

The distance variable is replaced by locational variables when establishment characteristics are added to the regressions. The north and west regions of the Standard Consolidated Area which are outside the important industrial concentrations had a nega-

TABLE 27.4 JANITOR REGRESSION EQUATIONS FOR THE ENTIRE SAMPLE AND FOR THE RACES SEPARATELY (t-VALUES IN PARENTHESES)

	All Janitors		Whites		Nonwhites	
	Coefficients Using Individual Characteristics Only	Coefficients Using Both Individual and Establishment Characteristics	Coefficients Using Individual Characteristics Only	Coefficients Using Both Individual and Establishment Characteristics	Coefficients Using Individual Characteristics Only	Coefficients Using Both Individual and Establishment Characteristics
Individual variables						
Negro race dummy	−.077 (−2.48)	−.090 (−3.31)	—	—	—	—
Age	.005	.013	.008	.014	.001	—
Age squared	−.0001	−.0002	−.0002	−.0002	−.0001	—
Seniority log*	.206 (12.34)	.202 (12.76)	.216 (11.71)	.206 (11.47)	.155 (4.26)	.173 (7.05)
Weight dummy	.079 (3.03)	.063 (2.69)	.042 (1.36)	.043 (1.49)	.162 (3.49)	.101 (2.73)
High school graduate dummy	.114 (3.04)	.073 (2.10)	.174 (3.56)	.114 (2.38)	—	—
Experience in Chicago	.168 (5.54)	.151 (5.50)	.092 (2.58)	.097 (2.87)	.304 (5.47)	.211 (4.59)
Distance traveled to work 70+ blocks	.096 (3.32)	—	—	—	.165 (3.56)	—

	(1)	(2)	(3)	(4)	(5)	(6)
Establishment variables						
Employment size (log)*	—	.028 (2.23)	—	.022 (1.45)	—	.068 (3.39)
Food industry	—	.404 (9.12)	—	.322 (5.36)	—	.445 (7.53)
Transportation and public utilities	—	.135 (3.31)	—	.111 (2.14)	—	.253 (4.59)
Other nondurables, trade and services	—	−.106 (−3.07)	—	−.106 (−2.70)	—	—
Region I	—	.119 (3.58)	—	.125 (3.62)	—	.224 (3.73)
Region II	—	.046 (1.30)	—	—	—	.310 (4.96)
Constant term	1.890 (12.79)	1.524 (10.79)	1.880 (9.85)	1.584 (8.60)	1.797 (7.06)	1.323 (16.53)
R^2	.317	.456	.338	.439	.376	.628
Standard error of $.YX$	.279	.248	.271	.251	.281	.219
N	473†		314		153	
Number of establishments	52		47		27	
Dependent variable						
Mean	2.390		2.378		2.406	
Standard deviation	0.335		0.329		0.349	

* Measured in natural log.
† The subgroups do not total to the all total because in six cases race was not determined.

tive sign and a high *t* value as expected. There were too few nonwhites employed in this region, however, to permit the use of the same variable in the nonwhite regression. Instead, we used a variable which measured the percent of Negro population in the establishment's general neighborhood. The negative sign of this coefficient reflects the fact that employers in areas heavily populated with Negroes do not face supply problems. Looked at another way, those nonwhites who are willing or able to find jobs outside their neighborhoods are paid a premium for doing so. Again, this is related both to housing and employment discrimination, and it would only be a guess as to how much of the coefficient is contributed to each factor.

Janitor Regressions

Tables 27.4, 27.5 and 27.6 present the results of the regressions run within the janitor occupation, and here the race variable performs differently.[27] It remains fairly steady between 8 and 9 cents per hour, both with and without the establishment characteristics. This suggests that the nonwhite janitors are not disproportionately represented in low-wage firms but rather that the differential arises because the employer gets better quality for the same wage when employing nonwhites. The fact that nonwhites and whites have about the same wage—$2.41 an hour for nonwhites and $2.38 for whites—is consistent with this.

Why does the race variable differ between the two occupations? A number of reasons can be proposed. Janitors are usually more isolated from the rest of the work force than material handlers and, on that count, pose less of a threat to fellow employees. Nonwhites in the janitorial occupations are in what may be considered traditional work for them, and employers worried about disrupting their current work forces would not face this hazard by hiring Negroes as janitors.

[27] The janitors in one establishment had to be excluded from the sample because there were a large number of them and job location was unknown for the entire group.

TABLE 27.5 AGE-EARNINGS FUNCTIONS FOR JANITORS

	All	White	Non-white
Mean age	47.1	50.2	41.0
Results of Regressions Using Individual Variables Only			
t value of age-earnings function at age			
25	−0.31	0.14	−0.33
35	−1.84	−0.96	−0.98
50	−4.83	−4.10	−1.46
Value of one more year at age			
25	$−0.001	$ 0.004	$−0.002
35	−0.004	−0.003	−0.003
50	−0.008	−0.007	−0.005
Age of peak earnings	21.1	26.9	—*
Results of Regressions Including Establishment Variables			
t value of age-earnings function at age			
25	1.46	1.19	—†
35	0.50	0.33	—†
50	−2.90	−2.95	—†
Value of one more year at age			
25	$ 0.004	$ 0.004	—†
35	0.001	0.001	—†
50	−0.004	−0.005	—†
Age of peak earnings	37.6	37.1	

* Peak lies below range of observations.
† Age variable not included in this regression.

Furthermore, there is some evidence which suggests that janitors of both races are not considered promotable by employers. As mentioned above, to some extent this is the case only with nonwhite material handlers. Thus, the mean age of the janitors is 47 years, with the whites over 50 and the nonwhites at 41. Only 15 percent of the janitors were high school graduates and mean school years completed were for all, 8.6; whites, 8.3; nonwhites, 9.1. For the material handlers, these figures were: all, 10.2 years;

TABLE 27.6 VALUE OF SENIORITY FOR JANITORS

	All	White	Non-white
Mean seniority (years)	7.8	7.9	7.7
Results of Regressions Using Individual Variables Only			
Value of			
One year	$0.143	$0.150	$0.108
Five years	0.369	0.387	0.278
Ten years	0.494	0.517	0.372
One more year at five	0.032	0.033	0.019
One more year at ten	0.018	0.024	0.013
Results of Regressions Including Establishment Variables			
Value of			
One year	$0.140	$0.143	$0.120
Five years	0.361	0.370	0.310
Ten years	0.483	0.495	0.415
One more year at five	0.031	0.032	0.027
One more year at ten	0.018	0.018	0.015

white, 10.2 years; nonwhite, 10.2 years. (The few white high school graduates were to some extent concentrated in high-wage establishments; the education coefficient drops from 17 to 11 cents when the establishment variables enter, and the t value drops from 3.6 to 2.4.)

The difference between the two occupations is also reflected in the operation of the experience variables. In the case of janitors, work experience restricted to the Chicago area was clearly the superior variable. This is probably because a substantial number of the whites were recent immigrants, displaced in many cases from Eastern Europe. Employers were interested in checking Chicago references on these applicants, and this is roughly comparable to the situation with nonwhite material handlers.

Taking all these factors into account, it seems clear that the difference in the way the race variable operates in these two occupations is attributable in large part to the promotability factor. White material handlers are considered promotable and hence are disproportionately in positions in high-wage firms. Nonwhite material handlers are not generally in the promotable category and, through the allocational effects of discrimination, are to a larger extent employed by low-wage firms.

This allocational effect does not seem to apply in the case of white and nonwhite janitors, and this is consistent with the view that promotion is a relatively minor factor in this occupation. The larger, high-wage employer does not hesitate to hire nonwhite janitors, since they probably will not be promoted and thus do not pose a threat to the current work force.[28] As a result, the morale problem, about which a number of the personnel people we interviewed were deeply concerned, does not arise.

In the case of janitors, a dummy for distance traveled to work was the best form of the distance variable. The t value is high, but the variable drops out in the white regression. This is undoubtedly related to the fact that the mean distance traveled to work for whites was fifty blocks, while for nonwhites it was eighty blocks.

The regional model was used for material handlers because it worked better than the percent Negro variable, and there were enough nonwhite observations in the north and west region. Because of this, the sign of the variable is reversed (the white coefficient was not significantly different from the base and was combined with it). That is, the usually low-wage north and west region had a strong positive effect, because it was a relatively high-wage region for nonwhites.

This area has a small nonwhite population, and the nonwhites who work there must travel long distances. The variable for this region thus has a strong positive simple correlation with the dummy for workers who

---

[28] This is also consistent with the behavior of the establishment size variable. It worked for janitors but not material handlers, and it worked primarily because of the nonwhite sample.

travel seventy blocks or more to work. Again this variable reflects both housing and employment discrimination.

The industry dummies, which are probably acting as proxies for both institutional and economic characteristics of the job, bear a heavy burden in these regressions as well as in those discussed above.[29] The dummy for the food industry stands out in this regard, undoubtedly because janitors in this industry must meet rigidly enforced standards of cleanliness.

Summary and Conclusions

Our concern here has been racial discrimination and its effects on the relative wages of whites and Negroes.

The regression analysis was designed to isolate the wage effects of this activity when a variety of nonrace characteristics of the worker and his job were taken into account. The size of the race coefficient for material handlers was surprisingly large as compared with our expectations based on census data. This resulted in large part because nonwhites were disproportionately relegated to low-wage establishments.

A different set of factors seems to be operating in the janitor occupation. Here, although the race coefficient was significantly negative and stable throughout the scores of regressions we ran, it was much smaller than in the material handler equations. The nonwhite janitors were not disproportionately represented in low-wage establishments, but rather they supplied the employer with higher quality personal characteristics than their white counterparts at the same wage.

We argue that the difference between the two occupations reflects primarily the promotability of the material handlers and the dead-end nature of the janitorial occupation. This argument can only be a tentative one, but it is supported by the behavior of the age, education, and prior work experience variables.

Even more important, however, we have found substantial evidence that racial discrimination has a marked effect on the wage levels of the workers considered. This is especially significant in view of the fact we are analyzing the wages and worker characteristics at only the lowest end of the occupational distribution—an area in which earlier research has indicated that discrimination has the least impact.

---

[29] Dummies for unionization were tried in both the janitor and material handler regressions and had negative signs in all cases. The t values were very low in the case of janitors but exceeded two for material handlers, due to interaction with the industry and locational variables.

E. UNION IMPACT ON WAGE DIFFERENTIALS

28
Marshall and Friedman on Union Strength

Lloyd Ulman[1]

In a recent essay Professor Milton Friedman claimed that ". . . laymen and economists alike tend . . . to exaggerate greatly the extent to which labor unions affect the structure and level of wages."[2] His estimate is that "probably not over 10 per cent and certainly not over 20 per cent of the labor force can be supposed to have had their wages significantly affected by the existence of unions."[3] This interesting conclusion is held to flow from a theoretical analysis of the determinants of union bargaining power, based in considerable part on Marshall's theory of joint demand. From this analysis Professor Friedman derives in substance the following conclusions:

1. Generally speaking, it can be predicted that craft unions are strong while industrial unions are weak, partly because, in the long run, the elasticity of demand for the labor of members of industrial unions can be expected to be much greater than the elasticity of demand for the labor of the crafts. This is significant for the empirical problem of assessing the magnitude of the impact of unionism upon the structure and level of wages, because the membership of the craft unions constitutes only a small percentage of the total labor force.

2. To be effective in raising and maintaining wage rates above the levels which would have prevailed in their absence, unions must be able to restrict the supply of workers or they "must be able to exercise control over employers—they must be able to prevent existing employers from under-

---

Reprinted from the *Review of Economics and Statistics*, Vol. 37 (November 1955), Harvard University Press, pp. 384–401, by permission of the publisher and author.

[1] The writer is most grateful to Professors O. H. Brownlee, John T. Dunlop, and Sumner H. Slichter, who were kind enough to read an earlier draft of this paper and to make valuable criticisms and comments thereon. He wishes also to acknowledge his indebtedness to the Social Science Research Council.

[2] Milton Friedman, "Some Comments on the Significance of Labor Unions for Economic Policy," in David McCord Wright (ed.), *The Impact of the Union* (New York, 1951), 204.

[3] *Ibid.*, 215. All page references hereafter in the body of this text are to the above article.

cutting the union wage rate, as well as the entry of new employers who would do so."

3. Wage increases in unionized sectors of the economy imply wage reductions elsewhere (page 216). This statement follows from Friedman's interpretation of the nature of the impact of unionism on the supply of labor.

4. In inflationary periods unions probably prevent wages from rising as rapidly as they otherwise would (pages 226–27). This statement follows from an argument which is not directly related to Friedman's analyses of demand and supply, although it rests upon the conclusions derived therefrom.

Friedman thus holds that craft unions are significantly stronger than industrial unions, that the over-all impact of unionism upon the structure of wages is weak (relatively few workers are organized in craft unions— pages 205–206), and that, by implication, the impact of unionism upon the general level of money wages is even weaker. Friedman sought to test his conclusions by comparing certain changes in wages and prices during three wartime inflationary periods (pages 217–21), and he found that the relative increase in money wages (and in prices) in the World War I period, when union membership reached a maximum of about one-eighth of the work force, was virtually identical with the relative increase in money wages (and in prices) in the World War II period, when union membership constituted about one-quarter of the work force (pages 216–21).

Professor Slichter, however, claims that it is incorrect to infer from such evidence that unions failed to exert an important influence upon money wage levels in the World War I period when their membership almost doubled, when the proportion of "employed wage-earners" on strike reached one-fifth (in 1919), and when many nonunion employers sought to keep out unions by adopting employee representation plans.[4] Nor do other recent empirical studies of the effects of unionism upon money wages tend to support Friedman's interpretation. Friedman confines this part of his analysis to an observation of money wages and prices during three wartime inflationary periods. Levinson, however, found that hourly earnings or wage rates of the entire group of union members rose while those of nonunion workers fell during the contraction of 1920–23, that hourly earnings or rates of union workers increased more rapidly than did those of nonunion workers during the noninflationary upswing of 1923–29, and that union wages fell less rapidly than did nonunion wages during the downswing 1929–33. On the other hand, during the period 1933–37 wages increased more rapidly in nonunion than in union sectors, while in the war boom periods, 1914–20 and 1941–47, wages in the two sectors rose at about the same rate. Levinson ascribes the latter phenomena in part to the influence of aggregate demand and in part to the influence of unions on wages in the nonunion sectors.[5] Slichter comes to a similar conclusion for the periods involved and concludes further that although "hourly earnings in poorly organized industries have risen almost as rapidly as in well-organized industries . . . the period 1946 to the present is one in which unions have exerted a powerful influence on the wages of nonunion workers."[6] Douty's analysis of wage rates for selected occupations within industries at given points in time finds that "union wages . . . do tend to be higher than nonunion in broadly comparable situa-

---

[4] Sumner H. Slichter, "Do the Wage-Fixing Arrangements in the American Labor Market Have an Inflationary Bias?" *American Economic Review,* XLIV (May 1954), 335.

[5] Harold M. Levinson, *Unionism, Wage Trends, and Income Distribution, 1914–1947* (Ann Arbor, 1951), 23–79. See also Levinson, "Collective Bargaining and Income Distribution," *American Economic Review,* XLIV (May 1954), 311–12, in which he points out that for the entire period 1934–52, as well as in each of the subperiods 1934–41 and 1941–52, average hourly earnings in the unionized sector industries rose considerably more than they did in nonunion sector industries.

[6] Slichter, loc. cit., 337.

tions."[7] Although he cautions that it is difficult to isolate the influence of unionism *per se,* the existence of positive union-nonunion wage differentials (and Douty found that such exist in 87 per cent of the 902 occupations which he analyzed and in 31 of the 32 industries in which those occupations were studied), imply a much greater union impact on the structure of wages than does Friedman's analysis, which contemplates only the alleged influence of unionism upon craft-noncraft differentials. And Maher concludes a detailed study of the effects of unionism on intra-industry wage differentials in 1950 by asserting that "within a given geographic area, possessing some homogeneity in the competitive nature of its markets," union wages do not exceed nonunion wages during periods of expansion, whereas "during the initial periods of contraction, wage differentials favoring unionized workers will appear."[8]

Friedman's estimate that membership in "old-line craft unions" and their equivalents (like the American Medical Association) constitutes a small proportion of the labor force is significant in the construction of his hypothesis, for his quantitative conclusion assumes that members in such organizations, and they alone, "can be supposed to have had their wages significantly affected by the existence of unions." This implies that unions have not been instrumental in raising nonunion wages. On this point we have already referred to studies citing historical evidence to the contrary. It also implies that craft unions are strong and industrial unions are weak, a point which Friedman seeks to establish both empirically and theoretically.

This latter point is essential to Friedman's argument about the impact of unionism upon the structure of money wages, for even if one were to agree that unionism has exerted only a weak effect upon the level of money wages, a weak impact upon the wage level is not inconsistent with a strong effect upon the structure of money wages, as we shall observe later and as Friedman's own analysis implies. His empirical evidence on this point consists in "a brief examination of three major apparent exceptions to the generalization that industrial unions are likely to be less potent than craft unions. In each case, it will be found that other economic changes tended to make the strength of the unions appear greater than it actually was" (page 208). Granted the last statement, it does not follow that the genuine strength of the industrial unions to which he refers (the miners', the men's and ladies' garment workers', and the auto and steel workers') was not considerable. Nor does it follow that other economic changes did not tend to make the strength of craft unions appear greater than it actually was; and Friedman, relying upon Kuznets' and his analysis of incomes from medical practice, attributes to the crafts the ability to raise wages by not more than "about 15 or 20 per cent above the levels that would have prevailed without unions" (page 216). The fortunes of industrial and craft unions alike waxed during "attendant favorable circumstances" and waned in their absence. During the period 1920–33, Friedman observes that the "Miners' Union practically went to pieces." The official membership figures reveal a decline of 25 per cent during that period—but so do those of the Locomotive Engineers. Friedman attributes the relative success (when measured against the miners' record) of the two garment workers' unions during the 1920's and early 1930's to the imposition of restrictions on immigration; it is equally necessary to view the relative success of the building trades against the background of the building boom of the 1920's. Friedman's examples do not illustrate a differential effect of environmental changes upon industrial unions, on the one hand, and upon craft unions, on the other.

---

[7] H. M. Douty, "Union and Nonunion Wages," in W. S. Woytinsky and Associates, *Employment and Wages in the United States* (New York, 1953), 493–501.

[8] John E. Maher, *Union, Nonunion Wage Rate Differentials* (Unpublished Ph.D. dissertation, Harvard University, 1954), 139.

The fact that the average annual earnings per full-time employee of soft-coal miners for the period 1939–48 rose virtually no more rapidly than did the annual earnings of domestic servants, and less rapidly than the wages of farm labor during the same period, is also interpreted by Friedman as evidence that there is less to unionism (and in particular, industrial unionism) than meets the eye. He attributes the above-average increases in all three groups to a common cause, the difficulty of attracting workers to and retaining them in relatively unpleasant occupations. (Incidentally, the fact that Marshall observed that wages of domestic servants were rising more rapidly than union wages in Britain in 1892 is eloquent alike of the persistence and pervasiveness of the servant problem and the perceptiveness of economists![9]) But, as Philip Taft indicates, Friedman points to no evidence of labor shortage in the coal mines. On the contrary, Taft notes that no claims of labor shortage were made during the war, when the union sought to break the little Steel Formula, although the Stabilization Act provided for extraordinary wage increases in cases of shortage, and such increases were granted in other cases. Moreover, the operators resisted increases.[10] Friedman argues that the percentage increases in the wage rates of nonunion coal miners exceeded those of union miners during World War I. However, that this is consistent with the view that the union was responsible for the more rapid increase in the nonunion rates is evident when one considers, first, that the membership of the United Mine Workers increased by one-third between 1915 and 1918 and, second, that nonunion miners' wages remained lower than union wages in 1920.[11] A recent study by Baratz cites the ability of this union to push up wages in the recessions of 1937 and 1948 as evidence that, since 1933, the union was a significant factor in the movement of wages in the industry.[12]

The finding that, at least during certain periods, wages in more heavily unionized industries generally rose more rapidly than wages in relatively unorganized industries and that union wages have tended to exceed nonunion wages within the same industry (although subject to considerable statistical qualification) would make it appear that the influence of unionism upon the structure of wages has been of greater magnitude than Friedman's analysis, which limits that impact to the effect produced only by craft unions upon unionized craft-noncraft differentials, would indicate. Moreover, the assertion that unions can and do significantly raise wages of nonunion workers implies that unions can affect the level of money wages without altering the structure of money wages. In this connection a study of occupational wage differences by Strain is of interest. He finds that, over the period 1929–49, the reductions in skill differentials in four industries in which "strong" industrial unions developed since 1930 (automobile, steel, meat packing, and West Coast saw-milling) were somewhat greater than those which occurred in two craft-union industries (building construction and book and job printing) and in two unorganized industries (cotton textiles and saw-milling in the South). Although he hesitates to assign an appreciable causal role to industrial unionism because in steel and autos and meat packing significant declines occurred before the late 1930's, he does acknowledge that employers might have raised wages in order to forestall unionization during the N.R.A. period; this of course is well known. In addition, this study provides evidence of the impact of unionism upon the wages of unskilled as well as of

---

[9] Alfred Marshall, *Elements of the Economics of Industry* (3rd ed., London, 1899), 389.
[10] Philip Taft, *Economics and Problems of Labor* (3rd ed., Harrisburg, 1955), 298–99.
[11] Gerald G. Somers, *Experience Under National Wage Agreements* (Morgantown, West Virginia, 1950), 22. Cited in Taft, op. cit., 299.

[12] Morton S. Baratz, *The Union and the Coal Industry* (New Haven, 1955), 95–99.

skilled workers both in industries in which industrial unions are organized.[13]

One cannot claim that the evidence cited above is conclusive. Nevertheless, when one considers the evidence and Friedman's interpretations of it in the construction and testing of his hypothesis, on the one hand, and when one considers the evidence and interpretations in the other studies referred to, we submit that it is reasonable to regard with considerable reserve Friedman's very low estimate of the magnitude of the impact of unionism—Bronfenbrenner calls it "close to a 'chanticleer' or 'illusion' theory"—upon the level and structure of money wages. For this reason, but also because Friedman's arguments are characteristically novel and stimulating, it might prove interesting to examine the theoretical components of his hypothesis and in places to widen its scope. In this connection, we shall discuss (1) the demand for union labor and the application of the Marshallian analysis of joint demand, (2) the supply of labor and freedom of entry, union and nonunion wages, and (4) unionism as a wage depressant. This discussion will be concerned only with the possible impacts of unionism upon the structure and level of money wage rates, since Friedman's article is for the most part similarly confined.

---

[13] Robert Strain, *Occupational Wage Differences: Determinants and Recent Trends* (Unpublished Ph.D. dissertation, University of Wisconsin, 1953). Bronfenbrenner cites this study to support the thesis that industrial as well as craft unions are weak. Martin Bronfenbrenner, "The Incidence of Collective Bargaining," *American Economic Review*, XLIV (May 1954), 302. This assumes that, to establish the case for strong industrial unionism, evidence must be produced to show that occupational wage structures have been compressed more in industries in which industrial unions are organized than in industries in which craft unions are organized. This might be true if unskilled workers were unorganized in the latter industries. But unskilled workers have been organized in both building construction and printing, which are the only craft jurisdictions chosen by Strain for purposes of comparison. Thus, only if it is assumed to be the policy of the industrial unions to compress occupational differentials by denying to their skilled members wage increases as great as they could obtain outside of industrial unions could a demonstration of the effectiveness of industrial unionism under these conditions require evidence that occupational differentials have been compressed more in industrial than in craft jurisdictions. Strain seeks to establish only that industrial unions have not altered intra-industrial wage structures; he does not deny that they have raised wage levels within their own jurisdictions.

Indeed, in several instances Strain asserts that unions did affect wages within their respective jurisdictions. He holds that one reason why the skill differential was compressed much more during the 1930's in the unorganized southern sawmilling industry than in the unionized western sector, and indeed in all other industries studied, was that the wages of the skilled workers in the South lagged far behind the northern skilled workers' wages because the latter were unionized and the former were not. (Another reason suggested was the greater impact of the establishment of the legal minimum upon the lower southern unskilled rate.) He also ascribes the fall in the skill differential in book and job printing in the late 1930's in part to increasing organization among the less skilled press assistants and feeders. The latter phenomenon is also held to account in part for the fact that the differential in book and job printing declined between 1935 and 1939 while his index of the differential in building construction continued to rise during this period. (The B.L.S. index of occupational differentials for building construction fell, while Strain's series rose during the period 1933 to 1943. This is partly attributed to the fact that the former series included the wages of helpers as well as unclassified common labor in its unskilled categories while the latter did not and that the unionization of helpers increased more rapidly than did the unionization of common labor during this period.)

Nor does Strain argue that parallel movements in the skill differential in unorganized and in organized industries imply the inability of unions independently to raise the wages of their members. While observing that the increase in the differential in the southern cotton textile industry was comparable to increases in building construction and book and job printing between 1930 and 1933, he also notes that the percentage reductions in wages in both the skilled and unskilled categories studied were much greater in the unorganized cotton textiles (South) than in the highly unionized construction and printing trades during this period.

I. Demand for Union Labor: Industrial and Craft

1.1. The Marshallian Analysis

Marshall, in seeking to identify the determinants of the elasticity of derived demand inquired into

the conditions, under which a check to the supply of a thing that is wanted not for direct use, but as a factor of production of some commodity, may cause a very great rise in its price. The first condition is that the factor itself should be essential, or nearly essential to the production of the commodity. . .

The second condition is that the commodity in the production of which it is a necessary factor, should be one for which the demand is stiff and inelastic. . .

The third condition is that only a small part of the expenses of production of the commodity should consist of the price of this factor. . .

The fourth condition is that even a small check to the amount demanded should cause a considerable fall in the supply prices of other factors of production.[14]

Marshall's analysis is clearly of some relevance to the problem involved in determining the bargaining strength of any given union, as he himself appreciated. Professor Friedman's contribution consists in part in utilizing this Marshallian framework in the determination of the aggregate impact of unionism in the economy upon "the structure and level of wage rates" in the long run. That impact, he argues in this part of his analysis, is small (although "by no means . . . unimportant"), primarily for two reasons. In the first place, "a factor is likely to be far more essential in the short run than in the long run" (page 207). Secondly, the strongest unions are those whose members account for only a small portion of the "total cost" of product; these are usually unions whose memberships also satisfy the first Marshallian criterion of essentiality and who constitute therefore only the small highly skilled fraction of the total

force (page 208). This analysis implies that craft unions are much stronger than industrial unions. Although Friedman qualifies this conclusion by adding that industrial unions are "by no means impotent," his estimate of the total effect of unionism is based primarily upon an estimate of the strength of craft unions and the proportion of their membership to the total labor force.

If one agrees (as this writer does) that the Marshallian analysis of joint demand is relevant to the investigation of the determinants of union bargaining power, one should consider some of the limitations of this approach. In this connection, we shall discuss, first, the Hicks-Robinson criticism of the Marshallian analysis and, second, unionism in more than one class of labor.

1.2. The Hicks-Robinson Criticism[15]

It was first demonstrated by Hicks that Marshall's statement that the elasticity of demand for a factor varies directly with the proportion of the outlay on that factor to total expenses of production holds only when the elasticity of substitution is less than the elasticity of demand for the final product, on the assumption of constant returns to scale. As Hicks put it,

It is "important to be unimportant" only when the consumer can substitute more easily than the entrepreneur. Further even if $\eta > \sigma$, but if the difference is small, the importance of this second rule will be negligible.[16]

Thus, whether a low labor-cost ratio is a bargaining asset at all, or whether it is a significant bargaining asset, cannot be determined *a priori*. It is frequently asserted, however, that the elasticity of substitution with respect to all labor is in fact very low in the short period. But even if we make an assumption to that effect, it by no means follows that the elasticity of substitution is

---

[14] Alfred Marshall, *Principles of Economics* (8th ed., London, 1938), 385–87.

[15] J. R. Hicks, *The Theory of Wages* (New York, 1948), Appendix III, 241–46; Joan Robinson, *The Economics of Imperfect Competition* (London, 1948), 257–62.

[16] Hicks, op. cit., 246; η designates the elasticity of demand, σ the elasticity of substitution.

always significantly less than the elasticity of product demand in industries whose output consists not in consumer goods but in products designed for consumption by other industries. The short-period elasticities of substitution with respect to the products in question might be as low, or virtually as low, for such industrial consumers as are the elasticities of substitution with respect to labor in the industries producing those products. This relationship might obtain in some of the so-called basic industries in which large industrial unions are organized. And although indirect negative "expansion effects" would remain, such unions might still find it unimportant to be important, given the existence of other factors which tend to make their bargaining power great. Moreover, Friedman must choose a time period sufficiently long for the difference in substitutability between unskilled and skilled labor to emerge. Then if, as he assumes, relevant labor-cost ratios are higher in the industrial than in the craft jurisdictions, it might be argued that this condition could mitigate, rather than aggravate, the greater substitutability in unskilled trades. But we must now call this assumption into question.

1.3. Unionism in More Than One Class of Labor

As Marshall indicated, "other classes of workmen" might be included among those factors demanded jointly with the class of labor whose elasticity of demand is to be determined. We have assumed that the latter group is unionized and that the "check" to its supply results from union policy. Now we shall assume that the other labor group (for convenience we suppose that only one such exists) becomes unionized. How does this affect the elasticity of demand for the labor of the original group and, therefore, its ability to raise wages within its own jurisdiction?

Let us suppose first that a union-secured wage rise in the original group will be largely "absorbed" by a consequent reduction in demand for and in the wages of the second group; this will be the case if the elasticity of substitution between the two groups is zero (fixed proportions) or, if positive, below some critical value, and if the supply of the second class of labor is not perfectly elastic at its original wage rate. Once the second group becomes organized, however, its members will probably refuse to accept wage reductions; that is, its supply curve becomes infinitely elastic at the prevailing wage rate. In this case a given reduction in the demand for the services of its members, occasioned by a rise in the price of its cooperant labor factor, will merely result in more unemployment. However, if wages in the now-unionized second group are prevented from falling, the rise in product price occasioned by a given rise in wages in the first group would be greater than it would have been in the absence of unionism in the second group. Thus the reduction in employment in the first group associated with any given wage increase therein would be greater, and, as a result, the union in the first group would be unable or unwilling to press for as large a wage rise as it could when its cooperant labor factor was unorganized. It is denied the channel of relief indicated in Marshall's fourth proposition.

Now let us suppose that the value of the elasticity of substitution between the two labor groups is such that a union-won rise in the wage rate in the first group results in an increase, rather than a decrease, in demand for the services of the second group. Here the bargaining power of the unionized group is limited by the availability of substitute labor. But if the second group is also organized and if its union secures a proportionate wage increase equal to that secured by the first union, the latter need fear no substitution effect, as discussed by Marshall in his first statement. Of course it is not necessary to assume that the second union would achieve an equal proportionate increase and that the substitution effect be eliminated completely; it is sufficient that it secure *some* increase above the equilibrium wage level for the substitution effect to be "softened" from the viewpoint of the first union.

However, it cannot be assumed that the effect of unionism elsewhere is to reduce the elasticity of the demand for labor in the first unionized group if both groups are employed by the same employer. For, although wages in the first group might constitute a very small fraction of "the expenses of production," if wages in the second group can be counted on to rise by union action whenever wages are raised in the first group, then neither management nor the policy-makers in the first union are justified in regarding the impact of any given wage increase in the first group as being limited by the proportion of total expenses of production constituted by the wage of the first class of labor alone. The greater the increase secured by the second union, the greater the total effect of the first union's wage rise upon product price. Thus, while the substitution effect of a rise in wages in the first group is mitigated by union activity in the second, the proportionate rise in labor costs and, therefore, in product price associated with a given rise in wages in the first group is increased.

Marshall might well have had these complications in mind when he wrote that "The relations between plasterers, bricklayers, etc., are representative of much that is both instructive and romantic in the history of alliances and conflicts between trades-unions in allied trades."[17] Certainly in our own time and country there exists ample evidence of the importance of the economic ties binding different organized groups in the same industry. Friedman limits long-run effectiveness in making wage rates "significantly different from what they otherwise would have been" to unions in "construction, railroads, printing trades, and in general the areas in which old-line craft unions are strong." In construction, unions in the six so-called basic trades (the operating engineers, carpenters, common laborers, teamsters, iron workers, and cement finishers), whose members work for the same employers (the general contractors), bargain as a group in some communities. The other trades bargain with their respective subcontractors. The latter thus deal with only one union each, but to such employers the cost of union labor constitutes a very high proportion of total cost. Moreover, so-called national contractors frequently influence local wage settlements involving both general contractors and subcontractors whom they hire.[18] And of course the existence of local building

[17] Marshall, *Principles of Economics*, op. cit., 387.

[18] I am indebted to an unusually reliable source, Professor Dunlop, for furnishing me with information on collective bargaining in the construction industry.

The writer would agree with Stephen P. Sobotka, "Union Influence on Wages: The Construction Industry," *Journal of Political Economy*, LXI (April 1953), 128–29, that the relevant denominator of the labor-cost ratio in construction is total construction costs, but only if the numerator consists of a larger fraction of the total cost of housing than that accounted for by a single craft only. If the latter be chosen as the numerator, however, then the more appropriate base would be the total cost of the subcontractor in question, for the general contractor's awareness of the interrelatedness of the different bargains would make it difficult for a minor subcontractor to "pass on" a given wage increase merely because that wage increase would constitute a much smaller percentage increase in total building cost. Sobotka finds a significant degree of correlation between the extent of organization and relative full-time earnings of skilled building trades workers, but virtually no correlation (.06) for common building laborers (page 134). However, his inference that unions of unskilled labor in this industry were unable significantly to affect the wages of their members overlooks the fact that the frequency of distribution of common labor unions with respect to degree of organization was markedly different from that of the unions of skilled crafts, in that a far greater proportion of unskilled unions than of skilled locals fell in the zero-to-25 (and zero-to-50) per cent organized group. Further, the data used in this portion of Sobotka's argument all refer to 1939, a year of high unemployment; and in periods of high unemployment, unemployment rates among unskilled labor are generally higher than in skilled trades. Professor Dunlop has suggested this latter point to me; it carries the interesting implication that unions composed predominantly of unskilled workers might labor under a greater handicap than others in periods of high unemployment.

trades councils and contractors' associations testifies to awareness on each side of the interrelatedness of all interests.

The railroads have a long tradition of "pattern increases" both within and between the operating and the non-operating groups of unions. Since 1937 all the operating crafts received increases totaling $1.245 per hour, while all the "non-ops" received $1.234.[19] Although, with one exception, every one of the nine "wage movements" which occurred since 1937 involved government intervention, the uniform cents-per-hour pattern of settlement owes its remarkable vitality to the support granted it by the unions and the carriers. When, in 1947, the differential between yard foremen and helpers was increased "in an effort to correct a supposed inequity," the Locomotive Engineers claimed that this created a new inequity in the differential between the yard engineers and the yard foremen. Their counsel warned that "the Carriers cannot expect the engineers' organization to watch the ground supervisors' basic rate rise and alter the differential, unless the engine supervisor's rate also rises. If they expect this they are in for a rude awakening." When, in 1954,

[19] These figures are inclusive of adjustments made when the work week was reduced from 48 to 40 hours in 1948. Below are listed the awards exclusive of that adjustment.

Awards granted in	Amount of award	
	Operating employees	Nonoperating employees
1937	5½ ¢	5 ¢
1941	9½ ¢	10 ¢
1942–3	9 ¢	9 ¢
1945–6	18½ ¢	18½ ¢
1947	15½ ¢	15½ ¢
1948	10 ¢	23½ ¢
1949–52	23 ¢	12½ ¢
1952–53	4 ¢	4 ¢
1953–54	5 ¢	5 ¢

SOURCE: National Mediation Board, Arbitration Board No. 192, Case A–4400; *In the Matter of a Dispute between Carriers Represented by the Eastern, Western and Southeastern Carriers' Conference Committees and Their Employees Represented by the Brotherhood of Locomotive Engineers, 1954, Brief on Behalf of the Carriers.*

the Engineers sought to increase the existing differentials between their craft and the other railroad groups, the carriers were wide awake. Their case in opposition to the Engineers' demand emphasized the importance of the "pattern" in collective bargaining on the railroads; one of their spokesmen said that "if the demand of the Engineers for a percentage increase should be granted by this board, it is certain that the remainder of the industry's operating employees would be keenly dissatisfied with their settlements. They would surely make further demands that the same amount of money increase be granted to them."[20]

It is interesting to note that, in the shipbuilding industry, collective bargaining is conducted between the employer and the local metal trades council in some shipyards, while in others the workers are organized in industrial locals. Local trades councils of different crafts also exist in printing, but joint bargaining between allied printing trades councils and employers is not typical (although not unknown). In both the newspaper and the book-and-job branches of this industry, however, the phenomenon of what Dunlop has termed "wage leadership" might be observed: ". . . the negotiations of the strongest craft frequently sets the stage for the others, which then get approximately the same settlement."[21] According to Emily Clark Brown, insistence by the followers in the book-and-job branch on the reestablishment of "proper" differentials after a wage increase is granted to a leader is responsible for the fact that "indexes of changes in wage rates for the separate crafts have moved closely together since 1907."[22] But each party's recognition of interdependence has typically led it to oppose joint negotiations in this industry. "Stronger unions hesitate to give up their special advantage in bargaining by cooperating with the weaker ones,

[20] Ibid., 6–7; Transcript of *Proceedings*, 1320.
[21] Robert K. Burns, "Newspapers," and Emily C. Brown, "Book and Job Printing," in *How Collective Bargaining Works* (New York, 1942), 77, 139.
[22] Brown, loc. cit., 156.

while the weaker sometimes fear inadequate attention to their interests in joint action." Moreover, employer interest in separate bargaining is clearly motivated by concern over intercraft relationships. According to Mrs. Brown, "Granting a demand of one craft at a crucial moment may prevent the development of a movement for more unity and militancy."[23] Case studies of collective bargaining in two firms, each negotiating separately with several craft locals, some of which were in the printing trades, reveal how the employer's awareness of the leader-follower relationship influences his negotiating policy when dealing with any one local. The following quotation from the study of the Marathon Corporation is clearly pertinent to our problem:

The small number of members of the printing unions, coupled with their important position in Marathon's connecting operations, suggests that the company could afford to comply with almost any demands of these unions, no matter how unreasonable, simply to avoid a stoppage. In practice, however, each of the unions watches the other negotiations carefully, and the company attempts to grant concessions which are relatively uniform.[24]

In view of what might be termed the "complementarity effect" of unionism in other groups in the same industry when substitutability between them and the group in question is sufficiently low, and in view of what might be termed the "effective labor-cost ratio effect" when substitutability is sufficiently high, it is probable that the bargaining power of a well-organized craft group is reduced if other groups in the same industry become organized (in the same or in separate unions). But we have not been describing an actual historic process, for we

[23] *Ibid.*, 141.
[24] R. W. Fleming and E. E. Witte, *Marathon Corporation and Seven Labor Unions*, Case Study No. 8, *Causes of Industrial Peace under Collective Bargaining* (National Planning Association, Washington, D. C., 1950), 19. See also Charles A. Myers and George P. Shultz, *Nashua Gummed and Coated Paper Company and Seven AFL Unions*, Case Study No. 7, same series, 35 and 74.

have assumed that the earliest organized group had been thoroughly organized by the time the other groups in the industries formed unions; historically this condition has rarely obtained. And so long as the older craft organizations remained only partially organized throughout their jurisdictions, employers could and did break their strikes and keep plants in operation by contracting out struck work. Hence the subsequent unionization and cooperation of other groups increased the actual bargaining power of the older organizations at the same time that they might have diminished their potential bargaining power. This explains the origin of many of our so-called multicraft unions. By the same token the latecomers did not regard themselves as organizing in self-defense against the ability of the established unions to secure wage increases at their expense. Hence what we have been describing must not be regarded in the category of those forces which sometimes tend, in the absence of offsetting changes, to undermine the strength even of well-organized unions *over time*—for example, shifts in product demand, technological change, and so forth. Conceptually the experiment must begin with all groups in an industry well organized, as historically it begins with some groups completely unorganized and the unionized sector only partially organized. Thus we do not assert as a generalization that the bargaining power of craft groups has been in fact reduced since the rise of industrial unionism in the past quarter century, for the organization of hitherto completely unorganized groups has been accompanied by the more complete organization of the older, craft jurisdictions; and this has tended to increase the bargaining strength of the older craft unions.

But our observations are relevant to Friedman's contention that craft unions are strong and industrial unions are weak and that differences in essentiality and especially in labor-cost ratio account for this disparity in bargaining power. The advantages of essentiality are reduced in two respects when other types of labor input become unionized:

in the first place, a rise in the wage of an "essential" unionized factor can no longer be offset by wage reductions in other labor groups; and in the second place, if the craft group in question is not very "essential" and if the potential substitutes are not employed by the same employer, unionism elsewhere tends to reduce the penalty which an easily substitutable group must otherwise pay for its temerity in pushing wages up by union action.

As for the labor-cost ratio argument, our analysis of the impact of unionism in more than one class of labor in the same industry leads us to believe that the relevant ratio is not the proportion of variable cost accounted for by the wages of only the particular unionized craft group under observation but rather the proportion of variable cost accounted for by the wages of all labor groups which must be presumed to increase when the observed union obtains a wage increase for its own members. If this is true, then one must take note of the fact that total-labor-cost ratios in the industries in which the unions of "highly skilled workers" are situated are, on the whole, certainly no lower than they are in industrial-union jurisdictions.[25] And, if Professor Friedman's estimate of the ability of the craft unions to raise the wages of their members (by 15 per cent, see page 216) holds after allowing for any possible effects of other unions in the industry upon their bargaining power, then it would appear that the analysis understates the bargaining power of the industrial unions and, therefore, the total impact of unionism upon the general level of money wages. If, on the other hand, it is held that the arguments and evidence produced in this section support the view that craft unionism is weaker than Friedman's application of the joint-demand analysis would lead one to suppose, then Friedman's estimate of the over-all impact of unionism is probably too high. We hold merely that the joint demand analysis does not justify the prediction that craft unions would tend to be "the most potent" (page 208), since it cannot be presumed that a high degree of essentiality is associated in fact with a low effective labor-cost ratio. And Professor Friedman places primary emphasis upon "the importance of the percentage of total cost accounted for by the factor" in predicting that craft unions would be more powerful than industrial unions.

II. Supply of Labor and Freedom of Entry

Even if the demand for the labor of its members is inelastic, high supply elasticity could undermine a union's bargaining power.

---

[25] In 1947 all salaries and wages accounted for 47.7% of total railroad operating revenues. (Computed from data in Harry E. Jones, *Railroad Wages and Labor Relations, 1900–1952*, New York, 1947.) In newspapers, wages of production workers constituted only 19.4% of value of products shipped, but in book-printing this ratio was 34.2%, and in commercial printing it was 29.8%. Site payroll accounted for about one-third of total construction cost of new housing. Construction costs, however, do not include sales profit, selling costs, cost of land, and site improvements and other nonconstruction expenses; on the other hand, site labor costs exclude wages paid to shop labor. See Adela L. Stucke, "Labor Share in Construction Cost of New Houses," *Monthly Labor Review*, 68 (May 1949), 517.

Although the above data on production labor costs in craft jurisdictions are not closely comparable, it is of some interest to compare them with wages of production workers relative to value of products shipped in the following industrial-union jurisdictions: tires and inner tubes 20.1%, petroleum refining 6%, tractors 20%, other farm machinery 22.9%, industrial trucks and tractors 18.2%, electric lamps 24.1%, pulp mills 13.6%, paper and board mills 13.6%, cigarettes 4.9%, men's and boys' suits and coats 23.5%, blouses and waists 19.6%, woolen and worsted fabrics 21.7%, cotton broad woven fabrics 21.2%, blast furnaces 5.4%.

Of course, it is not claimed that production labor-cost ratios are lower in all industrial jurisdictions. In steel foundries, the ratio was 37.2%, in flat glass 30.2%, in machine tools 33.1%, in electronic tubes 37.5%. In shipbuilding and repairing, a jurisdiction which is shared between craft unions and an industrial union, the ratio was 43.9%. (Percentages of production labor cost to value of products shipped computed from data in U. S. Department of Commerce, *Census of Manufactures: 1947*.)

Hence Friedman supplements his application of the Marshallian joint demand analysis with a discussion of the "supply of labor and control over wage rates." As noted above, he maintains that unions must be able either to restrict the supply of workers or to control the wage rate directly by (1) preventing existing employers from undercutting the union rate and (2) preventing the entry of new employers who would do so.

Friedman points out that union work rules and some membership regulations cannot restrict the supply of workers; they serve only to ration a limited number of jobs among job-seekers, given the existence of a union wage rate already in force. But direct control over the wage rate can be and sometimes is achieved, Friedman goes on to say, through "political assistance"; in this connection he mentions state licensure laws and the permission of mass picketing.

Can a union prevent an existing employer from undercutting the union wage rate in the absence of the first variety of "political assistance"? In such cases, an excess supply of labor would be associated with the union wage rate, and the employer would be free to exploit this situation by hiring nonunion labor at a lower rate of pay, if such is available and if he should choose to do so. Nevertheless, the union could confront the employer with an alternative to which the extra cost involved in paying the union wage rate might be preferable. That alternative consists simply in the cost to the employer of incurring a strike. If the employer decides to attempt to break the strike, the cost of a strike to him includes paying strikebreakers a sufficiently high wage to induce them to leave their present employments for jobs that entail social opprobrium and possible danger and that are likely to be temporary. Moreover, it must also include the cost of breaking in an entirely new work force on the job, even if the strikebreakers closely approach the strikers in individual "ability, merit, and capacity," which has rarely been the case. The more efficient the strikebreakers, the smaller the latter element in the cost of the strike (which is, however, positive even in the case of perfect individual substitutability), but the higher the cost of hiring the strikebreakers. If the employer decides to take a strike and not attempt to run his plant with strikebreakers, the cost of the strike becomes the cost of a complete shutdown.

But while established unionized employers might be unwilling to risk a strike, new firms might be attracted to the industry by the high prevailing product prices (due to high union wages), on the one hand, and the availability of a supply of nonunion labor, on the other. If the unwillingness of union employers to incur a strike is to constitute an absolute bar to the entry of new workers, the entry of new firms must also be precluded. Thus we now inquire whether unions can or must be able to prevent the entry of new firms which would undercut the union rate.

The condition of non-entry is satisfied if the elasticity of supply of labor has a zero or a very small positive value, but, of course, that is not a necessary condition of monopoly or oligopoly in the product market. However, the mere presence of monopoly or oligopoly would not ensure either the emergence or the success of unionism. So long as unions seek wage levels that are associated with excess supplies of labor, employer opposition to increased labor costs might be expected to materialize. Moreover, employers in what might be regarded as oligopolistic industries are often abundantly endowed with the sinews of war, if they choose to fight. The notable lack of success of American unions in organizing the mass-production industries prior to the New Deal period bears testimony to both the power and the will to fight possessed by the employers in these industries, the "theory of countervailing power" to the contrary notwithstanding.[26]

[26] John K. Galbraith, *American Capitalism* (Boston, 1952), 121–23. See George J. Stigler, "The Economist Plays with Blocs," *American Review,* LXIV (May 1954), 11.

But if, to return to our original assumption, such employers do not choose to fight, even unions of workers for whom substitute labor is easily available—mostly industrial unions—need not fear that many of those substitutes will find employment within their jurisdictions if entry by new enterprises is difficult. (Bargaining power would still be limited by demand elasticities, of course; but, as noted above, excess supplies could be blotted up by seniority or work rules, and, as some writers have pointed out, unions in monopolistic industries—and this refers to some of the large industrial unions—can extract wage increases from monopoly profits. See footnote 29 below.) Now there is some evidence that technical and especially pecuniary barriers to entry are rather formidable in the so-called heavy manufacturing industries.[27] And since the large industrial unions are based in those industries, it is probable that Friedman's analysis, which makes no reference to imperfections in product markets, understates their ability to raise wages.

To be sure, a union in such a sheltered jurisdiction could not raise wages without limit, for, as we have mentioned, the greater the difference between the union wage rate and the wage rate which a sufficient number of nonunion workers would accept, the greater the incentive to the entry of nonunion firms in the industry in question. Far from preventing "the entry of new employers," unions tend to facilitate their entry.[28] Nevertheless unions capitalize on imperfections; the United Steelworkers of America are not obliged to assume the policing chores which the organizer in the garment trades considers a fact of life.[29]

Thus, in answer to our first question, we conclude that unions can prevent existing employers from undercutting union wage rates. In answer to our second question we conclude that unions cannot prevent the entry of new employers unless the supply of labor within their jurisdiction is highly inelastic (as in the case of highly skilled crafts), or without legalized restriction on entry, which is available to relatively few unionists. (The laws on picketing have hardly sufficed to prevent the emergence of nonunion firms; if they could do so, one's

---

[27] Joe S. Bain, "Economics of Scale, Concentration, and the Condition of Entry in Twenty Manufacturing Industries," *American Economic Review*, XLIV (March 1954), 15–39.

[28] See Sumner H. Slichter, *Union Policies and Industrial Management* (Washington, 1941), 345–69, for examples of "encroachment of non-union upon union production." But Slichter also argues that even if a lower rate of profits in union plants (including negative profit rates) exists, this does not ordinarily imply the hasty exit of such plants from the industry since, for several reasons, "the rate of return necessary to cause a perpetual renewal of the capital in an industry is less than the rate of return necessary to attract additional capital into the industry" (page 346). He thus extends the time period during which the union can impose successive wage increases beyond that allowed by Marshall, who limited it to the period required to diminish entirely the stock of capital, which he regarded as a quasi-rent. (*Elements of Economics of Industry*, op. cit., 370, n. 1.)

[29] The studies of Ross and Goldner and of Garbarino are of interest in this connection, for they indicate a positive relationship between increases in hourly earnings and the degree of industrial concentration, and both studies suggest that the presence of unions, which can tap oligopoly profits, is a significant factor in explaining this relationship. Arthur M. Ross and William Goldner, "Forces Affecting the Interindustry Wage Structure," and Joseph W. Garbarino, "A Theory of Interindustry Wage Structure," both in the *Quarterly Journal of Economics*, LXIV (May 1950), 254–305. Christenson, on the other hand, attributes the great increases in wage rates in "oligopolistic" industries in the late 1930's to increases in "employment, business volume, and dollar profits." C. L. Christenson, "Variations in the Inflationary Force of Bargaining," *American Economic Review*, XLIV (May 1954), 348–52. It will be recalled, however, that great shrinkages in employment preceded the increases therein, so that these industries entered upon the latter phase with large pools of unemployed workers to draw on. It may be argued, therefore, that wage rate increases of the magnitude observed were not necessary to expand the volume of employment and that collective bargaining was indeed responsible for securing considerable wage increases under favorable conditions.

estimate of the total impact of unionism would have to be revised considerably upward, for such laws apply to unions in virtually all industries and trades in the community in question.) But we also conclude that, where pecuniary or technological barriers to entry do exist, unions can and do exploit such imperfections in product markets. Such a situation is stable only in the economic short run, but the short run might well, in the presence of sufficient frictions (see footnote 28), prolong itself in historic time. And, of course, unions in even the highly skilled crafts cannot maintain their own favorable circumstances indefinitely.

III. Impact on Structure and Impact on Level

3.1. Must Unions Reduce Nonunion Wages?

When we turn to consider the possible effects of whatever level of unionism exists throughout the economy upon the structure and level of wages therein, it is no longer always safe to rely upon the Marshallian analysis of joint demand which assumes that prices of all other products and factors (including wages in other jurisdictions) remain constant as the wage and (in consequence) the corresponding product price under consideration are changed. And when we consider the possible effect of unionism upon nonunion wages it becomes obvious that the problem of the effect of unionism upon the structure of wages is distinct from the problem of the effect of unionism upon the level of wages. Friedman contends, I believe, that if unions are too weak to exert an appreciable effect upon the structure of money wages, they are too weak to exert an appreciable effect upon the level of money wages. However, the failure of unions to affect the level of wages might be quite consistent with their ability to produce a strong effect upon the structure of wages. Nor must failure to affect the wage structure be taken to imply failure to affect the level of wages; hence the limited helpfulness of empirical studies based exclusively on comparisons between wage movements in heavily organized and in lightly organized sectors of the economy. Finally, it is possible, under certain circumstances, for unions to affect both the structure and the level of wages.

3.2. When Unions Can Affect Structure But Not Level of Money Wages

The impact of a union-secured wage increase in one industry or sector of the economy upon the wage levels in another industry or sector of the economy which is not unionized depends, among other things, upon the method employed by the union or unions in securing the given wage increase. Friedman discusses this problem in a footnote:

It is often asserted that nonunion members have had their wages raised because of the "pattern" set by the unions. This may have some validity for workers highly competitive with union workers, but in the main, the assertions are supported by neither economic analysis nor empirical evidence. The observed general similarity of money wage movements in union and nonunion areas is better interpreted as the result of common influences from the side of demand... In general, one would expect that any rise in the wage rates of certain classes of workers secured by unions would tend to lower wage rates of other workers because of the increased competition of workers for jobs.[30]

It will be noted that Friedman confines his analysis in two respects. He does not here consider the effect of the union-won wage increase upon the demand for goods produced under nonunion conditions. And, in referring to "the increased competition of workers for jobs," he assumes that the unions which secured the wage increases are able to exclude the excess of job-seekers from their respective jurisdictions. He does not consider either the method of securing wage increases by rationing the reduced amount of work among a fixed or increased force of union workers or the method of securing wage increases by regulations which are intended to oblige the employer to hire

[30] Friedman, loc. cit., 215–16, n. 6.

more workers than he would desire to hire at the going union wage.

Professor Friedman's omission of reference at this point to any effect of the union-won wage increase upon the demand for goods produced under nonunion conditions does not invalidate his conclusion so long as it is assumed that, as a result of the establishment of the union wage, the supply of labor in the nonunion sector is sufficiently increased. The increase in the supply of labor in the nonunion sector tends to drive down nonunion wages. This effect is countered to some degree by an increase in demand for goods produced in the nonunion sector which results from a rise in the prices of union-made goods (induced by the union-won wage increase). The increase in the demand for nonunion goods is translated into an increased demand for labor in those industries, which tends to offset the increase in supply of nonunion labor. Nevertheless, the increase in product demand cannot completely offset the increase in labor supply. If this were the case—so that wages in the nonunion sector either remained unchanged or increased following a rise in union wages —the average wage rate throughout the economy would increase. So would the price level, and, assuming unchanged conditions of aggregate demand and price elasticity of aggregate demand less than zero, a rise in the price level would imply a reduction in quantity demanded and employment. But if we assume that the unions are able to secure their wage increase solely by excluding excess job-seekers from their jurisdictions, the excess supply would be absorbed in the nonunion sector where competitive conditions prevail. And since unemployment is ruled out the average level of prices and wages must prevail after the unions secured their wage increases as before, so that nonunion prices and wages must be lower than they had been before the union wage increase.

Friedman's conclusion that union-won wage increases tend to drive down nonunion wages holds under the following conditions: (a) supply of nonunion labor is increased and there is no unemployment; (b) unionism is numerically weak or is not expanding, so that nonunion employers do not feel obliged to grant anticipatory wage increases to their employees in order to forestall unionism; and (c) the level of aggregate money demand at any given price level is not increased. Under these conditions the impact of unionism upon the general level of wages is zero, but its impact upon the structure of wages might be pronounced. When we relax any of the above conditions, the impact of the union upon the structure of wages is weakened, while its impact upon the general level of wages is increased.

3.3. When Unions Can Affect the Level of Money Wages

Consider now the case in which the union's wage increase is secured by work-sharing rules.

A. *Sharework, restriction of output, and makework.* Under such work-sharing rules, there need occur no net exodus of workers from the union trades following the union-won wage increase; indeed, a net influx of labor into the union trades from the nonunion sector might take place. Since the excess supply of labor is retained in the union sector, there is no increase in the supply of nonunion labor to offset the induced increase in demand for the goods produced in the nonunion sector, so that wages of nonunion workers would tend to rise. If substitution of machinery for labor occurs, demand for labor in the industries producing the substitutes would tend to rise. If the latter industries were in the union sector, the excess supply of labor there would be reduced; and if the unions involved held fast to their rationing devices, they might be able to increase further the wage rates of their members. If the industries producing the substitutes were in the nonunion sector, the increase in demand for their labor would tend to induce a rise in wage rates there. Hence, under these sharework assumptions, it is entirely possible that the wages of nonunion members could be maintained or raised "because of the 'pattern' set by the unions." Under such circumstances the average wage rate throughout the economy would rise and the number of man-hours hired would probably be reduced, but such reduction would be concentrated in the union sector where it would be absorbed in the form of restrictions on either output (under piecework) or hours worked, imposed by the unions upon employers and workers.

If the unions seek to secure their wage increases by makework rules—or by the guaranteed annual wage—three outcomes are possible. (1) Makework rules, as noted above, are designed to oblige the employer to hire more labor than he would be otherwise willing to hire at the union wage rate. Now if the union employers do in fact hire as much labor at that higher rate as at a lower rate and if, in response to higher labor costs, they raise their prices relative to nonunion prices, wage rates in the nonunion sectors would tend to rise. (2) To the extent, however, that makework devices force employers off their demand curves for labor, labor becomes for them a fixed cost; and, if they price their output according to marginal costs, they will not raise prices in response to union-won wage increases. In this case there may occur neither an increase in the demand for nonunion labor nor an increase in the supply; but wages in the nonunion sector would tend to fall, for reasons considered below. (3) Finally, it is possible that employers will in fact hire less rather than more labor at the going rate under makework restrictions than they would have otherwise hired. (Under conventional makework rules, an employer might be obliged to hire a minimum number of workers per machine, but he is not obliged to work any given number of machines. And the "pure theory of the guaranteed annual wage" makes it quite explicit that the employer is free to go out of business!)[31] Under such conditions, an unemployed surplus of union labor will develop, in which case the union might have to retreat from its newly-won wage position. Or it might be obliged to reduce employers' costs at the higher wage by substituting sharework for makework regulations (in whole or in part). Finally, some workers might depart for the nonunion sector, in which case the wages therein might decline.

Thus we observe that a union-won wage rate increase might spread to nonunion workers if it is secured by devices which effectively prevent an exodus of labor from the union sector to the nonunion sector of the economy and if it induces a sufficient increase in demand for nonunion goods. Indeed, *it is not necessary that no such exodus occur at all*; some movement out of the union sector and into the nonunion sector can be associated with a rise in nonunion wages or with the maintenance thereof.

It should be noted, however, that any rise in nonunion prices induced by wage increases secured by union-imposed work-spreading or, under certain conditions, makework devices, would be a net rise. Thus far we have considered only the effect upon the demand for nonunion goods exerted by an initial *relative* fall in their prices; this tends, as we know, to induce excess demand for nonunion goods and labor, which in turn induces increases in those prices. But the initial rise in union prices also raises the general price level and so tends to reduce the amounts demanded of all goods, nonunion goods included, assuming unchanged conditions of aggregate demand.[32] Whether or not money wage rates in the nonunion sector would increase would depend on the relative magnitudes of these two opposing tendencies. If they do, however, the induced rise in nonunion money wages and prices would not be as great as the rise in union money wages and prices. Under such circumstances, the effect of

---

[31] Wassily Leontief, "The Pure Theory of the Guaranteed Annual Wage Contract," *Journal of Political Economy*, LIV (February 1946), 76–79.

[32] See Oscar Lange, *Price Flexibility and Employment* (Bloomington, Ind., 1944), chs. I–IV.

securing union wages by the working rules discussed above would be to alter both the structure and the level of money wages.

One should note that not all unions can be expected to ration by sharework or by restriction of output under piecework; nor can all unions which do ration in this manner do so to the same degree. Demand elasticities differ, and jurisdictions characterized by high elasticities should possibly be regarded as not conducive to the flourishing of such work rules. In this connection, however, three cautionary remarks may be in order. First, if strong unionism is concentrated in jurisdictions where the demand for labor is inelastic, as Friedman implies, then one might expect that an important portion of the wage increase secured in the union sector is associated with makework, sharework, and equivalent practices. Second, some organized groups might adhere irrationally to a "lump-of-labor" philosophy, although their members might in fact better their position by working more at a lower wage rate. Third, since the worker's welfare is defined as a function of leisure as well as income, the institution of makework or sharework devices need not worsen the welfare position of the individuals concerned even if it does entail an income at the union wage rate lower than the income which they would receive at a lower wage rate in return for more work performed.

However, it should be noted that, whether or not wages rise in the nonunion sector, the magnitude of the union effect on the economy's money wage level might tend, under assumed static conditions, to dwindle over time as resources flow from the union sector to the nonunion sector, where, due to increase in product demand or labor supply, higher profits prevail. In other words, if it is assumed that unionism cannot spread to a certain sector of the economy, then it can be expected that, over time, the nonunion sector will expand and the union sector will contract—just as it has been observed that, if a union in a single industry is unable to organize a sizeable sector of that industry, the nonunion sector might "encroach" upon the union sector in that industry.[33]

B. Anticipatory wage increases. It should be noted that the type of "contagion increase" under discussion in the previous section is not the only type of money wage increase which might occur in nonunion firms as a result of increases secured by unions in organized firms. Friedman finds no "empirical evidence" that nonunion workers have had their wages increased as a result of union action elsewhere, but Slichter, Hicks, and Levinson maintain that nonunion employers have frequently granted wage increases to their employees (or have refrained from cutting their wages) in order to prevent unionism from spreading to their plants.[34] In some cases, such increases might indeed have taken the form of increases in equilibrium wage rates which would have occurred in the absence of threatened union activity or employer apprehension thereof. Such increases are somewhat akin to (but not identical with) the type of wage change, discussed by Friedman (page 222), for which unions may be generally but incorrectly held responsible. They are apt to occur in periods of rising demand. However, the fact that nonunion employers formed and granted substantial wage increases to company unions during the depression of the 1930's suggests that, during periods of rapid union growth, whether or not accompanied by rising aggregate demand, wage increases in union firms might well result in the establishment of wages in nonunion firms above the minimum levels necessary to attract and retain the required number of workers.

If employers grant such anticipatory wage increases in response to increases won by unions, encroachment of nonunion upon union sectors would not materialize, and the total impact of the unions upon the structure of money wages will have been reduced while the impact of unionism upon the level

---

[33] Slichter, op. cit., 347.
[34] Slichter, loc. cit.; also, Hicks, op. cit., 137; Levinson, op. cit., 69–73.

of money wages will have been increased. Since the anticipatory wage increases in the nonunion sector might raise prices there relative to prices in the union sector, it might appear that the nonunion wage increases would facilitate further union wage rises, so that the original union-nonunion wage relationship would be restored. However, the price rise in the nonunion sector raises the general level of prices which thus curtails over-all demand, including demand in the union sector. With conditions of aggregate demand assumed unchanged, the granting of anticipatory wage increases in response to a union wage rise raises the level of wages and the excess supply of labor throughout the economy. While this new situation will be as stable as the old one, owing to the willingness of the nonunion employers to administer the necessary job rationing in their sector, any further union wage increase would entail a further increase in unemployment and would be more difficult to obtain. Union employers' resistance to further increases (that is, their willingness to incur the cost of strikes) would presumably rise as the unions seek to raise money wages relative to prices, while the willingness of unionists to incur the cost of strikes for further increases might abate (due to decreasing marginal utility of real income, increased availability of strike replacements, or decreased opportunities for obtaining employment elsewhere).[35] A partially offsetting factor is the possibility that, as Slichter has suggested, union wage increases in excess of increases in productivity might make it profitable for firms to increase their expenditures on research out of which further increases in productivity will emerge—to make the next round of wage increases easier to achieve.

C. **Increasing aggregate money demand.** A rise in aggregate demand tends to reduce the impact of unionism upon the structure of wages in a partially organized economy. We have observed that, under given conditions of aggregate money demand, a union-won wage increase raises union wages relative to nonunion wages whether it is accompanied by a net exodus of workers from the union to the nonunion sectors of the economy or not. (In the latter situation, however, the union-won wage increase might affect the level, as well as the structure of money wages). Now if, other things being equal, the supply of money is increased at least in proportion to the initial rise in prices, the constraint exercised by the latter upon aggregate money demand would be neutralized, and nonunion wages might rise proportionally with union wages. The structure of wages prevailing before the union-won wage rise might be restored at a higher level of wages.

Of course, the same effect could be produced by an increase in the money supply without union action sufficient, in its absence, to affect wage structures and/or levels, but could unions be responsible for an increase in aggregate money demand at given price levels and thus for the resulting increase in the money wage level? Rees doubts whether mechanisms whereby this could be accomplished are "applicable either to recent experience in this country or to probable experience in the near future."[36] But Clark holds to the contrary, and Bronfenbrenner notes that "increased wage bills always embarrass some employers as to liquid assets, which they can and do replenish by increas-

---

[35] See Albert Rees, "Industrial Conflict and Business Fluctuations," *Journal of Political Economy,* LX (October 1952), 371–82. Rees discovered that the peak of the strike cycle (number of strikes) has tended to precede the peak of the Burns-Mitchell "reference cycle" and suggested that this may occur because employers might anticipate a future downswing in aggregate demand before unionists do. This is consistent with the argument in the text. So is Rees's further finding that a positive correlation exists between the number of strikes and the reference cycle; he attributes this to "changes in the propensity to strike" on the part of workers.

[36] Albert Rees, "Discussion." See Slichter, loc. cit., 365.

ing their credit accommodations at the commercial banks."[37] Slichter, in a recent paper, makes the same point but cautions that wage increases imply an increase in spending only "under the right circumstances."[38] Since, for this to occur, investment must not be depressed by the implied rise in labor costs or by any induced rise in interest rates and consumption must not be depressed by any actual or expected price increases induced by wage increases, "the right circumstances" are found in a period of economic recovery. In other words, it is probable that unions would be most effective in raising money income and wage levels when money income and wage levels are already on the rise.

The observed fact that wages have increased more rapidly in union than in nonunion sectors during periods of falling or stable price levels is consistent with the hypothesis that unions could and did raise wages in their jurisdictions above the levels which would have prevailed in their absence. In order to conclude that unions lose this power during periods of rising money demand, one might argue that the impetus for unionists to raise wages diminishes or that the willingness of employers to incur the cost of strikes increases during the upswing of the cycle. Following the argument at the conclusion of the previous section, it would appear, on the contrary, that, once money wage rates no longer rise relative to prices, the willingness of workers to incur the cost of strikes would increase while that of employers would diminish. Friedman, however, implies that employer resistance to union demands will at least remain high during a cyclical upswing; we turn now to a brief examination of this final point.

IV. Unionism as a Wage Depressant

Friedman believes that employers would be reluctant to grant wage increases even "in response to what they may regard as short-term improvements in their position, since they fear that they will be permanently saddled with the higher wage rate" (pages 226–27). For this reason, coupled with the fact that "union contracts must be negotiated at discrete intervals," it is argued that unions actually keep wages from rising as rapidly as they would otherwise rise during upswings in demand. Nevertheless employers are sometimes free to raise wages above contract levels, and they have done so. Nor is such action inconsistent with prudent regard for the future; for the wage rate which is subject to periodic renegotiation by union and management is the contract rate, and it is the contract rate alone which the union is prepared to defend. If an employer is indeed willing to take a strike to enforce a subequilibrium contract rate, he may, if successful, feel free both to raise wages to equilibrium levels and subsequently to reduce them to contract levels—if declining demand should reduce equilibrium levels that far.

But, even if willing, is he typically able to enforce a subequilibrium contract rate during a cyclical expansion? On this point one can only speculate, but Ree's evidence on the cyclical timing of strikes is of some relevance. It may be true that, in some instances, "strikes may be required to produce wage rises that would have occurred in the absence of the union," as Friedman claims (page 222). But strikes cost money and it would appear at least equally probable that wage rises higher than those which would have occurred in the absence of a union are granted in the absence of strikes and in order to avoid them. Moreover, the fact that employers take relatively more strikes in cycli-

---

[37] Bronfenbrenner, loc. cit., 304. Bronfenbrenner suspects that "the point is minor, but worth listing in this subordinate position." See also J. M. Clark, "Criteria of Sound Wage Adjustment, with Emphasis on the Question of Inflationary Effects," in Wright, op. cit., 5.

[38] Sumner H. Slichter, "Prospective Changes in the Economic Trend," *The Commercial and Financial Chronicle*, 4 November 1954, 10. J. R. Hicks, *A Contribution to the Theory of the Trade Cycle* (Oxford, 1950), 139, discusses the effects on money income of upward wage flexibility induced by a reduction in the interest rate.

cal upswings[39] suggests to this writer that the settlements emerging from such strikes yield wage rises greater rather than smaller than those which would have issued in the absence of unions.

V. Conclusions

1. We conclude that Friedman tends to understate the bargaining power of industrial unions and possibly to exaggerate the bargaining power of the crafts for the following reasons:

a. His analysis does not contemplate the possibility that the elasticity of substitution might not diverge substantially from and might even exceed the elasticity of demand in jurisdictions in which the relevant labor-cost ratios are relatively high.

b. His analysis overstresses the importance of Marshall's condition of essentiality insofar as it fails to consider the complications created when more than one labor group in an industry is organized.

c. For the same reason, Friedman assumes that the relevant labor-cost ratio is the proportion of "total cost" accounted for only by the wage bill of the members of the union under consideration. We suggest that the relevant ratio is the proportion to total variable cost of the wage income of all groups whose wage rates tend, for institutional reasons, to be interrelated. Such is the case with all the craft unions to which Friedman attributes significant bargaining strength. Thus, while we agree that the labor-cost ratio is indeed a significant factor in determining union bargaining strength, we deny that the joint-demand theory implies that craft unions are stronger than industrial unions.

d. Friedman's analysis omits reference to imperfections in product markets which tend to make it possible for unions—including industrial unions—to raise wages at the expense of profits without themselves restricting the supply of labor or the entry of (nonunion) firms within their respective jurisdictions.

2. The conclusion that unions tend to depress nonunion wages assumes that union-won wage increases are invariably accompanied by increases in the supply of nonunion labor; the implications of wage increases secured by sharework or makework or restriction of output are not explored. Neither is the possibility that nonunion employers might grant, as they have in fact granted, what we have termed anticipatory wage increases; or that, during periods of business expansions, unions might induce increased business borrowing and thus contribute to the inflation of money demand.

3. Friedman's empirical assessment of the impact of unionism upon the structure of money wage rates does not take into account the existence of union-nonunion differentials within the same industry.

For the above reasons, then, we submit that the impact of unionism upon the structure of money wages cannot be predicted by reference to the ratio of members of craft organizations to the total civilian labor force in the manner employed by Friedman.

4. Finally, we question that it "seems clear" (as Friedman claims) that employers' apprehension concerning future union opposition to future wage cuts has inhibited them from increasing wage rates (as, perhaps, distinct from contract rates) during the recent inflationary upswing.

5. The foregoing is not intended to deny

---

[39] Rees, "Industrial Conflict," loc. cit., 371–82. Rees found that a positive relationship between the strike cycle and the Burns-Mitchell reference cycle existed during the period 1915–38 but not for the period 1939–50. He cited the relaxation of wage controls and the passage of the Taft-Hartley Act as special factors which tended to obscure the impact of the cycle on the frequency of strikes. Friedman discusses the alleged depressant effect of unionism on wages in connection with the post-World War II period. However, his discussion runs in general terms, and for this reason I believe that consideration of Rees's cyclic pattern is relevant in this connection.

that "the most important forces responsible for the inflation of 1945 to 1949 operated from the side of aggregate money demand" (page 228). Nor is it my intention to minimize the novelty of Friedman's approach to the problem of union bargaining power or the importance of his theoretical contributions. He has attempted to provide a concrete estimate of the magnitude of the impact of unionism on the structure of money wages by combining theoretical analysis with empirical evidence in the construction of his hypothesis. But our admiration for the methodology cannot preclude rejection of the particular method employed and of the estimate which it provides. We agree wholeheartedly with Professor Friedman that "a major research project" is required and "very much needed to get a reasonably precise quantitative estimate" of the impact of unionism (just as it would require a major effort to get a similar estimate of the impact of enterprise monopoly). This paper has attempted to discuss the limitations of some of the methods employed thus far; we hope that it has served in addition to suggest some areas which further work might find it profitable to explore.

29
Unionism and Relative Wages in the United States

H. Gregg Lewis

1. Introduction

This is an empirical study of labor unions and relative wages in the United States. Its main purpose is to estimate the magnitude of the impact of unionism on percentage (relative) wage differentials among groups of labor. The principal questions for which the study attempts to give quantitative answers are:

By how much has unionism increased the average wage of union labor relative to the average wage of all labor, both union and nonunion? Reduced the average wage of nonunion labor relative to the average wage of all labor?

To what extent has unionism affected, in different proportions, the average wages of different industries?

How variable were the effects of unionism on relative wages from one date to another during the last forty years? How much of this variability can be explained by changes in the rate of inflation of the general price level or general money wage level? By changes in the degree of unionization of the labor force?

How much higher or lower is the relative inequality in average wages among industries than it would be in the absence of relative wage effects of unionism? The amount of relative inequality in the distribution of wages among all workers?

2. Relative and Absolute Wage Effects of Unionism

Labor unions may have three different kinds of "wage" effects that are often confused with each other. Unionism may change (a) the economy-wide average or general level of money wages per hour; (b) the economy-wide average or general level of real wages per hour; and (c) relative wages —the ratios of the wages per hour of particular groups of labor to the average wage per hour of all labor. The first two, (a) and (b), are *absolute* wage effects of unionism.

Reprinted from H. Gregg Lewis, *Unionism and Relative Wages in the United States* (1963), by permission of The University of Chicago Press. The portions reprinted here were excerpted by the author.

This study deals only with (c), the *relative* wage effects of unionism.

Unionism can affect the relative wages of different groups of labor only if it changes the wages of the groups by percentage amounts which differ from one group to another, that is, changes the percentage differences in wages among the groups. Furthermore, neither unionism nor anything else can raise (or, alternatively, lower) the wage of every different group of labor relative to the average wage of all labor. Therefore, all of the following statements have the same meaning:

Unionism has raised the average relative wage of union workers.
Unionism has lowered the average relative wage of nonunion workers.
Unionism has raised the average wage of union workers relative to the average wage of nonunion workers.
Unionism has lowered the average wage of nonunion workers relative to the average wage of union workers.

On the other hand, that unionism has raised the average *relative* wage of union workers—lowered the average *relative* wage of nonunion workers—does not mean that unionism has raised the average *absolute* wage (money or real) of union workers or lowered the average *absolute* wage of nonunion workers or changed in either direction the average *absolute* wage of all workers taken together. The effects of unionism on the general level of either money or real wages cannot be deduced from knowledge only of the *relative* wage effects of unionism. . . .

The effect of unionism on the average relative wage of a particular group of labor (the labor employed in a particular industry, occupation, city, etc.) is a weighted average of corresponding relative wage effects for (a) the union workers and (b) the nonunion workers in the group, where the relative weight for the union workers is the degree of unionization of the group. For example, if the degree of unionization were 50 per cent and if unionism had raised the relative wage of union workers in the group by 10 per cent and lowered the relative wage of the nonunion workers by 2 per cent, the effect of unionism on the average relative wage of the group would be a plus 4 per cent. Thus the differences among groups in the impact of unionism on their relative wages will be larger, the greater are the corresponding differences in degree of unionization and in the effects of unions on the relative wages of union workers and of nonunion workers. . . .

3. Empirical Studies of Unionism and Wages

Our knowledge of the relative wage impact of unionism in the United States stems almost entirely from research reported in the last decade and a half. Before 1945 there were, to be sure, many serious studies of wages and of unionism containing statements regarding the effects of unions on wage differentials, but in none of these studies, to the best of my knowledge, are there numerical estimates of the relative wage effects of unions.[1] Since World War II, on the other hand, a substantial amount of empirical research on one or another facet of

[1] Mention should be made, however, of Paul H. Douglas' *Real Wages in the United States, 1890–1926* (Boston and New York: Houghton Mifflin Co., 1930). This work was devoted almost entirely to the construction of historical statistics on wages and hours of work by industry, but in a brief discussion of unionism as a possible cause of the increase in real wages which occurred in the United States between 1890 and 1926, Douglas observed (p. 564): "Unionism, in other words, very probably does give an appreciable increase in earnings during the early period of effective organization, but during the later and more mature years of union development, the relative rate of further progress seems, to say the least, to be no more rapid on the whole for unionists than for nonunionists. Judging by our indexes, indeed, the nonunion trades have made slightly greater relative progress since 1914 than the union trades, although their average absolute earnings are still below those of the unionist." Nowhere in his study does Douglas replace the adjective "appreciable" in the above statement by a number or a set of numbers.

unionism and wages has been performed by economists; the findings given in this volume are based chiefly on the evidence presented in twenty of these recent studies.[2]

Twelve of them focus on relatively small segments of the U.S. labor force, ranging from barbers to steel workers. In addition, there are eight global studies dealing with large segments of the labor force. . . . From the evidence presented in each study and from supplementary data, I have drawn estimates of the impact of unionism on the relative wage of the union workers covered in the study. Table 29.1 displays these estimates in detail. . . .

. . . The table contains three types of information on the relative wage effects of unionism:

1. Numerical estimates, in decimal points, of the effects of unionism at specified dates on the average wage of the covered union labor relative to the corresponding average wage of nonunion labor. . . . Thus the first entry, 0.05, in the table is an estimate that in 1939 the average wage of union building construction common labor was 5 per cent higher relative to the average wage of nonunion building construction common labor than it would have been in the absence of unionism.
2. Numerical estimates, in decimal form, of the *change* from a base date to a given date in the union/nonunion relative wage effect. . . .
3. Directions of change in the union/nonunion relative wage effect between two dates.

In interpreting Table 29.1, it is important to recognize that there is some statistical dependence among the estimates from the separate studies. The dependence among the figures for the mid-1940's derived from the Levinson, Ross, and Ross and Goldner papers is almost perfect. There is also some dependence between the 1938 and 1941 Levinson estimates and the 1940 Garbarino estimate, and between the Tullock and the Lewis estimates. Moreover, the studies with broad coverage overlap in varying degree the other studies in the table.

The main task is to estimate from the data in Table 29.1 the size of the impact of unionism on the economy-wide average wage of union labor relative to the economy-wide average wage of nonunion labor during the last forty years. . . .

Although I show most of the numbers in Table 29.1 to two decimal places, many of the individual estimates undoubtedly contain large errors, stemming mainly, I judge, from incomplete control over factors other than unionism in the estimation procedures. Some of the differences between studies (or groups of labor) in the tabulated estimates no doubt consist more largely of errors of estimation than of real differences in relative wage effects of unionism. In some other instances the errors may hide real differences in effects that are not suggested by the table. Thus the errors of estimation impede the discovery of the factors causing dispersion in the relative wage effects among groups of labor, and the errors probably lead to over-estimation of the amount of the dispersion.

This chapter deals chiefly, however, with the *average* union/nonunion relative wage effect in the economy, rather than with dispersion in relative wage effects among groups of labor. The figures in Table 29.1, even though they contain substantial errors, will not lead to bias in the estimate of this

---

[2] I have endeavored to cover all of the reports of empirical research on unionism and wage differentials from which I could take directly or compute numerical estimates of relative wage effects of unionism or of directions of change in these effects. I have excluded, therefore, a good many studies in which there is evidence that unionism may have caused relative wage changes, but the evidence was of such nature that I could not estimate the size or direction of change of the wage effects. Much of the postwar research on unions and wage differentials has been reported only in unpublished or little-known papers and dissertations, some of which, no doubt, I have not covered simply because they were not known to me.

average if (a) the errors do not tend more or less consistently to be in one direction and (b) the industries and occupations covered in the table are not a biased sample from the whole population of industries and occupations. The data in the table, I fear, are defective on both of these scores.

First, it appears to be true of studies of the relative wage impact of unionism that the estimates of the relative wage effects typically tend to diminish in size as they become more refined, especially as the factors other than unionism affecting wages are more completely controlled. For example, the introduction of two new variables and weighting of the observations in the Goldner regressions reduced the relative wage effect estimate for the group of unskilled occupations by about 75 per cent. Other examples may be found in the reviews of the Scherer, Craycraft, Rapping, Friedman and Kuznets, Ross-Goldner, Ross, Tullock, and Lewis studies and in chapter vi. There are also counterexamples . . . but they are less numerous and less striking. This suggests that refinement of the estimation procedures underlying the figures in Table 29.1 would tend to reduce the figures on the average.

Second, I suspect that the estimates derived from the Levinson, Garbarino, and Bowen and Levinson data . . . contain a conceptual upward bias. . . .

Third, I judge from my experience as an onlooker and, sometimes, adviser in several of the studies covered by the table that the industries and occupations selected for study consisted disproportionately of those in which the relative wage effects of unionism were believed to be exceptionally large. These beliefs, of course, may have been wrong, but if they were right, the sample of estimates in Table 29.1 has an upward bias on this account.

4. The Average Union/ Nonunion Relative Wage Effect in the Economy

The range of the individual estimates of union/nonunion relative wage effects in Table 29.1 is very large: from zero to over 100 per cent. The figures for bituminous coal mining span the entire range. The estimates for this industry indicate that in 1921–22, immediately after the 1920–21 deflation, the relative wages of coal miners in unionized mines may have been more than twice as large as they would have been in the absence of unionization in coal mining. In contrast, it appears that near the end of World War II the relative wage position of unionized miners was *no* higher than in the absence of their unionization. Neither of these two extremes lasted very long. By the mid-1920's the estimated relative wage effect for coal miners, although large, was only about half that in 1921–22. Similarly, after 1945 the relative wage effect rose to a level in 1956–57 about the same as that in 1924–26.

An effect of the order of magnitude of 50 per cent or larger truly deserves to be called "very large." The data for bituminous coal mining thus tend to confirm the popular impression that the United Mine Workers has been exceptionally effective in raising the relative wage position of the unionized coal miners.

However, closer inspection of Table 29.1 reveals that the high figures for bituminous coal mining are really extreme. None of the other studies yielded estimates of the impact of unionism on wages of union workers relative to wages of nonunion workers as high as 40 per cent, and for only three of the other studies are there numerical estimates (or midpoints of estimate ranges) above 25 per cent:

Sobotka: During at least part of 1930–34, the relative wage effect for skilled building craftsmen may have exceeded 25 per cent slightly.
Rayack: Estimates for men's and boys' suits and coats manufacturing in the period 1928–32 ranged from 30 to 39 per cent.
Sobotka and others: The estimate range for 1956 for commercial airline pilots is 21 to 34 per cent.

TABLE 29.1 ESTIMATES OF THE RELATIVE WAGE EFFECTS OF UNIONISM DERIVED FROM EARLIER STUDIES (IN DECIMAL POINTS)

Author	Coverage	Estimated Effect	
		Date	Amount
Sobotka	Building construction, common labor	1939	0.05
Sobotka	Building construction, skilled craftsmen	1914	About equal to that in 1939
		1919	Less than in 1914
		1923	Greater than in 1919
		1929	About equal to that in 1939
		1931	Greater than in 1929
		1935	Less than in 1929
		1939	0.25
		1944–48	Less than in 1939
		1950	Greater than in 1945–48
Greenslade	Bituminous coal miners	1909–13	0.38–0.43
		1914–18	0.33–0.38
		1919	0.31–0.36
		1920	0.50–0.57
		1921	1.0–1.1
		1922	1.2–1.3
		1924	0.57–0.62
		1926	0.52–0.61
		1929	0.33–0.43
		1931	0.45–0.48
		1933	0.56–0.58
		1937–39	0.27–0.32
		1945	0.00
		1948–52	0.33–0.42
		1953–55	0.37–0.46
		1956–57	0.48–0.58
Rayack	Production workers in the manufacturing of men's and boys' suits and coats	1919	0.24
		1922	0.20
		1924	0.17
		1926	0.21
		1928	0.30
		1930	0.34
		1932	0.39
		1939	0.13–0.23
		1946–57	Approximately zero
Lurie	Motormen in the local transit industry	1920–23	About equal to that in 1925
		1925	0.15–0.20
		1929	0.15–0.19
		1933	0.22–0.24
		1937	0.12
		1939	0.03–0.06
		1948	0.07–0.18
		1958	About equal to that in 1948
Levinson (1951)	Wage-earners in selected mining, construction, manufacturing, transportation and public utility industries	1920	Less than in 1914
		1922	Greater than in 1914
		1929	Greater than in 1922
		1931	Greater than in 1929
		1933	Greater than in 1931

TABLE 29.1 ESTIMATES OF THE RELATIVE WAGE EFFECTS OF UNIONISM DERIVED FROM EARLIER STUDIES (IN DECIMAL POINTS) (*continued*)

Author	Coverage	Estimated Effect	
		Date	Amount
Levinson (1951)	Wage-earners in selected mining and manufacturing industries	1938 1941 1944 1945 1946	0.16 0.17 0.09 0.07 0.05
Rees	Production workers in basic steel manufacturing	1939 1945–48	Greater than in 1945–48 Approximately zero
Scherer	Employees of year-round hotels	1939 1948	0.00 0.06–0.10
Sobel	Production workers in rubber tire manufacturing	1936–38 1945–48	0.10–0.18 Less than 0.10
Maher	Employees in the manufacturing of paints and varnishes, footwear, cotton textiles, and automotive parts	1950	0.00
Maher	Employees in the manufacturing of wooden furniture, hosiery, and women's dresses	1950	0.07
Craycraft	Barbers in large cities	1948 1954	0.01 0.19
Sobotka and others	Commercial airline pilots	1956	0.21–0.34
Rapping	Seamen in East Coast ocean shipping	1950's	0.06–0.35
Friedman, Kuznets	Nonsalaried physicians	1929–34	Substantially less than 0.25
Lewis	Civilian physicians	1948–51	0.00
Ross	Wage-earners in selected mining and manufacturing industries	January 1945	About 0.10
Ross and Goldner	Wage-earners in mining, manufacturing, transportation and public utility industries	1933 1938–42 1946	Greater than in 1938–42 Greater than in 1946 0.04
Garbarino	Wage-earners in selected manufacturing industries	1940	0.15
Goldner	Unskilled workers in selected occupations	1951–52	Less than 0.15
Goldner	Skilled workers in selected occupations	1951–52	Less than 0.20
Tullock	All wage and salary employees	1948–52 1953–57	Much less than 0.25 Much less than 0.30
Bowen, Levinson (1960)	Production workers in manufacturing industries	1958	Exceeds effect in 1947–49 by 0.11–0.12
Lewis	All wage and salary employees	1957	Exceeds effect in 1948 by about 0.10

Moreover, the estimates for men's and boys' suits and coats manufacturing for the period 1947–57 were approximately zero.

Thus I strongly doubt that the effect of unionism on the average wage of all union workers relative to the average wage of all nonunion workers exceeded 25 per cent at any time since 1920 except, possibly, in 1921–22 and from about 1930 to about 1935. My doubts are reinforced by the following considerations:

1. The weighted average (with roughly estimated 1957 employment weights) of the following numerical estimates (or midpoints of estimate ranges) drawn from the "industry" studies reviewed in chapter iii was approximately 0.18, that is, about 18 per cent:

0.25, skilled building craftsmen in 1939 (Sobotka);
0.05, common building labor in 1939 (Sobotka);
0.53, bituminous coal miners in 1956–57 (Greenslade);
0.18, production workers in men's clothing manufacturing in 1939 (Rayack);
0.12, motormen in local transit in 1958 (Lurie);
0.08, hotel employees in 1948 (Scherer);
0.00, employees in paints and varnishes, footwear, cotton textiles, and auto parts manufacturing in 1950 (Maher);
0.07, employees in wooden furniture, hosiery, and women's dresses manufacturing in 1950 (Maher);
0.19, large-city barbers in 1954 (Craycraft);
0.27, commercial airline pilots in 1956 (Sobotka and others);
0.20, seamen in the 1950's (Rapping);
0.14, production workers in rubber tire manufacturing in 1936–38 (Sobel).

The estimate from each study included in this average, if Table 29.1 presented more than one estimate for the period after 1935, was the highest figure shown for this period. Furthermore, if only one estimate was available after 1935 and that figure was for any date in the period 1945–49, the estimate was excluded from the average. (The reason for this exclusion is that Table 29.1 shows that the period 1945–49 was one in which the relative wage impact of unionism was unusually low.) Thus the zero estimates for basic steel manufacturing and for physicians were not included in the average.

2. The estimates from the global studies reviewed in chapter iv were:

Levinson (1951): 0.17 (in 1941), the highest of the numerical estimates drawn from this study;
Garbarino: 0.15 (in 1940); and
Goldner: 0.15 for unskilled workers and 0.20 for skilled workers (in 1951–52).

(The figures from the Ross and Ross-Goldner studies were lower, but they pertained to the period 1945–46.) In addition, I estimated from the Bowen and Levinson (1960) data and independently from other data (Lewis) that the impact of unionism on the average wage of union workers relative to the average wage of nonunion workers was 10 to 12 per cent higher in 1957–58 than in 1947–49. I also have estimated (see the discussion below) that in 1945–49 this average relative wage effect of unionism did not exceed 5 per cent. These figures indicate that in 1957–58 the average effect was about 10 to 17 per cent.

3. The results yielded by my statistical study of "wage rigidity" effects of unionism in the next chapter indicate that the union/ nonunion relative wage effect probably was not greater than 20 per cent at any date in the period 1938–58.

There is a high degree of uniformity in the data summarized in the preceding paragraph that the average effect of unionism on the wages of union workers relative to the wages of nonunion workers in the United States since the late 1930's has not been larger than 20 per cent. Therefore, I put the upper-limit estimate of the average union/ nonunion relative wage effect . . . at 20 per cent for the period from about 1938 to date. Indeed, if my judgment that the estimates in Table 29.1 tend to be biased upward (see the preceding section) is correct, 20 per cent is an overestimate of the top value of the average union/nonunion relative wage effect in this period.

I noted parenthetically in the next-to-last paragraph that the relative wage impact of unionism in the period beginning about 1945 and ending about 1949 was apparently at an unusually low level. Nine of the studies provide estimates for this period as follows:

Basic steel manufacturing: 0.00 in 1945–48 (Rees);
Large-city hotels: 0.06–0.10 in 1948 (Scherer);
Rubber tire manufacturing: less than 0.10 in 1945–48 (Sobel);
Bituminous coal mining: 0.00 in 1945 (Greenslade);
Large-city barbers: 0.01 in 1948 (Craycraft);
Men's and boys' suits and coats manufacturing: 0.00 in 1946–48 (Rayack);
Motormen in local transit: 0.07–0.18 in 1948 (Lurie);
Physicians: 0.00 in 1948–51 (Lewis);
Economy wide: about 0.10 in January 1945 (Ross), 0.07 in 1945 (Levinson 1951), and 0.04–0.05 in 1946 (Ross and Goldner, Levinson 1951).

In addition, the data in the Sobotka study show a sharp fall from 1939 to 1945–48 in the relative wage position of skilled construction workers in large cities and the results of the "wage rigidity" study reported in chapter vi indicate that the relative wage impact of unionism in 1945–49 was probably close to zero. Hence I estimate that in 1945–49, unionism had little effect— 5 per cent or less—on the union/nonunion relative wage. There is much less evidence for the period at the end of and just following World War I, but what there is suggests that in this period, too, the relative wage impact of unionism was unusually low.

Except for the years in and near to these war and postwar inflationary periods, however, the estimates (or midpoints of estimate ranges) of the effects of unionism on wages of union workers relative to wages of nonunion workers are 10 per cent or larger, with two exceptions:

Motormen in local transit (Lurie): 3 to 6 per cent in 1938; and
Wage-earners in men's and boys' suits and coats manufacturing (Rayack): 0 per cent, 1946–57.

It appears, then, that "normally"—that is, apart from periods of unusually rapid inflation—the effect of unionism on the average wage of all union workers relative to the average wage of all nonunion workers was at least 10 per cent.

All of the studies (Sobotka; Greenslade; Rayack; Lurie; and Levinson 1951) spanning the 1920's and 1930's show that the union/nonunion relative wage effect was greater in the early 1930's than in the late 1920's and late 1930's. (The Ross-Goldner data go back only to 1933, but they also suggest a decline in the union/nonunion effect after 1933.) This finding is supported by the results of the wage rigidity study in chapter vi. The chapter vi estimates suggest that the union/nonunion relative wage effect may have been close to 20 per cent in 1923–29, increased to a peak well above 25 per cent in about 1932, and then declined to less than 20 per cent before 1940. . . .

The findings in chapter vi and those drawn from earlier studies point to a significant increase in the relative wage impact of unionism as the rate of inflation fell from 1945–48 to 1957–58. Nevertheless, the rate of inflation in 1957–58 apparently was still large enough, according to the chapter vi estimates, to hold the impact of unionism on the union/nonunion relative wage to a level of about 15 per cent. Because I suspect that the biases in the figures from which I have derived this estimate tend toward overestimation of the union/nonunion relative wage effect, I put the magnitude of this effect in the late 1950's at 10 to 15 per cent. . . .

Column (2) of Table 29.2 summarizes

TABLE 29.2   SUMMARY OF ESTIMATES OF AVERAGE RELATIVE WAGE EFFECTS OF UNIONISM IN SELECTED PERIODS (PER CENT)

		Average Relative Wage Effect of Unionism		
Period	Average Extent of Unionism in the Economy $100\bar{p}$	Union Labor Relative to Nonunion Labor $100(\bar{R}_{u/n} - 1)$	Union Labor Relative to All Labor $100(\bar{R}_u - 1)$	Nonunion Labor Relative to All Labor $100(\bar{R}_n - 1)$
	(1)	(2)	(3)	(4)
1923–29	7 to 8	15 to 20	14 to 18	−1
1931–33	7 to 8	> 25	> 23	< −1
1939–41	18 to 20	10 to 20	8 to 16	−4 to −2
1945–49	24 to 27	0 to 5	0 to 4	−1 to 0
1957–58	27	10 to 15	7 to 11	−4 to −3

my estimates of the effect of unionism on the average wage of all union labor relative to the average wage of all nonunion labor at key dates in the last forty years. Since the effect of unionism on the average *relative* wage of all labor in the economy is always zero and since this average is the weighted geometric mean of the average relative wage of union labor and the average relative wage of nonunion labor, the relative weight for union labor being the average extent of unionism, $\bar{p}$, in the economy as a whole, it follows that

$$\log \bar{R}_u = (1 - \bar{p}) \log \bar{R}_{u/n}$$
$$\text{and } \log \bar{R}_n = -\bar{p} \log \bar{R}_{u/n} \quad (1)$$

where $\bar{R}_{u/n}$ is the index of the effect of unionism on the average wage of all union labor relative to the average wage of all nonunion labor and $\bar{R}_u$ and $\bar{R}_n$ are the indexes of the effects of unionism on the average wage of union labor and nonunion labor relative to the average wage of all labor. The figures in column (2) are $100(\bar{R}_{u/n} - 1)$. Column (1) shows the estimates of the extent of unionism $100\bar{p}$, in the economy as a whole. ... The estimates of the effects of unionism on the average *relative* wage of all union labor, $100(\bar{R}_u - 1)$, computed from columns (1) and (2) by means of the above formula, are shown in column (3). The corresponding figures for nonunion labor are in column (4).

In the period 1931–33, unionism may have raised the average relative wage position of union labor by more than 23 per cent and lowered that of nonunion labor by more than 1 per cent. In the inflation at the end of and just following World War II, unionism had little effect on the relative wages of union and nonunion labor. More recently, unionism, I estimate, has raised the average relative wage of union labor by about 7 to 11 per cent and reduced the average relative wage of nonunion labor by approximately 3 or 4 per cent. . . .

5. Unionism and Money Wage Rigidity

The finding that the relative wage impact of unionism was greatest near the bottom of the Great Depression and was least during the periods of unusually rapid inflation and low unemployment following both world wars is not new. The authors of several of the studies reviewed in chapters iii and iv noted the phenomenon and commented on it. Albert E. Rees, Milton Friedman, Walter A. Morton,[3] and a number of

[3] Albert E. Rees, "Postwar Wage Determination in the Basic Steel Industry," *American Economic Review*, XLI, No. 3 (June, 1951), 395–99. Milton Friedman, "Some Comments on the Significance of Labor Unions for Economic Policy," in David McCord Wright (ed.), *The Impact of the Union* (New York: Harcourt, Brace & Co., 1951), pp. 226–31. See also Friedman's "Discussion" in In-

other economists have attributed the phenomenon to rigidities or lags in the adjustment of money wages introduced by collective bargaining: the collective-bargaining contract running for a year or more, the reluctance of unions to accept wage cuts during periods of deflation lest the deflation not continue, and the similar reluctance of employers of union labor to agree to unusually large money wage increases during periods of unusually rapid inflation.

In chapter vi, I report on a quantitative study in which I have attempted to measure the separate effects of changes in the general price level and changes in the rate of unemployment in the labor force on the average union/nonunion relative wage. The resulting estimates of the impact of unionism on the average wage of union workers relative to the average wage of nonunion workers agree fairly well, both in level and in directions of change over time, with those derived from the earlier studies. More importantly, the study indicates that during 1920–58, abnormally high rates of inflation strongly tended to reduce—and abnormally low rates of inflation to increase—the effect of unionism on the average union/nonunion relative wages. The study provides weaker evidence that changes in the rate of unemployment caused changes in the same direction in the relative wage impact of unionism.

6. The Extent and Locus of Unionism in the United States

To a significant extent, the differences among industries in the effects of unionism on their average relative wages stem from corresponding differences in their degree of unionization. . . .

In 1897, eleven years after the founding of the American Federation of Labor, union membership comprised less than 2 per cent of the labor force. By 1904 the proportion had risen to about 7 per cent, where it remained until 1917. From 1917 to 1920, union membership grew rapidly, but the increment in membership was short lived. In 1923 about one-twelfth of the labor force was unionized; a decade later the fraction was almost the same as in 1904.

In the decade beginning in 1935 the degree of unionization of the labor force approximately quadrupled to a level of about 25 per cent in 1945. The percentage rose slightly from 1945 to 1953 and since 1953 has declined by a small amount.

Before 1934 the degree of unionization was appreciable only in coal mining, contract construction, printing, men's and women's outerwear manufacturing, the railroads, local transit and trucking, the stage and theater, and the postal service, yet in 1929 only one-third of the persons engaged in this group of industries were union members. In 1929 these industries employed one-sixth of the U.S. labor force and three-fourths of all union members.

Since 1944 roughly half of the work forces in mining, contract construction, manufacturing, and communications and public utilities (except transportation) have been represented by unions in collective bargaining. In transportation the degree of unionization has been about 75 per cent. However, within each of these broad industry divisions there are wide differences in degree of unionization among detailed industries.

Both before and after 1934 the degree of unionization has been close to zero in agriculture, wholesale and retail trade, finance and insurance, and government (except government enterprises). The same is true of the service industries except for hotels and eating and drinking places in large cities, the entertainment industries, and some of the personal service industries. The agriculture, trade, finance, service, and government industry divisions have employed about half the labor force.

Between 1933 and 1945 the amount of inequality among industries in degree of

dustrial Relations Research Association, *Proceedings of the Eleventh Annual Meeting* (1958), pp. 212–16. Walter A. Morton, "Trade Unionism, Full Employment and Inflation," *American Economic Review*, XL, No. 1 (March, 1950), 18.

unionization doubled. Since 1945 the inequality in the distribution of unionism by industry has been approximately half as large as it could conceivably be. Thus, *as a matter of arithmetic,* another doubling, or close to it, of inequality in degree of unionization among industries is possible. For this extreme to occur, however, the extent of unionization of the labor force would have to rise to 50 per cent and, more importantly, all of the union workers would have to be employed in industries that were 100 per cent unionized.

Since 1945 there has been no persistent tendency for the degree of unionization of the labor force to increase, but even if it were to rise to 50 per cent, the dispersion among industries in degree of unionization would not increase substantially unless the growth of unionism were to consist much more largely than it has in the past of the unionization of supervisory and staff (nonproduction) employees in industries in which the production workers were already highly unionized.

7. Unionism and the Interindustrial Relative Wage Structure

Chapter viii deals mainly with the relative wage effects of unionism among industries. The studies reviewed in chapter iii provide estimates for various dates of relative wage effects for only a short list of industries. Moreover, it is not possible to deduce from these estimates and from other data presented in this study the relative wage effects, industry by industry, for the rest of the industries in the economy.

Nevertheless, some of the over-all characteristics of the distribution of the relative wage effects of unionism among industries can be gauged from the data on degree of unionization by industry given in chapter vii and the relative wage effect estimates drawn from earlier studies. The majority of workers, I judge, are employed in industries whose average relative wages have been raised or lowered by unionism by no more than about 4 per cent. However, in industries employing a quite small fraction of the labor force—considerably less than 6 per cent— the relative wage effect is 20 per cent or more.

I cannot, for lack of information, give a complete list of the industries in which the relative wage effects recently have been as high as 20 per cent. The studies covered in chapter iii suggest that the list includes bituminous coal mining, some of the building trades in some cities in which the trades are highly unionized, and possibly barbering in a few cities. The inclusion of the building trades, however, rests chiefly on data for 1939 and for both these trades and other industries the estimates of the relative wage effects of unionism may contain substantial errors.

It is likely that the industries which should be added to the list are highly unionized. However, a high degree of unionization does not guarantee that the relative wage effect of unionism is also large. For example, the manufacturing of men's and boys' suits and coats is a highly unionized industry, yet according to a study discussed in chapter iii the relative wages of union workers in the industry have been affected very little by unionism since World War II.

Only about 15 per cent of the females in the labor force are union members. The corresponding figures for males is 30 per cent. If there were no differences by sex in the average relative wage effects of unionism among either union workers or nonunion workers, I estimate that in recent years unionism has lowered the average relative wage of females by about 1 to 1.5 per cent and raised that of males by less than 1 per cent. However, in the occupations in which the impact of unionism on relative wages apparently has been greatest—coal miners, airline pilots, skilled building tradesmen, and seamen, for example—the ratio of female to male employees in very close to zero. For this reason, the above figures may underestimate somewhat the difference in relative wage effects by sex. But even if the effect

TABLE 29.3 DISPERSION OF AVERAGE ANNUAL FULL-TIME COMPENSATION AMONG INDUSTRIES, 1929–58

Year	Standard Deviation of		
	Relative Wages (Per Cent) (1)	Money Wages (Current Dollars) (2)	Real Wages (1947–49 Dollars) (3)
1929	29.6	445	608
1930	29.9	437	612
1931	32.1	442	680
1932	35.1	424	725
1933	34.4	389	704
1934	33.4	391	684
1935	33.1	407	693
1936	33.0	427	720
1937	31.8	439	714
1938	32.4	443	734
1939	31.9	449	756
1940	32.1	463	773
1941	32.0	501	796
1942	33.1	589	845
1943	31.7	637	861
1944	29.4	641	853
1945	26.6	610	793
1946	24.1	587	704
1947	24.2	649	679
1948	24.9	717	697
1949	25.4	755	742
1950	26.5	829	806
1951	27.7	933	841
1952	28.0	993	875
1953	28.7	1,068	934
1954	28.9	1,108	965
1955	29.7	1,192	1,041
1956	30.5	1,287	1,107
1957	30.9	1,365	1,136
1958	31.5	1,448	1,173

for women were the same as that estimated for *nonunion* workers—a minus 3 per cent to a minus 4 per cent—the corresponding effect for males would be no more than a plus 2 per cent. . . .

8. The Impact of Unionism on the Distribution of Wage and Salary Income

Column (1) of Table 29.3 shows the standard deviation of relative average annual full-time compensation per wage and salary worker, 1929–58, among the approximately seventy industry headings (excluding military and work relief) for which the U.S. Department of Commerce reports national income and its components by industry of origin. Columns (2) and (3) are the absolute money and absolute real counterparts of column (1). . . . (The 1929 and 1958 average annual full-time compensation figures for each industry heading are given in Table 29.4.)

Absolute money wage dispersion, column (2), increased in all except five of the twenty-nine years covered by the table and in 1958 was more than three times as great as in 1929. The upward trend in real wage dispersion was less great, but the standard deviation of real wages in 1958 was almost twice that of 1929.

My main interest, however, is with the relative wage dispersion figures in column (1). Throughout the whole period, 1929–58, the amount of relative wage dispersion was quite large.[4] Furthermore, only a small part of the observed dispersion was transitory. In general, the industries whose relative wages were high in any one of the thirty years also had high relative wages in the other years: the standard deviation among the industry groups of their thirty-year average relative wages was 28.6 per cent, which is only slightly lower than the thirty-year average, 30.1 per cent, of the figures in column (1). Thus the interindustrial relative wage structure was a highly stable one in the sense that the correlations among industries between relative wages in one year and relative wages in another year were very high.

The structure was also fairly stable in a second sense: there is no trend to speak of

---

[4] The standard deviations in col. (1) are probably biased upward by errors of measurement in the relative wage figures from which they were computed and by differences among industries in relative full-time hours worked per man per year. On the other hand, they are biased downward by their exclusion of relative wage dispersion among detailed industries within the broad industry headings used by the Department of Commerce.

TABLE 29.4 AVERAGE ANNUAL FULL-TIME COMPENSATION OF WAGE AND SALARY WORKERS BY INDUSTRY, 1929 AND 1958; EXTENT OF UNION ORGANIZATION OF WAGE AND SALARY WORKERS BY INDUSTRY, 1929 AND 1953

Industry	Average Annual Full-Time Compensation (Dollars)		Extent of Union Organization (Per Cent)		Weights	
	1929 (1)	1958 (2)	1929 (3)	1953 (4)	1929 (5)	1958 (6)
Farms	379	1,484	0	1	0.025	0.012
Agricultural services, forestry, fisheries	906	3,773	0	24	0.002	0.002
Metal mining	1,645	5,934	3	70	0.004	0.002
Anthracite mining	1,754	5,043	80	80	0.005	0.000
Bituminous coal mining	1,312	5,790	30	88	0.012	0.005
Crude petroleum, natural gas	2,050	5,970	1	14	0.006	0.007
Non-metal mining, quarrying	1,432	5,170	12	32	0.002	0.002
Contract construction	1,712	5,352	48	72	0.050	0.060
Food and kindred products	1,523	4,856	4	45	0.031	0.029
Tobacco manufactures	986	4,022	12	58	0.003	0.001
Textile mill products	1,161	3,608	3	30	0.029	0.014
Apparel, finished fabric products	1,366	3,402	29	53	0.021	0.016
Lumber and timber basic products	1,180	3,800	12	21	0.014	0.008
Furniture, finished lumber products	1,412	4,151	3	29	0.012	0.008
Paper and allied products	1,532	5,557	2	45	0.009	0.013
Printing and publishing	2,021	5,507	23	38	0.024	0.019
Chemicals and allied products	1,691	6,459	0	39	0.013	0.023
Petroleum and coal products	1,938	8,662	0	67	0.005	0.008
Rubber products	1,608	5,669	0	54	0.006	0.006
Leather and leather products	1,335	3,586	12	39	0.010	0.005
Stone, clay, glass products	1,580	5,326	9	45	0.012	0.011
Iron and steel and their products	1,765	6,223	5	58	0.042	0.048
Nonferrous metals and products	1,674	5,729	4	46	0.011	0.010
Miscellaneous manufacturing	1,579	5,083	3	18	0.009	0.013
Machinery, except electrical	1,843	5,962	13	45	0.028	0.037
Electrical machinery	1,672	5,760	12	56	0.017	0.027
Transportation equipment	1,760	6,463	0	52	0.005	0.026
Automobiles and equipment	1,819	7,024	0	80	0.019	0.018
Wholesale trade	2,083	5,803	0	4	0.067	0.068
Retail trade, including auto services	1,418	3,747	1	14	0.118	0.114
Banking	2,037	5,185	0	0	0.015	0.013
Security, commodity dealers, etc.	3,188	8,227	0	4	0.008	0.003
Finance, n.e.c.	1,977	5,834	0	0	0.005	0.005
Insurance carriers	2,293	4,768	0	0	0.016	0.016
Insurance agents, etc.	2,000	5,251	0	11	0.005	0.005
Real estate	1,629	3,645	3	15	0.009	0.007
Railroads	1,791	6,394	33	95	0.065	0.025
Local railways, bus lines	1,721	4,934	36	74	0.009	0.002
Highway passenger transportation	1,377	3,918	0	69	0.004	0.003
Highway freight and warehousing	1,322	5,727	38	78	0.007	0.017
Water transportation	1,287	7,081	16	76	0.004	0.004
Air transportation	2,624	6,785	0	51	0.000	0.004
Pipeline transportation	1,927	6,760	0	50	0.001	0.001
Services allied to transportation	1,441	5,134	22	61	0.005	0.004
Telephone and telegraph	1,416	5,124	1	69	0.015	0.016
Radio broadcasting and TV	2,513	7,192	0	52	0.000	0.002

TABLE 29.4 AVERAGE ANNUAL FULL-TIME COMPENSATION OF WAGE AND SALARY WORKERS BY INDUSTRY, 1929 AND 1958; EXTENT OF UNION ORGANIZATION OF WAGE AND SALARY WORKERS BY INDUSTRY, 1929 AND 1953 (continued)

Industry	Average-Annual Full-Time Compensation (Dollars)		Extent of Union Organization (Per Cent)		Weights	
	1929 (1)	1958 (2)	1929 (3)	1953 (4)	1929 (5)	1958 (6)
Electric and gas utilities	1,615	6,277	0	41	0.015	0.015
Local utilities, public services	1,152	4,200	0	0	0.001	0.000
Hotels and other lodging places	1,103	2,909	2	28	0.008	0.006
Personal services	1,224	3,197	9	29	0.015	0.011
Private households	732	2,150	0	0	0.034	0.014
Commercial and trade schools, etc.	1,700	4,302	0	0	0.001	0.001
Business services, n.e.c.	2,287	5,291	0	0	0.007	0.014
Miscellaneous repair services	1,831	4,805	0	0	0.002	0.003
Motion pictures	2,183	4,378	16	22	0.006	0.003
Amusement and recreation	1,277	4,352	25	29	0.006	0.004
Medical and other health services	927	2,820	0	0	0.008	0.016
Legal services	1,378	4,052	0	0	0.002	0.002
Engineering, other professional services	2,314	6,595	0	2	0.002	0.006
Educational services, n.e.c.	1,321	3,638	0	0	0.006	0.008
Non-profit membership organizations	1,723	3,844	0	0	0.012	0.012
Federal general government, civilian	2,062	5,959	11	15	0.011	0.040
Federal government enterprises	1,943	5,560	65	79	0.011	0.013
State, local general government, nonschool	1,589	4,326	1	11	0.036	0.042
Public education	1,483	4,712	0	2	0.032	0.039
State, local government, enterprises	1,609	4,655	0	30	0.003	0.006

in column (1). On the other hand, some of the short-run changes in relative wage dispersion were large: the standard deviation rose by almost one-fifth from 1929 to 1932, declined by more than one-fourth from 1942 to 1946, and increased by almost one-third from 1946 to 1958. . . .

To what extent was the relative wage dispersion among industries a result of relative wage effects of unionism? As the measure of the effect of unionism on relative wage dispersion among industries, I use the difference, $\Delta = \sigma_{\log v} - \sigma_{\log v_o}$, between the standard deviation of the logarithms of relative wages, v, in the presence of unionism and the standard deviation of the logarithms of relative wages, v_o, in the absence of unionism. Since the index, R, of the effect of unionism on the relative wage of an industry is the ratio v/v_o, and, therefore, $\log v_o = \log v - \log R$, it follows that

$$\sigma_{\log v_o} = (\sigma_{\log v}^2 + \sigma_{\log R}^2 - 2r_{vR}\sigma_{\log v}\sigma_{\log R})^{1/2}, \quad (2)$$

where r_{vR} is the simple correlation among industries between $\log v$ and $\log R$.

If the correlation, r_{vR}, were perfect and positive, then $\Delta = \sigma_{\log R}$. Similarly, if the correlation were perfect and negative, then $\Delta = -\sigma_{\log R}$. However, if the correlation is not perfect, $|\Delta| < \sigma_{\log R}$.

Columns (1) and (2) of Table 29.4 give the figures on average annual full-time compensation per wage and salary worker for 1929 and 1958 by industry group. These figures are the same as those used to compute the standard deviations for 1929 and 1958 in Table 29.3. Columns (5) and (6) show for each industry group, for the two years 1929 and 1958, the ratio of total employee compensation of wage and salary workers in the group to the corresponding total employee compensation of all industries included in the table. The numerators of the employee compensation ratios in columns (5) and (6) are also the numerators of the average annual full-time compensation estimates in columns (1) and (2). The standard deviations, $\sigma_{\log v}$, of the natural logarithms of the figures in columns (1) and (2) are:

1929: 0.324, with 1929 weights from column (5) of Table 29.4;
1958: 0.326, with 1929 weights from column (5) of Table 29.4; and
1958: 0.278, with 1958 weights from column (6) of Table 29.4.

These logarithmic standard deviations are close to the standard deviations of relative wages for the same years in column (1) of Table 29.3.

In chapter viii, I estimated that in recent years the standard deviation, $\sigma_{\log R}$, among industries of the logarithms of the relative wage effect indexes R was about 0.04 to 0.06. In 1929, the value of $\sigma_{\log R}$ was probably somewhat smaller, since the dispersion in extent of unionism among industries in 1929 was about half as large as that in the 1950's. Thus it is quite clear that even if the correlation among industries between relative wages and the relative wage effects of unionism were very high, the level of relative wage dispersion among industries shown in Table 29.3 must be accounted for mainly in terms of factors other than unionism.

More precise calculation of Δ requires estimation of the correlation r_{vR}. For 1958, I made two estimates of this correlation. The first estimate covers twelve "industries" for which I was able to calculate estimates of both the relative wage, v, and the index R: construction, bituminous coal mining, men's clothing manufacturing, local transit, hotels, rubber tire manufacturing, paints and var-

TABLE 29.5 ESTIMATES OF $\sigma_{\log v_o}$ AND Δ IN 1958

Weights	$\sigma\log R$	$\sigma\log v$	$\sigma\log v_o$	Δ
1929	0.06	0.326	0.292	0.033
1929	0.04	0.326	0.303	0.023
1958	0.06	0.278	0.244	0.034
1958	0.04	0.278	0.254	0.024

nishes manufacturing, footwear manufacturing, cotton textiles manufacturing, barbers, airline pilots, and seamen. . . .

The simple correlation between log v and log R in this sample of twelve industries was 0.63. This correlation, together with the figures for $\sigma_{\log v}$ and $\sigma_{\log R}$ given above, yields the estimates of $\sigma_{\log v_o}$ and Δ for 1958 in Table 29.5.

In the second estimate of r_{vR}, I assumed that the correlation among industries between log v and log R was the same as the correlation between log v and extent of unionism, p. For the purpose of calculating $\sigma_{\log v_o}$ and Δ, this assumption is equivalent to assuming that

$$\log v_o = \log v - (p - \overline{p})\sigma_{\log R}/\sigma_p, \quad (3)$$

where $\overline{p}$ is the average extent of unionism among all industries. I calculated log v for 1929 and 1958 for each industry heading in Table 29.4 from the average annual full-time compensation figures in columns (1) and (2) of the table. Columns (3) and (4) show estimates of extent of union organization of wage and salary workers, by industry group, in 1929 and 1953. In calculating log v_o for 1958 by equation (3), I assumed that the extent of union organization in 1958 differed little, industry by industry, from that in 1953. For both 1929 and 1958, I set the value of $\sigma_{\log R}/\sigma_p$ at 0.2.[5]

[5] For 1958, this estimate of $\sigma_{\log R}/\sigma_p$ was based on the value, about 0.05, of $\sigma_{\log E}$ estimated for recent years in chap. viii and the estimate, approximately 0.25, of σ_p for 1953 made in chap. vii. I assumed that the value of $\sigma_{\log R}/\sigma_p$ in 1929 was the same as that in 1958. [Mention of chapters made in this and subsequent footnotes in this article refer to H. Gregg Lewis', *Unionism and Relative Wages in the United States*—Eds.]

TABLE 29.6   ESTIMATES OF $\sigma \log v_o$ AND Δ CALCULATED FROM TABLE 29.4 BY EQUATION (1), 1959 AND 1958

Year	Weight	$\sigma \log v$	$\sigma \log v_o$	Δ
1929	1929	0.324	0.320	0.004
1958	1929	0.326	0.300	0.026
1958	1958	0.278	0.256	0.022

Table 29.6 shows the standard deviation, $\sigma_{\log v_o}$, among the industry headings of Table 29.4, where $\log v_o$ was calculated for each heading from the data in that table according to equation (3). The resulting values of Δ for 1958 are a bit lower than those in Table 29.5. For 1958, the correlation, r_{vR}, between relative wages and the relative wage effects of unionism implied by the figures in Table 29.6 is 0.50 to 0.58; the value of r_{vR} implied by the table for 1929, however, is only about 0.2.

The statistics in Tables 29.5 and 29.6 indicate that in the recent period, unionism may have made the relative inequality of average wages among industries, as measured by the standard deviation of relative wages, two to three percentage points, or about 6 to 10 per cent, higher than it otherwise would have been. The corresponding effect in and near 1929 probably was less than one percentage point (2 per cent). . . .

That unionism has increased the relative inequality (as measured by the coefficient of variation) of average wages *among industries* in recent years by roughly 6 to 10 per cent does not imply, of course, that unionism must also have increased the relative inequality of the distribution of wage and salary income (on a full-time equivalent basis) *among all individual workers* by 6 to 10 per cent, or even increased the latter inequality at all. The relative inequality of wages among all workers depends on both the relative inequality of average wages *among industries* and the average relative inequality of wages of individual workers *within industries*. Therefore, in principle, unionism could have reduced the all-worker inequality by reducing the average inequality within industries by more than enough to offset the increase in inequality among industries.

In a popular picture of unionism, collective bargaining has reduced relative wage inequality within the more extensively unionized industries by (a) raising the wages of unionized production workers relative to the higher wages of nonunion nonproduction workers, (b) equalizing occupational wage rates among firms within and between localities in nation-wide collective-bargaining agreements, (c) reducing occupational relative wage differences within firms by across-the-board cents-per-hour wage increases, and (d) eliminating or reducing interpersonal wage differences within occupations. This picture may fit some industries producing for a national market whose wage-earners are highly organized by industrial unions.

On the other hand, consider the commercial air transportation industry, about half of whose employees are represented by unions on a craft basis. I have estimated that in 1956 the average relative wage of commercial airline pilots was 21 to 34 per cent higher than it would have been in the absence of pilot unionization. The annual earnings of commercial airline pilots in 1956 averaged about $12,000, more than double the average annual full-time earnings of all employees in the commercial air transportation industry. Furthermore, there were large differences in salary among the airline pilots in 1956. Thus it is by no means obvious that unionism has reduced, rather than increased, relative wage inequality within the air transportation industry.

Air transportation, of course, employs only a small fraction of all union workers in the economy. About one-eighth of all union workers, however, are employed in contract construction. Construction workers are represented by numerous craft unions, collective bargaining typically is conducted on a locality basis, and there is some tendency for unionization to be more extensive among construction workers in large firms, large cities, and outside the South.⁶ Moreover, Sobotka's study of the building trades suggests that the relative wage effects of unionism in this industry group may have been much larger for skilled than for unskilled workers. Similarly, the popular picture does not appear to fit barbering, the printing, publishing, and allied industries, and the entertainment industries.

Thus even within the more or less highly unionized industries unionism probably has had mixed effects, reducing relative wage inequality in some industries and increasing the inequality in others.

Within industries in which the degree of unionization is low, the effects of unionism on relative wage inequality are mainly the indirect results of relative wage changes caused by unionism elsewhere in the economy.... I see no reason for expecting that within these industries the average change, either reduction or increase, in relative wage inequality has been more than trivial. Over half the wage and salary employees in the economy, I judge, are employed in industries in which less than a fourth of the employees are covered by collective-bargaining agreements. Most of these work in industries in which the degree of unionization is close to zero.

The preceding paragraphs suggest that the majority of employees work in industries within which unionism has had a negligible impact on relative wage inequality. The remaining minority are divided in uncertain ratio between industries (a) within which unionism has increased relative wage inequality and industries (b) within which unionism has decreased relative wage inequality. But this, in turn, implies that the average increase in relative wage inequality within the industries (a) in which unionism has increased inequality, or, alternatively, the average decrease in inequality in industries (b) in which unionism has decreased inequality would have to be quite large to change the economy-wide average *within-industry* relative wage inequality by as much as, say, 5 per cent.⁷

In the preceding section I estimated that unionism has increased the inequality of average relative wages *among industries* by about 8 per cent. If, in addition, unionism has changed the average relative wage inequality *among workers within industries* by less than 5 per cent, then I estimate that unionism has changed the relative inequality of the distribution of wages *among all workers* by less than 6 per cent.⁸

I conclude tentatively that the impact of unionism on relative wage inequality among

---

⁶ This tendency is not peculiar to construction. As I pointed out in chap. vii, there is a general tendency for unionism to be concentrated disproportionately within industries in large cities outside the South. This disproportionality probably works toward increasing relative wage inequality within industries.

⁷ For example, assume that:
a. Half the labor force is employed in industries within which unionism has had a negligible impact on relative wage inequality, 20 per cent in industries within which unionism has increased relative inequality by 5 per cent on the average, and the remaining 30 per cent in industries within which unionism has reduced inequality;
b. In the absence of unionism the average within-industry relative wage inequality in each of the three groups would have been the same.

Then in the group of industries within which unionism has reduced inequality, the amount of reduction would have to exceed 22 per cent in order to reduce the average within-industry inequality by 5 per cent.

⁸ The data in Table 29.7 in n. 9 below suggest that the standard deviation of relative wages on a full-time equivalent basis among all workers was less than 75 per cent in 1958. The standard deviation of average annual full-time compensation among industries was about 32 per cent in 1958 and would have been, I estimate, about 8 per cent lower in the absence of relative wage effects of unionism. If the standard deviations of relative wages within industries were uncorrelated with average relative wages among industries, then:
a. If unionism reduced the relative inequality of wages among all workers by as much as 6 per cent, it must have reduced the average within-industry inequality by more than 8 per cent;
b. If unionism increased the relative inequality of wages among all workers by as much as 6 per cent, it must have increased the average within-industry inequality by more than 5 per cent.

TABLE 29.7 RELATIVE WAGE DISPERSION AMONG INDUSTRIES AND AMONG ALL WORKERS, 1945–58 (COEFFICIENTS OF VARIATION OF WAGE AND SALARY INCOME IN PER CENT)

Year	Persons, Aged 14 and over, with Wage and Salary Income (1)	Full-Year Wage and Salary Workers (2)	Industry Average Wages (From Table 29.3) (3)
1945	80.7	—	26.6
1946	—	—	24.1
1947	74.3	—	24.2
1948	77.3	—	24.9
1949	76.7	60.5	25.4
1950	75.9	—	26.5
1951	76.5	—	27.7
1952	77.7	—	28.0
1953	84.8	—	28.7
1954	86.2	—	28.9
1955	86.9	—	29.7
1956	87.9	—	30.5
1957	87.7	—	30.9
1958	90.4	—	31.5

all workers has been small—under 6 per cent.[9] The direction of the effect, on presently available evidence, is ambiguous.

[9] Table 29.7 compares the relative inequality of wages among all workers with the relative inequality of average wages among industries in the period 1945–58. The coefficients of variation in col. (3) are the same as those in col. (1) of Table 29.3 in the text. Col. (1) shows estimates of the coefficient of variation of annual wage and salary income of persons fourteen years of age and over with wage and salary income. Assume that over the period 1945–58, unionism had *no* effect on the average inequality of relative wages *within* industries, but caused the relative inequality of average wages *among* industries to increase by about 5 per cent more than it otherwise would have between 1945 and 1958. Then this effect would cause the coefficient of variation of average wages among industries to rise by a bit less than 5 per cent relative to the coefficient of variation of wages among all workers. This is almost exactly the amount by which the ratio of col. (3) to col. (1) increased between 1945 and 1958. The data in Table 29.7, by themselves, are very inconclusive evidence, of course, that unionism was not a significant factor tending to change the economy-wide average inequality of relative wages within industries.

The figures in col. (1) overestimate the coefficient of variation of "full-time" wage and salary income among all workers, since the income distributions from which they were computed included, without adjustment, the wage and salary income of part-time and part-year workers. The figure in col. (2) is the coefficient of variation of wage and salary income of wage and salary workers in the experienced civilian labor force who worked 50–52 weeks in 1949. This coefficient of variation is 21 per cent lower than the figure for 1949 in col. (1).

The coefficients in col. (1) were computed from income distributions reported in various issues of Bureau of the Census, *Current Population Reports: Consumer Income*. The source of the income distribution underlying the figure in col. (2) is Bureau of the Census, *U.S. Census of Population: 1950*, IV, *Special Reports*, Part 1, chap. B, Occupational Characteristics, Table 23. All of these income distributions were open ended at the highest income class. I "closed" the open end by fitting a Pareto curve to the data for the top income classes.

References

William G. Bowen, *Wage Behavior in the Postwar Period* (Industrial Relations Section, Princeton University, 1960).

Joseph L. Craycraft, "A Cross-Section Analysis of the Effect of Unionism on the Relative Earnings of Barbers," (unpublished A.M. paper, University of Chicago, 1957).

Milton Friedman and Simon Kuznets, *Income from Independent Professional Practice* (New York: National Bureau of Economic Research, 1945).

Joseph W. Garbarino, "A Theory of Interindustry Wage Structure Variation," *Quarterly Journal of Economics,* Vol. 64 (May 1950), pp. 282–305.

William Goldner, "Labor Market Factors and Skill Differentials in Wage Rates," Industrial Relations Research Association, *Proceedings of the Tenth Annual Meeting* (1958), pp. 207–216.

Rush V. Greenslade, "The Economic Effects of Collective Bargaining in Bituminous Coal Mining," (unpublished Ph.D. dissertation, University of Chicago, 1952).

Harold M. Levinson, "Unionism, Wage Trends, and Income Distribution, 1914–1947," *Michigan Business Studies,* Vol. 10 (Ann Arbor: Bureau of Business Research, Graduate School of Business, University of Michigan, 1951).

Harold M. Levinson, *Postwar Movements of Prices and Wages in Manufacturing Industries* (Study Paper No. 21, Joint Economic Committee, 86th Cong., 2d sess.; Washington, 1960).

Melvin Lurie, "The Effect of Unionization on Wages in the Transit Industry," *Journal of Political Economy,* Vol. 69 (December 1961), pp. 558–572.

John E. Maher, "Union, Nonunion Wage Differentials," *American Economic Review,* Vol. 46 (June 1956), pp. 336–352.

Leonard A. Rapping, "The Impact of Federal Subsidies and Maritime Unionism on the Relative Earnings of Seamen," (unpublished Ph.D. dissertation, University of Chicago, 1961).

Elton Rayack, "The Impact of Unionism on Wages in the Men's Clothing Industry, 1911–1956," *Labor Law Journal,* Vol. 9 (September 1958), pp. 674–688.

Albert E. Rees, "Postwar Wage Determination in the Basic Steel Industry," *American Economic Review,* Vol. 41 (June 1951), pp. 389–404.

Arthur M. Ross, "The Influence of Unionism upon Earnings," *Quarterly Journal of Economics,* Vol. 62 (February 1948), pp. 263–286.

Arthur M. Ross and William Goldner, "Forces Affecting the Interindustry Wage Structure," *Quarterly Journal of Economics,* Vol. 64 (May 1950), pp. 254–281.

Joseph Scherer, "The Union Impact on Wages: The Case of the Year-Round Hotel Industry," *Industrial and Labor Relations Review,* Vol. 9 (January 1956), pp. 213–224.

Irvin Sobel, "Collective Bargaining and Decentralization in the Rubber Tire Industry, *Journal of Political Economy,* Vol. 62 (February 1954), pp. 12–25.

Stephen Sobotka, "Union Influence on Wages: The Construction Industry," *Journal of Political Economy,* Vol. 61 (April 1953), pp. 127–143.

Stephen Sobotka et al., "Analysis of Airline Pilot Earnings," (unpublished mimeographed MS, Transportation Center, Northwestern University, 1958).

Gordon Tullock, *The Sources of Union Gains* (Research Monograph 2, Thomas Jefferson Center for Studies in Political Economy, University of Virginia; Charlottesville, 1959).

30
Unionism, Concentration, and Wage Changes: Toward a Unified Theory

Harold M. Levinson

The issue of the relationship, if any, between the competitive character of the product market and the ability of a union to obtain wage increases continues to be characterized by differences of opinion among economists. On the one hand, several empirical studies have indicated that there has been a strong relationship over fairly long periods of time between interindustry rates of increase in wages, "degree of monopoly" in the product market, and extent of union strength.[1] Some writers, on the other hand, have continued to express serious doubts about the general validity of the relationship on both theoretical and empirical grounds.[2] This article is designed to investigate further the nature of the unionism-monopoly-wage increase relationship, with the objective of suggesting a more unified approach which can encompass and integrate both of these points of view.

Variables Affecting Wage Increases

The several studies cited in the first footnote in this article all indicate, on the basis of an examination of the available empirical

---

Reprinted from the *Industrial and Labor Relations Review*, Vol. 20 (January 1967), pp. 198–205. Copyright © 1967 by Cornell University. All rights reserved.

[1] See A. M. Ross and W. Goldner, "Forces Affecting the Interindustry Wage Structure," *Quarterly Journal of Economics*, Vol. 64, No. 2 (May 1950), pp. 254–281; W. Bowen, *Wage Behavior in the Postwar Period* (Princeton, N.J.: Princeton University, Industrial Relations Section, 1960), Chap. V; H. M. Levinson, *Postwar Movement of Prices and Wages in Manufacturing Industries*, Joint Economics Committee, 86th Cong., 2nd sess., Study Paper No. 21, 1960; and Martin Segal, "Unionism and Wage Movements," *Southern Economic Journal*, Vol. 28, No. 2 (October 1961), pp. 174–181.

In the following discussion, the term "rate of increase in wages" will refer to percentage increases in average hourly earnings, unless otherwise indicated.

[2] See esp. Albert Rees, "Union Wage Gains and Enterprise Monopoly," *Essays on Industrial Relations Research* (Ann Arbor and Detroit, Mich.: University of Michigan-Wayne State University, Institute of Industrial Relations, 1961); and H. G. Lewis, *Unionism and Relative Wages in the United States* (Chicago: University of Chicago Press, 1963), pp. 159–161 and 177–178.

evidence, that at least for certain time periods and industrial sectors, greater rates of increase in wages have been strongly correlated with three variables—relatively strong union strength (as measured by the proportion of production workers covered by collective agreements), relatively high "degrees of monopoly" (as measured by concentration ratios), and relatively high profit rates. Furthermore, attempts to isolate the separate effects of each explanatory variable on the wage by the use of multiple regression techniques have not been particularly helpful. This failure has been due to the high degree of intercorrelation among the explanatory variables themselves. Consequently, these results have been interpreted by some writers as suggesting that the three variables do not act independently of each other, but rather that it is the combined result of strong union power, facilitated by and functioning within a "permissive" product market environment, which *together* explain the more favorable wage movements. It should be noted that under this interpretation, strong unionism would still represent the primary or "initiating" force, since there is no reason to presume that more concentrated and more profitable industries would, on those accounts alone, continue to grant greater wage increases over time than would other industries.

In a perceptive critique of these studies, however, Albert Rees questioned the basic proposition that the ability of a union to achieve wage increases is in fact facilitated by the presence of a more monopolistic product market. He pointed out that because of the limitations of available data, these studies were confined almost exclusively to manufacturing industries and that

it just so happens that in manufacturing almost all strong unions deal with concentrated industries. . . . This is by no means true of the whole economy; indeed, for the rest of the economy the reverse is more nearly true. Trucking, bituminous coal mining, building construction, and entertainment are all highly organized . . . and all are competitive industries or would be in the absence of unionization. . . . In my judgment, data for the whole economy would be much less likely than data for manufacturing alone to show strong association between unionization, enterprise monopoly, and wage increases.[3]

Rees's skepticism regarding the nature of the unionism-concentration relationship was later given some empirical support in work done by H. G. Lewis with the basic manufacturing data. In a multiple regression analysis using the traditional unionism (u) and concentration (c) variables, Lewis added an interaction variable (uc) in order to test for the additional effect of the two variables taken together. The sign of the coefficient of the interaction variable was negative, suggesting the possibility (depending upon the size of the coefficients associated with each variable) that for a given degree of union strength, a greater degree of concentration in an industry may yield a smaller rate of increase in wages; thus, a union's ability to obtain wage increases may be hindered rather than helped by the presence of greater concentration in the product market. More recently, Lewis' results have been given additional support by Leonard W. Weiss, who found that during the year 1959, the interindustry level of annual earnings of several occupational groups was positively correlated with concentration and union strength, but also found the interaction effect of the latter two variables to be negative.[4] It

[3] Rees, *loc. cit.*, p. 133 (emphasis added).
[4] Leonard W. Weiss, "Concentration and Labor Earnings," *American Economic Review*, Vol. 56, No. 1 (March 1966), pp. 96–117 [Reading 22 in this text—Eds.]. It should be noted that Weiss's analysis differed from those previously cited in that he dealt with relative levels of annual earnings in 1959 rather than with relative rates of change in hourly earnings over a period of time.

A different type of criticism of the concentration-wage increase hypothesis has been raised by M. W. Reder, who pointed out that if greater wage increases were consistently correlated with concentration, it would be reflected in an ever-increasing differential between the wages paid by monopolists and by competitors for comparable labor; such an increasing differential has not in fact been observed over time. M. W. Reder, "Wage Differentials:

is interesting to note that Weiss also concluded on the basis of additional empirical investigation that while the more concentrated industries did pay higher annual incomes for given occupations, they thereby were able to obtain a superior "quality" of labor so that little or no monopoly rents or misallocation of resources resulted.

A Contrary View

Finally, a rebuttal to the Rees-Lewis position was made by M. Segal, who reiterated the point of view that concentration does indeed yield a wage-gaining advantage to the union.[5] Segal's case rested essentially on two propositions. First, that it is easier for a union, *once strongly organized*, to maintain its organizational strength in a non-competitive than in a competitive industry, because greater freedom of entry and greater mobility of capital in the latter situation tend to undermine the union's jurisdictional control; where entry is highly restricted, however, non-union competition is much more difficult to establish.[6] Second, a union in a monopolistic industry is in a much better position than in a competitive industry to make an aggressive wage policy "stick," since the existence of price leadership and the lack of downward price pressures in the former case preclude the possibility that individual locals might make special concessions to individual firms in order to permit them to attract more business by lowering prices. Segal most clearly rejected the Rees-Lewis position by asserting that competitive pricing pressures are such that "even in the improbable case of complete unionization, a union in a competitive industry would have less wage gaining ability than a union in a fully organized oligopoly or monopoly."[7]

Within this broader framework, Segal's analysis of the reasons for the apparent success of unions in competitive industries, such as the Teamsters, the building trades, and the Mine Workers is less clear. In some cases, as construction and local trucking, his explanation lies in the fact that the product market is local; hence these unions are better able to prevent the rise of non-union competition, despite the ease of entry. Furthermore, the limited areas of the product market makes it easier to prevent interlocal competitive wage pressures from developing. In the case of long-haul trucking, however, Segal suggests the explanation lies in the fact that entry is barred or restricted by regulatory authorities;[8] yet there are over 15,000 such regulated carriers operating in interstate commerce[9] in addition to the actual or potential competition from interstate carriers and from the use of private trucks. Nor does Segal deal with the bituminous coal case in which the product market is national in scope.

Towards Another Theory

Several important lines of analysis have been suggested by the work of the authors cited above; nevertheless, they do not fall into any internally consistent pattern and in some important respects, underlying causal

---

Theory and Measurement," *Aspects of Labor Economics* (National Bureau of Economic Research, 1962), pp. 291–296 [Reading 20, pp. 281–309, in this text—Eds.]. The explanation lies in the fact that during certain periods, particularly when the labor market is very tight, competitive pressures for the scarce labor supply pull the lower wages up to the higher level, thus narrowing or eliminating the previously developing differential. For a discussion of these differing types of wage interrelationships under differing labor market situations, see H. M. Levinson, *Unionism, Wage Trends, and Income Distribution* (Ann Arbor, Mich.: Bureau of Business Research, 1951), pp. 66–73. More recently, these varying types of interrelationships over time have been confirmed by Lewis, *op. cit.*, pp. 193 and 222.

[5] M. Segal, "Union Wage Impact and Market Structure," *Quarterly Journal of Economics*, Vol. 78, No. 1 (February 1964), pp. 96–114.

[6] As Segal points out, this does not mean it is easier for a union to organize a monopolistic industry in the first place; in the United States, such organization required strong government assistance.

[7] *Ibid.*, p. 105.

[8] *Ibid.*, p. 112, n. 4.

[9] American Trucking Association, *Trends*, 1965, p. 13.

relationships are still unclear. In the remainder of this article, an attempt will be made to develop a more unified analysis of the forces affecting the wage change–degree of monopoly relationship, into which these various points of view may be fitted.

We have observed that in the manufacturing industries of the economy, a strong correlation has been found over fairly long periods of time between rates of increase in wages and two "explanatory" variables, union strength and concentration ratios.[10] Rees has suggested, however, that "it just so happens" that union strength and high concentration are correlated in manufacturing, but that such a relationship is not generally true in other sectors of the economy and indeed the opposite may well be the case.

Segal's analysis, however, provides an explanation of the fact that the relationship between union collective bargaining coverage and an oligopolistic product market structure is not coincidental but follows rather from the relative ease of entry of new firms into production outside the jurisdictional control of the union. Thus, industries having high concentration ratios are characterized by entry barriers imposed by the nature of the industry itself—high capital requirements, patent controls, established brand names, and so forth. Given these entry barriers, a union, once firmly established within all or a large proportion of the existing firms in the industry,[11] is more able to maintain its jurisdictional control against the threat of erosion by the establishment of new non-union firms and hence (other things equal) can press more aggressively for greater wage adjustments. By contrast, a competitive product market implies a much greater ease of entry of new firms as well as a much higher degree of plant mobility among existing concerns, both of which contribute to a gradual erosion of union jurisdictional control and to a lowered ability to obtain wage gains. The high correlation observed in manufacturing between union strength and concentration is therefore not coincidental, but is systematically related by the structural interaction of entry barriers on the maintenance of union jurisdictional control.

A Cause of Union Strength

How then can the continuing presence—indeed in some cases the continuing expansion—of some of the strongest unions be explained, unions which are in industries characterized by large numbers of sellers, ease of entry, and strong competitive pricing pressures? Among the cases having these characteristics would be the Teamsters, the building tradesmen, the United Mine Workers, the offshore maritime seamen, the longshoremen, and some of the unions in the service industries.

The explanation suggested here lies in precisely the same logic as that relating to manufacturing, except that the protection against non-union entrants which is provided by concentration in the manufacturing industries is provided by an alternative characteristic of production—the spatial limitations of the physical area within which new entrants can effectively produce. In every one of the industries mentioned, the technological or physical character of production requires that any new entrant into production must either locate his plant within a specific and relatively limited geographic area or must physically enter such a specific area at some important phase of the production process. Under this type of industrial structure, the union need only achieve a high degree of organizational strength within the limited strategic areas involved in order to be protected against the undermining effects of new non-union entrants or of runaway shops, irrespective of how easy entry into the industry itself might be.

It should be noted that the point being

---

[10] Relatively high profit rates were also found to be correlated with wage increases; this variable, however, is not directly germane to the issue being analyzed.

[11] We omit for the moment the matter of the relationship between product market structure and the ability of the union to gain jurisdictional control in the first place.

made here regarding the importance of the spatial characteristics of the area of effective entry into production is not the same as the more commonly made point regarding the geographic area of the product market, though the two concepts are sometimes significantly related. In the construction and local service industries, for example, both the area of effective production and the product market area are local. In mining, however, the area of effective production is limited by the geographic location of the available mineral resources, but the product market is national in scope.[12] Similarly, the important limitation in maritime is related to the requirements of production rather than to the extent of the product market, since the limited geographic availability of adequate port facilities requires that entrants into stevedoring or ocean shipping must be established or at some point must operate within the unions' jurisdictional control. Finally, in long-line trucking it is only necessary that the union be firmly established within a few key cities throughout a region in order to exert control over the great bulk of new entrants, since any entrant wishing to engage in important over-the-road operations almost invariably must function within the union's jurisdiction at some point in his operations. In fact, the interrelationships among long-line carriers are such that the union is often able to extend its influence far beyond the specific areas in which it is established.[13]

Once this key relationship is seen between the maintenance of union strength and the conditions of entry of new firms into effective production, the reason for the differing experience of the manufacturing and non-manufacturing sectors with respect to the unionism-concentration relationship also becomes clear. This is because it is most commonly in manufacturing that concentration rather than spatial production limitations would be the dominant mechanism limiting the establishment of new firms outside the union's jurisdiction. For while it is true that the locational flexibility of some types of manufacturing operations is limited by high transportation costs, availability of raw materials, or other particular circumstances, the number of operations so limited is quite small relative to all manufacturing and even these few usually have a wide range of locational choices within broad regional limits. On the other hand, it is in mining, construction, transportation, and services where the spatial limitations on effective entry would most commonly be found. Hence, the primary reason for the strong relationship found in past studies between union strength and concentration was caused, as Rees suggested, by the reliance of the researchers on manufacturing data; once the analysis is broadened to include non-manufacturing, concentration is replaced by spatial characteristics as the primary mechanism for preventing entry outside the union's jurisdictional control, even in the face of a highly competitive product market structure.

Employer Resistance to Unionization

Up to this point, we have been concerned solely with the effect of product market structure on the strength of the union and on its ability to press aggressively for wage increases; we now suggest, however, that the competitive nature of the product market also has an important bearing on the employer's *ability to resist* such union pressure.

It is a commonplace observation that the history of the American labor movement indicates that oligopolistic industries have been more difficult to unionize than have competitive industries. With few exceptions, most of the earliest and strongest unions were to be found in such competitive indus-

---

[12] Where the spatial area of effective production has been quite wide, however, as in bituminous mining, the union's ability to control new entrants has often been correspondingly more difficult, as the history of the organizational strength of the Mine Workers clearly indicates.

[13] See Ralph and Estelle James, "Hoffa's Leverage Techniques," *Industrial Relations*, Vol. 3, No. 1 (October 1963), pp. 73–93.

tries as construction, printing, bituminous mining, men's and women's clothing, and a few local service industries such as local trucking and entertainment. Conversely, attempts to organize such oligopolistic industries as steel, automobiles, non-ferrous mining, meat-packing, machinery, and shipbuilding were largely abortive except under the extremely favorable conditions of World War I.

While several other factors have undoubtedly also played a role in explaining the differing degrees of success in organizing different industries,[14] one major consideration was the fact that the large oligopolistic employers had at their disposal substantial financial resources with which to resist union organizing efforts through such devices as the employment of spies and private police and the importation of strikebreakers; the funds available to smaller competitive employers for these purposes were usually much less. In addition, large financial reserves enabled the oligopolist to more easily absorb losses attendant upon a shutdown of operations caused by a lockout or a strike involving a demand for union recognition; here again, the small individual competitor was in a much weaker position to withstand such a loss of current revenue. Hence, other things equal, the ability of a union to *organize* a new plant successfully was considerably greater if the employer were a small competitor rather than a large oligopolist.

The passage of the Wagner Act in 1935, by making anti-union practices unlawful, virtually eliminated the advantages previously held by oligopolistic employers with respect to their ability to resist the unionization of their employees. There is no reason to presume, however, that the relative bargaining advantages of the oligopolist are not still present insofar as the ability to resist union bargaining demands is concerned.

A closer analysis of the nature of employer bargaining strength in some of the most strongly unionized competitive industries provides much support for this point of view.[15] In such industries as trucking, maritime, and construction, the great bulk of individual companies are small, with limited financial reserves with which to withstand a strike of any duration. Consequently, when faced with the threat of a work stoppage from such militant and organizationally strong unions as the Teamsters, the Longshoremen, the various seamen's unions, or the building trades, their ability to provide any significant resistance is very weak indeed.

Employers' Associations

As a result, employers in these industries and in others having similar characteristics have usually attempted to overcome this weakness by negotiating as a group through one or more employers' associations. An analysis of the actual bargaining policies of these associations in trucking, longshore, and maritime indicates, however, that they are often unable to maintain a "united front" in the face of a strike threat because of the large number of firms involved, the wide divergence of interests among them, and their generally poor financial resources. In trucking, for example, those firms whose operations are primarily intrastate are often subject to less stringent regulatory policies than those predominantly in interstate commerce; similarly, certain carriers are more affected than others by competitive modes of transportation, some handle types of freight more able to bear higher charges; etc. In maritime, there are strong internal differences between the subsidized and non-subsidized carriers, between those engaged in freight versus passenger operations, etc. Similarly, in construction the varying importance of the different skilled trades in different types

---

[14] Among the most important of these has been the skill of the workers involved.

[15] A fuller discussion of this question, based on a detailed analysis of collective bargaining policies in six major industries—long-line trucking, longshoring, offshore maritime, airframe, paper, and lumber—is provided in my book, "Determining Forces in Collective Wage Bargaining." [(New York: John Wiley & Sons, Inc., 1966)—Eds.].

of construction and the varying time pressures under which different groups of contractors may be operating creates sharply different views regarding appropriate bargaining policy. Under these circumstances, a particular set of demands will be less burdensome to some employers than to others or the potential losses from a strike will be much greater to some than to others. And given the large number of employers involved and the limited financial reserves of many of them, one or another group will be anxious to avoid a strike and a settlement favorable to the union is usually forthcoming.

By contrast, the larger and financially much stronger firms in oligopolistic industries are in a relatively better position to withstand the potential losses from a strike, even when facing such formidable unions as the Automobile Workers or Steelworkers. In addition, the fewer firms involved in negotiations makes it easier to develop and maintain a unified policy in any joint negotiating endeavor, whether formal or informal. This is not meant to say, of course, that internal differences do not arise or that a "divide and conquer" technique may not sometimes be successful. Relatively, however, the seriousness of these problems is much less under oligopolistic than under competitive conditions.

The generalization is suggested, therefore, that *given a similarly high degree of union organizational strength, employers in a more concentrated industry will be able to resist union pressures more effectively than employers in a more competitive industry.* This proposition is quite consistent with the related hypothesis discussed earlier that (at least in manufacturing) *the greater the degree of concentration in an industry, the greater will be the union's ability to maintain a high degree of organizational strength and consequently the greater will be its rate of increase in wages.* Thus a high degree of concentration in the product market has a two-edged effect. On the one hand, it can provide the union with greater protection against the entry of non-union competitors, and thus help to maintain the union's jurisdictional strength in the industry. Yet at the same time, it is associated with fewer firms of larger size and greater financial reserves which are able more effectively to resist union pressures. But where the union is able to maintain complete jurisdictional control *despite* the competitive product market, because of spatial types of entry limitations— as in trucking, maritime, construction, or mining—its bargaining position would be made even stronger by the weaker "resistance power" of the competitive employers. This would suggest that, other things equal, this latter group of industries would experience as great or greater wage increases over time than would the strongly unionized and more concentrated industries.[16]

Conclusion

The preceding discussion has attempted to provide an internally consistent explanation of the empirical results reported in the several studies noted at the beginning, including the positive correlation found in manufacturing between union strength and concentration and the negative coefficient associated with the interaction of unionism and concentration. It has also attempted to provide an underlying rationale for the observation—probably correct but as yet untested—that the unionism-concentration relationship is much less prevalent in the non-manufacturing sectors of the economy and for the further observation—also still to be tested—that, other things equal, wage increases in strongly unionized, highly competitive, non-manufacturing industries are at least as great as those in the strongly unionized, oligopolistic, manufacturing sectors.

[16] In this connection, it may be noted that the study referred to in n. 15 above indicates that over the entire postwar period from late 1945 to 1962, the rate of increase in *negotiated wage and major fringe benefits* was greater in over-the-road trucking, longshoring, and offshore maritime than in the automobile industry.

31
Changes in Wage Dispersion

Albert Rees • Mary T. Hamilton

During the early part of the postwar period, wage changes in the organized sector of the economy proceeded in a series of so-called "rounds" of wage increases. Each of these rounds began with a major agreement in a large manufacturing industry, usually automobiles or basic steel, after which the same or similar wage increases were quickly extended to many firms and industries not included in the original bargaining. The original agreements have become known as key bargains, or pattern bargains, and their extension to other areas as pattern following.

The extent of pattern following has important implications both for the effect of unions on relative wages and resource allocation[1] and for the effect of unions on the general level of wages. From the latter point of view, pattern following is important for the following reason: If initial union wage gains spread quickly and uniformly to a wide variety of industries, then unions are more likely to raise the general level of wages than if these gains are confined to specific industries where unions are strong, and have only a lagged and attenuated effect elsewhere. In the period 1946–48, the importance of pattern following seemed obvious, and its continuation was widely assumed. Political rivalries among union leaders were seen as creating "orbits of coercive comparison" that could not be escaped. More recently, the rounds of wage increases have been less visible, and somewhat less attention has been devoted to pattern following.

Published research on pattern bargaining has been largely concerned with the extension of the pattern within the jurisdiction of

Section III of Albert Rees and Mary T. Hamilton, "Postwar Movements of Wage Levels and Unit Labor Costs." Reprinted from *The Journal of Law and Economics* (October 1963), pp. 50–56, by permission of The University of Chicago Law School. Copyright © 1966. Tables 31.1 and 31.2 have been updated through 1969 by Mary T. Hamilton and revised to reflect more recent data for 1958–1962. No alterations have been made in the original text.

[1] Considered in Rees, The Effects of Unions on Resource Allocation, 6 J. Law & Econ. 69 (1963).

a given union. Seltzer's studies of the United Steelworkers show that the extent to which the basic steel pattern was followed by steel fabricators tended to diminish over the postwar period.[2] He also found that the pattern was followed most completely by the larger fabricators and those who were closest to the basic steel industry in terms both of their location in the labor market and of the nature of their products. These last findings were similar to those reached by Levinson in his study of pattern following by automobile parts manufacturers and the United Automobile Workers.[3] Carpenter and Handler, in their study of pattern following in the rubber tire and meat-packing industries, also find some deviation from patterns among the smallest unionized firms.[4] In all these studies, deviations in fringe benefits were more frequent than in money wages. In the farm equipment industry, students of collective bargaining have noted that UAW wage settlements have sometimes been above the automobile pattern.

Thus it has been demonstrated that, even within the jurisdiction of a single international union, pattern following is not automatic and complete. Nevertheless, the studies cited above do not preclude the possibility that small manufacturers still follow the wage changes of large companies in their own or related industries more closely than they did in the preunion period.

The balance of this section will use a somewhat different technique to obtain additional insight into the extent of pattern following. It will be concerned with the amount of relative wage dispersion among three-digit manufacturing industries since 1934. Measures of dispersion are relevant to pattern bargaining and the spread of union influence, since the uniform cents-per-hour wage increases characteristic of the early postwar patterns will narrow relative wage dispersion among the industries over which they are effective, and uniform percentage increases will keep relative dispersion constant. A widening of wage dispersion among industries would suggest that divergent economic forces in particular labor and product markets were not prevented by bargaining institutions from affecting wage levels, or that the impact of unionism on wages was becoming greater in high-wage than in low-wage industries. This analysis of dispersion is confined to three-digit industries, to avoid the double counting involved in mixing three- and four-digit industries. An insufficient number of wage series is available to permit the analysis to be conducted entirely at the four-digit level. The number of two-digit manufacturing industries is quite small, which would limit the value of an analysis of dispersion at the two-digit level.

Table 31.1 presents data on the relative dispersion of hourly earnings for two sets of three-digit manufacturing industries. The measure used is the coefficient of variation—the standard deviation divided by the mean. Column 2 gives data for sixteen industries having continuous earnings series for 1935–62, and column 3 gives data for all three-digit manufacturing industries for which data are available in each year from 1934 to 1961.[5]

Table 31.1 shows a rise in the dispersion of earnings from 1934–35 to 1937, a rough plateau from 1937 to 1941, and then a very sharp decline until 1946 or 1947. In the period 1948–51, both series show irregular movement at levels close to those of 1946–47. Beginning in 1952, both begin a rather steady rise that carries them well above the early postwar trough. The levels reached by 1961 are not far below those of 1935.

---

[2] Seltzer, Pattern Bargaining and the United Steelworkers, 59 J. Pol. Econ. 319 (1951), and The United Steelworkers and Unionwide Bargaining, 84 Monthly Labor Rev. 129 (1961).

[3] Levinson, Pattern Bargaining: A Case Study of the Automobile Workers, 74 Q.J. Econ. 296 (1960).

[4] Carpenter & Handler, Small Business and Pattern Bargaining (1961).

[5] The number of industries included in col. 3 at various dates is as follows: 1934–46, 21; 1947–50, 88; 1951–53, 130; 1954–57, 129; 1958–69, 118.

An improved understanding of the meaning of these movements in the coefficient of variation can be obtained by examining the actual earnings data for the sixteen industries for which continuous data are available.

TABLE 31.1 COEFFICIENTS OF VARIATION OF AVERAGE HOURLY EARNINGS FOR THREE-DIGIT MANUFACTURING INDUSTRIES

Year (1)	16 Identical Industries (2)	All Industries (3)
1934	n.a.	.200
1935	.233	.203
1936	.244	.213
1937	.257	.225
1938	.257	.222
1939	.253	.224
1940	.248	.217
1941	.252	.225
1942	.241	.220
1943	.232	.214
1944	.223	.211
1945	.205	.192
1946	.178	.161
1947	.162	.174
1948	.164	.161
1949	.169	.166
1950	.165	.161
1951	.167	.161
1952	.176	.166
1953	.183	.172
1954	.181	.175
1955	.194	.183
1956	.191	.178
1957	.196	.181
1958	.205	.179
1959	.214	.186
1960	.208	.185
1961	.213	.190
1962	.214	.190
1963	.217	.191
1964	.217	.190
1965	.218	.190
1966	.216	.189
1967	.207	.180
1968	.209	.175
1969	.211	.177

[The table in the original article presented figures in column 3 for 1958–61 based on data for 119 industries. All figures since 1958 have been revised by Mary Hamilton as necessary to reflect revisions in the published data—Eds.]

These are shown in Table 31.2 for selected years.

Table 31.2 suggests that much of the movement of the coefficient of variation in the years 1935–38 can be explained by events in the highest wage industries, particularly basic steel, motor vehicles, and petroleum refining. In each of these industries, earnings rose sharply relative to the all-manufacturing average from 1935 to 1938, presumably because of the pressure of new or growing unions. During World War II, the relative position of these industries and of two additional high-wage industries—shipbuilding, and tires and tubes—deteriorated as wages rose more rapidly in the rest of manufacturing. Especially after 1942, the lowest-wage industries improved their standing, perhaps because of special treatment by the War Labor Board or as a result of the shortage of manpower. The fall in the wage ratios of the high-wage industries by 1946 had not only erased the relative gains of the middle thirties but in each case had gone further. The 1946 ratios lie below those for 1935, often substantially below. After 1946, the behavior of wages in this group of industries begins to diverge. Relative wages rose sharply in basic steel from 1950 to 1958, surpassing their 1938 level by the latter date. Relative wages continued to fall in shipbuilding until 1950 and did not regain their 1946 level. In the rest of the high-wage group—motor vehicles, petroleum refining, and tires and tubes—relative wages remained about constant at the 1946 levels and below the levels of 1935. The relative wage position of the lowest wage industries tended to worsen after 1946; this is particularly noticeable in textile finishing and in footwear. Similar tendencies are shown by other textile and apparel industries not included in Table 31.2 and by industries in the lumber and wood products group. This worsening of the relative position of low-wage industries may account for much of the rise in relative dispersion, as measured by the coefficient of variation, from 1946 to 1962.

It is tempting to consider the 1934–35

TABLE 31.2 AVERAGE HOURLY EARNINGS IN 16 THREE-DIGIT MANUFACTURING INDUSTRIES—SELECTED YEARS, 1935–62 (RATIOS OF GIVEN INDUSTRY TO ALL-MANUFACTURING AVERAGE)

Industry	1935	1938	1942	1946	1950	1954	1958	1962	1966	1969
Cement, hydraulic	1.06	1.11	0.98	0.97	1.00	1.02	1.09	1.15	1.17	1.17
Structural clay products	0.82	0.83	0.81	0.90	0.92	0.92	0.91	0.89	0.86	0.84
Pottery and related products	0.93	0.96	0.87	0.91	0.93	0.92	0.93	0.92	0.92	0.90
Blast furnace and basic steel products	1.21	1.35	1.20	1.20	1.18	1.25	1.36	1.36	1.30	1.26
Metal cans	0.93	0.97	0.89	0.98	1.02	1.11	1.20	1.26	1.19	1.20
Motor vehicles and equipment	1.32	1.47	1.38	1.26	1.23	1.24	1.21	1.25	1.26	1.29
Ship and boat building and repairing	1.37	1.34	1.37	1.27	1.13	1.15	1.17	1.20	1.16	1.12
Watches and clocks	0.88	0.91	0.88	0.93	0.93	0.93	0.89	0.88	0.82	0.80
Canned and preserved food, except meats	0.66	0.72	0.71	0.83	0.81	0.78	0.78	0.79	0.78	0.78
Bakery products	0.94	0.93	0.81	0.87	0.89	0.90	0.90	0.95	0.95	0.94
Finishing textiles, except wool and knit	1.03	0.92	0.83	0.91	0.92	0.85	0.79	0.77	0.78	0.78
Paperboard containers and boxes	0.89	0.86	0.78	0.86	0.90	0.92	0.93	0.95	0.94	0.93
Petroleum refining	1.46	1.57	1.34	1.33	1.34	1.34	1.35	1.33	1.32	1.33
Tires and inner tubes	1.52	1.51	1.30	1.32	1.26	1.28	1.29	1.33	1.35	1.32
Leather tanning and finishing	1.01	1.00	0.94	0.99	0.98	0.97	0.93	0.91	0.92	0.92
Footwear, except rubber	0.91	0.79	0.77	0.85	0.78	0.74	0.72	0.70	0.69	0.72

observations in Tables 31.1 and 31.2 as reflecting some sort of preunion norm, since manufacturing unionism was so weak at that time. However, 1934 and 1935 were unusual years in at least two other respects: they were not far past the trough of the Great Depression and during much of the period wages were subject to the National Recovery Administration codes. For this reason, it is desirable to use other wage data to move backward into the twenties. Table 31.3 is based on the wage data of the National Industrial Conference Board covering twenty-five manufacturing industries for the period 1925–48. It should be noted that for the period covered by both the National Industrial Conference Board (NICB) and the Bureau of Labor Statistics (BLS) data, the movement of wage dispersion is very similar: a rise from 1934 to 1937, continuing to 1939 in the NICB series; then irregular movement at a high level until 1942; after which there is a steady and sharp decline, reaching very low levels in the years 1946–48. This similarity of movement lends support to the view that the NICB series can shed light on the meaning of the 1934–35 levels in the BLS series.

Table 31.3 shows that the initial effect of the depression on wage dispersion was to increase it sharply in 1931 and 1932, pre-

TABLE 31.3 COEFFICIENTS OF VARIATION OF AVERAGE HOURLY EARNINGS, 25 MANUFACTURING INDUSTRIES, 1925–48 (NICB DATA)

1925	.160	1937	.159
1926	.159	1938	.165
1927	.152	1939	.175
1928	.157	1940	.169
1929	.160	1941	.171
1930	.158	1942	.169*
1931	.177	1943	.156
1932	.196	1944	.155
1933	.186	1945	.136
1934	.154	1946	.116
1935	.162	1947	.116
1936	.155	1948	.108

* Data for 1942 cover only twenty-three industries.

sumably because wages fell sooner and more in the low-wage industries. In 1934 and 1935, however, relative wage dispersion returned to levels similar to those prevailing from 1925 through 1929. This return to "normalcy" may have been a result of the operation of the NRA codes, which were not present earlier in the depression period.

We are now in a position to summarize this discussion of the dispersion of relative wage levels among manufacturing industries. The late war years and the immediate postwar inflation were accompanied by an extraordinary narrowing of wage differentials among manufacturing industries. One factor in this narrowing was undoubtedly the establishment of patterns of wage increases that cut across industries, first by the War Labor Board and later through pattern bargaining. A second and perhaps equally important factor was the presence of labor shortages that tended to drive up wages most in low-wage industries experiencing the greatest difficulties in recruitment. As the postwar period wore on and the pace of inflation slackened, relative wage dispersion again increased, reaching levels not much short of those of 1934–35 and probably not much short of those of the late 1920's. This increase in dispersion occurred in the presence of strong unions in much of manufacturing. Its nature, insofar as it can be detected from the data for the separate three-digit industries, was of two kinds. First, a few unionized, high-wage industries, of which basic steel is the most important, had increases in average hourly earnings much beyond the manufacturing average.[6] The other industry experiencing sharp gains in relative wages in the postwar period—metal cans—is also in the jurisdiction of the steelworkers' union. Second, and at the opposite extreme, many low-wage industries, some weakly unionized, failed to keep pace with the manufacturing average. This was true in footwear, canning and preserving, in almost all branches of the textile and apparel industries, and in lumber and wood products.

All this confirms what may long have been obvious: the pattern following of the immediate postwar period, insofar as it transmitted patterns across major industry lines, is now greatly attenuated, though there is still pattern following within the jurisdiction of particular unions. Among the unions with control of most of their jurisdictions, the steelworkers are far out in front of the parade in the size of their increases in earnings; the apparel unions lag far behind. The low-wage, weakly unionized parts of manufacturing are no longer keeping up with the wage gains in the rest of manufacturing. It seems reasonable to infer from this that union wage gains now pose more of a problem of shifting relative costs and employment than they did in 1946–48, but much less of a problem of raising the entire level of manufacturing wages.

[6] This increase in relative earnings in basic steel is concentrated in the period 1956–59 and is related to the provisions of the three-year agreement negotiated in 1956. For full discussion see Livernash, Collective Bargaining in the Basic Steel Industry 149–50 (1961).

32
The Effects of Unions on Resource Allocation[1]

Albert Rees

The purpose of this paper is to suggest in highly condensed form the general order of magnitude of the effects of unions and collective bargaining on the allocation of resources. It is widely accepted that unions have the power to raise wages in the establishments where they have bargaining rights. (The term "wages" should be understood to include fringe benefits.) This power comes from their ability to impose costs on management through strikes, slow-downs, or other pressure tactics which, in the short run, are greater than the costs of the wage increases provided through collective bargaining. By changes in relative wages we shall mean changes in wages in establishments covered by collective bargaining relative to wages elsewhere. For the discussion of resource allocation it is not necessary to specify how much of the relative increase arises from an absolute increase in union wages and how much from any possible decrease in nonunion wages. (Such a decrease could occur if labor were displaced from the union sector by rising wages and were therefore in more plentiful supply to the nonunion sector.)

The existence of a relative wage effect implies the existence of a relative employment effect. If blue-collar labor is made more expensive in the union sector, management will have added incentives to save such labor through closer supervision and through the use of additional labor-saving capital equipment. Such substitution will minimize, but not eliminate, the addition to cost created by union wage gains. The remaining addition

Reprinted from *The Journal of Law and Economics*, Vol. 6 (October 1963), pp. 69–78, by permission of The University of Chicago Law School. Copyright © 1966.

[1] I am heavily indebted to H. Gregg Lewis for comments on an earlier draft of this paper and for permission to draw freely on two of his works: Unionism and Relative Wages in the United States (1963) [Excerpted in Reading 29 in this Text—Eds.] and Relative Employment Effects of Unionism, in Proceedings of Sixteenth Annual Meeting of Industrial Relations Research Association 104 (1964). However, he is in no way responsible for the opinions expressed here or for the deficiencies of my estimates.

to average unit costs will tend to increase the price of final products and services produced in the union sector and therefore to reduce their consumption. Relative employment in the union sector should therefore decline for two reasons: (*a*) the substitution of other factors of production for union labor and (*b*) the substitution by consumers of cheaper final products and services for the more expensive output of the union sector. Whether these effects are empirically important depends on the size of the relevant elasticities of substitution and of demand.

Empirical estimates of the effect of unions on relative wages and relative employment encounter many difficulties. The basic problem is to correct for factors other than collective bargaining that might have produced differences between the union and nonunion sectors in the movements or levels of wages and employment. The devices used to control for such factors in the estimation of wage effects are discussed in detail in *Unionism and Relative Wages in the United States*.[2]

Lewis' book reviews, criticizes, and amends the previous studies that have estimated union effects on relative wages. In addition, it includes very substantial new work. From all this evidence, Lewis concludes that the effect of unions on relative wages in the late 1950's was about 10–15 per cent (that is, wages of union labor had been raised by unionism 10–15 per cent relative to the wages of nonunion labor). The highest estimate for any part of the period considered is 25 per cent or more at the depth of the Great Depression of the 1930's. In the late 1940's, because of rapid inflation, the union effect is estimated at 5 per cent or less.[3] During rapid inflation, market wages in the nonunion sector tend to rise rapidly, while the rise in union wages is often slowed by rigidities inherent in the bargaining process.

In his paper on *Relative Employment Effects of Unionism*,[4] Lewis estimates that the order of magnitude of the relative employment effect is not significantly different from that of the relative wage effect. In other words, the effect of collective bargaining is to reduce employment in the union sector about 10–15 per cent relative to employment elsewhere. This estimate rests on a less substantial body of work than the estimate of the wage effect.

The effects of unions on resource allocation can be divided into three components: effects via the interindustry wage structure, effects via the intraindustry wage structure, and effects via direct restrictions on output. We shall consider each of these in turn.

Lewis' two works permit us to make a rough estimate of the loss in real output caused by the effects of collective bargaining on the interindustry wage structure. Under certain conventional assumptions, it can be shown that the loss of real output is approximately equal to one-half the product of the wage effect and the employment effect (see Figure 32.1). I have used this formula to make a rough estimate for 1957, the last nonrecession year covered in Lewis' estimates. This estimated loss turns out to be approximately 600 million dollars. Since gross national product in 1957 was 443 billion dollars, the loss is approximately 0.14 per cent of national output. This welfare loss is of the same general magnitude as that estimated earlier by Arnold Harberger for enterprise monopoly (0.1 per cent).[5] The method used here is an application of that used by Harberger and derived from Harold Hotelling.[6]

---

[2] Lewis, Unionism and Relative Wages in the United States, *op. cit. supra* note 1, at 45. A briefer and less technical discussion may be found in Rees, The Economics of Trade Unions, 73–75 (1962).

[3] These summary figures appear in Lewis, Relative Employment Effects of Unionism, *op. cit. supra* note 1.

[4] *Ibid.*

[5] Harberger, Monopoly and Resource Allocation, American Economic Association Papers and Proceedings, Am. Econ. Rev., May 1954, p. 77.

[6] Hotelling, The General Welfare in Relation to Problems of Taxation and of Railway and Utility Rates, 6 Econometrica 242 (1938).

The Effects of Unions on Resource Allocation 491

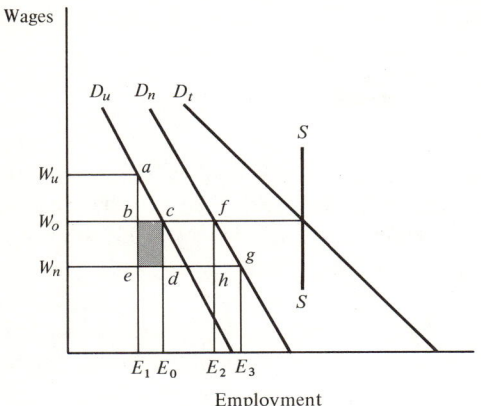

FIGURE 32.1 SS is the supply of labor, and D_u, D_n, and D_t are the demand for labor in the union sector, the nonunion sector, and both combined. Before the entry of the union, the wage is W_o. If the union raises the wage in its sector to W_u, employment in the sector declines from E_0 to E_1. This increases the supply of labor to the nonunion sector, raising employment from E_2 to E_3 and forcing the wage down to W_n. The areas under the demand curves are the real net product of labor. The loss in product in the union sector is $E_0 c a E_1$, the gain in product in the nonunion section is $E_2 f g E_3$. The difference between these areas is the loss of product shown by the shaded rectangle $b c d e$. This is equal to the change in employment times one-half the differences in wages. In the more general case, where the demand curves in the two sectors are nonlinear or do not have the same slope, the equality will be only approximate.

The estimated loss is arrived at as follows. Union membership in the United States in 1957 was approximately 17 million. A relative employment effect of 15 per cent implies a transfer of about 1.7 million workers out of the union sector as a result of bargaining, and a relative wage effect of 15 per cent implies an absolute wage effect of about 700 dollars per worker per year. One-half of 700 dollars times 1.7 million is approximately 600 million dollars.

This calculation assumes that the average compensation of union members is equal to the average compensation of all employees in the highly unionized industry divisions: mining, contract construction, manufacturing, transportation, and communications and public utilities. The last assumption involves offsetting errors. Among production workers, union members in these industry divisions have higher compensation than nonunion workers. However, in manufacturing, which accounts for about 70 per cent of total employment in these divisions, the compensation of nonproduction workers is substantially higher than that of production workers, and nonproduction workers are seldom unionized. Moreover, there are some union members in other industry divisions who will on the average have lower compensation than those in the divisions listed above.

In one very restricted sense, the estimate of 600 million dollars as the interindustry component of welfare loss for 1957 is an upper-limit estimate—it uses the upper limits of the ranges of relative wage effects and relative employment effects estimated by Lewis. Nevertheless, there are other assumptions embodied in the estimate that could lead it to be too low. First, since the estimate of employment effects rests on less evidence than that of wage effects, it is possible that they exceed the upper limit of the estimated range. An alternative method of estimation would be to combine the estimated relative wage effect with an assumed elasticity of demand for labor. This is the method used by Harberger in his study of enterprise monopoly, in which he assumed an average elasticity of demand for products of -1. The assumption of an elasticity of demand for labor of -1 would not change the estimate given above, since this is the elasticity implicit in the estimates used for the wage and employment effects.

The estimate also assumes that the relative wage and employment effects of unions are uniform within the union sector. The more realistic assumption that the size of these effects varies within the sector will not change the estimate provided that there is no correlation across unionized industries between the size of actual employment and actual wage effects. However, if in general large wage effects are associated with small employment effects, the estimate given above is too high; if large wage effects are associated with large employment effects, the estimate is too low.

In general, it seems reasonable to assume that large wage effects are associated with smaller-than-average employment effects— that is, that unions will raise wages most where the elasticity of demand for labor is smallest and the costs in reduced employment are lowest. There is, however, one important case that does not fit this generalization: the bituminous coal industry, where both the wage effect and the employment effect seem to be unusually large.

The estimated loss under discussion also assumes that no unemployment results from the employment effects of unionization. We should not, of course, charge the unions with the losses arising from general deficiencies in aggregate demand. However, the displacement of labor from one industry to another will give rise to frictional unemployment even under conditions of general prosperity, and the costs of this should be added to the interindustry component of welfare loss. These costs will be smaller if unionization is concentrated in expanding industries, since relative employment effects will then take the form of reducing the rate of hiring rather than requiring the dismissal of present employees. In fact, however, much of the strength of unions has been in contracting or stable industries, so that the unemployment costs of unionization are probably significant.

Professor Lewis has reported to me that he has made an unpublished estimate of the welfare cost of the interindustry component of relative wage and employment effects, using a somewhat more sophisticated method of calculation which allows for the dispersion of the relative wage effect within the union sector. The resulting measure of loss is almost the same as that reported above: 0.15 per cent of national product.

Not much is known about the relative wage effects of unions in particular industries. The available industry studies are summarized by Lewis in *Unionism and Relative Wages in the United States*, chapters iii and v, especially Table 49. These studies suggest that the unions of the following groups of workers had larger than average effects (20 per cent or more): skilled building craftsmen, bituminous coal miners, commercial airline pilots, and East Coast seamen. These estimates refer to the 1950's except that for building craftsmen, which is for 1939. The studies also show that one union, the Amalgamated Clothing Workers, had no appreciable relative wage effect in the period 1946–57, though it did in the years from 1919 to 1939. This loss of power was associated with declining demand for the product.

The list of cases with very large estimated wage effects includes three for craft unions and one for an industrial union. Economic theory suggests that craft unions will have larger relative wage effects than industrial unions because their wages constitute a smaller portion of total costs, except in the unusual case where there are very good substitutes for union craftsmen in production and the elasticity of demand for the product is low.[7] But this advantage holds only if the craft unions in an industry bargain individually. If they bargain as a group, or wage patterns are transmitted to all the occupations in the industry, the case becomes similar to that of industrial unionism.

It is possible to put together the available industry studies, the relevant economic theory, and data on wage movements to make informed guesses on which unions not mentioned in the preceding paragraphs have larger-than-average relative wage effects. My leading candidates would be the skilled craft unions in railroads, entertainment, and the printing trades; the teamsters; and the steelworkers. A list of candidates for additional unions with less-than-average relative wage effects would include the unions of ladies' garment workers, textile workers, shoe workers, and white-collar government workers. The first is included because of the similarity

---

[7] See Rees, *op. cit. supra* note 2, at 70–73, and the passages from Marshall and Hicks cited therein.

of the industry to men's clothing. The next two are examples of unions that have incomplete organization of industries with national product markets. The government unions are included because their political power is probably an inferior substitute for the use of the strike.

The relative wage and employment effects considered so far arise from the impact of collective bargaining on the interindustry wage structure. We turn next to the effects of collective bargaining on the wage structure within industries, which in some cases may be of considerable importance. Geographical wage patterns are one example. In the absence of collective bargaining, manual labor, and particularly unskilled labor, is appreciably cheaper in the South than in other regions. This regional wage differential arises from the more abundant supply of unskilled labor in the South. It tends to be reduced by the migration of labor to the North and of capital to the South, but such movements of resources have not been sufficient to offset the greater rate of natural population increase in the South.

Unions that bargain with multiplant employers or with associations of employers operating both in the South and elsewhere have attempted to eliminate regional wage differentials and frequently have succeeded. The union rate for unskilled labor in the southern operations of these employers is therefore further above the market rate than in their northern and western operations.[8] From this may flow a number of consequences: (1) national employers constructing new facilities both in the South and in the North would normally have an incentive to use somewhat more labor-intensive methods in the South; this incentive is eliminated by the uniform wage; (2) where plant location is oriented toward labor costs rather than access to markets or raw materials, an incentive to locate plants in the South is removed; (3) where plant location has been determined by access to southern markets or raw materials, the national employer may be unable to compete with local nonunion employers able to take advantage of low market rates of wages. Factors of this kind are unlikely to be important in the automobile or steel industries but are of considerable importance in meat packing. The displacement of national by local firms could retard the industrialization of the South to the extent that national firms have access to lower-cost sources of capital, both internal and external.

The elimination of regional wage differentials through collective bargaining benefits the southern workers already employed in the unionized sector. However, it injures those workers, not readily identifiable, who would have been employed in industry had incentives for the expansion of industrial employment in the South not been diminished. Equality is achieved within the union sector at the cost of increased disparity between the union plant in the South and the rest of the southern economy.

Another area in which collective bargaining affects the structure of wages is that of skill differentials. Such effects may be readily apparent to personnel people in industry. However, they have not been much studied by academic economists, and the discussion below is therefore somewhat conjectural. The effects seem from existing literature to be mixed and without a dominant pattern.[9]

In several industries represented by industrial unions, the effect of collective bargaining early in the postwar period appeared to be to compress skill differentials. The compensation of the least skilled workers was raised most by unions, that of the most skilled less or perhaps not at all. Such wage compression could affect resource allocation by reducing incentives to undertake training

---

[8] This is especially true in motor freight, where Hoffa has obtained the same mileage rates from southern as from midwestern truckers, removing traditional differentials. Because of superior weather conditions in the South, these bring higher weekly earnings to southern drivers.

[9] Reynolds & Taft, The Evolution of the Wage Structure 185–86 (1956).

and could lead to shortages of apprentices for the skilled trades. More recently, such compression has been limited or reversed by the actual or threatened secession of skilled workers to form separate unions of their own and by the operation of percentage wage increases such as annual improvement factors.

An opposite effect on skill differentials can occur under craft unionism if the unions representing the most skilled crafts are stronger than those representing the less skilled. This situation may prevail in portions of the railroad and printing industries. In such cases the effect of unionism is to prevent skill differentials from narrowing as much as would be expected from the general long-run trend; this provides incentives for employers to economize most in the use of skilled labor. However, the ability of employers to substitute other factors for skilled labor may be severely restricted by union rules.

Since union effects on intra-industry wage structures are more difficult to discern than effects on the interindustry structure, the costs of the former are probably less than those of the latter. This would suggest a combined cost of less than 0.3 per cent of gross national product. If this estimate seems low, it is because the social costs of transferring resources to less productive uses are far less than those of wasting resources altogether. This brings us to the third avenue of union effects on resource allocation: direct restrictions of output through control of manning requirements, the work pace, and work practices, often called "featherbedding." In the course of preparing this paper, I have reached the conclusion that losses of this kind—dead-weight losses—probably exceed the social losses from relative wage effects. Indeed, management in a single industry—railroads—claimed in 1959 that obsolete work rules were costing 500 million dollars a year, or over 0.1 per cent of national product. Although this may be an overestimate, particularly through the inclusions of some costs that are in reality higher compensation for necessary work, the comparison between this amount and those mentioned above suggests something about the general magnitudes involved.

The evidence available is not sufficient to permit any numerical estimate of the total costs of union control of manning practices and work rules. The published accounts suggest that a large part of the costs is concentrated in a few industries, especially railroads, printing, longshoring, entertainment, and some aspects of building construction. Costs are especially high in industries with craft union organization where each piece of work, however small, "belongs" to a particular craft, and a member of that craft must be called to do it. On the railroads such practices can result in the payment of a day's pay for a few minutes' work and sometimes in payment to two men for work done by one.[10]

It should be noted, however, that direct union impact on output is not always restrictive. Under some circumstances, unions have made significant contributions to efforts to raise output or productivity, especially where jobs have been threatened by competition from new products or products produced in other locations.

The practices bearing directly on resource use include apprenticeship rules, which can affect the number and quality of people trained, either by their effect on the size and nature of the entering group or by their influence on the percentage of entrants who complete the program. There seems to be general agreement that the number and quality of apprentices in many trades are inadequate to meet probable future needs. Such an effect could arise in any or all of the following ways: (1) the quality of the entering group can be lowered by nepotism or discrimination in the selection of entrants; (2) the number of apprentices can be limited by rules setting the ratio of apprentices to journeymen—this is the best known, but prob-

[10] Slichter, Healy & Livernash, The Impact of Collective Bargaining on Management, ch. 11 (1960).

ably not the most important, of the restrictive devices; (3) the numbers of people entering and completing programs will be held down if the programs are unnecessarily long or if the program content is poor; (4) the number entering and completing will be reduced if the apprentice's wage is too low relative to the journeyman's; (5) conversely, the willingness of employers to train apprentices will be reduced if the apprentice's wage rate is too high relative to the journeyman's. All of these observations apply in principle to training programs operated solely by management. However, when management is in sole control of a training program, it has greater freedom to take prompt corrective action if the number or quality of trainees is inadequate.

Union influence on resource allocation that arises from increases in relative wages works unambiguously in the direction of reducing relative employment. Practices that limit output or require unnecessary numbers of men have an unpredictable effect in the long run. In the short run, the effect may be an absolute increase in the employment of the group that institutes the restrictive practices; in the longer run, such practices may encourage types of substitution that the union is powerless to cope with, which will ultimately reduce employment. For example, an effective full-crew law or rule on railroads will increase the number of operating employees per train but may accelerate the substitution of other forms of transportation for rail transportation. In the long run, the number of jobs lost through such accelerated substitution could exceed the number created or preserved by the full-crew rule. The only unambiguous effect is to increase the cost of transportation.

Union restrictions on contracting out work traditionally done in the bargaining unit are less formalized than some other types of restrictions, but may be becoming more widespread. If the work can be done at less cost by the outside contractor, there is an obvious adverse effect on efficiency. In cases where the outside contractor also uses union labor (not necessarily from the same union), any shifts in employment arising from restrictions on contracting out will not be caught by estimates of changes in relative employment in the union sector as a whole.

Throughout the preceding discussion, the implicit comparison has been between the relative wages and distribution of employment existing under unionism and those which would exist under perfectly competitive labor markets. Since the allocation of resources by perfectly competitive markets is known to be optimal, by this standard the impact of the union is necessarily adverse. The standard must be modified to the extent that actual nonunion labor markets are monopsonistic. If nonunion employers, either singly or acting in concert, have the power to hold wages below the levels that would prevail under perfect competition, moderate union effects on relative wages may bring employment closer to an optimal configuration. The scanty available evidence suggests that monopsony power by employers in United States labor markets is small but not nonexistent.[11] However, in some markets where employers have such power (textile-mill towns, for example) there is little unionization, while in others where such power may once have existed (especially coal-mining areas), the union corrective may have gone too far.

If the entire impact of unions on our society could be subsumed under the heading of resource allocation, there would be little difficulty in reading the conclusions that the over-all impact is adverse and that union power is excessive. The difficulties for policy explored in Professor Meltzer's paper[12] arise because this is not the case. Important aspects of collective bargaining, such as grievance procedure, have only tangential implications for resource allocation, but strong

[11] Bunting, Employer Concentration in Local Labor Markets (1962) [chapter 1 is Reading 10 in this text—Eds.].
[12] See Meltzer, Labor Unions, Collective Bargaining, and the Antitrust Laws, 6 J. Law & Econ. 152 (1963).

effects on equity in work situations and on the meaning and status of manual work. Union representation of workers in political processes is largely noneconomic, yet could be affected by policies designed to deal with problems of resource allocation. The central policy issue is how to design measures that would reduce the adverse effects of collective bargaining on resource allocation while preserving those aspects of bargaining that are socially constructive. There remains much room for debate whether such goals can best be achieved by radical or by cautious measures.

PART VIII
GOVERNMENT POLICY—MINIMUM WAGE LAWS

Many families have such low incomes that they live in poverty. Often these poverty families include workers who have full-time jobs, but whose wages are so low they cannot earn an adequate income. Ergo, the solution to the poverty problem is to pass a law establishing a minimum hourly wage which will yield an adequate annual income.

If you can read the preceding paragraph without the slightest twinge of doubt, you might consider politics—but not economics—as a career. For the proposed solution to poverty is one that has evoked considerable controversy among economists, and while not all who have analyzed minimum wage laws have agreed on their inappropriateness as a poverty-reducing device, it is the rare (and unenvied) economist who has not been troubled by the approach.

The theory which would deny the relevance of minimum wage laws to the solution of the poverty problem is presented in the first reading in this part, George J. Stigler's "The Economics of Minimum Wage Legislation." Stigler argues that the obvious implication of economic theory is that, with one unlikely exception, an increase in wages will lead to a reduction in employment. An effort to use the minimum wage law to reduce poverty thus will be largely self-defeating, he predicts, for the law "will decrease the earnings of workers who had previously been receiving materially less than the minimum." This version of economic theory with its implications for the impact of minimum wage laws has not been without detractors, perhaps most notably Richard Lester.[1] Lester has argued that conventional economic theory is wrong in implying a determinative relationship between the wage rate and the level of employment; and he feels that in fact an increase in wages can be met, not by reducing employment, but by increasing employee productivity or by increasing employer efficiency through the "shock" of the minimum wage law.

One of our themes is that the proper arena for the resolution of economic controversies is not theoretical haggling but empirical test-

[1] *Economics of Labor,* 2nd ed. (New York: Crowell-Collier and Macmillan, Inc., 1964), pp. 516–518.

ing. Part VII suggested that the predictions concerning labor market behavior which result from competitive labor market theory have a mixed record: for some topics (long-run movements in occupational wage differentials) competitive theory provides verified hypotheses, while for others (short-run movements in interindustry wage differentials) it has not done as well. With this mixed record, some skepticism towards the predictions from competitive labor market theory about the results of minimum wage laws seems appropriate.

Fortunately, we need not confine ourselves to the implications of these studies of other facets of the labor market because a large number of empirical studies have specifically evaluated the economic impacts of minimum wage laws. Unfortunately, no consistent empirical answer has resulted from these studies. Most studies by the federal government have found increases in the legal minimum wage to have little impact on employment opportunities. These studies date from examinations of specific industries affected by the original act—passed in 1938—to the 1970 study of youth unemployment and minimum wages which concluded that "the magnitude of the employment effects of minimum wage legislation probably has been small . . ."[2] Richard Lester has also concluded that the data suggest minimum wage laws have little impact on employment.

Other scholars have found more substantial impacts on employment resulting from minimum wage laws. For example, John Peterson has examined the experience from increases in the federal minimum wage and in various state minimum wage laws and has found evidence of an association between wage increases and reductions in employment opportunities.[3] Yale Brozen and Milton Friedman have presented evidence which links increases in the federal minimum to the increased unemployment rate among Negro teenagers since 1955.[4]

Two recent studies have attempted to recapitulate the evidence on the employment effects of minimum wage laws. One, by John M. Peterson and Charles T. Stewart, Jr., concludes that the "weight of evidence" supports the view that adverse employment effects are related to the impact of statutory minimums and suggests that the policy implication of the findings is to bring into question "both the wisdom and equity of such minimums."[5] The other recent review, by Jacob J. Kaufman and Terry G. Foran, is reprinted here. This study concludes that the employment impacts of both the federal and

[2] Thomas W. Gavett, "Youth Unemployment and Minimum Wages," *Monthly Labor Review,* vol. 93 (March 1970), p. 11.
[3] John M. Peterson, "Employment Effects of Minimum Wages 1938–1950," *Journal of Political Economy,* vol. 65 (October 1957), pp. 412–430. For a study of the impact of massive minimum wage changes, see Lloyd G. Reynolds and Peter Gregory, *Wages, Productivity, and Industrialization in Puerto Rico* (Homewood, Ill.: Richard D. Irwin, Inc., 1965).
[4] Yale Brozen and Milton Friedman, *The Minimum Wage Rate* (Washington: The Free Society Association, Inc., April 1966).
[5] *Employment Effects of Minimum Wages* (Washington: American Enterprise Institute, August 1969), p. 15.

state minimum wage laws "are essentially consistent with the conclusions drawn from traditional economic theory." But the authors are skeptical of the evidence presented in support of such propositions as that the minimum wage has caused the deteriorating unemployment experience for nonwhite teenagers; and their conclusions stress that there are both costs and benefits of a policy of minimum wage laws. If the dichotomy between the Peterson-Stewart review and the Kaufman-Foran review is any guide to the future, the controversy in both positive and normative economics over minimum wage laws will outlast the binding on this book.

33
The Economics of Minimum Wage Legislation

George J. Stigler

The minimum wage provisions of the Fair Labor Standards act of 1938 have been repealed by inflation. Many voices are now taking up the cry for a higher minimum, say, of 60 to 75 cents per hour.

Economists have not been very outspoken on this type of legislation. It is my fundamental thesis that they can and should be outspoken, and singularly agreed. The popular objective of minimum wage legislation—the elimination of extreme poverty—is not seriously debatable. The important questions are rather (1) Does such legislation diminish poverty? (2) Are there efficient alternatives? The answers are, if I am not mistaken, unusually definite for questions of economic policy. If this is so, these answers should be given.

Some readers will probably know my answers already ("no" and "yes," respectively); it is distressing how often one can guess the answer given to an economic question merely by knowing who asks it. But my personal answers are unimportant; the arguments on which they rest, which are important, will be presented under four heads:

1. Effects of a legal minimum wage on the allocation of resources.
2. Effects on aggregate employment.
3. Effects on family income.
4. Alternative policies to combat poverty.

1. The Allocation of Resources

The effects of minimum wages may in principle differ between industries in which employers do and do not have control over the wage rates they pay for labor of given skill and application. The two possibilities will be discussed in turn.

Competitive Wage Determination

Each worker receives the value of his marginal product under competition. If a minimum wage is effective, it must therefore have

---

Reprinted by permission from the *American Economic Review*, Vol. 36 (June 1946), pp. 358–367, by permission of the author and publisher.

one of two effects: first, workers whose services are worth less than the minimum wage are discharged (and thus forced into unregulated fields of employment, or into unemployment or retirement from the labor force); or, second, the productivity of low-efficiency workers is increased.

The former result, discharge of less efficient workers, will be larger the more the value of their services falls short of the legal minimum, the more elastic the demand for the product, and the greater the possibility of substituting other productive services (including efficient labor) for the inefficient workers' services. The discharged workers will, at best, move to unregulated jobs where they will secure lower returns. Unless inefficient workers' productivity rises, therefore, the minimum wage reduces aggregate output, perhaps raises the earnings of those previously a trifle below the minimum, and reduces the earnings of those substantially below the minimum. These are undoubtedly the main allocational effects of a minimum wage in a competitive industry.

The second and offsetting result, the increase of labor productivity, might come about in one of two ways: the laborers may work harder; or the entrepreneurs may use different production techniques. The threat of unemployment may force the inefficient laborers to work harder (the inducement of higher earnings had previously been available, and failed), but this is not very probable. These workers were already driven by the sharp spurs of poverty, and for many the intensity of effort must be increased beyond hope (up to 50 or more per cent) to avoid discharge.

The introduction of new techniques by the entrepreneurs is the more common source of increased labor productivity. Here again there are two possibilities.

First, techniques which were previously unprofitable are now rendered profitable by the increased cost of labor. Costs of production rise because of the minimum wage, but they rise by less than they would if other resources could not be substituted for the labor. Employment will fall for two reasons: output falls; and a given output is secured with less labor. Commonly the new techniques require different (and hence superior) labor, so many inefficient workers are discharged. This process is only a spelling-out of the main competitive effect.

Second, entrepreneurs may be shocked out of lethargy to adopt techniques which were previously profitable or to discover new techniques. This "shock" theory is at present lacking in empirical evidence but not in popularity.

There are several reasons for believing that the "shock" theory is particularly inappropriate to the industries paying low wages. All of the large manufacturing industry categories which in 1939 paid relatively low wages (measured by the payroll of wage-earners divided by their average number) are listed in Table 33.1. A study of this table suggests two generalizations: (1) the low-wage industries are competitive, and (2) the ratio of wages to total-processing-cost-plus-profit is higher than in high-wage industries. The competitive nature of these industries argues that the entrepreneurs are not easy-going traditionalists: vigorous competition in national markets does not attract or tolerate such men. The relatively high labor costs reveal that inducements to wage-economy are already strong. These considerations both work strongly against the shock theory in low-wage manufacturing industries in 1939.[1] Since these industries were on the whole much less affected by the war than other manufacturing industries,

---

[1] The current extensive and confident uses made of labor productivity indexes seem to me inappropriate to their ambiguity and inaccuracy. For those who are less skeptical, I may add that for the period 1929 to 1937, output per worker can be approximated for 9 of the industries in Table 33.1 (using data from S. Fabricant's *Employment in Manufacturing, 1899–1939* [New York, Nat. Bur. of Econ. Research, 1942]). In 6 of the 9 industries the increase in labor productivity equalled or exceeded that of all manufacturing.

TABLE 33.1 EMPLOYMENT, AVERAGE ANNUAL EARNINGS OF FULL-TIME WAGE-EARNERS, AND PERCENTAGE WAGES FORM OF VALUE-ADDED, IN LOW-WAGE MANUFACTURING INDUSTRIES, 1939

Industry	Employment	Average Earnings	Wages as Percent of Value Added
Men's and boys' furnishings	166,945	$632	52.2
Canned and preserved foods	134,471	660	28.0
Cigars	50,897	673	42.0
Cotton manufactures	409,317	715	51.1
Fertilizer	18,744	730	24.0
Wood containers	45,070	735	47.2
Women's accessories	58,952	740	41.3
Misc. fabricated textiles	49,242	746	36.2
Misc. apparel	38,288	769	45.5
Rayon and silk manufactures	119,821	779	54.4
Animal and vegetable oils	21,678	781	25.1
Costume jewelry, etc.	25,256	782	43.5
Sawmills, etc.	265,185	810	52.0
Leather products	280,411	847	50.9
All Manufacturing		1,153	36.8

Source: *Census of Manufacturers, 1939.*

they will probably be present in the post-war list of low-wage industries. The low-wage industries in trade and services display the same characteristics and support the same adverse conclusion with respect to the shock theory.[2]

Employer Wage Determination

If an employer has a significant degree of control over the wage rate he pays for a given quality of labor, a skillfully-set minimum wage may increase his employment and wage rate and, because the wage is brought closer to the value of the marginal product, at the same time increase aggregate output. The effect may be elucidated with the hypothetical data in Table 33.2. If the entrepreneur is left alone, he will set a wage of $20 and employ 50 men; a minimum wage of $24 will increase employment to 70 men.

[2] We should perhaps also notice that, even if the shock theory were of general applicability, the maintenance or increase of employment would require also (1) that demand be elastic, and (2) low-efficiency workers continue to be used with the improved techniques.

This arithmetic is quite valid, but it is not very relevant to the question of a national minimum wage. The minimum wage which achieves these desirable ends has several requisites:

1. It must be chosen correctly: too high a wage (over $28 in our example) will decrease employment. The accounting records describe, very imperfectly, existing employment and wages; the optimum minimum wage can be set only if the demand and supply schedules are known over a considerable range. At present there is no tolerably accurate method of deriving these schedules, and one is entitled to doubt that a legislative mandate is all that is necessary to bring forth such a method.
2. The optimum wage varies with occupation (and, within an occupation, with the quality of worker).
3. The optimum wage varies among firms (and plants).
4. The optimum wage varies, often rapidly, through time.

TABLE 33.2 HYPOTHETICAL DATA ILLUSTRATING EMPLOYER WAGE DETERMINATION

Number of Workers	Wage Rate	Marginal Cost of a Worker	Value of the Marginal Product*
10	$12		$36
20	14	$16	34
30	16	20	32
40	18	24	30
50	20	28	28
60	22	32	26
70	24	36	24

* Or marginal value product, if this is less.

A uniform national minimum wage, infrequently changed, is wholly unsuited to these diversities of conditions.[3]

We may sum up: the legal minimum wage will reduce aggregate output, and it will decrease the earnings of workers who had previously been receiving materially less than the minimum.

2. Aggregate Employment

Although no precise estimate of the effects of a minimum wage upon aggregate employment is possible, we may nevertheless form some notion of the direction of these effects. The higher the minimum wage, the greater will be the number of covered workers who are discharged. The current proposals would probably affect a twentieth to a tenth of all covered workers, so possibly several hundred thousand workers would be discharged. Whatever the number (which no one knows), the direct unemployment is substantial and certain; and it fairly establishes the presumption that the net effects of the minimum wage on aggregate employment are adverse.

This presumption is strengthened by the existing state of aggregate money demand. There is no prospective inadequacy of money demand in the next year or two—indeed, the danger is that it is excessive. If the minimum wage were to increase the relative share of wage-earners and, hence, the propensity to consume—which requires the uncertain assumption that the demand for inefficient labor is inelastic—the increment of consumer demand will be unnecessary, and perhaps unwelcome.[4] (Conversely, the direct unemployment resulting from the wage law would diminish faster in a period of high employment.)

It is sufficient for the argument that no large increase in employment will be induced by the legislation. Actually, there is a presumption that a minimum wage will have adverse effects upon aggregate employment.

3. Wage Rates and Family Income

The manipulation of individual prices is neither an efficient nor an equitable device for changing the distribution of personal income. This is a well-known dictum that has received much documentation in analyses of our agricultural programs. The relevance of the dictum to minimum wage legislation is easily demonstrated.

One cannot expect a close relationship between the level of hourly wage rates and the amount of family income. Yet family

---

[3] One can go much farther: even administratively established minima, varying with firm and time, would be impossibly difficult to devise and revise, and their effects on private investment would be extremely adverse.

[4] This line of argument implies that a minimum wage is more likely to have beneficial effects in depression (if the demand for the relevant labor is inelastic), but it does not imply that the beneficial effects are likely.

TABLE 33.3 PERCENTAGE DISTRIBUTION OF WAGE-EARNER FAMILIES BY NUMBER OF EARNERS: MINNESOTA, 1939

Family Income	One Earner	Two Earners	Three Earners	Four or more Earners
$250–$500	94.5	4.6	.7	.2
500– 750	92.4	7.1	.3	.2
750–1000	86.7	10.7	1.5	1.1
1000–1250	88.5	10.4	1.1	.1

Source: *Minnesota Incomes, 1938–39,* Vol. II (St. Paul, Minnesota Resources Commission, 1942), p. 152.

income and needs are the fundamental factors in the problem of poverty. The major sources of discrepancy may be catalogued.

First, the hourly rates are effective only for those who receive them, and it was shown in Section 1 that the least productive workers are forced into uncovered occupations or into unemployment.

Second, hourly earnings and annual earnings are not closely related. The seasonality of the industry, the extent of overtime, the amount of absenteeism, and the shift of workers among industries, are obvious examples of factors which reduce the correlation between hourly earnings and annual earnings.

Third, family earnings are the sum of earnings of all workers in the family, and the dispersion of number of workers is considerable. The summary in Table 33.3 for low income wage-earner families in Minnesota in 1939, shows that in the $250–$500 income class one-twentieth of the families had more than one earner and in the higher income classes the fraction rose to one-eighth.

Fourth, although wages are, of course, the chief component of the income of low-wage families, they are by no means the only component. It is indicated in Table 33.4 that a tenth of the wage-earner families had cash investment income, a quarter had entrepreneural income, and a quarter owned their homes.

All of these steps lead us only to family

TABLE 33.4 COMPOSITION OF INCOME OF WAGE-EARNER FAMILIES: MINNESOTA, 1939

Income Class	Total	Wages and Salaries	Income		Investment Income	
			Entre-preneural Income	Room and Board	Cash	Total
1. Percentage of Families Receiving Income						
$250–$500		99.9	26.5	1.3	12.3	28.2
500– 750		100.0	25.2	1.7	10.1	24.2
750–1000		100.0	21.4	2.7	9.4	31.2
1000–1250		100.0	18.4	3.0	10.4	22.8
2. Average Amount						
250– 500	$ 387	$ 308		–$ 9	$64	
500– 750	631	560		62	82	
750–1000	865	766		53	82	
1000–1250	1124	1032		91	96	

Source: *Minnesota Incomes, 1938–39,* Vol. I (St. Paul, Minnesota Resources Commission, 1942), p. 42; Vol. II, p. 200.

income; the leap must still be made to family needs. It is argued in the next section that family composition is the best criterion of need, and whether this be accepted or not, it is clearly an important criterion. The great variation in family size among wage-earner families is strongly emphasized by the illustrative data in Table 33.5; an income adequate for one size is either too large or too small for at least half the families in that income class.

The connection between hourly wages and the standard of living of the family is thus remote and fuzzy. Unless the minimum wage varies with the amount of employment, number of earners, non-wage income, family size, and many other factors, it will be an inept device for combatting poverty even for those who succeed in retaining employment. And if the minimum wages varies with all of these factors, it will be an insane device.

4. The Problem of Poverty

Minimum wage legislation commonly has two stated objectives: the reduction of employer control of wages; and the abolition of poverty. The former and much lesser purpose may better be achieved by removing the condition of labor immobility which gives rise to employer control. Labor immobility would be reduced substantially by public provision of comprehensive information on employment conditions in various areas and industries. The immobility would be further reduced by supplying vocational training and loans to cover moving costs. But employer wage control is not the important problem; let us turn to the elimination of poverty.

Incomes of the poor cannot be increased without impairing incentives. Skillful policies will, for a given increase in the incomes of the poor, impair incentives less than clumsy policies. But the more completely poverty is eliminated, given the level of intelligence with which this is done, the greater will be the impairment of incentives. This is a price we must pay, just as impairment of incentives is a price we have willingly paid to reduce the inequality of income by progressive income and estate taxes. Society must determine, through its legislators, what minimum income (or addition to income) should be guaranteed to each family. We shall assume that this difficult decision has been made.

One principle is fundamental in the amelioration of poverty: those who are equally in need should be helped equally. If this principle is to be achieved, there must be an objective criterion of need; equality

TABLE 33.5 PERCENTAGE DISTRIBUTION OF WAGE-EARNER FAMILIES BY NUMBER OF PERSONS: CHICAGO AND ATLANTA, 1936

Income Class	Number of Persons in Family			
	2	3 or 4	5 or 6	7 or more
1. *Chicago*				
$ 0–$250	39.6	43.6	14.9	2.0
250– 500	35.3	45.8	17.6	1.3
500– 750	31.8	53.7	13.0	1.6
750–1000	29.0	56.5	12.4	2.1
2. *Atlanta*				
0– 250	30.	55.	15.	0.
250– 500	20.1	48.1	16.5	5.3
500– 750	22.6	46.9	24.4	6.2
750–1000	21.6	48.1	23.5	6.7

Sources: *Family Income in Chicago, 1935–36* (Bur. of Lab. Stat. bull. no. 642 [Washington, Supt. Docs., 194]), Vol. I, p. 117; *Family Income in the Southeastern Region* (Bur. of Lab. Stat. bull. no. 647 [Washington, Supt. Docs. 194]), Vol. I, p. 148.

can never be achieved when many cases are judged (by many people) "on their merits." We are driven almost inexorably to family size and composition as this criterion of need. It is obviously imperfect; the sickly require more medical care than the healthy.[5] But it is vastly easier to accord special treatment to certain families for a few items like medical care than to accord special treatment to every family for the sum of all items of expenditure.

It is a corollary of this position that assistance should not be based upon occupation. The poor farmer, the poor shopkeeper, and the poor miner are on an equal footing. There may be administrative justification (although I doubt it) for treating the farmer separately from the urban dweller, but there is no defense in equity for helping the one and neglecting the other. To render the assistance by manipulating prices is in any case objectionable: we help the rich farmer more than the poor, and give widely differing amounts of help to the poor farmer from year to year.

The principle of equity thus involves the granting of assistance to the poor with regard to their need (measured by family composition) but without regard to their occupation. There is a possible choice between grants in kind and in money. The latter commends itself strongly: it gives full play to the enormous variety of tastes and it is administratively much simpler. Yet it raises a problem which will be noticed shortly.

Even if these general observations be accepted, the structure of administration is of grave importance, and I do not pretend to have explored this field. There is great attractiveness in the proposal that we extend the personal income tax to the lowest income brackets with negative rates in these brackets. Such a scheme could achieve equality of treatment with what appears to be a (large) minimum of administrative machinery. If the negative rates are appropriately graduated, we may still retain some measure of incentive for a family to increase its income. We should no doubt encounter many perplexing difficulties in carrying out this plan, but they are problems which could not be avoided, even though they might be ignored, by a less direct attack on poverty.

One final point: We seek to abolish poverty in good part because it leads to undernourishment. In this connection, dietary appraisals show that in any income class, no matter how low, a portion of the families secure adequate diets, and in any income class, as high as the studies go, a portion do not. The proportion of ill-fed, to be sure, declines substantially as income rises, but it does not disappear. We cannot possibly afford to abolish malnutrition, or mal-housing, or mal-education, only by increasing incomes.

Either of two inferences may be drawn. The program of increasing income must be supplemented by a program of education—in diet, in housing, in education! Or the assistance to the poor should be given in kind, expertly chosen. The latter approach is administratively very complex, but quicker and in direct expenditure vastly more economical. These factors affect our choice, but a thought should be given also to the two societies to which they lead.

---

[5] One could argue that rural families should receive less help, to offset the lower prices at which food and housing are procured. The group is of sufficient size and perhaps sufficiently identifiable to justify separate treatment. But there are grounds other than political expediency for rejecting this proposal.

34
The Minimum Wage and Poverty

Jacob J. Kaufman • Terry G. Foran

Introduction

This paper examines the relationship between legislated wage minima and poverty. This is certainly not a novel context in which to view minimum wages since the Fair Labor Standards Act of 1938 stated that:

It is hereby declared to be the policy of this Act, . . . to correct and as rapidly as practicable to eliminate . . . labor conditions detrimental to the maintenance of the minimum standard of living necessary for health, efficiency, and general well-being of workers.[1]

In 1966, 28 years after the original Federal legislation, Congress amended the original Act for the fourth time by raising the minimum wage and extending its coverage. Its objective, as stated by the Congressman who brought the House bill from committee to the floor of the House, was: "this new reason for this legislation [is] the living power of our working people."[2]

From its inception up to the present the federal legislation in this field has been concerned primarily with the elimination of poverty. If raising the minimum wage would eliminate poverty, then the only argument remaining would be that of values. It is interesting to note that, according to one survey, 61 percent of university economists opposed the amendments to the minimum wage law even though 88 percent favored the so-called "War on Poverty."[3] Apparently, the majority thinks that minimum wage legislation is an inadequate tool for the elimination of poverty.

The primary concern of this chapter is the investigation of the role of a minimum wage

Reprinted from *Towards Freedom from Want*, edited by Sar A. Levitan, Wilbur J. Cohen, and Robert Lampman (1968), pp. 189–218, by permission of the Industrial Relations Research Association.

[1] Sections 2(a) and 2(b) Fair Labor Standards Act.

[2] John H. Dent, (D-Pa.), *Congressional Record*, Vol. 112, No. 85, p. 10740.

[3] *Business in Brief*, No. 68, June 1966, issued by the Chase Manhattan Bank. 79 percent of Business Economists opposed the legislation.

law as a vehicle for the elimination of poverty. No attempt is made to compare the efficacy of such legislation with other measures which are, or might be, employed to fight poverty. Such an undertaking is beyond the scope of the present paper.

The poverty group includes persons 65 years of age and older; residents in rural-farm areas; nonwhites; families headed by females; families headed by persons with limited education; and, the unemployed. To the extent that a minimum wage affects the individuals in these categories, it will have an impact on the structure of poverty. This paper, therefore, investigates the impact of minimum wages on unemployment in general, and, where possible, on unemployment of the disadvantaged groups. The ability of minimum wage legislation to raise wages and affect income distribution is also examined. As background to these problems a brief description of the legislation in this area is in order.

The Objectives and Theoretical Considerations of Minimum Wage Legislation

Federal Legislation

Minimum wage legislation has a long history, both foreign and domestic. Although the Fair Labor Standards Act of 1938 (FLSA) contained statutory minima, the administrator was allowed some discretion, reflecting, in part, a concern over the adverse employment effects of such legislation and an interest in spreading available work. The latter objective is revealed in the overtime provisions of the law.

It is important to point out that the coverage of the Act, even with its most recent amendments, is not universal and excludes certain industries engaged in interstate commerce and all industries engaged in intrastate commerce. There are about 41.4 million workers presently covered by the FLSA. Those covered are primarily nonsupervisory employees. The excluded nonsupervisory employees fall into the following categories: outside salesmen, domestics, agriculture, retail trade and services. Others not covered by the Act are: self-employed; governmental workers; unpaid family workers; and executive, administrative, and professional employees.

The minimum wage was originally set at 25¢ an hour in 1938. It was increased to 75¢ in 1949. The 1956 amendment raised it to $1.00. The 1961 amendments raised the wage of previously covered workers to $1.15 in 1961 and to $1.25 in 1963. The timing of the increases for newly covered employees was more gradual. The same is true of the timing provided for by the 1966 amendments. For the previously covered workers the legislated floor was raised to $1.40 in 1967 and will be increased to $1.60 by February of 1968.

The purpose of including this brief wage chronology is twofold. First, it provides a benchmark for later discussion, and, second, it demonstrates the concern on the part of advocates of the minimum wage over the possible unemployment effects of raising wages. The planned gradual wage increases attest to the fairly well grounded belief that too large an increase in the minimum wage might have serious unemployment repercussions.

State Legislation

Complementing the federal minimum wage legislation—in fact antedating it—is the minimum wage legislation in the individual states. Today, 38 states, the District of Columbia, and Puerto Rico have such laws. At first blush, it would seem that the state laws possess certain desirable qualities which are superior to the federal law. First, the federal law cannot consider the particular economic status of every state. Any given state may be justified in setting a minimum above that set by the federal government because of a better than average "economic condition." Second, a state may legislate a minimum for workers not covered under federal law. Third, more than one-third of the states set minima utilizing the wage board system, rather than setting a statutory minimum. This permits greater flexibility, particularly with respect to "area" conditions, than is provided for by the Fair Labor Standards Act. State minimum wage laws are capable, if properly formulated and conscientiously executed, of far greater flexibility than the federal law.

Unfortunately, the apparently superior avenues open to the states have been inadequately realized:

of the 40 jurisdictions with laws: 14 jurisdictions apply only to women and/or minors and do not cover men.
15 do not set a statutory rate.
3 states do not have minimum rates in effect for any occupation.
15 jurisdictions have statutory rates lower than $1.25 an hour.[4]

For example, New York which has one of the most enlightened minimum wage programs requires approximately 18 months to bring to fruition a wage order once it has been conceived.[5]

The New York law does, however, complement the federal law by covering employees outside the stipulations of the latter. The wage board system also enables the New York minima to account for "zone differentials," so that different wage floors exist in different areas in accordance with the different economic environments.

Theoretical Considerations

The standard argument of minimum wage proponents is that it raises the wages of the poorly paid and, therefore, boosts their incomes. Opponents retort that "It's better to receive a low wage than no wage at all," suggesting that a legislated minimum wage eliminates jobs. Although the arguments as stated in this fashion appear rather simple, they do, however, succinctly summarize the major area of conflict. This has been the primary issue in the literature to date. But it is not the only pertinent question. One question which does not appear to have received adequate attention is: What is the combined effect of the wage change and the employment change? That is, what is the effect on labor's share? This question is probably most relevant to the poverty problem.

Under competitive conditions each worker is paid the value of his marginal product. Therefore, given a normally downward sloping demand curve for labor, a minimum wage will cause the least efficient workers to be laid off, unless certain conditions hold. Although these conditions will be discussed below, at present, assume the competitive state.

Minimum wage regulation is not universal. Its coverage applies to specific industries within the economy, although it is likely that part of its effect is similar to that which would be generated from a general regulatory wage. The effect of the minimum wage as a specific regulatory device is the same as that which occurs from a decline in demand for labor in particular sectors.

In this case, it is not the unemployment which is economically speaking, the most significant effect of regulation (in an extreme case, where the affected firms are abnormally prosperous, and the rise in wages is only just sufficient to prevent their expanding employment or to diminish their expansion, there may be no net unemployment due to the regulation); the important effect is the redistribution of labor—the fact that some men are prevented from securing employment in a trade where they would be better off than they are otherwise condemned to be.[6]

However, if there are no industries available or suitable to absorb the unemployed, then the unemployment created will not be of a temporary nature. This unemployment "must go on until the artificial wages are relaxed,

---

[4] State Minimum Wage Legislation: *A Weapon in the War on Poverty*, U.S. Department of Labor, Women's Bureau (Washington: June 1966), p. 6.
[5] I. Lubin and C. A. Pearce, "New York's Minimum Wage Law: The First Twenty Years," *Industrial Labor Relations Review*, January 1958, p. 206.

[6] J. Hicks, *The Theory of Wages*, 2nd ed. (London: MacMillan & Co., 1964), p. 180.

or until competitive wages have risen to the artificial level."[7] Realistically, the former alternative may be discounted.

It is probably more realistic to assume, in light of the type of regulation provided for in the Fair Labor Standards Act and its evolution, that, if competitive conditions hold, there will be some redistribution of labor; but more predominantly there will be unemployment which will be eliminated only with the restoration of preexisting wage differentials. This is due to the imperfect mobility of labor, and the trend toward greater coverage under the federal minimum wage law.

Given the present assumptions, then, one can expect a certain amount of lengthy unemployment as a result of an increase in the minimum wage. The question thus becomes "how much unemployment?" This question really breaks down into two questions: (1) What percentage of workers lose their jobs? and (2) How does the increased unemployment compare to the increase in wages? The first is the traditional query; the second is relevant to the total wage bill, or labor's share.[8]

In the short-run, both answers are given by the elasticities of the relevant demand curves for labor. The relevant demand curves are the industry demand curves, because of the assumption of competitive conditions and, more realistically, because of the manner of coverage stipulated in the Fair Labor Standards Act and its amendments. The elasticity of the short-run demand curve for labor will depend on the technique of production, the demand for the product, and the supply curves of other (non-fixed) factors. The two pertinent factors for discussion are output market elasticity and percentage of labor cost to total cost, because they are the only factors amenable to empirical investigation. The more elastic the demand curve for labor the greater the unemployment which will result from any given wage increase. The demand curve for labor will be more elastic the greater the percentage of labor cost to total cost and the more elastic the demand for the product sold by the industry.

The evidence seems to indicate that those industries primarily affected by minimum wages have both a relatively high percentage of labor cost to total cost and have relatively elastic product demand curves. Four out of the five industries surveyed by the U.S. Department of Labor after the increase in the minimum wage in 1950 possessed a degree of monopoly power well below the average for manufacturing. As a general rule, the lesser the degree of monopoly the more elastic the product demand curve. A comparison of the lowest paying industries in 1954 showed that five out of the six had below average degrees of monopoly, and above average relative labor costs.

In general, the labor demand curves in those industries affected by minimum wage legislation will be more elastic than in other industries. This statement is made on the basis of the only observable parameters affecting these curves. The implications for employment changes and labor's share in the short-run are clear. Adverse employment changes will be relatively large and labor's absolute share will decline. These changes will be accentuated, the higher the minimum is above the old wage in any particular industry. If these assumptions are valid, the long-run results are the same. First, the increased ability to substitute factors increases the elasticity of the demand for labor. Thus, machinery may be used to replace labor. Second, certain types of product lines may be dropped because they are no longer profitable. Third, the least efficient firms in the industry may find their demise hastened by the added burden imposed by the minimum wage rate.

---

[7] *Ibid.*, p. 181.

[8] This discussion has ignored the question of a minimum wage setting a barrier to the expansion of further employment. This is, of course, an important aspect of the impact of a minimum wage. To the degree that a minimum wage causes workers to lose jobs, it must *a fortiori* be a barrier to further employment.

To what extent are these conclusions modified by relaxing the implicit assumptions of the above analysis? If the relevant laborers were not operating at peak efficiency before the establishment of the minimum wage, it is possible that they may subsequently do so, thus increasing their productivity and preventing unemployment. The only plausible reason for this occurrence is the spur of threatening unemployment. This particular influence, however, will probably not be great enough to save many jobs.

The second assumption to be dropped is that of the maximizing firm. This calls for the introduction of the standard textbook "shock effect." The basic premise underlying the shock effect is that management is too lazy and content to bother maximizing. The minimum wage thus "shocks" management out of its lethargy with the higher costs. It begins to alter its technique of production in an effort to cut costs, thus increasing worker productivity and preventing unemployment. However, as pointed out by Stigler,[9] and as argued above, the industries primarily affected by minimum wage legislation are, by and large, competitive and have a higher percentage of labor cost to total cost. Thus, it is unlikely that the managements in these industries have overlooked opportunities to minimize labor costs.[10]

In this same context, it might be noted that if one accepts Hicks' theory, then any sort of "shock" received by management as the result of a wage increase will result in "induced" innovation, as the result of the change in relative factor prices. "Its effect on the marginal productivity of capital is bound to be much more favorable than its effect on the marginal productivity of labour."[11] In other words, the types of inventions adopted because of higher minimum wages can be expected to be of a labor-saving type and, as such, they will have the least effect upon mitigating unemployment. The impact of this type of innovation would be to reduce labor's share.

A second factor which might mitigate against the unemployment effects of higher minima is the existence of monopsony in the labor market. When an employer has monopsony power he finds it necessary to increase wages to hire additional workers. If he cannot discriminate among his employees he must not only pay the new higher wage to the worker just hired, but also raise the wage of his other workers. Because of this, his additional labor cost of hiring one more worker is greater than the wage paid to that new worker. This will constrain the employer from hiring further workers. The effect of a minimum wage set above the old wage will, within a certain range, eliminate this constraint because now the cost of a new worker is simply the wage rate he gets paid. The result of this may be that a minimum wage will cause no unemployment and may even cause more workers to be hired.

However, it is unlikely that the monopsony element exists to any great degree in the low-wage areas covered under the Wage-Hour Act, and if it does, it is unlikely that a nationally set minimum will fall within the relevant range in many cases.

The primary emphasis of empirical studies on the effects of minimum wage legislation has been on the relevant labor market variables. A brief analysis of the possible effects of such legislation on non-labor market variables is in order.

It has already been pointed out, or implied, that the effects on the firms in the economy will be, in the absence of technological change, higher costs, higher prices, lower profits, and the possible elimination of some of the more inefficient firms.

It is also argued by some that minimum

---

[9] G. Stigler, "The Economics of Minimum-Wage Legislation," *American Economic Review*, June 1946, pp. 358–363. Reprinted in W. Bowen, *Labor and the National Economy* (New York, Norton & Co., 1965), p. 43.

[10] For a point of view different from this see the argument of R. Lester, *Economics of Labor* (2nd Edition, New York: MacMillan, 1964), pp. 516–518.

[11] J. Hicks, *op. cit.*, p. 204.

wage legislation may contribute to inflation (1) via the cost-push mechanism and (2) via an increase in demand, on the assumption of a redistributed income. One study has pointed out, however, that

> The wholesale price index remained stable through the last two increases in the minimum, and only recently has started to rise, at a time when there was no increase in the minimum. . . . The slight upward trend in the index of consumer prices, which may largely reflect an upward bias in the index, has shown no jump following increases in the minimum in the past. Increases in the past year certainly cannot be attributed to higher minima in 1961 and 1963.[12]

If the inflation argument is eliminated, so is the argument that an increase in the minimum wage is injurious to our balance of payments. If it does aggravate the problem, the damage is minor. Given the more powerful tools available to combat this problem, it is difficult to envisage the use of "not-passing-a-higher-minimum-wage" as a policy instrument to correct the balance of payments.

It is, of course, possible that increases in the minimum wage do contribute to, rather than cause, inflation. This, however, would be difficult to verify empirically. Even if this is the case the question to be considered is whether this cost—undoubtedly slight—offsets the benefits derived from legislated wage floors.

Impact Studies on Minimum Wages

There is no question that the immediate impact of raising minimum wages is to increase the wage of covered workers. There is also little question that given a once-and-for-all increase, pre-existing differentials eventually will be re-established. There may also be an almost immediate increase of the wages of non-covered workers due to personnel policies and a worker efficiency rationale. From the preceding discussion it has been shown that there will be some unemployment under a static situation. This unemployment will be greater, if entire firms are forced out of business, to the extent that they themselves are not dissolved by merger, and to the extent to which their shares of the market are lost to the industry. Further, this unemployment may either be accentuated or alleviated by technological changes introduced by the affected firms. The questions with regard to unemployment, therefore, are how much and for how long.

Naturally, the economy is not as static as is the theory. The difficulty of isolating the effects of minimum wages in a dynamic economy is obvious. Nonetheless, scholars, after stating this, proceed to do the best that is possible under existing conditions. It is to this research that we now turn.[13]

The first minima were the 25¢ and the 30¢ hourly rates, and finally the 40¢ hourly rate. In this early period there were not many special studies conducted to determine the impact of the legislation. "Of the 690,000 workers estimated to be receiving less than 30¢ an hour in the spring of 1939, 54 percent were in the South."[14] At the time, in the southern fertilizer industry, 17 percent

---

[12] *Legislative Analysis*, American Enterprise Institute (Washington, 1966), p. 10.

[13] At the outset of this discussion, it should be stated that much of the writing on the impact of minimum wages is in the nature of summarizing the studies that have been done. This discussion is in part a summary of summaries. For the sake of expediency the following borrows heavily from the summaries printed in:
  (1) Peck, *Economic Factors in Statutory Minimum Wages* (Washington: The Legis. Ref. Ser., L. of C. 1948).
  (2) J. F. Maloney, "Some Effects of the Federal Fair Labor Standards and upon Southern Industry." *Southern Economic Journal*, July, 1942, pp. 15–21.
  (3) H. Weiss, "Economic Effects of a Nationwide Minimum Wage," *Industrial Relations Research Association, Proceedings*, 1956, pp. 154–166.
  (4) H. M. Douty, "Some Effects of the $1.00 Minimum Wage in the United States," *Economica*, May 1960, pp. 137–147.

[14] Maloney, *op. cit.*, p. 17.

of common labor was receiving less than the minimum. About 55 percent of the common labor in the cottonseed crushing industry was also below the minimum. The increase in average hourly earnings in this industry between 1937–38 and 1939–40 was 30 percent. The wages of the unskilled workers rose more than the skilled. Despite a period of rising prosperity, employment decreased 19 percent. The indications were that, after the imposition of the minimum wage, labor-saving machinery was adopted in the industry.

The seamless hosiery industry was also rather severely affected by the initial minimum. Comparing employment in the industry for the first 9 months of 1938 with employment for the first 9 months of 1939, it was found that employment was 10.1 percent higher in the later years for the industry as a whole but 7.4 percent less for those establishments which were paying an average hourly wage below 25¢ before the minimum was set. Most of the plants which suffered the greatest declines were in the South. "Over the two-year period (1938–1940) employment in northern plants increased by 4.9 percent but decreased 5.5 percent in Southern plants."[15]

The firms in the industry made the predictable adjustments, following the legislation, of introducing labor-saving machinery and altering existing equipment to produce new lines of products.

The U.S. Department of Labor planned a rather extensive study as a follow up on the 1950 increase to 75 cents per hour. This study was focused primarily on five low-wage industries: southern sawmilling, fertilizer, men's dress shirts and nightwear, men's seamless hosiery, and wood furniture. Unfortunately the Korean War intervened, disrupting the economic forces then at work in the United States. "As a result, only the more immediate, short run effects of the 75-cent rate—those occurring during the comparatively stable economic climate of first half of 1950—are determinable with any degree of clarity."[16]

The results of the 1950 increase as presented by the U.S. Department of Labor are essentially of a standard nature. The wage impact was greatest in those industries with the lowest average hourly earnings at the beginning of the period. For example, in the short period covered by the study the increase in average hourly earnings was 16 percent in southern sawmilling, as opposed to a very small increase in wood furniture. Wage increases were also correlated with low wage regions—primarily the South.

There was, in addition, an indirect impact on the wages of workers getting paid above the minimum but this was quite small. This would indicate that a personnel policy of maintaining an internal equilibrium wage structure was not in effect in industries affected by minimum wage legislation. In three of the industries surveyed, no unemployment declines due to the higher minimum were apparent.

Peterson, using the 1950 survey and supplementary data and utilizing more sophisticated techniques, did not arrive at the same conclusions. In men's seamless hosiery he obtained a correlation coefficient of $-.476$ (significant at the 1 percent level) between percentage changes in average hourly earnings and percentage changes in manhours. "This relation does not appear to be explainable in terms of prior seasonal or cyclical patterns."[17] In men's cotton garments Peterson also found a negative correlation between the two variables, although it was not significant. There is a definite indication that low-wage plants suffered less favorable employment changes than high-wage plants. By

---

[15] See H. M. Douty, "Minimum Wage Regulation in the Seamless Hosiery Industry," *Southern Economic Journal*, Oct. 1941, p. 184.

[16] *Results of the Minimum-Wage Increase of 1950*, U.S. Department of Labor, Wage and Hour and Public Contracts Divisions, (Washington: 1954), p. 2.

[17] J. Peterson, "Employment Effects of Minimum Wages 1938–1950," *Journal of Political Economy*, Oct., 1957, p. 429.

disaggregating the Southern sawmill industry by type of mill and by state, Peterson again found a relationship between wage increases and adverse employment effects.

The 1950 study of the U.S. Department of Labor also noted a plant mortality of about two percent in men's dress shirts and southern sawmills. It is not at all clear whether or not these events were caused by the minimum wage or by other influences.

The next set of studies undertaken by the Department of Labor was designed to determine the impact of the $1.00 minimum wage. The major part of the survey program was directed toward 12 manufacturing industries which were known to come under the impact of the new increase.

In all of the industries studied there was an increase in the average hourly earnings immediately following the wage increase. These increases ranged from 5.3 percent to 21.7 percent. The wage structures in the industries were compressed, and the immediate indirect impact on the wages of non-affected workers was small. The re-establishment of pre-existing differentials was not particularly in evidence in the short-run. The evidence indicates that employers began to re-establish the differentials in the second payroll period following the increase in the statutory wage; this was continued into the third payroll period. In other words, the restoration of an equilibrium wage differential following the impact of a legislated disequilibrium is a slow process.

There did not appear to be any effect on workers in non-covered industries as a result of the wage increase in other industries.

The employment effects were adverse in all but one of the twelve industries, with employment declines ranging from 3.2 percent to 15 percent in the year following the increase in the minimum. A very small percentage of plants interviewed stated that the discharges were the result of the higher minimum wage, nonetheless the evidence is fairly convincing that this was the case. Certainly declining demand, inefficiency, substitution of machinery, or whatever reasons might have been offered by those interviewed, would not negate this conclusion.

The survey found that there were various degrees of non-wage adjustments by plants in eight affected industries and it is probable that some of these were precipitated by the minimum wage increase. It would be impossible to determine how many.

Richard Lester disagrees with the interpretation given above of the results of the B.L.S. study on the $1.00 minimum wage. Lester bases his disagreement primarily upon two tables which he has constructed. The first table presents the employment changes in the "high-impact" establishments as a percentage of the employment in all establishments in the study. "Thus, employment changes in high-impact establishments are being compared with employment changes in lower-impact establishments in the same sections of an industry."[18] Looking at Lester's table the employment changes are negative in 9 out of 13 observations. Admittedly a few of these declines are small. However, it would seem that the table, if anything, supports the conclusion of adverse employment changes created by increased minimum wages.

Lester's second table compares percentage changes in employment with percentage changes in earnings among high-impact, middle-impact, and low-impact industries. With 24 observations (using overlapping time periods) employment changes are negative in all but two instances. While it is true that the data "do not lend much support to the notion that a forced increase in the minimum wage will soon lead to a reduction in a firm's employment *in proportion to the relative size of the wage increase*,"[19] they do, nonetheless, add strong support to the hypothesis that an increase in the minimum wage will create unemployment.

Utilizing traditional data sources, such as the census of manufacturers, Kaun has conducted a study covering the post-war period

---

[18] R. Lester, *op. cit.*, p. 520.
[19] *Ibid.*, pp. 523–524. Emphasis added.

from 1947 to 1958, which included the increases to 75¢ and $1.00.[20] On the assumption that the low-wage industries would be most significantly affected by the statutory increases, Kaun found that there were greater increases in the capital-labor ratio over the period in those industries assumed to be primarily affected by minimum wages. Minimum wages cause a decline in labor intensity as a result of the substitution of capital for labor. Kaun also found that there were definite adverse effects on the number of establishments in five low-wage paying manufacturing industries.

The latest studies conducted by the U.S. Department of Labor are significant in that they, for the first time, due to the extension of coverage of the 1961 amendments, deal with the impact of minimum wage legislation on non-manufacturing industries (specifically retail and wholesale trade). They also, for the first time, attempt to assess the degree of influence of the maximum hours or overtime provisions of the Act.[21]

The 1961 amendments required the payment of time and one-half for hours in excess of 44 per week effective in September 1963 and after 42 hours the following September. The study cited covers only the first of these. The minimum wage of $1.25 was made effective in the newly covered establishments in 1961.

In the aggregate, there was no decline in employment in retail trade as a result of the 1961 increase. In fact, there was an increase in employment. Nevertheless, within certain categories and within certain regions, (particularly non-metropolitan areas of the South) there were declines in employment.

There appeared to be a general shortening of the work week in retail trade, despite being newly covered under F.L.S.A. and with, as yet, no overtime coverage. This result, as well as the increasing employment, is neither consistent with the conclusions derived from static theory nor is it consistent with previous studies on manufacturing. It is possible that the decline in the length of the work week may have been due to an anticipation of the impending overtime coverage so that a number of these establishments may already have begun adjusting their work procedures and recruiting the necessary additional work-force. This would also partially explain the growth of employment. This latter is probably better explained in terms of the generally favorable economic environment surrounding retail trade at the time of the increase.

The effect of the overtime provision would necessarily be small when finally instituted in 1963. In a matched sample study, in 1962 only 12 percent of employees were working beyond 44 hours a week. This percentage then decreased to 10 percent in 1964. The greatest declines were in the South and in non-metropolitan areas, which also had the greatest proportions of persons working overtime.

In addition to the impact studies dealing with the federal minimum wage, there have been a number of studies concerned with the impact of state minima. Peterson, employing data from three state studies undertaken by the U.S. Department of Labor, found that the inverse correlation between wages and employment seemed to result from changes in the state minimum wages.[22] The three state studies examined by Peterson were: Oregon retail stores, 1913–1914; New York power laundries, 1933–1935; and Ohio dry cleaning, 1934–1935.

Following the 1957 increase of the minimum wage to $1.00 for retail stores in New York State, a rather extensive follow-up

---

[20] D. Kaun, "Minimum Wages, Factor Substitution and the Marginal Producer," *Quarterly Journal of Economics*, 1965, pp. 478–486.

[21] *An Evaluation of the Minimum Wage and Maximum Hours Standards of the Fair Labor Standards Act*, U.S. Department of Labor (Washington: 1965) and "Report Submitted to the Congress in accordance with the Requirements of Section 4(d) of the Fair Labor Standard Act," U.S. Department of Labor (Washington: 1963).

[22] J. M. Peterson, "Employment Effects of State Minimum Wages for Women: Three Historical Cases Reexamined," *Industrial and Labor Relations Review*, April 1959, pp. 406–422.

study was undertaken. The impact of the increase was to raise payroll costs by about three percent in stores affected. The increase affected over 73,000 employees. The employment effect of this increase was that "24 out of every 10,000 retail workers lost their jobs by layoffs or failure to replace a worker who quit or retired."[23]

In addition, 55,000 paid manhours per week were eliminated to avoid the additional cost of overtime.

In relative terms these effects are minor. However, as pointed out in the New York State Report, it is probable, "in the light of the rise in retail trade volume that occurred in 1957, that the amount of offsets found in the survey is understated somewhat in the sense that it fails to reflect decisions not to increase the number of manhours used when larger business volume seemed to call for increasing the number."[24]

It appears that the experience of states with minimum wage laws has been essentially the same as it has been for the country under the F.L.S.A. Further, the experiences of both are essentially consistent with the conclusions drawn from traditional economic theory.

Given downward sloping demand curves for labor, when this labor is being hired under non-union, non-monopsony conditions, static economic theory postulates a fall in employment as the result of an increase in the wage. This unemployment will be greater in the more competitive firms which are affected. The unemployment which is thus created will be eliminated with the reestablishment of an equilibrium wage differential.

Further basic conclusions of economic theory are that factor substitution may occur following a wage increase, and that certain inefficient firms will be forced out of business. It should be noted that this theory and its conclusions are not restricted to the perfectly competitive state but hold equally well for an economy populated by various degrees of monopoly in the product market.

The overwhelming bulk of the evidence on the impact of minimum wages supports these conclusions. The fact that, in certain instances, adverse employment changes were noted as being rather minor in no way vitiates the theory. The theory assumes no changes in the variables, whereas in reality product demand may be expanding to such an extent that the impact of the minimum wage is the curtailment of the expansion of employment, rather than a rise in unemployment, as was the case in New York State following the 1957 increase.

Minimum Wage Legislation and Its Impact upon Disadvantaged Groups

Existing evidence indicates that younger and older workers, women, workers with little education, and non-white workers are "disadvantaged" in today's labor market. These people carry the burden of unemployment and poverty. The concern over poverty in recent years has drawn attention to these particular groups. Since minimum wage legislation is considered a tool to combat poverty, it is not unusual that attention has been drawn to its possible impact on the disadvantaged.

If minimum wage legislation causes adverse employment effects, then it seems to follow intuitively that these disadvantaged groups of workers will be most harmed by legislated wage floors. A number of economists have recently attempted to bolster their intuition with evidence. These include Arthur F. Burns, Milton Friedman and Yale Brozen.[25]

It is the contention of Friedman and Brozen that a disequilibrium wage differential has been created by the minimum wage

---

[23] *Economic Effects of Minimum Wages: The New York Retail Trade Order of 1957–1958,* New York State Department of Labor, Division of Research and Statistics (New York: 1964), p. 100.
[24] *Ibid.,* p. 74.

[25] Burns' discussion appears in Arthur F. Burns, *The Management of Prosperity,* Columbia University Press, New York, 1966, pp. 46–48. Burns' arguments echo those of Friedman and Brozen explored below.

law and its subsequent amendments, thus creating unemployment of covered workers.

The damage that has been done by the minimum wage has been caused, in large part, because the minimum has risen faster than the average manufacturing wage. The significant period is the last decade, 1955–1965, in which the minimum wage went up 67 percent while the average manufacturing wage went up only 40 percent.[26]

This is the first stage in the argument. The second stage is to single out the disadvantaged groups who are primarily affected by the disequilibrium in the wage structure created by the increased minima.

Friedman asserts that "The fact is—it can be demonstrated statistically—the minimum wage rate is a major cause of Negro teenage unemployment." This statement is supported with a chart graphing the unemployment rates for white male teenagers and non-white male teenagers. "It leaves out girls—and girls as we know always raise special problems." The chart shows "how a small gap opened up between unemployment rates for Negro and white boys in 1949–50, when the minimum wage was being increased from 40 cents to 75 cents. It closed temporarily during the Korean War emergency—so that in 1951–54 unemployment rates were about the same for both groups. But, at the end of the emergency, this small gap opened again. And then a much larger gap emerged. Today the unemployment rate is over 22 percent for non-white boys and under 12 percent for white boys." "This difference emerged all at once in 1956 and '57—with the 1956 increase in the minimum wage rate from 75¢ to $1.00 an hour."[27] Following this demonstration another graph is presented showing that a similar gap was created after 1956 between unemployment of adult males and teen-age males.

It may very well be that a disequilibrium wage differential is created by minimum wages and that this disequilibrium is the cause of teen-age unemployment and, more specifically, Negro teenage unemployment. However, if such a disequilibrium exists it is argued, that it is overstated by the authors cited; and if it increases the rate of unemployment of disadvantaged workers, a better demonstration will be required as proof than that which has been offered.

The measure of wage differential disequilibrium employed by Friedman and Brozen is the relationship between the minimum wage and the average wage in manufacturing. They examine wage rates rather than wage costs. In other words, the argument should be the relationship of the minimum wage to total employee compensation. It is probably the case that those people being paid the minimum wage do not receive as much in additional benefits as the more highly paid workers. Whereas the average manufacturing wage increased by 40 percent over the period 1955–1965, annual employee compensation per employee increased by 53 percent over the period. If this latter figure is employed then the differential disequilibrium postulated is not as drastic as it appears: the minimum wage increased 67 percent during the period. The figure of 53 percent is undoubtedly exaggerated for two reasons: (1) it is a yearly total and (2) it includes salaried workers as well as wage earners. The greater increase in this figure is not due completely to the salary component, however, because the wage and salary category increase was substantially less over the period. As for the fact that the figure is not an hourly figure, it appears that the total number of hours worked in manufacturing did not increase significantly over the period. The relevant figure probably lies somewhere between 40 percent and 53 percent.

Accepting the statement that the minimum wage has risen faster than the average hourly labor cost in manufacturing, it remains to be determined whether or not this disequilibrium has generated the results described by Friedman and Brozen.

---

[26] Yale Brozen and Milton Friedman, *The Minimum Wage Rate*, (Washington: The Free Society Association, Inc., April 1966), pp. 46–47.
[27] *Ibid.*, pp. 11 and 13.

In the period covered by Friedman and Brozen (1948–1965) there occurred four separate increases in the minimum wage—in 1950, 1956, 1961 and 1963. After the increases in 1949 and 1956 a gap widened between the rates of unemployment of white and non-white teenagers (male). The increases in 1961 and 1963 did not widen the already existing gap. With regard to the comparison of teenagers and adults (males) the gap was widened in 1956: it was not adversely affected by the two subsequent increases. With the increase in 1949, the unemployment gap between the two narrowed, rather than widened. In summary, with 4 observations, Friedman's contention shows up statistically 1 out of 4 times in one comparison; 1 out of 4 times in the second, and appears to be repudiated in at least one instance.

The bulk of the case presented by Friedman and Brozen relies on the minimum wage increase of 1956. Therefore, the following discussion is concerned with this period.

One must, of course, grant the fact that women have "special characteristics," but which one of these "special characteristics" is it that makes them immune to an increase in unemployment due to an increase in the minimum wage? For it is only on this basis that one has a rationale for excluding them from a study of this type. From 1956 to 1957 female white teenage unemployment rose from 8.9 percent to 9.4 percent whereas for non-whites in the same category the unemployment rate fell from 21.6 percent to 18.9 percent. The adult female unemployment rate rose from 3.7 percent to 3.8 percent over the 1 year period and the teenage female unemployment rate rose from 10.2 percent to 10.5 percent. These data indicate that the increase in the minimum wage in 1956 created no significant widening of the unemployment gap in Friedman's categories among the female members.

Turning now to the juxtaposition of white vs. non-white teenage unemployment among males (W.T.M. vs. N.T.M.) it might be pointed out that the type of statistic cited lends itself to a particular type of distortion. The finer the categories are drawn in this type of analysis, the greater the impact of the absolute change on the percentage change. From 1956 to 1957 unemployment of N.T.M. increased by 8,000 and by 28,000 in the category of W.T.M. In terms of percentages this translates into an increased unemployment of about 3 percent for N.T.M. and only about 1 percent for W.T.M. Even though the absolute unemployment created over the relevant period was distributed between the two groups in almost precisely the same proportion as it had been distributed before the increase in the minimum was put into effect, the unemployment *rates* indicate a worsening of the N.T.M. employment status relative to the W.T.M.

The point of this discussion has been to suggest that the use of unemployment rates in this case obscures the relative movements of absolute unemployment. When both comparisons are made, the minimum wage argument of Friedman is somewhat weakened.

Turning now to the second comparison made by Friedman and Brozen, that between adult males (A.M.) and teenage males (T.M.), one finds the gap between the two unemployment rates widening by about 1½ percentage points from 1956 to 1957 and by almost 3 percentage points from 1956 to 1958. This divergence, as a matter of course, is attributed to the implementation of the minimum wage increase of 1956. From 1948 to 1954 the labor force population of T.M. was declining but in the period 1955 to 1957 there was an increase of 5.7 percent. In contrast, throughout the early period, the labor force of A.M. increased steadily and in the 2 year period from 1955 to 1957 it increased by only 1.6 percent. Thus, the widening of the unemployment gap between the A.M. group and the T.M. group may well have occurred in the absence of a minimum wage increase after 1956 because of the greater number of teenage males who began to seek work during this period, relative to the increase in the number of adult males looking for work.

One might counter this argument by proferring the possibility that the increased number of teenagers might still have been able to find employment if the barrier of the new minimum wage increase had not existed. However, one study shows not only an increase in the number of teenagers in the labor force not hired in 1956 but also a decline in the number of job vacancies.[28] Further, it cannot possibly be argued that the decline in job vacancies was caused by the new minimum wage increase because the decrease occurred in the professional and managerial category and the skilled category, and subsequent to 1957 in all categories but the professional and managerial. Something other than the increase in the minimum wage was affecting employment adversely in 1956 and the years immediately following.

From the second quarter of 1956, the economy was following the road to recession: the inventory-sales ratio was increasing, investment in inventories was declining, and total output had leveled off. These changes would certainly dictate a degree of unemployment independent of a minimum wage increase.

The major changes in unemployment in Friedman's charts occur during the recession itself. The widened gap between N.T.M. and W.T.M. which occurred in 1949 and 1950 also took place during a downturn in the economy. In addition, this widening gap occurred *before* the minimum increase became effective, and began to narrow once it had become effective. It is not a new proposition that unemployment rates for the disadvantaged workers are the most greatly affected by downturns in economic activity. As pointed out before, one of the major reasons for this is difference in population size.

The major point is that out of 8 possible instances and with 4 increases in the minimum, Friedman and Brozen can cite only 3 of these instances to support their contention that Negroes and teenagers are the ones who suffer most from such increases. Of these three cited instances, one is not valid (1949–50) because the gap between the two groups compared actually narrowed after the increase. The two instances left are for the years 1956–58, a period of recession or almost recession. The general economic conditions existing in 1956 were such as to create the unemployment which resulted.

It may very well be, however, that the increase in the minimum wage in 1956 did add to the relative unemployment changes. If this is the case, it still remains to be demonstrated. The only instance where the minimum can possibly have had a definite adverse influence on the disadvantaged segments of the labor force under discussion was in the years 1956–58. The changes in these years are explainable without recourse to a change in the minimum wage; and this phenomenon of the effect of recession on disadvantaged workers is in evidence throughout post-war cycles. If the minimum wage does have the independent impact claimed, why then is this impact not in evidence with every increase? It is not only that the supposed impact occurs only in recession, it does not even occur in *every* recession. There appears to be nothing in the data to substantiate the claims of Friedman and Brozen.

In support of the above argument a recent study paper on "Employment Gains and the Determinants of the Occupational Distribution of Negroes" found, using multiple regression analysis, that

> Given the coverage that existed until 1967, minimum wages have played no part in the deteriorating employment picture for teenagers vis-à-vis adults or Negro teenagers vis-à-vis white teenagers. While the minimum wage variable is significant for adult Negro males, the size of the effect is small. . . . The income effects obviously outweigh the employment effects although the individuals who receive the income gains are not the ones who lose their jobs.[29]

---

[28] See Eleanor A. Gilpatrick, *Structural Unemployment and Aggregate Demand*, (Baltimore, Maryland, The Johns Hopkins Press, 1966), Table 46, p. 158.

[29] L. Thurow, paper presented in Madison, Wisconsin, May 12, 1967.

The Minimum Wage and Income Distribution

It has been asserted that "The manipulation of individual prices is neither an efficient nor an equitable device for changing the distribution of personal income."[30] It is of course true that a higher wage rate does not necessarily yield an adequate income. Nevertheless, it is one of the primary ingredients. In fact, wage income is the primary source of income of low-wage families. In 1955, 63.4 percent of the income of non-farm multi-person families with incomes under $4,000 was derived from wages and salaries. In 1964, of the 47.5 million families with incomes under $3,000, about 50 percent had one family member employed and 20 percent had 2 family members employed. In other words, a good deal of the poverty which exists today is wage related.

Therefore, if minimum wage legislation is a factor in redistributing factor shares in favor of labor, one possible inference might be that it is effective in redistributing the personal distribution of income toward the low income classes. A redistribution of income in favor of the low income classes is usually defined as alleviating poverty. If it can be shown that minimum wages do alter the personal distribution of income through its influence on factor shares in the manner suggested then it must be considered an effective weapon to combat poverty.

One major difficulty with this simple proposition is that the necessary data are not available to test it empirically. The least aggregative data available on labor's share is on the S.I.C. 2 digit classification level. The Labor's Share data utilized below are from Schultz and Tryon.[31] One caveat with respect to the data is that the employee compensation figures used to derive the estimates include both wages and salaries, so that a change in "labor's share" can be attributed to an increase in the salary component. The earnings and employment statistics are those presented in the B.L.S. series.

The basic assumption made for purposes of this analysis is that those industries which in 1947 had the lowest average hourly earnings would be the industries most affected by minimum wage increases. In other words, it is assumed that the dispersion of wages about the average is the same in all industries. It might be noted also that the B.L.S. average hourly earnings data include overtime hours, so that the changes in earnings figures used in the correlations below may be affected by this factor. There appears to be no relationship between amount of overtime and basic rates in the data, however, so that any bias which might exist is indeterminate.

Rank correlations were used because of the smallness of sample and the historical nature of the data. The value for the correlation of levels of earnings in 1947 (lowest to highest) against changes in labor's share for the period cited (highest to lowest) was $+.691$ which is significant at the 1 percent level. The relative increases in wages for the period correlated against wage levels was not significant $(+.196)$. If anything the sign of the coefficient would indicate that the higher paying industries experienced greater relative wage increases. Despite this, however, the low paying industries seemed to experience the smallest increases in employment: the rank correlation between wage levels and employment changes was $+.327$ (significant at the 5 percent level), indicating that the higher paying industries had the greatest increases in employment, or that the low wage industries experienced the least amount of increased employment over the period.

The conclusion must be then that the increase in labor's share in the low wage industries was not the result of increased labor productivity or product demand pulling up wages. The evidence of small employment changes indicates, to the contrary, that the relative wage increases, although not necessarily the highest in manufacturing were the result of a cost-push factor.

---

[30] G. Stigler, *op. cit.*, p. 44.
[31] U.S. Congress Joint Economic Committee, *Prices and Costs in Manufacturing Industries*, Study Paper No. 17 (Washington: GPO, 1960).

The villain most commonly sought in the case of a wage-push mechanism is unionism. Correlating wage levels in 1947 with degrees of unionism yields a coefficient of $+.503$, which is significant at the 1 percent level, and indicates that the higher paying industries have the greatest degree of unionism; or, conversely, that the low paying industries had the least amount of unionism. Such a correlation detracts considerably from unionism being the explanation of the cost-push factor in the low wage industries. Another possible, and traditional, explanation is the contagious nature of union increases; i.e., the "sympathetic pressure" which transmits wage increases in the organized sector to the unorganized sector. This factor, however, is to be doubted as an explanatory variable in the present case. If union wage increases in the high paying firms were transmitted to the low paying firms, then the percentage increases in the latters' wages would be greater. The evidence indicates that this is not the case for the period under study in which the low wage industries did not have greater relative wage increases.

A third possibility is that minimum wage legislation was a causal factor in the wage-push in the low wage industries in the postwar period, and that the result of this wage-push was a greater increase in labor's share than occurred in other, less affected industries.

One might ask at this point why did labor's share show the greatest increases in those industries with the lowest wage increases and the greatest amount of unemployment. In the short-run, a wage increase will result in an increase in labor's share. The more elastic the labor demand curve, the greater will be the resulting unemployment. As was argued earlier the more concentrated (monopolistic) industries will have the more inelastic demand curves. The high paying industries are the more monopolistic industries and, during this period, granted the greatest wage increases. The rank correlation between 1954 levels of concentration and wage changes for the period under consideration was $+.450$ and significant at the 1 percent level. Relative elasticities of labor demand, in the face of wage increases, easily explain the antithetical movement of employment and labor's share. In other words, the more elastic labor demand curves in the low wage industries would necessarily create more unemployment than in the high wage industries (with inelastic demand curves) for the same relative wage increase, and might very well do the same for differing relative wage increases.

In the long-run it can be argued that (assuming monopoly and size are synonymous): (1) there is more scope for the utilization of machinery in the larger firms; (2) large firms are able to purchase machinery at lower prices than smaller firms, because of a better bargaining position; (3) small firms are limited in their access to capital, whereas large firms are not.[32] In light of these considerations, one might expect that the larger firms are more readily able to innovate. Granting Hicks' argument that these induced innovations tend to be of a labor saving nature, they will provide for the employment of more labor.

Thus, both in the short-run and the long-run, the low-wage industries of the economy appear suited to the translation of minimum wage increases into a higher labor share and it is possible that they have done just that.

The connection between this increased labor's share in the low wage industries of the economy and the personal distribution of income is at best tenuous. In fact from 1947 to 1961 the percentage of total family income accruing to the bottom ⅖ of consumer units fell from 16 per cent to 15.6 percent, a slight movement toward greater inequality. If minimum wages have been effective in the manner postulated a movement toward greater equality in the distribution of income would be expected.

One explanation offered for the relative

---

[32] Tibor Scitovsky, "Economic Theory and the Measurement of Concentration": *Business Concentration and Price Policy*, National Bureau of Economic Research (Princeton: Princeton University Press, 1955), p. 130.

stability of the postwar personal distribution of income is that an increase in the wage and salary component tending to create more equality was offset by an increased share of wages and salaries going to the top 10 percent of consumer units. This latter development being primarily due to the increased number of high income salaried managers and professionals.[33]

Thus, the possibility presents itself that the increased labor share evidenced in low wage industries may be due primarily to an increase in the salary component. However, it is equally possible that this increased labor share is at the lower end of the distribution, but is not reflected in the personal distribution because it has been outweighed by the factors creating inequality.

This brief study of labor's share is far from adequate. In large part this is due to the paucity of appropriate data. The correlations above do not unequivocally demonstrate that minimum wage legislation has increased labor's share. However, they do hold out a fairly strong possibility that this may have been the case, and further that, even though this may not have created an increased equality in the distribution of income, it may have helped prevent a movement toward greater inequality.

Conclusion

The nexus between minimum wages and the problem of poverty is not easily demonstrated. The connection runs from increased wages through changes in employment to the aggregate effect of both on labor's share, and the effect of this on the personal distribution of income. Also important is the consideration of who the individuals are who are most affected by these changes.

The conclusions of this paper—which, it must be stressed, are not all conclusive—are:

(1) minimum wages raise the wages of workers;
(2) minimum wages create adverse employment effects, but there is no strong evidence that this unemployment is unequally distributed toward the "disadvantaged" groups in society;
(3) minimum wages may very well have the effect of redistributing income in favor of labor, thus creating a tendency toward less inequality in the personal distribution of income.

Many argue that the number of "poverty" families affected by minimum wage hikes is a small proportion of the total "poverty" category. This, however, is not a relevant argument. Granted, there are more efficacious means to eliminate poverty, but no comprehensive program is available. Social security goes *part* of the way; unemployment compensation goes *part* of the way; all welfare measures go *part* of the way; and minimum wage legislation goes *part* of the way.

Of all these means of eliminating poverty, the minimum wage is the only one which does not impair worker incentives. In fact, it will increase the incentive to work in most instances in a way that a negative income tax cannot be expected to do.

As with any other measure designed to reduce poverty, the benefits to society which result from a rise in the minimum wage must be weighed against the costs to society. This paper has attempted to point out these benefits and costs.

---

[33] W. Avril, *The Size Distribution of Income in the U.S.: 1947 to 1961.* An unpublished Master's Thesis at The Pennsylvania State University, 1965.

Date Due